Title Searching and Conveyancing in Ontario

Sixth Edition

Title Searching and Conveyancing in Ontario

Sixth Edition

Sixth Edition by
Marguerite E. Moore, B.A. (Hons.), J.D.

Janet M. Globe
(Founding Author)

LexisNexis®

Members of the LexisNexis Group worldwide

Canada	LexisNexis Canada Inc, 123 Commerce Valley Dr. E. Suite 700, MARKHAM, Ontario
Australia	Butterworths, a Division of Reed International Books Australia Pty Ltd, CHATSWOOD, New South Wales
Austria	ARD Betriebsdienst and Verlag Orac, VIENNA
Czech Republic	Orac, sro, PRAGUE
France	Éditions du Juris-Classeur SA, PARIS
Hong Kong	Butterworths Asia (Hong Kong), HONG KONG
Hungary	Hvg Orac, BUDAPEST
India	Butterworths India, NEW DELHI
Ireland	Butterworths (Ireland) Ltd, DUBLIN
Italy	Giuffré, MILAN
Malaysia	Malayan Law Journal Sdn Bhd, KUALA LUMPUR
New Zealand	Butterworths of New Zealand, WELLINGTON
Poland	Wydawnictwa Prawnicze PWN, WARSAW
Singapore	Butterworths Asia, SINGAPORE
South Africa	Butterworth Publishers (Pty) Ltd, DURBAN
Switzerland	Stämpfli Verlag AG, BERNE
United Kingdom	Butterworths Tolley, a Division of Reed Elsevier (UK), LONDON, WC2A
USA	LexisNexis, DAYTON, Ohio

National Library of Cataloguing in Publication Data

Globe, Janet M.
  Title searching and conveyancing in Ontario / Janet M. Globe. —
6th ed. / by Marguerite E. Moore.

Includes index.
ISBN 978-0-433-46131-9 (bound)
ISBN 978-0-433-46132-6 (pbk.)

  1. Title examinations — Ontario. I. Moore, Marguerite E. II. Title.

KEO274.G66 2003   346.71304'38   C2003-903869-6
KF678.G56 2003

Printed and bound in Canada.

For my parents, Ruth and John, from whom I inherited the love of the land, and for my sons, Bruce and Bill, from whom I have borrowed the land and to whom I entrust the land.

M.E.M.

About the Author

Marguerite E. Moore, B.A. (Hons.), J.D. is a graduate of Victoria College and the University of Toronto Law School, and has been a member of the Ontario Bar since 1977. She is a professor and past program co-ordinator of the Law Clerk Program in the Information Technology Division at Fanshawe Community College in London, Ontario. She specializes in teaching real property and real estate law, conveyancing, title searching, legal research, and legal technology. She has been a speaker and instructor on title searching and land registration records for the Office of the Director of Land Registration, the Ontario Association of Archivists, the University of Western Ontario, Historical and Archival Associations, and the Ontario Police College.

Ms Moore is presently renewing her love of real property law in her final year of the part-time LL.M. in Real Property Law at Osgoode Hall Law School.

Foreword

Presumably, editors the world over have the same dilemma when publishing successor editions of classic works: either maintain tradition and brand recognition by keeping the predecessor title (even if that existing title does little to incite the reader or does little to reflect the true nature of the work) or break with tradition to come up with a new title that is perhaps more reflective of the text between the covers (even if the new title alienates the long list of standing orders for just about anything that comes with a spine and a pedigreed title). It is with some sadness that I see that the publishers of the sixth edition of *Title Searching and Conveyancing in Ontario* have opted for the former naming protocol.

I say that this decision is misguided not so because *Title Searching and Conveyancing in Ontario* is any less a classic or as seminal a text as, say, a *Falconbridge* or an *Anger & Honsberger* or a *Ziff*. Indeed, *Title Searching and Conveyancing in Ontario* is every bit as true a classic as these other great works, whose very names scream "credibility". Instead, I say that the decision is misguided because the title itself is now worse than boring — it has become positively misleading by omission. True, the sixth edition of *Title Searching and Conveyancing in Ontario* deals exhaustively with title searching and conveyancing in Ontario — after all, where else can one find a how-to guide walking the practitioner through a forty-year search (a dying skill to be sure, but one that remains critical in quieting those titles that did not get automatically converted into LTCQ). Nonetheless, the choice of *"Title Searching and Conveyancing in Ontario"* ultimately does a disservice to the uninitiated because it unfairly under-values the true utility of this text, which is a whole lot more than a mere title searching manual.

Nowhere is the true scope of the text more apparent than in a list of the newest sections added to the text since the fifth edition came out in 2003. For instance, a huge section of the very first chapter is now dedicated to the enormous explosion in First Nations' real property rights in the past few years, replacing what was nothing more than a glorified footnote on Aboriginal title that stood in its place in the fifth edition.

Likewise, in an almost antithetical departure for a text ostensibly dedicated to "title searching", there appears a brand new chapter in the sixth edition devoted exclusively to "off-title searching", covering both the "usual" off-title letter inquiries, as well as a number of "unusual" off-title letter inquiries (and even some that this commentator would consider downright "exotic") off-title letter inquiries.

In the sixth edition of *Title Searching and Conveyancing in Ontario*, Marguerite Moore has revisited the topics contained in the predecessor edition through the multi-coloured glasses of the practicing real estate bar, managing to mix a surprisingly heady dose of substantive property law (a whole new chapter devoted exclusively to title and mortgage fraud) with the less glamorous but desperately necessary practice mechanics of getting deals closed (with what is still, in this commentator's opinion, one of the best "closing" checklists available today) and an exhaustive and up-to-date overview of modern title insurance. Even quasi-political issues so dear to the hearts of real estate practitioners and that are rarely covered in other legal texts (such as the role and governance of paralegals) are touched upon in this sixth edition of *Title Searching and Conveyancing in Ontario*.

Simply put, for those practitioners long enough in the tooth to make the reference relevant, "this ain't your grandfather's thin brown copy of *Globe on Title Searching*" (an ode to the founding author of *Title Searching and Conveyancing in Ontario*). Instead, the sixth edition of *Title Searching and Conveyancing in Ontario* has become a comparatively huge (888 pages) encyclopaedic tome on the practice of real estate law sharing shelf space right beside my OED and *Donahue & Quinn* (check your library — this latter text should now include a "Grandilli" or else you are out of date!) and in front of my copies of *Falconbridge, Anger & Honsberger* and *Ziff*. It is an indispensable resource for front-line practitioners who are increasingly expected to do much more for much less. Congratulations Marguerite and thank you from the profession.

Jeffrey W. Lem
April 2010

Preface

Land is sacred and of value beyond money

The goal of the sixth edition of *Title Searching and Conveyancing in Ontario* is to assist the practitioner/professional in navigating title and off-title conveyancing requirements in both a marketable title and an insurable title context. The writing of the sixth edition reflects the emergence of the combining of real property law and title insurance as a new area of legal specialization in Ontario. The focus of the book is on the law and practice related to land registration systems, electronic land registration, title and off-title inquiries, and title insurance from a proactive risk management perspective. Conscientious and knowledgeable title and off-title searching is a powerful proactive risk management tool and fraud avoidance tool. As in earlier editions, I have endeavoured to review in detail the law and practice, and to show how to search, transfer, and register land by way of example searches, screen captures, precedents, charts and checklists, file management software screens, title insurance documentation, and appendices and research tools. In particular, I have addressed in detail the legal and practical differences concerning Registry titles, Land Titles Absolute titles, Land Titles Conversion Qualified titles, Land Titles Absolute Plus titles, Parcelized Day Forward Registry titles, Registry Non-Convert titles, and Condominium titles.

The road to safe title and off-title searching and title conveyancing is — more than at any other time —littered with complex, demanding practice guidelines; unprecedented growth in the federal, provincial, and municipal governments' regulation of land; an electronic land registration system which contains multiple, often difficult to distinguish, variations in title rights and qualifications; developing and sometimes unsettling case law exploring the relationship of lawyer diligence duties and the evolving role of title insurance; exponential client expectations; unrealistic timelines; arguably insufficient economic reward in relation to the economic risk and the nature of the work; constant, fast-paced, legal and technological change; what has been referred to as an epidemic in title and mortgage fraud; and new market trends and economic pressures — all in an increasingly litigious landscape.

The sixth edition integrates title insurance applications throughout the text. It also contains new sections on hot topics such as mortgage and title fraud; government regulation of land and related off-title inquiries; Aboriginal ownership and treaty issues, including Internet resources for Treaty maps and status of Aboriginal claims; changes in client identification and verification rules; powers of attorney due diligence requirements; amendments to the *Land Titles Act* on the effect of fraud and forgery on ownership; fraud reduction strategies and reporting; changes to the Land Titles Assurance Fund; the two-lawyer requirement for transfers; life leases and fractional share ownership; conservation easements; and the interface of environmental law and real property ownership, including the *Green Energy Act* and Toronto's Green Roof bylaw. The sixth edition also incorporates more case law, particularly with respect to current topics such as the *Planning Act*, statutory notice provisions under the *Registry Act*, easements, access, possessory rights, and restrictive covenants, title insurance and title and mortgage fraud, and lawyer due diligence standards and liability.

On a more personal note, it is my belief that land registration or representational systems are essential to the political and economic well-being of countries. I also believe that land ownership and a passion for place are unique, and of great importance to the human spirit. I have given my best with the time and resources available to me and have been more ambitious with this edition. Although the book's main purpose is that of a practical tool, I hope that it may at the same time stand as a record of land registration past and present in Ontario.

Real property conveyancing is a complex area of law that presents increasing challenge and growing risk. I have worked hard to gather into one consolidated reference as much current information as possible about the law, the practice, and the technology related to land; it is, of course, impossible to cover fully all possible topics in a broad field that changes daily. This publication makes no attempt to offer legal or professional advice or to warrant the accuracy, the adequacy, or the currency of information. Legal advice, expert assistance, and the services of a competent legal professional are essential for all real property transactions.

I hope that the sixth edition of *Title Searching and Conveyancing in Ontario* will provide lawyers, law clerks, surveyors, and title insurers, as well as other professionals who work in fields related to the regulation and the management of land, with the tools as well as the information essential to practice safe title searching and careful conveyancing.

Marguerite E. Moore
London, Ontario
April 1, 2010

Acknowledgements

The magnitude, the complexity, and the unrelenting speed of change in real property law, real estate practice, conveyancing technology, and the now-pervasive impact of title insurance and insurance law throughout the transaction had almost persuaded me not to invest the necessary time, energy, resources, and the simply overwhelming amount of work required to produce the sixth edition of *Title Searching and Conveyancing in Ontario*. It is for this reason that the acknowledgements in the sixth edition are of special significance.

I wish to express my sincere appreciation to the following individuals who, by sharing resources, expertise, ideas, and encouragement, have played a bigger role than they know in the creation of the sixth edition.

My thanks to the LexisNexis Canada editors of the last three editions who have picked up the ball from the author and carried the book to publication. My special thanks to Stephanie Joisten, who finalized the sixth edition comma by semicolon, word by word, and line by line, and to Sheila Nemet-Brown, who guided the publication to completion and helped so much with the permissions. It is a pleasure to work with talented editors who strive for excellence.

My thanks to Kevin Rogers of Stewart Title, who has, without hesitation, for the last three editions provided me with precedents and a continuous flow of current information on the inter-relationship of real estate law and practice and title insurance, and to Karen Decker for sharing her expertise and expediting precedents and permissions.

My appreciation to Teranet for allowing me not only to explain title searching and land registration procedures but also to illustrate the mechanics of title searching and electronic land registration by allowing me to include so many examples of POLARIS searching and Electronic Land Registration System screens and printouts.

My appreciation to TitlePLUS and to the Law Society of Upper Canada for sharing resources and checklists.

My gratitude to my parents, no longer with me, whose unrelenting work ethic and passionate belief in the enduring value of quality education and the pursuit of knowledge for its own sake may explain why this edition was written.

My gratitude to my sons, Bruce and Bill, who continue to provide me with the motivation and the sense of purpose without which no major accomplishment can come into being.

My thanks to the friends, Elaine, Helen, Denise, Frances, Daisy, Cathy, Ruth, Martie, and Paula, to name only a few, who tirelessly encouraged me to continue working, writing, studying, and caring for family, and never doubted that the book would happen, despite not so subtle inquiries about how many chapters had been written.

My thanks to colleagues who have provided precedents and puzzled over potential *Planning Act* contraventions with me: Tom, Simone, Alex, Virginia, and Fay.

In addition, I wish to acknowledge the pivotal contribution of two individuals who made the sixth edition possible:

> Bernard Sandler, who shares my love of the land, and somehow persuaded me to complete a sixth edition when I had decided that I had neither the time nor the resources to write the book that was now needed in the new practice of real estate.

> Paddy Musson, who made the writing of the book possible by her efforts and interventions in arranging a sabbatical, without which it would have been impossible to accomplish the extensive research and writing required for the creation of a comprehensive, fully revised practice resource.

I wish to thank my professors and my colleagues at the Osgoode, part-time LL.M. in Real Property Law Program. I particularly wish to thank Jeffrey Lem for assembling and directing an unparalleled cast of real property stars. The program's outstanding courses and materials and the extraordinary combined expertise and experience of faculty, guest experts, and students have provided me with the much-appreciated opportunity to make the sixth edition of *Title Searching and Conveyancing in Ontario* a different and much better book than earlier editions.

With acknowledgement and
sincere appreciation,

Marguerite Moore

Disclaimer

The author and publisher of *Title Searching and Conveyancing in Ontario, Sixth Edition* acknowledge that the information herein will be used by legal practitioners and others in their practice. While every effort has been made to ensure the accuracy, completeness, and utility of the work (and the tables and figures herein), neither the publisher nor the author shall be responsible for any errors or omissions contained in the work and expressly disclaim liability whether under contract or in negligence to any user of the work whether a direct person, any person who may borrow or use it, or to any client of such person.

The law and materials contained in this work are, in general, those in force in November 2009. Figures have been updated to January 2010 where possible.

Table of Contents

**Chapter 2: Land Division and Geographical Referencing
in Ontario**

Chapter 3: The Registry System

Chapter 4: The 40-Year Registry Search

Chapter 7: Condominium Ownership and the Search

Chapter 14: Off-Title Inquiries

Chapter 18: Title Insurance

List of Abbreviations

20M-649	Subdivision Plan 649 in Registry Office #20 (Halton)
33R-1234	Reference Plan 1234 in Registry Office #33 (Middlesex)
AGRMT	Agreement
AGRMT SUBD	Agreement of Subdivision
APPL	Application to Register
Beno	Beneficial owner (abbr. used in POLARIS printouts and e-reg)
BLK	Block
BTN	Between
C	Certified (LT) or checked (RO) instrument on POLARIS printout
COMM	Commencing
CON	Concession
COND	Condominium
D	Deleted instrument on POLARIS printout
Dep.	Deposit
E&OE	Errors and Omissions Excepted
ELRS	Electronic Land Registration System, formerly e-reg
ER	Electronic Registration
E/S	East Side
FS	Fee simple ownership called absolute ownership in Land Titles

G.R.	General Register document
INST	Instrument (document)
JTEN	Joint Tenant
LawPRO	Lawyers' Professional Indemnity Company
LRO	Land Registry Office
LRRA	*Land Registration Reform Act*
LT	Land Titles
LT(S)	Lots(s)
LT Abs	Land Titles Absolute
LTCQ	Land Titles Conversion Qualified (land administratively converted from the Registry system to the Land Titles system)
LT PLUS	Land Titles Absolute Plus (LTCQ title upgraded to LT Absolute Plus)
M-Plan	Subdivision Plan
MRO	Mineral Rights Only
NTCE	Notice
OLS	Ontario Land Surveyor
PCL	Parcel
PDFR	Parcelized Day Forward Registry (automated Registry records as of the PIN creation date)
PIN	Property Identification Number (used in POLARIS)
PL	Plan
POB/POC	Place of Beginning/Place of Commencement

POLARIS	Province of Ontario Land Registration Information System (the computerized land records database)
POTL	Parcel of Tied Land
PPSR	Personal Property Security Registration
PREM	Premising
PSP	Personal Security Package is a personalized, specially encrypted floppy diskette or storage device (USB) and a unique pass phrase required for each person in a law firm using electronic land registration. The PSP provides access to Teraview.
PT(S)	Part(s)
R	Registry System
RDAL	Road Allowance
RDWY	Roadway
REG NUM	Registered Number
ROW	Right of Way
R-Plan	Reference Plan
RPR card	Real Property Registration card (debit card for automated LROs, more recently a Teranet Cash Card)
R.R.O.	Revised Regulations of Ontario
R.S.C.	Revised Statutes of Canada
R.S.O.	Revised Statutes of Ontario
SEC	Section
SRO	Surface Rights Only
S/T	Subject to

TCOM   Tenants in Common

TRANS   Transfer (deed or grant)

TRANS EASMENT   Transfer of Easement

TRANS PWR OF   Transfer under a power of sale in a mortgage
SALE

T/W   Together With

WID   Widening

List of Figures

Figure A

TERAVIEW ELECTRONIC REGISTRATION ROLLOUT MAP[*]

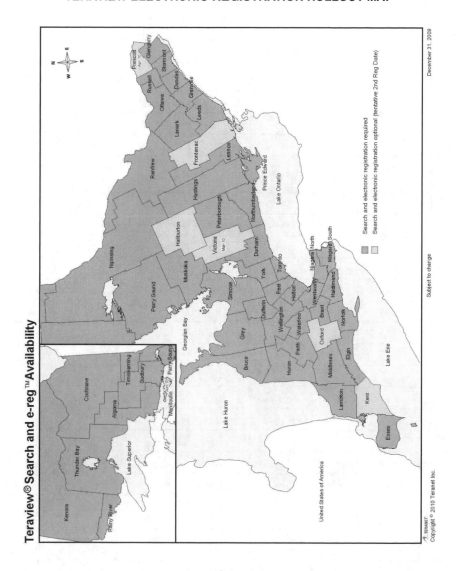

Figure B

TERAVIEW IMPLEMENTATION STATUS[*]

No.	Land Registry Office	POLARIS Title				MAPS	IMAGES
		Full Search	PDFR/Last Registered Owner	Percentage Complete	e-reg™	Percentage Complete Entire LRO	Documents Available
1	Algoma	100.0%	0.0%	100.0%	Required	Complete	Yes
2	Brant	100.0%	0.0%	100.0%	Required	Complete	Yes
3	Bruce	100.0%	0.0%	100.0%	Required	Complete	Yes
4	Ottawa/ Carleton	100.0%	0.0%	100.0%	Required	Complete	Yes
6	Cochrane	100.0%	0.0%	100.0%	Required	Complete	Yes
7	Dufferin	100.0%	0.0%	100.0%	Required	Complete	Yes
8	Dundas	100.0%	0.0%	100%	Required	Complete	Yes
11	Elgin	100.0%	0.0%	100.0%	Required	Complete	Yes
12	Essex	100.0%	0.0%	100.0%	Required	Complete	Yes
13	Frontenac	56.3%	43.7%	100.0%	Optional	Complete	Yes
14	Glengarry	100.0%	0.0%	100.0%	Required	0.0%	Yes
15	Grenville	100.0%	0.0%	100.0%	Required	100.0%	Yes
16	Grey	100.0%	0.0%	100.0%	Required	82.0%	Yes
18	Haldimand	100%	0.0%	100%	Required	Complete	Yes
19	Haliburton	37.2%	0.0%	37.2%	Optional	32.3%	Yes
20	Halton	100.0%	0.0%	100.0%	Required	Complete	Yes
21	Hastings	100.0%	0.0%	100.0%	Optional	Complete	Yes
22	Huron	100.0%	0.0%	100.0%	Required	Complete	Yes
23	Kenora	100.0%	0.0%	100.0%	Required	Complete	Yes
24	Kent	68.0%	32.0%	100.0%	Optional	Complete	Yes
25	Lambton	100.0%	0.0%	100.0%	Required	Complete	Yes
27	Lanark	100.0%	0.0%	100.0%	Required	Complete	Yes
28	Leeds	100.0%	0.0%	100.0%	Required	Complete	Yes
29	Lennox	100.0%	0.0%	100.0%	Required	Complete	Yes

Figure B (cont'd)

No.	Land Registry Office	POLARIS Title				MAPS	IMAGES
		Full Search	PDFR/Last Registered Owner	Percentage Complete	e-reg™	Percentage Complete Entire LRO	Documents Available
30	Niagara North	100.0%	0.0%	100.0%	Required	Complete	Yes
31	Manitoulin	39.3%	0.0%	39.3%	Optional	22.6%	Yes
33	Middlesex	100.0%	0.0%	100.0%	Required	Complete	Yes
**35	Muskoka	100.0%	0.0%	100.0%	Required	Complete	Yes
36	Nipissing	100.0%	0.0%	100.0%	Required	Complete	Yes
37	Norfolk	100%	0.0%	100%	Required	Complete	Yes
39	Northumberland	100.0%	0.0%	100.0%	Required	Complete	Yes
40	Durham	100.0%	0.0%	100.0%	Required	Complete	Yes
41	Oxford	74.9%	25.1%	100.0%	Optional	Complete	Yes
42	Parry Sound	100.0%	0.0%	100.0%	Optional	Complete	Yes
43	Peel	100.0%	0.0%	100.0%	Required	Complete	Yes
44	Perth	100.0%	0.0%	100.0%	Required	Complete	Yes
45	Peterborough	100.0%	0.0%	100.0%	Required	Complete	Yes
46	Prescott	69.0%	0.0%	69.0%	Optional	48.7%	Yes
47	Prince Edward	100.0%	0.0%	100.0%	Required	Complete	Yes
48	Rainy River	100.0%	0.0%	100.0%	Required	Complete	Yes
49	Renfrew	100.0%	0.0%	100.0%	Required	Complete	Yes
50	Russell	100.0%	0.0%	100.0%	Required	Complete	Yes
**51	Simcoe	100.0%	0.0%	100.0%	Required	Complete	Yes
52	Stormont	100%	0.0%	100%	Optional	Complete	Yes
53	Sudbury	100.0%	0.0%	100.0%	Required	Complete	Yes
54	Timiskaming	100.0%	0.0%	100.0%	Required	Complete	Yes
55	Thunder Bay	100.0%	0.0%	100.0%	Required	Complete	Yes
57	Victoria	91.1%	0.0%	91.1%	Optional	86.3%	Yes
58	Waterloo	100.0%	0.0%	100.0%	Required	Complete	Yes
59	Niagara South	100.0%	0.0%	100.0%	Required	Complete	Yes
61	Wellington	100.0%	0.0%	100.0%	Required	Complete	Yes
62	Wentworth	98.2%	1.8%	100.0%	Required	Complete	Yes

Figure B (cont'd)

		POLARIS Title				MAPS	IMAGES
No.	Land Registry Office	Full Search	PDFR/Last Registered Owner	Percentage Complete	e-reg™	Percentage Complete Entire LRO	Documents Available
65	York	100.0%	0.0%	100.0%	Required	Complete	Yes
80	Metropolitan Toronto	100.0%	0.0%	100.0%	Required	Complete	Yes

Legend

PDFR/Last Registered Owner - Parcelized Day Forward Registry and Last Registered Owner (Oxford & Kent).

Full Search - Land Titles, Land Titles Conversion Qualified, Registry non-converts or 40yr load Registry properties automated

Instruments Available - Documents available via viewing on screen or email

Shaded areas represent LROs with 1st and 2nd Regulations

**The remaining properties in the LRO may be automated at a later date

Figure C

ELECTRONIC REGISTRATION ROLLOUT SCHEDULE[*]

NOW AVAILABLE

OPTIONAL

Manitoulin JANUARY 2007	Notice
Haliburton OCTOBER 2006	Notice
Prescott JUNE 2006	Notice
Kent MARCH 2006	Notice
Oxford JANUARY 2006	Notice
Victoria OCTOBER 2005	Notice
Frontenac APRIL 2005	Notice

REQUIRED

Grenville NOVEMBER 2009	Notice
Grey DECEMBER 2009	Notice
Parry Sound DECEMBER 2009	Notice
Glengarry NOVEMBER 2009	Notice
Dundas AUGUST 2009	Notice
Leeds MAY 2009	Notice
Northumberland APRIL 2009	Notice
Hastings DECEMBER 2008	Notice
Stormont JUNE 2008	Notice
Bruce APRIL 2008	Notice
Haldimand MARCH 2008	Notice
Lennox MARCH 2008	Notice
Prince Edward DECEMBER 2007	Notice
Muskoka NOVEMBER 2007	Notice
Algoma OCTOBER 2007	Notice
Norfolk SEPTEMBER 2007	Notice
Lambton SEPTEMBER 2007	Notice
Peterborough AUGUST 2007	Notice
Elgin MAY 2007	Notice
Kenora FEBRUARY 2006	Notice
Timiskaming FEBRUARY 2006	Notice
Nipissing JUNE 2005	Notice
Thunder Bay MAY 2005	Notice
Sudbury MARCH 2005	Notice
Cochrane FEBRUARY 2005	Notice
Rainy River NOVEMBER 2004	Notice
Niagara North SEPTEMBER 2004	Notice
Niagara South SEPTEMBER 2004	Notice
Waterloo FEBRUARY 2004	Notice
Toronto DECEMBER 2003	Notice
Essex SEPTEMBER 2003	Notice

Figure C (cont'd)

NOW AVAILABLE

REQUIRED

Lanark JUNE 2003	Notice
Renfrew JUNE 2003	Notice
Russell JUNE 2003	Notice
Huron MAY 2003	Notice
Perth MAY 2003	Notice
Brant DECEMBER 2002	Notice
Wellington DECEMBER 2002	Notice
Simcoe NOVEMBER 2002	Notice
Ottawa MAY 2002	Notice
Durham MARCH 2002	Notice
York DECEMBER 2001	Notice
Dufferin NOVEMBER 2001	Notice
Peel OCTOBER 2001	Notice
Halton APRIL 2001	Notice
Hamilton JANUARY 2001	Notice
Middlesex MARCH 2000	Notice

CHAPTER 1

Land Registration in Ontario

INTRODUCTION

There are no simple property transactions.

Brandon v. Brandon, [2001] O.J. No. 2986 at para. 117 (Ont. S.C.J.)

The title inquiries required for a specific property depend on the wording of the contract, the nature of the property, the expectations of the client, the land registration system in which the property is registered, and the terms of the title insurance coverage including the search requirements for the policy. Lawyers and law clerks combine legal title searching and registration due diligence requirements in multiple, for the most part electronic land registration systems, with diverse off-title inquiries including survey and boundary investigations, and title insurance policy search requirements.

CURRENT ISSUES IN TITLE CONVEYANCING

In Ontario, title insurance is now the norm and in the opinion of the author necessary for residential real estate transactions, and appropriate for the majority of commercial transactions. Title and mortgage insurance is a value-added, after-the-fact indemnity that protects purchasers and lenders from the risk of fraud and losses caused by title defects that are either specifically listed or routinely covered in the wording of the policy. As with all insurance policies, standard policy coverage contains numerous exemptions and restrictions such as environmental risks, water quality, and Aboriginal rights, title, and treaty claims.

It is important to remember that only full title searches based on legal and professional due diligence standards can identify the title risks not covered by standard policy language and insurance search requirements and, as a result, protect lawyers from negligence claims. Title insurance provides market value compensation for unknown, narrowly defined, title deficiencies, such as executions, some work orders, and access. For example, title insurance would not address the loss of use and enjoyment and quality of life factors generated by an acrimonious, undetected boundary or access dispute. Title insurance does not guarantee or rectify title; it does not provide the same protections and choices as a full title search and a survey.

Not all real estate transactions close; requisitions must be made, contracts may be breached, and lawyers may need to tender on closing in order to protect their clients' interests. Only full title searches and surveys that meet legal due diligence requirements will reveal title defects in a timely manner, provide lawyers with the ability to make requisitions, prove title, effectively tender on closing, and protect clients, and themselves, when a deal does not close.

Current case law makes the importance of a full search of title and the difference between title insurance requirements and legal due diligence title investigation duties abundantly clear. In *Syvan Developments Ltd v. Ontario (Ministry of Government Services)*, [2006] O.J. No. 3765 at para. 48 (Ont. S.C.J.), the purchaser's lawyer did not confirm the legal validity of an access easement by completing an adjoining lands search on both the benefitted and the burdened lands. An adjoining lands search would have revealed that the easement had been expropriated. The Court agreed that "[t]itle insurance provid[ed] financial protection from the consequences of a purchaser's failure to exercise what would otherwise be due diligence"; however, it decided the case on the basis that "an act or omission that would otherwise be a neglect or default within the meaning of the provision will not cease to be so if it has been insured against" (*Syvan* at para. 48). In *Ruksc v. Hussein*, [2005] O.J. No. 5231 at paras. 16 and 17 (Ont. S.C.J.), the purchaser chose to sue the lawyer in negligence instead of making a title insurance claim for arrears of taxes not adjusted on closing. The Court stated that "the existence of insurance will not extinguish a plaintiff's cause of action against a defendant. The mere fact that the plaintiff has an alternate source [title insurance] from which to recover his loss does not extinguish his right to seek recovery from the negligent party" (*Ruksc*, at para. 16). In *Stewart Title Guarantee Co. v. Zeppieri*, [2009] O.J. No. 322 (Ont. S.C.J.), house purchasers chose to sue their lawyer in negligence for an alleged *Planning Act* contravention; the Court found that "[a]n obligation to defend ... in cases where it eventually turns out that an insured is not entitled to indemnification" under the insurance policy (*Stewart*, at para. 48). Simply put, a client's agreement to purchase title insurance does not release a solicitor from liability for negligence and the risk of litigation (*Solicitors Act*, R.S.O. 1990, c. S.15, s. 22).

TITLE SEARCHING: A PROACTIVE RISK MANAGEMENT TOOL

Title searching and real estate conveyancing have been consistently documented as high risk activities by errors and omissions excepted (E&OE) claims history, case law, and title insurance claims statistics. The automation of title searching and document registration combined with the legal conversion of Registry titles to Land Titles ownership have added many layers of legal and technological complexity to what was already a risky business. Title searching and the review of title is not the same as retrieving data. Conscientious and knowledgeable title searching practices provide lawyers with a powerful, proactive, risk management tool.

For the sake of the client and for the sake of the lawyer and law clerk, in a time of electronic land registration, title insurance coverage, heightened risk of fraud, and increasingly knowledgeable and potentially litigious clients, it is critically important to maintain a specialized knowledge of the law of real property, title registration systems, title investigation, real estate conveyancing, and real estate practice standards and technologies. The following chapters are meant to provide lawyers, law clerks, and title insurers with both a comprehensive reference source and a practical, risk management toolkit for title searching, title registration, and title insurance in Ontario.

Experienced, conscientious practitioners know that real estate law and practice is constantly changing, increasing in complexity, and relentlessly demanding in a competitive market environment in a time is of the essence world. Indeed the law of real property, title conveyancing, and the art of title investigation could be described as "a riddle wrapped in a mystery inside an enigma" (Winston Churchill, made in a radio broadcast in 1939). In response, the Law Society of Upper Canada (LSUC) has developed online practice resources including: the real estate practice portal; residential real estate transactions practice guidelines; real estate practice guide; and fraud prevention and money laundering reference materials. The title insurers have built fraud prevention questions and strategies into the policy application process, increased education and training opportunities to clients, and offered current awareness and practice alert services. In addition, Stewart Title now offers real estate file management software called Legal-STEPS in order to assist examining counsel, provide quality control, and reduce risk. The Ministry of Government Services has implemented its Real Estate Fraud Prevention Plan.

The goal of this book is to provide lawyers and law clerks with the information and the tools to practise safe title searching and conveyancing.

FEUDAL BEGINNINGS

> *The house of everyone is to him as his castle and fortress....*
>
> Sir Edward Coke, *Semayne's Case*, 5 Rep. 32b

Nearly 1,000 years ago, following the Norman victory at the Battle of Hastings in 1066, William the Conqueror's armies swept over England. The Norman

Conquest brought with it the French tenurial or feudal system of land holding. This system was based on the underlying principle that all land was held or owned by the Crown, and that individual citizens or property owners could only acquire specific rights with respect to the use and enjoyment of land in return for feudal services, often military in nature. Should a tenant or landowner not fulfil military, agricultural, or other required services to the satisfaction of the King, then the land would revert to the Crown, the residual owner, by a process of law called "escheat". To this day, in Canada, individuals do not own the land itself; instead they own estates in land.

THE DOCTRINE OF ESTATES IN LAND

As the centuries passed, the rights and interests of individual owners to enjoy degrees of exclusive use and control over land, subject to underlying Crown ownership, became known as "estates" in land. In time, an individual owner's interests in and rights of possession over land were enhanced in law by the ability to transfer or convey rights in land freely, either by will or by deed. A process of history had set the stage for the development of basic common law principles respecting the ownership of real property.

CANADIAN CONSTITUTIONAL FRAMEWORK

The law of real property ownership and land registration systems and the records they contain are a reflection of Ontario's and Canada's past.

In Canada, the federal parliament and the provincial legislatures share constitutional and law or legislation making powers. Canada's constitutional structure of federal and provincial divisions of legislative powers or jurisdictions was first set out in ss. 91 and 92 of the *British North America Act, 1867* (U.K.), 30 & 31 Vict., c. 3, now renamed the *Constitution Act, 1867*. The current federal and provincial division of legislative powers along with the *Canadian Charter of Rights and Freedoms* and the domestic amending formula comprise the *Canada Act, 1982* (U.K.), 1982, c. 11, now referred to as the *Constitution Act, 1982*. The federal government retains powers over such things as national parks and sites, "Indians, and Lands reserved for the Indians", harbours and airports, interprovincial roads and waterways, military lands, penitentiaries, some lighthouses and federally owned properties (*Constitution Act, 1867*, s. 91). Federal legislation includes the *Federal Real Property and Federal Immovables Act*, S.C. 1991, c. 50, which governs most dealings with federally owned lands. This Act modernized federal conveyancing practices by replacing the conveyancing regime under the earlier *Public Lands Grants Act*, R.S.C. 1985, c. P-30, the *Public Works Act*, R.S.C. 1985, c. P-38, and the *Surplus Crown Assets Act*, R.S.C. 1985, c. S-27 (now personal property only), and by removing the traditional requirement of letters patent for the transfer of federal Crown lands. In addition, federal legislation includes: the *Indian Act*, R.S.C. 1985, c. I-5; the *Indian Oil and Gas Act*, R.S.C. 1985, c. I-7; the *Canadian Environmental Assessment Act*, S.C. 1992 c. 37; the *Harbour Commissions Act*, R.S.C. 1985, c. H-1; *Heritage Railway Stations Protection Act*, R.S.C. 1985, c. 52 (4th Supp.); the *National Capital Act*, R.S.C. 1985, c. N-4; the *Canada National Parks Act*, S.C. 2000, c. 32; the *Historic Sites and Monuments Act*, R.S.C. 1985, c. H-4; the *Canada Lands Surveys Act*, R.S.C. 1985, c. L-6; the *Navigable Waters Protection Act*, R.S.C. 1985, c. N-22; the *Fisheries Act*, R.S.C. 1985, c. F-14; the *Criminal Code*, R.S.C. 1985, c. C-46; the *Proceeds of Crime (Money Laundering) and Terrorist Financing Act*, S.C. 2000, c. 17; and a multitude of other statutes that regulate the use and ownership of federally controlled lands and jurisdictions (*e.g.*, a national harbour, such as Toronto Harbour or a federal historic canal such as the Trent-Severn Waterway).

Provincial legislative jurisdiction is set out in s. 92 as being the right to pass laws regulating property and civil rights in the province and generally all matters of a merely local or private nature. Hence, the province legislates on real property ownership rights and has passed hundreds of statutes that in some way affect the use and ownership of land in Ontario. Title searching, land registration, and conveyancing in Ontario involve primarily provincial legislation; however, both federal and provincial legislation are often relevant to a specific property. As well, a person buying a cottage with docks and a boathouse on the Trent Severn Waterway Ontario may be affected by two systems of land registration, the Registry system governed by the *Registry Act*, R.S.O. 1990, c. R.20, and the Land Titles system governed by the *Land Titles Act*, R.S.O. 1990, c. L.5. The *Land Registration Reform Act*, R.S.O. 1990, c. L.4 has for the most part now modernized, automated, and integrated the two systems into one electronic land registration system.

A specific property in Ontario is frequently affected by both federal and provincial legislation. For example, a person buying a cottage with docks and boathouses on the Trent Severn Waterway which is a historic canal under the federal *Department of Transport Act*'s Historic Canal Regulations, SOR/93-220 may need to consider permit requirements under the Historic Canal Regulations (Parks Canada), the *Fisheries Act* if fish habitat is affected, the *Canadian Environmental Protection Act* if the shoreline is designated as a federal environmentally sensitive area, and if navigation is affected, the Canadian Coast Guard. From a provincial perspective, a purchaser might consider the need for approvals and permits from the Ministry of Natural Resources under the *Public Lands Act*, R.S.O. 1990, c. P.43, from the Ministry of Environment or the local Health Unit if the boathouse hooks up to a septic system or contains a residential unit, and of course from the municipality for building permits and zoning compliance. If the construction or the use of the boathouse might affect water quality, then additional permits and approvals under the *Ontario Water Resources Act*, R.S.O.

1990, c. O.40 and the *Lakes and Rivers Improvement Act*, R.S.O. 1990, c. L.3 may be required. When the boathouse or dock construction involves the removal of topsoil from Crown land, for example, the Crown shoreline allowance or bed of navigable water, then the *Aggregate Resources Act*, R.S.O. 1990, c. A.8 regulations require permits.

The *Constitutional Act, 1791*, 31 Geo. III, c. 31 gave birth to the provinces of Upper Canada (later Ontario) and Lower Canada (later part of Quebec). Upper Canada immediately established a legislature and, on October 15, 1792, passed its first statute, the *Property and Civil Rights Act*, Upper Canada, 1792, c. 1 (now R.S.O. 1990, c. P.29), which made English civil law the basic land law for what is now called the Province of Ontario.

Title to the land comprising the Province of Ontario today was originally claimed by the Crown in the right of Canada and later the Crown in either the right of Canada or the right of Ontario. Settlers who arrived in the late 18th century were issued Crown grants called Crown patents by the province under what is now the *Public Lands Act*. The Crown patent generally involved one or two, usually 100-acre or 200-acre, farm lots and retained timber and mineral rights as well as concession road and shoreline allowances. As a condition of receiving the Crown patent, the settler was required to clear a stated number of acres and build a shelter. Where no original Crown patent was issued for a piece of land, no private ownership can exist in law, even today.

FIRST NATIONS

In Ontario, as in Canada, ownership of land is always subject to current as well as historical Crown rights and, not to be forgotten, conflicting Crown obligations. For example, the relationship between "conquest" and "treaty" is becoming increasingly complex in Canada. How do these French-English concepts and procedures — and by 1760, these had become very different — relate to pre-existing Aboriginal law and to the land claims, Aboriginal rights, and treaty rights of First Nations? Much of southern Ontario in 1795 had been occupied by Ojibwa peoples who had moved south from the Algoma region in the late 1600s. What was "Huronia" to the French in the 1630s was conquered in 1648–1650 by the Iroquois, who then, 50 years later, lost two battles with Ojibwa forces near Southampton and Nottawasaga Bay. Had southern Ontario become Ojibwa by "conquest", or did different Nations still share the use of much of this land?

Constitutional Framework

In 1795, the British thought that the Ojibwa were the occupants and users of southern Ontario, and, although Britain claimed Crown rights to what became Canada, it also recognized, after the *Royal Proclamation of 1763*, R.S.C. 1985,

App. II, No. 1, that the First Nations were self-governing peoples with rights of occupancy and use, including Aboriginal title and Aboriginal rights recognized at common law. The British generally followed the practice of negotiating treaties with the different First Nations, increasingly for large blocks of land, before their officials surveyed or conveyed the land in Crown deeds or patents to the first Euro-American organized settlers. Section 35(1) of the *Constitution Act, 1982* constitutionalized both Aboriginal rights and title as well as treaty rights existing (not surrendered or extinguished by federal legislation as of April 17, 1982). Provincial legislation such as the *Registry Act* and the *Land Titles Act* and provincial Crown patents do not extinguish Aboriginal title or rights (*Delgamuukw v. British Columbia*, [1997] S.C.J. No. 108 (S.C.C.)). Since 1982, federal and provincial governments may infringe Aboriginal title and rights only when there is a substantive and compelling legislative need to balance the interests of the Canadian community as a whole. In addition, the Crown must act honourably and meet its fiduciary duties to Aboriginal peoples; infringe as little as necessary; participate in good faith in meaningful consultation, for example, in an environmental assessment of mining or development projects; and fulfil its duty to accommodate Aboriginal interests, including environmental protection concerns. Compensation may substitute for accommodation where accommodation is impractical (*Delgamuukw* and *R. v. Sparrow*, [1990] S.C.J. No. 49 (S.C.C.)). Refer to Chapter 2 and Appendix 5 for references to online sources for Aboriginal claims, including current claim status and mapping resources.

Difficult questions and conflicting perspectives remain. Did the treaties extinguish First Nations' rights to hunt, trap, fish, gather berries, or camp seasonally on what had become privately owned land? Do First Nations retain rights to hunt and fish "out-of-season" for commercial profit? Might First Nations harvest trees in the national and provincial parks, or elsewhere where the government has given a licence to a lumber company? Are First Nations bound by conservation laws? What is a First Nations' historical or sacred site, and who may interpret these sites in provincial parks? Are there continuing rights of private ownership once a court decision in a land claims case throws doubt on the existence of original Crown ownership as confirmed by a particular treaty, or in the absence of a treaty? These, and most issues relating to Canadian-First Nations relations, flow directly from differing conceptions of land-use and ownership.

Aboriginal Title and Rights and Comprehensive Land Claims

Aboriginal title is a proprietary right to the land itself whereas Aboriginal rights relate to activities such as hunting and fishing based on practices, customs, and traditions that are not linked to a specific location (*Delgamuukw*). Aboriginal title is a unique, communal title (*i.e., sui generis*) affecting surface and subsurface rights that give an Aboriginal group the right to use land for a variety of purposes that do not need to be based on distinctive Aboriginal practices and traditions. Aboriginal title remains subject to the inherent limitation that the land cannot be used in a manner that is irreconcilable with the group's original use and attachment to the land (*Delgamuukw*). Aboriginal title is communal and inalienable, although it can be surrendered to the Crown; it does not follow traditional real property rules. Communal decisions govern Aboriginal title. It is not based on Treaty rights. Aboriginal title is a burden which crystallized at the time sovereignty was asserted on the Crown's underlying title. It is dependent on exclusive possession at the time sovereignty was asserted and requires continuity between present and pre-sovereignty occupation. Aboriginal title or rights claims are based on inherit rights independent of government, legislation, or even sovereignty (see discussions in *Delgamuukw* and the *Mabo v. Queensland (No. 2)*, [1992] 5 C.N.L.R. 1 at 175 case in Australia); they may also be referred to as comprehensive title claims.

Treaty Rights and Specific Land Claims

The majority of land in Ontario is subject to treaties between First Nations and the Crown. Treaties exchanged land for reserves, treaty annuities, and off-reserve rights such as hunting, fishing and gathering rights. A land claim based on the non-fulfilment of a treaty obligation may be referred to as a specific land claim or a treaty land entitlement (TLE). A treaty land entitlement claim may address the failure to provide promised reserve lands, the accuracy of original reserve surveys and boundaries, Crown misadministration of reserve land and band funds, illegal sale of reserve lands without surrender, illegal occupation, or other treaty and *Indian Act*-related issues. Some claims challenge the fundamental validity of a First Nations treaty whereas others assert that the Crown has not met its fiduciary duties in accordance with the legal principle of "honour of the Crown".

Reserve Lands

The *Indian Act* provides that the Government of Canada hold title to reserve lands for the use and benefit of Indians (s. 18(1)). The Reserve Land Register records band certificates of possession and occupancy. The band council allocates reserve lands to band members; reserve land is exempt from taxation. The Minister of the Department of Indian and Northern Affairs may issue occupation permits to non-band members for up to a year and with the band council's consent for more than a year (s. 28). If a band wishes to sell or lease land to non-members, it must first surrender the land to the Crown. Any conveyance that does not follow *Indian Act* requirements is void.

The *First Nations Certainty of Land Title Act* (Bill C-63)

The *First Nations Certainty of Land Title Act* (Bill C-63) amends the *First Nations Commercial and Industrial Development Act*, S.C. 2005, c. 53 by establishing a land titles registration system for on-reserve commercial real estate developments and allowing bands to transfer property rights to non-Aboriginals. The new land registration system would allow non-Aboriginal third parties to register their legal interests and thereby facilitate commercial development and generate revenue, including tax revenue. The Act is optional legislation. A First Nation must request the Act's application by Band Council Resolution identifying a specific project and parcel of reserve land. In addition, the provincial government must agree to provide land registration administration and enforcement services on behalf of the federal government.

Aboriginal Rights in the Canadian Context

The balancing and reconciliation of Aboriginal rights and title with the competing interests of the Canadian community as a whole will continue as a dynamic, essential process in the management of real property rights and usage. Case law suggests, in theory, that consultation and negotiation are the best methods for determining and accommodating Aboriginal rights, Aboriginal title, and treaty rights. In Canada, there are complex historical, legal, economic, and political reasons why land ownership by its contemporary residents is never absolute or even clear. Unresolved disputes that involve Aboriginal land claims, be they treaty claims, Aboriginal title claims, Aboriginal land rights claims, failure to consult, or duty to accommodate claims, may generate devastating human and economic consequences for all stakeholders. Recent events in Caledonia, Brantford, questions concerning the Haldimand Tract, and the *Chippewas of Sarnia Band v. Canada (Attorney General)*, [2000] O.J. No. 4804 (Ont. C.A.), are all reminders that Aboriginal claims are serious title concerns and can affect urban areas as well as recreational and northern properties. In the *Chippewas of Sarnia* case, the Court was asked to divest private owners of their homes and businesses. Indian and Northern Affairs policy as of 2009 states on its website that Canada will not take away privately owned land to settle claims. Uncertainty in Aboriginal title, rights, and treaty rights may give rise to overlapping and conflicting claims. It is as essential as it is difficult to investigate, to the fullest extent possible, the nature of Aboriginal land claims that may affect a particular property.

Refer to Chapter 14 for off-title searches that address Aboriginal title, rights, treaty claims, and reserve lands. As well, Chapter 2 contains references for mapping resources that address Aboriginal treaties and claims in Ontario and Canada. Internet references for Aboriginal treaty locations and claims, including status of claim, are included in Appendix 5.

CROWN GRANTS AND LETTERS PATENT

In Ontario today, the Crown in the right of Ontario or, less frequently, in the right of Canada, retains residual ownership of land. As a condition of the existence of any privately owned estate in land, the Crown must first formally convey land to an individual by way of Crown patent or grant. Crown patents often contain reservations for timber and mineral rights, native rights such as hunting, fishing and gathering, road, beach and shoreline allowances, and navigable waters. Individuals may, subject to Crown rights, purchase, mortgage, and sell various estates in land, such as freehold (equity ownership) and leasehold estates. The Crown right of escheat remains and may be exercised by way of expropriation or, for example, by forfeiture of land for non-payment of taxes or when a property owner dies intestate without heirs.

Unless the Crown patent expressly grants the bed of navigable water or streams bordering or passing through a parcel of land, title to the bed or streams does not pass.

In order to ascertain the extent of title to any property, it is essential to review the Crown grant. Patents were not registered on title prior to the 1960s. Since 1991, the federal government no longer registers Letters Patent but instead registers transfers under the *Federal Real Property and Federal Immovables Act*. Crown patents should be carefully reviewed, particularly for cottage, mining, timber, rural, agricultural, undeveloped land, and lands bordering on water. The *Public Lands Act* has cancelled or changed many of the original reservations in Crown grants. Chapter 9 reviews reservations in Crown grants and the effect of the *Public Lands Act*. Appendix 5 provides references for obtaining Crown patents.

For a review of the law on how Crown patents affect the ownership of land and Aboriginal title and treaty rights in Ontario, refer to the Ontario Court of Appeal decision in *Chippewas of Sarnia Band v. Canada (Attorney General)*.

ESTATES IN LAND

It is essential to identify accurately an owner's exact interest or "estate" in land. An owner's interest in land is commonly referred to as ownership of or title to land. A search of title is completed in order to document an owner's interest in land as well as any restrictions and encumbrances, such as easements, restrictive covenants, liens, and mortgages which may be registered against the land.

The two basic categories of land ownership are freehold title and leasehold title. A freehold title or estate is an estate for an uncertain or indefinite duration. Fee simple estates and life estates are examples of freehold estates. A leasehold estate, which may also be purchased, is an estate for a certain or specified duration. For example, fixed-term leases and periodic tenancies (week to week, month to month, or year to year) are leasehold estates. Both freehold and leasehold estates or titles may be purchased, mortgaged, or leased.

Estates in Fee Simple (Allodial Title)

An estate in fee simple is the most comprehensive ownership right in land available in Ontario. An estate in fee simple is also referred to as allodial or ultimate title. An estate in fee simple is for an uncertain period of time and may, in theory, continue forever. In documentation, it may also be described by the terms "grant absolutely or grant to a person and his or her heirs forever or in perpetuity". In the Land Titles system, an estate in fee simple is called an absolute title. An estate in fee simple may be transferred by will, deed, gift, possession, or by operation of law. Most properties are owned in fee simple, although leasehold ownership is common in urban centres.

Although less common, conditional and determinable fee simple estates also exist. A conditional fee simple estate places a condition on the right to inherit or receive land, such as: "the family cottage will be granted to Ruth on condition that she earn a Masters in Real Property or Environmental Law". If Ruth does not succeed, the cottage will revert to its original owner (the reversionary interest) or pass on to a different person referred to as a remainder (the remainder interest). A determinable fee simple estate automatically terminates on the occurrence of a prearranged event, such as: "Naomi's ownership of the family farm will terminate should the farm cease to be used as a family farm". The farm would then revert to the previous grantor. Conditional and determinable fee simples may be created by *inter vivos* grant/transfer but are usually created by will.

Fee tails are an extinct form of fee simple estate ownership that could be inherited only by male persons. In Ontario, fee tails were abolished and converted to fee simple estates as recently as May 27, 1956. They were abolished in England in the 1920s.

Life Estates

An owner of land may grant the use and enjoyment of the land to a person for the duration of that person's life, or the life of some other designated person. This arrangement is referred to as a life estate. When the term is for the life of a named person other than the life tenant, the estate is called a life estate *pur autre vie*. Life estates are most often granted to spouses or heirs. When the life tenant dies, the life estate terminates and exclusive possession either reverts to the original grantor of the life estate or passes on to a different person or to a series of different persons referred to as a remainder(s). A life estate may be leased, mortgaged or transferred, but only for a period not exceeding the uncertain lifespan of the life tenant. Life estates may be created by will or by deed. They are usually non-arm's-length transactions and may carry similar risks of undue influence, duress, and even fraud as do grants of powers of attorney and wills.

Leasehold Estates

A leasehold estate provides a tenant or lessee with the right of exclusive possession over a property for a certain period, being the term of the lease. Leases and notices of lease may be registered in the Registry system, whereas in Land Titles longer term leases may be registered as a leasehold title in a separate register. Registered leases usually relate to commercial properties as residential leases are usually for a shorter term and often do not require registration to protect the interests of the tenant. When the lease expires, exclusive possession reverts to the fee simple estate owner. Periodic tenancies, which run from year to year, from month to month, or from week to week, are also leasehold estates.

Servitudes and Equitable Interests in Land

Freehold and leasehold estates comprise legal title. Other interests that affect land are referred to as equitable interests. Equitable interests that may be enforced against the owners of legal title include vendors' and purchasers' liens, mortgages, charges and liens, options and rights of first refusal, restrictive covenants, and easements and rights of way. Easements and restrictive covenants are extremely important real property interests. Chapter 9 reviews the extensive law and procedure concerning easements, restrictions, and access to land, including roads.

Methods of Alienation

Land may be transferred or alienated during life (*inter vivos* grant) or on death (testamentary grant). Land may be transferred by deed, by gift, by court order, by possession, by abandonment such as with an easement, or by operation of law. It may also be created through natural processes such as accretion, the slow, imperceptible build-up of a shoreline or delta, or lost through erosion or permanent flooding. A conveyancer must identify all owners, estates, and equitable interests which relate to the title of a particular property in preparation for purchasing, mortgaging, or leasing land.

Methods of Ownership

An individual may own or hold land in sole ownership, in trust ownership, or in "to uses" ownership. Land may be held in communal title, such as with Aboriginal title. Land may also be held in concurrent ownership, where an individual owns land together with one or more persons at the same time. Forms of concurrent ownership include joint tenancy with right of survivorship, tenancy in common, partnership, corporate, condominium, cooperative, time-share ownership, life lease, or fractional (interval ownership). Chapter 5 contains in-depth information on the methods of ownership and how they affect documentation and registration. Chapter 7 reviews various condominium ownership structures, and newer forms of concurrent ownership such as life lease ownership, and fractional (interval) share ownership including condominium/apartment hotel structures.

Title by Prescription/Adverse Possession

Where land is registered under the Registry system, title may also be acquired by prescription, often called adverse possession, under the *Real Property Limitations Act*, R.S.O. 1990, c. L.15, except in the case of road allowances, shoreline allowances, highways, and vacant land where the freehold is vested in the Crown or in the municipality.

If the occupant of the land can produce evidence by way of a declaration that he or she has been in possession and occupation of the land for ten years or more prior to the date of closing the transaction, that his or her possession has been undisturbed throughout the ten-year period by any claim and that he or she has made no acknowledgment in writing to any person of that person's right to the land, then the occupant can claim possessory title to the land. The declaration respecting possession should be deposited on title. Title by adverse possession is acquired by a negative right rather than a positive right. The registered owner loses his or her right to object to the trespasser's occupation after a time set by the *Real Property Limitations Act*. Adverse possession cases are difficult to predict; they turn on individual facts and what appear to be similar facts may produce different results. The Ontario Court of Appeal in *Elliot v. Woodstock Agricultural Society*, [2008] O.J. No. 3708 (Ont. C.A.) reviews the case law on adverse possession and how it affects ownership in Ontario. The Court held that holding land for future development is a current use that can rebut claims of adverse possession. Also, see *Bradford Investments (1963) Ltd. v. Fama*, [2005] O.J. No. 3258 (Ont. S.C.J.) for a comprehensive review of the case law on adverse possession and a different result on similar facts.

The acquisition of title by adverse possession is prohibited under the Land Titles system. However, land which has been transferred from Registry into Land Titles by administrative conversion, referred to as Land Titles Conversion Qualified (LTCQ) title, may bring with it mature adverse possession entitlements where there has been ten years of use prior to the conversion; no new possessory rights can be acquired once in Land Titles. However, in Land Titles, the fact that there is no guarantee as to the extent of land means that legal boundaries may be uncertain, particularly when owners have not obtained up-to-date surveys. The absence of possessory rights may increase the need for a survey to reconcile purchaser expectations with original legal boundaries. See Chapter 3 for a more in-depth review of the law of adverse possession in the Registry system and Chapter 8 for how mature possessory rights are dealt with when Registry land is transferred into Land Titles.

Easements by Prescription

Where land is registered under the Registry system, a possessory easement called an easement by prescription may be acquired after 20 years under s. 31 of the *Real Property Limitations Act* except in the case of road allowances, shoreline allowances, highways and vacant land where the freehold is vested in the Crown or in the municipality. Section 31 deems an easement by prescription to be an absolute right after 40 years of continuous use. Where a right of way or other easement has been enjoyed by a trespasser for 20 years or more continuously, without interruption, without the owner's consent or permission, without agreement in writing, and in good faith, the trespasser acquires title by possession, also called title by prescription.

Adverse possession and easements by prescription are unique to the Registry system. The acquisition of title by prescription is prohibited under the Land Titles system. However, land which has been transferred from Registry into Land Titles by administrative conversion, referred to as Land Titles Conversion Qualified title, may bring with it mature easement by prescription entitlements where there has been 20 years of use prior to the conversion; no new prescriptive rights can be acquired once in Land Titles. Chapter 9 has more on easements by prescription.

Title by Accretion

Water lines have changed considerably since the original Crown surveys were drawn. You may find that the 66-foot road allowance (shoreline allowance) along the shoreline of a lake reserved in the original Crown grant is now under water. Where land is extended beyond the shore by gradual and imperceptible retirement of water, the land so extended belongs to the owner of the adjoining land, be it the Crown or a private owner. If the extension is sudden and perceptible, it vests in the Crown. Alternatively, where water gradually encroaches on land, such land belongs to the owner of the shore between the low and high water marks. The water marks are established by an Ontario land surveyor.

REGISTRATION OF LAND OWNERSHIP

Rules, regulations and customs respecting the ownership of land differ greatly among nations, across cultures, and throughout history. Yet, the association of land ownership to wealth, status, power, political and economic structures, and the sense of personal identity represents a recurring theme in the affairs of humankind. Conflict and disagreement over ownership and boundaries of land may give rise to feuds and violent outbursts between neighbours in a suburban environment, or to wars of aggression on a global scale. As a result of the inherent social and economic importance of land ownership, detailed laws regulating the ownership of real property develop early in any legal system.

Ownership of real property may be defined as a collection of rights and responsibilities over the use and enjoyment of land and everything annexed to land (fixtures), *e.g.*, buildings and crops, which are protected by law, and enforceable against other persons. Fundamental real property rights include the right to use, possess and manage land, the right to exclude others from land, the right to transfer or alienate land during life or on death, and the right to the income from and the capital in land.

Modern common law jurisdictions require an owner of real property or land to register evidence of his or her title in a land registration system as a condition of being able to enforce private property rights against other persons with conflicting claims. Land registration systems provide a written framework for recording land ownership rights and for resolving disputes, competing claims, and uncertainties respecting ownership of real property.

In theory, the age-old common problem of two or more persons claiming conflicting rights to the same parcel of land might be settled in different ways. The law might favour the claimant with current or long-standing possession, or instead support the claimant who can document the earliest legal right, on a first come, first serve basis. Historically, the use of superior physical force created legal entitlement to land. Indeed, conquest, albeit indirectly, brought us the feudal system and many of our real property and land registration principles.

Modern legal systems prefer to use some form of land registration system as a means of settling priorities between competing claimants and resolving competing claims. Registration systems work on two basic legal premises. First, an owner of land must register evidence of ownership in a government regulated registration system in order to enforce property rights against other members of the community. Second, the order or sequence of registration of documents representing interests in land determines the priority of multiple or competing claims. Generally, the first person to register obtains a superior right to land over a person who registers an interest on a subsequent date. For example, a first mortgage will have an earlier registration time and date than a second or third mortgage. There are many exceptions to the priority of registration rule and these exceptions or qualifiers give rise to what is referred to as off-title inquiries, or rights that do not need to be registered in order to affect an owner's title.

The federal government maintains land registration records for federally controlled lands such as national parks and historic sites and all provincial governments maintain land registration records for lands within provincial boundaries. Throughout Canada, land registration systems create organized, accessible public records of ownership interests in land.

ONTARIO'S LAND REGISTRATION SYSTEMS

Currently, Ontario has two land registration systems which record registered documents/instruments that create or affect ownership rights in land: the Registry system and the Land Titles system. Information in Ontario's land registration records is public. The Registry system is governed by the *Registry Act* originally enacted in 1795. It is the older and less efficient of the two systems and requires a 40-year search and analysis of past title registrations each time a property is transferred. The Land Titles system was established in 1885 by the *Land Titles Act*. This system creates an up-to-date title register which mirrors and guarantees all current interests and instruments (registered documents) pertaining to the ownership of a parcel of land. Past registered instruments, which are no longer effective, are either ruled out or deleted from the current property register. Subject to the numerous exceptions set out in the *Land Titles Act* and other statutes, a conveyancer completes a search of current registrations listed on the present government guaranteed title register; however, it is also necessary to examine deleted or non-current documents for exceptions such as fraud, *Planning Act* violations, and escheats to the Crown.

Ontario's historical development of two separate land registration systems, based on paper records, was inefficient both legally and in terms of modern technology. As early as 1833, the Law Reform Commission and government studies in England and Ontario recommended that Ontario convert to a single government guaranteed land registration system similar to Ontario's Land Titles system. Since the late 1970s, the Province of Ontario's Land Registration Information System, known as POLARIS, now in partnership with Teranet Inc., has been in the process of: (1) converting all Registry system land to Land Titles; (2) automating all existing Registry and Land Titles paper records and registration procedures; and (3) building digitized or computer-generated maps for all land titles in the province. This fundamental change in both the law and the procedures involved in land records, ownership registration and title searching is driven by the *Land Registration Reform Act*.

The Ontario government, in partnership with Teranet Inc., has implemented POLARIS, in stages, throughout the province. As part of the computerization of land records and the conversion of land to the Land Titles system, Teranet has developed a computerized online title search and electronic land registration system called ELRS. ELRS, which was previously called e-reg, is based on a Windows-based software product called "Teraview". The Teraview gateway, allows execution searches (WritSearch), title searches, and document creation and registration (ELRS) to be completed online from any location, using a computer with Internet capacity. At the time of writing, over 95 per cent of all registrations are electronic and in Land Titles. Some properties have been automated, although they were left in various forms of Registry system. More than 95 per cent of searches are completed online using fax and courier back-up for delivery of difficult to scan records such as plans.

THE REGISTRY SYSTEM

The *Registry Act*, enacted in 1795, established the Registry system in Ontario. This system, originally developed in England, provides a means of registering and storing land ownership documents in a public office. The Registry system records documents evidencing title interests, according to a subdivision or a township lot on a register called the abstract index. The Registry system does not provide a statement of ownership or a government guarantee of title. In effect, Registry is simply a register or inventory of documents, not a register of ownership or title.

The legal effectiveness of documents or instruments recorded in Registry is in no way assured by the act of registration. Instead, lawyers must examine and assess all registered documents in order to give an opinion on the marketability of title to a purchaser or mortgagee. Each time a property is conveyed or mortgaged, a 40-year search of title is completed and a lawyer's written opinion on title is issued to the client. Title insurance is available for all registration systems as an alternative or a supplement for some but not all aspects of title.

Registry offices and Registry lands were found in those parts of Ontario that were settled early. Registry was found in the counties in the southern part of the province, particularly along early transportation routes, for example, the Great Lakes and the Ottawa, Thames, and Trent-Severn rivers. Registry land is less common in more northern districts and rarely reaches beyond traditional cottage country.

Regulation 992, R.R.O. 1990, under the *Registry Act*, provides that the land "registrar of a registry division to which a national park or Indian reserve is annexed shall keep an index book ... to be called the 'Canada Lands Index' in which he or she shall record plans, descriptions", orders and a record of subsequent dealings (s. 2). The Regulation includes a schedule listing the national parks and Indian reserves associated with specific Registry offices. For example, the Registry office for Bruce (No. 3) contains Flower Pot Island, part of Georgian Bay Islands National Park, and Essex (No. 12) contains Point Pelee National Park. Simcoe (No. 51) includes the Indian reserves of Rama No. 32, Christian Island, and Christian Islands No. 30. Plans of public lands under the *Canada Lands Surveys Act*, plans and descriptions of land under the *Navigable Waters Protection Act*, R.S.C.

1985, c. N-22, plans under the *Public Transportation and Highway Improvement Act*, R.S.O. 1990, c. P.50, and orders of the Governor-in-Council that transfer jurisdiction and control of land from the Government of Canada to the Government of Ontario are found in the Canada Lands Index.

Registry abstract books were originally indexed by township, also referred to as concession or farm, lot. Whenever a Crown patent was issued, the registrar would open a new page in a township abstract or index book and enter notice of the patent and the person receiving the patent at the top of the township lot page. Subsequent documents affecting the ownership of the lot were registered in chronological order by registration date. Registry documents were not restricted by statute as to kind or number, and were frequently unpredictable and ambiguous in nature. In addition, Registry instruments were not checked for legal validity or content, merely form and signing and description requirements, as part of the registration process.

Registered "metes and bounds" descriptions, made up of bearings and distances referenced to what were at the time landmarks, such as "the old elm tree", were subject to later acquired possessory title (*e.g.*, adverse possession after ten years of occupation, and easements by prescription (possession) after 20 years of continuous visible use). The Registry system was in need of improvement long before it found its way to Upper Canada.

THE LAND TITLES SYSTEM

In 1885, the *Land Titles Act* introduced the Land Titles system into Ontario. Land patented after 1885 was entered in Land Titles offices whenever Registry was not available. As a result, areas that were settled later, specifically most of the northern districts, are organized into Land Titles offices. Since 1973, all new subdivision and condominium developments have been required by law to be either registered in or transferred into the Land Titles system, whenever a Land Titles office existed in the region of the new development. Since the early 1980s, the POLARIS land registration reform initiatives have focused on converting Registry lands into the more modern and streamlined, and easier to automate Land Titles system. Most land is now in Land Titles, apart from areas that were left in Registry for various reasons and a few areas which are scheduled for conversion in the near future.

Land Titles is a form of "Torrens" or government guaranteed land registration system. The Torrens system — modelled on the International Ships' Registry — was originally designed in Australia by Sir Robert Torrens, next adopted in parts of England, and then established in British Columbia, followed by Canada's western provinces and Ontario. In a Torrens system, the title register mirrors currently active interests that affect a particular parcel of land, subject to numerous statutory exceptions referred to as qualifiers. The automation of Land Titles properties and the conversion of Registry properties to Land Titles has resulted in a variety of title categories that are subject to different legal qualifiers and as a result require different searching practices. Former no longer active interests, such as discharged liens and charges and transfers to previous owners, are cancelled and deleted, although they are still reviewed for qualifiers, fraud risk indicators, and title insurance policy application search requirements. The *Land Titles Act* and *Land Registration Reform Act* and regulations strictly regulate the form and number of all paper and electronic instruments or documents acceptable for registration. All registrations that comprise a title or parcel register are carefully checked for form and legal validity. Unlike Registry, the title register is therefore a register of title, guaranteed by the provincial government's Land Titles Assurance Fund, subject to statutory exceptions (qualifiers) called "overriding interests".

Each Land Titles property is indexed by a parcel number and allocated a separate parcel register. Parcel descriptions are usually based on registered reference, subdivision, or condominium plans. Unlike Registry, adverse possession and easements by prescription are prohibited in Land Titles, except for mature possessory claims in properties that have been converted from Registry to Land Titles and called LTCQ titles. Generally, in Land Titles, legal descriptions of land are simpler, usually illustrated by a Reference or registered plan, and less open to dispute than in Registry.

National parks and Indian reserves are recorded differently in Land Titles. Where a plan, description, or order relates to land that is the whole or part of a national park or Indian reserve and the land is registered under the *Land Titles Act* with Her Majesty in the right of Canada as the registered owner, the document shall be recorded in the Land Titles parcel register for the land.

LAND REGISTRATION REFORM

The historical and existing Registry and Land Titles systems were regional paper-based land registration and records management systems. Two land registration systems in one province created costly public and private resource duplication and a legal complexity that increased the risk of error.

Since the 1970s, Ontario has been involved in a massive land registration reform initiative called the Province of Ontario Land Registration Information System and referred to as POLARIS. The main goals of land registration reform in Ontario are to:

1. simplify conveyancing law and procedure;

2. standardize law, terminology, and procedure;

3. convert to one, automated Land Titles system;

4. reduce the costs of conveyancing;

5. save space;

6. computerize title and mapping information;

7. automate title searching and execution searching;

8. automate document creation and registration services; and

9. provide centralized, online title searching, execution searching, and registration services for land anywhere in Ontario.

POLARIS's long-range goal is to integrate fully all, not just title, land-related information and databases into one centralized, automated, online land information and mapping system. Today, most land-related documents are created, registered, stored, and searched electronically in a Land Titles system.

POLARIS: THE PROVINCE OF ONTARIO LAND REGISTRATION INFORMATION SYSTEM

Unprecedented growth in land transactions since the 1950s, coupled with the inability of land registration offices to keep up with modern technology, resulted in land records access and storage problems. In 1971, the Ontario Law Reform Commission recommended the conversion of all Registry system lands into Land Titles and the automation of all land ownership into one Land Titles or Torrens registration system. The Commission also recommended microfilm instead of paper records and the creation of province-wide, coordinate-based, computer-generated, digital, property maps.

By 1980, following a 1979 Ministry of Consumer and Commercial Relations Concepts Report, POLARIS was underway. By 1984, the *Land Registration Reform Act* was enacted to authorize POLARIS initiatives. The Oxford County Registry office at Woodstock was chosen as a test site for the automation of current records and the introduction of standardized documents. Following the successful completion of the Woodstock pilot project, the Middlesex County Registry office at London was selected in 1987 as the test site for a full Land Titles conversion combined with the automation of title and execution records. On April 1, 1985, standardized documents prescribed in the *Land Registration Reform Act* were implemented throughout the province.

In order to accelerate the POLARIS conversion, in 1991, the Ontario government, represented by the then Ministry of Consumer and Commercial Relations, entered into an equal partnership called "Teranet" with a private sector consortium representing computer, financial, legal, and project management expertise and resources. Teranet, under the POLARIS project, has since proceeded to automate land registration title and mapping records, convert Registry lands to Land Titles, and develop an online remote access title and execution searching and electronic land registration system called ELRS, formerly e-reg, and referred to as "Teraview". Today, Teranet Inc., in partnership with the Ministry of Government Services, has implemented the electronic land registration system throughout almost all of Ontario; although some automated areas have been left in Registry.

Teranet is in the process of moving the remaining registry offices from optional to mandatory, bringing the final registry offices online, converting automated Registry to Land Titles, and maintaining and continuously fine-tuning ELRS, the electronic land registration product. ELRS is a mandatory, fully electronic or paperless registration system that allows documents in electronic format with digital signatures to be created and registered online from a remote location, such as a lawyer's office. ELRS has replaced attendance for searching, closing, and registration at a Registry office. Teranet maintains a current, proposed roll-out schedule for the province-wide implementation of ELRS. The roll-out schedule is available on Teranet's website and is available in newsletters within the Teraview gateway. Mandatory electronic land registration started with a pilot project (beta-test) in 1999, in the Middlesex Land Registry Office (LRO) at London. Middlesex County was the first fully automated, mandatory, electronic search and registration district. Generally speaking, urban areas in southern Ontario were converted prior to less densely populated areas in northern Ontario.

Teranet Inc. has been designated by the Province as the sole service provider for electronic land registration and access to POLARIS. In 2014, the Province of Ontario is contractually scheduled to decide whether to continue with an exclusive service provider model or open the field to multiple providers. Should the province decide to terminate the exclusive provider arrangement in 2014, Teranet's exclusive rights would continue to 2017.

PRESERVATION OF ONTARIO LAND REGISTRY RECORDS

As Teranet converted Registry to Land Titles and automation progressed throughout the province, the decision was made that the original historical records, with microfilm back-ups, were no longer required for commercial purposes. In March 1990, the Ministry of Culture and Communications published the *Report of the Advisory Committee on Land Records for Ontario* in which the committee recommended that historic land registration records be transferred to appropriate local/regional archival repositories. Sections 53(1), (2), and (3) of the *Registry Act*'s Forms and Records, R.R.O. 1990, Reg. 995 authorizes the land registrar, with the concurrence of the Archivist of Ontario, to transfer any Registry or Land Titles to the Archivist of Ontario.

The Ministry of Consumer and Commercial Relations, the Real Property Registration Branch, and the Archives of Ontario were responsible for preservation of records pursuant to a working agreement entitled "A Plan for Ontario's Pre-1955 Land Registration Records: Joint Approach to Preservation and Placement by Archives of Ontario and Real Property Registration Branch, Ministry of Consumer and Commercial Relations". Provincially "significant material" was received by the Archives of Ontario, records essential to the operation of Land Registry offices remained in Land Registry offices, and remaining registers and documents were dispersed to local archival repositories or heritage groups, where available. Records were microfilmed; many original documents were destroyed.

TITLE INQUIRIES

By law, only a lawyer has the right to give an opinion on title. A purchaser or mortgagee of land will receive a lawyer's opinion on the marketability of title, setting out the nature and quality of the land ownership as well as any liens, encumbrances or restrictions that limit the title. In order to formulate an opinion on title, a lawyer must first complete a series of title/ownership inquiries in order to identify all rights and interests, and responsibilities and restrictions that affect the use and enjoyment of a particular property. The three main categories of title inquiry with examples are as follows:

1. Title Search in the land registry office records for all registered documents, required under the *Registry Act* and *Land Titles Act*, that affect ownership of land, such as deeds, mortgages, easements, liens, restrictive covenants, and development agreements;

2. Surveyor's Real Property Report illustrating actual possession, boundary and description information, and extent of the property; and

3. Off-title rights and restrictions that affect title but are not required to be registered under the Registry or Land Titles systems, such as short-term leases in possession, zoning, work orders, tax arrears, building restrictions, provincial, federal, and municipal land-use restrictions, Crown Patent reservations, for example, shoreline allowances, environmental risks, Aboriginal title, rights, and treaty rights, and a multitude of others.

Letter inquiry and online searches regarding zoning, municipal taxes, utility bills, work orders, and numerous other forms of government regulation are completed (see Chapter 14). Surveys are obtained in order to establish boundaries, actual possession, easements, existence and compliance with restrictions, adverse Aboriginal claims, riparian rights, *etc*. Other inquiries arise out of terms in the agreement of purchase and sale, the expectations and future use plans of the purchaser, and the nature of the property, and the nature of the risk.

The purchaser's or mortgage lender's decision to purchase title insurance potentially alters title, survey, and off-title search requirements. Title insurance may act as an alternative to completing certain title inquiries or as an additional protection for potential title deficiencies, assuming the deal closes.

RESIDENTIAL REAL ESTATE TRANSACTIONS PRACTICE GUIDELINES

The LSUC has developed a set of recommended residential real estate practice guidelines which address the title search, the off-title inquiries, and the effect of title insurance coverage on title investigation; the guidelines are posted on the LSUC website.

The Title Search

Lawyers must personally review title searches and all documents that may affect a client's interests and retain search notes in the file. The lawyer must also review title with purchaser, borrower, or lender clients specifically including the effect of easements, restrictive covenants, and subdivision and other agreements on title. The lawyer must request deleted documents and review title for fraud risk indicators mentioned in the following section on fraud. Suspicious transactions patterns and transfer and mortgage values should be reported to the purchaser/borrower client, the lender if the lawyer is acting for the lender, and the title insurer. Most title insurance policy applications incorporate a series of questions which address these suspicious transactions and values patterns and automatically flag the application for follow-up and a fraud due diligence or underwriter review. Some solicitors, particularly in Registry, document their review of title by completing a solicitor's chain and/or abstract, whereas others simply review and initial the title searcher's notes.

Off-Title Inquiries

The lawyer must also personally review all off-title searches and reports and retain search records in the file. The LSUC lists the following due diligence standards for off-title inquiries:

> The lawyer should discuss with the client and obtain instructions from the client regarding the off title searches that may be appropriate or advisable in view of the nature of the property, the circumstances of the transaction, the terms of the agreement of purchase and sale and the consequences of not conducting those searches.

> Where title insurance is being used, the lawyer should be cognizant of:

- what off-title searches relevant to the client or transaction are not covered by title insurance and make appropriate searches or obtain waivers from the client; and

- the inter-related nature of the following issues:

deciding not to make certain off-title searches; allowing the requisition date to pass without the results of those searches being available; the timing of receiving a title insurance binder or commitment (usually after the requisition date has passed); and the policy of the selected title insurer regarding 'insure over' requests for adverse circumstances which emerge before closing notwithstanding the lack of a search.

In summary, in terms of title inquiries, a lawyer is personally responsible for the following:

1. deciding the nature and extent of the title search;

2. deciding, in consultation with the client, which off-title searches will be completed;

3. reviewing the impact of title insurance coverage on decisions as to the nature and extent of the title search and the off-title inquiries;

4. the review of all off-title search reports; and

5. the review of draft title insurance policy exclusions and exemptions.

FRAUD PREVENTION AND TITLE SEARCHING

The risk of title or mortgage fraud is a serious problem with devastating personal, professional, and business consequences for clients, real estate lawyers, and law clerks in Canada today. All persons involved in the legal transaction will fall under scrutiny in the criminal, as well as the subsequent LSUC and title insurer investigations.

The risk of fraud is not restricted to the larger urban centres. Identity theft, fraudulent powers of attorney, and fraudulent certified cheques are common examples of fraud in real estate transactions. Unfortunately, fraudsters are sophisticated, organized, and are continually constructing new frauds schemes; organized crime is involved. The Ministry of Government Services has launched its Real Estate Fraud Action Plan which includes: changes in law to protect existing owners; simplified procedures for homeowners who have been the victims of title or mortgage fraud; tightened security requirements for access to Ontario's electronic land registration system; the requirement that the registration of most transfers of ownership be digitally signed by two independent lawyers, one acting for the purchaser and one acting for the vendor; and strict new practice standards requiring the verification of client identity through multiple sources.

Title insurance coverage for fraud is available to clients. Lawyers must carry fraud coverage as part of their practice insurance.

Thorough title searching practices provide a key, proactive risk management tool for fraud avoidance. All title searches should include a request for and review of deleted documents in the electronic record; insurer search standards require deleted documents. Lawyers who review deleted documents may identify suspicious patterns of transfers, mortgages, and discharges of mortgage. Unusual values in the context of fair market value in recent, prior transfers and mortgages, revealed by the search of title, may raise red flags, and trigger additional investigation. In addition, title searches reveal personal and business information that relate to the identity, such as age and spousal status, of clients. This information is useful as part of the verification requirements for client identity.

LAW SOCIETY OF UPPER CANADA RULES OF PROFESSIONAL CONDUCT AND REAL ESTATE CONVEYANCING

Permitted Areas of Practice

Real estate conveyancing is not a permitted area of practice for independent paralegals.

Relationship to Employee and Delegation to Non-Lawyers: The Requirement for Direct Supervision

Lawyers are professionally responsible to clients for the legal services including the acts of non-lawyer staff and are responsible for directly supervising the non-lawyers in their practice. Lawyers must ensure that non-lawyer employees do not give legal advice (Rule 5.01(2)). Lawyers must ensure that non-lawyer employees identify themselves as non-lawyers (law clerks) when dealing with clients, the public, and government officials (Rule 5.01(2)).

Lawyers may delegate to a non-lawyer matters of routine conveyancing, such as the title search and off-title inquiries, draft statements of account, routine documents and registrations. However, Rule 5 of the LSUC Rules of Professional Conduct requires that a lawyer must not delegate to a non-lawyer the ultimate responsibility for the review of a title search report, or of a document before signing, or the review and signing of the letter of requisition, the review and signing of a title opinion, or the review and signing of a reporting letter to the client. In addition, Rule 5.01(5) states that a lawyer shall not permit a non-lawyer to provide advice to the client concerning title insurance, without supervision. Only lawyers are permitted to sign for completeness electronic documents that contain compliance with law statements (legal opinions and statements in lieu of supporting documentation). Only lawyers are authorized to sign for completeness electronic transfers on behalf of clients. Most transfers are governed by the two-lawyer rule and require both a purchaser's and a vendor's lawyer to sign for completeness. Law clerks may sign electronic documents for release and complete the document registration process.

Electronic Registration of Title Documents

Users of ELRS need both the authorization of the Director of Land Registration and a licensing agreement with Teranet. Applicants are carefully screened and must prove identity, financial resources (insurance coverage) adequate to compensate victims of fraud, and good character and qualifications (lawyer in good standing) appropriate to registering documents in ELRS.

Teraview electronic registration security access keys (PSPs) are encrypted for either lawyer or non-lawyer use. Lawyers and non-lawyer employees have separate, personalized, specially encrypted diskettes or Universal Serial Bus (USB) for accessing Ontario's ELRS. Lawyers are responsible for the supervision of the use, security, and passphrases of both the lawyer and the non-lawyer electronic registration security access diskettes. A lawyer is prohibited from disclosing his/her passphrase to others. This includes employees and other lawyers; a lawyer must not allow other lawyers or a law clerk employee to use his/her personalized PSP. The lawyer is also responsible for ensuring that the non-lawyer does not disclose his or her passphrase to others or allow others to use his or her personalized PSP (Rule 5.01(4)).

The security of Ontario's electronic land registration system and the prevention of fraud depend on strict compliance by lawyers and law clerks with the rules governing the use of personal security packages. Lawyers are responsible for supervising the care and control of keys and may experience PSP compliance audits by the LSUC. Failure to comply with ELRS security requirements carries the risk of professional discipline, loss of access to ELRS resulting in the inability to practise real estate conveyancing, and potentially criminal consequences. The lawyer is responsible for the content of an electronic document, including when it is signed by a non-lawyer Rule (5.01(6)).

Title Insurance and the Professional Conduct Rules

Lawyers must be knowledgeable about title insurance in general as well as specific policies that they recommend and place on behalf of clients. Lawyers must discuss the "advantages, conditions, and limitations of the various options and coverages" of title insurance with the client.

The Rules of Professional Conduct require lawyers to advise clients that title insurance is an available option, although not the only option, for the protection of a client's property interests (Rule 2.02(10)). Although the rule states that the lawyer "shall advise the client that title insurance is not mandatory", today title insurance is placed on almost all residential transactions and most commercial transactions, although some larger developers self-insure. Twenty years ago title insurance coverage was rare. Now, many lawyers decline to act for a client who refuses to obtain title coverage. Increasingly, real estate lawyers in Ontario question whether a solicitor can adequately minimize a client's risk in a real estate transaction without obtaining title coverage for fraud and other title risks.

Rule 5.01(5) provides that under the supervision of a lawyer, a non-lawyer employee may advise clients about title insurance, give options and premium information, recommend a particular insurance product, and give legal opinions on the effect of the title insurance coverage obtained on the client's transaction. However, the practice guidelines emphasize that the lawyer must in consultation with the client and considering the nature of the property, the wording of the agreement of purchase and sale, the expectations of the client, and the potential risks, review the impact of title insurance search requirements and coverage and decide which title and off-title searches should be completed. In addition, results of the title search or the survey may affect the choice of appropriate off-title inquiries. For example, if the title search reveals that the property was previously owned and used as a gas station, the lawyer will know to complete full environmental off-title searches, arrange an environmental audit, and take other appropriate measures. The lawyer must directly supervise law clerks and title insurance activities in order to comply with Rule 5.01(5).

Rule 2.02(11) prohibits lawyers from receiving compensation from a title insurer for recommending a specific title insurance product to his or her client. A general prohibition exists that forbids lawyers, employees of the firm (law clerks), and related persons from receiving commissions, fees, or similar payments, be it directly or indirectly, from title insurers (Rule 2.02(12)). As well, lawyers must disclose to clients that TitlePLUS is a bar-related title insurance product associated with the Law Society and the Lawyers' Professional Indemnity Company/LawPRO (Rule 2.02(13)).

CATEGORIES OF TITLE SEARCHES IN REGISTRY, LAND TITLES, AND POLARIS

Most of Ontario's title information is now in electronic form in the POLARIS database. The computerization of Ontario's title records and registration procedures has greatly reduced the need to find and review historical registrations. Fewer and fewer 40-year Registry searches are necessary. Although POLARIS has reduced the length of many property searches, it has not reduced the legal complexity of the title search. All land automated in POLARIS is first parcelized as in Land Titles, mapped, and then assigned a property identification number referred to as a PIN. However, land, when automated in POLARIS, was sometimes left under the Registry system. Most often, when Registry titles were parcelized and automated, they were also converted to the Land Titles system. As a result, today POLARIS contains both Registry and Land Titles systems titles, and must be searched according to the appropriate Registry and Land Titles systems rules. In fact, lawyers and law clerks are now confronted with more title search scenarios than ever before, each with different legal requirements and administrative procedures. From a risk management point of view, it is arguably more difficult today than in the past for lawyers to review title search notes carefully.

In Ontario, lawyers and law clerks must be competent to complete title searches in any of the title search scenarios listed below. Electronic land registration is only available for Land Titles properties in POLARIS. Each category of title search presents different legal implications and requires markedly different practical title searching procedures. Each of these search scenarios will be explored in detail in later chapters.

Traditional Registry System Search (Paper Record)

A full 40-year search in the Abstract Index confirming the legal effect of all registered documentation is necessary. See Chapters 3 and 4.

Traditional Land Titles System Search (Paper Record)

Land Titles title registers are subject to ownership exceptions, called "qualifiers", listed in s. 44(1) of the *Land Titles Act*. A conventional Land Titles search in the Parcel Register reviews all active registered documents recorded on the current parcel page. It also reviews deleted documents for indications of fraud and statutory title qualifiers. See Chapter 6.

POLARIS Registry System Searches

Registry 40-Year Load

Early in the POLARIS conversion, an attempt was made simply to automate Registry titles by first creating and mapping a parcel and assigning a PIN, and then loading 40 years' worth of Registry records into the POLARIS database. This allows for a 40-year Registry search to take place within the automated system. In some cases (Chatham), the process included registering a Certificate of Title that shortened the 40-year search period. Registry system search and registration rules apply. See Chapters 3, 4, and 8.

Registry Non-Converts

On occasion, an apparent serious title defect prevented the POLARIS conversion process from converting a Registry title into a guaranteed Land Titles title. The property was parcelized, mapped and assigned a PIN, but left in Registry. Documents registered within the last 40 years were loaded on the automated record. A full 40-year search is required. It may be necessary to review the original Abstract books to identify the title problem. A Registry Non-Convert is not the same as a Registry 40-year load. They are found in Registry offices where Registry titles were converted to Land Titles ownership prior to automation. See Chapters 3, 4, and 8.

Parcelized Day (PIN Creation Date) Forward Registry Records (PDFR)

In some offices, Teranet parcelized, mapped and assigned a PIN and then computerized only the current Registry ownership document (deed) as of the date of automation, referred to as the PIN Creation Date. Following the PIN creation date, all new registrations are shown on the automated record (computer printout). PDFR was completed in two different ways. For example, in Mississauga, the last change in ownership document as of the PIN creation date was entered in POLARIS; however, any documents registered between that document and the date of automation were not recorded in POLARIS. These documents were left in the Abstract book. Other PDFR records automate the last change of ownership and all related title documents between the last change of ownership and the PIN creation date. Therefore the lawyer or law clerk must complete a full 40-year search using automated searching for recent information and checking the paper record back the full 40 years. Fortunately, PDFR is meant to be temporary and the Ministry plans to convert PDFR properties to Land Titles parcels. Registry search and registration rules apply. See Chapters 3, 4, and 8.

POLARIS Land Titles System Searches

Land Titles Absolute

Teranet simply automated and assigned a PIN to existing Land Titles parcels. This search is basically the same as a conventional Land Titles search, except that the title register and search procedures are fully automated. The Land Titles parcel is referenced by the PIN. The title searcher reviews all active registered documents recorded on the parcel print-out. Standard *Land Titles Act*, s. 44(1) title qualifiers apply and may require a review of deleted documents. Deleted documents also reveal fraud indicators. Title insurance search requirements require that both active and deleted documents be requested as part of the search. Land Titles Absolute parcels may be searched and documents registered electronically.

Land Titles Conversion Qualified (LTCQ)

This search relates to land that has been legally converted from Registry to Land Titles. It is similar to an automated Land Titles search, but is subject to different title qualifiers on the guarantee of ownership set out in ss. 44 to 46 of the *Land Titles Act* and listed on the new title register. For example, LTCQ titles are subject to mature claims for adverse possession, misdescription and some short-term unregistered *Registry Act* leases. LTCQ parcels require searches of adjoining lands descriptions, similar to Registry. However, some of the standard *Land Titles Act* exceptions to the guarantee of ownership in s. 44(1) qualifiers do not apply. For example, on a LTCQ parcel, it is unnecessary to check for succession duties and dower rights. It is also unnecessary to search for *Planning Act* contraventions, spousal rights, railway interests, and escheats to the Crown prior to the date of conversion. Except for the uncertainty of mature adverse possession and easement by prescription rights, a LTCQ title provides a title guarantee superior to that of a Land Titles Absolute. Prior to the POLARIS conversion, the majority of titles in Ontario were Registry titles. When the conversion is complete, a major portion of titles in Ontario will be LTCQ titles.

Land Titles Absolute Plus (LT PLUS)

A Land Titles Conversion Qualified title may on application be upgraded to a Land Titles Absolute Plus (LT PLUS) title in order to remove issues of adverse possession, easements by prescription, or misdescription. No possessory rights exist in an LT PLUS title. In order to register a new subdivision or condominium plan or to consolidate an existing parcel, the owner of an LTCQ parcel must first upgrade ownership to an LT PLUS parcel. A Land Titles Absolute Plus title has both the advantages of an LTCQ title and no adverse possession rights or description uncertainty. Since August 2001, new LT PLUS titles guarantee additional title qualifiers such as *Planning Act* compliance and the absence of corporate escheats as of the date of registration of the LT PLUS. It is the best of all titles.

Two different land registration systems, combined with the continuous change generated by the POLARIS land registration reform initiatives, have resulted in a complex and risky assortment of title searching procedures and related law. When the POLARIS conversion is complete, most land (other than problem non-converts) will be Land Titles Absolute, Land Titles Conversion Qualified, or LT PLUS. Lawyers and law clerks will need to determine the combinations of title variations found in a particular registry office and exercise caution when working in a registry office that they are not familiar with. For example, Middlesex which was originally a mixture of Registry and Land Titles properties was the first fully converted online land registry office. The Middlesex LRO contains the following:

- Land Titles Absolute (LT Abs)

- Land Titles Conversion Qualified (LTCQ)

- Land Titles Absolute Plus (LT PLUS)

- Registry Non-Converts

- Mandatory Electronic Land Registration

THE STAGES IN A TITLE INQUIRY

Registry office and Ministry staff and Teranet customer service representatives are not allowed by statute to give advice on ownership or title to a particular property, or on a particular search. They can assist only with the paper and electronic retrieval of records and the mechanics of title investigation and document registration requirements. Title searching procedures vary, firstly, depending on whether you are searching in the Registry or the Land Titles system, and, secondly, on whether you are searching in the paper or the automated system, and if in the automated system the nature of the title variation being searched. The following checklist provides a simplified overview of the basic stages in searching title to land in Ontario. Detailed checklists for the different categories of title searches and related law are set out in later chapters.

Preliminary Considerations

1. The lawyer in consultation with the client and considering the impact of alternative or supplemental title insurance coverage, the risks inherent in the specific property, and the expectations associated with the agreement of purchase and sale directs the nature and the extent of the title and the off-title searches.

2. The lawyer reviews and analyzes the title and off-title searches and in consultation with the client assesses the risk and decides whether to pursue additional title and off-title inquiries.

3. The lawyer reviews the results of title inquiries and how they relate to the covered risks, conditions, limitations, exclusions, exemptions, and additional coverage options of title insurance policy.

The Mechanics of Searching

☐ Identify and access appropriate physical or electronic Registry office.

☐ Determine if land is registered in:

- *Registry Act* system;

- *Land Titles Act* system; or

- POLARIS database accessed via Teraview.

□ Determine the category of search involved:

- 40-year Registry search (paper);

- Land Titles search (paper);

- POLARIS database accessed through Teraview:

  1. Land Title Absolute

  2. Land Titles Conversion Qualified (LTCQ);

  3. Land Titles Absolute Plus (LT PLUS);

  4. Parcelized Day Forward Registry (PDFR) under the *Registry Act* (two variations);

  5. 40-Year Load Registry with or without a Certificate of Title; or

  6. Non-Convert Registry.

□ Obtain short legal description or information to access records:

- Registry (paper system): lot, plan, city, township, county, *etc.*

- Land Titles (paper system): parcel, plan, city, township, county, *etc.* (Agreements of purchase and sale, tax bills, old documents, surveys, maps, assessment rolls, and notices, *etc.*, may provide short legal description information.)

- POLARIS database via Teraview:

  1. property identification number (PIN);

  2. owner's name (transferee's name on active transfers or documents general);

  3. current or previous title document registration number;

  4. municipal address;

  5. subdivision lot and plan numbers;

  6. condominium unit(s) and plan;

  7. reference plan number and Part number;

  8. physical location, particularly with reference to a road as POLARIS contains a search by road and map feature; and

  9. block and parcel maps, Teraview digital maps and road cross-references.

□ Complete Request for Service at Registry or Land Titles Office.

☐ Access Teraview online, if in POLARIS.

☐ Obtain parcel register in Land Titles or abstract book lot page in Registry.

☐ Access POLARIS parcel register. Print parcel register. Request deleted documents to see record of past transactions. If necessary, locate pre-conversion records by cross-reference on print-out.

☐ Identify relevant instruments from lot and parcel pages or print-outs. (This can be a slow and difficult process, particularly in Registry which requires that you sift through registrations by names and descriptions.)

☐ Obtain documents including related plans (paper, self-serve microfilm, or online (fax or courier) with Teraview).

☐ Read, copy, or summarize documents and plans.

☐ Complete search summary.

☐ Add search notes to the file.

☐ Review by lawyer of title and off-title searches.

☐ Review status of title with client and obtain written directions and waivers as needed.

☐ Complete additional title and off-title inquiries as needed.

☐ Incorporate search and title information into title insurance policy application.

☐ Customize title insurance coverage with underwriter as needed.

☐ Complete subsearches prior to or on closing.

☐ Confirm new title registrations following closing.

☐ Include title information, including restrictions, and insurance coverage in the report to the client. Report new registration particulars to the title insurer.

CHAPTER 2

Land Division and Geographical Referencing in Ontario

INTRODUCTION

Land registration systems record, organize, and provide title or land ownership-related information for the public. When title to a particular property is searched on behalf of a purchaser, a mortgagee checking collateral, or any interested person, the title searcher's job is to access and gather, from the appropriate registration system, all pertinent registered title documents and land-related information. In all Ontario land registration systems, title information, and registered documents are indexed geographically. The title searcher must first determine the geographical reference or description for any particular parcel of land before he or she may begin to locate and record the documents and plans that must be included in a title search.

Registry, Land Titles, and the automated records system, POLARIS, despite a common underlying framework of lots and plans, all work on different methods of geographical referencing. Registry indexes land by lot and plan. Land Titles indexes land by parcel. POLARIS uses a Property Identification Number (PIN) to identify a particular parcel. Today, it is essential for anyone conveying or searching title to land to develop not only a familiarity with lots and plans, but also a precise understanding of parcels, PINs, and POLARIS digital maps. Most land in Ontario is now in Land Titles in the POLARIS system. As a result, the majority of searches involve Teraview digital maps, parcels, PINs, and reference plans, although Land Titles Conversion Qualified (LTCQ) and the remaining registry titles still rely on traditional registry descriptions to determine property boundaries.

BACKGROUND

During the late 18th and early 19th centuries, the southern part of Ontario was organized first into large districts and later into counties. The northern part of the province was divided into districts. Frequently, counties and districts were redivided into five to ten townships. From each township, large blocks of land, being about one-seventh of the township lands, were reserved by the Crown as general reserves, revenue from the sale of which went into the Crown's general revenue funds. As well, a further one-seventh of township lands was set aside as clergy reserves for the support and maintenance of a Protestant clergy. In 1826, Crown reserve lands and other large blocks, including the Guelph and Huron Tracts, totalling about 2½ million acres, were granted to the Canada Company.

Crown surveyors divided the townships into concessions — often about 14 per township — containing large rectangular lots referred to as township, concession or farm lots. On Crown surveys, the concessions were identified by Roman numerals ("I", "II", "III", *etc.*), while the township lots were numbered with Arabic figures ("1", "2", *etc.*). Whenever a concession fronted, in whole or in part, on an irregular boundary, such as a lake, river, swamp, or escarpment, it was referred to as a "broken front" concession and identified by letters of the alphabet (*e.g.*, Broken Front concession "B"). Whenever a city, town, or village was incorporated, with reference to a registered plan, the land involved ceased to be referenced by township lot and concession. This underlying pattern, though often obscured by urban growth, remains with us today and is easily recognized when travelling on concession roads through agricultural regions in southern Ontario.

Initially, surveyors measured out distances, roads, and lots with a heavy metal chain, known as the Gunter's chain. One chain measured 66 feet and was divided into 100 links. In this system, acreage was established by multiplying the depth of a lot in chains by the breadth in chains and dividing by ten (10 square chains = 1 acre). Subsequently, the more familiar system of measurement using imperial units (feet and inches or tenths of a foot) for length and area was introduced. As a result of Canada's adoption of the metric system, land registrars have accepted descriptions of land and plans expressed in either imperial or metric units since July 1, 1976. At present, a search of title may involve careful time-consuming calculation, conversion, and plotting of descriptions in all three systems of measurement. A comprehensive list of measurements and conversion factors is included in the appendices as a convenient reference.

Road allowances, referred to as concession roads or lines, run between concessions and separate groups of township lots, often every five or six township lots, resulting in a grid pattern that allows access to properties. In addition, 66-foot road or shoreline allowances were laid out along the shorelines of lakes and rivers in parts of the province, particularly cottage country. Generally, road and shoreline allowances are one chain (66 feet) in width, although width may vary, as some allowances are 40 feet wide whereas others are 90 feet wide.

The actual location of shoreline allowances may be difficult to determine due to historical changes in water levels and reservoir and diversion projects. Often, road allowances have neither been constructed nor opened to the public and, as a result, they may have been mistakenly believed to be part of the township lot and occupied by adjoining owners. For example, it is extremely common for cottages and boathouses in the Muskoka Lakes to have been built on the 66-foot shoreline allowance, resulting in title, municipal zoning, and environmental issues. Road allowances may have been laid out as part of a township lot or they may have been laid out separately from the township lot, in which case the road allowance starts at the boundary of the township lot.

Whether open to the public or not, the freehold ownership in road and shoreline allowances is in most cases vested in the municipality by Part III of the *Municipal Act, 2001*, S.O. 2001, c. 25. Similarly, the *Beds of Navigable Waters Act*, R.S.O. 1990, c. B.4 reserves title to the bed of navigable water to the Crown in the right of Ontario (with some exceptions), unless there is an express grant to the contrary in the Crown patent.

The *Surveys Act*, R.S.O. 1990, c. S.30 describes several types of original township surveys. In practice, many original township surveys, based on unsettled and rugged topography, resulted in irregular patterns instead of uniform grids. Ontario contains front and rear townships, single front townships, double front townships, sectional townships with double fronts, sectional townships with single fronts, and sectional townships with sections and quarter sections. Single front and front and rear townships, as described below and illustrated in Figures 2.1 and 2.2, were common in the oldest townships and frequently had standard dimensions.

A typical single front township lot measured 20 chains (1,320 feet) wide by 100 chains (6,600 feet) deep and contained 200 acres. The first surveys of such lots were made in 1783 (see Figure 2.1).

As a result, lots usually contained 200 acres and were often patented or sold as 100-acre or 200-acre properties, no different than typical farm fields today. When a part of a lot, such as the north half or south half, was granted off, it was referred to as an "aliquot" part. The 66-foot road allowances ran between the concessions and between the lots. It was common for road allowances to be measured out, in accordance with Crown instructions, every five, six, or seven lots, often being every 100 chains or 1¼ miles.

A typical front and rear township lot measured 20 chains (1,320 feet) wide (frontage) by 50 chains (3,300 feet) deep and contained 100 acres. The first surveys of front and rear township lots were made in 1787 (see Figure 2.2).

Many township lots have irregular sizes and boundaries, *i.e.*, gore lots, which occur when the boundaries of lots and concessions are not at right angles to each other and a gore is created with the adjoining township. Similarly, natural features such as shorelines, swamps, and escarpments may form irregular lot boundaries, resulting in irregularly shaped lots known as broken front lots.

Irregular large lots may simply be laid out with reference to early transportation routes, such as rivers and original roads.

Unusual types of surveys related to settlement patterns have caused endless confusion for succeeding generations. One example is the upper part of the Grand River which was settled by different ethnic groups. One block, referred to as the German Company Tract, was divided into lots each containing 448 acres. As the usual creation of road allowances was disregarded, a complex system of private roads and rights of way developed, which resulted in endless boundary disputes before public roads could be built.

It is important to be aware that, by today's standards, many imperfect measurements were made in the original surveys due both to the rugged character of the land and the primitive nature of survey measurement tools. Technologically advanced surveys routinely reveal different measurements and are a necessary part of many real estate transactions.

Figure 2.1

SINGLE FRONT TOWNSHIP SHOWING BROKEN FRONT LOTS: LOTS POSTED AT FRONT OF EACH CONCESSION

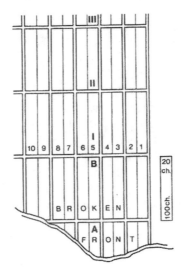

Figure 2.2

FRONT AND REAR TOWNSHIP:
LOTS POSTED AT FRONT AND REAR OF EACH CONCESSION

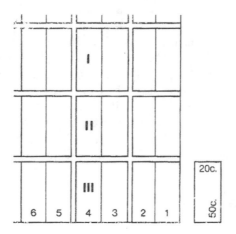

As the province's population grew, township lots were further subdivided into smaller lots that were surveyed and shown on often informal registered plans. The resulting lot and plan number then became the permanent description reference for the property. In 1946, the *Planning Act* was passed in order to control the subdivision and use of land. From that point on, division of land could occur only by registered plan of subdivision, by consent to sever land or according to a subdivision control exemption pursuant to the provisions of the *Planning Act*.

Few changes were made in the municipal organization of the province until 1953, when the Regional Municipality of Metropolitan Toronto was established (now restructured under the *City of Toronto Act, 2006*, S.O. 2006, c. 11, Schedule A). Numerous regional and district municipalities, such as the District Municipality of Muskoka or the Regional Municipality of Ottawa-Carleton, have been created. Ongoing annexation and amalgamation continue to affect municipal organization.

Historical boundaries and original names of counties, townships, cities, and towns have changed. Descriptions of land must refer to both the current appropriate municipal name and the original description. In the past, individual statutes, such as the *District Municipality of Muskoka Act*, R.S.O. 1990, c. D.14 would set out the land included by both former and new names, and the exact boundaries of a new municipality. For example, what were formerly the Town of Gravenhurst, the Townships of Morrison, Ryde and part of the Townships of Muskoka and Wood are now named the Town of Gravenhurst. Currently, the

Territorial Division Act, 2002, S.O. 2002, c. 17, Schedule E and O. Reg. 180/03 (under the same Act) divides Ontario into geographic areas in Schedules 1 and 2. Today, the geographic area of the Territorial District of Muskoka consists of the upper-tier municipality of Muskoka (pursuant to the *Municipal Act, 2001*), which is composed of the lower-tier municipalities of Bracebridge, Georgian Bay, Gravenhurst, Huntsville, Lake of Bays, and the Muskoka Lakes.

In order to ascertain municipal boundaries and current names, a conveyancer may refer to *Registry Act*, R.S.O. 1990, c. R.20 regulations (*e.g.*, O. Reg. 427/99, amended by O. Reg. 218/05) or research legislation creating specific regional and district municipalities. Copies of the original Crown survey and township plans are available for inspection in the appropriate Registry office and at the Ministry of Natural Resources. From a practical point of view, a telephone call to knowledgeable staff in the appropriate Registry office or to a land surveyor often provides the most efficient up-to-date determination of technical description requirements.

LAND ORGANIZATION IN REGISTRY

Land in the Registry system is referenced by lot or plan in a concession, or by lot and/or plan in a city, town, or township, county, district, municipality, or regional municipality. When a piece of land is first transferred to a private owner by Crown patent, the land registrar in the office in which the land is located will open a new index page in the abstract book for each lot that has been patented. The registrar will then enter a notice of the Crown patent, followed by any instrument registrations that relate to the lot or lots. As a result, each township lot is allocated a separate page in an abstract index relating to a particular concession in a township.

Whenever land in a township lot is subdivided by registered plan of subdivision, a new abstract index that allocates one separate page per individual subdivision lot is opened for the new subdivision plan. The *Registry Act* contains detailed sections and regulations relating to the description of land. Ontario Regulation 427/99 sets out the proper name, number, and land included in all Registry offices in the province (*e.g.*, the Land Registry office for the Registry division of Elgin (No. 11)). Ontario Regulation 43/96, also under the *Registry Act*, contains precise details on registered descriptions and plan registration requirements and includes the prescribed plan registration forms.

LAND ORGANIZATION IN LAND TITLES

The Land Titles system, which is found throughout northern Ontario, and in more recent (since the 1960s) subdivision and condominium developments in the south, retains the underlying original lot and plan numbers while superimposing a new primary description reference called a "parcel". All properties in Land Titles have been "parcelized" and are identified and indexed by parcel and section numbers instead of lots and plans. Land in a parcel is owned by an individual or by a group of concurrent or joint owners.

A parcel may be composed of any combination of whole or part lots in a concession or on a registered plan as well as Part(s) on a reference plan. A parcel may also be comprised of a public road. Although properties in Land Titles are identified and searched by parcel number, the legal description required in registered documentation retains the underlying lot, plan, concession, township, county, district, or regional municipality designations. Each parcel register sets out a stand-alone parcel or legal description stating the lot(s) and plan(s) and/or part(s) on reference plan(s) that are contained in the specific parcel. Parcel numbers often do not correspond to lots and plans, therefore some Land Titles offices provide informal cross-references between lot and plan numbers and parcel numbers.

In Land Titles, each separately owned property is identified by a parcel number regardless of the number of whole and/or part lots the parcel may contain. When a piece of land is first transferred to a private owner by Crown patent, the land registrar in the office in which the land is located will assign a parcel number and open a new index page called a parcel register. As a result, each parcel is allocated a separate parcel register on which all related title registrations are recorded. The process is similar when land is transferred from Registry to Land Titles by way of application for first registration in Land Titles. The *Land Titles Act*, R.S.O. 1990, c. L.5 contains detailed sections and regulations relating to the registered description of land. Ontario Regulation 428/99, under the *Land Titles Act*, sets out the proper name, number, and land included in all Land Titles divisions/offices in the province (*e.g.*, the land Registry office for the Land Titles division of Middlesex (No. 33)). When an allowance for a road forms a boundary of a Land Titles division, the centre line of the allowance is the boundary of the Land Titles division.

The use of parcels and parcel registers in Land Titles as the main form of indexing land and title-related information creates a far more efficient system for recording and searching title. The *Land Registration Reform Act*, R.S.O. 1990, c. L.4 retains the Land Titles system's concept of parcelization as a description reference.

LAND ORGANIZATION AND PROPERTY MAPPING IN POLARIS

Teranet, pursuant to the *Land Registration Reform Act*, has developed a comprehensive, province-wide, automated, title and property digital mapping database. The province has been divided into blocks identified by a five-digit number. Blocks are further divided into parcels (individual properties), each identified by a unique four-digit number. The property mapping database generates block and property index maps illustrating and referencing all parcels in Ontario in relation to adjoining parcels. The mapping database generates online, province-wide, digital maps in Teraview.

Parcel Types

There are a number of different parcel types in POLARIS. The most common type of parcel is referred to as a "property" parcel and includes single family homes, apartment complexes, and commercial and industrial properties. Road, railroad, and condo parcels are also common. Less common parcel types include: Indian land, Crown land, boundary undefined, disjoint, disjoint condo, complex relation, no POLARIS data available, not activated, and unknown.

Property Identification Numbers (PINs)

Each individually owned parcel is first identified and then assigned a unique nine-digit property identification number called a "PIN", which is a combination of the block number followed by the individual property number. The first five numbers of the PIN represent the related block number and the following four numbers identify the individual property number. PINs identify and index specific parcels. The property mapping database is continuously updated in order to illustrate current mapping information, including the creation of new PINs resulting from the subdivision or consolidation of existing properties.

The process of assigning PINs to individual properties is part of "parcelization". Each PIN is assigned a legal description. Unlike Land Titles parcel descriptions, a LTCQ (Registry conversion to Land Titles) parcel description may or may not include a stand-alone legal description. It is common for the parcel description for land that has been both converted from Registry to Land Titles and automated to be described "as in instrument number 123456", being the current deed at the time of the administrative conversion and PIN creation date. Therefore, it is necessary to review the deed mentioned in the parcel description to find the full legal description. Transfers following conversion may also describe land as "as in instrument number 123456".

Once a PIN is established, all title documents that affect ownership of the property are referenced to the PIN. In this manner, the title index database is linked to the mapping database. As a result, title information is indexed on a new property ownership basis, being that of the PIN. Although the PIN is the main title index reference, title information may also be accessed by municipal address, registered owners' names, registered instrument number and more recent subdivision lots and plans, or condominium units and plans. It is now possible to access title information by reference to a road or a location in the POLARIS database by way of an online Teraview digital map. POLARIS superimposes PINs on the older references of parcels, lots, plans, concessions, and roads. Some automated Registry offices contain informal indexes that cross-reference lots, plans, concessions, and parcels to modern PINs.

The content and form requirements for POLARIS parcelization and block and property maps are set out in full in Part VIII of O. Reg. 43/96, under the *Registry Act*.

Block Index Maps

A block is an area that contains at least one property and that is bounded by limits that the Director of Titles considers appropriate, such as Land Titles or Registry division boundaries, roads, railway lines, major utility corridors, water boundaries, and property limits.

Block index maps illustrate the location of numbered blocks in a municipality. Blocks are usually laid out using natural boundaries such as roads, railways, utility corridors, and bodies of water. Block index maps include block boundaries and numbers, roads and railways, underlying lots, plans and concessions, road allowances, bodies of water, legends, scale, north indicator, *etc*. In effect, the block index maps act as a reference to the property index maps.

Figure 2.3 illustrates the layout and contents of a block index map. If you look carefully, you will notice a broken front concession fronting on the Thames River. Small blocks, for example, blocks 08745, 08900, 08902, 08904, 08921, 08908, and 08864, represent separate blocks assigned to individual condominiums.

Property Index Maps

Property index maps illustrate the approximate location of PINs in relation to adjoining PINs, within a numbered block. Property index maps include description information such as underlying lots, plans, concessions, roads, street names, railways, bodies of water, major easements and rights of way, land registry division, county, district, regional or territorial municipality, the municipality or geographic township, current municipal names and boundaries, legend, scale, north indicator, the map's effective date and the Universal Transverse Mercator six-degree grid or the grid of the Ontario Co-Ordinate System established by R.R.O. 1990, Reg. 1028, made under the *Surveys Act*. The property map states that it is not a plan of survey and that it was prepared for property indexing purposes only. The map cautions that the registered dimensions of the property boundaries can be found only on the recorded plans and documents.

Separate property index maps, illustrating condominium units, do not exist for condominiums. Each unit, within the meaning of the *Condominium Act, 1998*, S.O. 1998, c. 19, or its predecessor, and the unit's appurtenant interest in the common elements is allocated a separate PIN.

In POLARIS, a PIN references a property made up of a specific legal description composed of lots and part lots on plans or concessions. Parcels, representing lots and plans or concessions in Land Titles, convert directly to PINs in POLARIS. Property index maps act as a main reference for PINs used in searching the automated title database.

Each PIN or property in POLARIS is allocated a separate parcel register printout, regardless of the number of whole and/or part lots the PIN contains. Similarly, each condominium is allocated a separate block number and each condominium unit is allocated a separate PIN resulting in a separate parcel register printout.

Figure 2.4 illustrates the layout and contents of a property index map. If you look carefully, you will notice some informal additions to the map. Handwritten additions represent recent changes or corrections made since the last printout of a property index map. Description changes contained in new registrations are entered into the mapping database following registration.

Figure 2.3
BLOCK INDEX MAP MIDDLESEX SHEET 15

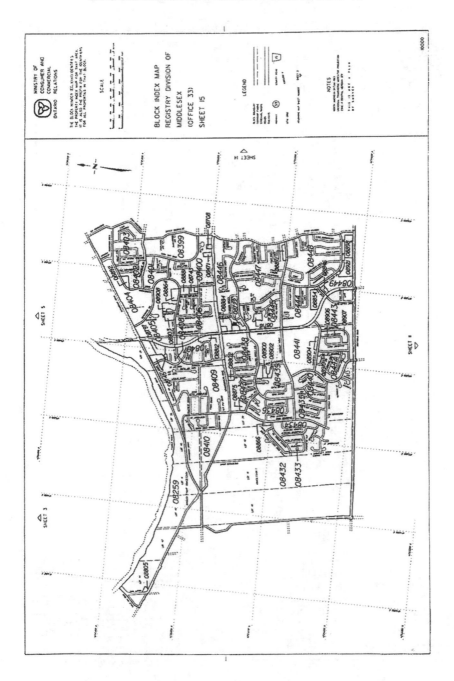

Figure 2.4

PROPERTY INDEX MAP BLOCK 08409

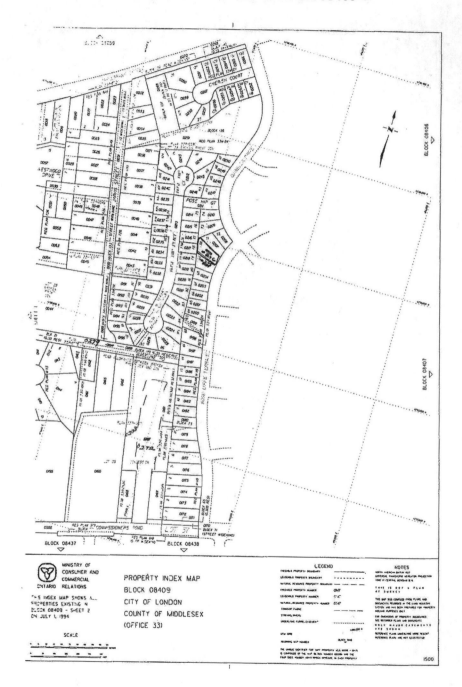

TERAVIEW DIGITAL PROPERTY MAPS

Teraview introduces a new generation of online, digital, property maps that illustrate land ownership (title) and description-related information. Teraview integrates the title information database with the geographical information digital property mapping database. POLARIS mapping is continuously modified to reflect new plans, new descriptions and changes in property ownership. Changes in ownership are entered into POLARIS first and then modified on the maps. As a result, the mapping database may not be as current as the title index database.

Earlier POLARIS block and property maps are constructed on the same underlying geographical information as the most recent digital property maps available through Teraview. However, the POLARIS block and property maps available in paper illustrate information that is different from that on the Teraview maps. For example, the block and property maps illustrate subdivision lot and plan locations (very useful to title searchers), whereas the Teraview maps do not. Teraview maps assemble adjoining lands and provide measurement and digital map manipulation tools, whereas the earlier paper block and property maps do not.

Teraview maps are compiled using title plans and documents recorded in the land registration systems in conjunction with underlying geographical information systems. These property maps have been prepared for property indexing purposes only and, therefore, should not be mistaken for plans of survey or for illustrating actual dimensions of property boundaries. In fact, Teraview map measurements are rounded to the nearest foot or metre. Teraview shows all measurement units initially in metres; however, a user may switch to imperial. For accurate legal description, measurement, and ownership information, it is essential to view and analyze registered plans and documents. Neither POLARIS nor Teraview mapping services can replace the need for a surveyor's real property report to establish boundaries, or for a title searcher's sketch illustration of the legal descriptions of land being dealt with in relation to adjoining lands. A title search requires assembling and plotting all description material from registered plans and documents that relate to the land being transferred or encumbered as well as registered legal description information concerning adjoining lands. Teraview maps provide an overview index that allows access to registered legal description and title information.

Teraview Map Features

Teraview provides the user with the ability to do the following:

1. search properties by location on maps;

2. search properties by location on roads;

3. search properties by PIN;

4. identify and display adjacent properties;

5. view key maps for entire land registry offices;

6. view key maps for specific areas in land registry offices;

7. view increasingly detailed maps in order to display a specific property or properties; and

8. print maps using options for scale, orientation and shading.

Teraview Map Manipulation Tools

Teraview contains map manipulation tools which allow the user to do the following:

1. zoom in and out generally or on a specific map area;

2. calculate approximate map area;

3. centre map;

4. fit all;

5. scale text;

6. retrieve parcel information;

7. place shape;

8. measure between points;

9. find road;

10. scale text;

11. display map legend; and

12. display underlying geographical information such as roads, secondary roads, road names, railways, rivers and lakes, block boundaries, land registry office boundaries, lot and concession fabric and easements.

The following five figures illustrate increasingly detailed Teraview maps as they progressively zoom in on a specific PIN in the central area of the Town of Georgetown, in Halton Hills, in Land Registry Office 20.

Figure 2.5
TERAVIEW DIGITAL MAPS FOR THE TOWN
OF GEORGETOWN, HALTON HILLS

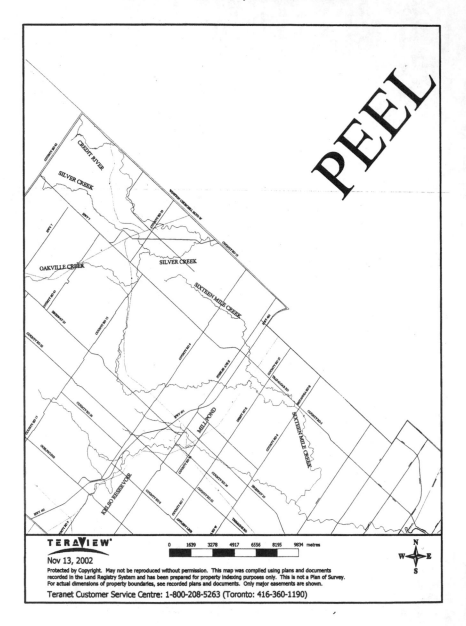

Figure 2.6

TERAVIEW DIGITAL MAPS FOR THE TOWN
OF GEORGETOWN, HALTON HILLS

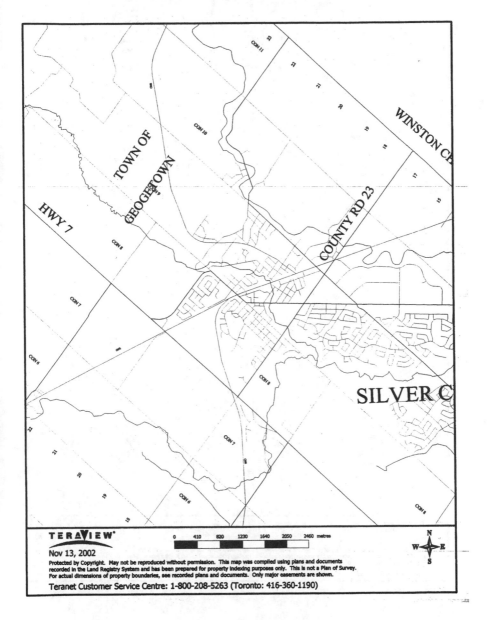

TERAVIEW®

Nov 13, 2002

0   410   820   1230   1640   2050   2460 metres

N
W—E
S

Protected by Copyright. May not be reproduced without permission. This map was compiled using plans and documents
recorded in the Land Registry System and has been prepared for property indexing purposes only. This is not a Plan of Survey.
For actual dimensions of property boundaries, see recorded plans and documents. Only major easements are shown.

Teranet Customer Service Centre: 1-800-208-5263 (Toronto: 416-360-1190)

Figure 2.7

TERAVIEW DIGITAL MAPS FOR THE TOWN
OF GEORGETOWN, HALTON HILLS

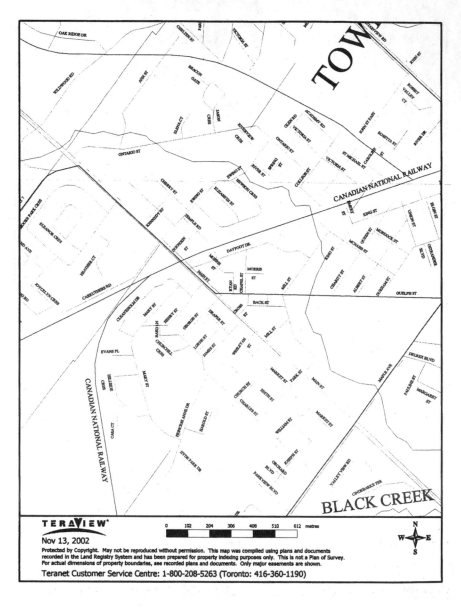

Figure 2.8

TERAVIEW DIGITAL MAPS FOR THE TOWN OF GEORGETOWN, HALTON HILLS[*]

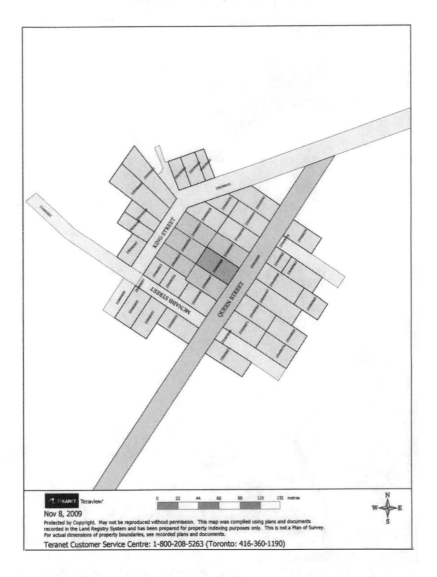

Figure 2.9

**TERAVIEW DIGITAL MAPS FOR THE TOWN
OF GEORGETOWN, HALTON HILLS***

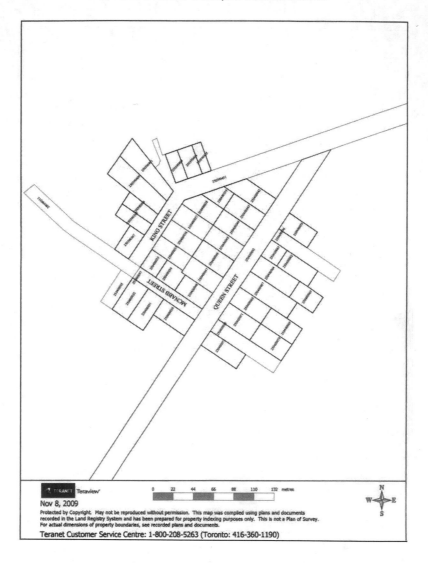

The following figure illustrates a Teraview search results window that displays the parcel map information for the selected active and adjacent PINs in the previous map figures. This search results window also displays the key map for Halton LRO 20 as well as the map toolbar and the parcel map legend.

---

*   © Teranet Inc. 2010. Reproduced with permission.

Figure 2.10

MAP SEARCH RESULTS SCREEN (TERAVIEW VERSION 6)*

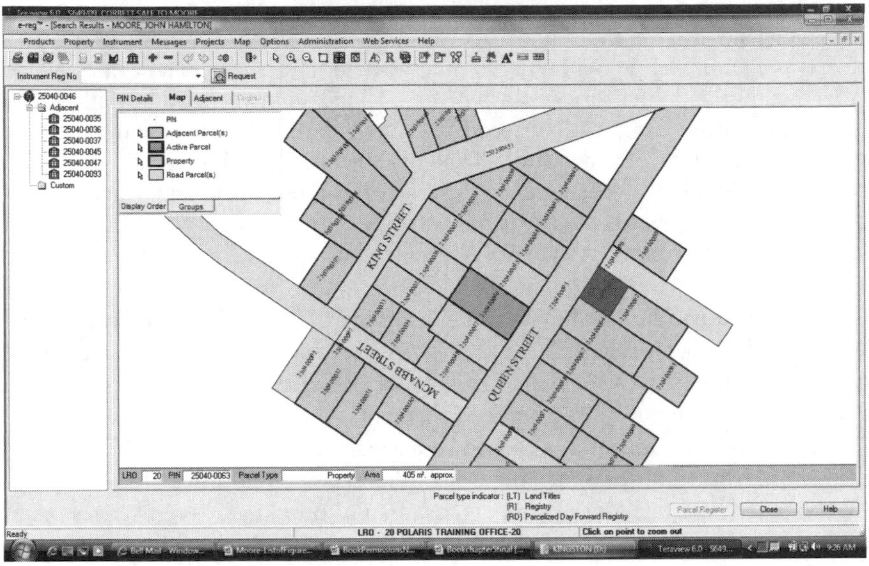

REGISTERED RIGHTS, BOUNDARIES, AND POSSESSORY TITLE

Lawyers investigate or search the quality of title, particularly registered title, whereas surveyors search, determine, and illustrate the extent of title, particularly the re-establishment of boundaries, including both property and lot lines. A surveyor will re-establish a boundary on the ground where it was first laid out. It is the surveyor's role to relate the written description of a parcel to the physical limits on the ground. The registered property description, as it is described on a registered deed or plan, is in reality only a written attempt to describe boundaries.

In Registry, additional ownership rights, which may have been acquired by adverse possession, will be documented on a survey. Even in Land Titles, where the acquisition of adverse possession is prohibited by statute, up-to-date surveys are essential in order to determine boundaries. Section 140(2) of the *Land Titles Act* clearly states that: "The description of registered land is not conclusive as to the boundaries or extent of the land." POLARIS parcel register printouts and block and property maps all caution that they in no way guarantee boundaries or possession. As a result, whether the registration system involved is automated or manual, purchasing land in Ontario without first obtaining a survey is a risky business.

---

* © Teranet Inc. 2010. Reproduced with permission

THE SURVEYOR'S REAL PROPERTY REPORT

A land surveyor investigates and illustrates the extent of title. A surveyor's real property report is a legal document that provides an owner, particularly a purchaser or lender, with an accurate visual representation of a property being purchased at a particular point in time. In order to determine the extent or title and the exact location and boundaries of a property, a land surveyor searches title as far back in time as is necessary. Title searches completed for the purpose of preparing a survey may extend beyond 40 years and document the original creation of a parcel of land, the Crown patent and historical maps, plans, documents, and descriptions. Surveyors investigate and document the effect of changes in topographical features, such as changes in water levels, shorelines, erosion, and accretion.

Only a trained and licensed Ontario land surveyor is qualified to prepare a surveyor's real property report. Such a report, sometimes referred to as a survey, a building location survey, or a mortgage survey certificate, consists of two parts: a plan document and a written report. The report portion may be endorsed on the face of the plan document or attached as a separate written report. A survey accurately illustrates, as of a specified date, the location and dimensions of property boundaries, related lots and plans, location of buildings, pools, fences, adjacent properties, roads, encroachments, easements, and setbacks to property boundaries.

Surveyors search title to a property, search abutting properties, investigate other boundary-related evidence, such as surveyors' files containing earlier surveys and plans, and complete field surveys as part of the preparation of a plan and written report. The survey is comprised of research, measurement, and monumentation in addition to the report and plan. The copyright for the surveyor's real property report remains with the surveyor, not the property owner.

Advantages of Obtaining a Survey

In recent years, title insurance has been held out and accepted, particularly by financial institutions, as a potentially less expensive alternative to an up-to-date survey in that title insurance may provide financial compensation when boundaries are not as represented in the agreement of purchase and sale or title documentation. Only a surveyor's real property report can assure a property owner of the location of all boundaries, compliance with zoning, and the extent of title, and identify possible conflicts with adjoining owners. Only a survey can assure a purchaser that their million-dollar, dream retirement home/cottage is not built on a shoreline allowance or a public beach, or that their new pool is not built on a utility easement. A lawyer can provide only a qualified opinion on title when an up-to-date survey is not available. Throughout history, property owners have been territorial in nature and surveys have ordered the delicate relationship between adjoining property owners. Good fences, not title insurance, make good neighbours.

Types of Surveys

The form of a survey varies depending on the client's reason for requesting one. Common reasons for obtaining a survey include purchasing or selling property, building a fence or an addition, subdividing an existing property or arranging or refinancing a mortgage. A survey may take the form of a surveyor's real property report, a plan of subdivision, a condominium plan, an expropriation plan or a reference plan. Registered plans such as plans of subdivision and reference plans must comply with additional *Registry Act* and *Land Titles Act* registration requirements. The original registered plan of survey is retained by the Registry office and the duplicate original is retained by the surveyor. Copies are issued to the property owner client. Plans of subdivision are registered on title, whereas reference plans are deposited on title.

A conveyancer, whenever possible, should review an up-to-date survey along with an agreement of purchase and sale as part of the title search process. The conveyancer should carefully reconcile the survey with registered descriptions, registered plans, POLARIS block and property maps, and online digital maps available on Teraview.

Figure 2.11 provides an example of a surveyor's real property report, which includes the municipal address, the legal description of the property, the dimensions and location of property boundaries and adjacent properties and roads, improvements, setbacks and projections of overhangs, any neighbour's rights of access, the location of all buildings relative to property boundaries and utility easements. Note that the plan in Figure 2.11 must be read in conjunction with an attached letter and that the plan was not prepared for registration purposes.

ONLINE MAPPING AND DESCRIPTION RESOURCES

Online maps are not a substitute for an up-to-date survey or registered descriptions. They do not indicate boundaries and come with no guarantee of accuracy. They may, however, alert the lawyer to potential title and description issues or provide information that relates to economic value and future land-use. For example, maps that outline Aboriginal treaty boundaries and land claims or future landfills, hydro-electric projects, water reservoirs, or proposed mines, parks or conservation areas and related flooding right, may be of great interest to purchasers. The following online mapping resources may also be of interest to real estate lawyers, developers, environmentalists, community groups, and surveyors, whether or not they relate directly to registered title rights:

- The Ontario Parcel Network (OPN)

<http://www.ontarioparcel.ca/english/pages/generalinfo/overview.asp>

- Ontario's Crown Land Use Policy Atlas (Ministry of Natural Resources)

  <http://crownlanduseatlas.mnr.gov.on.ca/clupa.html>

- Natural Resources Canada Mapping

  <http://www.nrcan.gc.ca>

  Natural Resources Canada provides online topographic maps, aerial photography, satellite imagery, geological maps, mining maps, forest maps, wetlands, groundwater and drainage pattern maps, and other Global Positioning System data.

- Canada Centre for Cadastral Management (Natural Resources Canada)

  <http://clss.nrcan.gc.ca/googledata-donneesgoogle-eng.php>

  This website contains maps for First Nations Land Management Areas, Indian Lands Registry Plans, Land Claim Settlement Maps, Canada Lands Index Maps, and other Canada Lands Survey System maps.

- Land Survey Records Inc.

  <http://www.landsurveyrecords.com/index.asp>

- Indian and Northern Affairs Geographic Portal (Indian treaty maps and information, including maps of specific claims)

  This comprehensive, integrated geographic portal is under development. It will provide location-based data and geographic map visualization available to Canadians and First Nations community with an interest in geomatics. The Indian and Northern Affairs Canada Geo-Portal project will contain the location of First Nations reserves, treaty boundaries, and claims area for Aboriginal title and rights.

  <http://geoviewer.inac.gc.ca>

- Indian and Northern Affairs Canada

  <http://www.ainc-inac.gc.ca>

- First Nation Information Project

  <http://www.aboriginalcanada.com/first nation/dirfnont.htm>

- Natural Resources Canada (maps of treaty and reserve lands)

  <http://wroc.nrcan.gc.ca>

LAND RECORDS: PAST, PRESENT, AND FUTURE

Township lots and concessions, measured out a century ago by Crown surveyors working with compasses, chains, poles and transits, and wooden or iron stakes instead of satellites and computers, survive today as required parts of registerable descriptions. It remains to be seen whether PINs, layered on top of parcels, layered on top of lots and plans, and entered into a digital mapping database, will endure as long. Hidden within the technical complexity of statute and conveyancing practice is the rarely appreciated broader principle that land division and geographical referencing parallel the social, political, legal, and technological history of Ontario.

Figure 2.11
SURVEYOR'S REAL PROPERTY REPORT

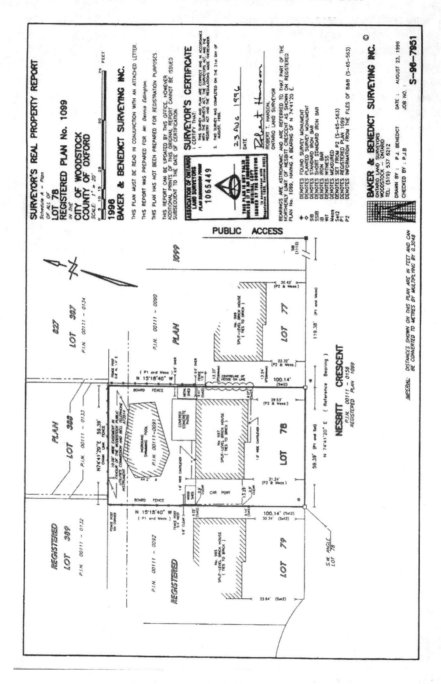

Table 2.1

DESCRIPTION REFERENCES REQUIRED TO ACCESS GEOGRAPHICALLY INDEXED TITLE INFORMATION

Registry System (Traditional)	Land Titles System (Traditional)	POLARIS/ Teraview

1. **Lot** and **Plan**, in a city, town, or township, in a county, district, municipality, or regional municipality.
 	
2. **Township,** farm, or concession **lot** in a **concession**, in a township, in a county, district, municipality, or regional municipality.
	1. **Parcel** and **Section** or **Plan,** in a city, town, or township, in a county, district, municipality, or regional municipality.
	
	2. **Parcel** and **Section** on a township, farm, or concession lot, in a township, in a county, district, municipality, or regional municipality.
	
	3. A **parcel:**
	(a) is a piece of land owned by one or more owners; and
	(b) may be comprised of any combination of:
	  • whole or part township lot(s) in a concession;
	  • whole or part subdivision lot(s) on a subdivision plan;
	  • Part(s) on a reference plan.
		1. Property Identification Number ("**PIN**") on Block/Property Maps. The PIN identifies a particular parcel of land (property) in both the mapping and title databases. The PIN references a parcel (property) owned by one or more owner(s) and represents a specific legal description comprised of lot(s), part lot(s), in concession(s), on plan(s), or part(s) on reference plans, or a description in a stated instrument.
		
		2. Search title record by:
		  • **municipal address**
		  • **owner name** (individual or corporate)
		  • **Registered instrument number** (including a reference plan number)
		  • **subdivision** or **condominium plan**
		  • **location on road**
		  • **location** on **digital map**

• Each **lot** is allocated a **separate page** in an **abstract index.** • A property may be comprised of one or more whole or part lots and title registered on one or more abstract pages.	• Each **parcel** is allocated a **separate page** in a **parcel register**, regardless of the number of whole and/or part lots on plans or in concessions, or reference plan parts, the parcel contains.	• Each **PIN** or **parcel** (property) is allocated a **separate parcel register printout**, regardless of the number of whole and/or part lots or parts the parcel contains. • Each **condominium unit** is allocated a **separate PIN** and a **separate parcel register printout.**

CHAPTER 3

The Registry System

INTRODUCTION

The Registry system is a rich historical archive of Ontario's land ownership past that contains maps, documents, and record books from the period of colonization in the 1700s to present. Registry is full of stories about transfers of land ownership, early trails, original town plans and urbanization, family histories, including inheritances, debts and financial ruin, fights with neighbours over fences, boundaries and rights of way, and the acquisition of land over time by squatters. Its maps may be works of art and its documents contain calligraphy, ribbons and seals. In 1985, the Province of Ontario entered a period of land registration reform that converted most land records from Registry to Land Titles as it automated Ontario's land records and land registration. This historic initiative called POLARIS provided Ontario with a state-of-the-art, modern, electronic, government-guaranteed system more suited to the realities of global markets and the information age. Legal philosophy associates private ownership of land with rights of freedom and liberty, individual status and self-determination, and security of the person in a property-owning democracy. The Registry system stands as a mirror of land ownership and socio-economic history reflecting who we were and who we have become.

APPLICATION OF THE REGISTRY ACT

Registry is simply a government regulated archive of land ownership records; registration does not guarantee title or the effectiveness of documents. Lawyers investigate and give opinions on the validity of registrations and marketability of title. Title insurance provides additional protection to purchasers and mortgagees.

A title search is completed according to Registry system procedures when land ownership is still registered under the Registry system. Registry system land is found in a few areas in which land records have not yet been automated and converted into POLARIS. The few remaining unconverted registry offices, for example, Prescott and Victoria, are scheduled for conversion and mandatory electronic land registration by spring 2010. However, in a few parts of the province, POLARIS has merely automated existing Registry title records as of a stated date instead of legally converting Registry ownership records into the Land Titles system. This form of POLARIS automation is referred to as "parcelized day (the PIN creation date) forward Registry records" and is found in small percentages in only four Registry Offices (Teraview Rollout Schedule, 2010). When problems arise as to quality of title, the legal description, or the accuracy of the conversion, conveyancers may need to search in earlier Registry records behind the PIN creation date for a POLARIS Land Titles conversion qualified title. Early in the conversion process, POLARIS experimented with loading 40 years of records into the automated record. This approach was quickly abandoned for the Land Titles Conversion Qualified (LTCQ) approach. A few properties with serious title or description problems were left in Registry and are called Registry Non-Converts. These are converted the next time a transfer takes place; *Land Titles Act* Bulletin No. 2004-02 sets out the requirements for upgrading a non-convert to an LTCQ.

Conveyancers and surveyors will continue to search in Registry for historical description information. Historical description evidence from the Crown patent forward incorporated into surveys is the only way to determine the actual location of a property "on the ground" for both Registry and Land Titles properties, despite the fact that Land Titles does not permit adverse possession. This historical description information is particularly important when dealing with valuable shorelines, mineral and resource rights, and Aboriginal title and rights. Lands that were transferred to Land Titles contain pre-conversion Registry documents. As duration of ownership is specific to a property, Registry documents will remain active in automated Land Titles for many years into the future. For these reasons, conveyancers must be familiar with the Registry system even in a fully electronic automated Land Titles system.

Only Land Titles documents can be registered on the electronic land registration system. As of March 31, 2008, approximately 92 per cent of total registrations flowed through the electronic land registration system (ELRS). Some of these registrations are land titles documents that cannot conform to the electronic format. Title insurance coverage provides a cost-efficient, alternative solution for some costly, time-consuming title deficiencies and impractical searches involving pre-POLARIS conversion problems. The very small percentage of Registry system paper registrations will continue to diminish. Nevertheless, Registry system search skills will remain important for researching the historical ownership of land.

THE REGISTRY ACT

Document Registration

Every instrument whereby title to land in Ontario may be transferred, disposed of, charged, encumbered or affected in any way may be registered in the Registry system. The *Registry Act*, R.S.O. 1990, c. R.20 imposes detailed registration requirements for all documents as well as additional requirements for specific kinds of documents, such as Crown grants and wills (s. 22). Ontario Regulation 20/995 provides detailed registration requirements for forms and records. In addition, Part I of the *Land Registration Reform Act*, R.S.O. 1990, c. L.4 implemented the standard, non-electronic *Land Registration Reform Act* documents as of April 1, 1985, thereby imposing additional document registration requirements.

A land registrar may refuse a registration when the document contains material that does not relate to an interest in land, such as Canada income tax residency statements. Generally, an instrument that refers to an unregistered instrument or to a notice or claim dependent upon an unregistered instrument may not be registered in the Registry system (*Registry Act*, s. 22(6)). However, notices of leases, subleases, assignments of lease, options to lease, determinations of lease, agreements to lease, mortgages of lease, and agreements, assignments and options for the purchase and sale of land may be registered in the Registry system (*Registry Act*, s. 22(7)). Notices of agreements of purchase and sale and related assignments and notices of options for purchase and related assignments expire one year after the date of registration, subject to the registration of a renewal notice, also good for one year (*Registry Act*, s. 22(8), (9)).

Registration Requirements for Descriptions

All instruments must contain a proper local description, including a PIN, when designated under Part I of the *Land Registration Reform Act*. Plans, general registrations for the general register index, by-laws that do not directly affect title to land, certificates of discharge of mortgage, and instruments and court orders with local descriptions attached by declaration do not need a local description (*Registry Act*, s. 25). "Where an instrument submitted for registration contains a description of land that in the opinion of the land registrar is complex or vague, [the registrar] may require a plan of the land to be deposited as a reference plan" (*Registry Act*, s. 81). The land registrar may accept "a sketch of the land prepared in accordance with the regulations" instead of a reference plan when the reference plan requirement would be unreasonable in the circumstances (*Registry Act*, s. 81(2)). The regulation to the *Registry Act*, entitled Surveys, Plans and Descriptions of Land, O. Reg. 43/96, provides detailed registration requirements for surveys, plans and descriptions of land.

Manner of Registration

An original instrument or an executed duplicate is registered on delivery to or deposit with the land registrar, accompanied by the payment of a prescribed fee (*Registry Act*, s. 22(2)). The date and time of registration is deemed to be the time that the instrument was received and accepted for registration by the land registrar (*Registry Act*, s. 77). On registration of an instrument, the land registrar endorses a certificate of registration on the original and on the duplicate, records the instrument in the proper index, and records the instrument on microfilm or by any other means of image recording that the Director specifies (*Registry Act*, s. 50). The original instrument remains available in the Registry office. A registrar has the discretion to refuse documents that are illegible or unsuitable for microfilming.

Effect of Registration

Land registration systems, by requiring the registration of interests in land, provide a written framework for recording rights and resolving disputes among competing claims. The rules and exceptions (qualifiers) concerning the effect of registration of instruments in the Registry system are set out in ss. 70 through 74 of the *Registry Act*.

In order to protect rights in land, a person claiming an interest or who wishes to enforce an interest in land must first register the interest at the Registry office. Unregistered instruments (documents) after the grant from the Crown are deemed to be void against a subsequent registered purchaser or mortgagee (*Registry Act*, s. 70). Under the *Registry Act*, the registration of an instrument constitutes notice of the instrument to all persons claiming any interest in the land, subsequent to such registration, subject to a number of exceptions (*Registry Act*, s. 71). For example, a person who paid full price but failed to register an interest in land may forfeit his or her ownership right to someone who later both purchased and registered the same piece of land. A subsequent registered owner or mortgagee takes title to land subject to prior registered documents. The order of registration date, time, and number, endorsed on each registered document, creates the order of priority of ownership among potentially conflicting claims to the same piece of land. In future, priorities will be determined according to the respective registration numbers (this change has received Royal Assent but is not yet proclaimed (*Registry Act*, s. 49(3))). For example, if an unscrupulous individual sold the same property twice to two innocent purchasers, the first purchaser, who in good faith registers ownership would own the land. Similarly, if a purchaser arranged both a first and second mortgage, the first mortgagee to register the mortgage, in good faith, would obtain a prior right to the land as collateral.

There are a number of exceptions to the basic registration principles. An instrument registered under the *Registry Act* is deemed to be notice of the instrument to all persons claiming an interest in the land, "subsequent to such registration" (*Registry Act*, s. 74). The first ownership right or claim registered against the land takes precedence over any subsequent registered rights and claims, except in the following circumstances as set out in ss. 70 through 74 of the *Registry Act*:

1.   where no Crown patent was granted (The Crown patent affects ownership of land whether or not it has been registered. If no Crown patent has been granted for a property, no private ownership exists, no matter how many registrations appear in the Registry system records. The

Act lists exceptions to this rule such as Crown leases under the *Mining Act*, R.S.O. 1990, c. M.14 and *Public Lands Act*, R.S.O. 1990, c. P.43, and licences of occupation for pipelines under the *Ontario Energy Board Act, 1998*, S.O. 1998, c. 15, Schedule B. It is essential to confirm the existence of the original Crown patent);

2.   where the Crown reserved conditions and reservations in the original Crown patent (Crown rights to timber, mining, fishing and hunting, and road, beach and shoreline allowances reserved in the original patent affect ownership of land whether or not they are registered in the Registry office);

3.   where a subsequent registered purchaser or mortgagee did not give valuable consideration (*e.g.*, a gift);

4.   municipal by-laws under the *Municipal Act, 2001*, S.O. 2001, c. 25 and the *Planning Act*, R.S.O. 1990, c. P.13 that affect the use of land but not the title to land. For example, road opening or closing by-laws must be registered in order to affect title, whereas zoning by-laws affect title whether or not they have been registered;

5.   short-term leases; leases for an original term not exceeding seven years where the actual possession goes along with the lease;

6.   *Planning Act* subdivision and part lot control by-laws;

7.   a spouse's possessory rights in the matrimonial home under the *Family Law Act*, R.S.O. 1990, c. F.3, s. 21;

8.   where there has been actual notice of a "prior instrument by the person claiming under the prior registration" (*Registry Act*, s. 71);

9.   where an instrument was merely deposited and not registered (*Registry Act*, s. 106(2));

10.   rights acquired by adverse possession and boundaries established by surveyors;

11.   Crown rights in general, such as escheat and expropriation legislation;

12.   instruments entered in the by-law index or as a general registration unless an entry of the instrument appears in the abstract index (Documents must be registered or cross-referenced in the abstract index in order to give notice to subsequent purchasers);

13.   public utility easements of a municipality or an easement of the Ministry of Government Services, including water works or water supply system, sewage works, steam or hot water distribution system, electrical power or energy generating, transmission or distribution system, street lighting system, natural or artificial gas works or sup-

ply system, or a transportation system that existed on the 31st day of July, 1981 continues until the 31st day of December, 1999 (*Registry Act*, s. 114). This exception includes public utility easements transferred to private companies under the *Electricity Act, 1998*, S.O. 1998, c. 15, Schedule A; and

14.   rights created by other statutes (*e.g.*, *Environmental Protection Act*, R.S.O. 1990, c. E.19 and *Beds of Navigable Waters Act*, R.S.O. 1990, c. B.4).

Rights that may affect title without being registered must be investigated in addition to the formal title search. These are called off-title inquiries. Surveys, numerous letter inquiries such as zoning, municipal tax and environmental inquiries, and other searches check for boundaries, liens, restrictions, and orders that might affect a property, as well as compliance with by-laws and federal and provincial legislation. Today, title insurance policies may offer a possible alternative to making certain costly, time-consuming title-related inquiries (refer to Chapters 14 and 18).

Notice Periods

Part III of the *Registry Act* contains the investigation of titles sections. These sections set out the 40-year title search period and the 40-year notice period. The investigation of titles sections were originally found in the *Investigation of Titles Act, 1929*, S.O. 1929, c. 41. They were moved to Part III of the *Registry Act* in 1966 and amended in 1981. Title searchers routinely started searches at what was referred to as a good root of title prior to the 40-year period and traced back any interest mentioned during the search. These sections have attempted to codify, simplify and shorten the common law 40-year title search and 40-year claim expiry periods. The *Consumer Protection and Modernization Act, 2006*, S.O. 2006, c. 34 is the most recent attempt to settle and simplify these notice periods.

Forty-Year Title Search Period

The search period limits most searches to a 40-year period subject to certain exceptions. Section 112(1) states that a person dealing with land "shall not be required to show that the person is lawfully entitled to the land as owner thereof through a good and sufficient chain of title during a period greater than the forty years immediately preceding the day of such dealing, except in respect of a claim referred to in subsection 113(5)."

Forty-Year Notice of Claim Expiry Period

The notice of claim period provides that a registered claim must have been registered within the preceding 40 years if it is to be enforceable against a conflicting claim. As a result, it is necessary to register notice of a continuing claim in the form prescribed by the *Registry Act* every 40 years, or at least prior to the registration of any conflicting claim. Section 113(1) states that "[a] claim that is still in existence on the last day of the notice period expires at the end of that day unless a notice of claim has been registered." A notice of claim may be registered at any time within the notice period, or at any time after the expiration of the notice period, but before the registration of any conflicting claim (s. 113(1)). When a notice of claim has been registered, the claim affects the land for the notice period of the notice of claim.

In 2006, the *Consumer Protection and Modernization Act, 2006* amended Part III of the *Registry Act* ending the uncertainty about the meaning of "notice of claim" in s. 113(2). The Act added s. 111(1) under definition and interpretation which contained the definition of notice of claim and for the purpose of the s. 113(2) notice of claim period. Section 111(1) states that "'notice of claim' means a notice of claim that is registered under subsection 113(2) and that is in the prescribed form and includes a notice registered under a predecessor of this Part or under *The Investigation of Titles Act*". In addition, the section defined "notice period" as meaning "the period ending on the day 40 years after the later of the day of, ... the registration of an instrument that first creates a claim, or the day of the registration of a notice of claim for a claim". A Notice of Claim must be registered by Forms 32 and 33 in R.R.O. 1990, Reg. 995. Notice of claim cannot be a reference or mention of a pre-existing right in a subsequent document that is still within the 40-year search period. Easements and restrictive covenants run with the land and are often meant to run in perpetuity. Easement and restrictive covenant rights must be carefully monitored and periodically renewed by registering a notice of claim (see *Registry Act* Bulletin No. 2007-02).

Prior to these sections, there had been debate about the meaning of "notice of claim" in the real estate bar and in the case law. *Pottruff v. Five Oaks Christian Workers Centre*, [1999] O.J. No. 795 (Ont. Gen. Div.) decided that a reference to a pre-existing restrictive covenant in a later deed during the 40-year period was not in the prescribed form under the Act and therefore did not constitute notice. Six years later, in *1387881 Ontario Inc. v. Ramsay et al.*, [2005] O.J. No. 2727 (Ont. C.A.), the Ontario Court of Appeal carefully reviewed the case law and a series of scholarly articles on the subject and decided that a claim to easement could be kept alive not only by registration of a notice of claim in the prescribed form but also by acknowledgement of or specific referral to a claim in a registered document. Leave to appeal the *Ramsay* decision was refused by the Supreme Court of Canada on March 23, 2006. Soon after, the Ministry amended the *Registry Act* to restrict a notice of claim to the prescribed form only. Special attention should be paid to easements and restrictive covenants when searching title and particularly when checking adjoining lands. Indeed, land owners, particularly corporate owners might consider checking their existing titles to determine the need for the registration of any notice of claim renewals. Easements and rights of way are of particular concern.

Leases

The term of a lease under the *Registry Act* is calculated by adding the original term of the lease to any option, renewal or right to purchase under the lease. If the term of a lease does not exceed seven years, where the actual possession goes along with the lease, it affects the ownership of land whether or not it has been registered on title. As a result, it is usually not necessary to register short-term, frequently residential, leases. If the term of a lease does extend for longer than seven years, it is necessary to register the lease in order to enforce the leasehold rights against the property. Seven years is a long time, particularly in a commercial transaction. From a practical point of view, registration is always prudent when you want to protect valuable, particularly commercial, property rights.

Deposits

It is possible to "deposit" instead of register a document that provides information relating to title but does not contain a registerable description (*Registry Act*, s. 106). These deposits are often in the form of statutory declarations and contain information, for example, about possessory title, boundaries, or the administration of past estates. Deposits are often identified by the prefix "Dep." and noted on the abstract index. Although deposits are deemed not to be registrations and do not receive the legal protection of registration, they should be reviewed as part of the title search as they frequently contain useful title information. The POLARIS conversion did not bring deposits forward onto the Land Titles Conversion Qualified parcel registers. Deposits, left in Registry, may provide helpful information when conveyancers encounter title or description problems in LTCQ titles.

Possessory Rights

Adverse possession comes from a time before formal registration systems, technologically advanced surveying tools, satellite imaging, geographical information systems, or for that matter, written land records. At one time, physical use and occupation of land and possession of title deeds determined ownership. Hence the expression, possession is nine-tenths of the law. This is not true under today's registration systems; however, possessory rights remain as a method of resolving boundary disputes and even determining ownership. Under the *Registry Act*, a property owner may acquire or lose rights to land by way of adverse possession, after ten years, or by way of an easement by prescription, after 20 years. These possessory rights may affect title without being registered. Only a survey can reveal the existence of possessory rights not reflected in registered documents and descriptions. Purchasers may demand declarations of possession setting out any possessory rights.

Adverse possession has a long history and has generated a large amount of complex law, much of it based on established equitable principles of fairness, notice, and good faith. A person claiming possessory rights must have demonstrated actual possession, a good faith (believed he had a legal right) intention of excluding the true owner from possession, and effectively excluded the true owner from possession. In addition, the possession must be open, notorious, constant, continuous, peaceful, and exclusive of the right of the true owner; it must not be equivocal, occasional, or for a special, temporary purpose. Many cases appear to turn on factual details relating to the use of the land. A recent Ontario case, *Bradford Investments (1963) Ltd. v. Fama*, [2005] O.J. No. 3258 (Ont. S.C.J.), provides a comprehensive review of the law of adverse possession. The Ontario Court of Appeal in *Elliot v. Woodstock Agricultural Society*, [2008] O.J. No. 3708 (Ont. C.A.) also reviews the case law on adverse possession and how it affects ownership in Ontario. See *Kaminskas v. Storm et al.*, [2009] O.J. No. 1547 (Ont. C.A.), in which the Ontario Court of Appeal interprets the effect of the 40-year search period and the 40-year notice period on a claim for a prescriptive easement concerning a single car driveway between two houses and the effect of written and verbal permissions from the true owners over a period of 50 years.

Possessory rights conflicts about boundaries, fences and rights of way are frequent, legally and factually complicated, and disproportionately important to clients. On a practical note, they have the potential for violence. Title insurance may provide monetary compensation when boundaries are uncertain or are being challenged. For those clients who wish to be informed consumers and know what they are getting, there is no substitute for a new survey prior to purchase. Robert Frost in *Mending Wall*, his famous metaphorical, blank-verse poem, written on the eve of World War I and published in 1914, understood the significance of boundaries when he said "Good fences make good neighbors".

Actual Notice

A purchaser or lender may have actual notice of an earlier unregistered claim to a property. A registered owner must have complete, accurate, actual knowledge of a prior claim in order to be affected by it. For example, on occasion, an unregistered mutual driveway has been found enforceable due to actual notice gained through a purchaser's inspection of a property. Actual notice comes from the law of equity and is based on principles of fundamental fairness. Equitable protections require a high level of good faith. Actual knowledge is difficult to prove and rarely alters registered title rights.

Fraud

Unlike Land Titles, fraudulent documents in Registry are simply void. In Registry, a void fraudulent document in the chain of title invalidates subsequent documents on the basis of *nemo dat non quod habet* (you cannot grant what you do not have). The effect of a fraudulent document in the chain of title is limited by the 40-year rule. For how to protect a client purchasing or mortgaging land in Registry from fraud, turn to Chapter 17 on title and mortgage fraud and Chapter 18 on title insurance.

CROWN PATENT

In Ontario, all land is owned, in theory, by the Crown in the right of the province, or, in the case of federal jurisdictions such as military lands, harbours or federal parks and sites, and Indian reserves in the right of Canada. Private ownership of land is conditional on the existence of an original Crown grant and, as a result, apart from a few statutory exceptions, any registration on unpatented land has no effect on ownership. Individuals do not hold absolute, private ownership of land. Instead, a private individual owns an "estate" or an interest, comprising a collection of rights related to the use, enjoyment and possession of land. Private ownership is subject to the right of the Crown and particularly to Crown rights reserved in the original Crown grant. Crown rights and restrictions continue to affect ownership of land whether or not they are registered within the 40-year limitation of claims search or notice periods. Crown patents are not on file in Registry offices, except in the case of those issued subsequent to October 1, 1965. Crown grants are now registered in the Registry system. Prior to that date, the original patent was given to the patentee, who frequently neglected to register it.

RECORD BOOKS IN THE REGISTRY SYSTEM

Registry office records are indexed by the abstract index, the general register index, the by-law index and the Canada Lands index. Additional informal and unguaranteed indexes and cross-references are available and vary greatly from office to office. When Registry land is automated by Teranet into the POLARIS database under Part II of the *Land Registration Reform Act*, such as with Parcelized Day Forward Registry titles, Registry Non-Converts, and Registry 40-Year Loads, Registry indexes are converted to an automated format including both a title and a mapping database, together with cross-references to prior paper records. Title searching procedures and examples for Parcelized Day Forward Registry titles and Registry Non-Converts are covered in Chapter 8.

Abstract Books

Notice of the granting of the Crown patent, not the Crown grant itself, is forwarded to the land registrar of the appropriate Registry or Land Titles office, who records the date, the patentee's name and a brief description of the land in an index referred to as an abstract book. If more than one lot is granted, a page is opened for each lot on which subsequent registrations are recorded. Crown land is owned by the province, and less frequently by the federal government, and patented lands by the registered owner. Subsequent grants of land are usually by conveyance, often referred to as an indenture, deed, grant, memorial, or instrument.

All registrations and deposits subsequent to the Crown patent are recorded on any affected lot page in an abstract book in the order of date and time of their registration. The abstract books contain a brief reference to every registered document commencing with notice of the Crown patent. The originals of the documents, except the patent, are filed in the Registry office and may be examined upon request or self-serve.

Prior to the subdivision of lands, the abstract books are referred to as concession books. After the registration of a plan of subdivision, the abstract book is referred to as a plan book. Searching title in the concession book is commonly referred to as "going behind the plan". Concession books usually comprise more than one volume, especially in offices where the old books have not been re-copied. At the top of each page, the concession and lot numbers are recorded for your convenience. Numerous individual properties may be registered on a concession lot. As a result, it can be both difficult and time-consuming for a title searcher to sort the property being searched from other properties registered on the concession lot pages.

A new abstract book is opened: (1) on registration of a plan of subdivision; (2) whenever new municipalities are incorporated or land is annexed into a new municipality; and (3) when Crown land is patented (concession lots).

Whenever an instrument (document) is registered, the land registrar makes a brief entry in the abstract book of the registration number, type of document or instrument, date of registration (and, in the past, date of execution of document), the owner(s) (grantor and grantee) or lender(s) (mortgagor and mortgagee), consideration, description, remarks, and, on occasion, the quantity of land involved. Upon making a written request (the form is provided by the Registry office) showing the lot and plan or concession and lot number and the municipality, and on paying the prescribed fee, one may have the use of the books. Most offices display signs to aid you in finding the various Registry office departments. In offices undergoing POLARIS conversion, abstract books and instruments are self-serve and on microfilm. Copies of abstract book pages and related plans may be purchased as part of a search. Sample pages from an abstract book are illustrated in Figure 3.1. The Registry search outlined in Chapter 4 was prepared based on this example.

Where Teranet has automated the abstract index but not legally converted ownership to Land Titles, Registry properties have been parcelized and allocated a PIN. When the same owner in the same capacity owns more than one whole or part lot that adjoin, all title information from the affected lot pages is consolidated into one parcel identified by a PIN and recorded on one parcel register. As a result, the abstract index is reorganized by giving each separately owned parcel of land a PIN and a separate parcel print-out in the automated POLARIS index. In POLARIS, Registry land is indexed by PIN and parcel and not by lot. Block and property maps in Registry offices as well as the Teraview automated index for POLARIS are available as a comprehensive index and cross-reference for all properties in the automated abstract index.

General Register Index

Section 18(6) of the *Registry Act* states that certain documents, because they do not contain a registerable land description, shall be registered as general registrations and, except as otherwise provided in the Act, shall not be recorded in the abstract index. General registrations often affect multiple parcels of land or land not yet ascertained, as with a will, a power of attorney, or a corporate change of name. The general register index is organized both alphabetically and chronologically. A land registrar may maintain a separate alphabetical index for any class of general registrations. Some offices keep a separate book for wills called the "wills book". General registrations are often identified by the prefix "G.R." followed by a registration number. It is common for the abstract index to contain a cross-reference to relevant general registrations. General registrations affect title and must be included in the title search. The following documents are commonly registered in the general register, although they may be registered in the abstract index when accompanied by a local description acceptable for registration:

1.   wills or notarial copies;

2.   certificates of appointment of estate trustee(s) with or without a will, previously called letters probate and letters of administration;

3.   general appointments of new trustees (notarial copies);

4.   certificates or certified or notarial copies of judgments or of court orders appointing or removing estate trustees (executors, administrators), guardians or trustees;

5.   powers of attorney or revocations or notarial copies;

6.   certificates of appointment of statutory guardians under the *Substitute Decisions Act, 1992*, S.O. 1992, c. 30 or notarial copies;

7.   certificates or certified or notarial copies of orders respecting mental incompetence;

8.   certificates or certified or notarial copies of orders of change of name;

9.   general bars of dower;

10. orders in council of Canada or Ontario, or certified copies thereof not containing local descriptions;

11. notarial copies of letters patent or certificates of incorporation, supplementary letters patent, or certificates of continuance;

12. notarial copies of letters patent or certificates changing names of corporations or amalgamating corporations;

13. notarial copies of certificates of amalgamation of loan or trust corporations;

14. general conveyances and transfers of assets of a corporation to another corporation;

15. notarial copies of licences in mortmain;

16. notarial copies of extra-provincial licences under the *Extra-Provincial Corporations Act*, R.S.O. 1990, c. E.27; and

17. instruments of a class prescribed by regulation.

By-Law Index

The by-law index contains a registration number, a by-law number, the name of the municipality and the title of the by-law, for every by-law registered after January 1, 1963. As the by-law index is a chronological index, it is usually easier to check for related land-use by-laws in the municipal records. By-laws that directly affect title to land, such as *Planning Act* subdivision control and road widening, closing by-laws, or heritage destinations, must contain a local description and be registered against the land affected in the abstract index. An order of the Ontario Municipal Board, or the Lieutenant Governor in Council under the old *Municipal Boundary Negotiations Act* or a certified copy of a quieting order under the current *Municipal Corporations Quieting Orders Act*, R.S.O. 1990, c. M.51 that changes municipal boundaries is registered in the by-law index.

Day Book/Fee Book

Registrations are entered immediately in the day or fee book. As soon as Registry staff are able, interim day book entries are transferred to the appropriate permanent register, *i.e.*, the abstract or general register. Depending on how busy the Registry office has been, entries of recent registrations, going back as far as two weeks, may be found only in the day book. Checking the day book for recent registrations is an essential part of any title search.

Patent Books

Informal, unguaranteed books may list original lots, Crown patents and patentees. As well, the original abstract page for a lot will indicate when land was patented and to whom. Complete Crown patent information is available from the federal and provincial governments.

Road Indexes

Separate books or abstract index pages, often at the beginning or end of subdivision plan books, are kept for roads and registrations that affect roads. Separate books may exist for concession roads. Informal books may be available recording road or street name changes and related by-laws. As well, large maps may provide road references.

Plan Index Book

An index book referencing all plans in an office may be available.

Copy Books

In the days before photocopying, microfilming and optical scanning, all registered instruments were painstakingly copied word for word into chronological copy books. These artifacts are finding their way into provincial and local archives and historical associations. At present, microfilm back-up records are required and available for all registrations.

Canada Lands Index

The land registrar of a Registry division to which a national park or Indian reserve is annexed maintains an index book called the "Canada Lands Index" in which he or she records plans, descriptions and orders filed, deposited or registered for the purposes of:

- the *Canada Lands Surveys Act*, R.S.C. 1985, c. L-6;

- the *Navigable Waters Protection Act*, R.S.C. 1985, c. N-22;

- the *Public Transportation and Highway Improvement Act*, R.S.O. 1990, c. P.50;

- orders of the Governor in Council that transfer jurisdiction and control of land from the Government of Canada to the Government of Ontario; and

- registering instruments that affect lands that were heretofore or are hereafter granted, in fee simple, by Canada.

Lands that comprise national parks and Indian reserves are annexed to their respective registry divisions in a schedule to the Canada Lands Regulation, R.R.O. 1990, Reg. 992. When land in a national park or Indian reserve is granted by the

Crown in fee simple, the grant will be cross-referenced from the Canada Lands Index to the new Registry abstract book or Land Titles parcel register. Unlike Registry, in Land Titles national parks and Indian reserves are not recorded in a separate index.

REGISTRY ACT RELATED LEGISLATION

The *Registry Act* affects more than 40 Ontario statutes, including:

Assessment Act, R.S.O. 1990, c. A.31

Boundaries Act, R.S.O. 1990, c. B.10

Certification of Titles Act, R.S.O. 1990, c. C.6

Condominium Act, 1998, S.O. 1998, c. 19

Construction Lien Act, R.S.O. 1990, c. C.30

Courts of Justice Act, R.S.O. 1990, c. C.43

Electricity Act, 1998, S.O. 1998, c. 15, Sched. A

Environmental Protection Act, R.S.O. 1990, c. E.19

Estates Administration Act, R.S.O. 1990, c. E.22

Evidence Act, R.S.O. 1990, c. E.23

Escheats Act, R.S.O. 1990, c. E.20

Execution Act, R.S.O. 1990, c. E.24

Expropriations Act, R.S.O. 1990, c. E.26

Family Law Act, R.S.O. 1990, c. F.3

Forestry Act, R.S.O. 1990, c. F.26

Land Registration Reform Act, R.S.O. 1990, c. L.4

Land Titles Act, R.S.O. 1990, c. L.5

Land Transfer Tax Act, R.S.O. 1990, c. L.6

Local Roads Boards Act, R.S.O. 1990, c. L.27

Mining Act, R.S.O. 1990, c. M.14

Mortgages Act, R.S.O. 1990, c. M.40

Municipal Act, 2001, S.O. 2001, c. 25

Niagara Escarpment Planning and Development Act, R.S.O. 1990, c. N.2

Ontario Water Resources Act, R.S.O. 1990, c. O.40

Personal Property Security Act, R.S.O. 1990, c. P.10

Planning Act, R.S.O. 1990, c. P.13

Provincial Land Tax Act, 2006, S.O. 2006, c. 33, Sched. Z.2

Public Lands Act, R.S.O. 1990, c. P.43

Social Housing Reform Act, 2000, S.O. 2000, c. 27

Surveyors Act, R.S.O. 1990, c. S.29

Surveys Act, R.S.O. 1990, c. S.30

Consolidated regulations under the *Registry Act* set detailed requirements for forms, descriptions, plans, registration requirements, records, indexes, and fees.

Registry Act Regulations

Registry Act Regulation	Subject
O. Reg. 427/99	Registry Divisions (current schedule of divisions)
R.R.O. 1990, Reg. 996	Registry Divisions
R.R.O. 1990, Reg. 992	Canada Lands
R.R.O. 1990, Reg. 993	Certification Areas
O. Reg. 43/96	Surveys, Plans and Descriptions of Land
R.R.O. 1990, Reg. 995	Forms and Records
O. Reg. 21/99	Registration of Instruments and Deposit of Documents in French
O. Reg. 22/99	Forms
R.R.O. 1990, Reg. 998	Transfer of Functions (where functions of Director of Land Registration transferred to or shared with Director of Titles under R.R.O. 1990, Reg. 998, s. 1)

Figure 3.1
ABSTRACT BOOK SAMPLE PAGES

	LOT 1	CONCESSION 2	WEST OF YONGE ST		TWP. OF YORK	
NO.	INSTRUMENT DATE	REG'N. DATE	GRANTOR	GRANTEE	CONSID'TION	DESCRIPTION
	PATENT	1 Nov. 1860	The Crown	Jos. Gray		All -200 AC.
234 MTG	3 Oct. 1895	31 Dec. 1895	Joseph Gray	Peter Kelso		W½ of N½ Ac. 50 Ac.
969 DEED	4 Jul. 1898	5 Oct. 1901	Joseph Gray	John J Long		PT.20 Ac-RESER'G A R.O.W.
1020 DISCH. MTG	3 Aug. 1901	1 Nov. 1901	Peter Kelso	Jos. Grey		MTG 234
TWP. NORTH YORK incorporated - 18 July 1922						
724 GRANT	3 Jan. 22	7 Feb. 22	Joseph Gray	Eldon Jones	$1	Pt. com'g 150'S. from N.W. <; TH SLY 510±; TH ELY 1650'; TH N.WLY 1560± to P.O.C. Subj. to restrictions.
1198 MTG	5 Jun. 48	9 Jul. 48	Joseph Gray	Royal Bank		Land in 234
PLAN 4340	7 Oct. 50	1 Dec. 50	Joseph Gray - owner Royal Bank - mtgee			Land in 234
102 DEPOSIT						Part
1945 EXOR.	2 Jun. 53	5 Aug. 1953	Joseph Acton	Peter Garnet	$1	Part inal - com'g. 70'W. from the N.E.<; TH N74°W 100'; TH S 16°W 100'; TH N 74° E 25'; TH S 17°E 10'; TH N 74°20'10"E 125'; TH N 16°W 100' to P.O.C.
345GR CONSENT	3 Jul. 53	5 Aug. 53	Treasurer of Ont.	Este. of Jos. Gray		Part

Figure 3.1 (cont'd)

NO.	INSTRUM'T	LOT 4 DATED	PLAN 4340 DATE	TWP. OF NORTH YORK GRANTOR	GRANTEE	CONSID''TION	DESCRIPTION
PLAN 4340		7 Oct. 56	1 Dec. 56	Joseph Gray - Owner			ALL INAL
1200	BY-LAW	1 Jan. 56	7 Jan. 56	THE CORP'N OF THE TWP. OF NORTH YORK		CREATING AN AREA OF SUBDIVISION CONTROL AND DEEMING LAND IN PLAN 4340 NOT TO BE WITHIN A REG'D PLAN OF SUBDIVISION	ALL INAL subj. to a MTG.
1215	GRANT	4 Jan. 56	5 Jul. 56	Joseph Gray	John Paul	$1	
1821	DISCHGE	1 Jul. 58	9 Jul. 58	Royal Bank	J. Long, Exec'or of Jos. Gray		MTG. 1198
2231	MTG	5 Jul. 58	9 Jul. 58	John Paul	Joy Builders Ltd.	30,000	ALL INAL
2304	M.L.	8 Dec. 58	8 Dec. 58	Star Lumber Co.	John Paul	6,000	ALL INAL
2799	CERT. OF ACTION ON M.L.	7 Jan. 59	9 Jan. 59	Supreme Court of Ontario	John Paul		M.L. #2304
3999	Grant under P. of S.	1 Aug. 1960	3 Aug. 60	John Paul	Joy Builders Ltd.	$1	ALL INAL
PLAN 6183		3 Jul. 75	4 Dec. 75	Joy Builders Ltd.			ALL INAL

Figure 3.1 (cont'd)

NO.	INSTRUM'T	LOT 22 DATE	PLAN 6183 DATE REG'N.	TWP. OF NORTH YORK GRANTOR	GRANTEE	CON.	DESCRIPTION
PLAN 6183		3 Jul. 75	4 Nov. 75	Joy Builders Ltd.			ALL INAL
8444	AGRT.	1 Nov. 75	6 Dec. 75	Joy Builders Ltd.	The Corp'n of Twp. of North York		ALL INAL
9302	MTG.	1 Nov. 75	7 Dec. 75	Joy Builders Ltd.	Eldon Troy	$25,000.00	ALL
17342	GRANT	7 Oct. 75	10 Dec. 75	Joy Builders Ltd.	John J. Jones	$1	ALL – subj. to MTG
28944	GRANT of Easm't	2 Jan. 76	7 Jan. 76	John J. Jones	Bell Telephone Co. of Canada		over rear 4'
82567	GRANT	8 Aug. 76	6 Sep. 76	John J. Jones	John Santos	$1	W½ - subj. to easement
103999	DISCHARGE	15 Jun. 77	15 Jun. 77	Eldon Troy	Joy Builders Ltd.		MTG. 9302

BOROUGH OF NORTH YORK – INCORPORATED Jan. 1, 1977 (actual date, 1967)

NO.	INSTRUM'T	DATE	DATE REG'N.	GRANTOR	GRANTEE	CON.	DESCRIPTION
64R2342	REFERENCE PLAN	1 Jul. 78	6 Jul. 78				PARTS 1 AND 2
1938768	GRANT	1 Jul. 78	10 Jul. 78	John Santos	Winston Croy	$1	PART 1 on R-PLAN 64R-3422 Subject to an easm't Over PART 2

CITY OF NORTH YORK - INCORPORATED Feb 14, 1979

CHAPTER 4

The 40-Year Registry Search

INTRODUCTION

Title searches are usually completed on behalf of purchasers, lenders (mortgagees) confirming good title to collateral, commercial tenants, existing owners, developers, expropriating authorities, environmental assessments and audits, oil and gas companies, or any other interested person. As well, title searches are a condition of submitting requisitions, giving an opinion on title, advising clients, completing a survey, or obtaining a policy of title insurance. A title search in the Registry system involves the finding and examining of all relevant indexes and all related registered instruments, including plans that affect the ownership of a property.

The responsibility for establishing and documenting the evidence of land ownership required to establish whether the owner has a good and marketable or an insurable title lies with the title searcher/conveyancer. A title searcher should have the ability to complete methodical, detailed, accurate work independently under demanding circumstances and time constraints. The search forms the basis for the lawyer's review of title, completion of *Planning Act*, R.S.O. 1990, c. P.13 compliance statements and other statements of law, and subsequent written opinion on title. The title searcher's search notes, along with the solicitor's review notes, must be retained and may provide important information when the client sells or refinances the property, particularly if subsequent purchasers or lenders find a title problem. If all the relevant title material has not been identified and retained, the lawyer may be liable to his or her client for professional negligence. In addition, title insurers audit search procedures of real estate lawyers in order to manage and reduce risk, including the decision not to place policies through individual lawyers.

Under the Registry system, a lawyer for a purchaser arranges for a 40-year search of title to be carried out for the lands the vendor claims to own and has promised to sell to a purchaser. The agreement of purchase and sale provides the lot and plan number, the owner's name, and particulars of charges/mortgages to be assumed and those to be discharged. The lawyer sends a memorandum requesting a search and setting the search requirements to the title searcher. Search requirements vary depending on the nature of the transaction and insurer preferences. The request sets out the type of search required, identified risks such as an access condition in the offer, and any relevant deadlines such as the requisition(s), condition(s), and closing dates. Whenever possible, the search request for a residential property should be accompanied by a copy of the agreement of purchase and sale along with a survey, if one is available.

REGISTRY SEARCH VARIATIONS

Land registration reform and POLARIS have resulted in a number of variations in Registry system title searching. It is critical for the lawyer and conveyancer to be able to identify from the outset the type of search required in order to ascertain ownership. Simply stated, a Registry search is a Registry search, whatever it is called, and whatever the environment, paper or electronic, that contains the Registry records. Search procedures may vary, but the law concerning title remains the same. The title searcher/conveyancer must research and document, and the real estate lawyer must review, a Registry title throughout the 40-year title search period required under the *Registry Act*, R.S.O. 1990, c. R.20. Today, real estate practitioners may encounter any of the following categories of Registry searches. Registry titles in POLARIS are indicated only by an "R" following the property identification number (PIN). The conveyancer or lawyer must review the parcel register and identify the nature of the Registry variation as this determines the search procedure. The following Registry variations require a full 40-year search:

1. **Traditional 40-Year Non-Automated (Paper Records) Registry Search** Some areas of Ontario, for example, Manitoulin Island and Victoria County, still contain Registry titles that have not been automated or converted to Land Titles. These areas require traditional Registry searches in paper records. These areas are interspersed among automated properties in POLARIS. Current planning still includes the retention of Registry titles in difficult or costly to automate areas.

2. **Automated Parcelized Day Forward Registry Search (POLARIS)** A "Parcelized Day Forward registry (PDFR)" title is when POLARIS parcelizes a Registry property and gives it a PIN. The automated PDFR parcel register contains only the ownership document at the date of automation (last transfer) and post-automation registrations. It does not include registrations, for example, mortgages and construction liens, between the transfer entered on the register and registrations that follow the PIN (parcel) creation date. Prior registrations in the 40-year title period and registrations between the last transfer and the PIN creation date remain in the paper records. For example, Frontenac, Wentworth, Oxford, and Kent have PDFRs. POLARIS plans to convert existing PDFRs to Land Titles Conversion Qualified (LTCQ) titles at a future date. A 40-year PDFR search requires the following:

a. Search of automated Registry records in POLARIS from the date the property was automated and the PIN was activated up to present.

b. Search of Registry paper records as far back as is necessary to document all title information within the 40-year search period.

c. The POLARIS PIN's property description line provides a cross reference to the property's lot and plan information as well as a reference to the previous Registry abstract book. In Registry, lot and plan information always allows the searcher the means of identifying earlier relevant paper records.

d. In theory, simply by passage of time, all records for the 40-year search period will transition into the automated POLARIS index.

3. **Automated 40-Year Load Registry Search (POLARIS)**

In a few areas of the Province, POLARIS simply parcelized and allocated PINs to Registry properties. Forty years of Registry records were then searched and loaded onto the automated parcel register. Some areas shortened the search period by issuing certificates of title under the *Certification of Titles Act*, R.S.O. 1990, c. C-6; it is unnecessary to search behind the date the certificate was issued. Other areas simply loaded 40 years of Registry records and did not issue a certificate of title.

4. **Automated Non-Convert, 40-Year Load Registry Search (POLARIS)**

In areas where Registry properties have been converted to Land Titles, the continuing presence of a Registry property raises serious title concerns. The only indication of a non-convert is an "R" following the PIN, same as with any Registry title in POLARIS. When Teranet was unable to confirm good title during the conversion process, it created a non-convert parcel. The Registry Office kept a file and made notes on all non-convert properties. In the past, information in this file helped lawyers who needed to rectify title on a purchase, mortgage, new development, or as a condition for closing or obtaining a title insurance policy. These files are no longer released to solicitors, although the information may still be available on a less formal basis. *Land Titles Act* Bulletin No. 2004-02 sets out the procedure for the conversion of a non-convert to an LTCQ title.

A particularly careful search of title is indicated as many non-converts involve potential *Planning Act* issues, breaks in the chain of ownership, or serious description deficiencies. In some parts of the Province, non-converts simply lack required legal age statements or spousal status statements or consents and are easily remedied. Often the solution is found in a deposit or other document still in the Registry records that was not brought forward in the conversion. A non-convert is an unknown; alert the title insurer and proceed with caution!

Registry searches in POLARIS are completed, at least in part, on Teraview. These Registry properties have been parcelized, assigned PINs and incorporated into the POLARIS mapping database, a geographic information system reference tool that in no way establishes or guarantees descriptions or boundaries. Current records are indexed and accessed online by PIN, owner name, municipal address, map, road, subdivision plan, but not by the traditional Registry lot and plan organization. Apart from working in the automated records, the searcher follows the basic steps for a Registry search. This chapter focuses on the traditional 40-year search in the paper records. Sample Registry parcel register printouts and generic procedures and for searching in an automated POLARIS environment are also described in Chapter 8. The following Figure is an example of a Registry parcel register. Note the "R" following the PIN. A Registry PIN does not indicate the nature of the Registry title. This example is a nonconvert. The lawyer would have to review the search and the documents to identify the reason for the non-convert status. The register alone does not contain enough information to indicate the title problem that stopped the parcel from being converted.

Figure 4.1

PARCEL REQUEST FOR REGISTRY PIN 21282-0485[*]

Figure 4.1 (cont'd)

Ontario | MINISTRY OF GOVERNMENT AND CONSUMER SERVICES | LAND REGISTRY OFFICE #66

ABSTRACT INDEX (ABBREVIATED) FOR PROPERTY IDENTIFIER 21782-0485 (R)

PAGE 2 OF 2
PREPARED FOR MOORE
ON 2008/11/20 AT 13:32:31

REG. NUM.	DATE	INSTRUMENT TYPE	AMOUNT	PARTIES FROM	PARTIES TO	CERT/CHKD
~~CA?????~~	~~1999/07/??~~	~~LIEN~~				C
CA100227	1990/07/17	LIEN				C
CA100228	1990/07/17	LIEN				C
CA105580	1990/08/28	CERTIFICATE				C
		REMARKS: CA100228				
~~CA?????~~	~~1990/07/??~~	~~LIEN~~				C
~~CA?????~~	~~1990/??/??~~	~~DISCHARGE~~				C
		REMARKS: CA99726				
~~CA?????~~	~~1990/10/11~~	~~SEARCH~~				C
		REMARKS: CA109169				
CA122378	1991/01/03	ORDER				C
		REMARKS: CA100127, CA105599				
CA443400	1996/12/12	TRANSFER	$495,000		GREEN ROOF INVESTMENTS LTD.	C
CA443401	1996/12/12	CHARGE	$250,000		MALDEN, SERENA	C
CA473000	1997/05/29	DEPOSIT				C
CA490451	1997/08/14	POSTPONEMENT				C
		REMARKS: CA443401, CA490526				
CA741600	2001/09/12	CHARGE	$225,000		HILL, JACK HILL, JILL	C
CA741601	2001/09/12	ASSIGNMENT GENERAL				C
		REMARKS: CA741600				
CA741602	2001/09/12	POSTPONEMENT				C
		REMARKS: CA443401, CA741600				

NOTE: ADJOINING PROPERTIES SHOULD BE INVESTIGATED TO ASCERTAIN DESCRIPTIVE INCONSISTENCIES, IF ANY, WITH DESCRIPTION REPRESENTED FOR THIS PROPERTY.
NOTE: ENSURE THAT YOUR PRINTOUT STATES THE TOTAL NUMBER OF PAGES AND THAT YOU HAVE PICKED THEM ALL UP.

THE FUTURE OF THE TRADITIONAL 40-YEAR REGISTRY SEARCH

Land registration reform has been actively phasing out the Registry system and the 40-year search since the 1960s. From the late 1800s, most land patented in northern Ontario was registered in the Land Titles system. From the late 1960s forward, almost all new plans of subdivisions and condominiums were registered in the Land Titles system, either by legislative requirement or developer choice. Today all Registry titles must be upgraded to Land Titles as a condition of subdivision or condominium development. As of the 1980s, Teranet has been systematically converting Registry titles to LTCQs. LTCQs must be upgraded to Land Titles Absolutes as a condition of subdivision. Although Teranet has simply parcelized, assigned PINs, and automated some Registry titles, now called PDFR titles, these automated Registry titles are scheduled to be converted into Land Titles at a later date.

Ontario is in the process of adopting mandatory electronic land registration (ELRS/e-reg). Electronic land registration is only available for land registered in the Land Titles system. Today, over 95 per cent of registrations take place in ELRS. The implementation of electronic land registration will result in the ongoing phasing out of the traditional Registry system.

THE PERMANENT NEED FOR REGISTRY SEARCH SKILLS

Registry skills will remain necessary for the foreseeable future. Although, traditional Registry searches are becoming increasingly less common, POLARIS has maintained Registry parcels in parts of Ontario. Even after the completion of the POLARIS initiatives, Registry searching will continue to take place, whenever it is necessary to check title back to the Crown for legislative exceptions to the 40-year title period or for exceptions to the Land Titles guarantees. For example, Crown grants prior to the most recent 40-year period may contain a variety of Crown reversions (reversionary rights) such as military easements (weapons/firing ranges) crossing agreements, easements, hydro/electric, water, canal rights, and transportation rights in general.

Registry searches will continue to be completed for historical and specialized informational purposes, such as, for the purposes of an environmental audit and assessment. In addition, surveyors also complete title searches in order to determine the extent (boundaries) of title and accurately locate shoreline and road allowances. Consequently, surveyors search back farther than 40 years to find historical description information such as, shoreline location, water levels, mining easements, and timber easements. Historical searching and description tracking for the purpose of supporting Aboriginal title, Aboriginal rights, and location of treaty areas often require Registry search skills, as do archeological assessments for development purposes.

Unfortunately, easements, restrictive covenants, registrations relating to encroachments, descriptions, and possessory rights, and other registration were not infrequently missed in the mass conversion from Registry to LTCQ titles. These rights can potentially be revived by a new registration as long as it does not conflict with an intervening registered interest. The Ministry has issued a bulletin setting out the options for reviving interests not brought forward in the POLARIS conversion. Registry searching is needed to identify rights missed in the conversion and provide the documentation required to revive the right by a new registration in Land Titles.

During the conversion of Registry titles to LTCQ titles, Registry documents were incorporated into Land Titles parcel registers. As a result, conveyancers must be familiar with Registry documentation when completing LTCQ searches.

CONTENTS OF A COMPLETED REGISTRY SEARCH

Although, historically, lawyers and title searchers have never adopted a uniform search format, the following rules are usually followed. Completed search notes are written in ink on one side of the page only. Pages are consecutively numbered and firmly attached. Most searchers use colour-coding to identify different properties and link their descriptions to related registered documents. A completed search contains the following information, usually in the order indicated below:

1. request for search and search requirements;
2. search summary;
3. execution (writ) search/certificate;
4. copies of all plans;
5. sketch (diagram) of main and adjoining lands, including access;
6. chain (tree) of title, if search is complex;
7. abstract of title (list of all registered documents within the 40-year search period);
8. adjoining lands abstracts, including roads, and copies of last registered deeds' descriptions; and
9. document summaries of all registered documents within the 40-year search period and photocopies of the most recent registered deed, outstanding mortgages and other encumbrances and documents such as court orders and *Planning Act* consents and validation certificates.

MAIN STEPS IN A REGISTRY SEARCH

The following steps are necessary to complete a search and detailed instructions are provided in subsequent paragraphs:

1. review the search request and requirements (consider title insurance search requirements, particularly concerning executions and escheat), diarize deadlines, and review the factual information contained in the request;
2. obtain the short legal description (lot, plan, *etc.*);
3. obtain the appropriate abstract book(s);
4. obtain copies of all related plans, including subdivision and reference plans;
5. establish a chain of title prior to the registered owner, for 40 years or more (for exceptions and when no transfer within 40 years), by owner name or property description or both;
6. establish the 40-year search period and identify a root or a starting point for the search (consider exceptions);
7. establish a chain of title subsequent to the starting point, by name and description;
8. prepare an abstract of title, being a list of all related documents;
9. requisition, read, and summarize or copy the documents;
10. search abutting lands for boundaries, description problems, easements, access, restrictive covenants, and subdivision control violations (*Planning Act*), where applicable;
11. prepare an illustration or sketch of the relevant lands and adjoining lands;
12. search roads and confirm access;
13. search executions (in WritSearch on Teraview);
14. complete subsearch (day book);
15. complete corporate, partnership, personal property security registration, Crown patent, and other inquiries as requested (relevant off-title inquiries will be completed separately);
16. organize search materials and prepare a search summary;
17. review of search by lawyer; and
18. arrange for retention and storage of the search records.

FINDING YOUR LEGAL DESCRIPTION

The following section is a sample, historical simulation, as this area of Toronto has now been automated by POLARIS. Dates have been altered for simulation purposes. The abstract index for this example property was illustrated earlier at the end of Chapter 3 (see Figure 3.1).

Presume that you were requested to complete a 40-year search of the east half of Lot 22, Plan 6183 in the City of Toronto, formerly in the City of North York, in the Municipality of Metropolitan Toronto, formerly in the Borough of North York, and that the registered owner is John J. Jones (see Figure 3.1). Normally, one determines which system land is registered under from the plan of subdivision. When the letter "M", or the Land Titles office number and the letter M, *e.g.*, "66M", or the letter "D" prefixes the plan number, the land is under the Land Titles system.

Plan 6183 was registered under the Registry system. Plans of subdivision under that system are numbered consecutively, followed by the municipality (*e.g.*, Plan 6183, Borough of North York). In the case of land that has not been subdivided, it is described by lot and concession number (*e.g.*, Lot 3, Concession VI, Township of North York).

Before starting a Registry search, you must first obtain a short legal description including the lot and plan, in order to find the proper abstract book, as abstract books are indexed by lot and plan. If, for example, you only have a municipal address instead of the necessary lot and plan, the Registry office may provide municipal maps illustrating concession lots and plans of subdivision including lot and plan cross-references. Failing that, a search of the local municipal assessment indexes, sometimes available at the Registry office, will provide a cross-reference from the municipal address to the lot and plan. As well, agreements of purchase and sale, vendors' deeds and previous title documents, tax bills and surveys contain lot and plan references.

OBTAINING THE ABSTRACT BOOK(S) AND RELEVANT PLAN(S)

Obtain the proper abstract book for a fee and purchase or make a copy of the white print of Plan 6183 (a white print is a copy of the original) at the beginning of your search. Books and plans are self-serve or obtained by the "Request for Service" form available in all Registry offices (see Figure 4.2).

You may wish to make a sketch of the relevant properties from the original plan — a time-consuming effort and usually only attempted when white prints are not available. The white print will provide you with the following information:

1. the boundaries of the plan drawn in a solid line;

2. the date of registration of the plan and the registered owner(s) and mortgagee(s) at registration;

3. the surveyor, survey monuments, and astronomic north;

4. the lands subdivided, *e.g.*, a plan of subdivision of Lot 4, Plan 4340, Township of North York;

5. the dimensions and bearings of the lot to be searched, and the adjoining lots, blocks and reserves;

6. easements;

7. road dedications, road widenings and closings, and one-foot reserves;

8. the relation of Lot 22 on Plan 6183 to Lot 4 on Plan 4340, *e.g.*, Lot 22 is situated in the south east corner of Lot 4 and commences 120 feet south from its north-west angle and runs southerly 60 feet by 45 feet easterly; and

9. *Planning Act* approval.

Presume that the subject land was subdivided by Plan 6183 in 1975. You will have to search prior to 1975 for a root of title. The white print indicates that Plan 6183 is a re-subdivision of Lots 4 and 5 on Plan 4340 of the Township of North York (Boroughs were established January 1, 1967).

Your next requirements are the abstract book and white print for Plan 4340. The white print indicates that Plan 4340 was registered in 1956, and that it is a sub-division of Lot 1, Concession II, West of Yonge Street. As you are already back more than 40 years, it is usually not necessary to search farther back unless you are looking for statutory exceptions to the 40-year rule. However, if you were instructed to search back to the Crown patent, you would next refer to the concession book for Lot 1, Concession II. Fortunately, at least in this example, the entries go back to the Crown patent so that there are no more books to examine. This process is called "going behind the plan".

Figure 4.2

REQUEST FOR SERVICE FORM

Please print clearly! *Veuillez écrire en lettres moulées!*

Ontario

Land Registry
Enregistrement immobilier ☐

Land Titles
Droits immobiliers ☐

P.P.S.R.
E.D.S.M. ☐

Request for Service
Demande de

WARNING / *AVERTISSEMENT*
$5,000 fine for alteration or removal of documents or records
Une amende de 5000 $ sera infligée à toute personne qui modifiera ou enlèvera des documents ou des dossiers

Firm Name
Nom de l'entreprise

Phone No.
N° de tél.

Address Street No.
Adresse N°

Street Name (in full)
Nom de la rue (au complet)

Reference
Référence

City/Town
Ville

Date

Name of Searcher
Nom du recherchiste

Municipality
Municipalité

Lot(s)		Plan

Parcel(s) *Parcelle(s)*	Section(s)	Concession	Range *Rang*
1			
2			
3			
4			
5			
6			
7			
8			
9			
10			
11			
12			

Fees for Searches:
Frais de recherche: _____

Documents: _____

Large Copies:
Copies grand format: _____

Small Copies:
Copies petit format: _____

Other Services
(specify):
*Autres services
(spécifier):*

White Prints:
Diazotypie: _____

_____

This is your Receipt
Conservez votre reçu

Total $ _____

10434 (08/86)

Once a plan has been registered, an entry is made in the concession and plan abstract books of the particulars of registration, the registered owner and prior mortgagees. At this point, dispense with the concession book because all the entries for the lands, now subdivided, are entered in the plan book, except for deposits. Since deposits, which are not "registrations", provide evidence of some fact relating to prior title, the description will be that of the prior title.

The white print of the plan of subdivision in this case indicates that the northwest angle of Lot 4, Plan 4340 commences 150 feet south from the north-west angle of Lot 1, Concession 2 and runs southerly 180 feet by 150 feet easterly. Figure 4.2 clarifies the relation of the plan's location to the underlying concession lot and the original road allowances. On referring to the concession book, in the description column you will find reference to all the north-west quarter of Lot 1. Plan 4340 will be contained in that description.

It is unusual for a plan to be re-subdivided as in this case. Frequently, it is un-necessary to refer to the concession book because many plans have been registered for 40 years or more. However, there are lands that have never been subdivided by plan of subdivision and in that case only the concession book is required.

THE 40-YEAR SEARCH PERIOD

The *Consumer Protection and Modernization Act, 2006*, S.O. 2006, c. 34 rein-forces the *Registry Amendment Act*, S.O. 1981, c. 17, which provided that the title search period be limited to and not exceed 40 years, except for statutory excep-tions, such as Crown rights and statutory rights set out later in this chapter. As a result, a chain of title does not depend upon and is not affected by any document registered before the commencement of the 40-year title search period except for statutory exceptions. The traditional real estate practice that required a title searcher to search for and establish the existence of a "good root of title" prior to the 40-year period has been eliminated, except as provided in the amendment in-corporated into the current *Registry Act*.

Fortunately, the *Consumer Protection and Modernization Act, 2006* and the Su-preme Court of Canada case, *Fire v. Longtin*, [1995] S.C.J. No. 83, [1995] 4 S.C.R. 3 (S.C.C.) have ended the earlier controversy around the interpretation and the application of the *Registry Amendment Act* sections. For an authoritative re-view of the law concerning the 40-year title search period, refer to *"Title Search-ing under the Ontario Registry Act* after *Fire v. Longtin*: A Consensus Position" (1996) 1 R.P.R. (3d) at 173-90 by R. Rosenblatt, Q.C.

Sections 111 to 115 of the *Registry Act* limit the title search period to the most recent 40-year period, immediately preceding the date of closing, subject to ex-ceptions stated in the statute. For example, if the closing date is set for May 4, 2005, the 40-year title search period will start on May 4, 1965. It is a common title searching practice to start 40 years prior to the date of the search as closing dates are frequently rescheduled. The safest practice is to start the search 40 years prior to the agreement of purchase and sale.

Establishing the Commencement Date for the Search of Title

The title searcher will identify the first conveyance of the freehold estate (not a mortgage) registered after the commencement date of the 40-year search period. Once the searcher has confirmed the existence of a conveyance of the freehold estate within the 40-year period, he or she will record all relevant registrations throughout the entire 40-year search period. This conveyance of the freehold estate is the starting point in the tree or chain of title (*Registry Act*, s. 112(1)).

Where there has been no conveyance of the freehold estate (other than a mortgage) within the title search period, the chain of title commences with the first conveyance of the freehold estate immediately preceding the 40-year period (*Registry Act*, s. 112(2)). This conveyance prior to the 40-year period forms part of the title and is also referred to as the root. The searcher will record this conveyance of the freehold as the root and then record all subsequent registrations within the 40-year period. Although the conveyance of the freehold forms part of the chain of title, registrations between this root and the start of the most recent 40 years do not form part of the title (*Registry Act*, s. 112(3)). Some lawyers still prefer that the title searcher record all registrations between the root conveyance and the commencement of the 40-year period as well as all registrations that fall within the 40-year period.

Section 112 of the *Registry Act* establishes the 40-year title search period as follows:

> Title search period
>
> 112. (1) A person dealing with land shall not be required to show that the person is lawfully entitled to the land as owner thereof through a good and sufficient chain of title during a period greater than the forty years immediately preceding the day of such dealing, except in respect of a claim referred to in subsection 113(5).
>
> Deemed commencement of chain of title
>
> (2) Where there has been no conveyance, other than a mortgage, of the freehold estate registered within the title search period, the chain of title commences with the conveyance of the freehold estate, other than a mortgage, most recently registered before the commencement of the title search period.
>
> Instruments registered prior to title search period not effective
>
> (3) A chain of title does not depend upon and is not affected by any instrument registered before the commencement of the title search period except,
>
> > (a) an instrument that, under subsection (2), commences the chain of title;

    (b)   an instrument in respect of a claim for which a valid and subsisting notice of claim was registered during the title search period; and

    (c)   an instrument in relation to any claim referred to in subsection 113(5) [Utility easement].

The 40-year search period is also subject to ss. 113(6) and 114(2).

Expiry of Claims to Title After 40 Years

Registered rights expire 40 years after the date of registration unless a new notice of claim has been registered. In order to preserve existing claims, a notice of a claim may be registered at any time within the notice period or at any time after the expiry of the notice period as long as there has been no registration of a conflicting claim. A Notice of Claim must be registered by Forms 32 and 33 in R.R.O. 1990, Reg. 995. It should be noted that a claim older than 40 years is no longer preserved by reference to it in a document registered within the search period (*e.g.*, a restrictive covenant or an easement). Any long-term owner, person, or corporation is vulnerable to losing ownership rights for failure to register a timely notice of claim. Property owners and their advisors must arrange for periodic searches and reviews of title in order to ensure that property rights do not inadvertently expire and are periodically registered within the 40-year notice period. Corporations, institutions, government bodies, and older individuals are more likely to have owned land for 40 years, and, as a result, are particularly at risk.

Chapter 3 contains a review of legislation and a discussion of case law, including *1387881 Ontario Inc. v. Ramsay*, [2005] O.J. No. 2727 (Ont. C.A.) leading up to the clarification of search and notice periods under the *Consumer Protection and Modernization Act, 2006*, which amended Part III of the *Registry Act*. The current legislation is set out below.

Section 111(1) defines a notice of claim as follows:

> "Notice of claim" means a notice of claim that is registered under subsection 113 (2) and that is in the prescribed form and includes a notice registered under a predecessor of this Part or under *The Investigation of Titles Act*. ...

Section 113 of the *Registry Act* provides for the expiry of claims, notice of claim and renewal of claim and effect of claim as follows:

Expiry of claims

113. (1) A claim that is still in existence on the last day of the notice period expires at the end of that day unless a notice of claim has been registered.

Notice of claim

(2) A person having a claim or a person acting on that person's behalf, may register a notice of claim with respect to the land affected by the claim,

    (a)   at any time within the notice period for the claim; or

    (b)   at any time after the expiration of the notice period but before the registration of any conflicting claim of a purchaser in good faith for valuable consideration of the land.

Renewal

(3) A notice of claim may be renewed from time to time by the registration of a notice of claim in accordance with subsection (2).

Effect of notice of claim

(4) Subject to subsection (7), when a notice of claim has been registered, the claim affects the land for the notice period of the notice of claim.

Exceptions to the 40-Year Search and Notice Periods

There are two types of exceptions to the 40-year search and notice periods. The first is referred to as off-title searches and the second is statutory exceptions that pre-date the 40-year period set out in the *Registry Act*.

Off-Title Inquiries

Both the *Registry Act* and other statutes set out numerous claims against land that are not required to be registered on title in order to affect the ownership of land. As a result, a lawyer/conveyancer must check for the existence of these unregistered claims against title in other locations, *e.g.*, the survey, municipal offices, utility offices, and federal and provincial government offices. These inquiries are referred to as "off-title" searches. Many off-title inquiries are now completed online. Chapter 14 focuses on off-title inquiries and Appendix 5 contains a list of online references, off-title inquiries, and Internet addresses.

Statutory Exceptions that Pre-Date the 40-Year Period

Important claims affect title to land even though they pre-date the 40-year search period; for example, claims of the Crown set out in the Crown patent. Chapter 3 provides a complete listing of claims that affect title but do not need to be registered within the 40-year period in order to affect title. The more common statutory exceptions to the 40-year title search period, found in s. 113 of the *Registry Act*, requiring additional investigation, include the following:

    1.   a claim to a freehold estate in land or an equity of redemption in land by a person continuously shown by the abstract index for the land as being so entitled for more than 40 years as long as the person is so shown;

2. claims of the Crown, such as Crown patent reservations and Crown claims in a public highway or lane, unpatented land and escheat (check Crown patent);

3. claims by possession, such as adverse possession and easements by prescription (only a survey can illustrate these possessory rights);

4. claims arising under any Act, such as statutory liens (*e.g.*, taxes, utilities) and spousal rights;

5. public utility easements or Ministry of Government Services easements, registered prior to July 31, 1941 and continuing until December 31, 1999. A notice of claim in respect of a public utility easement of a municipality or an easement of the Ministry of Government Services registered before the 31st day of December, 1999 is as effective as if it had been registered on the 31st day of July, 1981. Under s. 114(2.1), "a public utility easement of a municipality includes a public utility easement transferred by a municipality under a transfer by-law to a corporation established under the *Business Corporations Act* pursuant to section 142 of the *Electricity Act, 1998*";

6. a railway company right of way, in respect of lands acquired after July 1, 1930; and

7. Aboriginal title, Aboriginal rights, and treaty rights.

On a historical note, prior to the *Registry Amendment Act*, title searchers established a chain of title which commenced at a "good root of title" prior to the 40-year title search period and extended throughout that period. Conveyancers considered a "good root of title" to be the first conveyance in fee simple immediately prior to the 40-year period, for consideration, to a stranger, unsupported by any other document outside the 40-year period. Grants, deeds, indentures, bargains and sales, memorials and court orders were typical of good roots, whereas grants under power of sale (sale depends on a mortgage), quit claims (a release of someone else's interest), executor's or administrator's deed (rely on the terms of a will) were not considered good roots.

Short Roots of Title

When starting at a short root, a searcher must check the full 40-year period for any easements, restrictive covenants, adverse possession, and federal or provincial Crown rights and include them in the search. It is advisable to check with the lawyer in charge of the file prior to using a short root of title instead of searching the full 40-year period. The following, although registered within the 40-year period, are considered to be short or good roots of title and a point of commencement for the title search:

1. **A Crown patent**. Review the patent for Crown reservations and con-
    ditions, *e.g.*, road and shoreline allowances.

2. **A conveyance from the Director under the *Veterans' Land Act***. Af-
    ter World War II, the Director, under the *Veterans' Land Act*, R.S.C.
    1970, c. V-4, purchased lands for resale to veterans. Such grants had
    the same effect as a Crown grant and are considered by some lawyers
    to be a good root of title.

3. **A tax deed**. Under s. 379(7) of the *Municipal Act, 2001*, S.O. 2001, c. 25:

    > A tax deed, when registered, vests in the person named in it an estate in
    > fee simple in the land, together with all rights, privileges and appurte-
    > nances and free from all estates and interests, except,
    >
    > (a) easements and restrictive covenants that run with the land;
    > (b) any estates and interests of the Crown in right of Canada or in right of
    >   Ontario other than an estate or interest acquired by the Crown in right
    >   of Ontario because of an escheat or forfeiture under the *Business
    >   Corporations Act* or the *Corporations Act*;
    > (c) any interest or title acquired by adverse possession by abutting land-
    >   owners before the registration of the tax deed.

    Tax deeds under the *Municipal Tax Sales Act*, R.S.O. 1990, c. M.60
    (repealed S.O. 2001, c. 25, 484(2)) also vested title in the municipality
    or a purchaser.

4. **Expropriations**. Pursuant to the *Expropriations Act*, R.S.O. 1990,
    c. E.26, where a proposed expropriation has been approved under this
    Act or under the *Ontario Energy Board Act, 1998*, S.O. 1998, c. 15,
    Schedule B and its predecessor, the land vests in the expropriating
    authority on registration of a plan of the lands in the appropriate Reg-
    istry office. The plan must be signed by the expropriating authority
    and an Ontario Land Surveyor.

5. **Certificates under the *Certification of Titles Act***, the *Investigation of
    Titles Act*, R.S.O. 1960, c. 193 (repealed S.O. 1964, c. 48, s. 1) and the
    Quieting Titles Act, R.S.O. 1980, c. 427 (repealed S.O. 1984, c. 11,
    s. 208). A certificate of title is effective as of the certificate date. The
    certificate should be checked for any exceptions, conditions, out-
    standing rights and encumbrances, or qualifications on the title.

6. **Vesting orders** that vest title pursuant to a judge's order.

Figure 4.3

SUBDIVISION AND RE-SUBDIVISION OF PART OF A CONCESSION LOT

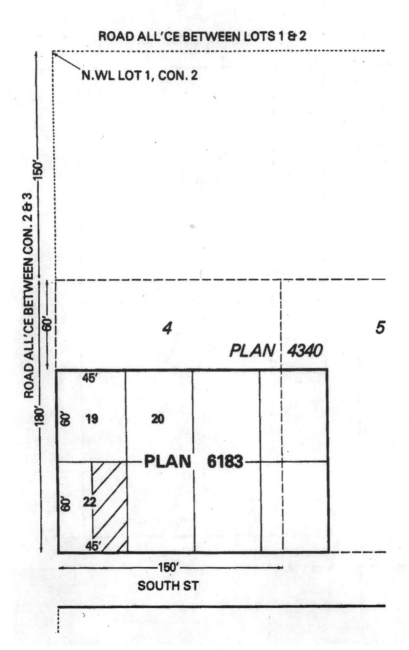

Figure 4.4
DIAGRAM ILLUSTRATING A CONCESSION LOT PARCEL

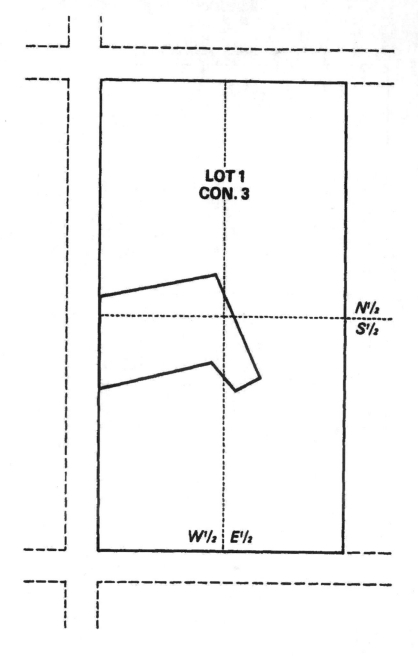

Certification of Title

The *Certification of Titles Act*, first passed in 1958, eliminates the 40-year search for Registry system lands which have received a certificate of title. This Act does not apply to land registered in the Land Titles system. In Ontario, it is compulsory for land in proposed plans of subdivision to be investigated and certified. As of January 1, 1982, a new plan of subdivision cannot be accepted for registration unless a certificate of title has been registered certifying that the subdivider is the owner of the land.

In addition, the Director of Titles may, without application, certify the title to land included in existing plans of subdivision registered under the *Registry Act*.

The certificate of title is conclusive evidence that the person named therein as owner has an absolute title to the lands described in the certificate as of the time named therein, subject only to the exceptions and encumbrances shown in the attached schedules.

Since a certificate creates a new root, it is unnecessary to search behind it. Consequently, the search need only check from the certificate up to the present and record the following information endorsed on the certificate:

1. particulars of documents affecting the land registered after the effective date of the certificate and prior to the registration date of the certificate (the effective date is the date that the certification office completed its search);

2. particulars of documents registered after the registration date of the certificate and new plan;

3. particulars of documents referred to in the certificate's schedule of encumbrances; and

4. particulars of the certificate number, time, effective date and registration date.

Plans prepared in support of an application under the *Certification of Titles Act* (CTA) are attached to the certificate of titles and copies are deposited as reference plans under Part II of the *Registry Act*. Lawyers may request a review of the patent for reservations, easements and road allowances, particularly when dealing with cottage and rural properties. Mortgages, liens, and agreements, which have been discharged or released and ruled out after the registration of the certificate may or may not be abstracted depending on a lawyer's request. It is unnecessary to read ruled-out documents.

Re-Abstracting of Documents Prior to Plan of Subdivision

Since 1978, the Director of Land Registration has authority to direct land registrars to include an abstract of all documents affecting the land to be subdivided in the abstract of the plan book immediately preceding the pages opened for lots on the new plan. As most new subdivisions are required to be registered in Land Titles, this process only applies to a few offices in which Land Titles is not available.

CHAIN OF TITLE BY NAME

The next step is to set up a chain or tree of title by tracing the names of the prior registered owners on title back 40 years, or as long as it takes to set up a commencement date of title. The chain is usually formatted as a flow chart or tree of title diagram, similar to a family tree. The chain diagram may demonstrate dates and information about deaths, spousal status, name changes, powers of attorney, corporate reorganizations, relevant instrument numbers, description changes and plans, outstanding mortgages and liens and *Planning Act* severances, consents and by-laws. A chain is a picture summarizing title throughout the 40-year search period.

Tracing a chain is usually a fairly straightforward exercise: from the grant to the vendor or most recently registered owner, *e.g.*, John Jones, follow the grants from one prior owner to the next until a search starting point is established. A meticulous investigation of all information in the books is necessary in order to avoid missing a document.

Occasionally, missing links occur and it is necessary to attempt to establish the starting point first. For example, where the next-of-kin of an intestate in whom the land vested after three years conveys, you will not find a grant to that person in the chain of title. A search in the general register index under the name of the previous registered owner will reveal if estate administration had been granted, or if a declaration stating the facts of the death of the intestate had been deposited on title.

Similarly, a change of name resulting from marriage or divorce can slow the pace when tracing names. The next deed on title or a deposit usually contains recitals or a declaration that clarifies the situation.

In the 19th and early 20th centuries, people were not too concerned about registering deeds. You may find a deed registered July 20, 1969 that was dated August 3, 1865, so it is often practical to check recent registrations when a link is missing.

In the past, properties could have been subdivided or assembled or both as illustrated in the chain of title in Figure 4.5. Prior title registrations may reveal that an owner (The Carson Company Limited) purchased all four parts of a current property from four different sellers in four different deeds. Similarly, the search may reveal that an owner in the chain of title (John Parks) divided and sold a property to four different purchasers in four different deeds. It is essential to track all of the parts of the land being conveyed and also all of the prior owners/ownership interests such as life tenants and remainder interests in a life estate. Subdivision and part lot control restrictions in the *Planning Act* may apply.

Figure 4.5

CHAIN OF TITLE

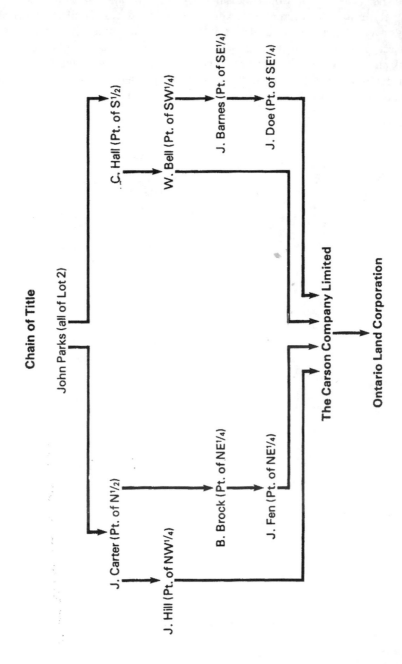

CHAIN OF TITLE BY DESCRIPTION

After a preliminary chain has been established by name, it is necessary to confirm the chain by checking the brief legal description in the abstract book for all possibly related instruments. List all entries that appear to affect the subject lands, and their registration numbers.

The abstract books contain only a condensed description of the land. Often, the description in the abstract book reads "part", meaning a part of the lot. To determine which part, it is necessary to requisition the documents and examine the descriptions. It may be frustrating but there is no other way of establishing whether the documents affect the subject lands. "Part inal" means part of the lands described in the document and other lands. As parts of the original lands are sold off, less land is usually granted in subsequent deeds, *e.g.*, the grantor owned the north half of the concession lot and sold only the west half of the north half, retaining the east half of the north half. Descriptions for lands that have been severed, particularly a parcel severed from a concession lot, are often difficult to plot, but the sections later in the chapter on land descriptions and metes and bounds descriptions should help to resolve any problems that arise.

Title searching is not an exact science but instead resembles a scavenger hunt, or possibly a game of hide and seek. Some documents may not cross-reference to the subject land by name or by description. Miscellaneous plans, deposits, by-laws, court orders, correcting deeds, and quit claims, containing neither name nor description references, may still affect the subject lands. Be sure to find and include all possibly related documents.

Review any reference plans noted on the abstract page as they may provide description or access information about both the subject lands and adjoining lands.

ABSTRACT OF TITLE

Once a chain of title has been established, copy all relevant or possibly relevant entries recorded in the abstract book onto your search paper (commonly referred to as abstract paper) in chronological order. Space is required for document summaries and lawyer's remarks, so for practical purposes, record one entry per page. Some searchers draft an index list of relevant documents and summarize documents on separate pages. Note the registration number of the last document recorded in the abstract book, whether or not it affects the subject lands, and the date of completion of the search, to indicate where and when a subsearch should commence. This list of relevant documents is called an abstract of title.

Documents recorded in an abstract of title may include: grants or deeds; grants under power of sale; final orders of foreclosure; mortgages, assignments and discharges; mortgages of mortgages; leases and releases; deposits; notices of conditional sales; construction liens; certificates of action and lien discharges; notices of pending litigation; cautions; tax arrears certificates; tax deeds; by-laws; agreements; certificates; consents; notices of security interest; annexation orders and plans.

Write in ink on one side of the page only and number the pages consecutively. Handwriting must be clearly legible and the layout must be well organized, as the title search is retained as a permanent record in the lawyer's file.

DELETION OF DISCHARGED DOCUMENTS (RULING OFF IN RED)

Section 56(11) of the *Registry Act* provides that after a discharge of mortgage has been registered for ten years or more, the land described in the mortgage is not subject to any claim under the mortgage, and the entries for the mortgage, discharge and related documents can be ruled off the abstract index. In the past, land registrars drew a line through the entries for mortgages and their discharges when the discharge had been registered for ten years or more. Documents ruled off in red in the abstract index need not be recorded on your search, provided the ruled line has been initialled and the registration number of the discharge has been noted in the margin.

Today, land registrars are required to rule off the entries for the mortgage, discharge and related documents, immediately after the discharge is registered, as a part of the abstracting procedure. The registration number of the valid discharge will be noted in the margin beside the mortgage and related document entries and signed by an authorized person. Earlier partial discharges and the original mortgage may be ruled off when a final discharge has been registered and the land registrar is satisfied that the *Planning Act* subdivision control provisions have been complied with. These rules also apply to mortgage-like documents such as debentures, deeds of trust, and lodgements of title documents.

Similarly, where a valid discharge of any of the following documents has been registered for two or more years, the land is not affected by any claim and the document may be ruled off the abstract page together with its discharge and all other related documents (*Registry Act*, s. 67).

- a certificate of pending litigation;
- a claim for a construction lien under the *Construction Lien Act*, R.S.O. 1990, c. C.30 or the *Mechanics' Lien Act*, R.S.O. 1980, c. 261;
- a certificate of action in respect of a construction lien under the *Construction Lien Act* or the *Mechanics' Lien Act*;
- a registered notice of a conditional sale contract;
- a registered gas or oil lease;

- a registered notice of security interest under the *Personal Property Security Act*, R.S.O. 1990, c. P.10;
- a certificate under s. 3(3) of the *Housing Development Act*, R.S.O. 1990, c. H.18;
- a registered notice of a lien under the *Legal Aid Services Act, 1998*, S.O. 1998, c. 26;
- a registered notice of a lien under the *Ontario Works Act, 1997*, S.O. 1997, c. 25, Schedule A; and
- a registered notice of a lien under the *Ontario Disability Support Program Act*, S.O. 1997, c. 25, Schedule B.

REQUISITION AND SUMMARIZE DOCUMENTS

All documents, including plans listed on the abstract of title, must be summarized or copied as part of the search. This process is referred to as abstracting documents; it provides the lawyer with the information needed to assess the legal effectiveness of the registered documents which constitute legal title.

Documents may be obtained by a request for service form provided by the Registry office or self-serve from microfilm records. When completing a request for service form, include the reference "G.R." (General Register document) or "Deposit/Dep." and any other document series references. There may be either a flat fee for the search or a fee for each document ordered. Documents ruled out in red on the abstract index do not need to be recorded.

If in doubt as to whether a document affects the subject land, record it and let the lawyer decide its validity. The most reliable way to decide if a document affects land is by description. It is safer to write too much rather than to miss a registration that affects title. It is easy to prove negligence, as the title record remains as proof of a title searcher's or lawyer's oversight.

Documents are read and summarized in chronological order. Document summaries vary widely in format and usually involve the use of standard abbreviations. Title searchers use a variety of private and commercially available pre-printed search papers that already contain pre-printed information boxes including standard abbreviations. Some title searchers use a stamp containing standard abbreviations.

The legal description in each document is summarized and reconciled with the descriptions in the first and last registered deeds. Many searchers photocopy last registered deeds and descriptions, outstanding liens and encumbrances, such as mortgages, and documents that are either complex or that raise title issues, such as sale papers and wills. Refer to Chapter 5 on documents, and Chapter 9 on easements, restrictive covenants, by-laws, development agreements and plans, and Crown grants. These chapters set out how to read and summarize documents in a search.

LAND DESCRIPTIONS

Land descriptions incorporated in a document, although interesting, often pose a special challenge. Fortunately, the advent of the requirements for reference plans in 1973 has greatly reduced the number of complex or ambiguous descriptions. At the beginning of a search, if a survey is not available, or if a plan or a sketch is not attached to a document, time may be saved by preparing a sketch from the description in the first deed and noting errors and omissions and changes in subsequent descriptions.

The description in subsequent deeds must be checked verbatim with the first deed and against the plans or sketches to ensure that exactly the same land is granted each time. For the sake of accuracy and time, obtain copies of long, complicated descriptions and particularly of those containing errors and inconsistencies. To determine if there are description inconsistencies and possible encroachments on your land, check the abutting lands descriptions against the description for the subject lands. The legal descriptions should coincide exactly.

Plans found on title are not always full plans of survey and may not contain sufficient information for a lawyer to form a title opinion. When placing new monumentation, the surveyor must attempt to re-establish the original boundary, not the limit described in the deed. Original boundaries are proven by evidence of natural boundaries (*e.g.*, lakes), or by proof of the location of the original undisturbed monumentation or other evidence as to where they were located and, as a last resort, by the limits as described in the deed. Only a survey can determine actual boundaries, possessory rights, encroachment, and the extent of a property.

The legal description in the deed, especially an old deed, may not correspond with the boundary the surveyor established. The descriptions in old documents and on old plans are usually in chains and links. A chart to facilitate conversion of chains, links, rods, *etc.*, to feet and inches or metric units has been included in Appendix 1. Notes should be made of any irregularities in dimensions and bearings.

The Surveyor's Real Property Report

A plan of survey is certified by an Ontario land surveyor who attends at the site and defines and documents the location and extent (boundaries) of a parcel of land. He or she is usually requested to site buildings, rights-of-way, easements, lanes, roads, fences, water courses, shorelines, trees, elevations, monumentation, and measurements. The description in the registered documents should conform to the survey. Additional online description and mapping information resources can be useful and is discussed in Chapter 2. Surveys avoid costly, acrimonious boundary disputes.

Registered Sketch

In the past, sketches were prepared by someone other than a surveyor, for the purpose of illustrating a description. They were often attached to old documents and deposits to illustrate a complex description that would require a reference plan today. Although deposits are not registrations under the *Registry Act*, title searchers check deposits as they may provide useful information on title and description problems.

Metes and Bounds Descriptions

Undeveloped lands are usually described in an uncomplicated manner such as:

1. the whole of the lot;
2. the south half of the lot; or
3. the south half of the north half of the lot.

Where land boundaries are parallel to the original lot line the description is easy to follow. A parcel having a frontage of 100 feet on the road allowance by 400 feet deep and running westerly from the north-east corner would be described as follows:

> commencing at the north-east corner of Lot 2;
> thence southerly along the east limit of the said lot, 100 feet to a point;
> thence westerly and parallel to the north limit of the said lot, 400 feet to a point;
> thence northerly and parallel to the east limit of the said lot, 100 feet more or less to a point in the north limit of the said lot;
> thence easterly along the north limit of the said lot, 400 feet more or less to the point of commencement.

The term "more or less" is a protection against minor discrepancies in legal descriptions; the measure is not as important as the fact that the line must reach the east limit, or the point of commencement, whichever it may be. There cannot be a gap.

In the case of a parcel of land where the boundaries are not parallel, a surveyor is engaged to prepare a metes and bounds description. The surveyor uses bearings, similar to compass directions, to define the relationship of a line to north and south. Bearings are stated as:

1. east or west of north
   e.g., north 74 degrees west on a description means a line which is 74 degrees west of north;

2. east or west of south
   e.g., south 18 degrees 16 minutes east means a line which is 18 degrees 16 minutes east of south.

The most common unit for measuring angles is the degree, which is defined as 1/360 of a circle.

Figure 4.6

DIAGRAM TO ILLUSTRATE BEARINGS

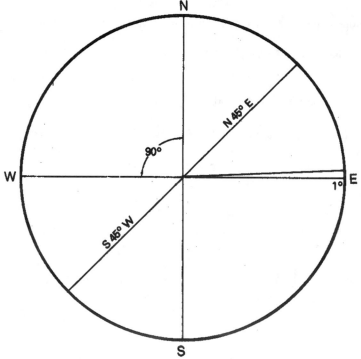

A circle contains 360 degrees (360°).
A degree contains 60 minutes (60').
A minute contains 60 seconds (6").

Every line has two directions (see Figure 4.6). The diagonal line proceeding towards the top of the page has a bearing of 45 degrees east of north, written as north 45 degrees east. When the line proceeds in the opposite direction, it has a bearing of 45 degrees west of south, written as south 45 degrees west.

Curved lines are often difficult to follow. The arc length, radius, and chord length and chord bearing are a part of the description. Note that a curve to the right will curve in a clockwise direction and a curve to the left will curve in a counter-clockwise direction. The arc of a curve to the right will always be to the left of a chord, when facing in the direction of the chord and vice versa.

The following description and Figure 4.7 illustrate bearings in a metes and bounds description:

> In the City of Brantford, in the County of Brant and being composed of part of Lot 61 according to Plan 141, registered in the Registry Office for the Registry Division of Brant.
> Premising that all bearings herein are referred to the western limit of Woodlawn Avenue, in the City of Brantford, being north 13°44'5" west.
> Commencing at the north-east corner of Lot 61, registered Plan 141; thence southeasterly on a curve to the right, having a radius of 150.00 feet, an arc distance of 20.23 feet (the chord equivalent being 20.23 feet measured north 17°36'4" west) to a point in the east limit of said Lot 61;
> thence south 13°44'5" east along the eastern limit of said Lot 61, a distance of 38.76 feet more or less to the south-east corner of said Lot 61;
> thence south 76°15'0" west along the southern limit of said Lot 61, a distance of 60.75 feet more or less to a point in the said southern limit;
> thence north 23°52'0" west, to a point in the north limit of said Lot 61, a distance of 30.00 feet more or less;
> thence north 62°58'5" east along the northern limit of said Lot 61, a distance of 80.13 feet to the north-east corner and the point of commencement.

Figure 4.7

METES AND BOUNDS DESCRIPTION DIAGRAM

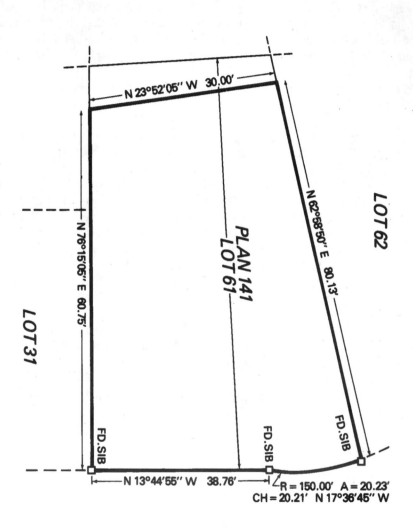

WOODLAWN AVENUE

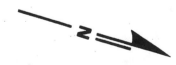

New Municipal Boundaries

Where new municipal boundaries have been established by dividing existing municipalities among two or more municipalities, an entry is made on the abstract book or parcel register.

If the land being searched is in the "Counties of Lincoln and Welland" and they have been renamed "Regional Municipality of Niagara", you will find "Regional Municipality of Niagara" noted on the book or register. Following that, the description in subsequent registered documents would contain the prior designation followed by "now in the Regional Municipality of Niagara". Record amendments of municipal boundaries on your search notes as they guide the way back into earlier records.

Description Registration Requirements

A description of land in an instrument, other than a plan, is referred to as a local description. The basic requirement for a local description is that it contain sufficient information to enable the land registrar to record the instrument in the proper abstract index or parcel register. Reference should be made to O. Reg. 43/96 and its predecessor regulation, R.R.O. 1990, Reg. 997. Ontario Regulation 997, although repealed, continues to apply to instruments and plans that were or are to be registered or deposited and that were executed before April 20, 1996. Also, O. Reg. 43/96, s. 67 sets out detailed requirements for descriptions in documents, including plans, tendered for registration in a land registration office.

Ontario Regulation 43/96 sets out the requirements for the preparation and registration of strata plans, reference plans, plans of subdivision, expropriation plans, municipal plans, correction of plans, sketches to illustrate descriptions, plans to illustrate descriptions, as well as the requirements for the POLARIS properties and property maps for land "in any part of Ontario designated under Part II of the *Land Registration Reform Act* [R.S.O. 1990, c. L.4]" (O. Reg. 43/96, s. 44). This detailed regulation also sets out the general requirements for the description of land in Registry documents (instruments) other than a plan. Where the deed/transfer to the vendor does not conform to description requirements, title search notes should indicate that the description is unacceptable for use in subsequent documents. Some of the more commonly referred to description registration requirements are the following:

1. The concession and township, the lot and plan number, the number and relevant parts on a reference plan, the name of the municipality and of the county, regional municipality or district, and the municipality where the land was included at the time of the execution of the instrument are included in a description acceptable for registration.

2. A local description shall mention every lot affected by the instrument and shall mention:

   (a) if the lot is according to a registered plan, the registration number of the plan;

   (b) if the land is a designated part on an expropriation plan, or is a portion of such a part, the number of the part and the registration number of the expropriation plan; and

   (c) if the lot is according to an original survey, the concession, tract, range, section or other designation in accordance with the original grant from the Crown.

3. Lots must be identified as: Lots 1, 2, 3, and 4, not as Lots 1 to 4.

4. Where the bearings of lines are in degrees, the origin of the bearings should be stated in the description and survey; they relate to the bearing of the road allowance.

5. Descriptions for curved boundaries shall include the arc lengths, the radius, the chord length and chord bearing.

6. The description for part of a lot shall refer to at least one of the corners of the lot, and shall give the distance from that corner to an angle of the part being described.

7. Symbols may be used in place of the words for degrees, minutes and seconds, but not for feet and inches.

8. Capital letters, N., S., E., and W. may be substituted for north, south, east, and west with respect to bearings and degrees. Other words in descriptions may not be abbreviated or contracted.

9. A local description shall not describe land by reference to a registered plan of subdivision that has been entirely superseded by a subsequent registered plan of subdivision.

10. Land shall not be described by exception, *e.g.*, "all Lot 10, Concession IV, except that part previously granted by document number 45789". A reference plan must now be prepared for the exception, except in the following cases:

    (a) a description repeated in a registered document prior to July 1, 1964;

    (b) the land excepted is the whole of the land shown on a registered plan;

    (c) the land excepted is a right-of-way of a railway company, or a public street, road or highway laid out by an original survey or shown on a registered plan;

(d) the land excepted is entirely surrounded by the land described in the instrument; or

(e) the land excepted is a designated PART on a reference plan or expropriation plan.

11. A local description shall not describe any boundary of the land affected by the instrument solely by reference to the registration number of a registered instrument or be dependent upon another instrument, unless the registered instrument is a registered plan.

12. A boundary line may not be described by reference to a registered document number, *e.g.*, "thence northerly to the south limit of land described in document registered number 16789".

13. Imperial units or metric units must be used. Subdivision of these units requires decimals to describe fractions, except that inches are still acceptable where the description is the same as in a previous document.

14. The new and former designation provided for reorganized municipal boundaries must be included in all future descriptions prepared for documents, *e.g.*, "in the Town of Halton Hills, in the Regional Municipality of Halton (formerly the Town of Acton in the County of Halton)".

15. Land may be described as the southeast 1/4 of Lot 14, Concession II, if it was so described in the Crown patent, and no adjoining part of the said lot is owned by the person dealing with such part.

16. A parcel of land may still be described as the north half of Lot 47 according to Registered Plan Number 2000, if it was previously so described in a registered document.

17. The description for part of a street or highway that has been stopped up or closed shall refer to the registration number of the by-law or other document by which it was stopped up or closed.

18. Notwithstanding any of the foregoing, an unacceptable description used in a deed/transfer to a person now deceased may be used in the estate trustee's (administrator's or executor's) deed/transfer; likewise in an assignment of a lease or charge/mortgage, an unacceptable description may be repeated.

19. Certain awards, certificates, releases, claims, consents, notices, orders, or other like instruments may be described by means of abbreviations, contractions, or references to registration numbers of previously registered instruments of the land affected, if the description is sufficient to enable the land registrar to record the instrument in the proper abstract index or parcel register for the land.

20. The description in a discharge of a charge or mortgage that purports to discharge all of the mortgaged land is sufficient for registration

purposes under the *Registry Act*, if it contains a reference to each lot and plan or lot and concession or to any other geographic designation of land as referred to in the mortgage. The full description as contained in the mortgage need not be repeated.

21. Descriptions must refer to and conform to a registered certified plan under the *Boundaries Act*, R.S.O. 1990, c. B.10.

22. If a plan or sketch is attached to the instrument, a description shall include a statement that the description is the same as that illustrated on the plan or sketch, if that is the case.

23. The following are deemed to be metes and bounds descriptions:

    (a) a description of a part of a lot lying to one side of a described line; or

    (b) a description by reference to the perpendicular width, either throughout or to a given perpendicular depth, of a rectangular part of a rectangular lot.

Reference to Registration Number for Most Recently Registered Deed Containing the Same Description

Pursuant to s. 61(2) of the *Registry Act* regulation, Surveys, Plans and Descriptions of Land, O. Reg. 43/96:

> If a description is by metes and bounds, in whole or in part, and appears in a previously registered deed, it shall include [a reference to the registration number of the most recent, previously registered deed] containing the same description unless,
>
> (a) the instrument is a certificate of discharge;
> (b) a property identifier has been assigned to the land; or
> (c) the land has been divided into parcels for abstract purposes under subsection 83 (3) of the *Registry Act*.

If a description sets out an easement and appears in a previously registered deed, it shall include the registration number of the most recent, previously registered deed containing the same description (O. Reg. 43/96, s. 61(3)).

"If the description does not appear in a previously registered deed but describes the same land as a description that appears in a previously registered deed, the description shall include" a reference to the registration number of the most recent, previously registered deed "containing the earlier description" (O. Reg. 43/96, s. 61(4)).

Land Registrar's Discretion Regarding Description Registration Requirements

The land registrar may choose to exercise some discretion in accepting documents that do not meet the formal description requirements. For example, if the description of land in an instrument presented for registration is not a local description or a description acceptable for registration, the land registrar, having regard to the circumstances, may register the instrument if the description accurately describes the land or the description is exactly or substantially the same as in a previously registered instrument.

POLARIS Block and Property Maps

Pursuant to s. 21(1) of the *Registry Act*, Registry land designated under Part II of the *Land Registration Reform Act*, as part of the POLARIS process, is divided into blocks and properties and assigned property identifiers. Once a property identification number (PIN) has been assigned to a property, subsequent deeds need not include a reference to the registration number of the most recent, previously registered deed containing the same description. Part VIII of O. Reg. 43/96, entitled Properties and Property Maps, sets out how registry land must be divided into blocks and properties and how property maps and block index maps are prepared and maintained. Schedule 1 of this regulation contains additional requirements.

Metric

The International System of Units known the world over as SI (from the French *Système International d'Unités*) is the modern version of the metric system. It was adopted in Ontario on July 1, 1976, and since that time, land registrars have accepted plans of subdivision, surveys and land descriptions in imperial or metric units. The metre (m) and decimals thereof are used to express distances, except for the occasional use of kilometres (km) on key maps. Conversion involves basic mathematics. Tables have been provided in Appendix 1 to facilitate the process of converting imperial to metric units.

Road Allowances

Frequently, road allowances shown on the original survey have never been opened, and new surveys show that what appeared to the purchaser to be private property is actually a road allowance. Crown patents usually contain the following reservation, "reserving a strip of land 66 feet in width, back from the water's edge for a road".

The *Municipal Act, 2001* provides that abutting owners have the first right to purchase, to the centre line of road allowances. If they do not exercise the right within the time period as set out in a by-law, then the municipality may sell the road allowance to other interested parties. The sale should be authorized by a by-law of the particular municipality. Similar provisions exist in the *Public Lands Act*, R.S.O. 1990, c. P.43 for stopping up any road allowance that was laid out by a Crown surveyor and that is not within a municipality. Common problems with waterfront properties and shoreline allowances in cottage country include older cottages built on the road allowance, changing water levels resulting in difficulty establishing the location of original shoreline allowances and water access rights. The Ministry of Natural Resources can assist in determining the existence, location and ownership of shoreline allowances; however, an up-to-date survey is the appropriate way of dealing with waterfront and road allowance issues.

Approvals must be obtained for the proper closing of any road allowance and it is important to note on your search the identity of the approving party and registration number of the closing by-law. Also, where part of a highway laid out on a plan of subdivision registered after March 27, 1946 is closed, the by-law is not effective until it has been approved by the Minister of Municipal Affairs and Housing, formerly the Minister of Housing.

Occasionally, you may find that part of the land that you have been requested to search forms part of a road allowance, and other lands, *e.g.*, parts of Lots 4 and 5, Concession 6, and part of the road allowance between the said Lots 4 and 5, in the said concession lot. Pages are designated for road allowances in the abstract books, and in small offices an entire book is set aside for all road allowances and concession roads. A particular sequence was never established and an entry for Concession 6 may be followed by an entry for Concession 12. By-laws authorizing the opening and closing of road allowances are recorded in the abstract books.

Plans of Subdivision

When a developer decides to construct houses on its land, it must register a plan of subdivision. The name of the person who signs the plan as owner will be recorded on the abstract book as the registered owner. After complying with both the *Registry Act* and the *Planning Act*, and obtaining the approval of the municipality and mortgagees, the subdivider lays out and names and numbers lots, blocks, streets, and reserves. The bearings of all the boundaries and the dimensions of all the lots, blocks, and reserves are shown on the plan. Every road allowance, highway, street, lane, walk, and common shown on a registered plan of subdivision is deemed to be a public road, highway, street, lane, walk, and common respectively. As well, spousal rights of possession are released from land dedicated by an owner for a street or public highway. A parcel of land on a subdivision plan can be referred to simply as being, for example, "Lot 5, Plan 649, City of London, County of Middlesex".

One-Foot Reserve

Subdividers are required to reserve a one-foot wide strip of land at the end of streets on the boundaries of the plan of subdivision to prevent anyone from using the streets until the requirements of the subdivision have been completed. Although a reserve has been granted or transferred to the municipality, it is not a public street or highway until it is dedicated as such by a municipal by-law or, alternatively, a notice has been typed on the plan of subdivision to the effect that the one-foot reserves thereon are dedicated.

The route from the subject land to a main access highway may be across one or more plans of subdivision. The reserves may be dedicated on the plan being searched but not on the adjoining plans, so that the client does not have the right of legal access to a main highway. Evidence of all reserve dedications should be recorded on your search. One-foot reserves are often created as a permanent arrangement in order to control access along the boundaries of lands adjacent to busy streets. The title searcher must check the pages at the back of the plan books for the roads, reserves, and related by-law entries. Include summaries of road-related entries in the search notes.

Reference Plans

The introduction of reference plans provided a significant improvement in title searching. The hours spent interpreting old, often inaccurate, descriptions have been greatly reduced. Most importantly, reference plans eliminate the possibility of error. In effect, reference plans both graphically illustrate and replace metes and bounds descriptions. Each Registry office maintains a "Reference Plan Index".

The *Registry Act* requires that a plan of survey certified by an Ontario Land Surveyor be deposited on title for every severance/subdivision, unless the land being conveyed or mortgaged is the whole of a lot, block, street, lane, reserve, or common, according to a registered plan of subdivision, judge's plan or municipal plan, or the whole part remaining to an owner (*Registry Act*, ss. 80 and 81). Reference plans are required when granting an easement or right of way. Reference plans are also required to replace existing metes and bounds descriptions which, in the opinion of the land registrar, are vague, complex or inaccurate.

A reference plan is usually referred to as a "R-Plan" and the land on which it is deposited is referred to as a "PART" or "PARTS" on a reference plan. All the PARTS are surveyed and monumented in accordance with the *Registry Act*. Each reference plan is allotted a number when it is deposited in the Land Titles or Registry office and the plan number is prefixed by the Registry office number and the letter "R", *e.g.*, 33R-2341. An appropriate description should read, "Parts of Lots 11 and 12, Plan 649, City of London, County of Middlesex, more particularly described as PARTS 7 and 8, 33R-649".

The land registrar may decide to waive the statutory requirements for a reference plan. In that event, an order, signed by the registrar, is stamped on the deed or other document indicating that the description is exempt from the requirement that a reference plan be deposited. A sketch, accompanied by a statement confirming that the sketch is not a survey, is acceptable under circumstances approved by the land registrar.

A reference plan is not a registered plan of subdivision for the purpose of the *Planning Act* and thus requires adjoining lands searches as whole PARTS are not exempt as whole lots. A "caution" is noted on all reference plans that: "This plan is NOT a plan of subdivision within the meaning of the *Planning Act.*"

Compiled Plans

The purpose of a compiled plan is to identify clearly property boundaries for parcels that were divided over the years by metes and bounds descriptions, and to assist in maintaining proper Registry office records. Compiled plans are classified according to the party who ordered their registration and include the following:

1. Judge's Compiled Plan, by Judge's order (discontinued January 1, 1980);

2. Municipal Compiled Plan;

3. Land Registrar's Compiled Plan (as required by the Examiner of Surveys).

On registration, each plan is assigned a registered plan number and each parcel, a lot number. Compiled plans are considered not to be registered plans of subdivision for the purpose of the *Planning Act* and thus require adjoining lands searches. To assist lawyers and conveyancers in identifying these plans, the *Registry Act* provides that a "caution" be noted on all compiled plans that: "This is NOT a plan of subdivision within the meaning of the *Planning Act.*" The land registrar is also required to make an entry in the abstract book that "the *Planning Act* may continue to apply as though this plan had not been registered".

Plans of Expropriation

As soon as a plan of expropriation has been registered in the appropriate Registry or Land Titles office, title automatically vests in the expropriating authority free of all encumbrances; a deed or transfer is not required to be registered. The plan should be signed by the expropriating authority and an Ontario land surveyor. Consent of the approving authority should be either endorsed on the plan, or reference made to the registration particulars, if the approval is registered separately. Expropriation plans identify parcels by numbered "PARTS", *e.g.*, PART 1.

Railway Abandonment Plans

Large tracts of land acquired by railway companies were seldom surveyed. As a result, descriptions were incomplete and are unacceptable for registration today. Much of this land is no longer required for railway purposes. Railway companies compiled railway property plans of their lands and prepared new plans showing the lands that they intend to abandon (Railway Abandonment Regulations, C.R.C. 1978, c. 1382). These plans, referred to as abandonment plans, are filed as deposits under Part II of the *Registry Act*. Railway abandonment plans, intended for the initial conveyance from the railway, identify each parcel as a "PART". A deed conveying railway abandonment land must include the portion of the plan showing the relevant "PART".

Boundaries Act **Applications and Plans**

Where doubt exists as to the true location on the ground of boundaries of a parcel of land, an owner, a municipality, a minister of the Crown, the Surveyor General of Canada or Ontario, or a surveyor with consent of the owner may apply to the Director of Titles under the *Boundaries Act* to have a new survey made and the present boundaries confirmed. As well, the Minister of Transportation may apply to confirm the true location of the boundaries on the ground of a public highway. The Director may require a hearing; affected parties may appeal to the Divisional Court. The Director reviews the application and confirms and certifies new boundaries as defined by the monuments shown on the *Boundaries Act* plan. These boundaries are deemed to be the true boundaries of the parcel, despite any other Act. Where a new survey is confirmed, a certified plan of survey is registered in the land Registry office and the land registrar records it in the title register or abstract index for each parcel that adjoins a confirmed boundary. This plan supersedes all corresponding portions of all former registered plans and descriptions. Once the certified plan has been registered, descriptions in documents for adjoining lands must both refer to and conform to the *Boundaries Act* plan. Adjoining land descriptions should be reviewed carefully as to whether they conform to the new survey.

ADJOINING LANDS AND PLANNING ACT COMPLIANCE SEARCHES

Adjoining lands may be checked for s. 50 *Planning Act* subdivision and part lot control violations, legal description inconsistencies and potential encroachments, easements and restrictive covenants, and access rights. Adjoining land searches are less common when dealing with the whole of a lot on a registered plan of subdivision, since whole lots rarely produce registered description problems and are usually exempt from *Planning Act* subdivision control provisions.

An adjoining lands search must include all properties that share a common boundary with the main property as well as all properties involved in an easement, a restrictive covenant, or a right of access. An adjoining lands abstract should be prepared for each adjoining owner, including any registrations that might affect boundaries, descriptions, easements, and restrictive covenants throughout the title search period.

Similarly, any registration that might affect the *Planning Act* subdivision and part lot control provisions must be included in the adjoining lands abstract. For *Planning Act* purposes, it is only necessary to check back to the appropriate *Planning Act* search commencement date, the earliest being June 15, 1967, the date prior to which all contraventions of the Act were forgiven. During the *Planning Act* search period, it is essential to establish that there was never common ownership between the main and the adjoining lands, as illegal subdivision results in the inability to convey title to subsequent purchasers.

Adjoining lands abstracts include grants to prior owners, leases and easements over 21 years, quit claims, correcting deeds, encroachment agreements, deposits, plans, particularly reference plans, and documents which include sketches. The descriptions in the last registered deeds of adjoining owners are copied and used to plot the title search sketch. Adjoining land searching is complex, legally and mechanically. Refer to Chapter 11 for a detailed review of *Planning Act* subdivision and part lot control legislation and detailed instructions and checklists on how to complete an adjoining lands search.

ACCESS AND ROAD SEARCH

The lawyer and conveyancer must review the relevant road pages in the abstract book. Road closings, openings, and widenings are registered on the road pages and road dedications are endorsed on registered plans. Each search must confirm legal access from the property to a public road. Access may involve public highways, easements by prescription, or private rights of way, which must be checked for registration on adjoining properties. Private roads raise issues of seasonal access and road maintenance costs and responsibilities. Access is critical to ownership and access disputes often lead to litigation. Detailed information on access law and searching requirements, including the effect of title insurance, is reviewed in detail in Chapters 9 and 11.

THE SKETCH

On completion of the search, the title searcher must draw a sketch or diagram illustrating the main and adjoining lands. This sketch will illustrate easements, legal descriptions and inconsistencies, possible encroachments, description gaps, overlaps, and errors, as well as legal access to the property being purchased or mortgaged. The searcher uses legal descriptions in the last registered deeds on the main and adjoining lands, combined with dimensions and description information found on subdivision and other registered plans to plot the descriptions. A sketch usually contains the following information:

1. north arrow and scale;

2. streets and street names;

3. all related subdivision and reference plan numbers, also concession lots and roads, concessions and townships;

4. dimensions bearings and description boundaries of lots;

5. dimensions bearings and description boundaries of main property and adjoining properties unless dealing with whole lots on registered plans of subdivision;

6. last registered deed number and registered owner name for descriptions plotted;

7. main property outlined in red and adjoining properties outlined and colour coded to the adjoining lands search (sketch is usually cross-referenced by colour or other codes to the search notes);

8. location and dimensions of encroachments and easements and rights of way;

9. legal access to the nearest intersection or public road; and

10. Property Identification Numbers (PINs) when assigned by the conversion into POLARIS.

Sketches may be completed to scale or superimposed on the existing subdivision or reference plans, or possibly POLARIS digital maps, depending on the level of difficulty involved in the search. In summary, the sketch process reconciles registered descriptions with survey and possessory evidence, with POLARIS mapping references, and with the description set out for the property to be purchased in the agreement of purchase and sale. The sketch also illustrates access, easements and description inconsistencies and potential adjoining land encroachments. Detailed instructions on search sketches and an example sketch are included in Chapter 11.

EXECUTION SEARCH

Writs of seizure and sale resulting from judgment debts may be registered against land. Conveyancers complete execution searches against the names of all owners as shown on the registered documents in the 40-year title search period as well as against a purchaser as he or she will appear on the registered documents, if he or she is financing the purchase by way of a mortgage. Execution searching is now completed online usually on WritSearch in Teraview. Today, most lawyers search executions only against the current owner and the purchaser/mortgagor and cover the risk of executions against prior owners in the 40-year search period with title insurance. Execution law and procedures and the searching and deletion of executions is described in detail in Chapter 12.

CORPORATE SEARCHES AND ESCHEAT

When a company fails to file annual returns or pay corporations tax or undergoes some form of involuntary dissolution, the *Business Corporations Act*, R.S.O. 1990, c. B.16 provides that the company will be dissolved and its lands will be forfeited to the Crown by way of escheat. A company must have been in existence throughout the time period it owned land in order to hold and transfer good and marketable title. Title depends on the absence of corporate escheat. As a result, corporate status is checked against all corporate vendors and any other corporate owners shown on title, in theory, as far back as the Crown patent for federal corporations. Lawyers may also wish to obtain corporate profile reports for current corporate owners. As with executions, most lawyers today search corporate status for the current owner and rely on title insurance to cover the risk of escheat for prior corporate owners in the 40-year search period.

On March 31, 1995, the Ontario *Business Corporations Act* was amended so as to limit the requirement for corporate searches to no more than 20 years before registration of a transfer to a subsequent purchaser for value (*Business Corporations Act*, s. 244(3)). Corporate searches for Ontario corporations are accessed through the Ontario Business Information System (ONBIS). ONBIS is Ontario's official record of business information and is available online and through online service providers, such as Cyberbahn (<http://www.cyberbahn.ca>), On-Corp Direct (<http://www.oncorp.com>), Dye & Durham (<http://www.dyedurham.ca>), or at the public search office at the Ministry of Government Services. A corporate status certificate will disclose the name and number of the corporation, its incorporation jurisdiction, and the date of incorporation and/or dissolution.

Corporate searches for companies under the *Canada Business Corporations Act*, R.S.C. 1985, c. C-44 are made at Corporations Canada. Certificates of compliance/ certificates of existence are available for corporations that are up to date with their statutory filing requirements. Corporate ownership search practice varies greatly as a result of the impracticality or impossibility of checking for corporate owners, particularly federal corporate owners, in deleted documents and non-active registers. Title insurance is available to cover the risk of corporate escheat in prior corporate owners.

OTHER INQUIRIES

A real estate purchase or mortgage transaction includes a multitude of possible "off-title" land-related searches and inquiries in addition to the Registry office title search and a surveyor's real property report. Frequently, Crown patents are checked for restrictions on ownership, such as road and shoreline allowances and mining, timber, and hydro-electric rights. Partnership searches may be completed for when the land has been owned in partnership. A personal property security registration search may reveal liens on chattels transferred with the land. Off-title searches may reveal liens, work orders, and restrictions on use, such as the placement of docks and boathouses on the Trent-Severn Waterway or access to provincial highways. Properties in designated heritage areas and environmentally sensitive zones are subject to additional restrictions.

A lawyer in consultation with the client decides which "off-title" searches to complete on the basis of the nature of the transaction, the nature of the land involved, client instructions (after a careful explanation of the risks and consequences involved in not completing the search, confirmed by a signed direction by the client(s) not to complete the search) and whether or not the client has decided to purchase title insurance. Title insurance provides an after-the-fact indemnity alternative for some off-title searches but not others. For example, title insurance does not cover environmental issues, Aboriginal rights, or water quality.

Inquiries differ depending on whether the land is residential, recreational, commercial, industrial, agricultural, or located in an unorganized territory. When the client purchases title insurance as part of the transaction, certain low risk, high cost off-title searches may be eliminated as the risks involved are covered by the title insurance policy. Increasingly, these off-title searches are made online directly from the lawyer's office. For example, it is now possible to search all of Hydro One's unregistered easements online and receive an up-to-date answer within minutes at: <http://unregeasement.hydroone.com/lvr/welcome.html>. Chapter 14 reviews the more common federal and provincial off-title searches and risks.

SUBSEARCH

At the end of the search, the conveyancer must check for recent registrations noted in the day (fee) book and not yet entered in the abstract index. Immediately before closing, the conveyancer will update the abstract and day books from the time of the original search. Execution searches, adjoining lands/ *Planning Act* searches and personal property security registration searches will also be updated at closing. Refer to Chapter 13 for detailed instructions and checklists on subsearching.

SEARCH SUMMARY

A brief summary or report of a title search should be prepared for the lawyer who reviews the search, prepares the requisitions, and gives an opinion on title. The summary often acts as a cover page for the title search. A search summary should highlight title issues and be cross-referenced to the search notes. An example search summary form is included below. Note that disbursements and fee information are also included in a separate invoice to facilitate billing/ accounting office procedures.

SEARCH SUMMARY

FIRM NAME _____

FILE NUMBER / CLIENT REFERENCE _____

MUNICIPAL ADDRESS _____

REGISTRY _____ LAND TITLES _____ POLARIS _____

PIN _____   _____ LAST REGISTERED INSTRUMENT _____

CITY/COUNTY/DIVISION _____ BOOK# _____ PAGE# _____

LEGAL DESCRIPTION _____

_____ ASSESSMENT ROLL #_____

LOT SIZE _____

DESCRIPTION APPROVED_____

REGISTERED OWNER(S) _____

TRANSFER#_____DATE REGISTERED _____ TITLE _____

CHARGES_____

_____

_____

ACCESS / ROADS

EASEMENTS _____

RESTRICTIONS _____

BY-LAWS _____

ADJOINING LANDS _____

EXECUTION SEARCH _____

CORPORATE OWNERS _____

OTHER _____

PROBLEMS _____

DISBURSEMENTS SEARCH FEE

COPIES _____ DISBURSEMENTS _____

WHITE PRINT _____ G.S.T _____

EXECUTION SEARCH _____

SEARCHED BY _____ DATE _____

COMPLETED TITLE SEARCH CHECKLIST

Completed search notes are written on one side of the page only, and pages are numbered consecutively and firmly attached. A completed search contains the following information:

☐ request for search/search instructions;
☐ search summary;
☐ execution search/certificate;
☐ copy of plan(s);
☐ sketch of main and adjoining lands, including access;
☐ chain, if search is complex;
☐ abstract of title;
☐ adjoining lands abstracts and copies of last registered deeds' descriptions;
☐ document summaries;
☐ photocopies of last registered deed, outstanding mortgages and other encumbrances; and
☐ copies of any document containing a title or description problem.

CHAPTER 5

Registered Documents

BACKGROUND

Ownership rights in land are evidenced by written agreements and recorded as documents in public, government-regulated, land registration records systems. History has provided Ontario with the Registry system, the Land Titles system and, more recently, the POLARIS database. Each system developed its own documentation rules which then underwent continuous change throughout the decades. As a result, real estate practitioners today are confronted by a challenging array of registered documents that relate to title to land. Lawyers and conveyancers, because of the historical nature of title, must be familiar with Registry, Land Titles, *Land Registration Reform Act*, R.S.O. 1990, c. L.4 (LRRA) documents, and the constantly changing electronic documents, online in Teraview. For example, a Land Titles Conversions Qualified (LTCQ) title will be based on still effective Registry documents, such as easements, deeds, mortgages, and restrictive covenants. Lawyers must review documents from the past, which may still be the current registration, as well as produce current documents in both the paper and electronic formats. From a practical point of view, today over 95 per cent of documents created and registered take place online in Land Titles, in the electronic land registration system.

Prior to 1985, the names, forms, contents, and registration requirements of documents were different in the Registry and Land Titles systems. As of 1985, the LRRA standardized the basic format of all documents in both systems. Nevertheless substantive law and statutory content requirements, and legal affect of documents remain different in Registry and Land Titles. Registry permits diverse documentation (instruments) subject to registration requirements, whereas Land Titles has always restricted documents to a limited number of forms prescribed by statute and regulation. The LRRA also prescribes document form and content by statute and regulation. Under the LRRA, the Director of Land Registration has the authority to allow the registration of documents that do not comply with the precise requirements of the prescribed forms. A court order may also authorize the registration of a document that does not meet registration requirements. Detailed document requirements are found under the *Land Registration Reform Act*, Form of Documents, R.R.O. 1990, Reg. 688 and Electronic Registration, O. Reg. 19/99. Sample LRRA standard forms for non-electronic registration are included at the end of this chapter as Figures 5.1 to 5.5.

Today, in Ontario, most documents are created and registered online in Teraview. Ontario's ELRS contains numerous detailed electronic forms. These forms contain relevant statements of law and fact relating to the particular transaction, which can be selected and sometimes amended by the conveyancer. The ELRS contains some artificial intelligence in that documents cannot be signed or registered unless they have been completed according to minimum standards. Nevertheless, the lawyer remains responsible for the proper drafting and legal effectiveness of the document.

DOCUMENT CREATION RESOURCES AND GUIDES

When working in the electronic system, practitioners rely on the Policy and Regulatory Services Branch of the Real Property Registration Branch of the Ministry of Government Services, including Land Registrars' Bulletins and the Ministry's *Electronic Registration Procedures Guide* for the precise legal requirements and examples for documents and registration. The *Electronic Registration Procedures Guide* contains hundreds of pages of instructions for completing specific documents. Document registration requirements change daily. Practitioners rely on the *Teraview Reference Guide* for how to work in the electronic land registration system environment. Both guides are available online on the Teraview website at <http://www.teraview.ca>. Electronic land registration is dealt with in Chapter 16 of the text, whereas the rest of this chapter focuses on paper documents and the content of documentation in general.

LAND REGISTRATION SYSTEMS DOCUMENT COMPARISON

Electronic land registration, or ELRS, offers approximately 100 online variations of the basic LRRA standard forms. The chart below illustrates the basic document forms under the three real property registration environments, but does not include the documents in electronic land registration.

Table 5.1

Registry	Land Titles	Land Registration Reform Act/1985
Deed	Transfer	Transfer/Deed of Land A (Form 1)
Mortgage	Charge	Charge/Mortgage of Land B (Form 2)
Discharge of Mortgage	Cessation of Charge	Discharge of Charge /Mortgage C (Form 3)
Other Documents	Other Documents	Document General D (Form 4)
Schedule	Schedule	Schedule S (Form 5)

REGISTRATION OF DOCUMENTS

Under the Registry system, registration constitutes notice to all persons claiming any interest in land subsequent to registration. Registration does not guarantee the effectiveness of the document. It simply makes it available for public scrutiny and gives the registration priority over subsequent registered interests. While registration is not necessary to make a document effective, it is necessary to protect the interest of a client in a conveyance or other dealings with land against subsequent dealing or conveyances. Documents are registered once they have been accepted by the land registrar and the appropriate fee is paid. A registration number, the date, and the land registrar's certificate are stamped on each registered document and duplicate as evidence of registration.

Under the Land Titles system, documents are accepted, paid for, and entered in the register if they are executed by the party recorded on the register as the registered owner. Once registered, a Land Titles document is guaranteed effective, except for statutory exceptions, and is given priority over subsequent registrations.

The LRRA provides for storage of title records in POLARIS. Most Registry and Land Titles records are now stored in POLARIS; however, a few registry offices are not yet automated. Only Land Titles documents can be registered electronically on ELRS through Teraview.

ABSTRACTING (SUMMARIZING) DOCUMENTS

Once a document has been registered on title, a conveyancer will include that document as part of the abstract of title. Each document affecting title must be read and summarized, or photocopied if it is complex or an encumbrance on title. Document summaries form the core of the title search. This process of summarizing documents is called abstracting documents.

Over the years, title searchers have developed many methods of summarizing documents. Numerous preprinted summary sheets, stamps, and special abstract paper were all in use. Most title searchers used a variety of easily understood abbreviations in order to speed up the abstracting process. In Land Titles, it is common to photocopy current registrations and highlight important points, whereas in Registry, searchers summarize all relevant registrations within the last 40 years. As a result of the simplified LRRA forms and the mass conversion of Registry properties to Land Titles, increasingly, title searchers are printing, photocopying, and highlighting shortened, current documents.

Individual styles can be confusing for the inexperienced title searcher. Fortunately, basic common sense rules apply in most situations. A title searcher records the who (parties and signatures), where (accurate description), what (content of document, including background recitals and related documents), and when (dates) of all registered documents. Unusual information is recorded and inconsistencies are noted. Confusing or complex documents (wills, sale papers, bankruptcies, *etc.*) are photocopied. In addition, the last registered deed, outstanding liens and encumbrances, particularly mortgages, and all plans are photocopied.

In Registry, registration requirements, such as signatures, witnesses, and affidavits/declarations, are checked and recorded. In Land Titles, the form and legal effectiveness of the document are guaranteed on registration and therefore signatures, *etc.*, do not require recording. When in doubt, it is always safer to include unnecessary information rather than run the risk of missing a title defect. The following is an example of a document summary sheet.

DOCUMENT SUMMARY SHEET

Document Type	Registration Number	Date of Document	Registration Date

From		To	

1)

2)
Date of Birth

3)　　　　　　　　　　　　　　　　Recitals/Mortgage Provisions/Other

SFCA	DEA	SFMA	NHA	SFLA	Description	PIN _____
Grant:	FS	JT	TinC	PP	Uses	

HAB: _____
4UC & Rel _____
Res Cov _____
Bar DOWER _____
SPOUSAL CONSENT _____

EXEC Wit / Corp Seal
Aff EXEC
Stat Aff AGE & MS /SS

Aff RESIDENCE (ITA)
Aff PLANNING ACT
PL ACT Decl (3)
PLANNING ACT Consent
Aff LAND SPEC
Aff MORTMAIN

Document Prepared By:	LAND TRANSFER TAX Aff
	Cash
	Mtge Assumed
	Mtge Back
	Chattels
	Other
	Total

Document Registered By:

Comments	Remarks

This document summary sheet illustrates some abbreviations commonly used in document summaries. The following are examples of commonly used abbreviations:

SFCA	*Short Forms of Conveyances Act*
DEA	*Devolution of Estates Act*
SFMA	*Short Forms of Mortgages Act*
NHA	*National Housing Act*
ITA	*Income Tax Act*
SFLA	*Short Forms of Leases Act*
FLA	*Family Law Act*
EAA	*Estates Administration Act*
PA	*Planning Act*
FS	fee simple
JT	joint tenants
TinC	tenants in common
PP	partnership property
HAB	habendum
4 UC	4 usual covenants
Rel	Release

Res Cov	Restrictive Covenants
B of D	Bar of Dower
Sp Cons	Spousal Consent
PA Cons	*Planning Act* Consent
Aff PA	Affidavit of *Planning Act*
Aff EXEC	Affidavit of Execution
Aff SW	Affidavit of Subscribing Witness
Aff AGE & MS /SS	Affidavit of Age & Marital Status/Spousal Status
Aff RES (ITA)	Affidavit of Residence (*Income Tax Act*)
Aff LTTA	*Land Transfer Tax Act* Affidavit of Value and Consideration and Residence
PA Decl (3)	3 *Planning Act* Declarations
Aff LSTA	Affidavit of *Land Speculation Tax Act*
CS	corporate seal
SS&W	signed sealed & witnessed

LAND REGISTRATION REFORM ACT DOCUMENTS

Part I of the LRRA legislated significant changes to the traditional documents presented for registration. The prescribed forms are standardized, shortened, and designed in box format. The following prescribed forms are permitted: Transfer/Deed of Land: A; Charge/Mortgage of Land: B; Discharge of Charge/Mortgage: C; Document General: D; and a Schedule: S. These documents have remained relatively unchanged, particularly when they relate to Registry land as the paper documents are used in a small percentage of transactions. On the other hand, electronic documents on Teraview undergo constant upgrading. Land registrars may, at their discretion, permit registration of a document that is not entirely in accordance with a particular form. Following registration, documents are microfilmed and, on completion, originals are destroyed.

Parties

Parties to a document must be described by their surname, followed by a comma, first name and another given name, if any, in that order. Evidence is not required to prove that a party has no middle name or only an initial(s), and a document will not be refused under these circumstances. All additional given names may be included. Transfers require the transferee's birth date. A transfer/deed in favour of a partnership or the name under which one carries on business must indicate the full names of the partners, whereas a corporation takes title in its legal corporate name. Corporate names must be entered in capital letters. The *Electronic Registration Procedures Guide* has an extensive section on how to name different types of owners, such as transfer by personal representative, by religious organization, by trustee in bankruptcy, or by power of sale. The name of a transferor must match exactly the name of the registered owner or it will not be accepted for document creation and registration. A change of name application is registered before a name other than the registered owner is accepted.

LRRA naming conventions aid in compiling a list of owners' names and facilitate the filing of writs of execution on a particular title. In the past, in Registry, parties to a document were described by their surname and at least one given name. Title searchers should ensure that the current parties' names are consistent with the prior registered owners' names.

Land Descriptions

LRRA forms include a short legal description as well as the Property Identification Number (PIN) in a separate box wherever land has been converted into POLARIS. Metes and bounds descriptions and all easement descriptions are referred to in the new forms by reference to the registration number of the most recent deed/transfer containing the same description. Metes and bounds descriptions may also be attached by schedule. Where a plan or sketch is appended to a schedule, a statement that the document description is the same as the drawing is required. Such statements should be confirmed by reference to the sketch and the description, as well as prior description references. The new forms may only refer to the full description; however, the title searcher must locate and analyze all description information.

LAND REGISTRATION REFORM ACT FORMS

Part 1 of the LRRA relates to document reform and standardization. The terms "document" and "transfer" replace "instrument" and "deed". Consideration, interest transferred, PIN (when available), addresses for the parties and the property, postal codes, and assessment roll numbers are required. Personal seals, witnesses and commissioners, and most affidavits have been eliminated and corporate seals are optional, although discouraged. Corporate seals may be replaced by the signatories, simply stating that they have the authority to bind the corporation. The *Land Transfer Tax Act* Affidavit regarding Value of the Consideration continues to be inserted by the purchaser into each transfer, and specific affidavits that apply to Sale Papers, Executions, Court Orders, and Transmission Applications are retained. Declarations of Age and Spousal Status and optional declarations under the *Planning Act* take the place of similar content affidavits. Transfers and charges include blank spaces for statements by the transferor(s) or chargor(s) that he or she is 18 years old, his or her spousal status, the status of the property as a matrimonial home, a spousal consent to the transaction, and whether or not the document is signed by way of a power of attorney (POA).

Standard Charge Terms

The intent of the LRRA is to reduce unnecessary paper in the title registration process. The LRRA implies certain standard covenants set out in the Act into all transfers and charges. The Act creates a scheme for the creation and filing of commonly used standard charge terms (SCT) as set out in O. Reg. 18/99. The terms are then simply incorporated into mortgages and charges for registration purposes by reference to a Ministry filing number. A charge can only refer to one set of SCTs. Additional or custom terms must be added either in a box specifically for additional terms or by schedule. Financial institutions are required to file standard charge terms for their standard loan contracts with the Ministry. Books of standard charge terms, published annually for purchase, are also available at the Registry office. Financial institutions post their standard charge terms and often their standard mortgage transaction documentation on their websites. Law firms download standard charge terms and standard mortgage documentation directly from the lenders' websites. The Teraview website also makes available standard charge terms, also known as FiDocs, and mortgage documentation for major lenders. Once standard charge terms have been filed with the Ministry, they are public and available for use by any lender.

LRRA forms are different in the ELRS. For example, electronic documents substitute a solicitor's electronic statements of law for paper document affidavit requirements, such as land transfer tax, power of sale papers and execution clearance affidavits. All possible standard declarations, such as age and spousal status, are built into the electronic form and are selected by the click of a mouse. The supporting documentation is retained by the lawyer in the client's file. In ELRS, a statement must always be made as to whether or not an electronic document is being signed by POA.

Transfer/Deed of Land

Transfers and the Two-Lawyer Rule

As of March 31, 2008, only lawyers are authorized to sign transfers for completeness, subject to certain exceptions. In addition, as of March 31, 2008 most transfers require that two different lawyers sign for completeness, one for the transferee and one for the transferor. Ontario Regulation 76/08 amended O. Reg. 19/99 to reflect the two-lawyer rule. Not all transfer documents require two lawyers. For example, one lawyer can sign and complete a transfer of easement. The following are exceptions to the two-lawyer rule.

- transfers to or from the provincial (Ontario) or the federal Crown or a municipality, Crown corporations, agencies, boards, and commissions;

- transferor and transferee is the same person who is transferring to change legal tenure or register a *Planning Act* consent;
- transfer from a personal representative (estate) to a beneficially entitled person;
- inter-family and related party transfers;
- transfers in remote communities; and
- transfers of easement.

Electronic transfer documents now contain additional statements that identify who the lawyer is acting for and the nature of the exception to the two-lawyer rule.

Lawyers apply to the Ministry and are issued access keys that permit document creation and registration. This restriction is part of the province's title fraud prevention strategy. Documents other than transfers may be registered by persons, such as law clerks, who have been approved and given access to Teraview.

Transfers convey freehold or leasehold interests in land and replaces the traditional Registry deed and Land Titles transfer. Transfers are comprised of pre-set boxes and may include optional schedules for additional parties, consents, signatures, metes and bounds descriptions, court orders, and background statements. Schedules may also contain additional information, plans, sketches, and exclusion or variation of covenants. A *Land Transfer Tax Act* affidavit is inserted into the transfer on registration. A Form 1 transfer contains the following statements that have the same force and effect as affidavits:

1. Statements as to age, spousal status, matrimonial home status, and spousal consents (*Family Law Act*, R.S.O. 1990, c. F.3) are incorporated into boxes 8 and 9 and should be dated and executed by the transferor(s).

2. Optional statements, signed and dated by the transferor, the transferor's lawyer, and the transferee's lawyer, stating that the conveyance does not contravene the subdivision control provisions under the *Planning Act*, R.S.O. 1990, c. P.13, s. 50(22) are incorporated into boxes 13 and 14. All three *Planning Act* statements must be completed before previous violations are rectified by statute. If the boxes are not completed, or only partly completed, a document will still be accepted for registration. It must be clearly recorded whether all three declarations were completed.

Electronic transfers contain additional statements relating to whether the document was signed by power of attorney and relating to the two-lawyer rule. See Bulletin No. 2009-01, which outlines the Real Estate Fraud Action Plan changes and example statements.

Charge/Mortgage of Land

A Charge/Mortgage of Land is a lien for the payment of a debt or other obligation secured on land, and replaces the old Registry mortgage and Land Titles charge. The document contains 18 boxes and usually an attached schedule for additional provisions, plans, sketches, and exclusion or variation of covenants implied under s. 7 of the LRRA. A Charge/Mortgage document summary should record all financial terms and the standard charge terms reference number (institutional lenders' loans) from box 8, or the payment provisions provided by lenders and inserted in box 9. A Charge may only refer to one standard charge terms reference number. Age, spousal status, matrimonial home status and spousal consents and power of attorney statements are executed and dated in boxes 11 and 12.

Discharge of Charge/Mortgage

A discharge sets out the registration number and date of the charge being discharged. It states whether the discharge is a complete, partial, or a final partial discharge. It must also refer to every other registered instrument relating exclusively to the charge, such as assignments, extensions, postponements, amendments, *etc.*, so that the registrar may delete the related documents at the same time as the charge being discharged is deleted. A discharge must contain a statement verifying that the person granting the discharge has the authority to grant it and is entitled to do so.

Document General

A document general is used for registration of all types of documents except transfers, charges, and discharges of charges; for example, plans, liens, leases, powers of attorney, changes of name, survivorship and transmission applications, cautions, notices, agreements, matrimonial home designations, plans, and court orders. A document general may comprise an original document or act as a cover page to which an original document is attached.

Schedule

A schedule provides space for additional information, descriptions, parties, executions, covenants, mortgage repayment provisions, and supporting documentation such as proof of death and court orders, *etc.*, and it may be attached to the other four LRRA forms. Record or copy all additional information in schedules.

DOCUMENTS PRIOR TO APRIL 1, 1985

Subject to statutory exceptions, Land Titles documents are guaranteed effective on the completion of registration. As a result, documents registered under the *Land Titles Act*, R.S.O. 1990, c. L.5 do not usually require reviewing for statutory compliance, such as signatures and witnesses. However, documents under the *Registry Act*, R.S.O. 1990, c. R.20 are not guaranteed, and as a result, must be reviewed for legal effectiveness and statutory compliance. Lands automated in POLARIS may be in either the Land Titles or the Registry system and must be checked accordingly.

EXECUTION OF PRE-1985 DOCUMENTS

Affidavits included in documents registered prior to April 1, 1985 should be checked. Inconsistencies in the name or names on the affidavit compared to the party or parties to the document should be recorded on the title search.

The signature on a document may be completed as follows:

1. in foreign characters;

2. signed by making his or her mark;

3. by recital that he or she was unable to read the document plus a statement made by a witness that he or she saw the individual sign the document after it had been read to him or her; or

4. even by initials that bear no significance to the name as set out in the document.

Documents must be properly witnessed and affidavits properly executed. Signatures of public officials such as the Public Guardian and Trustee, formerly the Official Guardian, do not require affidavits of execution or subscribing witness. Documents, other than a discharge of a mortgage presented for registration, prior to April 1, 1985, under the Registry system, required that a seal be affixed opposite the parties' signatures. Space was provided in the affidavit of execution for the insertion of a statement in respect to the residence of the vendor for the purpose of the *Income Tax Act*, R.S.C. 1985 (5th Supp.), c. 1 (a declaration to that effect is now provided by the vendor on closing), also, for the declaration in respect to recitals — "the recitals herein are true". In the past, other important background recitals were included in the affidavits, so conveyancers should review information contained in recitals in older documents.

AFFIDAVITS SWORN OUTSIDE ONTARIO

Under s. 31(2) of the *Registry Act*, affidavits on a document sworn outside Ontario, in another province or another country are required to be sworn in accordance with ss. 44 and 45 of the *Evidence Act*, R.S.O. 1990, c. E.23 before one of the following:

  (a) a judge;
  (b) a magistrate;
  (c) an officer of a court of justice;
  (d) a commissioner for taking affidavits or other competent authority of the like nature;
  (e) a notary public;
  (f)   the head of a city, town, village, township or other municipality;
  (g) an officer of any of Her Majesty's diplomatic or consular services, including an ambassador, envoy, minister, chargé d'affaires, counsellor, secretary, attaché, consul-general, consul, vice-consul, pro-consul, consular agent, acting consul-general, acting consul, acting vice-consul and acting consular agent;
  (h) an officer of the Canadian diplomatic, consular or representative services, including, in addition to the diplomatic and consular officers mentioned in clause (g), a high commissioner, permanent delegate, acting high commissioner, acting permanent delegate, counsellor and secretary; or
  (i)   a Canadian Government trade commissioner or assistant trade commissioner....

EXECUTION BY A CORPORATION

Before the LRRA, a corporation executed documents by affixing its corporate seal over the signatures of its signing officers. A corporate seal was accepted as evidence that the person signing had authority to act on behalf of the corporation. A witness to the signatures was not required, but the office held was indicated below the signatures. Accordingly, an affidavit of execution or subscribing witness was not required. The name on the corporate seal had to be identical to that set out in the document. Even a missing comma or period could nullify a document. Where a corporate seal was missing on a document executed by a foreign corporation, an affidavit as evidence that a seal was not required in the jurisdiction where the corporation was incorporated had to be attached; also necessary was an affidavit with respect to the signing officers.

AFFIDAVITS OF AGE AND MARITAL OR SPOUSAL STATUS

In the past, anyone who executed a document was required to complete an affidavit stating that he or she was of the full age of 18 years, except for: (1) a wife signing to bar her dower; and (2) an executor, or an administrator of an estate, the Public Trustee or any other trustee, or the Official Guardian.

Prior to the now-repealed *Family Law Reform Act*, which came into effect March 31, 1978, a widow had a right to dower in her husband's lands. A husband, who executed a document, completed an affidavit stating that he was married, unmarried, divorced, or widowed. Either the man or the wife could complete an affidavit that they were married at the time of execution of the document when the wife joined to bar her dower. The affidavit was not required when land was held by joint tenants or trustees, or as partnership property. Executor(s) and administrator(s) acting on behalf of an estate were exempt from marital status affidavits, whereas a person, acting in his or her personal capacity as well as in his or her capacity as an executor or an administrator, was required to complete an affidavit of age and marital status. Refer to Chapter 10 for a full discussion of dower rights and family law property rights. Chapter 10 contains the required *Family Law Act* statements of age, spousal status, matrimonial home status, and exemption statements for both the post-1985 LRRA paper and electronic forms.

LAND TRANSFER TAX ACT AFFIDAVIT/AFFIDAVIT OF RESIDENCE AND OF VALUE OF THE CONSIDERATION

In the past, under the *Land Transfer Tax Act*, R.S.O. 1990, c. L.6, transfers of land offered for registration had an Affidavit of Residence and of Value of the Consideration attached. The *Land Transfer Tax Act* Affidavit now relates only to the value of the consideration and not to residence. Similarly, in the past, this affidavit split into two separate affidavits called the *Land Transfer Tax Act* Affidavit and the Affidavit of Residence. The Act provides that a tax, payable to the Treasurer of Ontario, based on the consideration recited in the document, is due on tendering a document for registration. In the past, an executed copy, or a copy of the original, was left with the land registrar for forwarding to the Treasurer. The affidavit may be sworn by the purchaser, the purchaser's lawyer or an agent authorized in writing to act on his or her behalf. Lawyers are usually interested in the amount and method of payment disclosed in the affidavit and any additional remarks relating to title. Where a deed or transfer bears the stamp, for example, "Land Transfer Tax paid by the Treasurer of Ontario, receipt No. 2341", the consideration paid is not disclosed. However, it may be obtained by contacting the office of the Minister of Revenue, Land Transfer Section. The Ministry of Revenue website contains a detailed guide, including information on exemptions, on how to complete the *Land Transfer Tax Act* Affidavit and additional exemption and rebate affidavits, both in paper and in the ELRS.

AFFIDAVIT OF LAND SPECULATION TAX

This affidavit was short-lived, becoming effective on April 10, 1974, and repealed on October 24, 1978. This affidavit no longer has any effect on land and as a result most conveyancers no longer record its presence.

DEED OR TRANSFER

In Registry, the estate or title in land was passed by a deed, whereas in Land Titles, ownership was conveyed by a transfer. A deed may also be referred to as a grant, a conveyance, an assurance, an indenture or a bargain and sale. Deeds or transfers, registered prior to the LRRA forms, should be checked for the following:

1. The Act under which it was made (SFCA/*Short Forms of Conveyances Act*, DEA/*Devolution of Estates Act*, EAA/*Estates Administration Act*, etc.).

2. The document registration number, the date of the document, and the date of registration.

3. Full names of all parties, their capacity, and the relationship between them. The Grantor is the party of the first part; the grantee is the party of the second part; a person joining in or releasing an interest is called the party of the third part. For practical coding reasons, the parties to a document are referred to on the search as one, two, and three throughout, *e.g.*, one grants to two, three (a beneficiary) releases an interest, three (the spouse) consents.

4. All background information contained in recitals/statements, such as estate administration information.

5. The consideration as set out in the Affidavit of Residence and of Value of the Consideration.

6. The exact contents of the granting clause (the grantor grants to the grantee in fee simple, which means that he or she holds the absolute interest in the lands for himself or herself and his or her heirs, as joint tenants, tenants in common, as partnership property, to uses, or in trust).

7. A full description of the land together with or subject to easements or rights-of-way (once a description has been plotted and checked, it may be cross-referenced to the last registered description, *e.g.*, same as in instrument number 123456). Should there be description problems, the description should be sketched and photocopied and compared to earlier and subsequent document descriptions.

8. The four usual covenants: (1) the grantor has the right to convey; (2) the grantee will enjoy quiet possession of the lands; (3) the grantor will execute further assurances; and (4) the grantor has done no act to encumber the lands; and followed by a release of claim.

9. Subject to the reservations, limitations, provisos, and conditions expressed in the original grant from the Crown, means that the deed is subject to the reservations in the Crown patent.

10. Contents of the "habendum" or receiving clause, being a clause in the deed that sets out the interest (*e.g.*, fee simple) and tenure (*e.g.*, as joint tenants) received by the grantee (this should be identical to the granting clause).

11. Other restrictions, conditions, and covenants, such as restrictive covenants, that run with the land (photocopy restrictions that have not expired).

12. Spousal consents and releases or a wife's bar of dower (execution by the wife is sufficient evidence of bar of dower). Also note any other specific releases, for example, a release by a beneficiary.

13. Vendor's liens for the outstanding purchase price reserved by way of a mortgage (establish whether or not the mortgage is discharged).

14. Execution (signed, sealed, and witnessed) by the grantor(s) or anyone releasing an interest and possibly by the grantee(s) to observe covenants.

15. Affidavit of execution/affidavit of subscribing witness. Check that it refers to all the signatories and that it is commissioned.

16. Affidavit of age and marital/spousal status (see Appendix 4 for a checklist of dates for when this affidavit is required).

17. Combined Affidavit of Residence and of Value of the Consideration became mandatory May 1, 1979, replacing the old Affidavits of Residence and Land Transfer Tax (residence information is no longer required).

18. Affidavit of the *Planning Act*. Remember that this affidavit has no impact on the existence of a *Planning Act* contravention, unlike post-1985 *Planning Act* declarations.

19. Affidavit of *Land Speculation Tax Act* (in effect from April 10, 1974 to October 24, 1978).

20. Affidavit of residence for income tax purposes.

21. Other affidavits (*e.g.*, recitals are true or partnership property, mortmain).

22. Names of lawyers (optional).

Make notes of any of the above items that are missing, misspellings of names, handwritten alterations and lines typed over and any less routine information. Where recitals or statements relating to background facts (*e.g.*, that the grantor is a widower or that a joint tenant has died) are found in deeds, deposits, or other documents that are at least 20 years old, you have sufficient proof of the truth of the stated facts — you need not search for further evidence. However, if the recital draws a conclusion, it remains necessary to confirm the accuracy of the conclusion. If the recital information is less than 20 years old, it must be confirmed in affidavit form before it may be accepted as sufficient proof of the facts.

Land Titles' transfers do not require checking for proper form. However, particulars of restrictions or covenants that the register indicates are still in existence remain effective and must be recorded. Also, note spousal status, *Planning Act* information, and any other information that is not guaranteed under the *Land Titles Act*. (See Chapter 6.)

Appendix 4 provides a detailed list of significant title searching dates related to past statutory and registration requirements.

ESTATE TRUSTEE'S (EXECUTOR'S OR ADMINISTRATOR'S) TRANSFER/DEED

Estate legislation, taxation, and administration and conveyancing rules have changed a great deal over the years. Estate conveying is complex and a full discussion of the mysteries past and present of estate conveyancing is beyond the scope of this chapter. For an excellent, in-depth review of estate conveyancing, including wills, testacy and intestacy, transmission and survivorship applications, estate cautions, and the registration requirements and precedents for electronic documents in Land Titles, refer to the *Electronic Registration Procedures Guide*.

All estate trustees, as set out in the certificate of appointment of the estate trustee, must be named on and sign an estate transfer/deed. Estate transfers are subject to complex requirements in the *Estates Administration Act*, R.S.O. 1990, c. E.22, formerly the *Devolution of Estates Act*. When summarizing an estate transfer, note or photocopy the following information:

1. usual registration and deed particulars;

2. spousal status of the deceased at the time of death;

3. recitals regarding the deceased's date of death and the interest which the deceased held in the land being searched;

4. recitals outlining the registration particulars of the will or the certificate of appointment of the estate trustee/letters probate (the certificate is registered in the general register);

5. recitals regarding the registration particulars of Canada and Ontario (Succession Duty) estate tax releases;

6. registration particulars concerning court orders and estate trustee's caution, if applicable;

7. recitals regarding the purpose of the sale, such as for the purpose of paying debts, for the purpose of distribution to persons beneficially entitled, for the transfer of land to a person beneficially entitled, *etc.*;

8. recital stating that the estate's debts have been paid in full;

9. additional recitals where the estate trustees are selling to distribute the proceeds of sale among persons beneficially entitled;

10. spousal release under the *Family Law Act* (see Chapter 10 for family law matrimonial home requirements);

11. bar of dower by the widow, where applicable. Dower was abolished March 31, 1978. However, if a husband had died prior to this date, a widow was entitled to a vested dower right. A claim for dower must be made within ten years of a husband's death unless the doweress has remained in possession of the dower property, in which case, the ten-year time limit starts to run on the date the doweress ceases to be in possession of the property. Conveyancers must check for outstanding dower rights in Registry, although the likelihood of encountering dower rights today is highly unlikely;

12. all releases by a beneficiary and his or her spouse (regarding a specific bequest to named beneficiary(ies));

13. the Public Guardian and Trustee's approval on behalf of children under 18;

14. the signature of all estate trustees, as personal representatives of the deceased; their capacity should be noted after the signature (when an estate trustee releases a personal interest, and at that time only, an affidavit or declaration of age and spousal status is required by him or her); and

15. the signature(s) of all beneficiaries releasing an interest.

Recitals about the estate administration often required confirmation that they were true and there was usually a statutory declaration to that effect deposited on title or a sworn statement included in the affidavit of execution form, or, on the new documents, a statement prepared on a Form 5 schedule.

The payment of debts of a deceased is a lien against land specifically devised to an heir or heirs, or upon its becoming part of the residue of the estate. The debt must be paid, or the land released from the lien. A purchaser may get title free from debts in the following cases:

1.   Where a will contains an express power of sale or an implied power, which is a direction to the estate trustees to pay debts, a statutory declaration declaring that the debts of the estate have been paid, and that the sale of the property was for the purpose of paying debts should be provided.

2.   Where an estate trustee states that the deed is given for the purpose of paying the debts.

3.   Where an estate trustee states that the deed is for the purpose of distribution of proceeds to heirs and the majority of the persons beneficially entitled representing together not less than one half of all the interests in the estate consent in the deed. Special consents are required when the beneficiaries are minors (Children's Lawyer) or incompetent persons.

4.   Where lands are conveyed to beneficiaries, pursuant to a court order, within three years of the death or longer if a caution is registered.

5.   When lands have been purchased by a purchaser in good faith, without notice of debts, three years or more after the testator's death, where the estate trustees have not registered an estate trustee's caution and as long as a creditor has not registered a certificate of pending action (*lis pendens*).

Dealing with the person beneficially entitled to the land under the will or intestacy often creates a problem. Land vests in such a person three years after the death of the deceased person whether or not a deed has been registered. The estate trustee may register a caution on title which will postpone vesting for a further three years and enable him or her to pay the debts and dispose of the assets. In the past, property did not vest until the Ontario Succession Duty and the Federal Estate Tax consents, when required, had been registered. Succession Duty and Estate Tax have been revoked. Land that vests directly in beneficiaries remains subject to the debts of the estate.

A conveyance by the personal representatives for the purpose of distribution of real property to beneficiaries requires the consent of the majority of the persons beneficially entitled representing together not less than one half of all the interests in the estate as well as special consents when the beneficiaries are minors or incompetent persons. Unless a court order has been obtained, land conveyed to beneficiaries in this manner remains subject to the debts of the deceased owner up to three years or longer if an estate caution has been registered. After three years, a creditor must register a certificate of pending action or a caution in order to enforce its claim against a subsequent third party purchaser, in good faith, for value, without notice of the debt.

Lands held by two or more persons as joint tenants are not usually dealt with under a will. Except in special cases of land held in joint tenancy by a spouse with a person who is not his or her spouse, title passes automatically to the survivor(s). Post-March 1, 1986, when a person is a joint tenant with someone other than his or her spouse, the *Family Law Act* provides that the joint tenancy is severed on death and becomes a tenancy in common (see Chapter 10). The deed from the surviving joint tenant will recite the death of the other joint tenant, that the person was not a joint tenant with someone other than his or her spouse, and that he or she is the owner by right of survivorship. Succession duty consents were not required where real property interests passed by the law of survivorship. If the survivor was the spouse of the deceased, an affidavit to that effect was included with the affidavit of age and marital status prior to the new documents. Now an electronic statement is required.

Land Titles and ELRS

Under the Land Titles system, it is much less complicated for the searcher. Either a transmission application is made registering the title in the estate trustee's name or a survivorship application is made registering the title in the survivor's name. Where the will does not provide for an express or an implied power of sale, the land vests in the beneficiary, who may apply directly to the land registrar after three years to be entered on the register as the owner. The transfer from the estate trustee will contain statements relating to spousal rights and consents, and beneficiaries and consents, and that the estate trustee is entitled to transfer the land and has met the requirements under the *Estates Administration Act*, and the *Succession Law Reform Act*, R.S.O. 1990, c. S.26. The statements are statements of law and must be made by the estate's solicitor. Estate trustees no longer need to set out the purpose of the transfer. Chapter 6 deals in more depth with estate conveyancing in Land Titles and current electronic Land Titles registration requirements and precedents are set out in detail in the *Electronic Registration Procedures Guide*.

CERTIFICATE OF APPOINTMENT OF ESTATE TRUSTEE WITH OR WITHOUT A WILL (FORMERLY LETTERS PROBATE AND LETTERS OF ADMINISTRATION)

An Application for a Certificate of Appointment of Estate Trustee with or without a will, formerly referred to as Letters Probate or Letters of Administration, is the procedure by which the court approves a will to be the valid last will and testament of a deceased and confirms the appointment of the person named in the will as estate trustee, formerly referred to as an executor/executrix or administrator/administratrix. After a will has been validated, or an intestacy verified, a notarial copy of the certificate is registered in the General Register Index of the Registry office in which any land devised in the will or inherited by intestacy is situate. Different rules apply in traditional Land Titles and in ELRS. When the registration number of a certificate of appointment of estate trustee with or without a will (probate) or a will has not been recited in a deed or other instrument, search chronologically and alphabetically in the General Register Index.

Estate conveyancing is complex and a will should be carefully reviewed for any disposition of the land as well as for all possible liens affecting the estate's assets. Wills, when not photocopied, are summarized as follows:

1. In respect of the Certificate/Probate:

    (a) date and registration particulars;
    (b) the county and date of granting;
    (c) the name, marital status and the date and location of the death of the testator/testatrix; and
    (d) the names of the estate trustees/executors appointed.

2. In respect of the will and the codicil if applicable:

    (a) the testator's name (should match the name on the deed from the estate);
    (b) the estate trustees/executor(s) appointed;
    (c) all powers of sale express or implied to sell the property;
    (d) whether land has been devised to the executors upon certain trusts (trust will) or directly devised to named beneficiaries;
    (e) direction to pay debts (for land sold within three years of the death of the deceased);
    (f) any specific bequest affecting the land being searched and the persons named as beneficiaries;
    (g) any life interests;
    (h) disposition of residue;
    (i) any charge, legacy, condition (conditional or determinable fee simple), or reservation affecting the disposition of the land;
    (j) election by a surviving spouse not to claim under the *Family Law Act* or payment to a widow in lieu of her dower; and
    (k) when only the will is registered, the death certificate, and affidavits of death and execution of the will.

Similar information is summarized when dealing with intestacies and less routine estate administrations.

SUCCESSION DUTY ACT

The *Succession Duty Act*, R.S.O. 1970, c. 449 was repealed by the *Succession Duty Repeal Act, 1979*, S.O. 1979, c. 20. The *Succession Duty Act* required that where persons died between January 1, 1970 and April 10, 1979, a deed, mortgage, or other instrument must include a Succession Duty Consent of the Treasurer of Ontario (attached or endorsed). Land held in joint tenancy with a spouse is exempt from consent requirements. An original certificate or notarial copy may be registered separately and the registration date and number recited in the related document.

Succession duty is a first lien and charge on the property until a certificate is given to discharge it. Failure to obtain an Ontario Succession Duty release invalidates subsequent transactions and prevents land vesting in the proper beneficiaries. If the estate trustee's deed does not provide a cross-reference to the registered particulars of the tax releases, a search of the General Register Index will produce this information.

When summarizing a release, note the following:

1. a short description or a reference to a previously registered document's registration number;

2. the deceased's exact name should be described as in the document registered to him or her; and

3. the date of death and release number.

FEDERAL ESTATE TAX ACT

An estate tax release was required for persons who died between January 1, 1959 and January 1, 1972. However, under an amendment to the *Estate Tax Act*, R.S.C. 1970, c. E-9, a release is no longer required, and Revenue Canada will not issue a release for outstanding notices of lien registered on title. In effect, they can be ignored.

THE PUBLIC GUARDIAN AND TRUSTEE

The Public Guardian and Trustee (formerly the Official Guardian) is appointed by the provincial government to protect the interests, administer property, and concur in the sale of property devised on behalf of an infant (anyone under 18 years as of September 1, 1971) in a will or left to a trustee in trust, unless the trustee has been given the express power in the will to sell the property.

In the past, the Public Trustee was the "committee" for mentally incompetent persons under the *Mental Health Act*. Where real estate was involved, the committee had the power to sell or otherwise deal with the land, subject to the approval of the court. A certified copy of the court order was registered on title and the searcher examined it and made notes of the powers granted. Particulars of the order were also recited in the deed and the Public Trustee's consent endorsed thereon.

Pursuant to the *Mental Health Act*, R.S.O. 1990, c. M.7, the Public Guardian and Trustee may become the statutory guardian of property for a patient of a psychiatric facility who is found to be incapable of managing property under a certificate of incapacity (s. 54) unless

> (a) the patient's property is under guardianship under the *Substitute Decisions Act, 1992*; or
>
> (b) the physician believes on reasonable grounds that the patient has a continuing power of attorney under that Act that provides for the management of the patient's property.

The Public Guardian and Trustee may also become the statutory guardian of property pursuant to the *Substitute Decisions Act, 1992*, S.O. 1992, c. 30. Either an attorney under a continuing power of attorney or members of the immediate family may apply to replace the Public Guardian and Trustee. When a statutory guardian of property is dealing with the property of a legally incompetent person, a notarial or certified copy of the certificate or court order providing evidence of the guardian's power must be registered on title.

POWERS OF ATTORNEY

Special care must be exercised when taking instructions for powers of attorney, when registering powers of attorney, and when receiving and relying on documents signed and registered by power of attorney! A POA can no longer be taken at face value.

The Ministry has implemented sweeping changes to the registration requirements for powers of attorney as part of its Real Estate Fraud Action Plan. Powers of attorney are a real estate fraud "hotspot". The *Consumer Protection and Service Modernization Act, 2006*, S.O. 2006, c. 34 has amended the law relating to the registration requirements for powers of attorney. The Law Society of Upper Canada has set heightened due diligence requirements for lawyers when creating and acting pursuant to powers of attorney, including independent legal advice, donor inquiries, and, in general, inquiries going behind the power. The courts, when dealing with title and mortgage fraud, have vigorously cautioned the profession to exercise vigilance when relying on powers of attorney (*Reviczky v. Meleknia*, [2007] O.J. No. 4992 (Ont. S.C.J.)). Title insurance companies have added risk management guidelines for practitioners. The following section deals both with POA requirements on documents prior to recent legislation and with current requirements. Bulletin No. 2009-01 reviews the electronic registration requirements and statements for powers of attorney, revocations of powers of attorney, and transfers.

For various reasons, attorneys are appointed to execute documents on behalf of others. Of particular interest to conveyancers is the donor's (principal's) authorization to sell real estate and execute related documents. The original POA, or a copy, must be registered in the Land Titles office or in the General Register Index of the Registry office where the land is registered. The registration number and date of the power should be recited in the deed, or other document executed thereunder. If they are not, a search of the General Register Index should provide them. A search in that index should always be made to determine if the power was revoked prior to the registration date of the document executed thereunder.

When a document has been executed by way of POA, the attorney provides a statement (formerly an affidavit) that to the best of his or her knowledge and belief, the power was in full force and effect and not revoked, the donor/principal was at least 18 years old and had the legal capacity to give the POA when giving it, and the witness to his or her signature was not the attorney or the attorney's spouse at the time the document was executed. A POA must be witnessed by two witnesses. A POA automatically terminates on the death of the donor, unless it expressly provides that the power survives the grantor's death. Where the Public Guardian and Trustee becomes the committee for an estate, and upon appointment of a committee, a POA will terminate. A POA may terminate where the donor is declared mentally incompetent depending on whether the power is specifically drafted to survive mental incapacity.

An attorney may make exempting affidavits and statements concerning the principal's spousal status and the status of the principal's matrimonial home as long as the attorney states that the *Family Law Act* statements were made on the basis of personal knowledge. Spousal releases and consents may also be executed by way of POA.

The designation of attorneys for banks differs considerably from that for individuals or other corporations. Bank employees are usually authorized to conduct business on behalf of the bank, but because of frequent staff transfers, it would be impractical to register powers of attorney every time a transfer occurred. Accordingly, land registrars will register a POA which designates the office or position held in the bank but does not name the individual. When a document is made by a corporation by way of a POA, the document should contain a statement by the person acting for the corporation that the person is authorized to bind the corporation.

An affidavit of a subscribing witness must be attached to the document deposing that the person executing the document was authorized to do so as an attorney. Since April 1, 1985, a statement verifies the attorney's authority.

Note the following information when summarizing a POA:

1. the parties, the duration of power, the execution and registration requirements;

2. the acts that the attorney is authorized to perform (note any conditions and restrictions);

3. the express statement that the power survives mental incapacity or death;

4. the specific authorization to make matrimonial home statements (on the basis of personal knowledge only) and sign spousal consents under the *Family Law Act*;

5. statement that the POA is in full force and effect and not revoked; and

6. statement that the principal is at least 18 years old and had the legal capacity to give the POA when giving it.

The *Substitute Decisions Act, 1992* currently governs the use of continuing powers of attorney for property and statutory guardians of property.

Prior to the *Consumer Protection and Service Modernization Act, 2006*, s. 27 (now revoked) of the LRRA regulation entitled Electronic Registration, O. Reg. 19/99, required that a POA contain the following:

(a) the name of the person or the title of the office holder appointed under the power;

(b) a statement that the attorney is entitled to make statements of spousal status under the *Family Law Act* on behalf of the donor; and

(c) a statement that the giving of the power has been witnessed in accordance with the *Substitute Decisions Act, 1992*, if the power is given under that Act.

New Registration Requirements

Lawyers must discuss a POA with a client and make statements of law confirming the discussion and review of POA requirements in documents, particularly transfers, registered by the POA. The original power of attorney is registered in the POLARIS register for powers of attorney by county. POAs registered prior to POLARIS are now included in POLARIS and are available in Teraview. An original POA is now scanned into POLARIS. Revocations of POA are also registered and now scanned into POLARIS. Lawyers' law statements are required for documents signed by POA except for bank and corporate powers; these require a confirming statement by the attorney. Earlier POA statements have been replaced as of April 7, 2008.

Section 4 of O. Reg. 19/99 relates to powers of attorney and now requires the following:

    (i)   if the document is made by an attorney acting under a power of attorney given by a donor that is not a corporation,
        (i)   a statement by the attorney that, to the best of the attorney's knowledge and belief,
            (A) the donor was at least 18 years old and had the legal capacity to give the power when giving it, and
            (B) the power is in full force and effect,
        (ii) a statement by the solicitor submitting the document confirming that the solicitor has reviewed the power with the attorney who has confirmed that,
            (A) the attorney is the lawful party named in the power,
            (B) the attorney is acting within the scope of the authority granted by the power,
            (C) to the best of the attorney's knowledge, information and belief, the power was lawfully given and has not been revoked, and
            (D) if the attorney is a corporation, the person signing the document at the time the document was made was in the stated position at the corporation and had the authority to bind the attorney, and
        (iii) the registration number and date of the power;
   (i.1) if the document is made by an attorney acting under a power of attorney given by a donor that is a corporation,
        (i)   a statement by the attorney that,
            (A) to the best of the attorney's knowledge and belief, the power is in full force and effect,
            (B) the attorney is acting within the scope of the authority granted under the power, and
            (C) the attorney has the authority to bind the donor, and
        (ii) the registration number and date of the power....

Power of Attorney and Revocation of Power of Attorney Searches

Powers of attorney and revocations of powers of attorney are now required to be registered in the POA index in ELRS. Whenever a document is signed and registered by POA, the conveyancer must verify the existence and terms of the power by completing a search in POLARIS. The conveyancer must also search to determine whether or not the power has been revoked. Revocations must be registered to be effective. Conveyancers can search for POA and revocations in the power of attorney index in ELRS as follows:

1.   by instrument number;

2.   by donor name; and

3.   by attorney name.

DEED TO USES

In the past, a deed to uses was a common device to avoid a wife's right to dower in her husband's land. Dower was abolished under the *Family Law Reform Act* on March 31, 1978 and is no longer considered a title issue. In a deed or transfer, the words "to uses" replace "fee simple" and the granting clause includes the words, "grants limits and appoints" when selling to uses ownership.

MEMORIALS OF INDENTURES OF BARGAIN AND SALE

Registered occasionally during the 1800s and 1900s, memorials recited the parties and the land as in a deed, and included an affidavit by the witness to the signature of the party of the first part (grantor), that he or she saw the indenture to which the memorial related signed by the party of the first part and that he or she was a witness to the execution of the indenture.

QUIT CLAIM DEED

A Quit Claim Deed may release any claim or interest that a person may have in land registered under the Registry system. For example, a mortgagor may quit claim the equity of redemption to the mortgagee when a mortgage is in default and thus avoid power of sale proceedings. Quit claims frequently release potential possessory rights in order to settle boundaries and disputed easements by prescription.

TAX DEED

Tax deeds and tax arrears certificates registered on title prior to the introduction of the LRRA forms were brief. They provided a description of the land, the parties, required statutory declarations required by the relevant Act, all of which should be recorded on title. Form 1 is now used for a tax deed and a tax arrears certificate. Statutory declarations regarding notices and tax arrears cancellation certificates are registered by Document General. When summarizing tax sales, the following information is usually recorded in the title search:

1.   the statute authorizing the tax sale;

2.   the tax arrears certificate or certificate of cancellation of tax arrears;

3. statutory declarations by the treasurer regarding service of notice to assessed or registered owners and occupiers and spouses, and persons named on the abstract book or Land Titles register or the execution index as having an interest in the land;

4. recitals confirming date of registration of tax arrears certificate, duration of arrears, offering of land for public sale or auction; and

5. notice of vesting in the municipality.

When a tax sale does take place, a tax deed, or a notice of vesting if it goes to the municipality, should be registered on title and an estate in fee simple vests in the person named on the deed, or in the municipality subject to the following:

1. easements or restrictions that run with the land;

2. any estate or interest of the Crown in the right of Canada or Ontario; and

3. an interest or title acquired by adverse possession by abutting owners before registration of the tax deed or the notice of vesting.

DEED/TRANSFER UNDER POWER OF SALE

When a mortgagor/borrower defaults in making payments under a mortgage, the mortgagee/lender may sell the mortgaged land by way of power of sale as set out in the mortgage document in order to recover the unpaid debt. Following the sale, the lender may still sue the mortgagor for the difference between the mortgage debt and the net sale proceeds. The purchaser of a property under a power of sale takes title subject to prior registered encumbrances on title. Subsequent encumbrances and the mortgage itself are cancelled by a properly conducted sale proceeding.

In Registry, the sale papers, including the notice of sale and statutory declarations regarding service of the notice of sale, default under the mortgage, and compliance of the mortgagee with the *Mortgages Act*, R.S.O. 1990, c. M.40 are registered on title by Document General. The property is then transferred by a grant under power of sale, which is similar to other grants except that it contains recitals as to the sale and the granting clause grants by virtue of the power of sale and all other powers enabling the mortgagee to grant in fee simple.

Under the *Land Titles Act*, the power of sale papers, statutory declarations and transfer are combined and, once registered, are backed by the Land Titles Assurance Fund. When available, electronic registration permits compliance with law statements instead of statutory declarations and postal receipts.

When summarizing or, preferably, photocopying sale papers and a deed/transfer under power of sale, the following information is usually highlighted in the title search for review by the lawyer:

1. the registration date and number of the mortgage, mortgagor and mortgagee and any assignments and postponements, if applicable;

2. mortgage default provisions and a statement that default occurred (compare power of sale provisions in the mortgage with default statements in the deed); and

3. service of notice including parties served and notice to spouse, mortgagee and mortgage registration particulars, principal, interest and costs owing, time periods, demand for payment by a set date and notice of impending sale (reconcile post office registered mail receipts with affidavit of service).

FINAL ORDER OF FORECLOSURE

When a mortgagor has defaulted under a mortgage, the mortgagee usually chooses to enforce the mortgage security by exercising the power of sale in the mortgage contract. However, the mortgagee may choose to proceed by foreclosure and retain the property as an investment in a depressed real estate market. Mortgage foreclosure is a court-supervised and approved procedure ultimately resulting in the registration of a court-issued final order of foreclosure against the mortgagor and other subsequent registered encumbrancers. If the property is not redeemed within a time period set by the courts, the mortgagee becomes the registered owner of the property, free of interests that were registered after the registration of the mortgage that has been foreclosed. The final order of foreclosure is registered on title by Document General.

In Land Titles, an application to amend the register is registered by Document General, making the mortgagee the owner of the property.

When summarizing or, preferably, photocopying a final order of foreclosure, the following information is usually highlighted in the title search for review by the lawyer:

1. the parties, the description, the dates and lawyers;

2. all recitals relating to the mortgage and foreclosure; and

3. confirmation that all parties (including execution creditors) subsequent to the mortgage have been foreclosed.

CHARGE/MORTGAGE

In the past, a mortgage was a pledge of property to a creditor as security for the payment of a debt. The creditor/lender (mortgagee/chargee) then held title to the land, subject to the owner's/borrower's (mortgagor's/chargor's) right to redeem (the equity of redemption) the land upon payment of the principal and interest. The LRRA provides that a charge/mortgage no longer transfers a legal estate in land, but instead creates only a security interest that is discharged on payment of the principal and interest and agreed on fees.

Most mortgages are paid by monthly, bi-monthly, or weekly instalments. Mortgage repayment terms usually run between six months and five years, although they may run up to 25 years. It is a matter of contract. The term "amortization" refers to the length of time that it would take for the mortgage principal and interest to be paid in full pursuant to a fixed repayment schedule. Interest rates may be fixed or variable.

Mortgages may be open or closed and may either allow or not allow early prepayments of all or part of the outstanding principal on the loan, with or without notices and bonuses (penalties). An open mortgage provides that the mortgagor, when not in default, shall have the privilege of paying all or any part or parts of the principal sum secured under the mortgage at any time or times, without notice or bonus. The balance due on the maturity date at the end of the mortgage term is paid as a lump sum or balloon payment. A bonus is an extra payment of interest required before the mortgagee will accept prepayment of the principal before the due date. Contemporary mortgages contain a multitude of payment options and financial features and are subject to the standard charge terms registration requirements.

TYPES OF MORTGAGE

Blended Payment Mortgage: In a blended payment mortgage, regular instalment payments containing both principal and interest are fixed throughout an amortization term. As a result, with each successive payment, the principal portion of the payment increases and the interest allocation in the payment decreases. Blended payment mortgages are paid off by way of a declining balance calculation. Blended payment mortgages are the norm in Canada. However, in challenging economic circumstances, debt-stressed borrowers may resort to interest-only payment schemes, reverse equity payment plans, and longer amortizations.

Blended Rate Mortgage: A blended rate mortgage is a mortgage that combines the amount the borrower owes under an existing mortgage with additional mortgage money required by the borrower. The interest rate for the new amount borrowed is a combination of the interest rate of the old mortgage and the interest rate for the additional amount to be borrowed.

Bridge Financing: Bridge financing is a loan made for a short term to cover the time gap between purchasing a property and finalizing arrangements to pay for it. Bridge or interim financing is used when the closing date for the purchase of a new property precedes the closing date for the sale of an existing property. Bridge financing provides interim financing for mismatched closing dates. Bridge financing is more expensive than long-term loans and is much more common in economic downturns in which purchasers have difficulty selling their existing home.

Collateral Mortgage: A collateral mortgage is a loan based on a promissory note and backed by the collateral security of a mortgage on a property. The loan is usually for a purpose other than the purchase of a home, for example, home renovations, or business purposes.

Conventional Mortgage: A conventional mortgage is a first mortgage of up to a set percentage, currently 80 per cent, of the property's appraised value or purchase price, whichever is lower. A conventional mortgage does not require mortgage default insurance.

High Ratio Mortgage: A mortgage for more than 80 per cent or the lesser of the purchase price or the appraised value of a property. A high ratio mortgage requires default insurance.

Convertible Mortgage: A convertible mortgage is a mortgage that may be pre-paid or changed to another term at any time.

First Mortgage: A first mortgage is registered first on the title to the property and is paid first in the event of a sale or a default.

Second Mortgage: A second mortgage occurs when there is already a first mortgage registered against the property. It is paid after the first mortgage if a borrower defaults and the property is sold.

Fixed Rate Mortgage: In a fixed rate mortgage, the interest rate is fixed for the term or the mortgage (*i.e.*, a three- or five-year term).

Open Mortgage: An open mortgage can be prepaid or renegotiated in whole or in part at any time without notice or additional interest.

Variable or Floating Rate Mortgage: The interest rate fluctuates with the money market in a variable rate mortgage. The regular payments stay the same for the term of the mortgage. As a result, the amount applied toward the principal and the interest changes according to the change in the rate of interest.

Protected Variable Rate Mortgage: A protected variable rate mortgage is a mortgage in which the interest rate varies with money market conditions, but cannot exceed a pre-set maximum rate during the term of a mortgage.

Blanket Charge/Mortgage: A large blanket or developer's mortgage financing a development is placed on an entire subdivision. As individual properties are sold, a partial discharge of mortgage is registered. Partial discharges of mortgage must comply with the subdivision control provisions of the *Planning Act*. These are often exempt, as they relate to the whole of a lot on a registered plan of subdivision.

Building and Completion Loan: A mortgage referred to as a building loan is different in that advances are made as construction proceeds. The title should be subsearched and executions searched against the builder immediately prior to each advance. The lawyer holds the cheque for the advance until he or she is advised that the builder still owns the land and that no construction liens or other charges/mortgages have been registered since the last advance. On completion of construction, with the lender's approval, the full amount of the loan is advanced.

Vendor Take-Back Mortgage: When the vendor takes a mortgage as security for payment for part of an unpaid purchase price, it is referred to as a vendor take-back mortgage. Vendor take-back mortgages are used in commercial as well as residential real estate transactions. The vendor becomes the lender and the purchaser is the borrower. This type of seller financing is most common in economic downturns when credit is tight, houses are not selling, interest rates are high, or a purchaser does not qualify with conventional lenders. It is uncommon in strong markets with low interest rates.

Bond Charge/Mortgage or Trust Deeds: These charges/mortgages are usually for large sums of money and are given by the borrower to a trustee who holds title to the property in trust for several lenders who combine their moneys to lend a portion of the total amount. On repayment, the borrower is given a reconveyance and a release and a standard form discharge of charge/mortgage is registered, particulars of which should be recorded on the search.

OUTSTANDING MORTGAGES AND CHARGES

A charge/mortgage usually represents the most serious encumbrance registered on title. The agreement of purchase and sale will frequently state whether an outstanding mortgage will be assumed or discharged on closing. Where a mortgage or a charge has not been discharged or is not to be discharged on closing, it is either photocopied or summarized. The purchaser will require a copy of any mortgage assumed. Where a mortgage is to be discharged on closing, details from the mortgage and any related assignments are checked against the mortgage discharge.

When summarizing an outstanding mortgage, the following information is usually recorded in the title search:

1. the statute (*e.g.*, *Short Forms of Mortgages Act, Land Registration Reform Act, National Housing Act*);

2. the date of the document, the date of registration, and the registration number;

3. the names and signatures of the mortgagor, mortgagee and guarantor, if there is one, and their relationships;

4. the spouse of the mortgagor and spousal releases and matrimonial home and spousal status and legal age statements;

5. the description of the land;

6. full details of the repayment clause, *e.g.*, payment, date of payment, date of first and last payments, frequency of payment, maturity date, interest rate, interest adjustment date;

7. mortgage terms, *e.g.*, prepayment of principal privileges, notices and bonuses, interest differential clauses, assumption and assignment renewal and discharge provisions, provisions as to notice and procedure on default, any special provisions such as demolition of buildings, additional provisions added by schedule;

8. standard charge terms in post-1985 mortgages;

9. *Planning Act* consents to sever when dealing with a severance of land;

10. financial institution's internal loan number for easy reference;

11. address of the mortgagee/address for service; and

12. lawyer for the mortgagee.

TRANSFER OF CHARGE/ASSIGNMENT OF MORTGAGE

By an assignment of a charge/mortgage, the mortgagee assigns to the assignee its interest in the mortgaged land and all its rights to collect the outstanding principal and interest. If the charge/mortgage has been discharged or ruled out on the register, do not record the assignment's contents. When summarizing an assignment, the following information is usually recorded in the title search:

1. the names of the assignees;

2. the date and registration number;

3. any reassignment provisions;

4. the legal description; and

5. confirmation that the facts recited in the assignment match the mortgage.

DISCHARGE OF CHARGE/MORTGAGE

When registering a discharge of charge/mortgage, the registrar deletes or rules off the mortgage and related documents, such as assignments, amendments, and postponements, from the abstract book or the register. Under the *Registry Act*, if a mortgage has been discharged for ten years or more but it has not been ruled off, the registrar may rule it off on request as it no longer affects title. Post-1985, on registration of a discharge of charge/mortgage by Form 3, the duplicate charge/mortgage and related assignment(s) should be produced. If they are lost, a statement to that effect may be recited in box 7 of the form. By tracking all related assignments, a conveyancer can confirm that the proper party gives the discharge.

CONSTRUCTION LIEN

The *Construction Lien Act*, R.S.O. 1990, c. C.30 replaced the *Mechanics' Lien Act*, R.S.O. 1980, c. 261 on April 2, 1983. A construction lien is a lien in favour of a person who supplies services or materials relating to construction, repair, or improvement, provided to an owner, contractor, or subcontractor. The lien attaches to the interest of the owner in the premises which have been improved. It gives the claimant the right, in addition to his or her ordinary creditor's rights, in certain circumstances, to sell the land and to apply the proceeds against the debt.

The title searcher will provide both the name of the registered owner and the legal description of the lands, as part of the lien registration process. Usually, the person has a street address, and in that case it is possible to establish the lot and plan number from the assessment maps often provided by the Registry office, or locate the PIN when in POLARIS. The description in the lien may be by reference to the registration number of a previously registered document, so that you need not copy a long land description. If the lien has not been discharged, the following should be recorded in your search:

1. names and addresses of parties and lawyers;

2. legal description of land; and

3. when the work was done and the material supplied.

If payment is not made, a lien claimant perfects his or her lien by commencing an action and by registering a certificate of action on title. On payment, the court makes an order vacating the registration of a claim for lien and certificate of action. A Document General is used for the lien, the certificate of action, and the release of lien. The following information should be included in your search:

1. date lien obtained and date registered (note time period between date of lien and registration);

2. name and address of the parties which must be the same as those in the lien; and

3. evidence that the lien and certificate of action are discharged (confirm accuracy of recitals).

NOTICE OF SECURITY INTEREST

Fixtures are chattels attached to land or buildings in such a way that they become a permanent part of the land. A creditor who claims a security interest in a fixture may register a notice of security interest in the Registry office to protect its rights under the *Personal Property Security Act*, R.S.O. 1990, c. P.10, s. 54. Registration of a notice of security interest in consumer goods is effective for five years (*Personal Property Security Act*, s. 54(2)); an extension may be registered on expiry and, on discharge, a discharge of notice of security interest is registered. A notice of security deals with fixtures or goods that may become fixtures or crops, including minerals or hydrocarbons to be extracted, or timber to be cut.

NOTICE OF PENDING LITIGATION/LIS PENDENS

A notice of pending litigation warns would-be purchasers that there is litigation pending that might affect the title to land. The notice is registered under the Registry system, or a caution is filed under the Land Titles system. A certificate of a vacating order may be registered as a release of the land from the claims of the plaintiff. Court orders, registered on title, are usually photocopied as part of the search.

DEPOSITS

In the Registry system, documents, such as surveys and statutory declarations, often regarding possessory rights and which verify facts recited in documents or clarify defects in title, are deposited in the Deposit Index. The deposit of a document is not deemed to be registration and does not provide notice pursuant to s. 70 of the *Registry Act*. Prior to April 1, 1985, deposits were attached to a requisition which provided a description of the land and of the parties. Since that date, deposits are registered by Document General.

Deposits are indexed by number, rather than by municipality, and should be requisitioned by number, "2634 Deposit". Prior to 1937 they were not abstracted on the title; you may find it necessary to search in an alphabetical index. When summarizing deposits, record dates and relevant statutes, and either summarize or photocopy the contents (especially sketches). Deposits are not registrations under the *Registry Act* and for that reason they were not brought forward onto new LTCQ parcel registers when land was converted into POLARIS.

NOTICE OF AGREEMENT OF PURCHASE AND SALE

The *Registry Act* provides that a notice of agreement of purchase and sale or an assignment thereof, or a notice of an option to purchase or an assignment thereof will expire one year after the date of its registration. It may be renewed for an additional year. When these notices are outstanding on title, copy or record the particulars of the parties, purchase price, terms, and any clauses over and above the standard form. In Land Titles, rights in an agreement of purchase and sale are registered by caution.

LEASES

Under the Registry system, a leasehold interest may be created by the registration of a lease, or an agreement for lease. Leases or notices of lease exceeding seven years not registered on title are considered void against subsequent purchasers and mortgagees. Leases or notices of lease not exceeding seven years and not in possession must be registered or they are considered void against subsequent purchasers and mortgagees. Under the Land Titles system, an application should be made to register a notice of lease or of an agreement to lease exceeding three years on the register. Notices of lease not exceeding three years and not in possession must also be registered or they are considered void against subsequent purchasers and mortgagees. A release may be registered under the Registry system and an application for a notice of determination of lease under the Land Titles system. In Land Titles, if the term is in excess of 21 years (including any options or rights of renewal), the lessee may apply to the land registrar to be registered as the owner of a leasehold title. An executed copy of the lease must form part of the application.

When summarizing a lease, the following information is usually recorded in the title search:

1. the lessor, the lessee, and the guarantor, if there is one, and signatures, *etc.*;

2. the description of the leased premises;

3.   the commencement and expiry date/term of the lease;

4.   payment amounts, dates, and method of payment;

5.   assignment and sublet provisions, assignments of rent provisions;

6.   renewal clauses and options to purchase;

7.   notice provisions and penalties;

8.   proper execution by the parties;

9.   terms of interest depending on the circumstances; and

10. a photocopy of the lease if the lease is current.

NOTICE OF LIEN

A multitude of liens, certificates and notices may be registered under federal and provincial statutes. Copy or record the full particulars of these documents unless they have been already discharged, released, or ruled out on the register.

VENDOR'S/PURCHASER'S LIEN

Today, most vendors prefer to register a vendor take-back mortgage as security for any unpaid purchase price. Under the Registry system, when the balance of the moneys due to the vendor on delivery of the deed to the purchaser is secured on stated terms, the vendor has a lien on title for the unpaid purchase moneys. In the past, this vendor's lien was often referred to in the habendum of the deed and constituted notice on title to subsequent purchasers and mortgagees of the land. When it was secured by a mortgage given back to the vendor, the recital in the deed was usually "subject to a vendor's lien for unpaid purchase money to be secured by a mortgage in favour of John Smith and a discharge of the mortgage shall operate as a discharge of the lien". If the mortgage was not discharged, the lien was outstanding and an encumbrance against the land. When the terms of the lien were not specifically expressed in the deed, it was discharged from title by a release. In Land Titles, the lien is registered by a notice with a one-year registration life that can be extended for another year. These notices are by an application.

A purchaser's lien is subject to similar registration requirements as a vendor's lien and it protects money paid by a purchaser under an Agreement of Purchase and Sale. A purchaser's lien provides some protection to a purchaser who has not yet registered a deed or transfer. A purchaser can protect his or her equitable title under the Agreement of Purchase and Sale by registering a purchaser's lien. It is subject to the same time limits.

METHODS OF OWNERSHIP

Joint Tenancy and Tenants in Common

Where land is conveyed to two or more persons, they take title as tenants in common unless it is expressly stated in the deed that they take title as joint tenants. It is essential to check the granting clause and the habendum in the deed to determine if the deed conveys the entire estate in land or an undivided part interest of a tenant in common or a joint tenant. The undivided part interest of each tenant is specifically set out in the deed. The decision as to whether to hold land as tenants in common or as joint tenants affects ownerships rights and is a form of estate planning. The grantees' choice as to whether to take title as joint tenants or tenants in common is usually based on family relationships, estate planning, and tax considerations.

In a deed or will where title is taken as joint tenants, each joint tenant must have an equal share in the whole of the land, an equal right of possession and receive his or her part interest at the same time, in the same conveyance. Both the granting clause and the habendum recite as joint tenants and not as tenants in common. When one joint tenant dies, the entire interest automatically passes to the surviving joint tenant or tenants by right of survivorship. When the land is sold, the deed from the surviving joint tenant(s) should contain a recital to the effect that the land was held as joint tenants and that they are granting by right of survivorship. A joint tenancy may be severed by one joint tenant transferring his or her part interest to a stranger, to himself or herself, or by agreement between the joint tenants. When a person is a joint tenant with someone other than his or her spouse, s. 26(1) of the *Family Law Act* provides that the joint tenancy is severed on death and becomes a tenancy in common.

Tenants in common must share an equal right to possession but are not required by law to hold an equal ownership share. A tenant's in common share may be expressed as a fractional or as a percentage amount. As well, tenants in common may receive their undivided shares at different times in different conveyances. When a tenant in common dies, his or her share passes by will or by intestacy, as part of the estate administration. The *Conveyancing and Law of Property Act*, R.S.O. 1990, c. C.34 provides that co-owners hold land as tenants in common unless the deed expressly states that the co-owners hold land as joint tenants.

Corporate Ownership

Where title to land is registered in the name of a corporation, a conveyancer should establish whether or not it was an incorporated company at the time of both the purchase and sale of the land and whether it held an extra-provincial licence if it was a foreign company. The *Business Corporations Act*, R.S.O.

1990, c. B.16 was amended so as to limit the requirement for corporate searches to no more than 20 years before registration of a transfer to a subsequent purchaser for value (s. 244(3)). Corporate searches for Ontario companies providing the status and corporate profile of an Ontario company and particulars of incorporation or date of dissolution may be searched through online service providers, such as BAR-eX at <http://www.bar-ex.com>, Cyberbahn at <http://www.cyberbahn.ca/>, and ONCORP. These service providers provide access to the Companies Branch of the Ministry of Government Services, and the Government of Ontario's ONBIS electronic searching function. A certificate of status and possibly an extra-provincial licence is obtained for the current company selling or mortgaging land.

An extra-provincial licence permits an extra-provincial corporation to acquire, hold, and convey land in Ontario. A conveyancer may also be required to check whether a company incorporated outside Canada holds an extra-provincial licence under the *Extra-Provincial Corporations Act*, R.S.O. 1990, c. E.27 to carry on business including the holding of land in Ontario (s. 1(2)(b)).

When a corporation has changed its name, a notarial copy, or a certified copy of Articles of Amendment will be on file in the General Register Index in the Registry system. In Land Titles, an application to amend the register (Form 4) is registered.

Corporate searches for companies under the *Canada Business Corporations Act*, R.S.C. 1985, c. C-44 are made at Corporations Canada.

Corporations without share capital under the *Corporations Act*, R.S.O. 1990, c. C.38 and the *Canada Corporations Act*, R.S.C. 1970, c. C-32 require a special resolution (Ontario's *Corporation Act*, two-thirds vote of members present) passed at a members meeting to authorize dealings with land. A search of the letters patent will reveal what authority the company has to deal with land.

Refer to Chapter 4 for more detail on escheat and corporate searching.

Partnership Property

Two or more people or corporations may purchase land as partnership property. In order to carry on business, all partners must first register the name of the partnership pursuant to the *Business Names Act*, R.S.O. 1990, c. B.17. The registrar under the *Business Names Act* maintains a public record of every registration made under this Act or filed under either the *Partnerships Act*, R.S.O. 1990, c. P.5 or the *Limited Partnerships Act*, R.S.O. 1990, c. L.16. Conveyancers check the registration of partnerships that either hold title currently or held title in the past and review the contents of the partnership declarations with respect to the authority of a partnership to hold land.

The granting clause of the partnership deed reads, "in fee simple as partnership property", or, "as partners" and recites the partnership name, if there is one. Otherwise, the land will be considered as being held as tenants in common. The deed from the partnership must be signed by all the partners registered under the *Business Names Act* or its predecessors and include a declaration by one partner stating: the names of all the partners; that they were the only partners in the partnership; that the land was purchased as partnership land; and that the land was held as partnership land up to the date of the sale. The content of these statements has changed over the years. Refer to the *Electronic Registration Procedures Guide* for present wording.

Limited partnerships are less common. A declaration, which is filed with the Ministry of Government Services, sets out the names and addresses of both the general and the initial limited partners, the address of the limited partnership and the lawyers. Title is registered in the name(s) of one or more general partners and recites the partnership name. The land may also be registered in the name of the general partner or the nominee/trustee company authorized to sign documents on behalf of the limited partnership. When all partners (including limited partners) are listed on the deed or mortgage, all partners (including limited partners) execute the document. Unless a transfer or charge contains a declaration by the general partner that the conveyance is for a partnership purpose within the meaning of s. 8 of the *Limited Partnerships Act*, all partners must sign the document.

Trustees

The granting clause of a deed or mortgage may indicate that the land is held in trust, or by a trustee. Trust ownership may conceal the beneficial owner's identity or prevent land vesting in a minor or a person lacking legal capacity. Registration of trust ownership is permitted in Registry but not in the Land Titles system.

All trustees should sign the documents and convey on behalf of the trust. The trust instrument will set out the trust powers to deal with real property and the authority of the trustees. Charities may be organized as trusts.

Unincorporated Organizations

The by-laws and constitution of an unincorporated organization such as a club set out the power and procedure to deal with real property. Individuals must act on behalf of the organization.

Children

The Children's Lawyer's consent must be endorsed on all transfers and mortgages of land to or from individuals under the age of 18. All transfers and mortgages require a statement of age.

Charities Accounting Act

The *Mortmain and Charitable Uses Act*, R.S.O. 1980, c. 297 was repealed, effective June 15, 1982, and was replaced by an amendment to the *Charities Accounting Act*, R.S.O. 1990, c. 10, s. 8, which permits charities to hold land subject to the right of the Public Guardian and Trustee, formerly the Public Trustee, to register a notice vesting the land in itself for the purpose of selling it, if it finds that the land:

    (a) has not been actually used or occupied for the charitable purpose for a period of three years;
    (b) is not required for actual use or occupation for the charitable purpose; and
    (c) will not be required for actual use or occupation for the charitable purpose in the immediate future....

Conveyancers should copy a vesting notice and note it in the search summary.

Religious Organizations' Lands Act

Religious organizations are authorized to acquire land for specified religious purposes under the direction of the *Religious Organizations' Lands Act*, R.S.O. 1990, c. R.23. Under the Act, religious organization "includes an association of persons that is charitable according to the law of Ontario and that is organized for the advancement of and for the conduct of worship, services or rites of the Buddhist, Christian, Hindu, Islamic, Jewish, Baha'i, Longhouse Indian, Sikh, Unitarian, or Zoroastrian faith" (*Religious Organizations' Lands Act*, s. 1). Many churches are incorporated federally by private Act. For example, the United Church of Canada, the Anglican Church, the Baptist Union, the Methodist Church, and many others are incorporated by federal legislation. Federal incorporating legislation must be reviewed for additional requirements on the conveyancing of church-owned lands.

A religious organization may acquire and hold land for the following purposes:

- a place of worship;
- a residence for its religious leader;
- a burial or cremation ground;
- a bookstore or a printing or publishing office;

- a theological seminary or similar institution of religious instruction;
- a religious camp, retreat or training centre; or
- any other religious purpose.

The land is to be held in the name of trustees appointed by the organization and title vests automatically in their successors. Trustees may act only upon the resolution of the organization, adopted by the majority of those present at a meeting called for that purpose. A certified copy of the trustees' resolution should be deposited on title so that conveyancers can establish the trustees' exact authority. Also necessary is a resolution appointing the trustees. The property may be held under a deed of trust that sets conditions that must be complied with. Again, the conveyancer must confirm that the conditions have been met.

Bankruptcy

A court-appointed trustee in bankruptcy is registered as the owner of the bankrupt's interests in land. Registration of a trustee severs joint tenancies; the trustee and remaining owner are tenants in common. Land held by a trustee is not shown as subject to spousal rights. A trustee can register a caution to protect the creditors; subsequent registrations are subject to cautions until removed. A transfer by a trustee authorized under the *Bankruptcy and Insolvency Act*, R.S.C. 1985, c. B-3 does not require age, spousal status, or POA statements.

Concurrent Ownership Structures

Since the 1960s, there has been ongoing development of new forms of concurrent ownership. Condominium ownership, co-operative ownership, time share arrangements, life leases, and, most recently, fractional share ownership have become popular methods of ownership. Co-operative, life lease, and fractional ownership will be discussed in Chapter 7, which focuses on condominium ownership.

Figure 5.1*

TRANSFER/DEED OF LAND

Figure 5.2

CHARGE/MORTGAGE OF LAND

Province of Ontario

DYE & DURHAM CO. INC.
Form No. 975

Charge/Mortgage of Land
Form 2 — Land Registration Reform Act

B

FOR OFFICE USE ONLY

New Property Identifiers

Additional:
See
Schedule ☐

Executions

Additional:
See
Schedule ☐

(1) Registry ☐ Land Titles ☐ (2) Page 1 of _____ pages

(3) Property Identifier(s) Block Property

Additional:
See
Schedule ☐

(4) Principal Amount Dollars $

(5) Description

(6) This Document Contains (a) Redescription New Easement Plan/Sketch ☐ (b) Schedule for: Additional Description ☐ Parties ☐ Other ☐ (7) Interest/Estate Charged Fee Simple

(8) Standard Charge Terms — The parties agree to be bound by the provisions in Standard Charge Terms filed as number _____ and the Chargor(s) hereby acknowledge(s) receipt of a copy of these terms.

(9) Payment Provisions
(a) Principal Amount $
(b) Interest Rate _____ % per annum
(c) Calculation Period
(d) Interest Adjustment Date Y M D
(e) Payment Date and Period
(f) First Payment Date Y M D
(g) Last Payment Date
(h) Amount of Each Payment Dollars $
(i) Balance Due Date
(j) Insurance Dollars $

(10) Additional Provisions

Continued on Schedule ☐

(11) Chargor(s) The chargor hereby charges the land to the chargee and certifies that the chargor is at least eighteen years old and that

. . . .

The chargor(s) acknowledge(s) receipt of a true copy of this charge.

Name(s) Signature(s) Date of Signature Y M D

(12) Spouse(s) of Chargor(s) I hereby consent to this transaction.
Name(s) Signature(s) Date of Signature Y M D

(13) Chargor(s) Address for Service

(14) Chargee(s)

(15) Chargee(s) Address for Service

(16) Assessment Roll Number of Property Cty. | Mun. | Map | Sub. | Par.

(17) Municipal Address of Property

(18) Document Prepared by:

FOR OFFICE USE ONLY

Fees

Registration Fee

Total

Figure 5.3

DISCHARGE OF CHARGE/MORTGAGE

Figure 5.4

DOCUMENT GENERAL

Province of Ontario	**Document General** Form 4 — Land Registration Reform Act	DYE & DURHAM CO. INC.—Form No. 985 Amended NOV. 1992 **D**

(1) Registry ☐   Land Titles ☐   **(2)** Page 1 of   pages

(3) Property Identifier(s)   Block   Property   Additional: See Schedule ☐

(4) Nature of Document

(5) Consideration   Dollars $

(6) Description

New Property Identifiers   Additional: See Schedule ☐

Executions   Additional: See Schedule ☐

(7) This Document Contains: (a) Redescription New Easement Plan/Sketch ☐   (b) Schedule for: Description ☐   Additional Parties ☐   Other ☐

FOR OFFICE USE ONLY

(8) This Document provides as follows:

Continued on Schedule ☐

(9) This Document relates to instrument number(s)

(10) Party(ies) (Set out Status or Interest)
Name(s)   Signature(s)   Date of Signature Y M D

(11) Address for Service

(12) Party(ies) (Set out Status or Interest)
Name(s)   Signature(s)   Date of Signature Y M D

(13) Address for Service

(14) Municipal Address of Property | **(15)** Document Prepared by: | Fees and Tax

FOR OFFICE USE ONLY

Registration Fee

Total

Figure 5.5
SCHEDULE

CHAPTER 6

The Land Titles System: Torrens in Ontario

SEARCHING IN LAND TITLES

Chapter 6 focuses on the *Land Titles Act*, R.S.O. 1990, c. L.5 and the Land Titles registration system, with emphasis on the title qualifications under the Act, the certification of instruments, and title searching. There are now five different kinds of Land Titles parcels and searches, not including condominium parcels. They are as follows:

1. fee simple Land Titles Absolute;

2. fee simple Land Titles Conversion Qualified (LTCQ);

3. fee simple Land Titles Absolute Plus;

4. qualified title with a specific qualifier; and

5. leasehold title.

The nature of the title is determined by the timing and the circumstances of the first registration under the Act, or an application to remove qualifiers from an existing title, for example, when an LTCQ is upgraded to a Land Titles Absolute Plus (LT PLUS). Competent searching in Land Titles is based on a sophisticated understanding of the different kinds of title and the effect of the different legal qualifiers on the registered title search, the off-title searches, the survey, combined with when title insurance provides an alternative coverage for title risks, and more importantly, when it does not. Printing a Property Identification Number (PIN) register is not a search of title.

This chapter reviews the search requirements for and gives an example of a search of a Fee Simple Land Titles Absolute title in both the traditional paper environment and in the POLARIS record. Fee Simple LTCQ and Fee Simple Land Titles Absolute Plus have different qualifiers. Chapter 8 focuses on searching LTCQ and LT PLUS titles on Teraview in the context of their specialized title qualifiers and the procedures generated by the POLARIS conversion to the automated electronic land registration (ELRS) system.

THE LAND TITLES ACT

Today, most land in Ontario and all of the north is registered under the *Land Titles Act*. Since the late 1960s, all new plans of subdivision and condominium properties were registered in Land Titles whenever a Land Titles office was available (*Land Titles Act*, s. 31). The POLARIS project has now converted almost all Registry land to LTCQ titles through an administrative Land Titles conversion process (*Land Titles Act*, s. 32) and requires developers to upgrade an LTCQ title to an LT PLUS title as a condition for the registration of a new subdivision or condominium plan.

The fundamental principle behind the Land Titles system is that the government guarantees that title is vested in the current registered owner, subject to registered encumbrances, as shown on the parcel register, and subject to the numerous exceptions and qualifications listed in s. 44 of the *Land Titles Act*. In the event of error, a claim for compensation may be made to the Land Titles Assurance Fund. The fund offers compensation to a person wrongfully deprived of land by reason of some other person's being registered as owner through fraud, misdescription, or other error in an entry on the register. The *Consumer Protection and Service Modernization Act, 2006*, S.O. 2006, c. 34 (Bill 152) amended the *Land Titles Act* and reformed the claims process by creating two separate recovery streams. As of December 20, 2006, homeowners and innocent purchasers of residential property who are victims of fraud may apply immediately to the fund and receive a decision regarding compensation within 90 days. This new claim remedy is only available for claims that are based on a fraudulent instrument registered against land on or after October 19, 2006. Claimants who do not fall into these categories follow a different claims process that requires that potential claimants first seek any available compensation under the law before claiming against the fund. The fund will not compensate a person who has contributed to his or her loss by participating or colluding in the fraud (*Land Titles Act*, s. 59(1)(d)). In addition, the fund requires that claimants demonstrate that they have exercised due diligence as a condition for being compensated from the Fund. For example, a lender must "take reasonable steps" to verify the identity of both the borrower and the registered owner, and that they are the same person. Similarly, an innocent purchaser for valuable consideration must take reasonable steps to verify that the registered owner is the person selling the property. Title insurers who have paid out fraud claims under title and mortgage insurance policies are barred from seeking to be indemnified from the fund (*Land Titles Act*, s. 59(1)(e)). Information about how to make a claim, what happens at a hearing, the necessary procedures and forms, and earlier decisions are available online at the Ministry of Government Services at <http://www.gov. on.ca/MGS/en/ConsProt/107229.html>.

Land Titles is a register and partial government guarantee of ownership or title; whereas, Registry is a register of deeds and other documents, in which registered documents are merely evidence supporting the title. Relevant information from all documents registered subsequent to the patent is recorded, in the order of registration, in a series of books referred to as registers. As Teranet automates Land Titles registers, information is stored in and retrieved online from an electronic record (POLARIS), and registered online in ELRS using the Teraview software.

Plans of subdivision registered in Land Titles are identified by a number that is prefixed by the number of the particular Registry office and the letter "M", *e.g.*, 33M-2345. The same identification procedure is applied to reference plans, *e.g.*, 33R-630. A registered plan prefixed by the letter "D" relates to lands consolidated by a municipality or to several parcels owned by a developer in order to facilitate future transactions with the land. Miscellaneous plans with the prefix "MISC" are plans deposited, filed or registered by the Minister of Transportation.

There are also lots on concessions under the Land Titles system that have not been subdivided, or were subdivided prior to entry under Land Titles and have not been re-subdivided by an "M" plan. In that case, the original Registry office abstract book will disclose an entry by which the registered owner made application to register the land under the Land Titles system. The application will indicate the necessary Land Titles reference to obtain the register, *e.g.*, the parcel and section number.

PARCELS AND SECTIONS

All properties in Land Titles have been "parcelized" and are identified and indexed by parcel and section numbers instead of by lot and plan. A parcel of land may incorporate a lot, a block, a one-foot reserve, a road allowance, or a multiple thereof, or a part of a lot, or block, or reserve, or road allowance, or any other delineation of land on a plan. Frequently, parcels are made up of a Part or Parts on a reference plan. As well, a parcel may contain a combination of lot(s), part lot(s), block(s), road(s), reserve(s), and/or Part(s) on reference plans.

A page is opened in the register, and a particular parcel is identified by the number and section allotted to it and recorded at the top of each page, and not by the lot and plan as under the Registry system. Land Titles parcel registers are identified by a parcel number and contain a stand-alone parcel description.

The parcel and section numbers are required in order to obtain the parcel register. In the past, the system for establishing parcel numbers had no particular significance. However, in more recent years, a consecutive numbering system for all lands that are subdivided was established. For example, Lot 250 on Subdivision Plan M-1684 would be designated Parcel 250-1, Section M-1684 and subsequent subdivisions of the lot would be allocated new parcel numbers, *e.g.*, 250-2, 250-3. In this way, the parcel number corresponds with the lot number and the section number with the plan number. Another commonly used consecutive numbering system is one in which the parcel is given a number, or a letter and a number, and the section usually identifies with the municipality, *e.g.*, 88863 or Parcel S-8301, Section Sudbury East (S.S.E.).

Although properties in Land Titles are identified and searched by parcel number, the legal description required in registered documentation retains the underlying lot, plan, concession, township, county, district or regional municipality designations. As parcel numbers rarely correspond to lots and plans, some Land Titles offices provide cross-references between lot and plan numbers and parcel numbers. These cross-references are particularly useful when searching adjoining lands.

Where a registered owner owns more than one parcel under the Land Titles system, he or she may make an application to consolidate them in one parcel. The previous description may be retained, except where a part of a parcel is being consolidated; then a reference plan is usually required for the part.

Today, the automated POLARIS record assigns a Property Identification Number or PIN to each parcel. The PIN is now the primary description reference. The PIN adds another description layer and references the underlying parcel description references. The automated search and registration system and information about the new types of title and their qualifiers is found in Chapter 8.

REFERENCE PLANS

A reference plan must be registered when a parcel, lot, or block is subdivided. A surveyor's real property report may be deposited on title and referred to as a reference plan. A reference plan creates a new legal description based on parts laid out on a reference plan instead of lots on plans or metes and bounds descriptions. Much of the land registered in Land Titles is described by parts on reference plans. Reference plans are identified by a number that is prefixed by the number of the particular Registry office and the letter "R", *e.g.*, 33R-2345.

CERTIFICATE OF OWNERSHIP OF LAND AND OF CHARGE

The *Land Titles Amendment Act, 1979*, S.O. 1979, c. 93 provided that Certificates of Ownership and Certificates of Ownership of Charge would no longer be issued. Prior to the registration of new transfers or charges, the registrar may require the surrender of outstanding certificates. Certificates of ownership are not of practical importance today.

LEASES

In Land Titles, leases must be registered by an application to the land registrar, with permission of the registered owner, to register a notice of lease. A signed copy of the lease is usually included in the notice of lease application. If the full lease is not included in the notice as is often the case in more recent commercial leases, the lease must be produced on request or the notice is cancelled. Once a notice of lease has been registered, related notices of documents, such as sub-leases, assignments of lease, amendments of lease, determination/surrender of lease and charges of lease, may also be registered.

Land Titles provides for a separate leasehold register for long-term leasehold titles. The leasehold register contains "leasehold land held under a lease for a life or lives, or determinable on a life or lives, or for a term of years of which at least twenty-one are unexpired", including options and renewal rights (*Land Titles Act*, s. 38). Section 44(1) of the *Land Titles Act* states that short-term leases with an unexpired term, including options and renewal rights, for less than three years, where there is actual occupation, are encumbrances on title even though they are not registered on the parcel register (s. 44(1)4). Leases with an unexpired term, including options and renewal rights, for three years or more, must be registered as a notice of lease on the parcel register in order to protect the lessee's interest.

TRUSTS

The Land Titles system does not recognize trust ownership. Section 62(1) of the Act states that "notice of an express, implied or constructive trust shall not be entered on the register or received for registration". The current registered owner on the parcel page is the only registered owner whether or not he or she is described as a "trustee". Describing a registered owner as a trustee does not impose a duty on a subsequent purchaser or mortgagee to make an inquiry as to whether other persons may have a beneficial interest in the land. Pursuant to s. 62(3), "Where two or more owners are described as trustees, the property shall be held to be vested in them as joint tenants unless the contrary is expressly stated." The Act does allow for the registration of: (1) estate trustees in the place of a deceased owner; (2) trustees of a registered pension fund or plan; (3) trustees under the *Religious Organizations' Lands Act*, R.S.O. 1990, c. R.23; and (4) trustees on behalf of a bankrupt estate.

ADVERSE POSSESSION

In Ontario, acquiring ownership rights through possession is prohibited in Land Titles. Unlike in Registry, Land Titles does not permit either the acquisition of adverse possession after ten years of obvious, undisputed possession, or easements by prescription after 20 years of continuous, uninterrupted use. In the past, when an owner transferred land in Registry to Land Titles by an Application for First registration (*Land Titles Act*, s. 31), existing possessory rights were either extinguished or established as absolute title by the application process. Once in Land Titles, possessory rights were barred as long as adjoining owners had received notice in the application process. Not all Canadian Land Titles systems bar possessory rights.

One exception to the no adverse possession rule is when land has been transferred from Registry into Land Titles as part of the administrative Land Titles conversion as part of POLARIS reforms. The POLARIS conversion did not require surveys and did not give notice to owners. It does not guarantee boundaries. As a result, LTCQ title is subject to mature adverse possession and easement by prescription claims that were established while the property was still in Registry. However, once in Land Titles, no new possessory rights can be acquired. Land Titles Conversion Qualified parcel register printouts contain the warning that title is subject to adverse possession, prescription, misdescription or boundaries settled by convention. As well, the parcel register printout warns that adjoining properties should be investigated to ascertain descriptive inconsistencies, if any, with the description included on the parcel register printout.

Adjoining owners who wish to assert a possessory claim or a description error in LTCQ titles must act promptly as continuing possessory claims are barred and the *Real Property Limitations Act*, R.S.O. 1990, c. L.15 governs. The owner of an LTCQ title may apply to upgrade to a Land Titles Absolute Plus title. This process settles possessory claims or description disputes. An LT PLUS title bars possessory rights and verifies the description. The owner of an LTCQ title must upgrade to an LT PLUS title as a condition of registering a new subdivision or condominium plan.

Although, in general, Land Titles bars possessory rights, it does by s. 44 qualifiers create rights in land that are reminiscent of possessory rights. For example, s. 44(1)2 protects unregistered watercourses and right of water and other easements. These rights could include traditional well access or water licences or flooding rights and are the subject of off-title inquiries.

EXTENT OF LAND: SECTION 140

The absence of possessory rights in Land Titles does not guarantee the extent of the description or boundaries. Section 140(2) of the *Land Titles Act* clearly states that: "The description of registered land is not conclusive as to the boundaries or extent of the land." Only a survey can establish the extent of land and the boundaries of a property. It is critical that lawyers know that the *Land Titles Act* does not guarantee boundaries or extent of land; the parcel description is not conclusive as to boundaries. Physical location of land can only be established by a survey. A survey is as important in Land Titles as it was in Registry.

REGISTRATION AND CERTIFICATION OF INSTRUMENTS

Only the registered owner, as entered on the parcel register, is entitled to transfer or charge registered freehold or leasehold land. The registered owner of land or a charge, other than a corporation, must be described by surname and by the first given name in full, followed by another given name, if any, in full (*Land Titles Act*, s. 67). Land Titles staff completes only a preliminary check when an instrument is tendered for registration. If the land registrar decides that a proposed registration is in some way deficient, he or she may notify the lawyer any time within 21 days that the document will be rejected unless the deficiency is corrected. The registrar may allow "a period of time not less than seven days and not more than thirty days" for correcting the problem. If the request is not satisfied within the specified time, the instrument will be rejected and all rights of priority will be lost (*Land Titles Act*, s. 78(2)).

Registration in Land Titles is complete only when the instrument and its entry into the proper register are certified by the land registrar or an authorized signing officer. In the past, the day, hour, and minute of the receipt of each instrument was the official time of registration for the purpose of establishing priority among registered interests. Currently, registration is complete when the land registrar has certified the instrument and entered it in the proper register. The instrument is deemed to have been registered on the day that the registrar received it and in the order that the registrar entered it into the register. In effect, the Act has moved from time of registration to date and order of registration (*Land Titles Act*, s. 78(5)).

Instruments are registered on a parcel rank, in terms of priority, according to the order in which they are entered into the register. Agreements to change rights of priority, such as postponements of charge, may be registered and alter rights of priority originally acquired through order of registration. Lawyers should be aware of the potential risk that exists between the time when the Land Titles office receives an instrument and when it certifies the instrument's entry on the parcel register. Title insurance now offers coverage for this risk; it is called gap insurance.

When a document is submitted electronically, it undergoes a series of automated checks and is given a time and date. It is then certified by land registration staff and becomes effective as of the time and date submitted. A certified document is followed by a "C" on an automated parcel register. The same rules and time limits apply for rejection, return, and rectification of instruments. Lawyers must confirm that documents that they have registered electronically have been certified and that a new parcel printout indicates a "C" following the document registration particulars.

DOCUMENTS

The *Land Titles Act* and its regulations, together with the *Land Registration Reform Act*, R.S.O. 1990, c. L.4 ("LRRA"), prescribe in detail the type and content of forms and documents acceptable for registration in Land Titles. The ELRS has in excess of 100 core electronic document forms which are pre-populated with underlying parcel information. These documents have embedded legal requirements and a multitude of pre-populated factual and legal statement precedents that are governed by artificial intelligence and automated checks that enforce minimum standards and assist in the production of certifiable, registerable documents. Lawyers remain responsible for the content of documents. The *Land Titles Act* and regulations, particularly O. Reg. 27/99 and R.R.O. 1990, Reg. 690, prescribe the legal requirements for Land Titles documents. The LRRA, Form of Documents, R.R.O. 1990, Reg. 688, and Electronic Registration, O. Reg. 19/99 set the statutory requirements for electronic documentation.

The Policy and Regulatory Services Branch of the Real Property Registration Branch of the Ministry of Government Services produces Land Registrars' Bulletins and the Ministry's *Electronic Registration Procedures Guide*, which provide precise legal requirements and examples for documents and for registration. The *Electronic Registration Procedures Guide* contains hundreds of pages of instructions for completing specific documents. Document registration requirements change daily. Practitioners also rely on the *Teraview Reference Guide* for how to work in the ELRS environment. Both guides are available online on the Teraview website at <http://www.teraview.ca>.

Although the five standardized forms under the LRRA apply generally to both Land Titles and Registry, the *Land Titles Act* requires very different form and content within the LRRA standardized documents. Prior to the LRRA, Land Titles documents differed in name as well as in form. For example, a deed in the Land Titles system was called a transfer, a mortgage was a charge, an assignment of mortgage was a transfer of charge, and a discharge of mortgage was a cessation of charge. Land Titles documents, unlike Registry documents, did not require seals. Many other Land Titles documents are registered by a notice or by an application to amend the register.

Chapter 5 reviews documentation past and present for both Registry and Land Titles and highlights the information most commonly included in search summaries of documents.

Applications

In Land Titles, most documents, other than transfers, charges, and cessations of charge, are registered by application to amend the register. Applications to delete writs of seizure and sale, to register notices and cautions, to amend the register by entering or deleting restrictive covenants or easements, to remove outstanding interests such as debts, beneficiaries' interests, spousal rights, options, rights of first refusal, temporary rights, subject to rights as a result of conversion, and to change name are all common registrations. A certificate of pending litigation is registered by application.

Notices

A person with an unregistered interest in land may register a notice to protect that interest in Land Titles, without consent of the registered owner. The following interests are examples of interests registered by notice: notice of lease; notice of sublease or assignment of lease; notice of option to purchase; notice of vendor's lien; notice of purchaser's lien; notice of first refusal; notice of agreement amending charge; notice of development or subdivision agreement; notice of general assignment of rents; notice of site plan agreements; notice of property standards orders; notice of agreement amending charge; notice recreation of lien under *Homes for the Aged and Rest Homes Act*, R.S.O. 1990, c. H.13; postponement of execution to a charge; occupancy agreement; notice of agreement under s. 8 of the *Building Code Act, 1992*, S.O. 1992, c. 23; notice of agreement under the *Drainage Act*, R.S.O. 1990, c. D.17; notice of lease of chattels; an agreement specifically permitted to be registered by other legislation; cautions under the *Provincial Land Tax Act, 2006*, S.O. 2006, c. 33, Schedule Z.2; and encroachment agreements. *Planning Act*, R.S.O. 1990, c. P.13 sections generate many notices, for example: community improvement agreements (s. 28(10)); demolition permit conditions and liens (s. 33(7)); increased density agreements (s. 37(3)); site plan agreements (s. 41(7)); subdivision agreements (s. 51(26)); severance consent agreements (s. 53(12)); and property standards orders (Building Code, O. Reg. 350/06, and *Ontario Heritage Act*, R.S.O. 1990, c. O.18).

An application to register notice and an application to delete notice are registered by Document General. The application to register notice may contain a summary of the agreement or the agreement itself. The application must authorize the registrar to delete the notice at the end of a stated period, or on the consent of the specified parties, or that the notice will be effective for an indeterminate time. Online electronic documents are created through a series of screens and appear visually different from paper documents.

Restrictive Covenants

Refer to Chapter 9 for the requirements for registration and deletion of restrictive covenants.

Death of a Registered Owner

On the death of a registered owner, title will be transferred by way of a transmission application to the estate trustee(s) with or without a will, to the beneficiary(ies) under the will, or to the heir(s) at law. Land held in joint tenancy will be transferred to the surviving joint tenant(s) by way of survivorship application. Supporting evidence in transmission applications includes proof of death, a notarial copy of the certificate of appointment of estate trustee, the spousal election under the *Family Law Act*, R.S.O. 1990, c. F.3 and information relating to the administration of the estate. Transmission applications and survivorship applications are registered by Document General. Estate conveyancing is one of the more complex areas of conveyancing and is dealt with in more detail in Chapter 5. The Ministry's *Electronic Procedures Reference Guide* has an extensive section on estate conveyancing that includes background information and numerous precedents.

Cautions

Land Titles provides a protection, called a caution, for claims against land by a person other than the registered owner. Under the *Registry Act*, R.S.O. 1990, c. R.20, anyone may register a claim or agreement against property. Under the *Land Titles Act*, a person who claims to have an interest in land or in a charge of which he or she is not the registered owner may register a caution to protect that interest.

A caution is available to protect interests such as: a purchaser's interest in an agreement of purchase and sale; outstanding taxes; estate trustee's caution to prevent vesting; caution under the *Bankruptcy and Insolvency Act*, R.S.C. 1985, c. B-3; an optionee's interest under an option to purchase when the optionee has exercised the option; a beneficiary's request to transfer an interest in land under a trust agreement; an option to purchase; a claim by an execution creditor that the property has been conveyed with the intention to defeat creditors; a claim by a registered owner of property that power of sale proceedings are improper because he or she has redeemed the charge; and any interest that may be protected by way of a caution pursuant to any Act of Ontario or Canada, such as cautions under the *Provincial Land Tax Act*, the *Local Roads Boards Act*, R.S.O. 1990, c. L.27, and the *Estates Administration Act*, R.S.O. 1990, c. E.22. The Registrar may also register a caution. An application to register a caution accompanied by an affidavit or statements in support setting out the proprietary interest is registered by Document General or as a caution in electronic registration. Depending on the interest claimed under the caution, the registered owner of the land or charge may or may not be allowed to deal with the land or charge without the registered consent of the cautioner. As of June 18, 1999, cautions based on proprietary interests in land, being rights to receive or charge land, prohibit the registered owner from dealing with the land (*Land Titles Act*, s. 128). For cautions that prevent dealings, a "no dealings" indicator is displayed on the parcel register; the registered owner of the land or charge cannot deal with the land or charge without the consent of the cautioner.

The following cautions do not prohibit the registered owner from dealing with the land (*Land Titles Act*, s. 71). Cautions based on: agreements of purchase and sale; claims by execution creditors that the property has been conveyed with the intention to defeat creditors; claims by registered owners of property that power of sale proceedings are improper because they have redeemed the charge; the authority of a judgment or court order; the power of sale contained in a charge that is prior to the interest under which the cautioner claims and the cautioner has been served with a notice of power of sale; circumstances which do not detrimentally affect the interest of the cautioner; when the person registers subject to continuance of the caution; when a registered interest was acquired prior to the registration of the caution; and, in the case of statutory liens, construction liens, and tax arrears certificates.

Cautions registered prior to June 18, 1999 prohibited the registered owner from dealing with his or her land without the permission of the cautioner or having the caution withdrawn. Cautions registered prior to June 18, 1999 can be withdrawn by the cautioner, or removed on the caution's stated expiry date, or five years from June 18, 1999. Depending on the circumstances, a caution could be removed without an application or on application to the registrar following 60 days' notice to the person claiming an interest under the caution.

On June 18, 1999, the *Red Tape Reduction Act, 2000*, S.O. 2000, c. 26 changed the rules for the registration of cautions. Special rules apply for cautions that protect a purchaser's rights under an agreement of purchase and sale (*Land Titles Act*, s. 71). A caution based on an agreement of purchase and sale does not prohibit the registered owner from dealing with the land and must contain the closing date and a statement authorizing the registrar to delete the caution 60 days after the scheduled closing date. This type of caution cannot be renewed, although another caution may be registered if the agreement of purchase and sale has been extended.

Director's Fraud Caution

The Director of Titles may enter a caution on title, if the Director suspects that a title or mortgage fraud has taken place. This caution prevents dealings pending an investigation and a claim to the Land Titles Assurance Fund (*Land Titles Act*, s. 57(15) and (16)). The Director may by Order depending on the outcome of the investigation and hearing rectify the title by deleting the fraudulent registration(s) and remove the caution.

APPLICATION FOR FIRST REGISTRATION IN LAND TITLES

Owners may transfer land from Registry to Land Titles through a process called application for first registration. Since the 1960s, assuming a Land Titles office is available in the registration division, all new subdivision and condominium developments are required to be transferred into Land Titles prior to plan registration. Most of the land in the North was entered in Land Titles when it was originally conveyed by Crown patent. Most of the remaining Registry land underwent an administrative transfer to Land Titles as part of POLARIS and became LTCQ titles. LTCQ titles can be upgraded by an application to a Land Title Absolute Plus (LT PLUS) title and is required to be upgraded prior to the registration of a new subdivision or condominium plan registration.

The *Land Titles Act* regulations contain detailed forms and procedures for applications for first registration in Land Titles. The application procedure requires an application, an affidavit of the applicant, a solicitor's certificate, a surveyor's certificate, a solicitor's abstract for the subject lands, a solicitor's abstract with respect to adjoining lands, three working copies of a draft reference plan, a draft parcel register, a draft certificate of first registration, a sheriff's certificate, a notice of application to adjoining landowners, copies of all deeds of applicant, copies of all affected plans, a copy of the Crown grant, and other related material. The solicitor's abstract for the subject lands and adjoining lands is different from a conventional commercial search. Detailed rules for this type of search are set out in R.R.O. 1990, Reg. 690 and must be followed precisely.

As Teranet continues its mass conversion of all Registry land to Land Titles, applications for first registration, once important, will become a thing of the past.

EFFECT OF FIRST REGISTRATION IN LAND TITLES

The registered owner of land in Land Titles may be registered as the owner of an absolute title, a leasehold title, a qualified title, or a possessory title. There are different kinds of qualified titles, for example, LTCQ, LT PLUS, or a qualification that is specific to a particular property. "No person, other than the registered owner, is entitled to transfer or charge registered freehold or leasehold land by a registered disposition" (*Land Titles Act*, s. 68(1)).

Section 78(5) of the *Land Titles Act* states that the order in which documents are entered in a parcel register, and not the order in which they were created, determines the priority of a registered right or interest in land. Ownership interests in land must be entered on the parcel register in order to affect title, subject to listed exceptions in s. 44.

In Land Titles, registered title overrides express, implied, or constructive notice of unregistered ownership rights and interests. Some case law exists that recognizes that actual notice of an unregistered interest is an exception to the rule that a subsequent purchaser or mortgagee takes title subject only to registered interests. For example, in *Gawalko v. Sullivan*, [1990] O.J. No. 658, 68 D.L.R. (4th) 765 (Ont. C.A.), the Ontario Court of Appeal held that a purchaser bought land subject to an unregistered easement agreement in the form of an obvious travelled road.

Special rules, including recent amendments to the Act, apply to fraudulent transactions and will be dealt with later in the chapter. Chapter 17 addresses the law governing title and mortgage fraud.

ABSOLUTE TITLE

An absolute title represents a fee simple estate in land. It is the highest form of ownership available within the legislative jurisdiction of Ontario. An absolute title is subject to encumbrances entered on the register and overriding interests set out in s. 44 of the *Land Titles Act*. Absolute title may be held in sole or concurrent ownership such as tenancy in common, including part or percentage shares, or joint tenancy. Absolute title may be held by corporations, partnerships or any other legal entity.

LEASEHOLD TITLE

Leasehold title may be registered separately from the freehold title and entered into a new leasehold parcel register. Long-term leases, the "term" of which is not less than 21 years, and leases for a life or lives, or determinable on a life or lives, qualify for a separate leasehold register. The term of a lease is calculated by adding the unexpired portion of the lease's term, called the reversion, to any options or rights of renewals included in the lease agreement. A leasehold title receives a title guarantee backed by the assurance fund.

POSSESSORY TITLE

An applicant for first registration may transfer a good possessory title — being ten years of open, uninterrupted possession — from Registry to Land Titles. The applicant may be registered as either the owner in fee simple with an absolute title or the owner of a possessory title, which may be upgraded to an absolute or qualified title after ten years. Anyone who goes to the time and expense of processing an application for first registration invariably chooses to be registered as the owner of an absolute title. As a result, possessory title is extremely rare in Land Titles.

QUALIFIED TITLE

A qualified title has the same effect as an absolute title except for any qualifier or limitation entered on the parcel register. The qualifier may be specific to a particular parcel or standard to a class of titles, for example, properties transferred from Registry to Land Titles under the POLARIS conversion are entered as a special qualified title called a "conversion qualified title". Conversion qualified titles are subject to a different set of title qualifiers. Conversion qualified titles and related searching procedures are covered in detail in Chapter 8. Qualified title may, on application, be upgraded to an absolute title.

Land Titles Conversion Qualified Title

An LTCQ is a qualified title. Section 44(1)11 provides that an LTCQ is not subject to some of the standard s. 44 Land Titles qualifiers that apply to a Land Title Absolute Plus title. An LTCQ is not subject to dower rights or provincial succession duties. It is not subject to corporate escheats and forfeitures to the Crown that took place prior to the date of conversion. An LTCQ is not subject to a *Planning Act* violation that took place prior to the date of conversion. On the other hand, an LTCQ is subject to additional qualifiers brought forward in the administrative conversion from Registry. An LTCQ is subject to residual Registry rights such as rights through adverse possession, prescription, misdescription or boundaries settled by convention, and unregistered leases with terms up to seven years that are in possession (*Registry Act*, s. 70(2)). The new qualifiers are listed near the top of the LTCQ parcel register. Different qualifiers result in a different title search, particularly in terms of descriptions and *Planning Act* compliance checks.

APPLICATION TO UPGRADE LAND TITLES CONVERSION QUALIFIED TITLE (LTCQ) TO LAND TITLES ABSOLUTE PLUS TITLE (LT PLUS)

LTCQ titles are subject to legal description uncertainty and also possessory claims that have matured by the time of administrative conversion to Land Titles. Description uncertainty and mature possessory rights are special title qualifiers on an LTCQ that present an exception to the general Land Titles policy that bars possessory rights. As a result, registered owners of LTCQs now have the option under s. 46 to make an application to upgrade a Land Titles Conversion Qualified Title (LTCQ) to a Land Titles Absolute Plus Title (LT PLUS). Registered owners may choose to upgrade an LTCQ in order to resolve adverse possessory claims and description disputes, to settle any "subject to" title problems brought forward in the conversion, and to remove the description and possessory rights qualifier as a condition for obtaining consent for a new subdivision or condominium plan. In addition, a person who is not the registered owner and who is in possession of LTCQ land may apply to claim and perfect an ownership right based on a pre-existing period of possession under s. 36 of the Act. A claim for possessory rights requires declarations of possessions that cover 20 years when requesting an absolute title, or ten years if requesting only a possessory title. An online guide for this application process is available under Land Registration Information through Service Ontario for residents at: <http://www. ontario.ca/en/information_bundle/land_registration/guides/index.htm>.

The application process requires a survey, a draft reference plan, a solicitor's search and review of title with special emphasis on *Planning Act* compliance and easements, a solicitor's declaration of title, the application, a notice list and service of notice of the application and draft reference plan on all affected persons, including government authorities such as Ontario Hydro Networks or the Trent-Severn Canal Waterway System, objections by affected persons, government authorities, utilities, and the government authority over access roads, a hearing when indicated, a resolution, a draft amended LT PLUS parcel register, and an indemnity for the Land Titles Assurance Fund if it is a possessory claim. The notice of application includes a copy of the property index map, the parcel register, draft proposed Land Titles Absolute Plus parcel register, copies of all relevant registered plans and documents, the notice list, copies of objections and/or consents and waivers from potential objectors, and an indemnity covenant for possessory claims in favour of the Land Titles Assurance Fund. The solicitor's declaration of title and the solicitor's certificate contain the solicitor's opinion based on the review of title that there are no *Planning Act* contraventions and no escheats and forfeitures.

The application removes the uncertainty of the LTCQ description qualifier and applies the superior LTCQ-type qualifiers to the new LT PLUS title up to the date of registration with an absolute title. Dower, succession duties, escheats claims, and usually *Planning Act* contraventions (see below) are cancelled up to the date of registration with an absolute title. In addition, in more recent applications to upgrade to LT PLUS (since August 2001), *Planning Act* violations and escheats prior to the date of registration of the new Land Titles Absolute Plus title are cancelled. It is essential to check the specific qualifier in each Land Titles Plus parcel register. A Land Titles Absolute Plus title is superior to both the traditional Land Titles Absolute title and to the Land Titles Conversion Qualified title. It is the best of all the titles.

Land Titles Absolute Plus Title

An LTCQ can be upgraded to an LT PLUS; this results in the removal of the Registry-like description qualifier, the retention of the new LTCQ qualifiers, and, for upgrades after August 2001, the addition of new Land Titles Plus qualifiers. A Land Titles Absolute Plus is mixture of absolute and qualified title characteristics. An LT PLUS title is subject to the same title qualifiers as an absolute title except it is clear of all possible historical dower and succession duties claims. It is also clear of any corporate escheats and sometimes *Planning Act* contraventions up to the date of registration with an absolute title. An LT PLUS will be subject to potential corporate escheats and *Planning Act* contraventions from the date of registration with an absolute title to present.

Special rules apply for *Planning Act* contraventions and LT PLUS parcels. The LT PLUS parcel is clear of any *Planning Act* contraventions prior to the date of conversion for the parent LTCQ parcel. For parcels created since August 2001, it often has a special qualifier added to the face of the LT PLUS parcel register that clears it from any *Planning Act* violation prior to the date of creation of the new LT PLUS parcel. Careful review of the LT PLUS parcel will show whether a *Planning Act* qualifier was added to cover the time between conversion to Land Titles and the creation of the LT PLUS parcel. On an LT PLUS parcel, it is necessary to check for *Planning Act* contraventions from, either the date of conversion to the original LTCQ parcel, or the date of creation to the LT PLUS when there is a new *Planning Act* qualifier added to the register, up to present. Since August 2001, most new LT PLUS parcels have a special qualifier that clears potential *Planning Act* contraventions prior to the date of registration of the LT PLUS parcel. Current applications require evidence that there are no *Planning Act* contraventions between the LTCQ conversion date and the registration of the new LT PLUS parcel. As a result, most searches of LT PLUS parcels will only require a *Planning Act* compliance search from the date of registration of the new parcel.

When an LT PLUS parcel register contains the following wording, the lawyer can start *Planning Act* compliance searches as of the date of registration with a Land Titles Absolute Plus title:

> Subject to subsection 44(1) of the *Land Titles Act*, except paragraphs 3 and 14 and Provincial Succession Duties and except paragraph 11 and Escheats or Forfeiture to the Crown up to the date of registration with an absolute title.

OVERRIDING INTERESTS/TITLE QUALIFIERS

The design of a Land Titles system is to certify titles, guarantee that the title register mirrors all current interests that pertain to a parcel of land, and thus greatly simplify the conveyancing of land. Unfortunately, s. 44 of the *Land Titles Act* creates a large number of serious exceptions/qualifiers to the Land Titles guarantee. Although these title qualifiers affect and can cancel ownership, they are not registered on the register page. Different categories of title as mentioned above, such as LT Absolute, LTCQ, LT Qualified, and LT PLUS, are subject to different exceptions and qualifiers (see Chapter 8 for details).

Each parcel register contains the warning that "title of the said owner is subject to the exceptions and qualifications in the *Land Titles Act*". These exceptions, often referred to as overriding interests or qualifiers, must be investigated in addition to completing a search of all interests entered on the parcel register. Land Titles qualifiers generate the need for a multitude of potential off-title searches and inquiries. Lawyers consider the nature of the property and the availability of title insurance coverage as an alternative and then consult with clients about the nature of the risk and which off-title searches to complete. Aboriginal claims and environmental restrictions and liabilities are examples of overriding interests. Chapter 14 deals with off-title searches and inquiries in depth.

In Land Titles, there may be additional equitable remedies and rights, and doctrines such as actual notice that may affect registered ownership. For an illustration of equitable remedies in a Land Titles registration context, see *Save the Heritage Simpson Covenant Society v. Kelowna (City)*, [2008] B.C.J. No. 1534 (B.C.S.C.). In the *Heritage Simpson Covenant* case, the British Columbia Supreme Court enforced a restriction that land donated be used in perpetuity only for municipal purposes as a term of a charitable trust created by the covenants, despite the fact that the conditions were not enforceable restrictive covenants as there was no reference to the dominant lands in the registered Simpson Covenants. For a review of the impact of actual notice on title in the Land Titles system, refer to *United Trust Co. v. Dominion Stores Ltd.*, [1976] S.C.J. No. 99 (S.C.C.).

The following are the statutory listed exceptions/qualifiers to the Land Titles guarantee (*Land Titles Act*, s. 44(1)-(6)):

Liability of registered land to easements and certain other rights

44. (1) All registered land, unless the contrary is expressed on the register, is subject to such of the following liabilities, rights and interests as for the time being may be subsisting in reference thereto, and such liabilities, rights and interests shall not be deemed to be encumbrances within the meaning of this Act:

1. Provincial taxes and succession duties and municipal taxes, charges, rates or assessments, and school or water rates. [Succession duties were repealed and only relate to deaths and incomplete estate administrations between January 1, 1970 and April 10. 1979. Municipal taxes can contain various charges, including local improvements, water charges, development charges, *etc.*]
2. Any right of way, watercourse, and right of water, and other easements. [Consider flooding or drainage rights and access to wells and water agreements, rights related to mining and hydro generation, and portages. Crown patents and related rights to navigable waters should also be investigated. References to shorelines and water are frequently found in old documents and plans that pre-date the current parcel register. This section does not permit the acquisition of easements by prescription on an absolute title (*Land Titles Act*, s. 51).]
3. Any title or lien that, by possession or improvements, the owner or person interested in any adjoining land has acquired to or in respect of the land. [The Ontario Court of Appeal in *Gatz v. Kiziw*, [1957] O.J. No.

195 (Ont. C.A.) decided that this section did not create adverse possession rights in Land Titles. When land is transferred into Land Titles,
notice to adjoining owners bars future possessory claims based on possession prior first registration in Land Titles (s. 44(1)3). Mortgagees
and tenants may acquire some rights or lien for improvements under
this section.]

4.   Any lease or agreement for a lease, for a period yet to run that does not
     exceed three years, where there is actual occupation under it. [Purchasers
     and mortgagees would need declaration evidence and off-title inquiries
     to track unregistered leases.]

5.   Any right under Part II of the *Family Law Act*, of the spouse of the per-
     son registered as owner. [Spousal rights in a matrimonial home are
     protected under the *Family Law Act*. Subsequent purchasers and mort-
     gagees take subject to spousal rights unless the transaction was exempt
     or contained a spousal release. Most conveyances require spousal
     statements or consents to exempt or release spousal rights. Spousal
     rights may also be protected by registrations such as a notice of desig-
     nation of a matrimonial home. When a property is transferred without
     the required statements or consents, it will be marked by the Registrar
     as being "subject to spousal rights".]

6.   A construction lien where the time limited for its registration has not ex-
     pired. [A construction lien claimant has 45 days to register the lien af-
     ter completion or substantial completion. Purchasers can make off-title
     inquiries of the seller and require declarations and warranties.]

7.   Any right of expropriation, access or user, or any other right, conferred
     upon or reserved or vested in the Crown by or under the authority of
     any statute of Canada or Ontario. [For example, Crown patent reserva-
     tions, escheats under s. 244(3) of the *Business Corporations Act*,
     R.S.O. 1990, c. B.16, mining rights, rights under the *Public Lands Act*,
     R.S.O. 1990, c. P.43, and a multitude of rights and restrictions that are
     examined in more detail in Chapter 14. This section creates an open-
     ended exception for all levels of government activity and requires re-
     view and consultation with the client, and consideration of available ti-
     tle insurance coverage. Lawyers in consultation with clients decide
     when to complete off-title inquiries that might reveal Crown rights and
     restrictions on a particular property. For example, property that abuts
     on water is subject to multi-layered restrictions that require additional
     off-title searches, be it for dock and boathouse restrictions and work
     orders, or for environmentally sensitive zone designation that restricts
     shoreline use. Aboriginal rights are linked to the Crown rights and re-
     sponsibilities and can result in unregistered claims that affect title.]

8.   Any public highway. [The extent of a highway may not be registered
     on title. Only a survey can adequately assess the risk of the highway
     exception.]

9.   Any liabilities, rights and interests created under section 38 of the *Pub-
     lic Transportation and Highway Improvement Act*. [Restrictions regu-
     lating access to highways and signage and construction adjacent to
     highway and related permits are not registered on title. Off-title
     searches are necessary.]

10. Any by-law heretofore passed under section 34 of the *Planning Act*, or
     a predecessor of that section, and any other municipal by-law hereto-
     fore or hereafter passed, affecting land that does not directly affect the

title to land. [For example, municipal zoning by-laws that range from use and building standards and parking and garage safety and anti-mugging by-laws to tree preservation and light pollution.]

11. Sections 50 and 50.1 of the *Planning Act*. [The subdivision and part lot control provisions. Non-compliance extinguishes title; see Chapter 11.]

12. Where the registered owner is or a previous registered owner was a railway company, any interest that may be or may have been created by any instrument deposited in the office of the Secretary of State of Canada or the Registrar General of Canada, as the case may be, under section 104 of the *Canada Transportation Act* (Canada), or any predecessor of it, but, where the previous registered owner was a railway company, this paragraph does not apply to a subsequent registered owner, except a railway company, unless a note of the previous ownership of the land by the railway company has been entered in the title register. [This is a difficult exception to deal with as railway rights may date back to Crown patents and railway rights of way are not necessarily visible on the ground in terms of extent; they may not have been developed. Descriptions and railway surveys may be difficult and/or vague; a current survey is indicated when dealing with this qualifier.]

13. [Repealed: S.O. 1997, c. 24, s. 214, effective June 17, 1998 (O. Gaz. 1998, p. 1006)]

14. Any right of the wife of the person registered as owner to dower in case of surviving the owner. [The *Family Law Reform Act* abolished a widow's dower right which had not vested on her husband's death as of March 31, 1978. Vested dower rights are extinguished ten years after a widow ceases to occupy land subject to the dower rights. The risk, 30 years later, is remote.]

Effect of registration of land upon timber licences

(2) Where a licence under Part III of the *Crown Forest Sustainability Act, 1994* has been or is granted and the land is registered under this Act, the land shall be deemed to have been and to be subject to the rights of the licensee or the assigns of the licensee for the current licence year under the licence, and to the rights of Her Majesty in the pine trees under the *Public Lands Act*, without the fact of the land being so subject being expressed in the entry in the register.

Where owner of adjoining land has no right

(3) A parcel of land registered under this Act is not subject to paragraph 3 of subsection (1) if a notice of the application for first registration that contained an accurate description of the parcel, or of a former larger parcel of which the parcel is a part, was served upon the person who at the time of giving the notice was the owner, mortgagee, chargee or purchaser, or assignee thereof, under a registered instrument of adjoining land and no objection to the first registration was filed with the land registrar within the time allowed by the notice.

Application under s. 30 deemed action for recovery of land

(4) An application under section 30 shall be deemed to be an action for the recovery of land within the meaning of the *Real Property Limitations Act*.

Application of subs. (1), par. 6

(5) Paragraph 6 of subsection (1) does not confer upon a person claiming a construction lien any greater right than the person would have if the land were registered under the *Registry Act*.

Writs of execution

(6) The title of the registered owner for the time being of land is subject to enforceable writs of execution against the owner that have been recorded under section 136, but no writ of execution against a prior registered owner is enforceable in respect of the land unless a note of such writ has been entered in the title register.

THE EFFECT OF FRAUD ON REGISTRATION

Bill 152, known as the *Consumer Protection and Services Modernization Act, 2006*, and the Ministry's Real Estate Fraud Action Plan are a response to an increase in title and mortgage fraud, high-profile title fraud cases, and consumer confidence concerns. This Bill amends the fraud and Land Titles Assurance Fund sections in the *Land Titles Act*, particularly ss. 78(4.1), (4.2), and 57(13).

Section 78 was enacted to incorporate the common law doctrine of deferred indefeasibility as set out in the *Lawrence v. Wright*, [2007] O.J. No. 381 (Ont. C.A.) case into the *Land Titles Act*. The *Lawrence* case resolved a series of earlier, at times conflicting, cases. Section 78 states that fraudulent documents do not affect title and can be removed from title by rectification of the register (*Land Titles Act*, s. 57(13)). The true registered owner(s) will not lose his or her title, in a practical sense his or her home, as a result of a fraudulent document registered on or after October 19, 2006. The doctrine of deferred indefeasibility has a similar result on fraudulent documents registered prior to October 19, 2006. The act of registration does not validate an instrument that, if unregistered, would be fraudulent and void (*Land Titles Act*, s. 78(4.1)). However, an instrument that is not fraudulent that is registered subsequent to a fraudulent document is valid and good as against the world (*Land Titles Act*, s. 78(4.2)). As a result, a subsequent or deferred owner, in good faith, and without notice of the fraud, may acquire an interest in the property that is good against the world. Current case law indicates that uncertainty continues to exist in the appreciation of the *Land Titles Act* amendments and the doctrine of deferred indefeasibility. For a more detailed examination of the effect of fraud in Land Titles and recent cases, refer to Chapter 17 on title and mortgage fraud. The section 78 subsections set out below appear to codify the common law doctrine of deferred indefeasibility:

Effect of registration

(4) When registered, an instrument shall be deemed to be embodied in the register and to be effective according to its nature and intent, and to create, transfer,

charge or discharge, as the case requires, the land or estate or interest therein mentioned in the register.

Exception

(4.1) Subsection (4) does not apply to a fraudulent instrument that is registered on or after October 19, 2006.

Non-fraudulent instruments

(4.2) Nothing in subsection (4.1) invalidates the effect of a registered instrument that is not a fraudulent instrument described in that subsection, including instruments registered subsequent to such a fraudulent instrument.

PROCEDURE SUBSEQUENT TO FIRST REGISTRATION IN LAND TITLES

The registrar may enter land directly into the Land Titles system on receipt of a Crown patent under s. 37 of the *Public Lands Act*, R.S.O. 1990, c. P.43 (*Land Titles Act*, s. 33(1)). Where land is transferred from the Registry system to the Land Titles system, the owner of the land must make an application for first registration. If the Land Titles office is already automated, the land on first registration undergoes a similar process and will be issued a PIN and entered into the POLARIS record, and subsequent registrations will be online in ELRS. Once land has been accepted into Land Titles, the following procedures are initiated:

1. Where land is on a lot on a concession, a register is allotted for the particular municipality until further dealings with the land commence.

2. A parcel and section number is designated and recorded at the top of the page. The application number, the registered owner(s), the land description, and particulars of encumbrances, *etc.*, that the land is subject to, follow in that order. However, the Registry reference (*e.g.*, Plan 345, City of London) for land subdivided prior to first application is incorporated in the Land Titles reference.

3. The register is signed by the land registrar or a deputy certifying that, *e.g.*, John Edward Smith is the owner with an absolute title, subject to the encumbrances.

4. A plan of subdivision is usually registered immediately after the registration of the owner's application and, in that event, what is referred to as a "parcel plan" is set up and designated Parcel Plan 1. The section is allotted the registration number of the plan, *e.g.*, M-678. An inhibiting order, whereby the owner is obligated to comply with certain responsibilities, is registered by the municipality and is a part of the plan document. Reference to prior parcels and sections and to corporate owners is made in the margin.

5.   When all the lots, blocks and reserves are sold and transferred to new parcels, the parcel plan is closed. Several lots are often transferred to one person, usually a builder. They are re-entered in Parcel Plan 2, Section M-678. Individual lots as sold are re-entered in separate parcels; *e.g.*, Lot 24 would be designated as Parcel 24-1. When parts of that lot are sold, *e.g.*, the west half, a reference plan is deposited on title showing the part to be transferred and it is re-entered as Parcel 24-2.

6.   Between the date of registration and the entry of a document on the register a few days may elapse. Therefore, a temporary note of the registration number only is made in pencil on the register in most offices; in others it is recorded on a day sheet. The document is available for inspection in the meantime. Even after it is recorded in full in the register, a document is not considered registered until an authorized signing officer (A.S.O.) signs the entry.

7.   A note is made in the margin, opposite the transfer, *e.g.*, "Lots 90-100 transferred". Thus, one can tell at a glance what lots have been transferred and severed from the original parcel.

8.   The new parcel is set out in the register, on the next page, *e.g.*, the parcel, Parcel 90-100-1, and section, Section M-678, recorded at the top of the page.

9.   The prior parcel number is recorded at the top left corner of the page, *e.g.*, originally Parcel E-l, Section London. This is only for identification of prior parcels.

10. The new parcel is identical to the original parcel in that the owner, encumbrances and description are recorded on the new parcel register.

11. The names of the prior owners are ruled off Parcel Plan 1 when all the lots are severed, except where the transfer is subject to an easement, conditions, *etc*.

12. Where cessations of charges, compliance with agreements and inhibiting orders, releases of cautions and discharges of construction liens and their certificates of action are registered, the registration number, date, and signing officer's signature are noted in the margin opposite the entry for the registration. The particulars, parties, *etc.*, are not recorded in a separate entry as in the case of other registrations. Such a registration is then ruled off and of no further interest.

13. Where a caution is superseded by a transfer, that notation is made in the margin with the registration number of the transfer, date and the signing officer's signature.

14. The new parcel is issued a PIN and an automated parcel register.

RECORD BOOKS IN LAND TITLES

Land Titles offices are required to maintain the following record books. In the past, R.R.O. 1990, Reg. 690 set out the required record books and the procedures for keeping them. Under s. 163.1(1) of the *Land Titles Act*, the Minister of Government Services may make Minister's orders as opposed to regulations related to the following:

6. specifying the manner in which the abstract index is to be created and maintained;

7. specifying other indexes and records and the manner in which they are to be maintained;

8. specifying the manner in which instruments are to be entered for the purpose of subsection 141(7); ...

10. specifying the form and manner in which entries in the records of land registry offices are to be made; ...

11. specifying the manner in which instruments and entries in the register are to be certified at registration;

12. governing the mode in which the register is to be made and kept;

13. governing the mode in which any special register is to be made and kept;

14. specifying methods and standards for computer entry, storage and retrieval of information;

15. governing the custody, disposition and destruction of instruments and records of land registry offices;

16. specifying the manner in which instruments, books, public records and facsimiles of them are to be produced for inspection;

17. specifying the manner in which copies of instruments, books and public records are to be produced and certified;

18. requiring that printed copies of the parcel register relating to land in the parts of Ontario designated under Part II of the *Land Registration Reform Act* be produced at specified times and specifying the times at which they are to be produced; [and]

22. requiring land registrars to assign to persons who ask to search the records of the land registry office account numbers and other identification to enable them to do so.

Parcel Register (Freehold Title)

The parcel register is the main title register in Land Titles. This register records all transactions that affect the title of an individual parcel. The parcel register relates to freehold, such as absolute or fee simple ownership, as opposed to leasehold ownership. It records LT Absolute, LTCQ, and LT PLUS titles. The parcel register in Land Titles corresponds to the abstract index in Registry.

As each new registration is certified by the land registrar, former registrations are cancelled (ruled out), added to or modified. Documents that are no longer active are shown as deleted ("D") on the electronic register. As a result of continuous updating, the parcel register mirrors current registered title. Even instruments in the process of registration are shown as temporary pencilled-in entries or uncertified instruments in ELRS.

Each distinct property, which is owned by an owner or a group of owners, comprises a parcel. A parcel is identified by a parcel and section number and each parcel is allocated a separate page in the parcel register. The legal description for the freehold land in each parcel is entered at the top of the first page of the parcel register, *e.g.*, all of Lots 2 and 3 and part of Block A on Plan M-340 (City of Brampton) registered in the Land Titles Office for the Land Titles Division of Peel (No. 43) at Brampton, designated as Parts 1, 2, and 3 on a plan of survey of record in the said office as Plan 43R-8278, subject to a right of way in favour of the Corporation of the City of Brampton to enter upon that part of the said Block A on Plan M-340, designated as PART 2 on the said Plan 43R-8278.

When an existing parcel is subdivided, a new parcel is created and numbered and a new parcel register is opened. The new parcel register will refer to any previous as well as the original parcel registers. Similarly, the previous parcel will include a cross-reference to the new parcel. In the automated system, each parcel is identified by a PIN and each PIN accesses the parcel register printout.

Leasehold Parcel Register

The owner of a leasehold title may apply to have a leasehold title designated as a leasehold parcel, separate from the underlying freehold parcel, under s. 38 of the *Land Titles Act*. The leasehold parcel is then entered into a separate leasehold register. For example, registration entries for a freehold parcel of land on which a developer proposes to construct a large office building are transferred to a leasehold register, when the owner of the land provides the developer with a long-term ground lease. Similarly, the Ontario Housing Corporation, Local

Housing Corporations, the Ontario Land Corporation, or the Crown under the *Mining Act*, R.S.O. 1990, c. M.14, or the *Public Lands Act* often hold leasehold estates. Any subsequent registrations affecting the leasehold title, *e.g.*, assignments or mortgages of lease, will be registered on the leasehold parcel.

Leasehold parcels are set up in the same manner as freehold parcels, except that leasehold is noted on the register at the top of each page. An entry is made on the freehold parcel, *e.g.*, "Entered in leasehold parcel 112-1, Section M-893 under Lease #A-3468." The original parcel and recent parcel number, *e.g.*, the freehold parcel that the leasehold parcel came from, are noted in the upper left corner.

As new leasehold parcels can be opened, so too can leasehold parcels merge into the original freehold parcel. Where the owner of the leasehold parcel (the lessee) acquires the freehold estate, the leasehold estate merges into the freehold and becomes subject to any interest to which the leasehold estate was subject prior to the merging and in the same ranking as to priorities. Note the abstracting procedure that follows:

1. A new parcel is opened to combine the freehold and leasehold estates. Prior encumbrances affecting both estates are entered in order of registration followed by the Transfer.

2. The Transfer is entered on the previous freehold parcel with a notation, "together with the leasehold estate in the said land lease number __ having merged under the said Transfer".

3. The prior leasehold parcel is closed out with a notation, "re-entry, the above parcel and lease having merged under Transfer number __ and entered as parcel __ ".

Mineral Lands Parcel Register

The land in Northern Ontario is usually registered under the *Land Titles Act*. Frequently, the surface rights of such lands are severed from the mining rights and all ores, mines, and minerals on or under the lands are conveyed with the mining rights land. When only surface rights are transferred, a new parcel is opened in the Land Titles office. The mining rights remain vested in the owner and a notation is made on the original parcel to indicate that it now contains mining rights only.

There are likely to be numerous easements for mining rights registered on the surface rights land register, since right of access for mining is reserved to the vested owner. The agreement of purchase and sale should make reference to exactly what rights are to be sold. Consent to sever such rights pursuant to the

Planning Act is not required because lands that abut only on a horizontal plane are exempt (*Planning Act*, s. 50(2)).

Highways Register

Every Land Titles office is required to keep a highways register for recording plans deposited, filed, or registered by the Minister of Transportation under the *Public Transportation and Highway Improvement Act*, R.S.O. 1990, c. P.50. The registration number allocated to such plans is prefixed by "MISC.", for miscellaneous, *e.g.*, MISC. 345. Note that the land registrar enters documents registered for highway lands on that register only; they are not repeated in the freehold register. The purchaser is deemed to have notice of highway register documents. It is important to search both.

TransCanada Pipeline Register

A TransCanada Pipeline register is kept in every Registry office through which a pipeline constructed or owned by TransCanada Pipelines Limited passes. "MISC." prefixes the plan number allocated. Note again that the land registrar makes TransCanada Pipeline entries on this register only, even though the documents may affect freehold land. The purchaser is deemed to have notice; therefore, both registers must be examined.

Fee and Receiving Book

The fee and receiving book contains an entry for every document received for registration. When a document has been certified and signed by the registrar or other signing officer and has been entered into the proper Land Titles register, such as the parcel register, a notation of the completed entry is entered opposite the entry of the document in the fee and receiving book.

When registration of a document has been delayed due to some deficiency, a re-entry is made in the suspense book described below. On registration of all the documents on a page, or re-entry in the suspense book, and where preceding pages have been ruled out, the land registrar rules the page with a diagonal line to indicate that the documents entered thereon, and on preceding pages, have been registered, rejected, or entered into the suspense book.

Suspense Book

A suspense book is kept for all documents for which registration has been delayed. When the documents have been registered or rejected, the pages are finalized in the same manner as in the fee and receiving book.

Powers of Attorney Register

A power of attorney (POA) or a certified copy may be registered in a powers of attorney register. The automated system, ELRS, has a separate electronic index for powers of attorney. This index is searchable. All electronic documents must state if they are registered under a POA. All powers of attorney and revocations of powers of attorney that relate to land must be registered in the ELRS system. Documents executed by POA pose a higher risk of fraud. All powers of attorney relating to title documents must be searched and carefully checked against the registered document. When relying on powers of attorney, it is prudent to confirm identity and capacity of both the grantor and the grantee of the power.

Register for Cautions

A register for cautions under s. 43(1) of the *Land Titles Act* is kept although cautions are registered on the relevant parcel register.

Executions Book

In the past, the land registrar kept a book for recording writs and renewals of executions received from the sheriff's office. Today, the sheriff maintains an electronic database (MAG) for all writs of execution and all renewals of writs of execution (*Land Titles Act*, s. 136(1)) and gives the land registrar of each Land Titles division wholly or partially within the sheriff's territorial jurisdiction access to the electronic database. Today, executions are searched online in Writsearch or OWL, available through Teraview and BAR-eX.

Condominium Register

The condominium register is discussed in detail in Chapter 7. The four separate condominium indexes in the paper system are now amalgamated into the electronic unit register. All condominium documents are entered on the unit registers.

Automated/Electronic Registers in POLARIS: ELRS

Most Land Titles registers have now been automated into POLARIS. Fortunately, the electronic parcel register consolidates information from the various paper registers, although powers of attorney are in a separate electronic index in ELRS. Land in Registry was first converted from Registry to Land Titles and then automated as part of the POLARIS Land Titles conversion — LTCQ. The searching of automated Land Titles parcel registers and LTCQ land that has undergone a conversion into POLARIS from Registry is dealt with in Chapter 8. New registrations are done in the ELRS.

REGULATION BY AND UNDER THE LAND TITLES ACT

Land Titles Act and Regulations	Subject Matter
Land Titles Act, R.S.O. 1990, c. L.5	
Land Titles Act, O. Reg. 26/99	General
Land Titles Act, O. Reg. 27/99	Forms
Land Titles Act, O. Reg. 428/99	Land Titles Divisions
Land Titles Act, R.R.O. 1990, Reg. 690	Forms, Records and Procedures
Land Titles Act, R.R.O. 1990, Reg. 693	Transfer of Functions

LEGISLATION AFFECTED BY THE LAND TITLES ACT

Regulations and Minister's Orders and Land Registrar's Bulletins under the *Land Titles Act* set detailed requirements for forms, descriptions, plans, registration requirements, records, indexes and fees. The *Land Titles Act* affects numerous Ontario statutes, including the following:

- the *Assignments and Preferences Act*, R.S.O. 1990, c. A.33;
- the *Boundaries Act*, R.S.O. 1990, c. B.10;
- the *Cemeteries Act (Revised)*, R.S.O. 1990, c. C.4;
- the *Certification of Titles Act*, R.S.O. 1990, c. C.6;
- the *Condominium Act, 1998*, S.O. 1998, c. 19;
- the *City of Toronto Act, 2006*, S.O. 2006, c. 11, Schedule A;
- the *Construction Lien Act*, R.S.O. 1990, c. C.30;
- the *Courts of Justice Act*, R.S.O. 1990, c. C.43;
- the *Electricity Act, 1998*, S.O. 1998, c. 15, Schedule A;
- the *Electronic Registration Act (Ministry of Consumer and Business Services Statutes), 1991*, S.O. 1991, c. 44;
- the *Environmental Protection Act*, R.S.O. 1990, c. E.19;
- the *Escheats Act*, R.S.O. 1990, c. E.20;
- the *Estates Administration Act*, R.S.O. 1990, c. E.22;
- the *Execution Act*, R.S.O. 1990, c. E.24;
- the *Family Law Act*, R.S.O. 1990, c. F.3;
- the *Forestry Act*, R.S.O. 1990, c. F.26;
- the *Land Registration Reform Act*, R.S.O. 1990, c. L.4;
- the *Land Transfer Tax Act*, R.S.O. 1990, c. L.6;
- the *Local Roads Boards Act*, R.S.O. 1990, c. L.27;
- the *Mining Act*, R.S.O. 1990, c. M.14;
- the *Mortgages Act*, R.S.O. 1990, c. M.40;
- the *Municipal Act, 2001*, S.O. 2001, c. 25;

- the *Personal Property Security Act*, R.S.O. 1990, c. P.10;
- the *Planning Act*, R.S.O. 1990, c. P.13;
- the *Provincial Land Tax Act, 2006*, S.O. 2006, c. 33, Schedule Z.2;
- the *Public Lands Act*, R.S.O. 1990, c. P.43;
- the *Registry Act*, R.S.O. 1990, c. R.20;
- the *Surveyors Act*, R.S.O. 1990, c. S.29; and
- the *Surveys Act*, R.S.O. 1990, c. S.30.

THE LAND TITLES TITLE SEARCH

Searching title under the Land Titles system is frequently believed to be relatively simple compared to the Registry system. It is not necessary to complete a 40-year search in Land Titles as prior defects in title are cleared when the land is transferred from the Registry system to the Land Titles system under the procedure of first registration. Only current ownership and outstanding encumbrances are reflected on the parcel register at that time of first registration. However, it is critical to understand the practical impact of the overriding interests and qualifiers and complete the appropriate off-title inquiries, potentially as far back as the Crown patent. In addition, it is essential to recognize the different types of title, know the different qualifiers for each type, and search accordingly. Title information is organized and presented differently in the paper system compared to the POLARIS record. The distinctions can be subtle; yet, they carry serious consequences. A Registry search was often longer, but not necessarily more difficult.

The distinguishing feature about searching in Land Titles is that the current parcel register certifies that the present registered owner holds an absolute title, a leasehold title, a qualified title including an LTCQ or LT PLUS, or a possessory title subject to outstanding charges, agreements, leases, easements, restrictions, by-laws, cautions, *etc.*, that are noted on the parcel register. Past registrations are cancelled and shown as ruled out or as deleted on the register. Particulars of the legal description, special title qualifiers, such as "subject to" executions and spousal rights, or estate interests, and part shares and legal capacity, such as joint tenants, partners, and estate trustees, are noted on the parcel register.

Each parcel is subject to the exceptions and qualifications listed in s. 44 of the *Land Titles Act*. These title qualifiers or exceptions, *e.g.*, *Planning Act* violations, Crown rights, and writs of execution, must be checked in addition to the outstanding instruments showing on the current parcel register. LTCQ and LT PLUS titles have different qualifiers than the traditional Land Titles Absolute title.

As in the Registry system, there is a fee for searching each parcel in the register. Plans and documents may be available by a form called a request for service or self-service, in paper or microfilm form, or online or by courier when searching in Teraview. Each office has its own rules and fee arrangements for examining and copying documents. Teranet and POLARIS have standard procedures throughout the Province. Forms for requisitioning parcels, plans, and documents, provided by the land registrar, should be completed in detail in order to save time at the counter. Documents are viewed, printed, or ordered online in Teraview. Registry offices are primarily self-serve and provide access to plan and document copiers, microfilm readers and copiers, and computer terminals for online title and execution searching. Almost all searching is done online using Teraview in the lawyer's office.

It is customary to order a copy of (or when searching online, to print) all relevant register pages. However, if you wish to study it and make notes from it, you may do so. The mechanics of searching online in POLARIS through Teraview are outlined in detail and illustrated with numerous screen captures in Chapter 8, which deals with electronic searching, and has an emphasis on searching LTCQ titles. The procedure in the traditional paper environment is as follows:

1. Obtain particulars or copies of all plans that affect the subject lands and outstanding documents, such as the current transfer, charges, encumbrances, easements, restrictive covenants, cautions, notices, agreements, and *Planning Act* consents and by-laws, shown on the current parcel or referred to on a prior parcel.

2. Check for the Land Titles signing officer's signature on the register after each document to confirm document certification. In the electronic parcel register, a "C" following the document entry indicates that the document has been certified. It is unnecessary to check signatures and requirements of form as Land Titles documents are certified as to legal effectiveness during the registration process.

3. Request a day sheet for current registrations from the counter staff if the office has not adopted the practice of pencilling them in on the register at the time of registration. In the electronic record, an uncertified document shows on the parcel register but is not followed by a "C". Subsearches can be done during the registration process and show all documents received in priority sequence. The automated system has reduced the risk of missing documents that have been submitted for registration but have not yet been certified.

4. Remember to check other relevant registers, such as the Highways and TransCanada Pipeline registers, as these entries are not made on freehold register; yet, you are deemed to have notice of any registration entered into them. Again, the electronic record has reduced this risk by integrating multiple paper registers onto a printable, consolidated, property parcel register indexed by PIN.

ADJOINING LANDS SEARCHES IN LAND TITLES

Section 44 of the *Land Titles Act* states that s. 50 of the *Planning Act* is an exception to the Land Titles guarantee. Absolute, leasehold and qualified titles must all be searched for *Planning Act* contraventions. The starting points for a *Planning Act* compliance search are different in LT Absolute, LTCQ, and LT PLUS properties. As in Registry, a *Planning Act* violation in Land Titles will result in a nullity no matter what the register page says. *Planning Act* contraventions that were missed during the adjoining lands search continue to result in negligence suits against real estate lawyers and title insurance claims, and litigation.

Fortunately, although not always the case, large portions of Land Titles land are within subdivision or condominium plans. Usually, parcels within a subdivision plan are comprised of whole lots. Hence, the whole lot or whole unit exemption may make the *Planning Act* search unnecessary, although a *Planning Act* by-law may be registered that revokes the whole lot exempt status for listed subdivision plans. It is therefore essential to determine what a parcel is made up of prior to deciding whether to complete a *Planning Act* search. A parcel that contains a part lot, which is not otherwise exempt, must be checked for *Planning Act* violations.

Unfortunately, prior to POLARIS, Land Titles parcels were not numbered sequentially and it can be very difficult to find adjoining land parcel numbers. Some offices make informal, unguaranteed indexes available and some do not. Tax information and assessment rolls may be of assistance. Teraview digital maps and POLARIS property maps illustrate adjoining PINs, which greatly simplifies the adjoining land search. Watch for the term "M-Plan", as this indicates a plan of subdivision in the Land Titles system. Never assume that a lot is a subdivision lot. Lastly, never assume that the whole of a parcel is the same as the whole of a lot.

When completing a *Planning Act* search, first establish the parcel and section numbers for all abutting lands, either by identifying them with the lot and plan numbers, *e.g.*, Lot 41, Plan M-234, which would be parcel 41-1, Plan M-234, or from the cross-reference index provided for that purpose. In Teraview, request that adjoining properties be selected and highlighted on digital maps and listed by PIN on search screens. Check the parcel registers or printouts for abutting lands and record all conveyances and prior owners throughout the proper *Planning Act* search period, at most back to June 15, 1967 (see Chapter 11 for detailed law and *Planning Act* search procedures, particularly start dates, for all title variations). Record and read all *Planning Act* by-laws, consents, validation certificates, compliance statements, and agreements. Note on your search whether or not the registered owner of the subject lands owned any of the abutting lands within the prescribed search period (see Chapter 11 for details on the *Planning Act* search period).

Special rules apply for *Planning Act* contraventions and LTCQ and LT PLUS parcels. An LTCQ parcel is clear of any *Planning Act* contraventions prior to the date of conversion. An LT PLUS parcel is always clear of any *Planning Act* contraventions prior to the date of conversion for the parent LTCQ parcel, and since 2001 it is usually clear of *Planning Act* violations prior to the date of registration of the LT PLUS parcel. The *Planning Act* compliance search for an LT PLUS parcel can start at the date of registration of the LT PLUS, instead of the date of conversion to the parent LTCQ parcel, as long as it has the following qualifiers listed on the face of the LT PLUS parcel register:

> Subject to subsection 44(1) of the Land Titles Act, except paragraphs 3 and 14 and Provincial Succession Duties and *except paragraph 11* and Escheats or Forfeiture to the Crown up to the date of registration with an absolute title. [emphasis added]

The *Planning Act* compliance search is as high-risk as it is complicated. Land Titles Absolute titles are subject to the same *Planning Act* rules whether in the traditional paper record or in POLARIS. Lawyers may need to search back to 1967 in the paper record or in Teraview to determine *Planning Act* compliance on an LT Absolute title. Automation does not change the effect of the *Planning Act* on LT Absolute titles. This is a common and dangerous misconception. Some title insurers do not require a full *Planning Act* search for some types of transactions. They provide alternative coverage. Again, consider the risk. If the deal does not close and there is a *Planning Act* violation, title insurance is not a substitute for proof of title or timely requisitions, a substitute for title documentation in a tender, or a defence to a subsequent negligence claim by a client.

Confirm legal access to a public road and confirm the registration and validity of easements and restrictive covenants on both adjoining dominant and servient tenements. Although, technically not a title or contract issue, consider reviewing adjoining lands for registrations that may have an impact on the use or generate risk on the land being purchased, for example, an environmental work order. It can be wise to "look over the fence" and see what is happening next door.

EXECUTION SEARCHING IN LAND TITLES

Under the Land Titles system, the only executions that affect a parcel of land are those filed in the Land Titles office by the sheriff in accordance with a paid request by the execution creditor (*Land Titles Act*, s. 136). Executions or writs are stored in MAG, the Ministry of the Attorney General's writ database, although they are searched through Teraview, BAR-eX, or OWL. All execution searches and certificate requests are completed online. Execution searches are part of the title search, and the subsearch, which is completed on the same day as or just prior to presenting a document for registration. Teraview contains an execution search feature called WritSearch. Writs can be deleted as part of an electronic land registration.

In the paper system, the registration clerk will complete the box provided for executions and the registration number, located in the upper left corner, with an "O.K." if a certificate of clearance results from the search. If the document is otherwise in order, it will be registered clear of executions. If, however, the search reveals that an execution is registered against the exact name of the registered owner or mortgagor, then the title searcher may obtain a writ abstract or particulars of the execution from the execution database, using a self-serve terminal at the Land Titles office or through online services. The lawyer may choose to register subject to an execution, although this is unusual. In that case, the land registrar will make the following note on the parcel register, "subject to execution number ___".

The *Land Titles Act* does not require execution searches against prior owners unless the parcel register is expressly marked subject to a prior execution (*Land Titles Act*, s. 44(6)). The guarantee against prior executions or executions not properly shown on a certificate of clearance is backed by the Land Titles Assurance Fund. Therefore, on completion of a search of title under the Land Titles system, a search of executions is required only against the exact name(s) of the registered owner(s), exactly as they are entered on the current parcel register and any "subject to" executions listed on the parcel register. If a purchaser is financing a purchase by way of a charge, then a search of executions should also be completed against the purchaser, exactly as he or she will be shown on the register as chargor.

Detailed rules which apply as to the manner in which executions are searched against registered owners are included later in this chapter in the Land Titles Search Checklist. Refer to the Land Registrars' *Land Titles Act* Bulletin No. 98003, "Writs of Execution" (December 14, 1998) for detailed Land Titles execution searching and clearance procedures.

Generally, a lawyer will search executions prior to a purchase or prior to an advance of funds on a charge. When the request for search results in a certificate of clearance, the transaction proceeds smoothly. If, instead, a search reveals similar or identical name executions against the exact name of the current registered owners, then different remedies apply depending on the circumstances. Normally, executions are removed by an application to delete executions or by statements of law contained in an electronic transfer.

In the case of transfers of freehold land, transfers of leaseholds, transfers of easements, vesting orders, foreclosures, power of sale transactions, survivorship applications and transmission applications, a certificate of execution on the parcel will result in the parcel register being marked, "subject to execution ___, if enforceable". The purchaser/transferee may choose to purchase the land subject to executions or require that a release of writ be obtained prior to purchase. An application to delete writs of seizure and sale may be registered later in order to clear title. Refer to Chapter 12 for the law and procedure for searching and deleting executions in all land registration systems.

TITLE SUBSEARCHES IN LAND TITLES

Under the *Land Titles Act*, a subsearch is less complicated and more reliable than in Registry. A subsearch of title may be made at the time a document is presented at the registration counter or submitted electronically for registration. Subsearch capability is built directly into the electronic document registration process, although subsearching on adjoining land must always be done separately in the search function. As part of the registration process, a registration clerk will work with both the parcel register and the new document. A document will not be accepted by the registration clerk if the parcel register indicates that the vendor, or chargor named in the document, is not identical to the owner indicated on the parcel register. A parallel document certification process takes place behind the scenes in the ELRS. Subsearches of adjoining lands and for executions are also completed.

Under the Land Titles system, a lawyer is required to update a full search as follows:

1. Check the paper or electronic parcel register before or during registration to determine if any registrations have taken place since the original search.

2. Check the parcel register for pencilled-in notations of documents as these indicate a recent, prior registration in the process of being entered into the parcel register. This pencilled-in, conditional registration will not be legally certified until it has been properly entered into the property register and signed by or on behalf of the registrar. Section 78 of the *Land Titles Act* allows the registrar a maximum of 21 days to accept or reject a Land Titles registration. Registrations in process appear on the electronic parcel register; they are identified by the absence of a "C" following the document entry. The automatic subsearch feature within the electronic registration sequence also indicates all pending, uncertified registrations, and refers to them as uncertified. The introduction of electronic land registration has in a practical sense closed the gap between document submission and certification. The risk has been greatly reduced; there is "gap" title insurance coverage now available.

3. Note, examine, summarize, report, and in the ELRS print any documents found registered against your parcel since the initial search.

4. Record the date and registration number of your document on both your search and closing memorandum or checklist. In ELRS, print the registration report and print the electronic document.

5. Confirm the signed, certified entry of the registration. This may require an additional subsearch at a later date. Depending on the circumstances, a lawyer may obtain a current paper copy of the parcel register reflecting the new registration. In the ELRS, always access and print the revised parcel register and confirm that the new registration is followed by a "C". In the ELRS, certification may be in place almost immediately; however, if not, monitor the electronic parcel register and print confirmation as soon as practical.

CORPORATE OWNER STATUS SEARCH

When a company fails to file annual returns or pay corporations tax or undergoes some form of involuntary dissolution, the *Business Corporations Act* provides that the company will be dissolved and its lands will be forfeited to the Crown by way of escheat. As escheat and Crown rights are a s. 44 exception to the Land Title's guarantee, a lawyer must record all corporate owners, in theory, as far back as the Crown patent when dealing with a Land Titles Absolute title. A company must have been in existence throughout the time period it owned land in order to hold and transfer good and marketable title. Title depends on the absence of corporate escheat. On March 1, 1995, the Ontario *Business Corporations Act* was amended so as to limit the requirement for corporate searches to no more than 20 years before registration of a transfer to a subsequent purchaser for value (s. 244(3)). Corporate status certificates, *Personal Property Security Act* (PPSA), and NUANS searches for Ontario corporations may be made through online service providers, such as Cyberbahn, OnCorp Direct, Dye & Durham (now associated with Teranet), or the Government of Ontario's ONBIS electronic searching function, maintained by the Ministry of Government Services' Companies Branch. A corporate status search will disclose the name and number of the corporation, its incorporation jurisdiction, and the date of incorporation and or dissolution. Corporate certificate of compliance and certificate of existence searches for companies under the *Canada Business Corporations Act*, R.S.C. 1985, c. C-44 are made at Corporations Canada.

Corporate ownership search practice varies greatly as a result of the impracticality or impossibility of checking for corporate owners, particularly federal corporate owners, in deleted documents and non-active registers. Title insurance is a practical alternative for covering the risk of corporate escheat in prior corporate owners.

It is not necessary to search corporate owners prior to the date of conversion for a LTCQ title. Corporate searches are required for corporate owners from the date of conversion to the present. Title insurance coverage is available for other than the current corporate owner.

It is now not necessary to search corporate owners prior to the date of registration for a Land Titles Absolute Plus title. Corporate searches are required for corporate owners from the date of registration to the present. Title insurance coverage is available for other than the current corporate owner.

CERTIFICATE OF SEARCH

A registrar will provide, on request and payment of a prescribed fee, a certificate of search made up of a dated, certified copy of a parcel register. A certificate of search may be relied on as proof of the matters contained therein, only in the absence of evidence to the contrary. A certificate of search does not provide copies of plans and documents and adjoining land and execution information, which are necessary to complete a standard search. Certificates of search are often used for evidentiary and litigation purposes.

TITLE INSURANCE REQUIREMENTS AND LAND TITLES SEARCHING

Most insurers only require lawyers to review the parcel register; title insurers recommend particular attention to the "subject to" documents in the property description line. Insurers provide alternative coverage for corporate profile and status inquiries for past corporate owners that might reveal a corporate escheat. Insurers require adjoining land searches to confirm *Planning Act* compliance, easements and restrictive covenants, and legal access. When working in ELRS, insurers require that lawyers always request deleted documents as this reveals heightened fraud risk patterns and also ownership information back to the required *Planning Act* start date. *Planning Act* violations are an identified high risk area for lawyers. They result in no title for the client and may not be curable. Apart from the effect of title insurance policies, a *Planning Act* violation can provide grounds for a purchaser to refuse to close the transaction and for a client to sue the lawyer in negligence. Insurer requirements vary and are subject to change. Full searches are not required on refinance transactions.

PRACTICE SUMMARY

The following is a checklist that reviews the general requirements of searching in Land Titles and focuses on the steps for searching a Land Titles Absolute title. The checklist list includes comparisons to the procedures in the automated record. The checklist is not specifically designed for LTCQ or LT PLUS properties that have been automated or converted from Registry under the POLARIS project. Refer to later chapters, particularly Chapter 8, for more detail on electronic searching mechanics that focus on title variations found in POLARIS, and also procedures in the electronic system for adjoining lands searches, execution searches, and subsearches.

LAND TITLES SEARCH CHECKLIST

☐ **Identify appropriate Registry office**. The Teranet website has a search tool that cross-references names of towns and cities to a registry office name and number. The Teraview search tool allows the lawyer to select any automated registry office in the Province. (Appendix 5 contains a list of Registry Offices.)

☐ **Determine if land is registered in the Land Titles system**. In POLARIS, the parcel register indicates whether land is in Land Titles or Registry by placing either a "LT" or an "R" immediately following the PIN at the top of the printout.

☐ **Obtain the Land Titles description reference in order to access the parcel register**, such as the M-Plan, section, city, township, county, district, regional municipality, *etc*. In POLARIS, identify the PIN, the municipal address, the last registered instrument, the current owner's name, or the lot and subdivision plan as this information will access the parcel register in Teraview. The agreement of purchase and sale, the vendor's lawyer, tax bills, old documents, surveys, maps, assessment rolls, the Ministry of Revenue, the municipal tax office, and Registry office cross-references and microfiche assessment rolls, *etc*. may provide short legal descriptions.

☐ Complete request for service and pay cashier prescribed fee or access the PIN on Teraview.

☐ **Obtain a copy or a printout of the parcel register** by reference to the land's parcel and section numbers, or on Teraview by municipal address, PIN, owner name, last registered instrument number, or subdivision lot and plan.

☐ Examine, copy, and search, when necessary, **other related registers**, *e.g.*, the Mineral Lands parcel register, the Highways register, the Trans-Canada Pipeline register, *etc*. In Teraview, print the parcel register.

☐ **Search the online Powers of Attorney Register** when relying on a power of attorney. The electronic registration system requires statements in documents as to whether they are executed by power of attorney. Powers of attorney are registered and searched online.

☐ **Identify the specific Land Titles title**, whether absolute title, leasehold title, or qualified title, and note any title qualifiers listed on the parcel register, *e.g.*, subject to execution number ___, or subject to spousal rights. Identify whether the title is an LT Absolute, an LTCQ, or an LT PLUS; this information is listed beside the heading "estate qualifier". Review the listed qualifiers on the parcel printout as they can affect *Planning Act* compliance, corporate status, description matters, mature possessory rights (LTCQ), and adjoining land searches.

☐ **Obtain a copy (white print) of the relevant M-Plan (plan of subdivision) and R-Plan (reference plan)**. In Teraview, some plans are available online; they are most often couriered or faxed, following an online request.

- Compare the dimensions on the plans to the dimensions in the agreement of purchase and sale and survey, if available. When in Teraview, also reconcile information in the property description line with the digital maps.
- Confirm that streets and reserves (one foot) have been dedicated as public streets. Verify road widenings. In Teraview, find and check separate PINs for parcel registers for streets, roads, and reserves.
- Check front of plans for compliance with plan requirements, *e.g.*, mortgagee's consent.
- **Confirm legal access to a public road**.

☐ **Review the parcel register and identify current registered documents**, such as outstanding transfer and charges/mortgages, liens, leases, agreements, notices, cautions, easements, restrictions, restrictive covenants, by-laws, *etc.* which affect or encumber title. Also always review deleted documents for transactional patterns that indicate a potential fraud risk, or an environmental hazard, a *Planning Act* violation, or prior corporate owners. Deleted documents may indicate prior owners with a higher risk of environmental contamination, for example, a gas station, a car wash, or a dry cleaning business. In Teraview, always request deleted documents and print the parcel register. Current, certified documents are identified by a "C" following the document entry on the register. Deleted documents are noted as deleted on the face of the register.

☐ Examine, summarize, copy, or **print outstanding documents** for specific terms. Documents may be available by request for service or self-service, in paper or microfilm form. Each office has its own rules about using documents. It is unnecessary to check signatures and requirements of form as Land Titles documents are certified as to legal effectiveness during the registration process. In Teraview, documents can be viewed online, printed, or requested by fax or by courier. (See Chapter 5 for guidance on the form, content, and effect of pre-POLARIS and post-POLARIS documents.)

☐ Check partially **ruled-out or deleted documents**, usually "transfers" for information on outstanding easements and restrictive covenants that were created in now-deleted transfers. Teraview notes these types of interests in the property description line as "subject to" instruments. Teraview also shows interests such as easements and restrictive covenants from earlier transfers on the parcel register.

☐ *Planning Act* **search**: When searching a parcel containing a part lot that is not exempt from subdivision or part lot control provisions under the *Planning Act*, complete a search of adjoining lands for *Planning Act* violations.

- Check the information on the face of the plan to determine whether you are dealing with a subdivision plan or some other kind of plan. "M-Plan" indicates a subdivision plan in Land Titles.
- Determine whether you are dealing with a whole lot or block, or a part lot or block on a registered plan of subdivision.
- If the parcel is exempt from the *Planning Act* part lot control provisions, the most common exemption being a parcel that is comprised of one or more whole lots or blocks on a registered plan of subdivision, then a *Planning Act* search may not be necessary. Check for by-laws, consents, and validation certificates that can affect exempt status.
- Identify abutting lands and record all conveyances and prior owners throughout the proper *Planning Act* search period (see Chapter 11 for detailed procedures). Note on your search the starting point for the *Planning Act* search and whether or not the registered owner of the subject lands owned any of the abutting lands within the search period.
- When searching back to the proper *Planning Act* search start date, the searcher often records ruled-out document entries.
- In Teraview, request adjoining lands in the digital mapping feature and print the map that shows the adjoining lands. Also print the parcel registers, including deleted documents, for all adjoining properties, including roads.

☐ **Other Adjoining Lands searches**: Confirm legal access to a public road and confirm the registration and validity of easements and restrictive covenants on adjoining dominant and servient tenements.

☐ **LTCQ titles carry mature possessory rights into Land Titles**. As a result, when searching an LTCQ title, it is necessary to complete Registry-type adjoining land searches for description discrepancies and potential encroachments as far back as necessary, including in pre-conversion records.

☐ Search **executions** online in WritSearch as follows:

- Search the exact name(s) of the registered owner(s) as they appear on the parcel register.
- Search the current purchaser names, exactly as they will appear on the parcel register, if the purchase is being financed by a mortgage.
- Search beneficiaries releasing their interest when registering a transmission application.
- Search the deceased's name, and any beneficiaries releasing their interests when registering a transfer from estate trustees, or when the devisee applies to be registered as owner. When searching the deceased's name, the automated WritSearch system will also search for any capacity of the deceased's name, *e.g.*, "Estate of" or "Estate Trustee of ...".
- In a survivorship application, search the deceased joint tenant in his or her personal capacity and not the estate.

- Search executions against the exact name of a corporation registered as owner as set out on the parcel register.
- Search executions against the exact name of a partnership registered as owner, as set out on the parcel register. Search names of partners as they appear on the parcel register.
- Search the general partners and the name of a limited partnership as they appear on the parcel register.
- Search executions against the registered owner when registering an application to change the name of the registered owner.
- Search executions against the registered owner when registering applications to release or abandon an easement.
- Search executions against a transferor who is transferring an interest in land from himself/herself to himself/herself.
- Search executions for inter-spousal and inter-family transfers as well as transfers of municipal land. See Registrars' Bulletin No. 98003/98.

☐ **Complete an illustration of the parcel**, often by simply outlining or highlighting the land being acquired and adjoining lands on the M-Plan or R-Plan. Illustrate dimensions, easements, and access. Colour-code main land and adjoining lands. In POLARIS, you may print digital maps that highlight and distinguish land being searched and adjoining lands. The digital map printout could form the base for the illustration. Easements and description information from documents could be superimposed on the digital map. However, it is essential to understand that digital maps do not represent boundaries or legal descriptions. They are for reference purposes only and must not be relied on. Legal descriptions in Land Titles do not determine the extent of the land "on the ground". The absence of adverse possession in Land Titles does not mean that the legal descriptions accurately identify the land owned; ONLY a survey can determine the extent of land.
Note that an LTCQ requires the same adjoining lands description searches and sketches as a Registry search. For description and boundary purposes, an LT PLUS is treated the same as an LT Absolute.

☐ **Update search** depending on the amount of time that has passed since the beginning of the search. Teraview has a date forward search feature that simplifies search updating.

☐ **Complete search summary**: The summary acts as a review of title.

☐ Do not remove documents from the Registry office. Return all documents properly. ($5,000 fine for removal, damage or loss.) Intentional harm to electronic records is a computer crime under the *Criminal Code*.

☐ Make sure the completed search contains the following:

- search summary or cover page, noting the last instrument number on the search and the date and time the search was completed in order to facilitate subsearching;
- copy/printout of parcel register and adjoining parcel registers when searching a part lot, which is not exempt from the *Planning Act*;
- copies of related M-Plans and R-Plans, including illustration;

- copies/printouts or summaries of outstanding documents (may be written onto copy of the parcel register);
- copies of documents on adjoining lands that might affect land being purchased, such as reference plans, *Boundaries Act* plans, encroachment agreements, or *Planning Act* consents; and
- execution/writ certificate.

☐ **Overriding interests**: Consider whether depending on the nature of the property it is prudent to check for overriding interests prior to the current parcel register. For example, proximity to navigable waters, railways, hydro-electric sources, or mining operations may raise the risk of overriding interests registered prior to the active parcel register.

☐ **Check Crown patent** for restrictions on ownership, such as road or shoreline allowances, Aboriginal rights, resource restrictions, *etc*.

☐ **Complete corporate status searches** for possible Crown escheats against present and past (starting at the Crown patent) corporate owners on title. Ontario companies under the *Business Corporations Act* need be checked only for the 20-year period prior to closing. Most lawyers prefer to rely on title insurance coverage for past corporate owner, corporate search, due diligence requirements.

☐ **Complete off-title searches** depending on the terms of the contract, the nature of the land, the choice of alternative title insurance coverage, and instructions from the client.

☐ **Complete subsearches** immediately prior to closing:

- **main search**: Record new or pencilled-in entries on the parcel register since the last registration (noted on search summary) on the original search in order to update the main search. In Teraview, update the search using the date forward search feature or subsearch during the registration process.
- **adjoining lands search**: Update adjoining lands search by checking new or pencilled-in entries on the parcel register for the adjoining lands. In Teraview, you can only subsearch adjoining lands in the POLARIS search function. There is a date forward search option.
- **execution search**: Update execution search against the exact name(s) of the registered owner(s) as they appear on the parcel register. If the purchase is being financed by a mortgage, update the current purchaser names, exactly as they will appear on the parcel register.
- **other searches**: Update, when relevant, inquiries such as corporate status searches.
- **off-title searches**: Update off-title inquiries depending on the time between the initial search and closing.

☐ Review the effect of title insurance coverage on the search. Complete a full search of the land being purchased, request deleted documents, complete a *Planning Act* search, and report search results to the insurer and specific search concerns to an underwriter.

LAND TITLES ABSOLUTE: PAPER RECORD SEARCH EXAMPLE

Figure 6.1 illustrates the layout and contents of a Land Titles Absolute traditional (paper) parcel register. The following title information should be reviewed when searching this parcel register:

1. The Land Titles division (office).

2. Original and previous parcel and section references.

3. Current parcel and section.

4. Registered title and estate in land (*e.g.*, absolute title).

5. Legal description. This parcel is a part lot and thus raises the question of whether a *Planning Act* search must be done. A *Planning Act* exemption by-law has been registered on this M-Plan; however, check the by-law for an expiry date. Assuming the by-law is still active, it is unnecessary to complete the *Planning Act* compliance search.

6. Copies of 11M-48 (M-Plan is a subdivision plan) and 11R-5649 (reference plan). Check plan validity. Superimpose sketch of subject land on the reference plan.

7. Application for first registration now ruled out and cancelled.

8. Notice #20611, which is an encumbrance on title and must be summarized or copied. A notice may contain many different documents, *e.g.*, development or subdivision agreements, notice of easement, easement maintenance agreements.

9. *Planning Act* By-law #20630, which exempts the property from the part lot control provisions and removes the requirement for a *Planning Act* search. *Planning Act* by-laws must be summarized or copied. Always check for an expiry date in a *Planning Act* exemption by-law.

10. Ruled out previous transfer. This transfer has been cancelled; however, a previous corporate owner usually requires a corporate search for escheat. Most lawyers rely on title insurance to provide coverage for prior corporate owners.

11. The signature of an authorized signing officer, as is required for each registration, confirming the registration of the instrument.

12. The current transfer, which is usually photocopied. Search executions against the name of the current registered owner as he or she appears on the parcel register. If the purchase is being financed by a mortgage, search the current purchaser names, exactly as they will appear on the parcel register.

13. The current charge, which is usually photocopied, as it is an encumbrance that will be either assumed or discharged. (This is a first charge.)

14. Outstanding Notice #22239, which relates to the outstanding first charge. It might contain an assignment of rents or possibly an amendment of charge. The notice must be summarized.

15. Current restrictive covenants noted in the remarks column which were attached to now-ruled out and cancelled registrations. The restrictions are still current although the transfer is not. This kind of entry is easy to miss in the paper record.

Figure 6.1

LAND TITLES PAPER PARCEL REGISTER SEARCH EXAMPLE

Parcel Register
Registre des parcelles

(2)

Original Parcel: 9-1, & 9-20, Section YAR-9
Description d'origine: & Parcel 96, St. Thomas

Recently: Part of Parcel #4-1
Description recante: Section 11M-48

(1) ELIGIN (NO. 11)

Land Titles Division of
Division d'enregistrement
des droits immobiliers de

(4) Estate in Fee Simple with an Absolute Title
Domaine en fief simple à titre absolu

(3) Page 1
Parcel
Parcelle 18-2
Section 11M-48

Ontario

Subject to subsequent entries this parcel comprises the following land
Sous réserve des inscriptions ultérieures, cette parcelle se compose du bien-fonds suivant

Registration Number / Numéro d'enregistrement	Instrument Type / Type d'acte	Registration date / Date d'enregistrement YY | MM | DD	Parties la / Parties	(Applicant, Creditor, etc.) / (Demandeur, titulaire del'avertissement, réclament, etc.)	Consideration / Contrepartie	Land/Remarks / Bien-fonds/Observations
	LEGAL DESCRIPTION: (5)		PART OF LOT 24, PLAN 11M_48 (6)	(City of St. Thomas), County of Elgin, DESIGNATED AS PARTS 7 & 8, PLAN 11R-5649.		
00470-11543	Application (7)	91 07 03	MID-ERIE DEVELOPMENTS LIMITED (OWNER)			
20811	Notice (8)	92 11 23	THE CORPORATION OF THE CITY OF ST. THOMAS THE PUBLIC UTILITIES COMMISSION OF THE CITY OF ST. THOMAS			
20630	By-Law (9)	92 12 29				
21430	Transfer (10)	93 05 30	NONAME SALES (ST. THOMAS) INC.		$80,000.00	Subsection 5 of Section 50 of the Planning Act, RSO 1990 does not apply. (11) restrictions (15)
21711	Transfer (12)	93 06 30	HANES, JESSIE SELENA		$200,000.00	
21548	Charge (13)	93 06 30	MONTREAL TRUST COMPANY OF CANADA		$150,000.00	
22239	Notice (14)	93 09 15	MONTREAL TRUST COMPANY OF CANADA			Re: 21548
23116	Notice	94 03 03	ZORO, MARK GOODMAN			Part 8, 11R-5649

FORM 2

10312(88)

LAND TITLES ABSOLUTE: ELECTRONIC RECORD EXAMPLES

Figure 6.2

POLARIS/TERAVIEW: EXAMPLE LAND TITLES ABSOLUTE SEARCH*

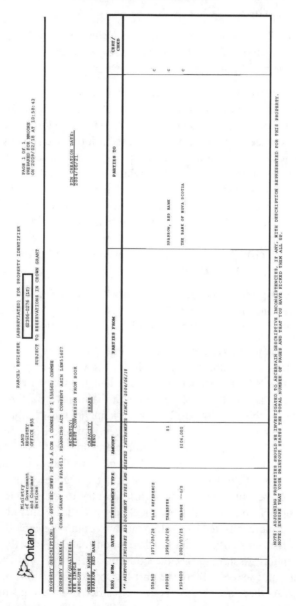

Figure 6.2 is a Teraview printout of a Land Titles Absolute electronic parcel register. The following title information should be reviewed when searching this parcel register:

1. **PIN 62306-0264** is followed by (LT). This is a Land Titles property that is found in Block 62306 and has been allocated 0264 as its property number.

2. Land Titles parcels are subject to **Crown reservations** found in the Crown patent. The patent must be reviewed to determine the specific Crown reservations that affect this parcel.

3. The **property description line** contains the parcel's description reference. PIN 62306-0264 indexes parcel 6907, section DFWF, which is made up of Part of Township Lot A in Concession 2, in the Township of Conmee. A township or concession lot is usually described by letter when it has an irregular boundary and is referred to as a broken front lot. Regular shaped township lots are usually numbered. Fortunately, this part concession lot is described as a Part 1, on Reference Plan 55R550, which avoids working with metes and bounds descriptions. Although less common than in Registry, Land Titles does contain metes and bounds descriptions. This PIN represents a part lot which normally requires the lawyer to complete a *Planning Act* compliance search of adjoining lands.

   The property description line often contains easements, restrictive covenants, and "subject to" claims, such as spousal rights, and executions. This property description line only deals with the description.

4. The **property remarks** line is often empty; however, it may contain critical information that is not shown elsewhere on the register printout. On this PIN, property remarks contains the Crown patent registration number and a reference to a transfer that contains a *Planning Act* consent for this part lot. Both these documents must be printed as part of the search. Crown patents have been registered in Land Titles since the 1960s; these patents are available from Teraview. The patent must be checked for conditions and reservations that continue to affect the property's title. Usually, the patent is not registered in the system and has to be obtained by an off-title inquiry to the Province. The *Planning Act* consent must be checked for validity including conditions and time limits for use. The transfer containing the consent must be checked to confirm that its decription matches exactly the PINs description. Assuming that the consent is effective, this PIN, although a part lot, is exempt from the part lot control provisions of the *Planning Act*. As there are no easements or restrictive covenants on the register, it is unnecessary to complete an adjoining lands search. Of course, it is always necessary to confirm legal access to the nearest public road.

The property remarks line can contain title problems that do not show in the main part of the register.

5. The **estate qualifier** line indicates that this PIN is an LT Absolute title. This line might identify an LTCQ, a leasehold, a qualified, a possessory, or an LT PLUS title. Different types of title have different qualifiers. The type of title determines the search requirements.

6. **"Recently"** provides a cross-reference to earlier parcel or book references. It may refer to earlier parcel numbers when there has been subdivision or consolidation of earlier parcels. It may refer back to the original Registry records prior to first registration.

7. **The PIN creation date** refers to the date the PIN was created and activated. It may not be the original POLARIS PIN. The PIN creation date is not the same as the date of the original conversion to POLARIS. The date of conversion on the face of the register is a starting point for a *Planning Act* search with an LTCQ title, but not with a Land Titles Absolute title. The PIN creation date does not provide a starting point for a *Planning Act* search, unless it coincides with the date of conversion.

8. **Owners' names** should correspond with registered document information. Documents are part of the parcel register. The execution search should be done on WritSearch against Red Hawk Sparrow, assuming the registered owner names matches the registered owners on the current title document. If a new mortgage is being placed, executions will be searched against the name(s) of the purchaser as they will appear on the register.

9. **Capacity and share**: Red Hawk Sparrow is the beneficial owner of this property. Owner capacity, such as joint tenants and tenants in common or as partners, and percentage shares are included under this heading. The capacity and shares should match the registered documents.

10. **This printout includes deleted documents**. There are no deleted documents on this register. Lawyers should always request deleted documents to check for patterns of fraud and for prior corporate owners for escheat purposes, and prior owners for *Planning Act* compliance searches.

11. **Request reference plan**: The reference plan provides the description information. Plans and documents can be viewed or ordered online. Plans are usually couriered.

12. F80069 is the current transfer. Print the transfer and check content.

13. F104600 is an outstanding first mortgage. Print the charge and review content, particularly information relating to discharge and assumption.

14. **"C"** in the far right column indicates that the documents are certified. No "C" means that a document's registration is pending.

Figure 6.3

POLARIS/TERAVIEW: EXAMPLE LAND TITLES ABSOLUTE SEARCH*

Ontario
Ministry of Government and Consumer Services

PARCEL REGISTER (ABBREVIATED) FOR PROPERTY IDENTIFIER

LAND REGISTRY OFFICE #12

75118-0119 (LT)

SUBJECT TO RESERVATIONS IN CROWN GRANT

PAGE 1 OF 2
PREPARED FOR MMOORE
ON 2009/02/18 AT 10:32:14

PROPERTY DESCRIPTION: PT LTS 98,99,100,101 PL M86 PT 2 12R10806 LEAMINGTON

PROPERTY REMARKS:

ESTATE/QUALIFIER
FEE SIMPLE
ABSOLUTE

RECENTLY:
RE-ENTRY FROM 01481-0581

PIN CREATION DATE:
2002/07/26

OWNERS' NAMES
MOORE, RUTH MARGUERITE
MOORE, JOHN ELLIS

CAPACITY   SHARE
JTEN
JTEN

REG. NUM.	DATE	INSTRUMENT TYPE	AMOUNT	PARTIES FROM	PARTIES TO	CERT/ CHKD
** PRINTOUT INCLUDES ALL DOCUMENT TYPES AND DELETED INSTRUMENTS SINCE: 2002/07/24 **						
R286888	1963/08/27	BYLAW		SEE DOCUMENT		C
	CORRECTIONS: 'DATE OF REGN.' CHANGED FROM '1963/08/23' TO '1963/08/26' ON 1996/03/05 BY MICHAEL CARR. 'DATE OF REGN.' CHANGED FROM '1963/08/26' TO '1963/08/27' ON 1996/03/26 BY GRAZIA GREGORIO.					
R463888	1970/04/01	BYLAW		SEE DOCUMENT		C
LT11088	1988/12/09	BYLAW		SEE DOCUMENT		C
12R10559	1990/06/05	PLAN REFERENCE				C
LT259559	1999/10/19	TRANSFER		*** COMPLETELY DELETED *** HAYNES, JESSIE SELENA HAYNES, ROBERT JOHN	CORBETT, HAMILTON LEWIS	
	REMARKS: PLANNING ACT STATEMENTS					
LT153500	1999/10/29	CHARGE		*** DELETED AGAINST THIS PROPERTY *** CORBETT, HAMILTON LEWIS	SCOTIA MORTGAGE CORPORATION	C
LT168557	2000/03/14	NOTICE	$235500	CORBETT, HAMILTON LEWIS	SCOTIA MORTGAGE CORPORATION	
	REMARKS: LT235500					
CE724455	2004/04/28	TRANSFER	$114,000	CORBETT, HAMILTON LEWIS	MOORE, RUTH MARGUERITE MOORE, JOHN ELLIS	C
	REMARKS: PLANNING ACT STATEMENTS					

NOTE: ADJOINING PROPERTIES SHOULD BE INVESTIGATED TO ASCERTAIN DESCRIPTIVE INCONSISTENCIES, IF ANY, WITH DESCRIPTION REPRESENTED FOR THIS PROPERTY.
NOTE: ENSURE THAT YOUR PRINTOUT STATES THE TOTAL NUMBER OF PAGES AND THAT YOU HAVE PICKED THEM ALL UP.

Figure 6.3 (cont'd)

Ontario

Ministry
of Government
and Consumer
Services

LAND
REGISTRY
OFFICE #12

PARCEL REGISTER (ABBREVIATED) FOR PROPERTY IDENTIFIER

| 75118-0119 (LT) |

SUBJECT TO RESERVATIONS IN CROWN GRANT

PAGE 2 OF 2
PREPARED FOR MMOORE
ON 2009/02/18 AT 10:32:14

PROPERTY DESCRIPTION: PT LTS 98,99,100,101 PL MB6 PT 2 12R10806 LEAMINGTON

PROPERTY REMARKS:

ESTATE/QUALIFIER
FEE SIMPLE
ABSOLUTE

RECENTLY:
RE-ENTRY FROM 01481-0581

PIN CREATION DATE:
2002/07/26

OWNERS' NAMES
MOORE, RUTH MARGUERITE
MOORE, JOHN ELLIS

CAPACITY   SHARE
JTEN
JTEN

REG. NUM.	DATE	INSTRUMENT TYPE	AMOUNT	PARTIES FROM	PARTIES TO	CERT/CHKD
CE72456	2004/04/28	CHARGE	$111,820	MOORE, RUTH MARGUERITE MOORE, JOHN ELLIS	FIRST NATIONAL FINANCIAL CORPORATION	C
CE75088	2004/05/10	DISCH OF CHARGE		*** COMPLETELY DELETED ***		
				REMARKS: RE: CE255500		
CE139780	2005/04/11	CHARGE		*** COMPLETELY DELETED *** MOORE, JOHN ELLIS MOORE, RUTH MARGUERITE	SCOTIA MORTGAGE CORPORATION	
CE216690	2006/05/31	CHARGE	$24,221	MOORE, JOHN ELLIS MOORE, RUTH MARGUERITE	CITIFINANCIAL CANADA, INC.	C
CE216900	2006/06/01	DISCH OF CHARGE		*** COMPLETELY DELETED ***	CITIFINANCIAL CANADA, INC.	
				REMARKS: RE: CE139780		

NOTE: ADJOINING PROPERTIES SHOULD BE INVESTIGATED TO ASCERTAIN DESCRIPTIVE INCONSISTENCIES, IF ANY, WITH DESCRIPTION REPRESENTED FOR THIS PROPERTY.
NOTE: ENSURE THAT YOUR PRINTOUT STATES THE TOTAL NUMBER OF PAGES AND THAT YOU HAVE PICKED THEM ALL UP.

Figure 6.3 is a Teraview printout of a Land Titles Absolute parcel register in POLARIS.

- PIN 75118-0119 is a Land Titles Absolute parcel. It is comprised of four part lots on a subdivision (M) plan. PIN 75118-0119 represents Part 2 on 12-R1006. PIN 75118-0119 was created July 7th 2002. The parent PIN was 01481-0581.

- PIN 75118-0119 is made up of part lots and for that reason it requires a *Planning Act* compliance search. The first step would be to read the three by-laws on title to determine if they are *Planning Act* implementation or exemption by-laws. The parcel register shows that the current transfer contains the *Planning Act* compliance statements. The *Planning Act* is an overriding interest or exception to the *Land Titles Act* guarantee. For this reason, it is necessary to read the transfer, not just the register, and confirm that all three *Planning Act* declarations have been properly completed. On this PIN, the *Planning Act* search starts at the last transfer as it contains three completed *Planning Act* statements; otherwise, it is possible that in on a Land Titles Absolute title the lawyer might have to go as far back as 1967 on all adjoining properties. Without the declarations in the active and deleted transfers, the start date for the *Planning Act* search would have been 1967 as the 1963 by-law implemented the part lot control provisions on this property. Deleted documents may contain *Planning Act* statements; this is one reason for always requesting deleted documents. This PIN is an excellent illustration as to why it benefits all parties to complete *Planning Act* statements on all transfers.

- The parcel printout contains examples of notices, deleted documents, and by-laws.

- The parcel does not contain registered easements and restrictive covenants. Easement and restrictive covenant registrations are common in Land Titles. They may be included in either the property description line or as a document on the parcel register, or as a notation in the right-hand column. It is necessary to check that easements are registered on the subject land and also on the adjoining land. Easements require a search of both the dominant and servient tenements whether or not the lawyer is dealing with a part lot.

- Many Land Titles parcels contain notices, agreements, and cautions. The parcel register does not indicate the nature of these documents. The lawyer must read the documents, as with by-laws. Sometimes notices are cross-referenced to a prior instrument and this may indicate the nature of the instrument. For example, LT268557 is a notice that relates to charge number LT255500. This notice is a notice of agreement amending charge LT255500. An examination of the register reveals that the charge has been deleted and the notice is no longer effective. It will have been missed in the electronic discharge when the registrant was required to include all related documents so they could also be deleted. Again, this is another example of the importance of requesting deleted documents.

- The parcel register illustrates deleted document notations and also how a deleted document does not have a "C" after the document entry. The lawyer will match up deleted documents such as charges and discharges. This parcel illustrates two outstanding mortgages and two discharged mortgages.

CHAPTER 7

Condominium Ownership and the Search

CONDOMINIUM SEARCHING: AN OVERVIEW

A condominium title search is different from a typical title search. A condominium unit search combines the following:

1. search of Land Titles system registrations;

2. off-title searches;

3. review of condominium creation documents such as the declaration, descriptions, by-laws, and rules; and

4. review of condominium administrative and disclosure documents, for example management agreements, shared facilities, cost sharing and mutual use agreements and easements, budget statements, reserve fund studies, disclosure statements, status certificates, and related condominium documents, such as s. 98 (*Codominium Act, 1998*, S.O. 1998, c. 19) common elements alteration agreements.

Search requirements vary among the different types of condominiums; for example, lawyers examine ground lease terms in leasehold condominiums, whereas they may focus more on *Planning Act*, R.S.O. 1990, c. P.13 compliance and restrictions on parcels of tied land in common elements condominiums. Case law indicates that risk hotspots such as parking allocation, special assessments, and reserve funds are common to all condominiums. Title insurance coverage and search requirements also vary among the different forms of condominiums. Timeshare, fractional share, life lease, and condominium hotel projects add an additional layer of complexity and risk to condominium title inquiries.

CONDOMINIUM LEGISLATION

The *Condominium Act, 1998* regulates condominium development, ownership, and management in Ontario. Ontario's current *Condominium Act, 1998* replaced the *Condominium Act*, R.S.O. 1990, c. C.26 as of May 5, 2001 (and as of July 4, 2001, respecting the timing of annual general meetings). The new Act provides increased consumer protection and disclosure for purchasers and owners of condominium units. It also establishes several new types of condominiums. Today the creation and regulation of condominium ownership is found in:

- *Condominium Act, 1998*;
- O. Reg. 48/01 (General); and
- O. Reg. 49/01 (Description and Registration).

Corporations created under the previous *Condominium Act* are continued as corporations under the new Act and are now classified as "standard condominium corporations" (O. Reg. 48/01, s. 3).

Today, a conveyancer may encounter condominiums registered under both the old and the new Acts. Condominium documentation, registration records, and the very nature of condominium ownership varies from one condominium to another despite an identical or similar physical appearance. Lawyers must be competent in both the Registry and the Land Titles systems as well as the pre-POLARIS paper records and the automated POLARIS records accessed through Teraview. Today, almost all condominiums have been converted to the electronic land registration system (ELRS). The title search is completed in combination with detailed off-title inquiries, the most important being a careful review of the title register and the condominium status and/or disclosure statements, including a careful examination of attached documentation. Competent condominium searching requires a great deal of background knowledge, accurate reading of detailed documentation, and a significant time commitment.

CONDOMINIUM CREATION AND REGISTRATION

Condominium ownership, first introduced in Ontario in the 1960s, has long existed in other parts of the world. Today, condominiums represent a large percentage of new home development, over 40 per cent according to some estimates. Condominium ownership is a creation of statute law. A condominium corporation, without share capital, whose members are the owners, is divided into units and common elements in accordance with the description and is created on the registration of a declaration and description in the Registry office in which the land is situated. A condominium corporation is managed by a board of directors elected by the unit owners. The board of directors must consist of at least three persons or such greater number as the condominium corporation's by-laws may provide.

Condominiums comprise a distinct form of property ownership rather than a particular style of building. Today, condominiums may include: apartment buildings; row housing; shopping malls; commercial or industrial complexes; golf courses; ski hills; trailer parks; marinas; recreational property; agricultural property; wilderness preserves; water sources; vacant land; leasehold land; or a mixture of uses. Prior to the current Act, condominium ownership was only permitted for freehold or fee simple ownership, and although individual units could be leased to a tenant, condominiums based on leasehold ownership were prohibited. Today, condominium ownership, documentation and regulation are extremely complex and vary depending on the legal nature of the condominium being purchased. Condominium conveyancing and title searching require a careful reading of registered documents such as the declaration and description and by-laws, as well as unregistered documents such as the disclosure statement, the status certificate, reserve fund reports, budget statements, and performance reports. Only a detailed review of both registered and unregistered condominium documentation will reveal the ownership rights and obligations of a potential purchaser and the current financial and management status of the condominium corporation.

The registered owner of the condominium unit, whether residential, commercial, industrial, or mixed-use property, holds title to a particular unit or units, while sharing with fellow owners the title to the common areas, and the costs, called common expenses, of the common elements of the condominium property. The owner(s) of each of the units must contribute to the common expenses of the condominium corporation according to their percentage share in the common interest, as set out in the declaration. Failure to do so creates a common expense lien against the defaulting owner's unit. Common elements condominiums are an exception to the general structure and comprise common elements and parcels of tied land instead of units.

Since September 1, 1967, in counties, districts, or regional municipalities where a Land Titles office is maintained, all condominium declarations and descriptions must be registered under the *Land Titles Act*, R.S.O. 1990, c. L.5. In areas where Teranet has converted Registry to Land Titles, a Land Titles Conversion Qualified (LTCQ) title must be upgraded to a Land Titles Absolute Plus title prior to the registration of a new condominium corporation. In areas where Land Titles is not available, land in Registry must first be certified under the *Certification of Titles Act*, R.S.O. 1990, c. C.6 before being accepted for registration as a condominium corporation. The certificate of title must show the proposed condominium declarant to be the owner in either fee simple or a leasehold title.

TYPES OF CONDOMINIUMS

The *Condominium Act, 1998,* which came into force in 2001, continues the traditional freehold condominium and also provides for several new kinds of condominium developments. The current Act provides for both freehold and leasehold condominiums. Under the current Act, freehold condominiums consist of common elements condominiums, phased condominium corporations, vacant land condominium corporations, and the traditional standard (freehold) condominium corporations. Two or more existing, same-type condominiums can reorganize as an amalgamated condominium. Leasehold condominiums are new in Ontario, although they are common in other places. Common elements condominiums, vacant land condominiums, and phased condominiums cannot be registered as leasehold condominiums.

The condominium declaration must state whether the corporation is a freehold condominium corporation or a leasehold condominium corporation, and, if the corporation is a freehold condominium corporation, must state the type of freehold condominium corporation. In addition, the disclosure statement must state the type of condominium.

Freehold Condominiums

Freehold (Standard) Condominium Corporation

The traditional condominium combines separately owned residential, commercial, industrial, or mixed-use units with shared common areas (elements) such as parking, storage, green space, recreational facilities, common walls, roofs, elevators, services, sidewalks, and roads.

A freehold (standard) condominium corporation is defined as a corporation in which all the units and their appurtenant common interests are held in fee simple. The purchaser purchases a unit in fee simple together with a common interest expressed as a percentage share in the common elements for which the unit owner will contribute a common expense payment. This category includes corporations created under the previous *Condominium Act* and continued as corporations under the new Act as "standard condominium corporations".

Common Elements Condominium Corporations

Common elements condominiums offer some interesting lifestyle choices. For example, a person could purchase a separate single-family home, or perhaps a ski chalet, linked to a share (common interest) in a private golf course, ski hill, tennis court, park, lake, or other recreational property. The owner has control over the design and maintenance of his or her home, subject to registered restrictions, and the advantages of a shared private recreational facility. Common elements condominiums provide a creative legal structure for designing planned, gated communities that cater to a wide range of lifestyle preferences traditionally related to recreational facilities. In theory, a common elements condominium could focus on a private road, a small lake or water resource, or a unique natural feature. The parcels of tied land linked to the common area could be developed in the future as standard, leasehold, or phased condominiums, resulting in clusters of condominiums sharing common facilities and features. However, this type of condominium also offers special interest groups a private legal structure in which to pursue, for example, an environmentally responsible, sustainable community, or possibly a private wilderness preserve.

A common elements condominium corporation is defined as a corporation in which a declaration and a description create common elements but do not divide the land into units. Each owner of a common interest in a common elements condominium must also own the freehold estate in a parcel of land that is not included in the land described in the condominium's description. The common interest of an owner in the corporation attaches to the owner's freehold parcel of land and is registered on the title of the owner's parcel. The parcel of tied land is referred to as the "POTL". The ownership of the POTL cannot be conveyed separately from the ownership of the linked common elements. The POTL does not have to adjoin the common elements condominium (for example, a ski hill); it can be miles away, although the tied parcels and the common areas must all fall within the boundaries or jurisdiction of a single registry office (*Condominium Act*, s. 139). POTLs are not governed by the condominium declaration and rules; however, they are usually subject to an extensive restrictive covenant scheme. Positive covenants set out in the registered declaration run with the parcels tied to the common elements, in perpetuity. The owners of the POTLs are individually responsible for the repair and maintenance of their properties including landscaping and snow removal. A common elements condominium is prohibited from contracting for services to POTLs and including them in the common expenses.

In effect, the owner of a common elements condominium owns both a common interest in the common elements and a freehold interest in the parcel of land to which the common interest is permanently attached. The common interest of the owner in the corporation cannot be terminated or severed from the attached or tied parcel except on termination of the condominium. As a result, when the purchase of a common elements condominium takes place, the purchaser's solicitor must complete two separate title searches, one for the POTL and one for the common elements condominium.

A common expenses lien will be registered against the owner's parcel of land if an owner defaults on a common expenses payment (*Condominium Act*, s. 139(5)).

The POTL is not a unit and is therefore not exempt from s. 50 *Planning Act* part lot control unless exempted by by-law. However, subdivision control provisions under s. 50 of the *Planning Act* do not apply to dealings with common interests in a common elements condominium corporation (*Planning Act*, s. 39.1). As a result, an owner of a common elements condominium can transfer or mortgage its interest in the common elements when the POTL adjoins the common areas.

A common elements condominium corporation cannot be a vacant land condominium corporation or a phased condominium corporation (except as provided in the regulations made under the *Condominium Act, 1998*).

Phased Condominium Corporations

A phased condominium corporation is a freehold condominium in which the declarant may create additional units or common elements in subsequent phases, over a ten-year period, after the registration of the condominium. New phases are added to the original condominium by registering an amendment to the existing declaration and description. Information about the planned phases is included in both the declaration and the disclosure statement and must be included in status certificates. The registration of an amended declaration for a new phase does not require the consent of the existing owners, although changes in the planned phases require the consent of the existing owners. In the past, new phases were legally structured and registered as a separate condominium corporation. A phased condominium corporation cannot be a vacant land condominium corporation or a common elements condominium corporation (except as provided in the regulations made under the Act). Generally, phased condominiums are standard condominiums. Standard, legally separate condominiums built in sequence may share costs and recreational facility maintenance. These condominiums are often referred to in promotional material as phased or phase 1 and 2 *etc.*, despite the fact that they are not phased condominiums under the Act, and thus subject to the regulation and disclosure requirements for phased condominiums under statute.

Vacant Land Condominium Corporations

A purchaser of a vacant land condominium can purchase a unit representing a vacant (building) lot and later build a dwelling subject to the restrictions in the declaration. The declaration of a vacant land condominium contains detailed covenants and restrictions that control the future buildings. A vacant land condominium corporation is defined as a freehold condominium in which, at the time of registration, one or more units are not part of a building or structure and do not include any part of a building or structure, and in which none of the units is located above or below any other unit. Owners in a vacant land condominium purchase a unit and a common interest in the common elements, and are responsible for common expense payments.

Section 156(1) of the *Condominium Act, 1998* states:

Contents of declaration

156. (1) If a unit in a vacant land condominium corporation is to include a building or structure constructed after the registration of the declaration and description, the declaration may contain restrictions with respect to,

    (a) the size, location, construction standards, quality of materials and appearance of the building or structure;

    (b) architectural standards and construction design standards of the building or structure;

    (c) the time of commencement and completion of construction of the building or structure; and

    (d) the minimum maintenance requirements for the building or structure.

The owner of a unit in a vacant land condominium corporation maintains the unit and repairs it after damage. The vacant land condominium corporation maintains the common elements and repairs them after damage. A vacant land condominium cannot be a phased, a common elements, or a leasehold condominium.

Leasehold Condominiums

Institutions such as universities, churches, hospitals, government (affordable housing initiatives), or First Nations (reserve lands) may wish or only be able to lease long-term instead of selling lands that they own. Another example of a leasehold condominium is a condominium hotel based on a ground lease. Condominium hotels are often recreational properties, such as The Rousseau at Red Leaves in Muskoka. Leasehold condominiums are built on land leased from a freehold owner pursuant to a ground lease instead of on land owned by the developer. Unit owners pay common expense payments which include ground lease rent to be paid to the ground lease landlord. When the underlying ground lease expires, the unit owners will cease to own an interest in condominium lands, buildings, or units.

The declarant of a leasehold condominium registers a declaration and description that divide the leasehold estate in the land described in the description into units and common elements. The declaration for a leasehold condominium corporation must contain the terms, such as rent, of the ground lease and the provisions of the leasehold interests that affect the property, the corporation, and the owners. Provisions of the leasehold interests in the property are not binding on the property, the corporation, or the owners unless the declaration sets them out and states that they are binding. The ground lease cannot be less than 40 years less a day and not more than 99 years (*Condominium Act, 1998*, s. 165). It can be renewed for at least ten years or for a greater term (*Condominium Act, 1998*, s. 174(2)). If the lessor does not give notice of renewal, the lease is deemed to be renewed for ten years. A purchaser buys a leasehold interest for a fixed number of years in the unit and appurtenant common elements. All leasehold interests in units in a leasehold condominium corporation and their appurtenant common interests must be for the same term. The unit purchaser should read the lease as well as the declaration to determine how it may affect the unit. For example, the ground lease will have terms that govern rent increases and these increases will in turn trigger increases in common expenses. A unit owner may not transfer, charge or lease less than the whole leasehold interest in the unit and its appurtenant common interests. A unit owner may transfer, mortgage or lease his or her unit without the consent of the lessor of the ground lease. Unit common expense payments include a *pro rata* share for the ground lease rent. Phased condominiums, vacant land condominiums and common elements condominiums may not be registered as leasehold condominiums. Part XIII of the Act deals with leasehold condominiums.

The *Residential Tenancies Act, 2006*, S.O. 2006, c. 17 does not apply to the leasehold interest of an owner of a unit in a leasehold condominium; but it does apply to a lease of an owner's leasehold interest in a unit.

Amalgamated Condominiums

Standard or leasehold condominiums, registered as separate condominium corporations, may amalgamate for the purpose of sharing and reducing costs. Only same form condominiums such as several standard freehold condominiums can amalgamate. The new amalgamated condominium documents are on the current condominium Property Identification Number (PIN) registers.

IMPORTANT TERMS

Units

Each owner is entitled to the exclusive ownership and use of the owner's unit, subject to the *Condominium Act, 1998*, the declaration, and the by-laws. The condominium declaration and description define and designate units in a condominium. Section 1(1) of the Act defines "unit" as "a part of the property designated as a unit by the description and includes the space enclosed by its boundaries and all the land, structures, and fixtures within this space in accordance with the declaration and description". Units represent those parts of the condominium that are individually owned; for example, the personal living, parking allocations, and storage space in a town house or apartment development, or a vacant lot in a vacant land condominium corporation. The configuration, location, and size of a unit vary and should be determined by reference to the condominium declaration and description schedules and to the floor plans. A standard unit extends from the upper surfaces of the concrete floor to the lower surface of the concrete ceiling or roof joists, and the backside of the interior drywall, including interior surfaces of exterior doors and windows.

Depending on how a condominium has been organized, a purchaser may purchase one unit that contains residential, parking, and storage space or instead may purchase three separate units, one for residential purposes, one for the garage or parking space, and one for a storage area. Often a purchaser will purchase additional parking units, depending on personal lifestyle. Again, it is necessary to refer to the declaration and description for a specific condominium in order to determine the exact nature and extent of units because identical structures may be organized differently. Parking space allocation requires special attention, including client/lawyer review, as it is often misunderstood by purchasers and has proven to be at higher risk of a potential title insurance or lawyer negligence claim. Parking may be structured as a separate unit, a common elements exclusive use area, or simply part of the common elements to be allocated at the discretion of the board. Clients should initial parking space allocations on condominium plans.

Common Elements

Depending on the structure of the condominium, common elements might include foundation and superstructure, roofs, external walls, elevators, heating systems, lobbies, hallways, laundry rooms, party rooms, recreational facilities, parking lots, gardens, private roads, and a variety of other common areas and facilities. Common elements condominiums are composed of common elements only; these common elements are tied to separately owned, freehold parcels.

Common elements include all condominium property except the units. The unit owners are tenants in common of the common elements and an undivided interest in the common elements is appurtenant to each owner's unit. The condominium declaration sets out the common elements and any conditions or restrictions that affect the occupation and use of the common elements. The ownership of a unit cannot be separated from the ownership of the common interest in the common elements. The common elements cannot be partitioned or divided other than by a sale approved by the owners. Section 98 of the *Condominium Act, 1998* sets out the circumstances under which either the condominium or the owner may make an addition, alteration, or improvement to the common elements that is not contrary to the Act or the declaration. The board may by resolution approve a proposed addition, alteration or improvement by an owner and enter into an agreement with the owner setting out the conditions of the change to the common elements. Construction liens relating to common areas may not be enforced against the common elements; instead, the Act provides that they are enforceable against the individual units proportionate to their common interests.

Exclusive Use Areas

The declaration may designate certain parts of the common elements, such as balconies, front yards and/or back yards, gardens, patios, locker and parking spaces, and boat slips for the exclusive use of an owner of a particular unit or a group of unit owners. Exclusive use areas are set out in a schedule to the declaration and illustrated on the condominium plan. It is important to reconcile unit description, common elements, and exclusive use common elements in the declaration with what is listed on the agreement of purchase and sale, disclosed in the status certificate, and with what the purchaser believes he or she is purchasing. It is prudent to have the purchaser initial the location of unit-related exclusive use areas on the condominium plan sheet.

Common Expenses

Common expenses are defined as the costs of performance of the objects and duties of a condominium corporation. Permitted common expenses are specified in the *Condominium Act, 1998* and in a specific condominium's declaration.

Common expenses may include maintenance and repair of the common elements, management, legal fees, insurance, banking and accounting fees, landscaping, snow removal, garbage disposal, lighting, and security. In leasehold condominiums, ground lease rent payments are factored into the common expenses. Common expenses can be based on usage of the common elements as long as the declaration authorizes usage formulas (bifurcated common expenses) and the usage calculation scheme is in the disclosure documents. Common elements condominiums and vacant land condominiums often have complicated formulas that calculate and assess common expenses based on usage and percentage of buildings ready for occupation, particularly in staged developments.

The condominium prepares an annual budget estimate and the unit owners contribute monthly one-twelfth of their annual proportionate share as set out in the declaration. This proportionate percentage share in the common expenses, which is assigned to each unit, is set out in a schedule to the declaration. The unit owners' proportionate share in the assets of the corporation is called the common interest. If a unit owner is in arrears for more than 30 days, the owner loses the right to vote (*Condominium Act, 1998*, s. 49).

Common Expense Liens

Sections 85 and 86 of the *Condominium Act, 1998* create a special lien and enforcement procedure for common expense arrears. Common expense arrears attach to the unit, not a specific owner. Purchasers and lenders require disclosure of arrears in common expenses in status certificates. The condominium must, within three months of a default in the payment of common expenses by a unit owner, register a notice of lien against the unit on the unit register. Once registered, the lien, interest owing, reasonable legal costs and collection expenses, and any future defaults are secured against the unit. When, prior to the registration of a lien, a condominium corporation gives notice by personal service or registered mail to unit mortgagees, the lien will acquire priority over the mortgages. A Form 14 (notice) must be given to the owner ten days before the registration of the lien. The lien can be enforced in the same manner as a mortgage; for example, by foreclosure, by power of sale, or by redirecting rent from the tenant of a leased unit.

In a common elements condominium, a common expenses lien is registered against the owner's POTL.

Repair and Maintenance

Unit owners are responsible for the maintenance and normal wear and tear of their units. The condominium corporation is responsible for the maintenance of the common elements as well as the repair of units and common elements after damage. Section 91 of the Act allows the declaration to alter the obligation to maintain or to repair units or common elements after damage. Condominium ownership demands collective financial responsibility. The condominium may levy special assessments for repair and maintenance purposes or to build up an inadequate reserve fund. Proposed and current special assessments should be disclosed in the status certificate. Special assessments and disclosure requirements in status certificates and agreements of purchase and sale have generated considerable case law often focused on when and whether the condominium or seller had knowledge of proposed special assessments.

Reserve Funds

Section 93 of the *Condominium Act, 1998* requires all condominiums to establish and maintain one or more reserve funds for major repairs and replacement of the common elements and assets of the condominium, such as roofs, roads, underground parking, elevators, building exteriors, recreational facilities, and heating, electrical and plumbing services, *etc*. The corporation collects contributions to the reserve fund as part of unit owners' contributions to the common expenses. Generally, reserve funds are not and should not be adjusted on closing; however, parties may agree separately by contract (agreement of purchase and sale) how to deal with reserve fund adjustments. Standard condominium agreements of purchase and sale such as the Toronto Real Estate Board Form specifically state that reserve funds will not be adjusted on closing. Reserve funds should be considered as part of the "bricks and mortar"; they can only be distributed to owners on the termination of a condominium.

Reserve fund studies are required to assess the adequacy of existing reserve funds and to determine the contribution rate necessary to create an adequate reserve fund in future. Condominium boards must produce a plan to ensure the adequacy of reserve funds. The board must give all owners and the condominium auditor a summary of the reserve fund study and the board plan, and disclose any areas in which the proposed plan differs from the study. Prior to the completion of a reserve fund study and plan, the contribution to the reserve must be not less than ten per cent of the contribution to the common expenses exclusive of the reserve fund. The Act requires that all new condominiums must complete a reserve fund study within a year of registration of the declaration and description. Following a reserve fund study, the reserve fund contribution must be the greater of the amount that is reasonably expected to provide sufficient funds for the major repair and replacement of the common elements and assets of the corporation, calculated on the basis of expected repair and replacement costs and the life expectancy of the common elements and assets of the corporation, or ten per cent of the budgeted amount required for contributions to the common expenses exclusive of the reserve fund (*Condominium Act, 1998*, s. 93(6)). Existing condominiums must complete a study by May 5, 2004. Periodic studies are required every three years. Ontario Regulation 48/01 sets out detailed requirements for reserve funds and reserve fund studies.

Performance Audit

Residential condominiums and common elements condominiums require the completion of a performance audit (engineering study) involving an inspection of the common elements, such as underground parking garages, roof, walls, foundation, elevators, heating, electrical and water systems, and an owner survey. The purpose of the audit is to reveal deficiencies in the common elements. The performance audit must take place between six and ten months following the registration of the condominium (*Condominium Act, 1998*, s. 44). The performance audit should reveal any major problems prior to the 12-month deadline for submitting warranty claims under the Ontario New Homes Warranty Program.

Compliance and Enforcement Remedies

Part IX of the *Condominium Act, 1998* offers stakeholders in a condominium the following options for resolving disputes:

1. Appointment of an inspector — A lessor of a leasehold condominium corporation, an owner or a mortgagee of a unit may apply to the Superior Court of Justice for the appointment of an inspector. An inspector has the power to investigate condominium administration, corporation records, or the actions of a condominium unit owner, mortgagee or declarant. An inspector may conduct an audit of the accounts and records. An inspector has the same powers as the commission under Part II of the *Public Inquiries Act*, R.S.O. 1990, c. P.41.

2. Appointment of an administrator — An administrator may be appointed when it is found to be in the best interests of the owners.

3. Mediation and arbitration — Mediation and arbitration are available to resolve disputes involving agreements affecting condominium corporations and unit owners.

4. Compliance order — An owner, an occupier of a proposed unit, a corporation, a declarant, a lessor of a leasehold condominium corporation or a mortgagee of a unit may make an application to the Superior Court of Justice for an order enforcing compliance with any provision of the *Condominium Act, 1998*, the declaration, the by-laws, the rules or an agreement between two or more corporations for the mutual use, provision, maintenance or cost-sharing of facilities or services of any of the parties to the agreement.

5. Oppression remedy — The stakeholders in a condominium, for example, a unit owner, a corporation, a declarant, or a mortgagee, may make an application to the Superior Court of Justice for an order for compensation or prohibiting conduct on the grounds that the conduct of an owner, a corporation, a declarant or a mortgagee of a unit is or

threatens to be oppressive or unfairly prejudicial, or unfairly disregards the interests of the applicant.

6. Offences — When a person knowingly contravenes certain sections of the Act, there is a fine of not more than $100,000 for a corporation, and a fine of not more than $25,000 for a person.

Construction Liens

Pre-POLARIS, a construction lien against the condominium was registered in the Common Elements and General Register. Now a construction lien against a condominium is entered on all the PIN registers. Construction liens are not enforced against the common elements; they are the combined financial responsibility of all the unit owners and are enforceable against the units (*Condominium Act, 1998*, s. 13). Section 13 of the Act allows the proportionate discharge of encumbrances registered prior to the registration of the declaration and the description; it does not permit the proportionate discharge of encumbrances registered after the registration of the declaration and the description. Holdbacks or adjustments or abatements in the purchase price can also be used to deal with construction liens.

CONDOMINIUM DOCUMENTS

A condominium is created by the act of registering condominium documents in a land registration system. Registered condominium creation documents combined with unregistered documents and agreements, within the environment of condominium legislation and case law, structure the rights and responsibilities of owners in a particular condominium corporation. New forms of condominium ownership introduced under the *Condominium Act, 1998* have added an additional layer of complexity to condominium documentation and conveyancing.

Condominium conveyancing involves complex specialized documents, combined with additional searches and file procedures. Contrary to public opinion, it is more challenging for the lawyer and presents greater risk of client dissatisfaction, than the routine residential real estate transaction. The client often lacks both understanding of condominium documentation and knowledge of the complicated rights, risks, and obligations inherent in condominium ownership, and particularly communal financial responsibility.

Declaration

On registration, the declaration and description provide the legal foundation for the condominium corporation. The declaration contains: a description of the units and common elements; an allocation of ownership of the common elements and common expenses; a designation of exclusive use areas; a specification of common expenses; restrictions on use and occupation of units; restrictions on pets; restrictions on leases; sales and gifts of units and common elements; repair and maintenance allocations; and service and mailing addresses. Declarations contain a series of required schedules, being Schedule A through Schedule G (O. Reg. 48/01). Schedule A describes the land and easements. Schedule B contains the consent of the mortgagees. Schedule C contains the unit boundaries. Schedule D contains each unit's proportionate share in the common interest and contribution to the common expenses. Schedule E sets out what is covered by the common expenses. Schedule F lists the exclusive use common elements. Schedule G is the engineer and architect's certificate of *Condominium Act* compliance parking space allocation and organization, be it a unit, a common elements exclusive use area, or part of the common elements subject to a user/rental fee is set out in the declaration and is of special importance to most purchasers. Leasing restrictions, adult-only restrictions, pet restrictions, and parking allocation, be it for owners, visitors, or the disabled, have all generated an increased risk of litigation.

The *Condominium Act, 1998* requires that a condominium declaration must state whether the corporation is a freehold condominium corporation or a leasehold condominium corporation. If the condominium corporation is a freehold condominium corporation, the declaration must state which type of freehold condominium corporation it is. Additional information is found in the declarations, particularly the schedules of leasehold condominiums, common elements condominiums, vacant land condominiums, and phased condominiums.

Leasehold Condominium

The declaration of a leasehold condominium includes a statement that the registration of the declaration and description create a leasehold condominium corporation, the term of the leasehold interests of the owners, the amount of the rent payable, the dates the rent is payable for the first five years, a formula for calculating the rent payable for the remainder of the term of the lease, a schedule stating all provisions of the ground lease that affect the property, the corporation and the owners (for example, renewal terms), and a statement that the lease may be terminated according to its terms and the *Condominium Act, 1998*.

Common Elements Condominium

The declaration of a common elements condominium includes a statement that the registration of the declaration and description creates a common elements corporation, a statement that the common elements are included for the use and enjoyment of the owners, and a legal description of the tied parcels. In addition to the legal description of the tied parcels, it contains a list of the common interest percentages that attach to each tied parcel, and detailed information on all buildings, structures, facilities, and services that are part of the common elements. It contains a list of any common elements that are restricted to the use of one or more POTLs. The declaration contains the consent of all mortgagees of the common elements and the POTLs and all owners of the POTLs to the registration of the condominium.

Phased Condominium Corporation

The declaration of a phased condominium corporation includes a statement that the registration of the declaration and description creates a phased condominium corporation. The declaration and description must describe the developer's land available for future phases. New phases containing additional units and common elements are created by registering an amendment to both the existing declaration and the description. The amendment outlines the changes in units, common interests and common elements, including easements and exclusive use areas.

Vacant Land Condominium

The declaration of a vacant land condominium corporation includes a statement that the registration of the declaration and description create a vacant land condominium corporation. When a vacant land condominium plans for the construction of buildings following registration, the declaration sets out restrictions respecting size, location, construction standards, quality of materials, building appearance, architectural and construction design standards, commencement and completion times for buildings, and minimum maintenance standards for the buildings. Additional restrictions are usually registered on title as with restrictive covenants for plans of subdivisions. The declaration and description of a vacant land condominium may not be registered until all common elements buildings and structures (for example, a recreational facility such as a golf club) have been completed, or the developer has provided security such as a performance bond or security units to the municipality.

Description/Plan

The description includes a survey showing the perimeter of the land and buildings, architectural and structural building plans, the boundaries of each unit, and diagrams showing the shape and dimensions of each unit and the approximate location of each unit in relation to the other units and the buildings, and the exclusive use areas of the common elements.

Additional information is found in the descriptions, particularly the schedules of leasehold condominiums, common elements condominiums, vacant land condominiums, and phased condominiums. A common elements condominium description does not contain architectural plans unless the common elements include buildings or structures. A phased condominium description sets out the original phase and the land available for future phases. A vacant land condominium description includes plans for existing or future buildings and structures on the common elements.

By-Laws

The condominium board can pass by-laws governing the day-to-day conduct of the condominium. Developers are not required to create by-laws. By-laws involve: governance and management matters including directors, officers, agents and employees of the corporation; indemnification of directors; meetings; owners' meeting quorum; management of the property; insurance perils and deductibles; leases over the common elements; maintenance of units and common elements; use and management of condominium assets; restrictions on use of common elements by non-residents; occupancy standards (maximum number of occupants for each unit); mediation and arbitration procedures; duties of the corporation; assessment collection and contribution towards the common expenses; and borrowing of money. By-laws often govern the use of the common elements; easements and licences over the common elements must be authorized by by-law.

By-law No. 1 usually relates to the general administration/operation of the condominium. By-law No. 2 is normally the borrowing by-law. Additional by-laws may relate specifically to management agreements, reciprocal agreements for phased condominiums, insurance trust agreements, *etc.* Specific by-laws authorize mediation and arbitration forums for unit owners and shared facilities agreements. By-laws must be reasonable and consistent with the *Condominium Act, 1998* and the declaration. For a by-law to be legally effective it must be passed by the board of directors and confirmed by the owners of a majority of the units at a meeting duly called for that purpose, and registered in the Registry office. By-laws are repealed by the registration of by-laws. Registered by-laws may be unenforceable depending on enforcement practices and case law. For example, by-laws containing prohibitions on keeping animals and on sales and leases to persons with children have been held to be invalid.

Rules

The condominium board may make reasonable rules respecting the use of common elements and units to promote the safety, security, or welfare of the owners and the property, and for the purpose of preventing unreasonable interference with the use and enjoyment of the common elements and of other units (*Condominium Act, 1998*, s. 58). Section 58(2) requires rules to be "reasonable and consistent" with the Act, the declaration, and the by-laws. Typically, these rules regulate what may become emotionally charged issues, such as pets, noise, garbage, parking, moving, security and access, and use of pools and other recreational facilities.

Rules are not required to be registered on title although the original rules may be attached to a registered by-law. Each owner must be given notice of the rules for them to be legally effective. As rules may create important restrictions on an owner's use of a unit and the common elements, the purchaser's lawyer must obtain the up-to-date rules in a condominium status certificate formerly called an estoppel certificate.

Management Agreement

Condominiums may be self-managed by members (unit owners) or professionally managed by way of a management agreement. Some lenders will lend only to professionally managed condominiums. It is useful to remember that the quality of management is essential to financial well-being as well as to the quality of life in a condominium development. Management agreements are not registered on title.

Insurance Trust Agreement

A condominium corporation must obtain insurance, on its own behalf and on behalf of the owners, for damage to the units and common elements that is caused by major perils or other perils specified in the declaration or by-laws. A condominium may retain an insurance trustee by way of an insurance trust agreement to receive and distribute impartially condominium corporation insurance proceeds, or the board of directors may receive and distribute the moneys directly. Lenders may require the existence of an insurance trust agreement both as a condition of lending on a unit and as an assurance of a well-run condominium. Insurance trust agreements are not registered on title. The condominium corporation may terminate an insurance trust agreement by giving at least 60 days' notice in writing of the termination date to the trustee, despite the wording of the agreement (*Condominium Act, 1998*, s. 114). In the last decade, most insurance trust arrangements only take effect when the damage is in excess of 15 per cent of the fair market value of the property. The unit holder and condominium coverage are interlocking and a unit holder must carefully reconcile personal unit coverage with corporation coverage.

Agreements Concerning Alteration of Common Elements by Unit Owners

Additions, removals, and improvements to units need board approval, compliance with condominium documents, and potentially municipal approval. Unit owners may enter into agreements between the unit owner and the condominium to alter a unit or unit-related common elements, such as the building or extension of a deck, patio, or fence, or changes in windows and doors. Agreements to alter common elements set out the conditions of the change to the common elements and the responsibilities of the unit owner to repair and maintain these alterations. These agreements and compliance with these agreements should be disclosed in the status certificate (*Condominium Act, 1998*, s. 98(1)). Agreements that allow unit owners to alter common elements become effective when registered on title and bind subsequent owners.

Status Certificate (Estoppel Certificate)

Condominiums are required by law to provide, on request, a status certificate, previously called an estoppel certificate, to purchasers and lenders (*Condominium Act, 1998*, s. 76). Anyone can order a certificate but only a purchaser or lender has the right to rely on the contents of the certificate. Purchasers require status certificates on final closing. A condominium resale agreement of purchase and sale should be conditional on review and approval of a status certificate.

The status certificate discloses detailed information about the financial and business status of the condominium. The status certificate includes: information about the description of all relevant units including parking units and storage units; parking allocation and storage area when part of the common elements or exclusive use areas; monthly common expenses; any arrears in common expenses; increases in common expenses; the absence of common expense liens; the number of units leased; the current mailing and service addresses; the most current budget statement; types of reserve funds; the existence of a reserve fund study; the amount in the reserve funds within the past 90 days; any indication that the reserve fund is inadequate; an intent to increase the reserve fund; reserve fund assessments and annual contributions; prospective common expense increases; the specifics of anticipated increases in utility costs; special assessments current or contemplated; proposed changes to the common elements; current or pending involvement in legal action; changes in the common elements under consideration; proposed applications to amend the declaration; confirmation of appropriate insurance and certificates of insurance; unauthorized use(s) by owners; names, addresses and phone numbers of the directors, officers and property manager of the condominium; and a copy of the current declaration, by-laws, and rules. The *Condominium Act, 1998* regulations may require additional information (*Condominium Act, 1998*, s. 76(1)). The status certificate must disclose any agreements to alter unit-related common elements such as an extension of a deck, patio, or fence between the owner and the condominium and set out the conditions of the change to the common elements. This agreement should be registered on title. The information disclosed in the status certificate must conform to the warranties and representations in the agreement of purchase and sale.

The status certificate is signed by an officer of the condominium and incorporates copies of up-to-date condominium documents, including: the current by-laws and rules; the management agreement; the insurance trust agreement and insurance certificates; the current budget statement; reserve fund studies and plans; the most recent audited annual financial statement (condominium of less than 25 units can vote annually not to audit statements); court applications; court orders (appointment of inspector); and outstanding judgments.

A purchaser or lender may rely on a current status certificate, dated no earlier than 60 days prior to closing, regardless of who actually obtained it. The condominium must give the status certificate within ten days of a request accompanied by payment of the corporation's fee. The Act limits condominium corporations to a maximum charge for a status certificate of $100, inclusive of all taxes (G.S.T.) (O. Reg. 48/01, s. 18(2)). If a status certificate is not delivered within the ten days (*Condominium Act, 1998*, s. 76(5)), then a certificate is deemed given on the day immediately after the required time has expired (day 11) stating that:

(a) there has been no default in the payment of common expenses for the unit;

(b) the board has not declared any increase in the common expenses for the unit since the date of the budget of the corporation for the current fiscal year; and

(c) the board has not levied any assessments against the unit since the date of the budget of the corporation for the current fiscal year to increase the contribution to the reserve fund.

If the certificate does not contain the required information, it is deemed to include a statement that the omitted information does not exist.

Section 76(1), O. Reg. 48/01, and Form 13 set out in detail the required format and the required content of a status certificate. Copies of the condominium documents (declaration, description, by-laws, and rules), budget statement, audited financial statements and auditor's report, applications to amend the declaration, schedule that defines the standard unit, s. 94(8) agreements that bind the unit (alteration agreements), notice of plan for future funding of a reserve fund, order appointing and inspector (*Condominium Act, 1998*, s. 130) or an administrator (*Condominium Act, 1998*, s. 131) are attached to the status certificate. In addition, the status certificate contains a list of relevant documents, copies of which must be made available on request. The condominium can charge a reasonable amount for copies of these agreements. This list includes condominium agreements such as management agreements and mutual use agreements.

Additional statements are required for leasehold condominiums, phased condominiums, common elements condominiums, and vacant land condominiums. For example, the status certificate for a leasehold condominium contains a statement as to whether the provisions of the leasehold interests in the property are in good standing, any unregistered lease renewal provisions, or whether the landlord has applied for a termination order (*Condominium Act, 1998*, s. 170). The status certificate for a common elements condominium refers to common interests and tied parcels instead of units. The status certificate for a phased condominium contains a disclosure statement for the phase containing the unit unless all phases have been completed and the declarant does not own any units in the condominium (*Condominium Act, 1998*, s. 148). As well, a phased condominium status certificate indicates which phases have and have not been completed.

Budget Statement

The budget statement sets out each unit's common expense allocation and the formulas involved in assessing common expenses. Common expenses assessments are based on units. The individual owner's assessment will be based on the aggregate of the residential unit and any related parking and storage units.

Interim Occupancy Licence

New condominiums have a two-stage closing: the interim or occupancy closing and the final transfer of title closing. Interim occupancy is governed by s. 80 of the Act. TARION allows for the extension of interim occupancy dates. Between interim and final closing, the occupant pays the builder an occupancy fee, usually by post-dated cheque that cannot exceed monthly interest of the unpaid purchase price, estimated monthly unit taxes, and projected monthly common expense fees (*Condominium Act, 1998*, s. 80(4)). Builders grant a contractual licence interest in the unit to the purchaser that governs utilities, assignment, and in general the period up to the final closing. Interim occupancy fees are estimated and re-adjusted on final closing.

Disclosure Statement

Disclosure statements are a form of consumer protection for purchasers of a complex, highly regulated form of property ownership, that of condominium units and common interests. They provide the purchaser with comprehensive, detailed information about a specific condominium project and an opportunity to rescind or vary an existing purchase agreement. Under the new Act, disclosure statements are required for all types of condominium corporations, whereas under the previous Act, they were only required for residential condominium corporations.

The declarant (developer) of a condominium project must deliver a copy of the current disclosure statement to every person who purchases a new unit or proposed new unit from the declarant. The purchaser of a new unit or new common interest in a common elements condominium is not bound by the agreement of purchase and sale until delivery of the current disclosure package. The purchaser has a ten-day cooling-off period, from the date of receiving the disclosure statement or a material amendment to a disclosure statement, in which to rescind or renegotiate the purchase agreement. Section 72 of the Act, O. Reg. 48/01, and Form 12 outline the content and form requirements for a disclosure package.

A disclosure statement is a massive document. It starts with a table of contents that contains pages of detailed information and it includes all significant documents that affect the creation and governance of the corporation and the ownership rights and responsibilities of the unit owners. A disclosure statement includes the name and address of the declarant and the property, a description of the property and recreational facilities, and a statement as to the type of condominium, and whether it is a conversion. It includes information about common interests and common elements; units designated for investors; units designated for commercial use; prohibition on gambling, adult entertainment, and alcohol sales in commercial units; units and common areas for proposed leases; minimum length leasing requirements; restrictions on use of the units or common elements; restrictions on pets; parking arrangements; type, frequency and level of services; whether utilities are "smart" metered separately (required by December 31, 2010 by the *Energy Conservation Responsibility Act, 2006*, S.O. 2006, c. 3) or included in the common expense fee; whether the water heater is rented or owned; coverage and enrolment under the *Ontario New Home Warranties Plan Act*, R.S.O. 1990, c. O.31; by-laws; rules; significant terms of current contracts such as management, service, mutual use, common elements leases, and insurance trust agreements; budget statement details; reserve fund studies and plans; amalgamation plans; and a schedule for completion. The disclosure statement includes copies of the declaration and description, rules, and insurance trust agreement.

The disclosure packages for leasehold, phased, common elements, and vacant land condominiums must contain additional information. For example, the disclosure statement for a leasehold condominium must contain a statement as to whether the provisions of the leasehold interests in the property are in good standing. The disclosure statement for a phased condominium contains information about each phase that the declarant plans to create and a statement that no amendments to the declaration creating new phases can be registered after ten years from the registration of the original condominium. The disclosure statement for a common elements condominium contains a list of buildings, structures, facilities, and services to be included in the common elements. A vacant land condominium disclosure statement includes a statement setting out the restrictions with respect to the construction of a building following registration of the declaration.

CONDOMINIUM CORPORATIONS INDEX

The land registrar maintains a Condominium Corporations Index listing in a land registration division all registered condominiums by assigned name and number and address for service. The land registrar also maintains a Condominium Register, which contains declarations, descriptions, by-laws, and notices of termination.

CONDOMINIUM NAMING

On registration of the declaration and description of a new condominium, the land registrar assigns to the declaration and description an identification in the form of "Condominium Plan No.__" with the next available consecutive number. The condominium description is given a name that includes the Land Titles or Land Registry division, excluding the number of the division, *e.g.*, "Middlesex Condominium Plan No. 678". The condominium declaration and description include the type of condominium, such as leasehold or common elements condominium.

The new condominium is registered on the relevant parcel that contains the registration history of the parcel prior to the creation of the condominium. Following the creation of the condominium by registration of the declaration and the description, each unit is given a PIN and all current registrations are brought forward and all new registrations are entered on the condominium PIN registers. Depending on the structure of the condominium, it is allocated level identifications such as Level 1, 2, 3, *etc.* Levels below grade are named Level A, B, C, *etc.* Levels and unit numbers may or may not be related to suite or residence numbers.

Under the new Act, the type of corporation is now included in the name of the condominium as follows:

- "Standard"   for a standard, phased, or amalgamated condominium corporation;
- "Common Elements"   for a common elements condominium corporation;
- "Vacant Land"   for a vacant land condominium corporation; and
- "Leasehold"   for a leasehold condominium corporation.

Condominium names are referred to by prefixes in condominium registers, descriptions, documents, and Teraview (POLARIS records) search inquiries. Under the new Act, the prefix for the type of corporation is now included in the name of the condominium as follows:

- "S"   for a standard, phased, or amalgamated condominium corporation;
- "CE"   for a common elements condominium corporation;
- "VL"   for a vacant land condominium corporation; and
- "L"   for a leasehold condominium corporation.

In addition, the Ministry has also assigned specific land registry office prefixes, which are available on the Teraview website (see Figure 8.4 in Chapter 8 on automated searching). Some land registry offices have several prefixes depending on location and date of registration. For example, the prefix for York Region is "YRCP". The prefix for Middlesex is "CONDO". Halton uses three different prefixes — HCP, HC, HSTC — depending on the plan number. The combined new naming and numbering systems produce condominium names and references such as the following:

Halton Condominium Corporation (Plan) No. 649   HC No. 649

Halton Standard Condominium Corporation (Plan) No. 649   HSTC No. 649

Halton Common Elements Condominium Corporation (Plan) No. 649   HCEC No. 649

(The parcel of tied land is often referred to as a "POTL")

Halton Vacant Land Condominium Corporation (Plan) No. 649   HVLC No. 649

Halton Leasehold Condominium Corporation (Plan) No. 649   HLC No. 649

CONDOMINIUMS AND PLANNING ACT COMPLIANCE

Condominium units are exempt from compliance with the part lot of control provisions in s. 50 of the *Planning Act*. POTLs are parcels of freehold land in a common elements condominium; they are not units and are therefore not exempt from s. 50 of the *Planning Act*. Section 50 does not apply to "dealings with common interests in a common elements condominium" (*Condominium Act, 1998*, s. 142). The conveyancer must do *Planning Act* compliance searches when dealing with POTLs. POTLs may be exempt as whole lots on an underlying registered plan of subdivision or they may be covered by a part lot control exemption by-law. However, these exemption by-laws are registered to facilitate the launching of the condominium and often expire within two years. Be sure to complete *Planning Act* compliance searches on adjoining lands whenever purchasing, mortgaging, or leasing POTLs. If you are relying on an exemption by-law, be sure to confirm that the by-law was or is in effect at the time of any conveyance where an owner or past owner also retained ownership in an abutting property. Refer to Chapter 11 for a full discussion of how to complete a *Planning Act* compliance search.

THE CONDOMINIUM REGISTER

The condominium register is called a register in Land Titles and an abstract index in Registry. Prior to the POLARIS conversion, the condominium register was made up of four separate registers. When a condominium is automated into the POLARIS record, the four paper registers are consolidated into one condominium parcel (unit) register.

Pre-POLARIS Condominium Register

The pre-POLARIS condominium register consists of four parts: the Property Parcel Register; the Constitution Index; the Common Elements and General Index; and the Unit Register. A conveyancer copies or summarizes the contents of all four registers. After the declaration and description are registered in Land Titles, the land registrar carries out the following:

1. Enters the registration particulars for the declaration and description in the existing parcel register. Where the condominium lands comprise the whole of that parcel, a closing entry is made on the parcel.

2. Opens a new register under the *Condominium Act, 1998* and re-enters the land on the Property Parcel Register. All the documents affecting the land at the time the condominium was registered, such as blanket mortgages, easements, restrictive covenants and development agreements, as well as the new declaration and description, are entered in order of their registration.

3. Opens the Constitution Index and enters the declaration, description and by-laws, including rules and any subsequent amendments.

4. Opens the Common Elements and General Index and enters the declaration, description, and any document that affects all units in the condominium, *e.g.*, documents already entered on the Property Parcel Register. Documents that affect all the units and that are registered after the condominium, such as new blanket mortgages, easements, and construction liens regarding the common elements, are also entered in this register.

5. Opens a Unit Register. The units and levels are recorded in numerical sequence, similar to that of the Land Titles parcel page. To conduct a search, it is necessary to have the name and number of the condominium corporation and the number assigned to each unit and level. The Unit Register contains transfers, charges, assignments of charge, leases, liens, including common expense liens, and other documents that affect only the individual unit. Partial discharges (for individual units) of blanket mortgages and partial discharges of common elements liens recorded on the Property Parcel Register and Common Elements and General Index are entered on the Unit Register.

Where a condominium is registered under the *Registry Act*, R.S.O. 1990, c. R.20, the land registrar proceeds as follows:

1. Enters the declaration and description in the existing abstract book for the condominium property.

2. Opens a Property Abstract Index for the condominium property and abstracts the following:

    •   Certificate of Title as registered under the *Certification of Titles Act*. (It is registered prior to the condominium.)
    •   All documents referred to in Schedules B and C of the certificate of title that are outstanding interests encumbering ownership in the certificate.
    •   The declaration, description and all intervening registered documents affecting the property.

3. Opens a Constitution Index and abstracts the declaration and description.

4. Opens a Common Elements and General Index and records the declaration and description.

5. Opens a Unit Index, *i.e.*, a page for each unit of each level of the condominium property.

THE PRE-POLARIS CONDOMINIUM TITLE SEARCH

It is usually not necessary to search prior to the registration of a condominium either in Land Titles or in Registry. In Registry, a certificate of title must be registered before a condominium declaration may be accepted. Registry condominiums are rare. They existed in a only a few areas where no Land Titles office existed. As well, since condominiums convert easily into POLARIS, they were slated for early conversion. Today, very few condominiums remain in the paper systems. However, pre-POLARIS skills are necessary for historical, environmental, and forensic searching. This section is also useful as a guide to older documents that were brought forward into the new system. For these reasons, most of the search information in this chapter uses examples of condominiums registered in Land Titles under POLARIS.

All condominium registers as well as all relevant Unit Registers must be searched and subsearched. It is important to remember that outstanding blanket charges, agreements, construction liens, easements, condominium by-laws, *etc.*, are not carried forward to the Unit Register.

CONDOMINIUM TITLE SEARCH CHECKLIST

☐   Purchase or compare the registered plan with the copy of the condominium plan from the disclosure statement or status certificate. However, some condominium plans, particularly those illustrating more complex and less regular high-rise projects, contain many pages and you should confirm with the lawyer which plan sheets should be copied, *e.g.*, the base reference plan sheet, the sheet for the first floor, and the sheet for the unit(s) being purchased.

Take care to obtain any plan sheets that show location and dimensions of the unit or units being purchased, including parking, storage, access and exclusive use areas. Obtain a unit sketch and horizontals. Confirm that the units in the agreement of purchase and sale match the plan layout and have the purchaser initial the location of the units (residential, parking, storage) on the plan.

Reference plans laying out easements and rights of way affecting the condominium may also be purchased. Outline/highlight in a contrasting colour

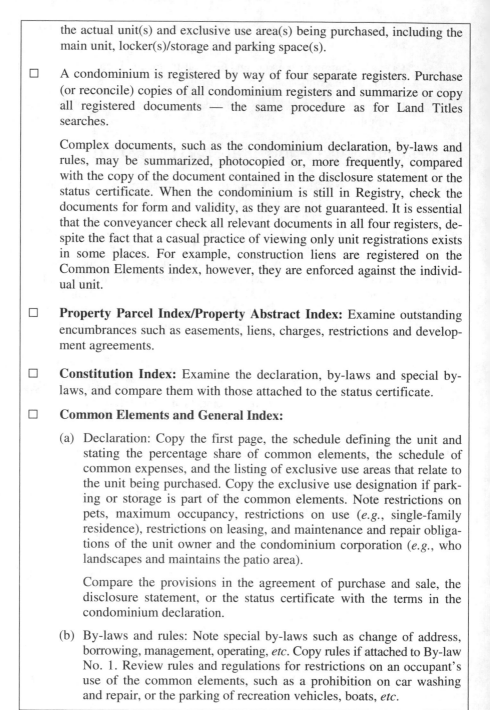

the actual unit(s) and exclusive use area(s) being purchased, including the main unit, locker(s)/storage and parking space(s).

☐ A condominium is registered by way of four separate registers. Purchase (or reconcile) copies of all condominium registers and summarize or copy all registered documents — the same procedure as for Land Titles searches.

Complex documents, such as the condominium declaration, by-laws and rules, may be summarized, photocopied or, more frequently, compared with the copy of the document contained in the disclosure statement or the status certificate. When the condominium is still in Registry, check the documents for form and validity, as they are not guaranteed. It is essential that the conveyancer check all relevant documents in all four registers, despite the fact that a casual practice of viewing only unit registrations exists in some places. For example, construction liens are registered on the Common Elements index, however, they are enforced against the individual unit.

☐ **Property Parcel Index/Property Abstract Index:** Examine outstanding encumbrances such as easements, liens, charges, restrictions and development agreements.

☐ **Constitution Index:** Examine the declaration, by-laws and special by-laws, and compare them with those attached to the status certificate.

☐ **Common Elements and General Index:**

(a) Declaration: Copy the first page, the schedule defining the unit and stating the percentage share of common elements, the schedule of common expenses, and the listing of exclusive use areas that relate to the unit being purchased. Copy the exclusive use designation if parking or storage is part of the common elements. Note restrictions on pets, maximum occupancy, restrictions on use (*e.g.*, single-family residence), restrictions on leasing, and maintenance and repair obligations of the unit owner and the condominium corporation (*e.g.*, who landscapes and maintains the patio area).

Compare the provisions in the agreement of purchase and sale, the disclosure statement, or the status certificate with the terms in the condominium declaration.

(b) By-laws and rules: Note special by-laws such as change of address, borrowing, management, operating, *etc.* Copy rules if attached to By-law No. 1. Review rules and regulations for restrictions on an occupant's use of the common elements, such as a prohibition on car washing and repair, or the parking of recreation vehicles, boats, *etc.*

(c) Review all documents that affect all units as well as the common elements, *e.g.*, blanket mortgages, easements, restrictions, notice of termination of the condominium, construction liens, notices of pending litigation, cautions, *etc.*

(d) Although construction liens are registered on the common elements register, the Act provides that they take effect against individual units proportionate to their common interest.

☐ Unit Register/Unit Index:

(a) The Unit Register page number is made up of a combination of the unit and the floor or level numbers. In a residential condominium, parking, lockers and storage may be set up and conveyed as separate condominium units or they may be assigned to the main units as exclusive use common elements. The offer to purchase should disclose the number and type of units being purchased. Plans of survey are also available showing a detailed description of all the units. For example, when a condominium structures parking as separate units, which may be purchased, a search of the particular parking space unit is also required. Reference to the agreement of purchase and sale will assist a conveyancer in identifying and searching all relevant units.

(b) Examine all registered documents or instruments that affect the unit or units being searched, *e.g.*, transfers, leases, charges, common expense liens, partial discharges on the unit of construction liens or blanket mortgages registered on the Common Elements and General Index, or the Property Parcel Register.

☐ In addition to the registered condominium documents, obtain the up-to-date management and service agreements, the insurance trust agreement, reciprocal use agreements, current disclosure statements, and other related agreements for review by the lawyer. These agreements and statements are obtained from the developer or condominium corporation as part of the status certificate.

☐ Complete an execution/writ search against the exact name(s) of the registered owner(s), as they appear on the Land Titles register, the condominium corporation, and if a mortgage is being placed the purchaser(s) mortgagor(s) as they will appear on title. When acting on the purchase of a new as opposed to a resale condominium unit, the developer will be the registered owner. In Registry, complete an execution search of prior registered owners since the certificate of title; however, today, title insurance provides alternative coverage and does not require an execution search of the condominium corporation, or of the prior owners in Registry. (See Chapter 12 for detailed procedures.)

☐ Whole units, condominium easements, and common interests and dealings with common interests in a common elements condominium are exempt from *Planning Act* s. 50 subdivision control restrictions. *Planning Act* compliance searches and declarations are not required except when dealing with the parcels of tied land (POTLs) in common elements condominiums. POTLs are not exempt and require *Planning Act* searches and compliance. (See Chapter 11 for detailed explanations on the *Planning Act*.)

☐ Confirm legal access from common areas to the nearest public road. Indeed, there have been cases where luxury condominiums did not have legal access. (See Chapter 9.)

☐ Check the survey, which forms part of the condominium description, for encroachments, easements, placement of buildings, set-backs, and other possible zoning requirements.

☐ Complete a Personal Property Security Registration (PPSR) search against the vendor/registered owner and the condominium corporation to find any security interests or liens registered against chattels, including common elements chattels such as furniture and pool equipment. Common elements condominiums can have significant chattels (consider a ski hill or a golf course). Appliances included in the unit purchase could also be subject to executions and security interests against the vendor or the condominium.

☐ Immediately prior to closing, complete a subsearch for title, executions, PPSR, and other off-title inquiries. (See Chapters 13 and 14 for detailed procedures.)

☐ Update status certificates if they were issued more than 60 days prior to closing. Contact the title insurer if the status certificate was issued more than 60 days prior to closing as it may choose to provide coverage between the 60 days and closing. Consider the effect of a delayed closing on the currency of a status certificate.

☐ In addition to the title search: complete other inquiries relevant to a condominium transaction regarding: status certificates; common expense levies and arrears; reserve funds; special assessments for major repairs; insurance; authorizations on exclusive use area common elements improvements; utilities; municipal taxes; Ontario New Home Warranties Plan unit and common elements enrolment; Ontario New Home Warranties Plan deposit receipts; warranties; and certificates of completion, zoning work orders, *etc*. Obtain current status certificates and/or disclosure packages. See below for information on title insurance coverage as an alternative for some off-title inquiries. There are many off-title risks that title insurance does not cover, particularly regarding recreational and common elements properties, such as environmental, water, aboriginal rights, and shoreline issues. Chapter 14 reviews off-title risks and inquiries in detail.

Note: New forms of condominium ownership under the *Condominium Act, 1998* involve modified or additional parcel registers, additional information and additional documents, such as the ground lease and related documents in a leasehold condominium, or the parcel register for the POTL in a common elements condominium. Most new forms of condominiums are recorded within POLARIS The section on searching condominiums in POLARIS, through Teraview, deals more directly with searching the new forms of condominium ownership.

SEARCHING CONDOMINIUMS IN POLARIS

The automated registration system, ELRS, under Part II of the *Land Registration Reform Act*, R.S.O. 1990, c. L.4, consolidates the four condominium registers and their documents into one unit property register printout. This arrangement is much more efficient, since the first three pre-POLARIS registers were common to all unit owners, yet had to be searched separately apart from the unit registers. All information pertaining to a unit is now included on the Teraview printout for the unit's PIN.

The unit is identified by a unique nine-digit PIN. Each condominium is a separate block in POLARIS. During automation, each condominium is assigned a unique five-digit block number. No new block map is created as the existing condominium plan is adequate. The four-digit property identification number is composed of a combination of the condominium unit and level (if available) numbers. For example, Unit 30 on London Condominium Plan No. 649 might convert to PIN 00239-0030 (LT).

The Registry office provides a county-wide paper condominium cross-reference that indexes the condominium unit and level to a PIN. The Teraview website, <http://www.teraview.ca>, under the "Reference Material" heading, provides a province-wide condominium electronic registration cross-reference that indexes condominium unit and level to a PIN.

In Teraview, it is now possible to search by condominium plan. The searcher selects the property search function and then selects "Search by Condominium". The searcher must enter the registration number of the condominium plan and the appropriate office-specific prefix in the search window. A complete list of office-specific condominium prefixes is available on the Teraview website (see Figure 8.4). For example, in order to search Halton Condominium Plan No. 306, Unit 1, Level 1 in Land Registry Office #20, you would enter HC306 in the "Search by Condominium" window (see Figure 7.1). Teraview would then display the cross-reference for Halton Condominium Plan No. 306. Double-click on the line for Unit 1, Level 1 and Teraview then displays the unit's parcel register. When searching other types of condominiums, such as a leasehold condominium, the searcher uses Registry-office-specific and condominium type-specific prefixes according to established condominium naming practices. For example, in order to search a Toronto common elements condominium, you would enter the prefix TCECP13 in the "Search by Condominium" window. These prefixes are constantly changing, so refer to the Teraview website and newsletters for help.

A condominium unit may include storage and a parking space or a garage; however, many condominium corporations contain separate units for the main unit, the storage unit, and the parking unit(s). Each unit has its own PIN and all PINs included in the purchase must be searched. Unfortunately, agreements of purchase and sale do not always list all the units involved in the purchase; it is necessary to confirm units with the purchaser. The condominium declaration and description, as well as cross-references in the property description line for the unit PIN, will allow you to identify all the PINs involved in a particular purchase. A close examination of all condominium plan sheets obtained from the Registry office or couriered from Teranet will assist you in identifying and confirming the exact limits of all units, exclusive use areas, common elements facilities, and POTLs involved.

When searching POLARIS records using Teraview, the searcher has the option of requesting active documents or both active and deleted (since the PIN creation date) instruments. When completing a full search, the required practice is to request both current and deleted instruments despite the fact that condominium units are exempt from the *Planning Act*. Title insurers require a deleted document search as a fraud risk identification condition in the application for coverage. As well, the Ministry advises requesting deleted documents as part of its Real Estate Fraud Action Plan, as does the Law Society of Upper Canada.

Once you have obtained a copy of the condominium plan, the Teraview map for the whole condominium, and the printouts of all the units involved in the purchase, you will review the registered documents for the same information as you do with condominiums that have not been automated. Simpler, one-page documents, such as transfers, charges, construction liens, and common expense liens, are usually photocopied. Long, complex documents, such as the condominium declaration, description, and by-laws, are compared with the copies of the condominium documents contained in the status certificate and/or the disclosure statement. For a discussion of development agreements, airport zoning, and Crown reservations, see Chapter 9.

The new forms of condominiums under the current Act have different title documentation and therefore require additional searching practices.

Leasehold Condominiums

The ground lease and any documents that relate to the ground lease, such as a notice of termination or a notice of renewal, are listed on the unit printout(s) and must be reviewed. The terms and schedules of the ground lease and the description of the ground lease in the declaration should be compared. For example, it is important to note whether the ground lease is for 40 years or for 99 years. Current and future rent calculations are also important.

Common Elements Condominiums

You must complete a full search of both the condominium PIN that lists the documents related to the condominium as a whole and the PIN for the POTL that contains documents related to the POTL. Obtain the PIN, plan, and description for the common elements and the description and subdivision or reference plan illustrating the boundaries of the POTL. A common expense lien is registered on the POTL register. The property description line on the printout for the POTL contains a cross-reference to the common elements condominium PIN and states that the POTL is "together with an undivided common interest in, for example, HCECC No.__". It also includes a remark indicating the condominium number and block number, and that there are additional encumbrances registered on the condominium PIN. A condominium parcel also contains a notice of attachment indicating that the POTLs are joined with the common elements condominium.

When dealing with common elements condominiums, watch for detailed restrictions and covenants registered against the POTL. As well, complete a full *Planning Act* compliance search for the POTL and check any *Planning Act* exemption by-laws for expiry dates. Review *Planning Act* consents for conditions and watch for agreements on title that relate to the conditions.

Phased Condominiums

The property description line on the printout for a phased condominium contains a reference to the registration number(s) for the amendment(s) to the declaration and description adding additional units and common elements. Watch for registrations related to easements and merger of easements and also reciprocal cost-sharing agreements.

Vacant Land Condominiums

Watch for restrictions registered on title.

Amalgamated Condominiums

Watch for registrations related to easements and merger of easements and reciprocal cost-sharing agreements.

EXAMPLE OF TERAVIEW (POLARIS) CONDOMINIUM SEARCH

The following Teraview screen captures, digital map, and unit parcel register printouts illustrate how to assemble the title information for Halton Condominium Plan No. 317, Unit 1, Level 1 in Land Registry Office #20. PIN 25618-0000 represents the PIN for Halton Condominium No. 317 (see Figure 7.4). PIN 25618-0001 represents Unit 1, Level 1 in a conventional freehold condominium corporation registered prior to May 5, 2001. Condominiums of this type, as well as phased and amalgamated condominiums registered after May 5, 2001, will be referred to as standard condominiums. The parcel registers for leasehold condominiums, common elements condominiums, and vacant land condominiums have a slightly different appearance and contain additional information.

Figure 7.1

SEARCH BY CONDOMINIUM*

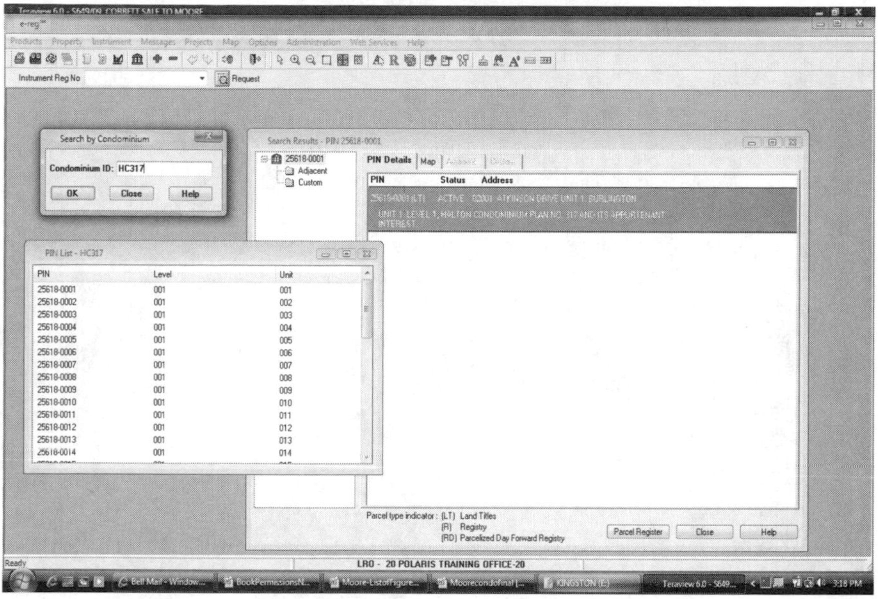

Figure 7.1 illustrates the search by condominium box, the condominium unit/PIN cross-reference, the search results for PIN 25618-0001, and the parcel register request box. Use the proper Registry office-specific and condominium type-specific prefixes when requesting the condominium corporation cross-reference. Request the search results for all the PINs (unit, parking, storage, *etc.*) involved in the purchase. View and print all the PIN parcel registers and always request deleted documents. Deleted documents may reveal prior corporate owners (usually covered by title insurance) and explain problems and, occasionally, errors on the registers. More importantly, deleted documents reveal title and mortgage fraud patterns and are required as part of the title insurance application process. It is unnecessary to complete either a *Planning Act* search or the *Planning Act* declarations in the transfer because condominium units are exempt from the part lot control prohibitions in s. 50 of the *Planning Act* (except for POTLs). Read the PIN details carefully, as they confirm the municipal address, the unit and the level.

---

* © Teranet Inc. 2010. Reproduced with permission.

Figure 7.2

PARCEL REGISTER AND INSTRUMENT REQUEST*

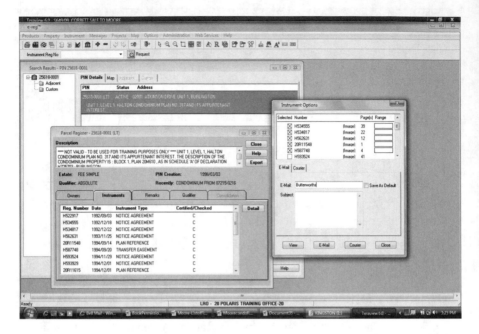

Figure 7.2 illustrates the parcel register screen and the instrument request box. Read the parcel register description carefully, as it will note additional plans and related PINs/units, and will include a reference to the POTL when dealing with a common elements condominium. Print the parcel registers and request plans and documents. Plans will be couriered, although some plans are available online. Documents may be viewed, printed, faxed, or couriered. Condominium creation and governance documents are very long and are usually compared with documents delivered with the status or disclosure statement. You may view and select specific pages for printing.

---

*   © Teranet Inc. 2010. Reproduced with permission.

Figure 7.3

TERAVIEW DIGITAL MAP SCREEN FOR
HALTON CONDOMINIUM NO. 317*

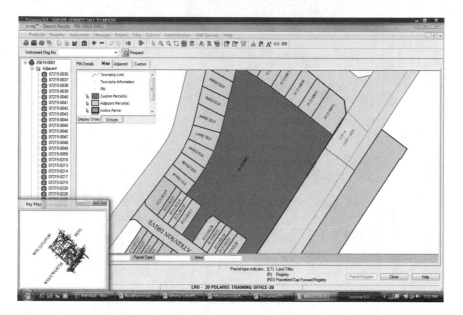

Figure 7.3 illustrates the digital map screen for Halton Condominium No. 317. The map includes the description details for HC317 as well as the description details for the adjacent PINs. The map and the condominium plan sheets illustrate access to a public road. It would show land held for future phases in a phased condominium and POTLs in a common elements condominium.

Figure 7.4

DIGITAL MAP PRINTOUT FOR HALTON CONDOMINIUM NO. 317*

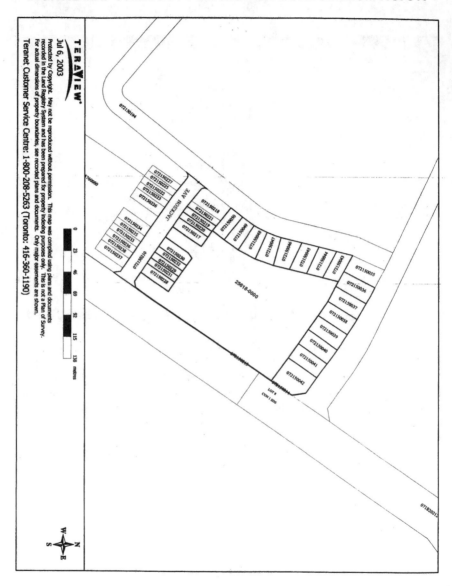

Figure 7.4 illustrates the digital map printout for the previous figure.

Figure 7.5

CONDOMINIUM UNIT PARCEL REGISTER PRINTOUT INCLUDING DELETED DOCUMENTS FOR PIN 25618-0001 (TERAVIEW)*

PARCEL REGISTER (ABBREVIATED) FOR PROPERTY IDENTIFIER

PAGE 1 OF 2
PREPARED FOR
ON 2003/05/04 AT 10:20:43

MINISTRY OF CONSUMER AND BUSINESS SERVICES — TRAINING

LAND REGISTRY OFFICE #20

25618-0001 (LT)

SUBJECT TO RESERVATIONS IN CROWN GRANT

PROPERTY DESCRIPTION: **** NOT VALID – TO BE USED FOR TRAINING PURPOSES ONLY **** UNIT 1, LEVEL 1, HALTON CONDOMINIUM PLAN NO. 317 AND ITS APPURTENANT INTEREST. THE DESCRIPTION OF THE CONDOMINIUM PROPERTY IS : BLOCK 1, PLAN 20M610 , AS IN SCHEDULE 'A' OF DECLARATION H725703 ; BURLINGTON .

PROPERTY REMARKS:

ESTATE/QUALIFIER:
FEE SIMPLE
ABSOLUTE

RECENTLY:
CONDOMINIUM FROM 07215-0216

PIN CREATION DATE:
1998/03/03

OWNERS' NAMES
PRUFROCK, ALFRED HEATHCLIFF
RIGBY, WOOLF CATHERINE

CAPACITY SHARE
JTEN
JTEN

EFFECTIVE 2000/07/29 THE NOTATION OF THE "BLOCK IMPLEMENTATION DATE" OF 1998/03/02 ON THIS PIN

WAS REPLACED WITH THE "PIN CREATION DATE" OF 1998/03/03

** PRINTOUT INCLUDES ALL DOCUMENT TYPES AND DELETED INSTRUMENTS SINCE: 1998/03/03 **

REG. NUM.	DATE	INSTRUMENT TYPE	AMOUNT	PARTIES FROM	PARTIES TO	CERT/CHKD
H522917	1992/09/03	NTCE AGRMT		THE REGIONAL MUNICIPALITY OF HALTON		C
H534555	1992/12/18	NTCE AGRMT		THE CORPORATION OF THE CITY OF BURLINGTON		C
H534817	1992/12/22	NTCE AGRMT		THE REGIONAL MUNICIPALITY OF HALTON		C
H562631	1993/11/25	NTCE AGRMT		THE CORPORATION OF THE CITY OF BURLINGTON		C
20R11548	1994/09/14	PLAN REFERENCE				C
H587748	1994/09/20	TRANS EASMENT			THE CORPORATION OF THE CITY OF BURLINGTON	C
H593524	1994/11/29	NTCE AGRMT		973511 ONTARIO LIMITED	THE CORPORATION OF THE CITY OF BURLINGTON	C
H593929	1994/12/01	NTCE AGRMT		973511 ONTARIO LIMITED	THE REGIONAL MUNICIPALITY OF HALTON	C
20R11615	1994/12/01	PLAN REFERENCE				C
H594246	1994/12/02	TRANS EASMENT			THE CORPORATION OF THE CITY OF BURLINGTON	C
H704194	1997/10/08	CHARGE		*** DELETED AGAINST THIS PROPERTY *** 1189286 ONTARIO INC.	BANK OF MONTREAL	C
HC317	1998/03/02	PLAN CONDOMINIUM				

NOTE: ADJOINING PROPERTIES SHOULD BE INVESTIGATED TO ASCERTAIN DESCRIPTIVE INCONSISTENCIES, IF ANY, WITH DESCRIPTION REPRESENTED FOR THIS PROPERTY.
NOTE: ENSURE THAT YOUR PRINTOUT STATES THE TOTAL NUMBER OF PAGES AND THAT YOU HAVE PICKED THEM ALL UP.

Figure 7.5 (cont'd)

MINISTRY OF CONSUMER AND BUSINESS SERVICES

TRAINING

LAND REGISTRY OFFICE #20

PARCEL REGISTER (ABBREVIATED) FOR PROPERTY IDENTIFIER

25618-0001 (LT)

SUBJECT TO RESERVATIONS IN CROWN GRANT

PAGE 2 OF 2
PREPARED FOR
ON 2003/05/04 AT 10:20:43

REG. NUM.	DATE	INSTRUMENT TYPE	AMOUNT	PARTIES FROM	PARTIES TO	CERT/CHKD
H725703	1998/03/02	DECLARATION CONDO		1189286 ONTARIO INC.	1189286 ONTARIO INC.	C
H726333	1998/03/06	BYLAW		HALTON CONDOMINIUM CORPORATION NO. 317		C
REMARKS: NO. 1						
H726334	1998/03/06	BYLAW		HALTON CONDOMINIUM CORPORATION NO. 317		C
REMARKS: NO. 2						
H726335	1998/03/06	BYLAW		HALTON CONDOMINIUM CORPORATION NO. 317		C
REMARKS: NO. 3						
H726336	1998/03/06	BYLAW.		HALTON CONDOMINIUM CORPORATION NO. 317		C
REMARKS: NO. 4						
H732172	1998/04/23	DISCH PART CHRG		*** COMPLETELY DELETED ***	BANK OF MONTREAL	C
REMARKS: RE: H704194						
H732173	1998/04/23	TRANSFER	$500,500	1189286 ONTARIO INC.	PRUFROCK, ALFRED HEATHCLIFF RIGBY, CATHERINE WOOLF	C
H732174	1998/04/23	CHARGE	$400,500	PRUFROCK, ALFRED HEATHCLIFF RIGBY, CATHERINE WOOLF	SCOTIA MORTGAGE CORPORATION	C
H746378	1998/07/22	NTCE CHNGE ADDRSS		HALTON CONDOMINIUM CORPORATION NO. 317		C

NOTE: ADJOINING PROPERTIES SHOULD BE INVESTIGATED TO ASCERTAIN DESCRIPTIVE INCONSISTENCIES, IF ANY, WITH DESCRIPTION REPRESENTED FOR THIS PROPERTY.
NOTE: ENSURE THAT YOUR PRINTOUT STATES THE TOTAL NUMBER OF PAGES AND THAT YOU HAVE PICKED THEM ALL UP.

Figure 7.5 illustrates the parcel register printout for PIN 25618-0001. The unit printout includes deleted documents since the PIN creation date. The following information is illustrated on the unit register printout for 25618-0001:

1. 25618-0001 (LT) indicates that the PIN is in the Land Titles system and is subject to the reservations in the Crown grant.

2. The property description line includes the unit, level, condominium name and plan number, and related subdivision plan number and block. It refers to the schedule in the declaration that contains the full legal description. The prefix "M" before a plan number (20M-610) indicates a Land Titles plan in the Halton registry office. When a unit is stated to be subject to executions at the time of automation, the statement "subject to execution # 12345 if enforceable", will be included in the property description line. Additional related units, declaration amendments for phased condominiums, and POTLs for common elements condominiums may also be included in the property description line. This line also includes any underlying easements or restrictions to which the condominium is subject ("subject to …") and easements and restriction that are appurtenant to the condominium ("together with …"). Note that lengthy easements located in the declaration will be included by reference to Schedule A of the declaration only.

3. Cross-reference to the pre-automation register ("recently: CONDO-MINIUM FROM 07215-0216").

4. Date the property was converted/implemented to POLARIS ("PIN CREATION DATE", formerly called the block implementation date).

5. The title of the owner, in this case, is an absolute or fee simple title. Since May 2001, it could also be a leasehold interest in a leasehold condominium.

6. "Names of the registered owners" is followed by their capacity and share ("JTEN" for joint tenants).

7. There are a series of development agreements with the municipality, two reference plans, and a transfer of municipal easement.

8. H704194 is a deleted developer's blanket mortgage, now discharged against this PIN by H732172, a partial discharge of charge. Both of these registrations are now deleted and no longer affect the unit.

9. HC317 is the condominium plan. Obtain a copy of the plan in order to confirm the location and extent of the unit, parking and storage space, exclusive use areas, and the common elements. Note that parking may be a separate unit.

10. H725703 is the condominium declaration. The declaration should be compared to the copy attached to the status or disclosure statement.

11. All condominium by-laws should be reviewed.

12. H746378 is a notice of change of address for service for the condominium. A condominium change of address must be registered.

13. Photocopy the current transfer and charge.

14. Search executions against the registered owners as they appear on the parcel register. Search the condominium corporation for executions affecting the condominium and the common elements, as s. 23 of the Act states that a judgment against the condominium is a judgment against each owner for its proportionate share in the common interests. Search the purchasers if they are assuming or purchasing a mortgage, since they will take title. When acting for a lender, search the condominium corporation, the registered owners as they appear on the unit register, and the mortgagors as they will appear on the unit register. Search executions within ELRS/e-reg or in WritSearch. At this time you are only able to search and subsearch executions against the registered owners within the ELRS. A purchaser or lender can require a release from the condominium of a unit's proportionate share liability in an execution.

15. Search PPSA (*Personal Property Security Act*, R.S.O. 1990, c. P.10), depending on the age and value of the appliances and the chattels that are part of the common elements.

16. Search corporate status for prior corporate owners, in this case, 1189286 ONTARIO INC. This is unnecessary if the purchaser has obtained title insurance.

17. Carefully review the status certificate, the disclosure statement, and other condominium documents, such as agreements to alter the common elements.

Tips and Traps

- Conduct a full detailed search of condominium documents!
- Watch for restrictions on gifting, selling, and leasing; on occasion a condominium retains a right of first refusal in its declaration. Also, declarations may restrict the sale of parking and storage units separately from the residential or commercial unit. Note pet restrictions, business use in residential unit restrictions, parking restrictions on trucks, trailers, campers, and visitor parking spaces.
- Confirm that a partial discharge of the developer's blanket mortgage has been registered against the unit PIN register.
- Reconcile exact boundaries of units, common elements, and exclusive use areas and particularly parking and storage spaces with the agreement of purchase and sale and declaration and description.

- Watch for parking allocations and special assessments, as these generate litigation. Confirm whether parking is a unit, part of the common elements, an exclusive use area, or rented by the month subject to availability.
- Watch for alteration agreements registered on title (common elements) and compare to status certificate. Watch for extensive unit alterations, possibly moving of internal walls, installation of flooring, plumbing renovation; these require board approval and agreements that should be attached to the status certificate.
- Note whether units are individually metered or assessed as part of the common elements and whether parking garages comply with safety standards in by-laws, such as the Toronto anti-mugging by-law.

Figure 7.6

BLOCK INDEX MAP ILLUSTRATING CONDOMINIUM BLOCK(S) (POLARIS)

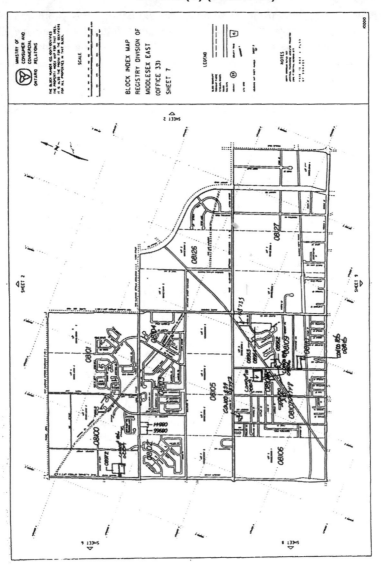

Figure 7.6 is an example Block Index Map illustrating condominium blocks. Each condominium is a separate block. Only the condominium plan sheets illustrate the location unit PINs and common elements. Condominium plan sheets substitute for the POLARIS property map.

TITLE INSURANCE REQUIREMENTS FOR CONDOMINIUM SEARCHES

Title insurance provides an alternative to completing routine, lower risk, off-title inquiries. Coverage varies depending on the insurer, and the nature of the property and the policy (owner or lender, or combined (TitlePLUS)). Insurer search requirements are subject to change. Most title insurers provide alternative indemnity coverage and do not require searches for the following routine off-title inquiries:

- writ search against the condominium corporation and prior owners in Registry (very rare as few condominiums in Registry);
- corporate status (escheat) searches;
- unregistered hydro easement searches;
- municipal realty taxes (obtain verbal or vendor's undertaking);
- utility (hydro, water, gas, oil) arrears certificates (obtain verbal or vendor's undertaking);
- subdivision and development agreement compliance certificate; and
- building and zoning compliance searches.

Insurers require status certificates within 60 days of closing, unless the lawyer obtains an extension. Insurers do not require a status certificate for a residential unit refinancing. Consider the many off-title risks that title insurance does not cover, particularly regarding recreational and common elements properties, such as environmental, water, Aboriginal rights, and shoreline issues. Chapter 14 reviews off-title risks and inquiries in detail.

Lawyers must request a condominium endorsement when arranging an owner or lender policy. Endorsements are specific to the different types of condominiums (see Chapter 18).

OTHER FORMS OF CONCURRENT OWNERSHIP AND COMMUNAL LIVING

Communal living and communal financial responsibility and decision-making are one person's dream and another person's nightmare. Purchasers decide before or after the purchase of a form of concurrent ownership such as a condominium, time-share, life lease, or fractional ownership cottage, into which group they fall. Life leases and fractional share ownership are descriptive terms that do not represent uniform legal relationships. Each development must be carefully investigated for title and contractual rights and obligations. Unlike condominiums, these newer forms of concurrent ownership are basically unregulated other than by existing conventional contract and property law principles. Only title, off-title inquiries, and a review of the development's creation documents will reveal the ownership structure and potential risks of a specific development. Communal financial responsibility for the development as a whole falls on the occupants or shareholders.

The Life Lease Lifestyle

Not all life leases are alike in terms of title or ownership structure. For that matter, not all life leases are leases. Most life leases are based on the long established real property concept of the life estate which is a freehold or equity estate in land and a greater title than a leasehold estate. Life leases are sustained on trust, a sense of community, and common lifestyle goals, the most common being retirement housing for seniors. Persons who purchase life lease interests are subject to a life lease occupancy agreement that sets out the rights and obligations of the purchaser. Contract, not legislation, governs life lease relationships. The *Residential Tenancies Act, 2006*, S.O. 2006, c. 17 does not govern life lease projects. The *Human Rights Code*, R.S.O. 1990, c. H-19 permits restrictions on occupancy of accommodation for preferential treatment of persons 65 years or older. Many life lease projects set an age restriction of 55 or over, which, in theory, may be subject to challenge. Unlike with condominiums, life leases lack consumer protection regulation such as disclosure duties and Ontario New Home Warranty Program new home warranties and deposit protection. Note that life lease deposits are often 25 per cent.

The sponsor of a life lease development is usually a non-profit or charitable organization, or a subsidiary of a non-profit or charitable organization. In exchange for a lump sum payment, the sponsor sells for the life or joint lives of the purchaser(s) the right to exclusive occupation of a designated property, such as an apartment or townhouse, together with shared use of common areas, such as recreational or dining facilities. Life lease developments set unit occupancy criteria such as minimum age, ability to function independently, and number of occupants per unit. Most life leases provide care services packages that include meal plans, housekeeping, emergency health monitoring response, and nursing care. In addition, life tenants pay monthly fees, similar to common expense payments, toward the maintenance and operation costs, such as taxes, utilities, landscaping, and snow removal, of the property. As with condominiums, life lease developments build reserve funds from monthly payments.

The sponsor owns the freehold or fee simple absolute title. Death of the life tenant or the survivor of joint life tenants (usually life partners), or the loss of the ability to function independently terminates the life lease. Life tenants also have the right to terminate the life lease on a specified notice. On termination, a redemption formula calculates a termination entitlement that recognizes equity values and appreciation in the living unit. Redemption formulas vary greatly and must be carefully considered in relation to the initial lump sum payment. Many life lease developments allow a life tenant to transfer his or her interest to a new tenant. The sponsor's written approval is a condition to the transfer of a unit.

Each life lease development must be carefully researched, as they differ widely in legal framework. The following are the types of life lease presently available in Ontario:

- Future Market Value Redemption — The sponsor redeems the unit or the life occupant sells the unit at market value. The occupant pays the sponsor a set value for expenses generated by transfer to a new occupant such as approval of the new purchaser and checking that they meet occupant age and health criteria, and also repair and decorating costs. This model provides investment potential to purchasers although there are restrictions on resale.
- Declining Balance Redemption — The life tenant occupies the unit until termination by death or inability to live independently; however, the redemption value and monthly payments decline over the occupation period, in a sense similar to a reverse equity financing structure based on life expectancy. On termination, depending on the length of occupancy, there may or may not be a redemption payment.
- Fixed Value Redemption — The sponsor sets a fixed re-purchase amount for the life of the life tenant's occupancy.
- Indexed Redemption — Indexed redemption models tie the redemption value to an economic index, often with a cap tied to unit market value.
- Zero Balance Life Lease — This relatively rare life estate model terminates on death or incapacity and is not transferable; there is usually no right to sublet or assign. It does not have a redemption value. The price is lower than other ownership models and the monthly payments reflect actuarial projections for life expectancy.

Prior to the building of the project, life lease purchasers enter into a reservation agreement accompanied by a deposit. Available disclosure information should be reviewed by a lawyer. The boundaries of the unit, the nature of the shared facilities, occupancy charges, reserve funds, and whether the sponsor is obligated to sell other units as life leases or simply rent them are particularly important considerations. Unlike in condominiums, the sponsor has full discretion over the management of the project and the life lease occupant may have no contractual or statutory means of influencing the project's governance.

Title Registration and the Life Lease

Life lease projects may be based on freehold or leasehold title. The lawyer for the purchaser will search and review registered title as with any other property, including mortgages, non-disturbance agreements, liens, restrictive covenants, easements, access, municipal and development agreements, and *Planning Act* compliance. If the project is based on a leasehold title, the lawyer will review the terms and conditions of the leasehold title, particularly the term, the rent, and rights of renewal. Individual life leases do not have a separate unit register as with condominiums; instead, life leases for all units are registered against the underlying parcel register. This makes for a long and complicated search of all registrations on the parent parcel, as there is no standard convention for describing or naming life lease units. The choice of off-title searches will be based on the nature of the property and the title insurer's search requirements. For life leases, the lawyer will contact an underwriter to customize coverage.

Life lease purchasers register the life lease on the parent parcel owned by the sponsor. Purchases of life leases are financed through the registration of leasehold mortgages using the assignment of the life lease as collateral. Some sponsors forbid the registrations of the life lease; this provision may be open to negotiation if the client seeks legal advice early enough in the transaction.

Planning Act Compliance and the Life Lease

There is some uncertainty as to how s. 50 of the *Planning Act* affects life leases. Life leases that are structured to be for less than 21 years or 21 years less a day escape the definition of a conveyance. Hopefully, s. 50(9) exempts life leases as being for "the use of or a right in a part of a building or structure for any period of years". On the other hand, if the lease is a freehold life estate, it requires a consent or an exemption by-law. *Planning Act* compliance should be confirmed for life lease projects.

Fractional (Interval) Ownership: Living the Dream

Fractional or interval ownership is the new entry into the concurrent ownership race, initiated by the coming of condominiums to British Columbia and Ontario in the 1960s. Fractional ownership offers flexibility, a maintenance-free vacation experience, and equity ownership. Fractional owners usually have the option of renting any or all of their weeks privately or through the management services and sometimes have the option of exchanging their unit at similar developments. Fractional share developments include new projects and also existing vacation resorts and trailer parks that have been converted to fractional ownerships projects. The rights and liabilities of fractional ownership are determined by owner agreement. At this time, some fractional ownership transactions are processed by the developer's lawyer directly to the purchaser. This developer-driven transfer transaction is in some ways similar to the early years of condominium conveyancing, when the public purchased new condominium units from the developer without the benefit of an independent purchaser's lawyer. Some might argue that this practice brought us the extensive consumer protection provisions now embedded in the *Condominium Act, 1998*, such as cooling-off periods, disclosure statements, reserve funds, and status certificates. For many fractional share developments, no such ownership-specific consumer protections are in place, although the *Consumer Protection Act, 2002*, S.O. 2002, c. 30, Schedule A may provide some generic protection.

Fractional Share Cottage Ownership

Fractional share ownership may refer to a fractional share in a condominium unit where the share is registered on title in the owners' names. The fractional owners are tenants in common of the condominium unit. Fractional share ownership may also refer to being a member and owning a share in a not-for-profit association. These members collectively own the property (such as cottages) and are collectively financially responsible for any liability generated by the project; they do not register an interest on title. Fractions are often five-week intervals (1/10 share) or four-week intervals (1/12 share), with the remaining weeks set aside for maintenance and repair, and/or separate purchase, often at Christmas and New Years. Fractional share ownership may be associated with a resort which includes rental cottages and resort services. For example, the Cottages at Port Stanton on beautiful Sparrow Lake, the Muskoka set for the television show *Paradise Falls*, are associated with the Bayview Wildwood Resort. The Cottages at Port Stanton offer fractional cottage ownership that consists of a voting membership in a not-for-profit association that holds the deed to the land and buildings in trust for the owners. Each owner purchases a share in the property in perpetuity, which can be sold or willed according to the association's by-laws. They are also affiliated with the global exchange network Interval International, which allows owners to exchange opportunities with over 2,000 Interval International exchange properties.

Fractional shares differ from traditional time-shares as the fractional share owners own the property, whereas the developer owns the timeshare property. Fractional share ownership is subject to numerous restrictions, such as pets and smoking; fractions can be sold or transferred by will. A management company deals with the day-to-day administration and maintenance of the property. Fractional share ownership enjoys both the advantages and disadvantages of communal living, including affordable luxury, maintenance-free vacations, and the risks of sharing a property with others (such as needing unanimous consent to affect upgrades, even to the shared furniture and dishes). Fractional share owners pay an annual maintenance fee that covers expenses such as taxes, utilities, maintenance, security, cleaning, and the contribution to reserve funds for major repairs.

Purchasers of fractional shares need to make both title and off-title inquiries for the property. In addition, they need to examine the owner agreement and the not-for-profit association creation documents and by-laws for the terms, conditions, and restrictions on owner/occupants. The absence of statutory protections similar to those in the *Condominium Act, 1998* combined with the collective responsibility for risks, such as environmental work orders, make title and off-title inquiries and the services of a lawyer particularly valuable.

Condominium Hotels

Condominium hotels, such as The Rousseau at Red Leaves in Muskoka and One King West in Toronto, are sold to unit investors who have a right to use the unit for specified time periods. When the owner/investors are not using their units, they are placed in a managed rental pool that generates income toward their shares of the operating expenses. Owners can sell their units. The hotel is operated by a hotel management company.

CHAPTER 8

Electronic Title Searching under the Land Registration Reform Act (POLARIS)

LAND REGISTRATION REFORM IN ONTARIO

The *Land Registration Reform Act*, R.S.O. 1990, c. L.4 (LRRA) implemented the Province of Ontario Land Registration Information System, known as POLARIS. POLARIS has been implemented in stages throughout Ontario. Most of Ontario has now been converted to POLARIS. Over 94 per cent of documents are now registered in POLARIS using the electronic land registration system, referred to as ELRS or e-reg. Searches and registrations are completed using Teraview software. The Teraview website contains an up-to-date geographic coverage and functionality chart and map illustrating conversion and ELRS status of land in the 54 registry offices. Chapter 1 outlines the history and background of the Registry system, the Land Titles system, and Ontario's *Land Registration Reform Act*. The main features of land registration reform are listed below.

Electronic Documents and LRRA Forms

Part I of the LRRA prescribes five standardized document forms, common to Registry and Land Titles. These *Land Registration Reform Act* forms are described in Chapter 5. They are available in electronic and paper format. ELRS contains many online variations of the five basic forms. Electronic forms and registration are available only in Land Titles. Documents are created, signed, and registered online in ELRS. POLARIS paper forms account for less than five per cent of registrations and are used wherever electronic land registration and Land Titles have not been implemented or when a particular document is not suited to electronic registration.

Automation of Title and Mapping Records

Part II of the LRRA governs the designation of properties in POLARIS and provides for a computerized version of title records and an automated title searching and electronic document registration system. POLARIS also contains a computerized property mapping system in which all lands designated in POLARIS are identified by a nine-digit property identification number (PIN). Chapter 2 includes a description of POLARIS block and property maps, Teraview digital maps, and the method of assigning PINs. Land originally in Land Titles is simply automated, whereas land in Registry is first parcelized, then either simply automated, or first converted to Land Titles and then automated.

Conversion to Land Titles

The goal of POLARIS is to convert land under the Registry system into the Land Titles system at the same time as the ownership and mapping records are computerized. As a result, almost all land records in Ontario (except for problem non-converts) will be both automated and in Land Titles when the POLARIS conversion process is complete. Registry properties that have been converted into Land Titles during automation are registered as being Land Titles Conversion Qualified titles (LTCQ). LTCQ titles are subject to different legal qualifiers under the *Land Titles Act*, R.S.O. 1990, c. L.5. As a result, title search rules are different for LTCQ titles compared to traditional Land Titles titles. Land Titles Conversion Qualified titles can be upgraded to a Land Titles Absolute Plus title (LT PLUS). An LT PLUS title is also subject to different legal qualifiers and title searching rules.

Some Registry properties were automated but not converted to Land Titles. These automated Registry properties are called Parcelized Day Forward Registry (PDFR) Records and they will be converted to Land Titles at a later date. Other automated Registry variations exist. In some areas early in the conversion, 40 years of Registry documents were entered on the parcel printout (Registry, 40-year load). On occasion, properties, referred to as non-converts, were not converted due to title problems.

Electronic Land Registration System

Part III of the LRRA governs the creation of a fully electronic or paperless land registration system. Teraview's electronic land registration system, referred to as ELRS, represents the final and most ambitious stage of the POLARIS initiatives. Electronic land registration is only available for land registered under the *Land Titles Act*. Once complete, Teraview software combined with the POLARIS database will provide fully automated title searching, electronic document production, and document registration throughout Ontario. Chapter 16 outlines the design and implementation of ELRS.

TYPES OF TITLE SEARCHES IN POLARIS

Automated title searching in POLARIS includes several variations on Registry and Land Titles searches. The following variations have resulted from different title conversion and automation projects:

POLARIS Registry System Searches

    1.   Registry 40-Year Load

    2.   Registry Non-Converts

    3.   Parcelized Day (PIN creation date) Forward Registry Records

POLARIS Land Titles System Searches

    1.   Land Titles Absolute or Leasehold

    2.   Land Titles Conversion Qualified

    3.   Land Titles Absolute Plus

    4.   Condominium searches (see Chapter 7)

Automated Land Titles referred to as Land Titles Absolute, and Land Titles Conversion Qualified where Registry titles were both automated and legally converted from Registry to Land Titles, are currently the most common searches. When POLARIS and Land Titles conversion is complete, a fully automated registry office will contain Land Titles Absolute titles, Land Titles Conversion Qualified titles, Land Titles Plus titles, and a few non-convert titles that will be required to be converted to Land Titles Absolute Plus titles when next transferred.

Applicable law and procedure relating to title searching in POLARIS varies greatly among Registry offices and even within a particular Registry office. As well, the POLARIS conversion causes constant change. Lawyers must familiarize themselves with the legal nature of the POLARIS conversion in each office before starting a search, in order to avoid the ever-present risk of negligence. All POLARIS search variations are completed in the Teraview environment and require expertise in retrieving title information using Teraview software. The long-range plan is to convert all the land in Ontario to Land Titles and to offer fully automated online searching, document production, and registration services using ELRS via the Teraview Gateway. Local Registry offices will provide limited back-up access.

Each category of title search presents different legal implications and requires markedly different practical title searching procedures. It is essential to identify the nature of the title before completing the title search. For example, a *Planning Act*, R.S.O. 1990, c. P.13 part lot control search may be required back to 1967 in Land Titles Absolute, Parcelized Day Forward Registry, Non-Converts, and Registry 40-Year Loads, whereas a *Planning Act* part lot control search need not go behind the date of conversion in a Land Titles Conversion Qualified or behind the date of registration in a Land Titles Absolute Plus (post-August 2001) search. Similarly, it may be necessary to complete abutting land searches back 40 years for description and boundary problems arising from possessory rights in Parcelized Day Forward Registry, Non-Converts, Registry 40-Year Loads, and Land Titles Conversion Qualified which allows mature unregistered possessory claims, whereas possessory rights are prohibited in Land Titles Absolute and Land Titles Absolute Plus. It can be difficult to distinguish the different title categories from the POLARIS printout and online screens; it requires a careful examination of listed title qualifiers and a familiarity with the characteristics of the title variations. Title searching in POLARIS requires the same detailed title investigation work as in the paper systems. Plans, documents, and descriptions must be examined; adjoining lands searches must be completed and documented whether or not title insurance is involved.

REGISTRY SEARCHES IN POLARIS

Land registered pursuant to the *Registry Act*, R.S.O. 1990, c. R.20 that has been parcelized, given a PIN, and entered into POLARIS may be searched in whole or in part via the Teraview Gateway. POLARIS contains Registry Non-Convert parcels, Parcelized Day (PIN creation date) Forward Registry Records (PDFR), and Registry 40-Year Load parcels. Registry in POLARIS is indexed by parcel and PIN, not by lot, and may be searched, but not registered, using Teraview. Registry searching, be it in the Abstract books or in POLARIS, is simply Registry. Chapter 4 deals with Registry searching in detail. A 40-year search is required; all documents registered within the 40-year period must be checked for validity. Executions are searched against all owners within the 40-year period unless the lawyer is relying on alternative title insurance coverage. Adjoining lands searches and *Planning Act* searches are completed as with a traditional Registry search. Descriptions must be sketched and reconciled in order to identify potential descriptive inconsistencies and possessory claims. Teraview simplifies Registry searching by: providing digital maps that illustrate the location and PIN for adjoining lands; organizing title documents by parcel and PIN instead of lot; making documents and property parcel printouts available online; and providing property search information by municipal address, PIN, registered owner, subdivision plan, condominium plan, instrument number, map, and road.

Registry titles in POLARIS are identified by the heading "Abstract Index (Abbreviated) for Property Identifier ..." located at the top of the POLARIS printout. The PIN at the top of the parcel printout is followed by an "R". The "Estate/ Qualifier" field is left blank on printouts for Registry titles in POLARIS.

Registry 40-Year Load

A few areas have parcelized, assigned PINs, and loaded 40 years of Registry documents onto the POLARIS parcel index. The POLARIS printout for a 40-Year Load contains the heading, for example, "-Date of Earliest Registration Loaded: 1960/06/06-", just above the list of registered documents, as well as being called an "Abstract Index (Abbreviated) for Property Identifier". The PIN is followed by an "R". Forty-Year Loads were sometimes combined with the registration of a certificate of title that shortened the 40-year search period by creating a short root of title.

Registry Non-Converts

Registry Non-Converts are found in Registry offices where Registry titles were converted to Land Titles ownership prior to automation. Registry Non-Converts are created whenever a serious title defect prevents the POLARIS conversion process from converting a Registry title into a guaranteed Land Titles Conversion Qualified title. Non-Converts are parcelized, mapped, and assigned a PIN, but left in Registry. Documents registered within the last 40 years are loaded on the automated record. The date of earliest registration loaded is set out near the top of the printout. The estate/qualifier field is left empty. A full 40-year search is required. It may be necessary to review the original Abstract books to identify the title problem. Unfortunately, POLARIS printouts for Registry Non-Converts look the same as POLARIS printouts for Registry 40-Year Loads. However, Non-Converts are found in Registry offices where Registry titles were converted to Land Titles Conversion Qualified titles prior to automation. Great care should be taken when searching a Registry title surrounded by LTCQ titles. Figure 8.1 is an example of a Registry Non-Convert. Chapter 4 also contains an example of a Non-Convert printout (see Figure 4.1).

Figure 8.1

REGISTRY NON-CONVERT PARCEL PRINTOUT 26050-0076(R)

MINISTRY OF CONSUMER AND BUSINESS SERVICES

TRAINING

LAND REGISTRY OFFICE #20

ABSTRACT INDEX (ABBREVIATED) FOR PROPERTY IDENTIFIER

26050-0076 (R)

PAGE 1 OF 2
PREPARED FOR
ON 2003/07/06 AT 12:08:38

PROPERTY DESCRIPTION: **** NOT VALID - TO BE USED FOR TRAINING PURPOSES ONLY **** PT LTS 10 & 11, PL 36 , NW OF ERNEST ST ; HALTON HILLS

PROPERTY REMARKS:

RECENTLY:
FIRST CONVERSION FROM BOOK

ESTATE/QUALIFIER:

PIN CREATION DATE:
1996/12/16

EFFECTIVE 2000/07/29 THE NOTATION OF THE "BLOCK IMPLEMENTATION DATE" OF 1996/12/16 ON THIS PIN
WAS REPLACED WITH THE "PIN CREATION DATE" OF 1996/12/16
** PRINTOUT INCLUDES ALL DOCUMENT TYPES AND DELETED INSTRUMENTS SINCE: 1996/12/13 **

DATE OF EARLIEST REGISTRATION LOADED: 1959/08/05

REG. NUM.	DATE	INSTRUMENT TYPE	AMOUNT	PARTIES FROM	PARTIES TO	CERT./ CHKD
100781	1959/08/05	TRANSFER	$2			C
227008	1967/07/04	TRANSFER	$2		WYNDHAM, NICHOLAS ALAN	C
228163	1967/07/19	QUIT CLAIM N TRNS			RIGGS, ROBERT MICHAEL WILLIAMS, SELENA KAREN	C
279490	1969/08/29	TRANSFER	$2		KNIGHT, PETER DAVID KNIGHT, SARAH ANN	C
280096	1969/09/08	DEPOSIT				
651046	1986/09/30	CHARGE	$65,000		THE TORONTO-DOMINION BANK	C
20R7993	1987/03/19	PLAN REFERENCE				C
662873	1987/03/30	TRANSFER	$159,000		KRAMER, PETER RICHARD	C
662929	1987/03/31	CHARGE	$145,000		MIDLAND DOHERTY CAPITAL CORPORATION	C
690445	1988/04/28	CHARGE	$46,000		THE TORONTO-DOMINION BANK	C
765526	1991/06/20	ASSGMT CH REMARKS: 724143 AND OTHERS (MULTI) AMENDED 97 12 22 NM.TOWNS DLR.			CENTRAL GUARANTY TRUST COMPANY	C
825641	1994/07/15	CHARGE	$45,000		TD TRUST COMPANY	C

NOTE: ADJOINING PROPERTIES SHOULD BE INVESTIGATED TO ASCERTAIN DESCRIPTIVE INCONSISTENCIES, IF ANY, WITH DESCRIPTION REPRESENTED FOR THIS PROPERTY.
NOTE: ENSURE THAT YOUR PRINTOUT STATES THE TOTAL NUMBER OF PAGES AND THAT YOU HAVE PICKED THEM ALL UP.

Figure 8.1 (cont'd)

TRAINING

MINISTRY OF
CONSUMER AND
BUSINESS
SERVICES

LAND
REGISTRY
OFFICE #20

ABSTRACT INDEX (ABBREVIATED) FOR PROPERTY IDENTIFIER

26050-0076 (R)

PAGE 2 OF 2
PREPARED FOR
ON 2003/07/06 AT 12:08:38

REG. NUM.	DATE	INSTRUMENT TYPE	AMOUNT	PARTIES FROM	PARTIES TO	CERT/ CHKD
847911	1995/12/29	TRANSFER	$265,000		NAKINA, GERALD JACKSON NAKINA, SCARLETT TARA	C
847912	1995/12/29	CHARGE	$235,750		ROYAL BANK OF CANADA	C
852869	1996/06/17	POSTPONEMENT				C
	REMARKS: 825641, 847912					
852860	1996/06/17	DISCHARGE				C
	REMARKS: 662929					

NOTE: ADJOINING PROPERTIES SHOULD BE INVESTIGATED TO ASCERTAIN DESCRIPTIVE INCONSISTENCIES, IF ANY, WITH DESCRIPTION REPRESENTED FOR THIS PROPERTY.
NOTE: ENSURE THAT YOUR PRINTOUT STATES THE TOTAL NUMBER OF PAGES AND THAT YOU HAVE PICKED THEM ALL UP.

Parcelized Day Forward Registry

Relatively few Parcelized Day Forward Registry (PDFR) titles exist in Ontario today. PDFR titles were meant to be temporary, and Teranet plans to convert the remaining PDFR properties to Land Titles parcels at a future date. In some offices, Teranet parcelized, mapped, and assigned a PIN, and then computerized only the current Registry ownership document (deed) as of the date of automation, now called the PIN Creation Date. Following the PIN creation date, all new registrations are shown on the automated record (PIN printout). The automation of PDFR title was completed in two different ways. In some areas, the last change in ownership document as of the PIN creation date was entered in POLARIS, but any documents registered between that document and the date of automation were not recorded in POLARIS. These documents were left in the Abstract book. Other PDFR records automated the last change of ownership and all related title documents between the last change of ownership and the PIN activation date. In both cases, the lawyer must complete a full 40-year search using automated searching for recent information as well as checking the paper record for the full 40 years. The parcel printout contains a cross-reference back to the appropriate Abstract index. Registry search and registration rules apply.

The heading "Abstract Index (Abbreviated) for Property Identifier" is found at the top of a PDFR parcel printout, and the PIN is followed by an "R". The POLARIS printout for a PDFR parcel contains the words, "This Abstract includes all instruments and documents from Y/M/D (PIN Creation Date)", just above the list of registered documents. The "Estate/Qualifier" is left blank on PDFR titles in POLARIS. It is the Property Remarks line on the POLARIS printout that distinguishes a PDFR title from other POLARIS Registry titles. The Property Remarks line on a PDFR parcel states: "THIS PARCEL WAS CREATED BASED ON INFORMATION CONTAINED IN DOCUMENT(S) 689763, WHICH IS (ARE) RECORDED FOR PIN IDENTIFICATION ONLY." Figure 8.2 is an example of a PDFR parcel printout.

Figure 8.2

PARCELIZED DAY FORWARD REGISTRY (PDFR) PARCEL PRINTOUT 00209-0209 (R)

LAND TITLES SYSTEM SEARCHES IN POLARIS

Different title qualifiers and different search requirements apply for each of the three POLARIS Land Titles system searches. It is essential for a lawyer to identify the nature of a POLARIS Land Titles parcel before completing or reviewing the search. Chapter 6 covers the Land Titles system in detail, including the title qualifiers in all Land Titles title variations. Chapter 6 also contains an example of a Land Titles Absolute search in the traditional paper format and two examples of automated Land Titles Absolute searches in POLARIS, as well as search checklists. This chapter contains an example of an LTCQ search and checklist.

Land Titles Absolute

Teranet simply automated and assigned a PIN to existing traditional Land Titles Absolute parcels. A Land Titles Absolute search in POLARIS is basically the same as a conventional Land Titles search, except that the title register and search procedures are fully automated. A Land Titles Absolute parcel is subject to the standard *Land Titles Act* s. 44 qualifiers unless otherwise stated on the parcel register printout. The Land Titles parcel is referenced by PIN, and Teraview digital maps and documents are available online. As in paper Land Titles, only current registrations are recorded as active on the parcel register. Prior transfers of ownership and discharged or no longer effective documents are noted as deleted from the parcel register. It is essential to request deleted documents when completing a Land Titles search. Title insurers also require deleted documents as part of an application for coverage.

When land under the Land Titles system is automated, the entries on the current parcel register are loaded onto the computer under the PIN assigned to the particular parcel. Teraview search software generates an up-to-date parcel register printout. The parcel register printout states the date the parcel was automated (PIN creation date) and cross-references back to the prior parcel register book.

The lawyer requests and reviews all active and all deleted registered documents recorded on the parcel register printout. The lawyer must request deleted documents prior to retrieving the parcel register as the Teraview default setting displays only active registrations on-screen or on the printouts. When viewing the parcel register, the lawyer should note whether a registration has been certified by checking for a "C", meaning certified, in the last column of the parcel printout. A transfer must be certified before "OWNERS' NAMES" is updated on the parcel register. Land Titles Absolute parcels may be searched and registered electronically.

Figure 8.3 is an example of an automated Land Titles Absolute parcel register printout. It refers to parcels, sections, and M-Plans. The PIN at the top of a Land Titles parcel register printout is followed by "LT", indicating the Land Titles system. Teraview screens and printouts contain the property description; the estate qualifier (Fee Simple Absolute); previous parcel references, PINs, and register books; the PIN creation date; owners' names, capacity and share; and whether the register includes deleted documents. Document registrations are listed on the parcel register printout by instrument number; however, they may also be noted in the Property Description and Property Remarks lines. The status of documents is important and may be indicated by a "C" for certified, by a document deletion notation, or by the absence of a notation, which means the document is not yet certified. Parcel registers that were converted to POLARIS early may refer to "Block Implementation Date"; whereas properties converted later refer to the PIN creation or activation date. PIN creation date is the current term. Figure 8.3 is an example of a Land Titles Absolute parcel printout. Chapter 6 contains two more examples of Land Titles Absolute printouts and searches accompanied by explanations and search checklists.

Figure 8.3

LAND TITLES ABSOLUTE PARCEL PRINTOUT 24935-2269 (LT)

MINISTRY OF CONSUMER AND BUSINESS SERVICES

TRAINING

LAND REGISTRY OFFICE #20

PARCEL REGISTER (ABBREVIATED) FOR PROPERTY IDENTIFIER

PAGE 1 OF 1
PREPARED FOR
ON 2003/07/06 AT 12:17:59

24935-2269 (LT)

SUBJECT TO RESERVATIONS IN CROWN GRANT

PROPERTY DESCRIPTION: **** NOT VALID - TO BE USED FOR TRAINING PURPOSES ONLY **** LOT 1, PLAN 20M701, OAKVILLE. S/T RIGHT H782026

PROPERTY REMARKS:

ESTATE/QUALIFIER:
FEE SIMPLE
ABSOLUTE

RECENTLY:
SUBDIVISION FROM 24925-1916

PIN CREATION DATE:
1998/08/27

OWNERS' NAMES
WAYNE, DAVID ROBERT
WAYNE, ROBIN MICHELLE

CAPACITY   SHARE
JTEN
JTEN

REG. NUM.	DATE	INSTRUMENT TYPE	AMOUNT	PARTIES FROM	PARTIES TO	CERT/CHKD
EFFECTIVE 2000/07/29 THE NOTATION OF THE "BLOCK IMPLEMENTATION DATE" OF 1996/03/25 ON THIS PIN						
WAS REPLACED WITH THE "PIN CREATION DATE" OF 1998/08/27						
** PRINTOUT INCLUDES ALL DOCUMENT TYPES (DELETED INSTRUMENTS NOT INCLUDED) **						
20M701	1998/07/29	PLAN SUBDIVISION				C
H751148	1998/08/21	NTCE AGRMT		METARA HOLDINGS INC.	THE REGIONAL MUNICIPALITY OF HALTON	C
H751764	1998/08/25	NTCE AGRMT		METARA HOLDINGS INC.	THE CORPORATION OF THE TOWN OF OAKVILLE	C
H769847	1998/12/17	APPL ANNEX R C		METARA HOLDINGS INC.	THE CORPORATION OF THE TOWN OF OAKVILLE	C
	REMARKS: UNTIL EARLIER OF 10 YEARS FROM 98/12/17 OR ON COMPLETE ASSUMPTION OF SUBDIVISION WORKS & SERVICES BY THE AND THE REGIONAL MUNICIPALITY OF HALTON.					
H782026	1999/03/31	TRANSFER	$208,037	METARA HOLDINGS INC.	WAYNE, DAVID ROBERT WAYNE, ROBIN MICHELLE	C
H782027	1999/03/31	CHARGE	$162,743	WAYNE, DAVID ROBERT WAYNE, ROBIN MICHELLE	BANK OF MONTREAL	C

NOTE: ADJOINING PROPERTIES SHOULD BE INVESTIGATED TO ASCERTAIN DESCRIPTIVE INCONSISTENCIES, IF ANY, WITH DESCRIPTION REPRESENTED FOR THIS PROPERTY.
NOTE: ENSURE THAT YOUR PRINTOUT STATES THE TOTAL NUMBER OF PAGES AND THAT YOU HAVE PICKED THEM ALL UP.

Condominiums

In the automated system, condominium ownership was traditionally registered in Land Titles as a "Fee Simple Absolute". Condominium reform permits different kinds of condominiums, including leasehold condominiums. Refer to Chapter 7 for the details of condominium legislation, practice, and searching; it also contains condominium search examples and checklists.

Each condominium corporation has a Condominium Plan number and is assigned its own separate block number. Individual units are assigned PINs. The location of unit PINs is not shown on block index maps. Separate property maps, which normally indicate PIN property lines, are not generated for condominiums. Instead, the condominium plan provides the necessary description information for condominium searching. The property number for a condominium unit (the last four digits of a PIN) often corresponds with the condominium unit number. The Registry office provides a county-wide paper condominium cross-reference that indexes condominium unit and level to a PIN. The Teraview website <http://www.teraview.ca>, under the "Reference Materials" heading, provides a province-wide condominium electronic registration cross-reference that indexes condominium unit and level to a PIN. The following is an example of a cross-reference for Halton Condominium Corporation No. 306:

HALTON CONDOMINIUM PLAN NO. 306

UNIT	LEVEL	PROPERTY ID. (PIN)
1	1	25607-0001
2	1	25607-0002
3	1	25607-0003
4	1	25607-0004
5	1	25607-0005
6	1	25607-0006
7	1	25607-0007
8	1	25607-0008

In Teraview, it is now possible to search by condominium plan. The searcher selects the property search function and then selects "Search by Condominium". The searcher must enter the registration number of the condominium plan and the appropriate office-specific prefix in the search window. A complete list of office-specific condominium prefixes is available on the Teraview website (see Figure 8.4). For example, in order to search Halton Condominium Plan No. 306, Unit 1, Level 1 in Land Registry Office #20, you would enter HC306 in the search window. Teraview would then display the cross-reference for Halton Condominium Plan No. 306. Double-click on the line for Unit 1, Level 1 and Teraview then displays the unit's parcel register. Similarly, the office-specific prefix for Toronto is MTCP and for York is YRCP.

A condominium unit may include storage and a parking space or a garage; however, many condominium corporations contain separate units for the main unit, the storage unit, and the parking unit. Each unit has its own PIN and all PINs included in the purchase must be searched. In the past, condominiums were registered by way of four separate Land Titles registers. Fortunately, POLARIS has consolidated these earlier registers and all information pertaining to a unit is now included on the printout for the unit's PIN.

Figure 8.5 is an example of a Teraview printout for PIN 33813-0050 Halton Condominium Plan No. 13, Unit 20, Level 1, in Land Registry Office #20. This printout includes deleted documents.

Figure 8.4

SEARCH BY CONDOMINIUM/CONDOMINIUM PLAN PREFIXES[*]

Teraview Tips - Search by Condominium   Updated April, 2008

The following chart contains some guidelines to help you search by condominium plan number through Teraview.
From the menu "Search by Condominium", in the search window enter the registration number of the
condominium plan. The office specific prefix is listed below.

Land Registry Office	Condominium Plan Prefix	Plans available through search by Condominium
01 Algoma	ACP	1 to 3, 5 to 10, 13 to 17 and future plans
02 Brant	BCOND	49 to 58
02 Brant	BCP	59, 69, 71, 72, 74 to 77
02 Brant	BSCP	60 to 61, 64 to 66, 70, 73
02 Brant	BVLC	62
02 Brant	BSC	63
04 Ottawa-Carleton	OCCPNO	568 to 641 except 635
04 Ottawa-Carleton	OCSCPNO	642 to 671 except 645, 652, 659, 663, 666, 723 & 724
04 Ottawa-Carleton	OCVLCP	652
04 Ottawa-Carleton	OCCEPNO	659, 663 & 666
04 Ottawa-Carleton	OCCP	635, 675 to 722, 725 to 729
06 Cochrane	CCP	1 to 10 & future plans
07 Dufferin	CONDO	15 to 18 & future plans
11 Elgin	ECP	1 to 25 and future
12 Essex	ECP	100, 107 to 117 & future plans
13 Frontenac	FCP	54 to 62 & future plans
20 Halton	HCP	271
20 Halton	HC	272 to 399
20 Halton	HSTC	400 to 406, 410 to 414, 416 to 418, 420 to 423, 425 to 432, 434, 436 to 449, 452 to 457, 459, 461 to 464, 468, 472, 475, 476, 478, 479, 481 to 484, 486 to 488 & 490, 494
20 Halton	HVLC	407, 415, 435, 466 & 477
20 Halton	HCEC	408, 409, 419, 424, 433, 450, 451, 458, 460, 465, 467, 469, 470, 471, 473, 474, 480, 485, 489, 491 to 493, 495, 498
21 Hastings	CONDO	1 to 42
21 Hastings	HSCP	43
22 Huron	CONDO	0
23 Kenora	KCP	1 to 8
23 Kenora	KSTCP	9
24 Kent	KCOND	3 to 6, 8 to 22 & future plans
27 Lanark	L8CC	12 & 13
27 Lanark	L8CNO	14
28 Lennox	LCP	future plans
30 Niagara North	NNCONPL	124 to 130, 132, 135, 136, 139, 150 & 154
30 Niagara North	NNCPL	141 to 143 & 145
30 Niagara North	NNCP	131, 133, 134, 137, 138 & 140
30 Niagara North	NNCON	122, 123, 144, 151 to 153, 155 to 162, 164 to 185 & future plans
30 Niagara North	PLCON	163
30 Niagara North	CONDO	148
33 Middlesex	CONDO	147, 148, 150 to 622 & future plans
35 Muskoka	MCP	1 to 51 & future plans
36 Nipissing	CONDO	1 to 40
36 Nipissing	NIPCONDO	41
39 Northumberland	CCP	10 to 44, 47, 48 & future plans
39 Northumberland	NSCP	45 & 46
40 Durham	DCP	145 to 174 & 186 to 196
40 Durham	DSCP	175 to 180, 183
40 Durham	DCECP	181, 182 and 185
41 Oxford	OXCON	37 & 38
41 Oxford	OXCOND	5 to 36, 39 to 56 & 61
41 Oxford	OXSCON	57 to 63, 65 to 67
41 Oxford	OXFSTCON	60
41 Oxford	OXVLCON	64
41 Oxford	OXS	68
41 Oxford	OXC	69 to 78
42 Parry Sound	PSCP	1 to 6 & future plans
43 Peel	PCP	501 to 767 & future plans
44 Perth	PERCON	14 to 25 & future plans
45 Peterborough	PCC	52 & 53
45 Peterborough	PCP	47 to 51, 54 to 66 & future plans
46 Prescott	PCP	1 to 19 & future plans
48 Rainy River	CONDO	1 & future plans
49 Renfrew	RSCP	10
49 Renfrew	RSCPNO	11
50 Russell	CONDO	17 to 25
50 Russell	RSCPNO	26 & 29 & future plans
51 Simcoe	SCP	201 to 305 & future plans
53 Sudbury	SUDCON	15
54 Timiskaming	TCP	1 & future plans
55 Thunder Bay	CONDO	1 to 38
55 Thunder Bay	TBVLCP	39 & 40
55 Thunder Bay	TBCP	41 & 42
57 Victoria	VCP	17 to 23 & future plans
58 Waterloo	WCP	246 to 430 & future plans
59 Niagara South	CONDO	53 to 83 & future plans
61 Wellington	WCP	95 to 134 & future plans
62 Wentworth	WCP	207 to 399 & future plans
65 York	YRCP	869 to 871, 873 to 1062 & future plans
65 York	YRC	872
80 Toronto	TCP	1633 to 1782 & future plans
80 Toronto	MTCP	958, 966, 988, 990, 992, 994, 1000, 1006 to 1418
80 Toronto	MTSCP	1419
80 Toronto	TSCP (Standard)	1420 to 1435, 1437 to 1448, 1451, 1452, 1454 to 1488 & 1491 to 1507, 1509 to 1511, 1513, 1515 to 1519, 1521, 1523 to 1532, 1535 to 1557, 1559 to 1566, 1568 to 1579, 1581 to 1583, 1585 to 1589, 1591 to 1603, 1606 to 1618, 1620 to 1622, 1625 to 1630, 1632
80 Toronto	TCECP (Common Elements)	1436, 1449, 1450, 1453, 1489, 1490, 1508, 1512, 1514, 1520, 1522, 1534, 1558, 1567, 1580, 1584, 1590, 1604, 1605, 1619, 1623, 1624, 1631
80 Toronto	TLCP (Leasehold)	1533
80 Toronto	TVLCP (Vacant Land)	

In order to search by condominium plan number, the condominium plan must have been opened and carried forward onto the individual
PINs for unit and level in POLARIS

* The prefixes may vary depending on the condominium being searched. If a search is unsuccessful, please contact Registry Office

---

Figure 8.5

HALTON CONDOMINIUM PLAN NO. 13, UNIT 20, LEVEL 1, PIN 33813-0050 (LT)[*]

Figure 8.5 (cont'd)

Ontario
Ministry of Government Services

LAND REGISTRY OFFICE #20

PARCEL REGISTER (ABBREVIATED) FOR PROPERTY IDENTIFIER

33813-0050 (LT)

SUBJECT TO RESERVATIONS IN CROWN GRANT

PAGE 2 OF 2
PREPARED FOR henry123
ON 2008/03/14 AT 13:35:14

PROPERTY DESCRIPTION: UNIT 20, LEVEL 1, HALTON CONDOMINIUM PLAN NO. 13 AND ITS APPURTENANT INTEREST. THE DESCRIPTION OF THE CONDOMINIUM PROPERTY IS: PT LT 12, ALL OF LT 13,
W/S SPARROW ST SOUTH, PT 1, 3R6925; PAISLEY, MORE FULLY DESCRIBED IN SCHEDULE 'A' OF DECLARATION LT432472; GEORGETOWN

PROPERTY REMARKS:

ESTATE/QUALIFIER
FEE SIMPLE
ABSOLUTE

RECENTLY:
CONDOMINIUM FROM 33883-0000

PIN CREATION DATE:
2006/06/19

OWNERS' NAMES
7774715 ONTARIO LTD.

CAPACITY   SHARE
ROWN

REG. NUM.	DATE	INSTRUMENT TYPE	AMOUNT	PARTIES FROM	PARTIES TO	CERT/CHKD
LT759082	2006/01/26	NO ASSGN RENT GEN				C
	REMARKS: LT759061					
LT759181	2006/01/31	CHARGE	$300,000		BEAR, YOGI	C
LT759402	2006/03/15	NO CHGN ADDR CONDO		HALTON CONDOMINIUM CORPORATION NO. 13		C
BR6290	2007/08/28	CONSTRUCTION LIEN		*** COMPLETELY DELETED *** ALGONQUIN CONSTRUCTION LIMITED		
BR8780	2007/11/15	DIS CONSTRUCT LIEN		*** COMPLETELY DELETED ***	ALGONQUIN CONSTRUCTION LIMITED	
	REMARKS: RE : BR6290					
BR8785	2007/11/15	CONSTRUCTION LIEN	$450,000	ALGONQUIN CONSTRUCTION LIMITED		C
BR9992	2007/12/31	CERTIFICATE		ALGONQUIN CONSTRUCTION LIMITED		C

NOTE: ADJOINING PROPERTIES SHOULD BE INVESTIGATED TO ASCERTAIN DESCRIPTIVE INCONSISTENCIES, IF ANY, WITH DESCRIPTION REPRESENTED FOR THIS PROPERTY.
NOTE: ENSURE THAT YOUR PRINTOUT STATES THE TOTAL NUMBER OF PAGES AND THAT YOU HAVE PICKED THEM ALL UP.

Land Titles Conversion Qualified Title

A Land Titles Conversion Qualified title (LTCQ) search is for land that has been legally converted from Registry to Land Titles. It is similar in procedure to an automated Land Titles search, but is subject to different title qualifiers on the guarantee of ownership as set out in ss. 44 to 46 of the *Land Titles Act*. Additional LTCQ qualifiers are listed on the parcel register printout. The legal qualifiers and the government assurance fund ownership guarantees involved in an LTCQ search are different from a conventional Land Titles Absolute search and result in different search requirements. For example, LTCQ titles are subject to mature claims for adverse possession, misdescription, and some short-term unregistered *Registry Act* leases. Therefore, LTCQ parcels require searches of adjoining lands descriptions similar to those required by Registry. An LTCQ is not subject to *Planning Act* part lot and subdivision control contraventions or corporate escheats and forfeitures to the Crown that took place prior to the date of the conversion. A LTCQ is not subject to provincial succession duties or dower rights.

LAND TITLES CONVERSION

Due to cost, volume, and time restrictions, the Teranet administrative conversion search is radically different from the standard 40-year Registry search. Specifically agreed upon search procedures for administrative conversion of Registry land to Land Titles are authorized under s. 32 of the *Land Titles Act*. In order to convert a property from Registry to Land Titles, Teranet staff establishes ownership through a search of title for either a period of ten years immediately preceding the search date or back three deeds, whichever happens to be the longer time period. No survey was completed and no notice of the conversion was given persons with interests in the land or to adjoining owners.

Administrative Conversion Search

The administrative conversion search includes only registered documents and ignores deposits (not registrations under the *Registry Act*), which in the past frequently shed light on boundaries and possessory claims, and other title deficiencies. Encumbrances and restrictions registered and still outstanding on the abstract within the 40-year period are brought forward and listed as current on the new parcel register, but not necessarily checked for current validity. For example, mortgages are not examined and restrictive covenants, easements, by-laws, and *Planning Act* consents are not checked for expiry dates. Consequently, documents containing expired interests, such as restrictive covenants, are frequently listed in the property description line as active on the new parcel register. On the other hand, encumbrances such as easements and restrictive covenants that were incorporated in older transfers or other documents were not infrequently missed. Easements and restrictive covenants that were not registered within the last 40 years by a separate document or a notice of claim are not brought forward to the new LTCQ parcel register. A full *Planning Act* search is completed. Executions are searched against only the last registered owner(s) and previous owners if the current title is non-arm's-length at the time of conversion, and corporate status searches are not done.

"Subject to" Interests and Documents Brought Forward on Conversion

Documents and "subject to" interests that no longer apply may have been brought forward to LTCQ parcels by expedited administrative conversion procedures. Ministry of Government Services Bulletin No. 2008-05 explains the reasons for bringing forward no longer effective interests and how to delete these interests. It also sets out procedures for how to bring forward documents that were missed in the conversion. A separate bulletin exists for easements (Chapter 9). "Subject to" interests may refer to the related document in a generic way, such as "subject to" instrument number 12345, or may be more specific by setting out that the interest concerns a description, debts, spousal interest, a beneficiary's interest, or an execution.

"Subject to" interests are deleted by an Application to Amend the Register under s. 75 of the *Land Titles Act* in the non-electronic environment, or by an Application General, specific to the type of interest in the electronic environment. The application is made by an interested party and contains a solicitor's statements or affidavits, and may be based on a solicitor's opinion, evidence in the solicitor's possession, a consent of a third party, case law, or limitation periods under the *Real Property Limitations Act*, R.S.O. 1990, c. L.15. The most common "subject to" interests are executions, easements, restrictive covenants, description notices, beneficiaries' interests, debts, construction liens and certificates of action, agreements of purchase and sale, certificates of pending litigation, mortgage related documents such as assignments and amendments, leases, life interests, and vendors' liens.

Creation of the Land Titles Conversion Parcel Register

When Teranet converts Registry lands to Land Titles, it creates computerized maps using only registered description materials; no survey is done. Properties are parcelized and assigned a PIN. Teranet staff generates a new parcel register from the conversion searches. Each new LTCQ parcel register is identified by a PIN and includes the statement that it is "certified by the land registrar in accordance with the *Land Titles Act*". The parcel's estate qualifier is described as "FEE SIMPLE LT CONVERSION QUALIFIED". The parcel register sets out the new title qualifiers, the date of conversion to Land Titles, the PIN creation date and the property description, owners, and registered documents. The property description line contains either a stand-alone legal description as in traditional Land Titles or a reference to the description in the last ownership document, usually the deed that was current at the time of conversion, for example "as in instrument number 123456". The "as in" description document as of the date of conversion is the only document that contains the full legal description. All registrations following conversion need only be described by the PIN and a short legal description that refers to the "as in" description document. At the top of the new parcel page, the title is noted as being subject to any executions revealed by the conversion search, including similar name executions, against the last registered owners. These outstanding executions are cross-referenced by registration number.

Occasionally conversion searchers will find a title problem. If the title problem is minor, it may be noted as a special qualifier or notice on the title. If, however, the title deficiency is serious, Teranet will classify the title as a "non-convert" and automate the property as a Registry title.

The accuracy of the new parcel register is guaranteed by the Land Titles Assurance Fund, subject to the new title qualifications in s. 44 of the *Land Titles Act* and listed on each LTCQ parcel register printout. These modified title qualifiers are unique to LTCQ titles. Each LTCQ title is subject to the new title qualifications as of the date of conversion to Land Titles. For example, LTCQ parcels are guaranteed against *Planning Act* contraventions, outstanding dower rights, succession duty liens, and previous corporate escheats and forfeitures to the Crown up to the date of conversion. Hence, it is unnecessary to search behind the PIN's date of conversion and the POLARIS record for any of these title issues. From the PIN's date of conversion to Land Titles until the present, an LTCQ title is subject to the usual Land Titles qualifiers for a Land Titles Absolute Title (see Chapter 6). As a result, it is necessary to search for corporate escheats and *Planning Act* contraventions from the PIN's date of conversion up to the present, but not for dower and succession duty, as they are now abolished. Except for the uncertainty of mature adverse possession and easement by prescription rights which must be searched as in Registry and unregistered leases in possession, an LTCQ title provides a title guarantee superior to a Land Titles Absolute.

Land Titles Conversion Qualified Qualifiers

Land Titles Conversion Qualified (fee simple) titles are subject to the following qualifications:

1. *Provincial succession duties and escheat or forfeiture to the Crown,* created prior to conversion, do not affect the new LTCQ title at the time of registration in Land Titles. Note, however, that an escheat that took place after the date of conversion could give rise to a title defect. Succession duties are abolished, so no new claims can arise.

2. *Planning Act subdivision and part lot control contraventions,* which took place prior to the PIN's date of conversion, no longer affect title at the date of conversion to Land Titles. Note, however, that a *Planning Act* subdivision or part lot control violation that takes place after the date of conversion could invalidate title (see Chapter 11).

3. *Mature claims of adverse possession* are defined as the rights of any person who would, but for the *Land Titles Act*, be entitled to the land

or any part of it through length of adverse possession, prescription, misdescription, or boundaries settled by convention. Mature adverse possession or easements by prescription that are fully enforceable in Registry at the PIN's date of conversion are carried forward into Land Titles and create an encumbrance on title. All automated LTCQ parcel register printouts contain the warning that "ADJOINING PROPERTIES SHOULD BE INVESTIGATED TO ASCERTAIN DESCRIPTIVE INCONSISTENCIES, IF ANY, WITH DESCRIPTION REPRE- SENTED FOR THIS PROPERTY". Note, however, that claims based on possession that takes place after the PIN's date of conversion are barred in Land Titles. Keep in mind that even in Land Titles there is no guarantee as to extent of land. Only a survey can determine extent of title.

4. *Dower rights* that vested prior to the PIN's date of conversion no longer affect title on conversion to Land Titles. Dower rights are abol- ished and do not affect LTCQ titles in any way.

5. *Spousal rights under the Family Law Act*, R.S.O. 1990, c. F.3 that were generated prior to the PIN's date of conversion no longer affect title on conversion to Land Titles, unless the property was marked subject to spousal rights on the parcel register. Note, however, that spousal rights claims that are generated after the PIN's date of conversion may affect title.

6. *Existing unregistered leases under the Registry Act* that are for a term of up to seven years and that are in possession are brought forward into Land Titles during conversion on a one-time-only basis. These unregistered, in possession, *Registry Act* leases are no longer a prob- lem once seven years have passed from the date of conversion. Note, however, that unregistered leases that were entered into after the PIN's date of conversion fall under the usual Land Titles rules that provide that only leases for a term/reversion of three years or less, which are in possession, need not be registered in order to be an en- cumbrance on title.

7. *Writs of execution not recorded on the parcel register at the PIN's date of conversion* that relate to registered owners prior to the PIN's date of conversion no longer affect title on conversion unless the property was marked subject to executions listed on the parcel register. This notation is placed at the end of the description line on the parcel printout. Note, however, that executions are searched following conversion against the current registered owner as per the parcel register.

The sample POLARIS simulation searches and parcel register printouts found later in this chapter are based on Land Titles Conversion Qualified parcels.

Land Titles Absolute Plus

An Application to Upgrade Land Titles Conversion Qualified Title to a Land Titles Absolute Plus title can upgrade an LTCQ to a Land Titles Absolute Plus (LT PLUS). An owner must complete an Application to Upgrade to Absolute Title in order to: register a new plan of subdivision or a condominium plan on an LTCQ parcel; consolidate an LTCQ parcel with a Land Titles Absolute parcel; remove issues of mature adverse possession, easements by prescription, misdescription and description inconsistencies; settle any "subject to" title problems; or remove the qualifier for pre-conversion *Registry Act* leases, which are in possession but unregistered. Chapter 6 elaborates on the application process.

The application removes the uncertainty of the LTCQ description qualifier as no adverse possession exists in an LT PLUS title. Dower, succession duties, escheat claims, and in the majority of titles, *Planning Act* contraventions are cancelled up to the date of registration with an Absolute Plus title. As a result, LT PLUS land is searched in a similar manner as for an LTCQ title, except that adjoining lands are no longer checked for boundary discrepancies and potential encroachments. In addition, the parcel description is guaranteed and the title is free of escheats, dower, succession duties, and usually *Planning Act* violations up to the date of registration of the Absolute Plus title (for post-August 2001 registrations). A Land Titles Absolute Plus title offers a more comprehensive title guarantee than either an LTCQ or a conventional Land Titles Absolute. Land Titles Absolute Plus is the best of all titles.

The "Estate/Qualifier" on an Land Titles Absolute Plus parcel is either "FEE SIMPLE LT ABSOLUTE" or "FEE SIMPLE LT ABSOLUTE PLUS". The estate/qualifier in early LT PLUS registers did not distinguish between an Absolute and an Absolute Plus. Registers created by more recent applications state that the estate qualifier is a Land Titles Absolute Plus. On older LT PLUS registers, it is only the Property Remarks line on the POLARIS printout that sets out the applicable qualifiers that distinguishes a Land Titles Absolute Plus parcel from a Land Titles Absolute parcel.

Not all LT PLUS parcels are created equal! It is critically important to review the specific qualifiers listed on an LT PLUS parcel. They are not always the same, particularly in relation to the *Planning Act*. Special rules apply for *Planning Act* contraventions and LT PLUS parcels. The LT PLUS parcel is always clear of any *Planning Act* contraventions prior to the date of conversion for the parent LTCQ parcel. For parcels created since August 2001, it often has a special qualifier added to the face of the LT PLUS parcel register that clears it from any *Planning Act* violation prior to the date of creation and registration of the new LT PLUS parcel. Careful review of the LT PLUS parcel will show whether a *Planning Act* qualifier was added to cover the time between conversion to Land Titles and the creation of the LT PLUS parcel. On an LT PLUS parcel, it is necessary to check for *Planning Act* contraventions from either the date of conversion to the original LTCQ parcel, or the date of creation to the LT PLUS when there is a *Planning Act* qualifier added to the register, up to present. Since August 2001, most new LT PLUS parcels have a special qualifier that clears potential *Planning Act* contraventions prior to the date of registration of the LT PLUS parcel. Current applications require evidence that there are no *Planning Act* contraventions between the LTCQ conversion date and the registration of the new LT PLUS parcel. As a result, most searches of LT PLUS parcels will only require a *Planning Act* compliance search from the date of registration of the new parcel.

When an LT PLUS parcel register contains the following wording, the lawyer can start *Planning Act* compliance searches as of the date of registration with an absolute title.

> SUBJECT TO SUBSECTION 44(1) OF THE LAND TITLES ACT, EXCEPT PARAGRAPHS 3 AND 14 AND PROVINCIAL SUCCESSION DUTIES AND EXCEPT PARAGRAPH 11 AND ESCHEATS OR FORFEITURE TO THE CROWN UP TO THE DATE OF REGISTRATION WITH AN ABSOLUTE TITLE.

In older LT PLUS titles, if the property remarks line does not include the *Planning Act* exemption qualifier, it is necessary to start the *Planning Act* search as of the date of conversion for the parent LTCQ parcel. The wording in this situation is as follows:

> SUBJECT ON THE DATE OF REGISTRATION DECEMBER 21, 1999 WITH AN ABSOLUTE TITLE TO SUBSECTION 44 (1) OF THE LAND TITLES ACT, EXCEPT PARAGRAPHS 3 AND PROVINCIAL SUCCESSION DUTIES.

Figure 8.6 is an example of an older Land Titles Absolute Plus parcel printout. Note that the parcel register printout does not state Land Titles Absolute Plus after "estate/qualifier. This LT PLUS does not except the *Planning Act* s. 11 qualifier as of the date of registration. It does not exclude escheat to the Crown as of the date of registration. On this parcel, a lawyer would check for *Planning Act* contraventions starting at the date of conversion to the original LTCQ parcel. The lawyer would also check for corporate escheat from the date of conversion of the parent LTCQ, unless using title insurance for alternative coverage.

Figure 8.6

LAND TITLES ABSOLUTE PLUS PRINTOUT 08149-0183 (LT)

Ontario

MINISTRY OF
CONSUMER AND
COMMERCIAL
RELATIONS

LAND
REGISTRY
OFFICE #33

PARCEL REGISTER (ABBREVIATED) FOR PROPERTY IDENTIFIER

08149-0183 (LT)

SUBJECT TO RESERVATIONS IN CROWN GRANT

PAGE 1 OF 2
PREPARED FOR:
ON2000/02/25 AT 10:20

PROPERTY DESCRIPTION: LOT 32, PLAN 33M-361, LONDON TOWNSHIP. S/T EASE OVER PT 10 PL 33R-13268 AS IN L7508483

PROPERTY REMARKS: *SUBJECT, ON THE DATE OF REGISTRATION (97/08/26) WITH AN ABSOLUTE TITLE, TO SUBSECTION 44(1) OF THE LAND TITLES ACT, EXCEPT PARAGRAPH 3 AND (CONT. BELOW)

ESTATE/QUALIFIER
FEE SIMPLE
ABSOLUTE

RECENTLY
SUBDIVISION
FROM 08139-0150

PIN ACTIVATION DATE
1989/12/11

OWNERS' NAMES
RADCLIFFE, RICHARD MICHAEL
RADCLIFFE, EMMA SIMONE

CAPACITY SHARE
JTEN
JTEN

REG. NUM.	DATE	INSTRUMENT TYPE	AMOUNT	PARTIES FROM	PARTIES TO	CERT/CHKD	FILM	FUTURE OFFICE USE
** PRINTOUT INCLUDES ALL DOCUMENT TYPES (DELETED INSTRUMENTS NOT INCLUDED)**								
118888	1999/04/09	BYLAW				C		
CORRECTIONS: THIS INSTRUMENT" WAS DELETED FROM PROPERTY 08072-0175 IN ERROR AND WAS RE-INSTATED ON 1993/03/17 BY BRUCE BURT.								
33R3360	1982/09/07	PLAN REFERENCE				C		
33R13058	1997/08/26	PLAN REFERENCE				C		
L7487026	1997/08/26	NOTICE		WALDEN ESTATES LIMITED		C		
REMARKS: APPLICATION TO ABSOLUTE TITLE								
L7494474	1997/10/21	NOTICE		WALDEN ESTATES LIMITED		C		
L7500930	1997/12/04	PLAN DOCUMENT		WALDEN ESTATES LIMITED	THE CORPORATION OF THE TOWNSHIP OF LONDON	C		
REMARKS: L7487775								
33R361	1997/12/04	PLAN SUBDIVISION				C		
L7501971	1997/12/11	APPL ANNEX R C		WALDEN ESTATES LIMITED		C		
REMARKS: EXPIRES 10 YEARS FROM DECEMBER 4 1997								
33R13268	1998/01/30	PLAN REFERENCE	2			C		
L7508483	1998/02/05	TRANS EASEMT	$	WALDEN ESTATES LIMITED	THE CORPORATION OF THE TOWNSHIP OF MIDDLASEX CENTRE	C		
L7512355	1998/03/12	POSTPONEMENT		DOYLE LTD. NANABUSH PROPERTIES LIMITED	THE CORPORATION OF THE TOWNSHIP OF MIDDLASEX CENTRE	C		
REMARKS: L7487777,L7503017,L7505260 TO L7508483								

NOTE: ADJOINING PROPERTIES SHOULD BE INVESTIGATED TO ASCERTAIN DESCRIPTIVE INCONSISTENCIES, IF ANY, WITH DESCRIPTION REPRESENTED FOR THIS PROPERTY.
NOTE: ENSURE THAT YOUR PRINTOUT STATES THE TOTAL NUMBER OF PAGES AND THAT YOU HAVE PICKED THEM ALL UP.

Figure 8.6 (cont'd)

Ontario

MINISTRY OF
CONSUMER AND
COMMERCIAL
RELATIONS

LAND
REGISTRY
OFFICE #3

PARCEL REGISTER (ABBREVIATED) FOR PROPERTY IDENTIFIER

08149-0183 (LT)

PAGE 2 OF 2
PREPARED FOR:
ON2000/02/25 AT 10:20

PROPERTY DESCRIPTION:

PROPERTY REMARKS: RECENTLY

PIN ACTIVATION DATE

ESTATE/QUALIFIER

REG. NUM.	DATE	INSTRUMENT TYPE	AMOUNT	PARTIES FROM	PARTIES TO	CERT./ CHKD	FILM	FUTURE OFFICE USE
ER411b	1999/03/01	CHARGE	$ 405,000	RADCLIFFE CONSTRUCTORS LIMITED	MEADOWCREEK ESTATES LIMITED	C		
ER4117	1999/03/01 REMARKS: ER4176	ASSGMT CH		WALDEN ESTATES LIMITED	CANADIAN IMPERIAL BANK OF COMMERCE	C		
ER48749	2000/02/04	TRANSFER	$ 45,000	RADCLIFFE CONSTRUCTORS LIMITED	RADCLIFFE, RICHARD MICHAEL RADCLIFFE, EMMA SIMONE	◊		

CONTINUATION OF PROPERTY REMARKS: PROVINCIAL SUCCESSION DUTIES."

NOTE: ADJOINING PROPERTIES SHOULD BE INVESTIGATED TO ASCERTAIN DESCRIPTIVE INCONSISTENCIES, IF ANY, WITH DESCRIPTION REPRESENTED FOR THIS PROPERTY.
NOTE: ENSURE THAT YOUR PRINTOUT STATES THE TOTAL NUMBER OF PAGES AND THAT YOU HAVE PICKED THEM ALL UP.

Figure 8.6.1 is an example of recent LT PLUS parcel printout. Note that the parcel register printout states LT PLUS after "estate/qualifier". This LT PLUS does except the *Planning Act* s. 11 qualifier as of the date of registration. It also excepts escheats to the Crown. On this parcel, a lawyer would check for *Planning Act* contraventions and escheats starting at the date of registration as an Absolute Plus title (2007/02/23). Note also that the current transfer on this parcel is accompanied by a *Planning Act* consent. It would be necessary to check this consent for conditions and time limits.

Figure 8.6.1

LAND TITLES ABSOLUTE PLUS PARCEL PRINTOUT 71007-0007 (LT)[*]

Ontario — Ministry of Government and Consumer Services

LAND REGISTRY OFFICE #61

PARCEL REGISTER (ABBREVIATED) FOR PROPERTY IDENTIFIER

71007-0007 (LT)

SUBJECT TO RESERVATIONS IN CROWN GRANT

PAGE 1 OF 1
PREPARED FOR henry123
ON 2008/05/27 AT 13:26:29

PROPERTY DESCRIPTION: PT BKLKS 1,2,3,4 PL WESTERN CANADA LOAN & SAVINGS COMPANY PALMERSTON - PT 1 , 61R10007; MINTO

PROPERTY REMARKS: FOR THE PURPOSE OF THE QUALIFIER, THE DATE OF REGISTRATION OF ABSOLUTETITLE IS 2007 02 23

ESTATE/QUALIFIER:
FEE SIMPLE
LT ABSOLUTE PLUS

RECENTLY:
DIVISION FROM 71007-46

PIN CREATION DATE:
2008/01/02

OWNERS' NAMES:
HALIBURTON CORPORATION

CAPACITY   SHARE

REG. NUM.	DATE	INSTRUMENT TYPE	AMOUNT	PARTIES FROM	PARTIES TO	CERT/CHKD
** PRINTOUT INCLUDES ALL DOCUMENT TYPES AND DELETED INSTRUMENTS SINCE: 2008/01/02 **						
** SUBJECT TO SUBSECTION 44(1) OF THE LAND TITLES ACT, EXCEPT PARAGRAPHS 3 AND 14 AND *						
** PROVINCIAL SUCCESSION DUTIES AND EXCEPT PARAGRAPH 11 AND ESCHEATS OR FORFEITURE **						
** TO THE CROWN UP TO THE DATE OF REGISTRATION WITH AN ABSOLUTE TITLE. **						
61R10555	2007/02/23	PLAN REFERENCE				C
WC165455	2007/02/23	APL ABSOLUTE TITLE		NEW GREEN HOMES LIMITED SOLAR LIMITED WINDPOWER CONSTRUCTION LIMITED	NEW GREEN HOMES LIMITED SOLAR LIMITED WINDPOWER CONSTRUCTION LIMITED	C
61R10007	2007/11/16	PLAN REFERENCE				C
WC197500	2007/12/20	TRANSFER	$10,147,485	WINDPOWER CONSTRUCTION LIMITED SOLAR LIMITED NEW GREEN HOMES LIMITED	HALIBURTON CORPORATION	C
REMARKS: PLANNING ACT CONSENT						

NOTE: ADJOINING PROPERTIES SHOULD BE INVESTIGATED TO ASCERTAIN DESCRIPTIVE INCONSISTENCIES, IF ANY, WITH DESCRIPTION REPRESENTED FOR THIS PROPERTY.
NOTE: ENSURE THAT YOUR PRINTOUT STATES THE TOTAL NUMBER OF PAGES AND THAT YOU HAVE PICKED THEM ALL UP.

ELECTRONIC SEARCHING IN POLARIS

Teraview permits online search and registration access to all Ontario Registry offices that contain POLARIS designated land. Almost all Registry offices have POLARIS search capability. All searches on Teraview involve the use of the POLARIS ownership database as well as POLARIS block and property maps, or Teraview digital maps. Lawyers search from their offices using the online Teraview search and registration software.

A Teraview self-serve search station called a ROSCO workstation is available for the public at local Registry offices. Clients can search and print writ clearance certificates and abstracts, search and print parcel registers, view and print electronic documents, and print activity and fee summaries. Other self-serve search services include Registry office photocopiers, plan copiers, and microfilm readers. Search related services require a Teranet Cash Card (available at the Registry office) or a major credit card. A service fee is charged for issuing a Teranet card. Block and property maps may be purchased from Teranet and are available at the Registry office, whereas Teraview digital maps are available to be viewed and printed online. Teraview search procedures will continue in a state of change, at least until the POLARIS conversion is complete. New properties are being designated and coming online on an ongoing basis. The Teraview website contains a list of Registry offices currently on POLARIS as well as a roll-out schedule for the Registry offices next in line for automation.

POLARIS PARCEL REGISTER PRINTOUT (LTCQ)

Figure 8.7 illustrates the layout and contents of the Land Titles Conversion Qualified parcel register for PIN 08242-0006 (LT), *not including deleted documents*, generated by the Teraview online search service. Figure 8.8 illustrates the layout and contents for the same LTCQ parcel register, also generated on Teraview; however, it *includes deleted documents*. Full searches and title insurers require deleted documents. When relying on a printout, always confirm that it contains deleted as well as active documents. Figures 8.9 and 8.10 illustrate the related block and property maps for PIN 08242-0006 (LT). Review the following when searching this parcel register:

1. PIN and Land Titles division (office);

2. registered title and estate in land (*e.g.*, fee simple, LTCQ) and general and special title qualifiers;

3. registered owners' names and capacity, and reconcile to information in the instruments;

4. *date of conversion* to Land Titles. The date of conversion is different from the PIN creation date, the PIN activation date, or the block activation date; and

5. current legal description, as in 764392, being Part Lots 40 & 41 on Plan 68(W) and Part Lot 43 on Plan 649(W). Make copies of Plans 68(W), 649(W) and all reference plans indicated on the parcel register. Also make a copy of the relevant property index map or Teraview digital map. Note that this LTCQ PIN is made up of part lots and that an adjoining lands search for both *Planning Act* violations and boundary encroachments must be completed.

Follow the procedures below when searching this parcel register:

1. Copy the legal descriptions of the PIN from instrument number 764392 and the legal descriptions for all adjoining PINs. The property index map or Teraview digital map provides the adjoining PINs. Teraview will generate an adjoining owner list and the adjoining owner PIN printouts provide the instrument numbers for the adjoining descriptions. Sketch the PIN and adjoining PINs to scale from the document descriptions. Superimpose the sketch on the property index map or Teraview digital map, if the descriptions are simple and if it is practicable. Otherwise, produce an illustration to scale as you would in a Registry search. Check whether the property descriptions reveal overlaps, gaps, inconsistencies, easements, or potential encroachments. Reconcile description information with the POLARIS maps, the agreement of purchase and sale, and, when available, the survey.

2. Complete an adjoining lands search for PINs 0005, 0007, 0015, 0016, and the adjoining street, being PIN 0105.

    For *Planning Act* purposes, check for common owners and *Planning Act* by-laws, consents, validation certificates, and declarations back to 1992/06/08, being the date of conversion. Be sure to check back to the date of conversion and not a PIN creation or activation date.

    For boundary purposes, check the adjoining lands for registrations that might affect boundaries, including easements and encroachment agreements. Go back into Abstract book 148 if necessary to resolve description inconsistencies.

3. View and print online from Teraview instrument numbers LT 595686 and LT 595687, being the current transfer and outstanding charge. Some documents can be ordered online and couriered, for example, plans. Pre-conversion documents are available in the Registry office on microfiche or microfilm and can be copied or summarized.

4. Search executions against the name of the current registered owner, Jessie Ruth Corbett, as it appears on the parcel register, assuming it is the same as the registered owners in the documents. Note that the parcel is not marked subject to additional executions at the top of the printout.

Figure 8.7

LTCQ PARCEL REGISTER PRINTOUT WITHOUT DELETED DOCUMENTS (TERAVIEW)

Figure 8.8

LTCQ PARCEL REGISTER PRINTOUT WITH DELETED DOCUMENTS (TERAVIEW)

Figure 8.8 (cont'd)

MINISTRY OF
CONSUMER AND
COMMERCIAL
RELATIONS

LAND
REGISTRY
OFFICE #13

PARCEL REGISTER (ABBREVIATED) FOR PROPERTY IDENTIFIER

08242-0006 (LT)

PAGE 2 OF 2
PREPARED FOR kpap-001
ON 1999/06/18 AT 13:48:59

* CERTIFIED BY LAND REGISTRAR IN ACCORDANCE WITH LAND TITLES ACT * SUBJECT TO RESERVATIONS IN CROWN GRANT *

REG. NUM.	DATE	INSTRUMENT TYPE	AMOUNT	PARTIES FROM	PARTIES TO	CERT/CHKD
LT554109	1997/01/22	APPL CT ORDER		*** COMPLETELY DELETED *** ONTARIO COURT	SAUNDERS & TIGGER INC., TRUSTEE ESTATE OF BUTTERWORTHS, WILLIAM MOORE BANKRUPT	D
LT555675	1997/10/29	APPLICATION		*** COMPLETELY DELETED *** IROQUOIS TRUST COMPANY		D
		REMARKS: RE: 454191				
LT555686	1997/10/29	TRANS PWR OF SALE	$ 400,000	IROQUOIS TRUST COMPANY	CORBETT, JESSIE RUTH	C
		REMARKS: RE: CHARGE 512791				
LT555687	1997/10/29	CHARGE	$ 300,000	CORBETT, JESSIE RUTH	MONTREAL LIFE TRUST COMPANY	C

NOTE: ADJOINING PROPERTIES SHOULD BE INVESTIGATED TO ASCERTAIN DESCRIPTIVE INCONSISTENCIES, IF ANY, WITH DESCRIPTION REPRESENTED FOR THIS PROPERTY.
NOTE: ENSURE THAT YOUR PRINTOUT STATES THE TOTAL NUMBER OF PAGES AND THAT YOU HAVE PICKED THEM ALL UP.

NOTE: EFFECTIVE 2000/07/29 THE NOTATION OF THE BLOCK IMPLEMENTATION DATE OF 1992/06/08 ON THIS PIN WAS REPLACED WITH THE PIN CREATION DATE OF 1992/06/08.

Figure 8.9
BLOCK INDEX MAP

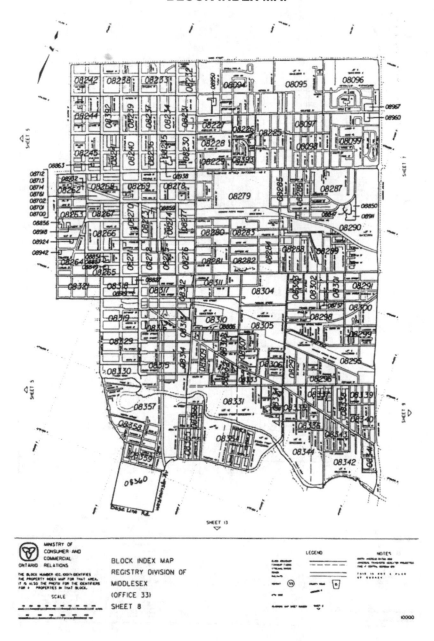

BLOCK INDEX MAP
REGISTRY DIVISION OF
MIDDLESEX
(OFFICE 33)
SHEET 8

Figure 8.10
PROPERTY INDEX MAP

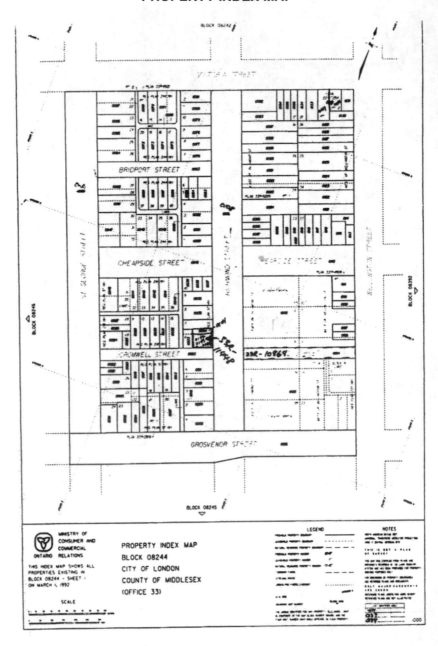

ERRORS IN THE ELECTRONIC RECORD

The creation of the POLARIS title and mapping databases is a massive transition that is subject to demanding time and financial restrictions. On occasion, inaccuracies in data acquisition and entry may cause errors and omissions in the new electronic title record. Lawyers often refer back to the prior paper records when confronted with title problems. Easements, including access rights, and restrictive covenants may not have been brought forward in the conversion. Chapter 9 deals with this problem and includes recent Ministry bulletins that set out how to register easements and interests that were not brought forward in the conversion. Chapter 9 includes a case law reference on the topic. The notice of claim period and the recent cases and registration of claim *Registry Act* amendments are also discussed. This law affects the Ministry's obligation as to whether to bring forward interests and the definition of when an error may have taken place. The Land Titles Assurance Fund applies to errors in the electronic record in the same manner as it does to paper records.

TERAVIEW ONLINE SERVICES

Teranet offers exclusive access to POLARIS and to Ontario's Electronic Land Registration System through "Teraview", a remote-access, online, Windows point-and-click title searching and land registration program. The POLARIS search function is part of the larger Electronic Land Registration System, known as ELRS. Any person who accesses ELRS must have a personal security package or PSP, often referred to as a key. The key is personal to the individual and must only be used by the authorized keyholder. Lawyers' keys allow more functions (law statements) than law clerk keys. Access and security for POLARIS and ELRS is being continuously upgraded and reviewed. The Ministry's Real Estate Fraud Action Plan identifies tightened access and security to ELRS as a fundamental fraud reduction strategy. Teraview also offers WritSearch, a remote-access, online search program for writs of execution databases, maintained by the Ministry of the Attorney General. Once Teraview is installed on a personal computer, you can search online for title information involving POLARIS-designated land located anywhere in Ontario.

The Teraview Gateway offers additional services including electronic data interchange and electronic funds transfer for search and registration costs and Land Transfer Tax payments, property information, transaction management, collateral risk management, geospatial information, workflow software, and enterprise solutions. Teranet also provides "CLOSURE" a secure service with financial (insured) guarantees that manages the transfer of the closing funds. The CLOSURE service reduces the need for and the risks associated with certified cheques, bankdrafts, direct deposits, and couriers. CLOSURE services are only available to other CLOSURE participants, which now include the major Canadian lenders, lawyers, and some builders and smaller lenders. Teraview also provides extended hours of service, training, and ongoing client support.

In order to search in POLARIS with Teraview, the client must first purchase the necessary Teraview-compatible computer hardware and then purchase and install the current Teraview software, available from the online software download centre. Teraview users purchase accounts and subaccounts, receive personal security packages for each account holder, and access to the Teraview Subscriber Reference Guide. Subscribers undergo identity checks and security clearances, and enter into the Teraview Access Agreement that includes a pre-authorized payment plan agreement reflecting current transaction pricing and connect time fees as well as security and use restrictions. Subscribers are required to update software regularly and work in the current program. Real estate transaction file management programs such as Stewart Title's Internet-based LegalSTEPS and Teranet's desktop application Conveyancer provide import and export capabilities, and access links with Teraview/ELRS/POLARIS.

Once online with Teraview, clients can access property ownership information, property maps, document images, and writ information. Documents, particularly maps, may also be provided by fax or by courier.

Using WritSearch, clients can access and search executions (writs) relating to land anywhere in Ontario (see Chapter 12 for a detailed discussion of searching executions using WritSearch, OWL, and BAR-eX).

Teraview users rely on the Teraview Training Manual, the Teraview e-learning course, the Teraview Reference Guide, the Ministry of Government Services *Electronic Registration Procedures Guide*, and customer service available online or by phone.

TERAVIEW ONLINE SEARCH PROCEDURES

A title search is completed within ELRS, Teraview's electronic land registration service. Most title searches are completed within the electronic land registration service as part of a purchase, a mortgage, or a lease transaction. A conveyancer first selects a specific automated Registry office and then searches a property by reference to one of the following search methods:

1. PIN (property identification number);

2. municipal address;

3. name of owner(s);

4. prior registered instrument number, including a reference plan number (must be active documents);

5. condominium plan number (requires Registry office prefix, *e.g.*, MTCP50);

6. subdivision plan number (33M649);

7. digital map index interface service connecting the Property Index Database to the Title Index Database; and

8. road (the search by map option contains an extremely useful search by road feature).

Once the parcel record has been located, the title searcher can access full property descriptions, maps, owners' names, and a list and images of all registered documents. Whenever an adjoining lands search is required for boundaries, easements, restrictive covenants, access, or *Planning Act* purposes, similar inquiries with respect to adjoining lands can be made by using the Teraview map feature and adjoining land search feature. Teraview clients can both display and print parcel registers, maps, search screens, and documents. Copies of instruments may be requested online and faxed or delivered by courier.

Teraview software leads the searcher through a series of search inquiry screens, prompts, and information tabs. A Teraview online search incorporates standard Windows features, such as multiple windows, point-and-click selection, menu bars, drop-down lists, and HELP options.

TERAVIEW TITLE SEARCH CHECKLIST (LTCQ)

The following checklist outlines the steps for completing an LTCQ search on Teraview within the electronic land registration system. Although the mechanics of the information retrieval process on Teraview are the same for all POLARIS parcel types, the legal requirements for title searching vary greatly depending on whether you are dealing with a PDFR, a Registry Non-Convert, an LT Absolute, an LTCQ, or an LT Absolute Plus parcel. Adjoining land searches may or may not be required depending on a number of factors, such as whether you are searching a parcel containing a part lot. The sample search checklist below is based on an LTCQ parcel that comprises two part lots.

☐ Log on to Teraview using the personal security key and select e-reg/ ELRS when completing the search within the electronic land registration system. Create or open an existing docket and select the appropriate Registry office from the administration drop-down list. The active docket is displayed at the top of the screen and the active Registry office is displayed at the bottom of the screen (see Figure 8.14). When possible, have the agreement of purchase and sale, survey, or vendor's transfer/ deed available for property information.

☐ Choose "Property" on the ELRS toolbar and search the property by:

PIN:	The first five digits of the PIN identify the block; the next four digits identify the property.
Multiple PIN Properties:	Some properties are made up of multiple PINs. It is necessary to identify a multiple PIN property and search all the PINs. For example, side by sides are properties that have not been consolidated into one new PIN by an application for consolidation. Condominium purchases often involve the purchase of multiple PINs and multiple units for the living unit, the parking, and the storage units. Leases for 21 years or more may have a separate leasehold parcel and PIN. It is necessary to search both the freehold and leasehold PINs when a separate leasehold parcel has been created. Subsurface and surface rights may have separate PINs. When dealing with multiple PINs, there is a higher risk of a *Planning Act* violation; multiple PINs often require adjoining lands searches.
Address:	Not all PINs can be referenced by municipal address. Only the exact street name and spelling will provide an accurate response. Always confirm the accuracy of the PIN by cross-referencing the search using different property information (see Figure 8.13).
Name:	Given names, surnames, and corporate names, particularly common names, such as Lee or Moore, may turn up multiple responses. These multiple responses include lot, plan, and address information. Use your background information to sort out which responses are relevant. This process may involve trial and error. Searching by PIN or document registration number tends to be more efficient. Name searches are based on transferees on active transfers and parties on documents general only (see Figure 8.14).
Instrument:	The registration number of a recent, preferably last registered transfer; a reference plan number may also be entered to find the PINs relating to the parts on a reference plan.
Condominium:	A condominium unit may be searched by PIN or by condominium plan. Request the condominium plan using the proper prefix and Teraview will display all units and PINs.
Subdivision:	A lot on a subdivision plan may be searched by PIN or by subdivision plan. Request the subdivision plan using the proper prefix, such as 20M649 for a Halton subdivision, and Teraview will display all lots and PINs on the subdivision plan.
Map:	Teraview will display a series of digital maps that will find the property by location and display the PIN. It is possible to search by road using search by map and map tools. Block index and property index maps, available in large books in the Registry office, will also locate PINs.
☐	The search inquiry often returns multiple names and multiple properties owned by the same person. Select the appropriate owner name and property, and request the parcel register (see Figure 8.13).

☐ Request the parcel register, including active documents, deleted documents, or documents within a specified date range (*e.g.*, updating a search from the date it was first completed or updating from a particular registered document). Deleted documents must always be requested when completing a full search. This option displays deleted documents, such as discharged mortgages and prior transfers, as well as current registered interests. Deleted documents may reveal corporate owners subsequent to the date of conversion or the PIN registration date. Deleted documents reveal transaction patterns that indicate a higher risk of fraud. Also, when a part lot is searched, deleted documents will reveal prior owners subsequent to the date of conversion. These prior owners are checked against prior owners of adjoining lands for *Planning Act* violations. Figure 8.13 illustrates the selection of the deleted document option.

☐ Print the parcel register. Figure 8.15 is a parcel printout that contains deleted documents. Figure 8.16 is a parcel printout that contains only active documents and does not contain deleted documents. Parcel register information may also be viewed online (see Figure 8.17). Review the parcel register printout (see Figure 8.16) for the following information:

- PIN;
- whether the PIN is in Registry (R) or in Land Titles (LT);
- property description and related subdivision and reference plans (Also check for easements that affect the property. The property description contains a reference to the registration number of the transfer containing the PIN's description. Include in your search all documents mentioned in the description line including "subject to" documents such as easements, *Planning Act* consents, restrictive covenants, executions, spousal rights, estate interests, *etc.*);
- whether the parcel is described in the property description line as containing a part lot;
- whether the parcel is subject to executions (the execution number is included);
- type of parcel, referred to as estate/qualifier (*e.g.*, fee simple, LTCQ);
- date of conversion, which may be different from the PIN creation date (formerly called the PIN activation date or block implementation date);
- whether the "Recently" field contains previous PIN references; all PINs in the recently field must be printed as part of the search. Note re-entry, splits and consolidation PINs; they will be part of the adjoining land search for descriptions and *Planning Act*, when an adjoining land search is required. The "Recently" field also contains inactive or closed PINs, such as when a property is divided or severed into two new PINs. It is often necessary to print inactive PINs to review deleted documents which are necessary for *Planning Act* and description searches, and other overriding interests.
- owners' full names and capacity, such as beneficial owner (BENO) or joint tenants (JTEN);
- statement as to whether deleted documents are displayed;

- statement as to standard Land Titles qualifiers or any special qualifiers; and
- listing of all current and still relevant deleted documents, including registration number and date, instrument type, amount of money involved (not for deleted documents), and the names of the parties to the transaction.

☐ Obtain a copy of all plans mentioned on the parcel register printout. These plans may be requested online and faxed or couriered.

☐ View all active registrations on the parcel printout. Document images may be requested, viewed, and printed online. Copies of documents may be ordered online and faxed or couriered. Documents may also be available on microfilm/fiche at the Registry office. The Registry office supplies self-serve microfilm/fiche readers that allow the searcher with a Teranet Cash Card to make copies (see Figure 8.17).

☐ When researching the cause of an apparent title problem, a description problem, or a "subject to" interest that has been brought forward in the conversion, locate pre-conversion records by the cross-reference on the printout to the earlier index. View/print all parcel registers for the PIN and necessary adjacent lands PINs. Print the Teraview digital map illustrating the PIN and all adjacent PINs.

☐ Teraview simplifies the adjoining lands search. The search results screen allows the searcher to view search results, the parcel register, and document images simultaneously (see Figure 8.17). The Teraview search screen allows the searcher to switch between the PIN details, the digital map for the PIN and the adjacent lands PIN details, parcel registers, and map detail. Teraview automatically selects adjoining lands on the digital map and the adjoining lands list. However helpful, do not rely on the list! It is for reference purposes only and does not in any way guarantee that the selection of PINs includes all PINs necessary from a legal point of view to do a *Planning Act* or description search. Figure 8.18 illustrates the list of adjacent PINs. Note that two of the adjacent PINs are Registry parcels which indicate a title problem sufficiently serious as to prevent conversion to Land Titles. These parcels are Non-Converts, and list 40 years of Registry documents. Figure 8.19 illustrates the parcel registers for the adjacent PINs. Figure 8.20 illustrates the map for the property being searched combined with the adjoining properties, including roads. Teraview provides map tools (see Figure 8.21) and permits the searcher to add and remove PINs (Custom) depending on the nature of the search. You may have to supplement the adjoining lands list with additional PINs selected using the "Custom" tool. This is often the case when dealing with access easements and private roads.

☐ Complete an adjoining lands search for potential *Planning Act* violations and for description discrepancies and potential boundary encroachments when searching a PIN/parcel containing a part lot that is not exempt from subdivision or part lot control provisions under the *Planning Act*. Print the parcel registers for all adjacent PINs, including roads. It is necessary to check adjoining lands for *Planning Act* violations only from the date of conversion to Land Titles, or when possible a later start date such as three signed *Planning Act* declarations or a *Planning Act* consent. It is also necessary to review the deleted documents in the *Planning Act* searches. Note in your search whether the registered owner of the subject lands owned any of the abutting lands between the date of conversion and the date of the search.

☐ Check the descriptions of adjoining lands for description discrepancies and potential boundary encroachments, since mature adverse possession claims are carried forward as part of an LTCQ title. The PINs of all the adjoining lands are indicated on the property map and the adjoining lands list. Print the list of PINs for the adjoining lands and print their parcel registers, including deleted documents. The description line in the parcel registers for the adjoining lands provides you with a reference to a document containing the parcel description. You can use these descriptions to draft a sketch that will illustrate description gaps and overlaps and possible encroachments. Parcel registers for adjoining lands must also be checked for reference plans, easements, quit claims, encroachment agreements, and any other registration that might affect boundaries. It may be necessary to refer back to the pre-conversion Registry abstract index to track down information on boundary disputes. Remember that mature adverse possession claims may still require a full Registry-type, 40-year search (see Chapter 11 for full details on adjoining lands searches, including those for Registry and LTCQ titles).

☐ Confirm legal access to and from the property. The property map provides PINs for roads, lanes, reserves, and some major easements. Print and review the parcel registers for adjoining roads and reserves, and roads and reserves that provide or affect access. Review the road registers for plans, by-laws, agreements, expropriations, and other documents that might open, close, divert, or affect roads, reserves, and access. (Refer to Chapter 9 for full details on issues of access.)

☐ If you are dealing with simple descriptions, superimpose a sketch of the parcel by simply outlining or highlighting the main land and the adjoining lands on the Teraview property map or M-Plan or R-Plan. Illustrate dimensions, easements, and access. Colour code main land and adjoining lands. If you are dealing with a complex, such as a metes and bounds description in a township lot, complete an illustration to scale as you would in a Registry search.

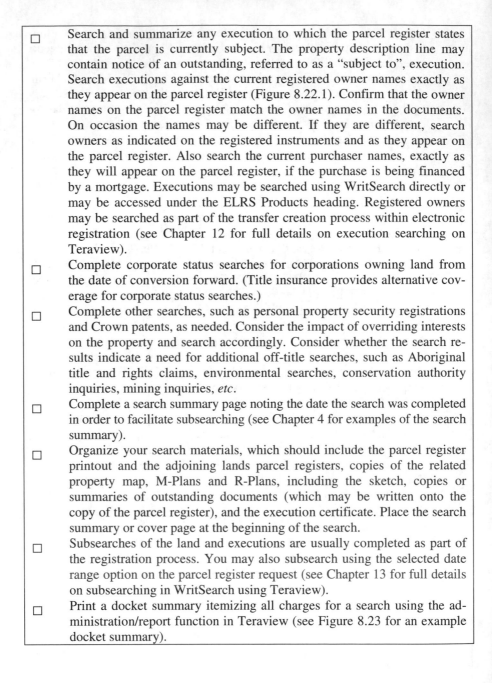

☐ Search and summarize any execution to which the parcel register states that the parcel is currently subject. The property description line may contain notice of an outstanding, referred to as a "subject to", execution. Search executions against the current registered owner names exactly as they appear on the parcel register (Figure 8.22.1). Confirm that the owner names on the parcel register match the owner names in the documents. On occasion the names may be different. If they are different, search owners as indicated on the registered instruments and as they appear on the parcel register. Also search the current purchaser names, exactly as they will appear on the parcel register, if the purchase is being financed by a mortgage. Executions may be searched using WritSearch directly or may be accessed under the ELRS Products heading. Registered owners may be searched as part of the transfer creation process within electronic registration (see Chapter 12 for full details on execution searching on Teraview).

☐ Complete corporate status searches for corporations owning land from the date of conversion forward. (Title insurance provides alternative coverage for corporate status searches.)

☐ Complete other searches, such as personal property security registrations and Crown patents, as needed. Consider the impact of overriding interests on the property and search accordingly. Consider whether the search results indicate a need for additional off-title searches, such as Aboriginal title and rights claims, environmental searches, conservation authority inquiries, mining inquiries, *etc.*

☐ Complete a search summary page noting the date the search was completed in order to facilitate subsearching (see Chapter 4 for examples of the search summary).

☐ Organize your search materials, which should include the parcel register printout and the adjoining lands parcel registers, copies of the related property map, M-Plans and R-Plans, including the sketch, copies or summaries of outstanding documents (which may be written onto the copy of the parcel register), and the execution certificate. Place the search summary or cover page at the beginning of the search.

☐ Subsearches of the land and executions are usually completed as part of the registration process. You may also subsearch using the selected date range option on the parcel register request (see Chapter 13 for full details on subsearching in WritSearch using Teraview).

☐ Print a docket summary itemizing all charges for a search using the administration/report function in Teraview (see Figure 8.23 for an example docket summary).

LAND TITLES CONVERSION QUALIFIED SEARCH ILLUSTRATIONS (TERAVIEW)

Figure 8.11

SEARCH BY ADDRESS SCREEN

Search by Address ☒

Street Number: 69	Suffix:	OK
Street Name: JACKSON AVE		Cancel
Area: (ALL) ▼		Help
Unit Type: (NONE) ▼ Unit Number:		

* Search will identify properties where this address appears on registered instruments.

Figure 8.12
SEARCH RESULTS SCREEN*

Figure 8.13

NAME LIST, SEARCH RESULTS, AND PARCEL REGISTER OPTIONS SCREENS*

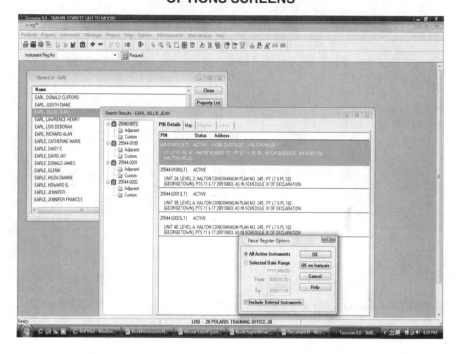

Figure 8.14

PARCEL REGISTER SCREEN[*]

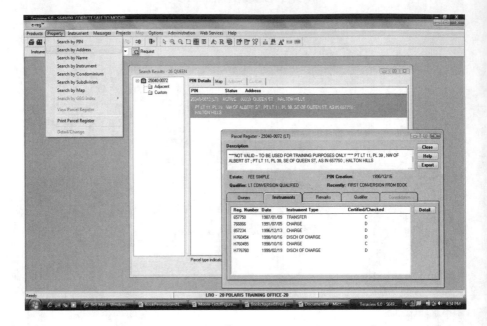

Figure 8.15

PARCEL REGISTER PRINTOUT WITH DELETED DOCUMENTS*

PARCEL REGISTER (ABBREVIATED) FOR PROPERTY IDENTIFIER

PAGE 1 OF 2
PREPARED FOR
ON 2003/07/06 AT 10:53:28

TRAINING	LAND REGISTRY OFFICE #20	25040-0172 (LT)

* CERTIFIED BY LAND REGISTRAR IN ACCORDANCE WITH LAND TITLES ACT * SUBJECT TO RESERVATIONS IN CROWN GRANT *

PROPERTY DESCRIPTION: ***** NOT VALID - TO BE USED FOR TRAINING PURPOSES ONLY ***** PT LT 11, PL 37 , NW OF ALBERT ST ; PT LT 11, PL 37 , SE OF JACKSON AVE AS IN 657760 ;
HALTON HILLS

PROPERTY REMARKS:

RECENTLY:
FIRST CONVERSION FROM BOOK

PIN CREATION DATE:
1996/12/16

ESTATE/QUALIFIER:
FEE SIMPLE
LT CONVERSION QUALIFIED

CAPACITY	SHARE
JTEN	
JTEN	

OWNERS' NAMES
EARL, BOBBIE RIGGS
EARL, BILLIE JEAN

REG. NUM.	DATE	INSTRUMENT TYPE	AMOUNT	PARTIES FROM	PARTIES TO	CERT/CHKD
				EFFECTIVE 2000/07/29 THE NOTATION OF THE "BLOCK IMPLEMENTATION DATE" OF 1996/12/16 ON THIS PIN		
				WAS REPLACED WITH THE "PIN CREATION DATE" OF 1996/12/16		
				** PRINTOUT INCLUDES ALL DOCUMENT TYPES AND DELETED INSTRUMENTS SINCE: 1996/12/13 **		
				**SUBJECT, ON FIRST REGISTRATION UNDER THE LAND TITLES ACT, TO:		
				** SUBSECTION 44(1) OF THE LAND TITLES ACT, EXCEPT PARAGRAPH 11, PARAGRAPH 14, PROVINCIAL SUCCESSION DUTIES *		
				** AND ESCHEATS OR FORFEITURE TO THE CROWN.		
				** THE RIGHTS OF ANY PERSON WHO WOULD, BUT FOR THE LAND TITLES ACT, BE ENTITLED TO THE LAND OR ANY PART OF		
				** IT THROUGH LENGTH OF ADVERSE POSSESSION, PRESCRIPTION, MISDESCRIPTION OR BOUNDARIES SETTLED BY		
				CONVENTION.		
				** ANY LEASE TO WHICH THE SUBSECTION 70(2) OF THE REGISTRY ACT APPLIES.		
				**DATE OF CONVERSION TO LAND TITLES: 1996/12/16 **		
657760	1987/01/09	TRANSFER	$300,000		EARL, BOBBIE RIGGS EARL, BILLIE JEAN	C
766867	1991/07/05	CHARGE		*** COMPLETELY DELETED ***	MEDORA FINANCIAL SERVICES	
857235	1996/12/13	CHARGE		*** COMPLETELY DELETED ***	MEDORA FINANCIAL SERVICES	
H760455	1998/10/16	DISCH OF CHARGE *REMARKS: RE: 857235*		*** COMPLETELY DELETED ***	MEDORA FINANCIAL SERVICES	
H760456	1998/10/16	CHARGE	$200,000	EARL, BOBBIE RIGGS EARL, BILLIE JEAN	MEDORA FINANCIAL SERVICES	C

NOTE: ADJOINING PROPERTIES SHOULD BE INVESTIGATED TO ASCERTAIN DESCRIPTIVE INCONSISTENCIES, IF ANY, WITH DESCRIPTION REPRESENTED FOR THIS PROPERTY.
NOTE: ENSURE THAT YOUR PRINTOUT STATES THE TOTAL NUMBER OF PAGES AND THAT YOU HAVE PICKED THEM ALL UP.

Figure 8.15 (cont'd)

PARCEL REGISTER (ABBREVIATED) FOR PROPERTY IDENTIFIER

MINISTRY OF
CONSUMER AND
BUSINESS
SERVICES

LAND
REGISTRY
OFFICE #20

PAGE 2 OF 2
PREPARED FOR
ON 2003/07/06 AT 10:53:28

25040-0172 (LT)

* CERTIFIED BY LAND REGISTRAR IN ACCORDANCE WITH LAND TITLES ACT * SUBJECT TO RESERVATIONS IN CROWN GRANT *

REG. NUM.	DATE	INSTRUMENT TYPE	AMOUNT	PARTIES FROM	PARTIES TO	CERT/ CHKD
H776761	1999/02/19	DISCH OF CHARGE		*** COMPLETELY DELETED ***	MEDORA FINANCIAL SERVICES	
	REMARKS: RE: 766867					

NOTE: ADJOINING PROPERTIES SHOULD BE INVESTIGATED TO ASCERTAIN DESCRIPTIVE INCONSISTENCIES, IF ANY, WITH DESCRIPTION REPRESENTED FOR THIS PROPERTY.
NOTE: ENSURE THAT YOUR PRINTOUT STATES THE TOTAL NUMBER OF PAGES AND THAT YOU HAVE PICKED THEM ALL UP.

Figure 8.16
PARCEL REGISTER PRINTOUT WITHOUT DELETED DOCUMENTS*

```
MINISTRY OF
CONSUMER AND          LAND                  PARCEL REGISTER (ABBREVIATED) FOR PROPERTY IDENTIFIER        PAGE 1 OF 1
[TRAINING]  BUSINESS   REGISTRY                                                                          PREPARED FOR
            SERVICES   OFFICE #20                                                                        ON 2003/07/06 AT 11:17:38
                       * CERTIFIED BY LAND REGISTRAR IN ACCORDANCE WITH LAND TITLES ACT * SUBJECT TO RESERVATIONS IN CROWN GRANT *

PROPERTY DESCRIPTION:  **** NOT VALID - TO BE USED FOR TRAINING PURPOSES ONLY **** PT LT 11, PL 37 , NW OF ALBERT ST ; PT LT 11, PL 37 , SE OF JACKSON AVE,AS IN 657760 ;
                       HALTON HILLS

PROPERTY REMARKS:

ESTATE/QUALIFIER:      RECENTLY:                                                      PIN CREATION DATE:
FEE SIMPLE             FIRST CONVERSION FROM BOOK                                     1996/12/16
LT CONVERSION QUALIFIED

                                                              25040-0172 (LT)

OWNERS' NAMES                          CAPACITY   SHARE
EARL, BOBBIE RIGGS                     JTEN
EARL, BILLIE JEAN                      JTEN
```

REG. NUM.	DATE	INSTRUMENT TYPE	AMOUNT	PARTIES FROM	PARTIES TO	CERT/CHKD
EFFECTIVE 2000/07/29 THE NOTATION OF THE "BLOCK IMPLEMENTATION DATE" OF 1996/12/16 ON THIS PIN						
WAS REPLACED WITH THE "PIN CREATION DATE" OF 1996/12/16						
**PRINTOUT INCLUDES ALL DOCUMENT TYPES (DELETED INSTRUMENTS NOT INCLUDED) **						
**SUBJECT, ON FIRST REGISTRATION UNDER THE LAND TITLES ACT, TO:						
** SUBSECTION 44(1) OF THE LAND TITLES ACT, EXCEPT			PARAGRAPH 11, PARAGRAPH 14, PROVINCIAL SUCCESSION DUTIES *			
** AND ESCHEATS OR FORFEITURE TO THE CROWN.						
** THE RIGHTS OF ANY PERSON WHO WOULD, BUT FOR THE			LAND TITLES ACT, BE ENTITLED TO THE LAND OR ANY PART OF			
** IT THROUGH LENGTH OF ADVERSE POSSESSION, PRESCRIPTION, MISDESCRIPTION OR BOUNDARIES SETTLED BY						
** CONVENTION.						
** ANY LEASE TO WHICH THE SUBSECTION 70(2) OF THE			REGISTRY ACT APPLIES.			
**DATE OF CONVERSION TO LAND TITLES: 1996/12/16 **						
657760	1987/01/09	TRANSFER	$300,000		EARL, BOBBIE RIGGS / EARL, BILLIE JEAN	C
H760465	1998/10/16	CHARGE	$200,000	EARL, BOBBIE RIGGS / EARL, BILLIE JEAN	MEDORA FINANCIAL SERVICES	C

```
NOTE: ADJOINING PROPERTIES SHOULD BE INVESTIGATED TO ASCERTAIN DESCRIPTIVE INCONSISTENCIES, IF ANY, WITH DESCRIPTION REPRESENTED FOR THIS PROPERTY.
NOTE: ENSURE THAT YOUR PRINTOUT STATES THE TOTAL NUMBER OF PAGES AND THAT YOU HAVE PICKED THEM ALL UP.
```

Figure 8.17

PARCEL REGISTER AND INSTRUMENT DETAIL SCREEN*

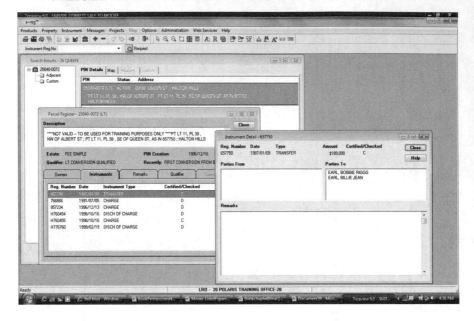

Figure 8.18

LIST OF ADJACENT PINS*

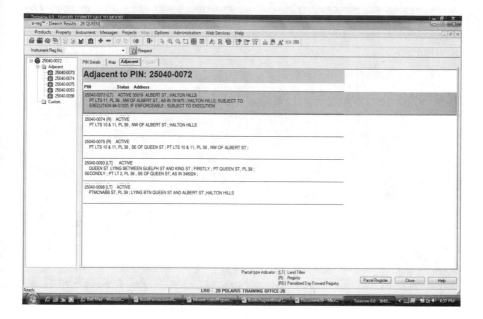

Figure 8.19
PARCEL REGISTERS FOR ADJACENT PINS[*]

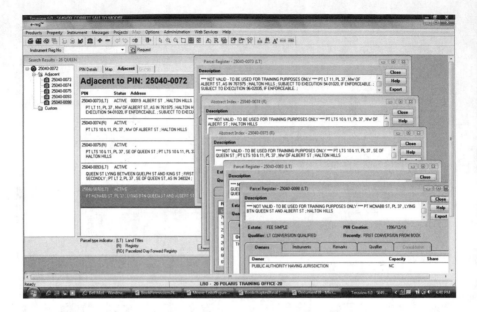

Figure 8.19.1

PARCEL REGISTER SCREEN*

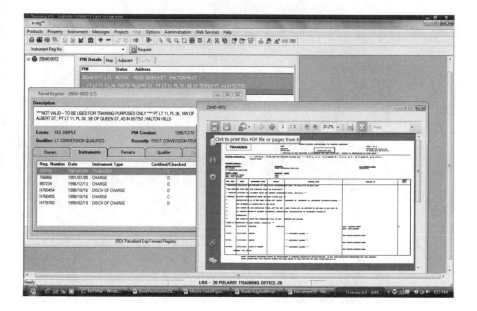

Figure 8.20

PROPERTY MAP INCLUDING ADJACENT PINS[*]

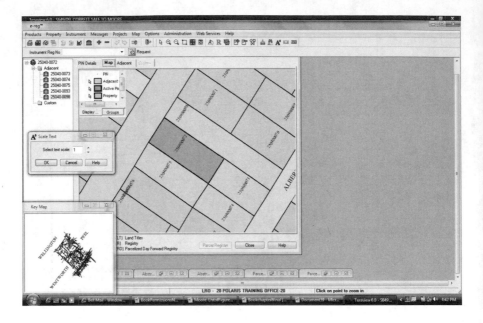

Figure 8.21
MAP TOOLS*

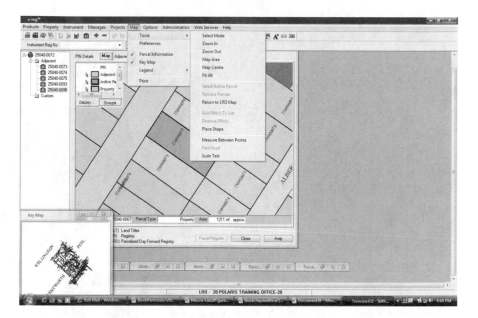

Figure 8.22.1

WRITSEARCH*

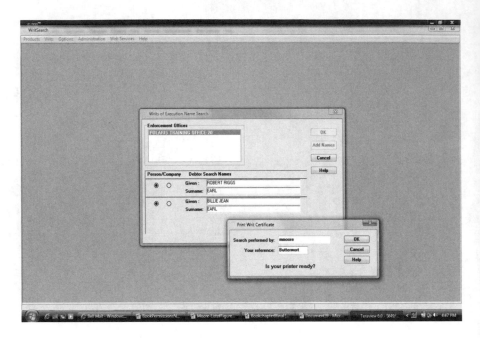

Figure 8.22.2
"CLEAR" CERTIFICATE*

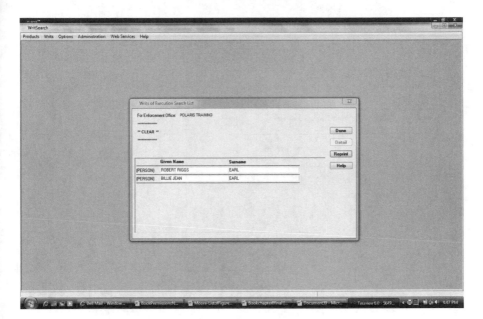

Figure 8.23

DOCKET SUMMARY REPORT*

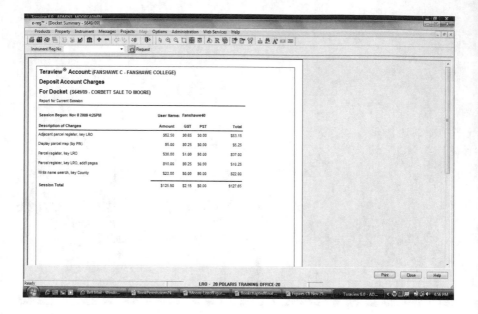

POWERS OF ATTORNEY SEARCHES IN ELRS

Land Titles searches in POLARIS may require an additional search in the new Powers of Attorney Index maintained in POLARIS. Powers of attorney records/indices are being automated in stages. The Teraview website contains a current list of search starting dates for automated power of attorney indices. These dates are included in Appendix 4 at the end of the book.

Powers of attorney under which a document is registered must be registered. All Land Titles registrations in ELRS must state whether a document is or is not signed by power of attorney. When a document is signed by power of attorney, the lawyer must search and review the operative power of attorney in the ELRS powers of attorney register. The lawyer must also check for revocations of powers of attorney that might affect the execution of a document.

A higher risk of fraud exists when documents are signed by power of attorney. The Ministry's Real Estate Fraud Action Plan has increased due diligence registration requirements and the LSUC has set higher professional due diligence standards for lawyers relying on powers of attorney.

TITLE INSURANCE AND LAND TITLES CONVERSION QUALIFIED TITLE

Always request deleted documents. Deleted documents may reveal a series of transactions that carry a higher risk of fraud. Policy applications usually contain questions that require a review of deleted documents. Review documents on the parcel register and "subject to" documents or executions brought forward in the property description line. Complete an adjoining land search for *Planning Act* compliance and description discrepancies, easements and restrictive covenants, and access. The date of conversion is a new starting point for *Planning Act* searches. If there are description issues, contact the insurer. Insurer requirements differ and change depending on the nature of the property. Search requirements need to be checked regularly. Unless the parcel register reveals a problem, usually the lawyer does not have to go behind the parcel register. However, depending on the title circumstances and the wording of the offer, it may be necessary to search prior to the LTCQ register for overriding interests or explanations for "subject to" documents.

DUE DILIGENCE IN THE TIME OF ELECTRONIC SEARCHING

Title searching and real estate conveyancing are high risk activities. E&OE claims history, case law, and title insurance claims statistics all consistently document this fact. Conscientious and knowledgeable title searching practices are a powerful proactive risk management tool. Automation and conversion have added a layer of legal and technological complexity combined with a layer of risk to title searching and conveyancing. For example, the complexity of so many title variations and the subtlety and impact of the differences in title qualifiers (consider the *Planning Act*) and system disclaimers have set a trap for anyone who has been lulled into a false sense of security by a point-and-click mentality or over-reliance on title insurance. Title searching and review of title is not the same as retrieving data.

There are no safe shortcuts.

COMPARISON CHART FOR THE TITLE VARIATIONS IN POLARIS

Title Variation	Registry Non-Converts and 40-Year Loads	Parcelized Day Forward Registry (PDFR)	Land Titles Absolute	Land Titles Conversion Qualified (LTCQ)	Land Titles Absolute Plus (LT PLUS)

Title Qualifiers	No title guarantee. Subject to *Registry Act* ss. 70-74 exceptions to 40-year search period. (See Chapters 3 and 4)	No title guarantee. Subject to *Registry Act* ss. 70-74 exceptions to 40-year search period. (See Chapters 3 and 4)	Guarantees current ownership interests and encumbrances subject to *Land Titles Act* s. 44(1) qualifiers. Not subject to possessory or prescriptive rights. (See Chapter 6)	Guarantees current ownership interests and encumbrances subject to LTCQ special qualifiers. Subject to *Land Titles Act* s. 44(1) qualifiers except:
				• Not subject to:
				  • Dower
				  • Provincial Succession Duties
				• Up-to-date of conversion not subject to:
				  • *Planning Act* violations s. 44(1)(11)
				  • Escheats and forfeitures
				• Subject to mature possessory rights, misdescriptions, and description issues
					Guarantees current ownership interests and encumbrances subject to LT PLUS special qualifiers. Subject to *Land Titles Act* s. 44(1) qualifiers except:
					• Not subject to:
					  • Dower
					  • Provincial Succession Duties
					  • Possessory rights (descriptions settled during application to upgrade to absolute
					  • *Registry Act* leases
					For post-August 2001 parcels, usually but not always, up-to-date

Title Variation	Registry Non-Converts and 40-Year Loads	Parcelized Day Forward Registry (PDFR)	Land Titles Absolute	Land Titles Conversion Qualified (LTCQ)	Land Titles Absolute Plus (LT PLUS)
				• Subject to unregistered *Registry Act* s. 70(2) leases in possession with original terms up to seven years. Seven years after conversion, no longer an issue. After date of conversion subject to *Planning Act*, escheat and forfeiture, *Registry Act* s. 70(2) leases.	of registration not subject to: • *Planning Act* violations s. 44(1)(11) • Escheats and forfeitures Pre-August 2001 LT PLUS parcels are subject to *Planning Act* contraventions from the date of conversion to parent LTCQ parcel forward. This is true of escheats and forfeitures as well. Be sure to read the qualifiers.
Search Period	40-year search period subject to *Registry Act* ss. 70-74 exceptions such as Crown rights,	40-year search period subject to *Registry Act* ss. 70-74 exceptions such as Crown patents, Crown rights created by statute, *etc.*	Current registered rights subject to *Land Titles Act* s. 44.1 overriding interests such as *Planning Act*,	Current registered rights and listed "subject to" interests in the property description line, subject to LTCQ special qualifiers/overriding interests	Current registered rights and listed "subject to" interests in the property description line, subject to LT PLUS special qualifi-

Title Variation	Registry Non-Converts and 40-Year Loads	Parcelized Day Forward Registry (PDFR)	Land Titles Absolute	Land Titles Conversion Qualified (LTCQ)	Land Titles Absolute Plus (LT PLUS)
	created by statute, *etc.* Start at date of certificate of title if one has been registered.		Crown patents and rights created by statute, watercourses and rights of water, spousal rights in the matrimonial home, *etc.*	such as *Planning Act*, Crown patents and rights created by statute, watercourses and rights of water, spousal rights in the matrimonial home, *etc.* Start at date of conversion for special qualifiers such as *Planning Act* and escheats and forfeitures, and matrimonial home rights. May need to search prior to conversion for possessory rights information, misdescriptions, and description inconsistencies and easements and other interests not brought forward in the conversion.	ers/overriding interests such as *Planning Act*, Crown patents and rights created by statute, watercourses and rights of water, spousal rights in the matrimonial home, *etc.* Start at date of registration for special qualifiers such as *Planning Act* and escheats and forfeitures (sometimes: see below). With pre-August 2001 parcels may have to start at date of conversion of parent LTCQ parcel for *Planning Act* and escheat.
Deleted Documents	Review deleted documents for	Review deleted documents for fraud	Review deleted documents for fraud	Review deleted documents for fraud patterns.	Review deleted documents for fraud

Title Variation	Registry Non-Converts and 40-Year Loads	Parcelized Day Forward Registry (PDFR)	Land Titles Absolute	Land Titles Conversion Qualified (LTCQ)	Land Titles Absolute Plus (LT PLUS)
	fraud patterns	patterns.	patterns. Review deleted documents for overriding interests such as *Planning Act* and escheat.	Review deleted documents for overriding interests such as *Planning Act* and escheat, usually back to the date of conversion.	patterns. Review deleted documents for overriding interests such as *Planning Act* and escheat, usually back to the date of registration.
Document Validity	Review all documents except deleted documents for legal validity.	Review all documents except deleted documents for legal validity.	Active, certified document validity guaranteed. Review for *Land Titles Act* s. 44(1) overriding interests.	Active, certified document validity guaranteed Review for *Land Titles Act* s. 44(1) overriding interests.	Active, certified document validity guaranteed. Review for *Land Titles Act* s. 44(1) overriding interests.
Descriptions	Subject to possessory rights, description conflicts, encroachments, and survey issues.	Subject to possessory rights, description conflicts, encroachments, and survey issues.	Subject to the extent of property qualification in *Land Titles Act* s. 140 (location on the ground).	Subject to the extent of property qualification in *Land Titles Act* s. 140 (location on the ground). Subject to mature possessory rights, misdescription and survey issues.	Subject to the extent of property qualification in *Land Titles Act* s. 140 (location on the ground).

Title Variation	Registry Non-Converts and 40-Year Loads	Parcelized Day Forward Registry (PDFR)	Land Titles Absolute	Land Titles Conversion Qualified (LTCQ)	Land Titles Absolute Plus (LT PLUS)
	PIN As in description document	PIN As in description document	PIN Parcels, M-Plans, and R-Plans	PIN As in description document	PIN Parcels, M-Plans, and R-Plans
Adjoining Lands Search (See Chapter 11)	Confirm easements and restrictive covenants, and access-related registrations on adjoining lands. Search and sketch description inconsistencies, overlaps, gaps, and boundary-related information as in a Registry search. Sketch current owner and adjoining owner descriptions and trace back as necessary.	Same Search behind POLARIS records for full 40 years in Registry books. Search and sketch description inconsistencies, overlaps, gaps, and boundary-related information as in a Registry search. Sketch current owner	Same Parcels on R-Plans and M-Plans; however, some metes and bounds in older *Land Titles Act* parcels (rarely need sketch of description).	Same Search and sketch description inconsistencies, overlaps, gaps and boundary-related information as in a Registry search. Sketch current owner and adjoining owner descriptions and trace back as necessary, including into old *Registry Act* books.	Same Parcels on R-Plans and M-Plans (do not need sketch of description).

Title Variation	Registry Non-Converts and 40-Year Loads	Parcelized Day Forward Registry (PDFR)	Land Titles Absolute	Land Titles Conversion Qualified (LTCQ)	Land Titles Absolute Plus (LT PLUS)
		and adjoining owner descriptions and trace back as necessary.			
Planning Act Compliance (See Chapter 11)	Search may go back on all adjoining owners as far as June 15, 1967 unless the property is exempt or unless there is a later starting point on title such as three *Planning Act* declarations, an unqualified consent, an exemption by-law, or a new subdivision plan, *etc.* Caution: non-converts may signal a *Planning Act* contravention.	Search may go back on all adjoining owners as far as June 15, 1967 unless the property is exempt or unless there is a later starting point on title such as three *Planning Act* declarations, an unqualified consent, an exemption by-law, or a new subdivision plan, *etc.* May have to go back into *Registry Act* books.	Search may go back on all adjoining owners as far as June 15, 1967 unless the property is exempt or unless there is a later starting point on title such as three *Planning Act* declarations, an unqualified consent, an exemption bylaw, or a new subdivision plan, *etc.* May have to cross-reference back into earlier *Land Titles Act* parcel registers.	Start *Planning Act* search as of the date of conversion unless the property is exempt or there is a later starting point on title such as three *Planning Act* declarations, an unqualified consent, an exemption by-law, or a new subdivision plan, *etc.*	Not all LT PLUS properties have the same *Planning Act* qualifier. Read the qualifier statement on the parcel register. Pre-August 2001 LT PLUS properties do not contain a new *Planning Act* exemption qualifier. The *Planning Act* search starts at the date of conversion for the parent LTCQ unless the property is exempt or there is a later starting point on title such as three *Planning Act* declarations, an un-

Title Variation	Registry Non-Converts and 40-Year Loads	Parcelized Day Forward Registry (PDFR)	Land Titles Absolute	Land Titles Conversion Qualified (LTCQ)	Land Titles Absolute Plus (LT PLUS)
					qualified consent, an exemption by-law, or a new subdivision plan, *etc.* Most, *but not all,* post-August 2001 LT PLUS properties contain a new, as of the date of registration, *Planning Act* exemption qualifier. The *Planning Act* search starts at the date of registration of the LT PLUS unless the property is exempt or there is a later starting point on title.

Title Variation	Registry Non-Converts and 40-Year Loads	Parcelized Day Forward Registry (PDFR)	Land Titles Absolute	Land Titles Conversion Qualified (LTCQ)	Land Titles Absolute Plus (LT PLUS)
WritSearch (See Chapter 12)	All registered owner names as they appear on the registered documents for full 40-year period unless relying on alternative title insurance coverage for prior owners.	Same as Registry. Search registered owner(s) from both POLARIS and paper registers unless relying on alternative title insurance coverage for prior owners.	Current registered owner(s) and a search of any "subject to" executions listed on the parcel register.	Current registered owner(s) and a search of executions listed on the parcel register.	Current registered owner(s) and a search of any "subject to" executions listed on the parcel register.
Escheat	Corporate owners for full 40-year search period. Ontario business corporations require only 20-year searches. Corporate escheat is an exception to the *Registry Act* search period and, in theory, is an issue	Same	Same Corporate escheat and forfeiture is *Land Titles Act* s. 44 qualifiers/ overriding interest and in theory is an issue back to the Crown patent. Ontario business corporations require only 20-year searches. Title in-	Special LTCQ qualifier guarantees no escheats as of the date of conversion. Corporate escheats are searched from the date of conversion forward subject to the OBCA 20-year limitation and alternative title insurance coverage.	Special LT PLUS qualifiers differ. Review the specific qualifiers on the printout. Recent LT PLUS titles guarantee that a parcel is free of escheats as of the date of registration of the Absolute Plus title. Start corporate escheat searches as of the date

Title Variation	Registry Non-Converts and 40-Year Loads	Parcelized Day Forward Registry (PDFR)	Land Titles Absolute	Land Titles Conversion Qualified (LTCQ)	Land Titles Absolute Plus (LT PLUS)
	back to the Crown patent for federal companies. Title insurance provides alternative coverage for past corporate owners.		surance provides alternative coverage for past corporate owners.		of registration. Older LT PLUS titles did not guarantee escheat as of the date of conversion. Corporate escheat checks must be done from the date of conversion of the parent LTCQ parcel forward.
Access (See Chapter 9)	Legal access to a public road throughout the search period. Check adjoining lands for confirmation of easement validity. Check property description line and review roads and reserve PINs, reserve PINs, and adjoin-	Same	Same	Same May need to search behind PIN register for description information and access based on easements and possessory claims. Consider the possibility that access easements were not carried forward in the conversion.	Same Description and possessory claims settled.

Title Variation	Registry Non-Converts and 40-Year Loads	Parcelized Day Forward Registry (PDFR)	Land Titles Absolute	Land Titles Conversion Qualified (LTCQ)	Land Titles Absolute Plus (LT PLUS)
	ing lands. PINs as required				
Electronic Searching	available	available	available	available	available
Electronic Registration (ELRS, formerly e-reg)	not available	not available	available	available	available

Notes

Refer to Chapter 7 for electronic condominium searching.

An LTCQ title offers superior title guarantees to a Land Titles Absolute title except for mature possessory rights, description inconsistencies and misdescriptions, and *Registry Act* s. 70(2) leases in possession.

A Land Titles Absolute Plus title offers superior title guarantees to an LTCQ title as it is not subject to mature possessory rights and *Registry Act* s. 70(2) leases, and the post-August 2001 Land Titles Absolute Plus titles guarantee *Planning Act* compliance and freedom from escheats and forfeitures as of the date of registration of the Land Titles Absolute Plus title.

CHAPTER 9

Easements, Access, and Restrictions on Use

EASEMENTS AND RIGHTS OF WAY

Easements and rights of way are rights or interests of use or passage of persons, vehicles, and animals over another person's owned or leased property. Utility lines, laneways, mutual drives, shortcuts, paths to the beach, cottage roads, and even drainage ditches are all examples of easements in common use. Statutory easements, such as easements to dump waste under the *Mining Act*, R.S.O. 1990, c. M.14, are surprising in their extent and affect over privately owned adjoining lands. Easements are a form of servitude or right to use over property. They are known as corporeal hereditaments. Access easements are often in perpetuity. The grant of an easement for 21 years or more is subject to the part lot control provisions in the *Planning Act*, R.S.O. 1990, c. P.13 and may require a *Planning Act* consent. Profits à prendre, the right to come onto land and to take some sort of profit, such as topsoil, blueberries, or grass; and Aboriginal rights, the right to come onto land to fish, hunt, and trap resemble easements but are a distinct property right. Conservation easements are a recent form of easement structured by statute that function more like a restriction on use. Conservation easements are dealt with later in the chapter in the section on restrictions on use.

Current Issues

Easements and restrictive covenants may have been missed in the conversion from Registry to Land Titles. The expedited search requirements for Land Titles Conversion Qualified (LTCQ) titles may have missed easements in perpetuity and access easements. In addition, frequently the registration of the original easement is now outside the 40-year search and notice periods. Easements are often only referred to in other documents, for example, the description in a subsequent deed. This is common practice; however, it is not notice under the *Registry Act*, R.S.O. 1990, c. R.20. As a result, these easements were not included in the property description on the new LTCQ parcel register. Careful searching is particularly important at this time as there may still be time to revive older easements, particularly access easements. The Director of Titles has issued *Registry Act* Bulletin No. 2007-02 setting out four options for owners of property whose easements were not brought forward in the government's automation and conversion program. Time is of the essence as owners will lose the right to revive an easement if a conflicting claim is registered before the easement interest is re-registered.

The Creation of an Easement

Easements may be established by:

1. express registered transfer of easement (An easement can be created in a separate transfer or as part of an original transfer of land. An easement cannot be created in an agreement or a lease. Since 1984, an easement cannot be created in a charge.);

2. express reservation (an interest retained by a grantor) of easement in a registered transfer of land for the benefit of an adjoining property that has been retained by the grantor;

3. prescription, also known as possession;

4. implication of law, such as an easement by necessity or estoppel, or an easement normally enjoyed by a property and not specifically excluded from a conveyance (*Conveyancing and Law of Property Act*, R.S.O. 1990, c. C.34, s. 15);

5. court order, expropriation plan, or condominium description; or

6. by statute, for example, the *Mining Act*. Section 175 of the *Mining Act* authorizes an easement to dump tailings, slimes or other waste products on the land of any person, subject only to right of compensation as determined by the Commissioner of Mining. The *Mining Act* also creates easement rights for roads and access, and draining and flooding rights on privately owned adjoining land subject only to the right of compensation determined by the Commissioner.

Once an easement has been legally established, it is automatically conveyed, in subsequent deeds and transfers, whether or not it is specifically referred to in the registered document. For this reason, easements are said to run with the land. Whenever the land benefitting from the easement (the dominant tenement) is sold, the purchaser receives any rights that the vendor possessed. When the land over or through which the easement runs (the servient tenement) is sold, the purchaser buys subject to the easement. Because an easement is created to benefit one or more specified dominant tenements, other properties have no right to use an existing easement. Properties acquired after the creation of the easement do not have the right to use the easement. An easement must be created for a specific property.

Merger of Easements

If the same person buys both the dominant and the servient tenements, the easement merges into that person's fee simple and ceases to exist. An easement which has merged, even when it remains physically visible as, for example, a road, must be recreated by a new registration. Conveyancers must be on the lookout for easements which have merged and ceased to exist.

Legal Requirements

Easements and rights of way are subject to the following legal requirements:

1. An easement affects a dominant and a servient tenement. The dominant tenement must benefit from the easement. The easement should be referred to in registrations on both the dominant and servient tenements. The dominant tenement is referred to as being together with a right of way, and the servient tenement is referred to as being subject to a right of way. The land registrar registers the easement on both the dominant and servient lands. The dominant and servient tenements must be owned by different individuals or owned in a different capacity by the same individual. Easements in gross such as utility easements and water and sewage easements, and conservation easements do not require a dominant tenement. It is not necessary for the lands to physically adjoin each other, although they must have some sort of proximate relationship.

2. An easement is attached to and passes or runs with the land; it is not a personal agreement. Easement rights are automatically transferred when the dominant and servient tenements are transferred.

3. The purpose, the rights involved, the parties, and the location of the easement must be clear.

4. Section 26 of the *Registry Act* provides that approximate descriptions in older easement documents, for example, "a right-of-way over a lane way now in existence and leading to the road allowance between Lots 5 and 6", is no longer acceptable. A reference plan or a metes and bounds description which complies with the local description regulations should be submitted on registration of easements. Ontario Regulation 43/96 sets out the description requirements for an easement.

5. A transfer of an easement for 21 years or more must comply with the s. 50 subdivision control provisions of the *Planning Act*.

6. Easements and rights of way may be modified or terminated by court order, released by the dominant tenement in a quit claim deed, or lost by

abandonment or merger. In Land Titles, an application for release of easement must be registered by way of Document General.

7. In Land Titles, prior to registering a transfer of easement, a search for writs of executions should be made. The transfer will be entered on the register subject to any outstanding writs.

8. In Registry, an easement is valid for only 40 years after the registration date of the original easement or for 40 years after the registration of a Notice of Claim that renewed the original easement. Easements must be registered every 40 years to retain legal enforceability under the *Registry Act*. The *Consumer Protection and Service Modernization Act, 2006*, S.O. 2006, c. 34 (Bill 152) came into effect on December 20, 2006. It amended Part III of the *Registry Act* and reversed the Ontario Court of Appeal decision in *1387881 Ontario Inc. v. Ramsay*, [2005] O.J. No. 2727 (Ont. C.A.) on easement enforceability and entrenched the Ministry's position by statute. See Chapter 3 for more information on *Registry Act* notice periods. Also see the recent case of *Phinny v. Macaulay*, [2008] O.J. No. 3629 (Ont. S.C.J.) for an extensive review of law concerning the 40-year search and notice periods in the context of easements under the *Registry Act*.

9. Easements may be terminated by a power of sale by a prior mortgagee. The mortgagee often postpones the charge to the easement in order to avoid terminating an easement.

10. When the Crown creates an easement across unpatented land, the Land Titles system creates a new "easement parcel" and Property Identification Number (PIN).

The Termination (Removal) of an Easement

An easement can be terminated by the following:

1. the owner of the benefitted land (dominant) releases the easement to the owner of the burdened land (servient);

2. the easement expires as per its expiry or condition date. Easements may have a specific time limit or expire when a condition has been met;

3. the servient land is expropriated and the easement is inconsistent with the purpose of the expropriation or specifically stated as being part of the expropriation;

4. the benefitted and burdened lands are acquired by the same owner and the easement merges. The new owner must register an application to amend the parcel register indicating the merger and termination of the easement;

5. easements can be released in part, as to purpose, as to persons affected, or as to location, as long as it complies with the *Planning Act*;

6. an easement must be released in a separate document;

7. abandonment; or

8. automatic expiry under the 40-year *Registry Act* search and notice periods.

Abandonment of an Easement

An easement can be released or abandoned by the consent of all benefitted persons. Abandonment can be inferred when a change in the dominant or servient tenement makes the easement useless and the dominant owner acquiesces in the change. Non-use of an easement does not imply abandonment. There must be evidence of intent of the easement owner to abandon the easement right. See *Overs v. ten Kortenaar*, [2006] O.J. No. 822 (Ont. S.C.J.) for a review of the legal criteria for abandonment of easements.

Automatic Expiry under the 40-Year *Registry Act* Search and Notice Periods

In Registry, an easement ceases to be enforceable 40 years after the registration date of the original easement or for 40 years after the registration of a Notice of Claim that renewed the original easement. The easement can be revived by registration as long as a conflicting claim has not been registered. Easements must be registered every 40 years to retain legal enforceability under the *Registry Act*. Registry easements were often missed in the conversion from Registry to Land Titles. If these easements are not revived by registration in the Land Titles system prior to the registration of a conflicting claim, they will be lost through operation of law.

Modification in the Use of an Easement

The law permits a modification or extension in the use of an easement as long as it was within the original intent of the parties. These cases turn on individual facts. For example, in *MacKenzie v. Matthews*, [1999] O.J. No. 4602 (Ont. C.A.), the Ontario Court of Appeal decided that the "grant of an easement includes a grant of ancillary rights which are reasonably necessary to the use and enjoyment of the easement which was contemplated by the grantor" (*MacKenzie*, at para. 8). The easement was specifically intended to afford owners of the islands access to their cottage properties by boat and the installation and maintenance of a dock is implicit in such an easement. Depending on the facts, courts sometimes allow increase or change in traffic and parking.

Important Terms

A conveyancer should list all easements on the summary of the completed search and record the following information when reviewing an easement:

1. the purpose and nature of the easement;

2. the exact dimensions and location of the easement;

3. the original term, conditions, rights of renewal, or if it is in perpetuity;

4. restrictions on use, building and encroachment;

5. obligations to maintain, repair, restore or resurface;

6. *Planning Act* compliance, declarations, consents, and exemptions, however, easements transferred to or reserved by the condominium are exempt (*Condominium Act, 1998*, S.O. 1998, c. 19, s. 9(1)(b));

7. execution of the document, schedules, declarations, and affidavits where necessary;

8. full description, including parts on reference plan, any attached sketch and reconciliation of subsequent descriptions;

9. confirmation of registration of the easement on all servient lands;

10. confirmation of validity of grant of the easement from all servient lands;

11. in Registry, confirmation that easement has been registered within the 40-year period by express grant or by Notice of Claim and how much time is left before the easement must be re-registered. Note that a mere reference to an easement within a different document does not meet registration and validity requirements; and

12. easement is included in the property description line on the dominant and servient tenements.

Under the Land Titles system it is not necessary to confirm the form and legal validity of a registered document, although the *Planning Act* remains an exception to the Land Titles guarantee.

TYPES OF EASEMENTS

Express Easements

Access to land, *e.g.*, a cottage or a beach, may be created by the registration of an express grant of right of way. A search must confirm that the right of way is registered on all lands subject to the right of way (servient tenements), as well as the land benefitting from the right of way (dominant tenement). In addition, the searcher must confirm the servient tenement's initial right to grant a right of way. In Registry, the easement must be registered every 40 years in a separate easement document.

Mutual Drives

It is important to establish access and ownership of driveways. A mutual drive is a strip of land shared by adjoining neighbours. Mutual drives are not unusual in the older parts of cities and in high-density multi-family housing. Title documents should include a reference to the mutual drive. A mutual drive may be described as follows: The whole of Lot 16, Plan 2345; together with a right of way over the northerly four feet of the lands lying immediately to the south of the lands described herein; and subject to a right of way over the southerly four feet of the lands described herein.

Party Wall Agreements

Party wall agreements relate to both commercial and residential attached buildings, frequently found in the older sections of cities where houses were built with common walls on the property line. The common wall is considered a right of way of mutual support. A searcher should record all description references, including sketches, responsibility for maintenance costs, provisions for termination, and restrictions on use.

Easements by Prescription

Where land is registered under the Registry system and a person has continuously used a neighbour's property as a shortcut, or as an access, for a minimum of 20 years, without interruption, without objection of the servient owner, without permission of the true owner, or without acknowledgment or agreement in writing from the proper owner, he or she may have established a permanent easement by possession or prescription. When the use is secretive, it does not generate possessory rights. A true owner who places a barrier, or closes a gate from time to time, such as once a year, interrupts the acquisition of an easement by prescription. The custom in some parts of cottage country has been to place a barrier the weekend after Thanksgiving and the weekend before May 24th in order to prevent the establishment of easements by prescription. Similarly, the request for periodic payments, periodic permissions and written notices, and periodic acknowledgements from the user prevent the establishment of easements by prescription.

Section 31 of the *Real Property Limitations Act*, R.S.O. 1990, c. L.15 is the authority for an easement by prescription. This section deems an easement by prescription to be absolute after 40 years of continuous use. Section 31 reads as follows:

> No claim that may be made lawfully at the common law, by custom, prescription or grant, to any way or other easement, or to any water course, or the use of any water to be enjoyed, or derived upon, over or from any land or water of the Crown or being the property of any person, when the way or other matter as herein last before-mentioned has been actually enjoyed by any person claiming right thereto without interruption for the full period of twenty years shall be defeated or destroyed by showing only that the way or other matter was first enjoyed at any time prior to the period of twenty years, but, nevertheless the claim may be defeated in any other way by which it is now liable to be defeated, and where the way or other matter as herein last before-mentioned has been so enjoyed for the full period of forty years, the right thereto shall be deemed absolute and indefeasible, unless it appears that it was enjoyed by some consent or agreement expressly given or made for that purpose by deed or writing.

Easements for wires and cables may not be acquired by prescription, only by grant from the owner of the property or buildings (*Real Property Limitations Act*, s. 35). Easements by prescription and adverse possession may not be acquired against the Crown or Ontario Hydro and its successors, against public roads or highways, or against a 66-foot Crown shoreline (road) allowances.

Rose v. Krieser, In Trust, [2002] O.J. No. 1384 (Ont. C.A.) contains an up-to-date Ontario Court of Appeal review of the law of easement by prescription in the context of a cottage access easement in the form of a mutual drive.

Section 51(1) of the *Land Titles Act*, R.S.O. 1990, c. L.5 prohibits the acquisition of easements by prescription. Similarly, once land has been converted under the *Land Registration Reform Act* into Land Titles, the acquisition of any new rights by prescription or possession is barred by statute. As a result, an LTCQ property may be subject to an easement by prescription that had been perfected prior to conversion; but, new prescriptive easement rights are barred. For example a potential easement by prescription that has been in use for 15 years on a parcel that is then transferred to Land Titles is lost forever. An application procedure is available for entering existing easements by prescription, which had been legally acquired in Registry prior to conversion into Land Titles, onto an LTCQ parcel.

Easements of Necessity

Occasionally, when an agreement of purchase and sale does not include an express right of access to a public road, *e.g.*, when a farmer sells farm lake frontage to a cottager and retains the rear part, the law will imply access or a right of way of necessity as part of the agreement, particularly when the farmer induced the purchase by the oral promise of an access easement. Implied easements by necessity are based on implied intentions of parties to a contract based on the particular facts. This right of way of necessity should not be confused with simply needing to use a road to access a cottage, or a path to access a beach.

An implied grant of easement may be created when an owner of a parcel of land fronting on a highway sells the rear part without providing the purchaser access to the highway. The law may imply a right of way of necessity. The right to visit and maintain a grave has also been treated as an implied easement by necessity when access to the grave is separated from a public road by private property.

Utility Easements

Large utility easements are referred to as easements in gross. The transfer of easement document usually names the utility's head office as the dominant tenement. Section 91(2) of the *Municipal Act, 2001*, S.O. 2001, c. 25 exempts public utilities provided by a municipality from the need for a dominant tenement. The same is true for municipal water and sewage easements (*Ontario Water Resources Act*, R.S.O. 1990, c. O.40, s. 27). Bell Canada, Consumers Gas, the local hydro commission and the local municipality may all have easements, often over the rear four or six feet of each lot in new subdivisions. Never assume the location or size of an easement. Utility easements may be ten feet wide, run along the side of a lot or through the middle of the backyard. Resurfacing provisions vary depending on circumstances and the nature of the housing involved. A property owner should not build or encroach upon utility easements. Occasionally, in special circumstances, a property may be subject to encroachment or maintenance agreements with a utility.

A searcher should determine the exact nature and location of utility easements in order to identify current encroachments by the property owner onto the easement (such as a pool built into the hydro easement or a driveway built on a gas easement) and restrictions on future use of the property. The purchaser's conditions in the agreement of purchase and sale and future plans for pools, garages, additions, and formal gardens depend on it.

Transfers of easements for a period of 21 years or more require *Planning Act* consents to subdivide unless exempt, *e.g.*, easements to and from Ontario Hydro or its successors (Hydro One Inc.). Easements granted or reserved by condominiums are exempt.

Underground Sewer and Water Lines

The description for an underground sewer and water line easement may be difficult to plot. A survey can assist the searcher both in determining the exact location of the easement and in revealing any encroachments by buildings, driveways, *etc.*

Unregistered Hydro Easements

Unlike most easements, Ontario Hydro (now called Hydro One Inc. under the *Electricity Act, 1998*, S.O. 1998, c. 15, Schedule A) may enforce easement rights without having first registered the easement at the Registry office. As a result, when searching non-urban lands, title searchers should consider checking for unregistered hydro easements at Hydro regional offices. It is also necessary to check for unregistered utility easements at the local Public Utilities Commission or Hydro Electric Commission.

Section 46 of the *Electricity Act* deals with unregistered rights:

46. (1) If, immediately before the repeal of section 48 of *the Power Corporation Act* under the *Energy Competition Act, 1998*, land was subject to a right referred to in subsection 48(2) or (3) of the *Power Corporation Act*, the land continues to be subject to the right until the right expires or until it is released by the holder of the right.

Transfer of right

(2) A right referred to in subsection (1) may be transferred to,

(a)   Hydro One Inc.;

(b)   Ontario Power Generation Inc.;

(c)   a subsidiary of Hydro Inc. that is authorized to transmit or distribute electricity;

(c.1) a subsidiary of Ontario Power Generation Inc. that is authorized to generate electricity.

(d)   a corporation established pursuant to section 142 that is authorized to transmit or distribute electricity; or

(e)   a subsidiary of a corporation established pursuant to section 142, if the subsidiary is authorized to transmit or distribute electricity.

Information

(3) On the request of the owner of land or a person intending to acquire an interest in land, the holder of a right referred to in subsection (1) shall make a search of its records and, within 21 days after receiving the request, shall inform the owner or person whether or not it has a right affecting the land that is not registered under the *Land Titles Act* or the *Registry Act* and, if it has such a right, shall also inform the owner or person of the term and extent of the right.

Compensation

(4) A person who suffers loss or damage due to the failure of the holder of a right to comply with subsection (3) is entitled to compensation for the loss or damage from the holder of the right.

Developer's Right of Re-Entry

A developer of a new subdivision will reserve a right of re-entry in the subdivision agreement in order to be able to complete its obligations under the agreement, such as grading and drainage.

REGISTRATION REQUIREMENTS OF EASEMENTS

Registration and Removal of Easements

Easements should be noted in the property description (thumbnail) for both the dominant and the servient property identification numbers or PINs. Ministry of Consumer and Business Services' Bulletin No. 2005-02 sets out the procedures for the registration and the removal of easements in Land Titles and Registry. This bulletin contains sample property descriptions for both dominant and servient tenements and reviews electronic registration procedures for creating and removing easements. It emphasizes that conveyancers must search the servient lands as well as dominant lands to confirm easements and to determine any prior interests related to an easement.

Bringing Missed Easements Forward from Registry to LTCQ

Registry Act Bulletin No. 2007-02 sets out the following options for when land has been converted to Land Titles and an easement interest has not been brought forward from Registry and entered on the new LTCQ parcel register:

1. The owner of the servient parcel can apply to add the easement to the parcel description. The application must contain descriptions of the dominant and servient lands, consent of any encumbrancer since automation, and a statement by a solicitor that the easement is in full force and effect. The application adds the easement to both parcels.

2. The owner of the dominant parcel which has the notation "except the easement therein" can apply to add the easement to the parcel description. The application must contain descriptions of the dominant and servient lands, consent of any encumbrancer since automation, and a statement by a solicitor that the easement is in full force and effect. The application adds the easement to both parcels.

3. The owner of the dominant PIN may register a *Registry Act* s. 71 notice against both the dominant and the servient PIN. The notice must

contain the registration particulars of the original easement and an explanation why the easement is still valid. This registration does not affect the wording of the property description. It can be followed by an application to amend the register. The owner of the dominant parcel may apply to amend the property description with the consent of the servient parcel and the consent of any subsequent encumbrancers since conversion. In addition, the owner of the servient property can apply to have a notice of easement removed.

4.   The owner of the dominant parcel can apply to amend the register on the same grounds as would have been available under s. 113(2)(b) of the *Registry Act* as long as there have not been any subsequent conflicting registrations and the owner of the dominant parcel agrees to indemnify the Land Titles Assurance Fund.

5.   The best approach, when possible, is to register a new transfer of easement.

Deleting Easements Brought Forward from Registry to LTCQ

Land Titles Act Bulletin No. 2008-05 sets out general guidelines for how to delete easements and other "subject to interest" documents brought forward during the conversion either in error or that are no longer applicable. An interested person in consultation with the registrar may bring an application to amend the register based on a solicitor's opinion, a consent of a third party, case law, expiry dates, time limits and limitation periods, or other evidence. A fee may or may not be required depending on the reason for the application. When an easement could not be verified on a servient PIN, a notice in the form of a "save and except easement or right of way as in number" was entered in the property description line on the new parcel register for the dominant lands only. *Registry Act* Bulletin No. 2007-02 has additional information on the removal of easements from parcel registers.

ACCESS TO LAND

The Importance of Access

Access is very important! For whatever reason, some conveyancers fail to perform what can be time-consuming, costly, legally complicated, access searches, particularly when these searches involve adjoining lands. Access affects value and owner satisfaction, and commercial viability. With or without title insurance, what new purchaser wants to learn that the neighbour owns what they thought was their driveway, or that their dream cottage has no access to the water, or, for that matter, only water access. Developers of commercial properties count on access to specific streets. At this time, access disputes represent not only a disproportionate number of title insurance claims but recent Ontario

Court of Appeal decisions. In human terms, access disputes have the potential for violence.

In addition to searching title to the land, a title searcher should gather information relating to legal access to property throughout the full search period. Many properties, particularly in cottage country and Northern Ontario, simply do not have legal or year-round access. Cottages that appear to enjoy the use of a shoreline, may not have legal access to the water. What appears to be a road on the ground, may not be access in law. Title searchers and conveyancers should determine whether access is by road or water, seasonal or year-round, public or private, or maintained by public or private funds. Access and road information should be noted, under a separate heading, on the search summary and access should be illustrated on the search sketch. Access may require a specific title requisition and/or a title insurance endorsement.

Access may be based on an express grant of right of way, an easement by prescription (not available in Land Titles), an original Crown road allowance, a dedication of a public road on a registered plan of subdivision, or even statutory rights relating to common and access roads under the *Road Access Act*, R.S.O. 1990, c. R.34 and *Public Lands Act*, R.S.O. 1990, c. P.43.

An access search should include a review of registrations on roads pages, by-laws relating to the opening and closing of streets, subdivision and reference plans dedicating and illustrating roads, and original road and shoreline allowances in patents, or those shown on municipal and township plans.

POLARIS block maps and Teraview digital maps illustrate roads and easements. Block maps provide references to PINs for roads and sometimes instrument numbers relating to the roads. In Teraview, a conveyancer may choose to search by road as well as by PIN, name, subdivision plan, or address. A searcher may then select a road by name or location on a map, allowing him or her to easily identify and search the adjacent PINs. Teraview indexes and maps have made searching road information much more efficient.

Access by Easement

When relying on an easement for access, both the dominant and servient tenements should be searched to a public highway to confirm the registration and enforceability of the easements. Easements must be registered on both the dominant and servient lands. In Land Titles, they must be shown in the property description line on the parcel register and in Registry and they must have been registered within the 40-year title search and notice periods.

In Registry, a reference to an easement in a deed is not notice to subsequent purchasers. An easement must be registered by the original grant from the servient tenement and/or renewed in a notice document within the 40-year title search period. Recent amendments to the notice provisions in the *Registry Act* may have invalidated access easements that are referred to only in the descriptions of subsequent deeds. It is essential for conveyancers to confirm a separate notice registration of an easement within the 40-year period. The search will also reveal whether the existing easement needs to be re-registered by notice for it to remain enforceable. Past conveyancing practice relied on a reference to an easement in a subsequent deed. As a result, recent amendments to the *Registry Act* have potentially invalidated access rights based on easements. Access easements require close attention, full adjoining land searches, and potentially additional registrations.

Easements and restrictive covenants were often missed in the POLARIS conversion to Land Titles. Consequently, access searches for LTCQ titles may require searching in the original Registry parcel and a correction of the POLARIS parcel register. The Director of Titles has issued *Registry Act* Bulletin No. 2007-02 setting out four procedures for bringing missed easements onto an LTCQ parcel. One option is for the owner of the dominant parcel to register a notice under s. 71 of the *Registry Act* against both the dominant and servient lands but this will not result in an amendment to the property description. (The notice should set out the original registration number and date of the easement and the rationale for the easement being valid.) This notice can remain on the parcels indefinitely until an application to amend the register to include the easement in the property description is registered by either the owner of the dominant or servient lands. Where the document that created the easement has been registered for over 40 years, a registered Notice of Claim may only be valid if there are no conflicting claims.

Planning Act approval is required when creating an access easement for 21 years or more. Rights of renewal are included in the calculation of the easement's term. An easement that violates the *Planning Act* is void.

Maintenance responsibilities and costs for private roads are a common area for conflict and non-compliance; they should be carefully recorded and communicated to the client.

In summary, a conveyancer completes a full adjoining land search in order to determine the location and nature of an easement, and to confirm that an access easement is registered on the dominant and all servient tenements to a public highway, that the easement is registered within the 40-year notice period, and that the easement complies with the *Planning Act*. Refer to Chapter 11 for how to complete adjoining land searches for easements, access, and *Planning Act* purposes.

Confirming Legal Access

The following legal principles relating to roads and access frequently assist the conveyancer in confirming legal access to land. A large body of statute and case law governs roads and access, including original road and shoreline allowances, easements by prescription, the *Road Access Act*, trespass and diversion roads, and opening, closing, and widening road allowances under the *Municipal Act, 2001*. Section 26 of the *Municipal Act, 2001* defines the term highway. Title to municipal roads is vested in the appropriate municipality. Title to provincial roads, referred to as King's Highways, is vested in the Crown in the right of the Province and subject to the *Public Transportation and Highway Improvement Act*, R.S.O. 1990, c. P.50. The Ministry of Transportation administers provincial highways. Conveyancers must confirm access for properties purchased, leased, optioned, or mortgaged.

Public Roads

Every road allowance, highway, street, lane, walk, and common shown on a plan of subdivision shall be deemed to be a public road, highway, street, lane, walk, and common, respectively, and is public and vested in the municipality until closed (*Surveys Act*, R.S.O. 1990, c. S.30, s. 57). Section 57 (initially s. 13(2)) was first enacted in the *Surveys Act* in 1920. Note that this section does not make one-foot reserves or road widenings public. The reserves must be opened by by-law. Section 57 is retroactive in effect and it affects plans registered before 1920. Section 26 of the *Municipal Act, 2001* has replaced s. 57 of the *Surveys Act* and states that highways on a plan of subdivision are public unless closed by by-law. Highways are owned by the municipality subject to rights reserved by the person who dedicated the land for road purposes (*Municipal Act*, s. 30). The original owner of land on a plan of subdivision owns the road allowance if it has not been dedicated to the municipality.

In addition, rights to a public road, lane or highway cannot be lost by adverse possession or acquiescence or estoppel. Lack of use cannot make a public highway private. The recent case of *Cornwall (City) v. Geneau*, [2000] O.J. No. 4270, 51 O.R. (3d) 460 (Ont. S.C.J.) reviews the law dealing with roads laid out on registered plans of subdivision.

When searching, particularly on older plans, note whether the plan includes a dedication of roads being public, and consents by the mortgagees. Review all by-laws registered on title. Check the status of one foot reserves and confirm whether or not they have been opened by by-law. Check with the municipality if it has closed the road, whether it has plans to close the road, and whether it maintains the road.

Prior to January 1, 2003, municipalities could establish a road as public either by using public funds for road maintenance or by passing a by-law declaring a road to be a public highway. After January 1, 2003, a by-law is required to create a public highway and for the municipality to assume the maintenance.

Controlled Access Highways

Controlled access provincial (King's) highways require a Ministry of Transportation permit for driveways or entrances which create access for adjoining properties. Similarly, municipalities can designate streets and roads to be controlled access (*Municipal Act*, s. 35). Conveyancers must complete an off-title search to confirm the existence of an access permit for a controlled access highway. Highway access can be critical to the success of gas stations and commercial ventures.

Easements by Prescription

Section 31 of the *Real Property Limitations Act* is the authority for easements by prescription. Generally, access by prescription may not be acquired against the Crown, Ontario Hydro or its successors, or in Land Titles. Special rules for LTCQ titles apply. Easements by prescription that had been perfected prior to POLARIS conversion are enforceable in LTCQ titles. Once in Land Titles, an owner can never acquire new prescriptive rights.

The Province downloaded ownership in roads to the municipality in 1913. Since June 1, 1922, statute states that possessory rights cannot be acquired against a road owned by the municipality. It was at least in theory, possible prior to 1922 to acquire possessory rights in limited circumstances to a municipal road, following 60 years of unequivocal, good faith possession.

Section 31 of the *Real Property Limitations Act* makes easements by prescription after 40 years absolute and indefeasible, unless the easement was used by consent or agreement. Easements by prescription, acting as roads, may be assumed by the municipality. See the section on easements earlier in this chapter.

Shoreline (Beaches) and Road Allowances

Sixty-six foot shoreline and concession road allowances, reserved in Crown grants, whether or not in use, are public roads. Road allowances are owned by the Crown. They do not provide legal access to adjoining owners or the public, other than with permission. In the recent case of *Lantry v. Ontario (Minister of Natural Resources)*, [2006] O.J. No. 239 (Ont. S.C.J.), a cottager on Wasaga Beach claimed that she had a legally enforceable right to drive her vehicle over 150 feet of public beach to reach her cottage in Wasaga Beach Park. She argued easement by necessity, by prescription, public rights to beach/shoreline allowance, and public highway rights, public road rights under the *Municipal Act, 2001*, and access rights under the *Road Access Act*. The Crown patent reserved the beach and free access to the shore of Lake Huron, for all vessels, boats, and persons, and retained a shoreline allowance. The Court held that Lantry had no legal access rights as the Crown was the owner of the beach and had revoked permission and that possessory rights do not accrue against the Crown. In addition, the *Public Lands Act* states that "[a]ny part of the public lands that is a beach and is used for travel by the public is not by reason only of such use a highway within the meaning of any Act" (s. 63).

Water levels change and as a result the shoreline allowance may now be under water or well back from the current shoreline. The Crown may have acquired land by accretion between the original shoreline allowance and the current water's edge. Only a survey can determine the location of the original shoreline allowance and its relationship with the current water's edge. As water levels continue to change, surveys will become increasingly important for waterfront properties.

Shoreline allowances and road allowances may not be legally encroached upon by adverse possession or prescription. In the past cottagers have frequently built or driven on the shoreline allowance. Check to see if the municipality has closed and conveyed the allowance to the adjoining owner.

Original road and shoreline allowances are vested in the local municipality, an upper-tier municipality (regional government), or a single-tier municipality (Toronto). The municipality is not required to maintain the allowance unless it has assumed it by by-law or demonstrated intent to maintain it on a continuous basis. The public must obtain municipal approval before using or improving unopened allowances. Road and shoreline allowances can be closed by by-law.

Road Closing By-Laws

A municipal by-law closing a street shown on a plan of subdivision, an access road to a Queen's Highway, or an original shoreline allowance requires approval from the municipality and in the past from the Minister of Municipal Affairs. Confirm that the municipality has registered a by-law closing the road and authorizing the sale, as well as a transfer including approvals and notice declarations to a private owner, usually the adjoining owner. Cottage owners often purchase the 66-foot shoreline allowance from the municipality. A conveyancer must confirm that the allowance has been closed and transferred to the adjacent owner.

The *Road Access Act*

The *Road Access Act* sets out the rules for closing common and access roads that are not based on a registered right. Its purpose is to substitute a judicial determination for self-help measures and reduce the risk to personal safety and the potential for violence. The definition of access road under the Act includes a road that provides motor vehicle access to one or more parcels of land that is not dedicated to a municipality, not on municipally owned land, or not, by law, deemed to be a public road, in other words, a private road. The finding of an access road is a question of mixed law and fact and is largely fact-driven. An access road under the Act must meet the following criteria:

- road meets the Act's s. 1 definition;
- road is on land that is not owned by a municipality;
- road is not a public highway;
- road used as a motor vehicle access route;
- road is used to access one or more properties; and
- closure of the road would prevent all vehicular access to the property (no alternative access).

Unless a private access road agreement contains a termination provision, s. 2 of the *Road Access Act*, stipulates that no person shall construct, place or maintain a barrier over an access road that "prevents all road access to one or more parcels of land" or to a boat docking facility unless: (1) a judge has granted an application to close the road; (2) all owners affected have agreed in writing; (3) the closure is temporary for the purpose of repair; or (4) the closure is for no more than "twenty-four hours in a year for the purpose of preventing the acquisition of prescriptive rights".

Section 3 provides the following requirements for a judge's order closing an access road:

- the road closure is "reasonably necessary to prevent substantial damage" to the owner of the land the road is on;
- closure is in the public interest;
- persons who are using the road "do not have a legal right" to use the road; and
- the road closuring order may include conditions.

Case law restricts the use of an access road to the right to enter and leave property. The *Road Access Act* has no effect on existing common law rights of acquisition for rights of way or easements. The Act places no obligation on the owner of the land to maintain or repair an access road over the property. Persons who use an access road over the property of another have no right to maintain or repair the road. As a result, current access roads may deteriorate through non-maintenance and cease to provide access.

In the past, many owners of recreational and northern properties have relied on informal access arrangements over private roads. Change of ownership predictably disrupts these loose, often personal, arrangements. The following recent Ontario Court of Appeal decisions provide a detailed review of access principles, private roads, and the *Road Access Act*:

1. *Blais v. Belanger*, [2007] O.J. No. 1512 (Ont. C.A.).

2. *2008795 Ontario Inc. v. Kilpatrick*, [2007] O.J. No. 3248 (Ont. C.A.).

3. *992275 Ontario Inc. v. Krawczyk*, [2006] O.J. No. 1730 (Ont. C.A.).

4. *Cook's Road Maintenance Assn. v. Crowhill Estates*, [2001] O.J. No. 360 at para. 28 (Ont. C.A.).

In summary, owners of land who have not acquired legal access rights but instead drive over the land of another often argue that the road has become public or an easement by prescription. The Ontario Court of Appeal has commented on this attitude as follows (*Cook's Road*, at para. 28):

> In these circumstances the owner of the property may well, in a neighbourly spirit, permit local residents to use a way across it for their convenience without having any intention of dedicating the road as a public highway.

Public Lands Act and Forest Roads

Nothing in the *Public Lands Act* prevents the temporary closing of a public forest road or a private forest road within the meaning of the *Public Lands Act* where, in the opinion of the district manager, an emergency exists. Section 48 of the *Public Lands Act* defines private and public forest roads as follows:

> "private forest road" means a road occupied under the authority of a document issued under this Act or the regulations;

> "public forest road" means a road, other than a private forest road, that is designated by the Minister as a public forest road; ...

Section 52 of the *Public Lands Act* deals with the temporary closing of forest roads.

RESTRICTIONS ON USE OF LAND

Restrictions on use might take the form of restrictive covenants, building schemes, zoning by-laws, development agreements, official plans, by-laws under the *Ontario Heritage Act*, R.S.O. 1990, c. O.18, airport zoning, or reservations in the original Crown patent. In addition, there is a multitude of diverse federal and provincial statutes that regulate the use of land. For example, land that is environmentally sensitive and shorelines are subject to extensive multi-jurisdictional regulation of use. Some restrictions are registered on title and others require off-title investigation. Chapter 14 provides additional information on legislation that regulates land use, generates the need for searches, fines, restrictions on use, and potentially criminal and regulatory strict liability offences.

A conveyancer should record in full the nature and duration of any registered restriction on use that might affect an owner's title to land. Restrictions on use should be listed under a separate heading in the search summary. Copies of restrictions are usually attached to the completed search. Registered restrictions often give rise to further investigation, often related to compliance.

Restrictive Covenants

Restrictive covenants were an early form of private zoning before the introduction of zoning by-laws. They were first recognized in 1848 in the landmark case of *Tulk v. Moxhay*, [1843-60] All E.R. Rep. 9 (L. Ch.), which dealt with covenants requiring what is now Leicester Square Garden in London to remain a park forever. Today, restrictive covenants can supplement or exceed public planning standards but cannot be in direct conflict with planning restrictions. The balancing of private property entitlements such as restrictive covenants with modern zoning, and the interests of the broader community from a land-use planning perspective, including densification and mixed use development, is becoming an increasingly important and contentious area in real estate practice.

Restrictive covenants restrict land (the servient tenement) to certain uses for the benefit of the neighbouring land owners (the dominant tenement), for a defined period of time, or in perpetuity. Today, most restrictive covenants form part of subdivision agreements and are included in a one- or two-page schedule in the transfer from the developer to the first owner. Some restrictive covenants are registered as separate documents. In Land Titles, the parcel register states in the property description when title is subject to or together with a restrictive covenant.

Restrictive covenants deal with a multitude of routine land-uses, such as pools, fences, clotheslines, satellite dishes, trailers in driveways, house size and height, *etc*. Covenants may restrict land to single family residential or low density developments or prohibit commercial uses. Another common theme, particularly in British Columbia is the protection of existing views and privacy by the use of height and density restrictions. More recently, restrictive covenants provide creative methods of regulating the environmental character of a neighbourhood. For example, some subdivisions now have restrictive covenants which prohibit the use of pesticides for purely ornamental purposes.

Restrictive covenants run with the land and can be enforced against subsequent owners. As with easements, most restrictive covenants must involve dominant and servient tenements. They must be negative in nature and transfer a benefit onto the dominant tenement. For example, a restrictive covenant may prohibit building a pool or fence, carrying on a turkey or pig farming operation, or operating a dry cleaning business or gas station. A vendor selling part of his or her land may prohibit the purchaser and successors on title of the adjoining land from carrying on an identical or similar business. This type of restrictive covenant is called a non-competition covenant. Statutory conservation easements are easements in gross and are exempt from the dominant/servient tenement requirement.

Registration of a restrictive covenant does not make it legally valid if it does not meet common law and statutory requirements. Instead, where a condition or restriction has been registered as annexed to land, "the condition or restriction is as binding upon any person who becomes the registered owner of the land or a part thereof as if the condition or restriction had been in the form of a covenant entered into by the person who was the registered owner of the land at the time of the registration of the condition or restriction" (*Land Titles Act*, s. 119(10)). Simply put, restrictive covenants run with the land. Subsequent owners take title subject to existing covenants as long as the covenants continue to meet underlying legal requirements. Both the statutory regulation of and the common law relating to restrictive covenants is highly technical and considered to be in need of reform. The law concerning covenant validity and enforceability and particularly modification and termination of covenants is complex. Cases appear to be fact-driven and outcomes difficult to predict.

Essential Requirements of a Restrictive Covenant

The following legal requirements must be present in order to enforce a restrictive covenant (*Crump v. Kernahan*, [1995] A.J. No. 704 at para. 10 (Alta. Q.B.)):

- "the covenant must be negative in nature". The covenant can be positive in form and in wording but must be negative in substance. Negative in substance means that compliance with the covenant requires no action on the part of the burdened owner;

- "the covenant must be must be made for the protection of land retained by the covenantee or his assignees". In other words, the covenant is not meant to be personal in nature;

- the covenant involves a dominant tenement that is benefitted by a servient tenement that carries the burden. The properties do not have to actually adjoin but they must be proximate. The definition of proximate is vague; however, dominant and servient tenements in different provinces are not enforceable. As well, the description of the dominant and servient tenement must be identifiable; some extrinsic evidence is permitted to clarify the description.

- "the burden of the covenant must have been intended to run with the covenantor's land". The covenant must "touch and concern" the land meaning, affect how the land is used and enhance the value of the land;

- the benefit must have passed to the covenantee by, for example, annexation or assignment under a building scheme. The covenant must demonstrate intent to pass the benefit; and

- subsequent owners and mortgagees must have notice of the covenant. Meeting registration requirements in the relevant land registration system or proving actual notice both provides notice to subsequent owners.

Specialty covenants created by statute, such as conservation easements are exempt from some of the common law requirements; however, they must meet additional requirements set out in statute. For a detailed analysis of restrictive covenant law in Ontario in the context of a condominium and a building scheme, refer to the Court of Appeal decision in *Durham C.C. No. 123 v. Amberwood Investments Ltd.*, [2002] O.J. No. 1023 (Ont. C.A.). For a detailed analysis of both the law of restrictive covenants that run with the land and the law relating to personal covenants and charitable trusts that can be enforced against land, see the recent British Columbia case of *Save the Heritage Simpson Covenant Society v. Kelowna (City)*, [2008] B.C.J. No. 1534 (B.C.S.C.).

Restrictive Covenants and Public Policy

Restrictive covenants, past or present, which purport to restrict ownership of land on the basis of race, creed, colour, marital status, nationality, place of origin, *etc.* have been void since March 24, 1950 (*Conveyancing and Law of Property Act*, s. 22). The *Human Rights Code*, R.S.O. 1990, c. H.19 and the *Canadian Charter of Rights and Freedoms*, Part I of the *Constitution Act, 1982*, being Schedule B to the *Canada Act 1982* (U.K.), 1982, c. 11 extend the protection to additional ground such as occupancy of accommodation, disability, and receipt of public assistance.

Public policy can void covenants for many reasons. For example, the regulation first made under the *Green Energy Act, 2009*, S.O. 2009, c. 12, Schedule A invalidates restrictive covenants and by-laws that prohibit clotheslines and clothes trees despite any restriction imposed at law that would otherwise prevent or restrict their use, including a restriction established by a municipal by-law, a condominium by-law, an encumbrance on real property, or an agreement (Designation of Goods, Services and Technologies, O. Reg. 97/08).

Variation and Termination of Restrictive Covenants

Restrictive covenants often stand in the way of development, re-subdivision and in-fill, multi-use and commercial projects, building permits, and, in general, someone's ability to profit. As a result, the law dealing with variation and termination of restrictive covenants has become increasingly important as the awareness that land is finite grows. Restrictive covenants may terminate on the basis of law or contract. In addition, a person with an interest in land affected by a restrictive covenant may apply to the court to discharge or modify the restriction in whole or in part.

Termination by Unity of Ownership (Merger)

When an individual acquires both the dominant and servient tenement, the restrictive covenant merges and is extinguished. It does not revive in the future should the land be once again owned by separate individuals. A restrictive covenant that has been extinguished by merger still appears on the title register. Conveyancers when searching title must confirm that there has been no common ownership of a dominant and servient tenement following the creation of the restrictive covenant. If there has been common ownership in the past, the restrictive covenant must have been re-registered for it to be valid. Extinguishment of restrictive covenants and easements through common ownership is one of the main reasons that conveyancers must search title on adjoining lands as well as the land being purchased, mortgaged, or leased.

Variation or Termination by Consent of All Benefitted Parties

The owner(s) of the dominant lands can expressly release at any time a restrictive covenant that runs with the land. All interested parties can agree to modify or terminate a restrictive covenant. Termination or modification of restrictive covenants by agreement is also referred to as discharge or modification *inter partes*.

Termination by Expiry Date in the Contract

Restrictive covenants most often contain an expiry date from 20 to 40 years, or they are to run in perpetuity as the rule against perpetuities does not limit their duration. Each restrictive covenant must be checked for the expiry date.

Termination by Waiver Clause in the Contract

Original, common vendors, often developers, sometimes attempt to reserve, usually in building schemes, the authority to waive restrictions to particular purchasers or lots. This type of clause in a restrictive covenant may invalidate the scheme as a court may decide that there is no common scheme. The case law is unsettled on this question. Waiver clause should be located and reviewed for legal effect by the conveyancer.

Tax Sales and Expropriations

Section 388(5)(a) of Ontario's *Municipal Act, 2001* states that a purchaser under a tax deed takes subject to easements and restrictive covenants that run with the land. As a result, under Ontario's Registry system, conveyancers must search back a full 40 years for easements and restrictive covenants, even though a tax deed provides a new starting point for most title investigation purposes.

Expropriation whether under legislation or agreement may or may not terminate a restrictive covenant on a servient tenement. For example, s. 9(2) of Ontario's *Expropriations Act*, R.S.O. 1990, c. E.26 states that lands may be "required for a limited time only or only a limited estate, right or interest therein". When an expropriating authority acquires dominant land, it acquires the benefit of a restrictive covenant. If the expropriating authority takes lands for a use that is inconsistent with an existing restrictive covenant or easement on a servient tenement, then the owner of the dominant tenement has the right to claim compensation for the taking of the interest (*Expropriations Act*, s. 21).

Expiry by Operation of Recording Statute

There are two basic kinds of land recording statutes. The first and the oldest is a registry system which is in essence a register of documents with no guarantee as to document validity; the second and the more modern is a Torrens or land titles system which is a register of current title backed by a government assurance fund. Increasingly, these recording statutes have incorporated and modified common law rules governing the modification and termination of restrictive covenants.

Registry System

Section 113 of the *Registry Act* in Ontario alters the common law by providing for the automatic expiry of claims following the expiry of the 40-year investigation of title period unless the claim is re-registered within the 40-year notice period by way of a notice prescribed under the *Registry Act* (see the combined effect of ss. 111(1) and 113(3)). Restrictive covenants in perpetuity must be registered in a separate document, at least every 40 years; a reference to the restrictive covenant in a more recent deed will not revive a restriction in perpetuity or provide notice. This legislated change in law has the potential to terminate older, in perpetuity, covenants. Ontario has nearly completed a historic modernization of the land registration system in which it both automated records and registrations and performed a massive, administrative legal conversion of lands in its original Registry system, a register of documents, to its current Land Titles system, a guarantee-backed register of titles. During the conversion, it was common for expired restrictive covenants to be brought forward and valid covenants to be missed during legislatively permitted expedited title search requirements. In a recent case about a 1950s Ottawa subdivsion, the Province of Ontario under the Province of Ontario Land Registration Reform System transferred 39 properties from Registry to Land Titles. The Province as an administrative decision, without notice to the property owners, failed to record the restrictive covenants on the new Land Titles parcel registers, even though they were recorded in the Registry deeds. The judge concluded that even though the restrictions were not recorded in Land Titles, they were not annulled (*Girard (Re)*, [2007] O.J. No. 5216 (Ont. S.C.J.)).

Changing notice periods in land registration statutes have the capacity to terminate restrictive covenants that had the potential to endure in perpetuity. Conveyancers must confirm and monitor expiry dates and may need to periodically re-register covenants to ensure that continuing registration requirements are met.

Land Titles (Torrens) System

The Land Titles system strives to mirror only current, enforceable title interests and encumbrances. In Land Titles, restrictive covenants are initially registered as encumbrances and, then, like descriptions, embedded in the title on the parcel register. They provide statutory procedures for deleting expired restrictive covenants from the register. An interested party such as the registered owner of the dominant or the servient tenement may apply to delete restrictive covenants from the register. Often, a registrar has the discretion to remove an expired restrictive covenant with or without an application. For example, s. 119(8) of Ontario's *Land Titles Act* states that "[w]here a condition or covenant has been entered on the register as annexed to or running with land for a fixed period and the period has expired, the land registrar may, at any time after ten years from the expiration of the period, remove the entry from the register" with or without an application to delete.

The *Land Titles Act* allows an owner or owners benefitted by a restrictive covenant to register an application to delete or modify restrictive covenants by the owner(s) of the servient lands, supported by the consent of all interested parties. If there is ambiguity about the identification of all interested parties, the applicant will proceed by consent court order under either s. 61 of the *Conveyancing and Law of Property Act* or under s. 119 of the *Land Titles Act*.

From a practice perspective, it is important to note that expired, fixed term restrictions often remain on the register unless deleted by application. Section 119(9) of the *Land Titles Act* states that covenants with no fixed expiry date are "deemed to have expired forty years after the condition, restriction or covenant was registered, and may be deleted from the register" by the land registrar with or without an application.

Variation or Termination by Court Application

Most reported cases involve challenges to existing covenants that prohibit other than single family residential, low density developments, in order to subdivide existing lots, allow in-fill developments, increase density by building multi-unit dwellings or apartments, or allow mixed residential commercial uses. Existing owners object on the basis that the modification will harm the character and ambiance of the existing neighbourhood by, for example, increasing noise and traffic or by reducing privacy, restricting views, and generally reducing the quality of life.

Statutory Framework for the Variation or Termination of Restrictive Covenants

In Ontario, the court can modify or discharge a restrictive covenant under s. 61 of the *Conveyancing and Law of Property Act* when dealing with land recorded under the *Registry Act*, or under the differently worded s. 119 of the *Land Titles Act* when dealing with land recorded in land titles. The older *Conveyancing and Law of Property Act* simply provides that "[w]here there is annexed to land a condition or covenant that the land or a specified part of it is not to be built on or is to be or not to be used in a particular manner, or any other condition or covenant running with or capable of being legally annexed to land, any such condition or covenant may be modified or discharged by a court order". This Act relies fully on the common law criteria to guide court decisions. Ontario's *Land Titles Act* deems registration of restrictive covenants to be notice to every person who derives title from the first owner. This Act provides for "modification or discharge by order of the court on proof to the satisfaction of the court that the modification will be beneficial to the persons principally interested in the enforcement of the condition or covenant" (*Land Titles Act*, s. 119). Decisions based on this section also follow the traditional common law criteria.

Courts exercise the jurisdiction to modify or discharge restrictive covenants with the greatest caution. The court will sever an unenforceable covenant from valid covenants. If the modifications are so substantial that they destroy the mutuality of a building scheme, the court will terminate the scheme rather than sever the unenforceable clauses. For the court to order termination or modification, the applicant must establish one of the following generic grounds:

- there has been a material change in the property or the neighbourhood or other circumstances that render the restriction obsolete;

- the continued existence of the restriction would impede the reasonable user of the land without securing practical benefit or real or substantial benefit to other person(s);

- the proposed modification will not substantially injure the persons entitled to the benefit of the restrictions; or

- all beneficiaries of the covenant agree expressly or by implication by acquiescence or delay. The doctrine of acquiescence is an equitable defence. For acquiescence to deprive an owner of a property right, it must be unconscionable for the owner to enforce the right. Generally, the occasional failure to enforce a restrictive covenant is unlikely to extinguish it as long as the original purpose of the covenant continues to benefit the interested parties. However, caution is indicated as there are cases where property owners who acquiesced on one earlier occasion to a breach of a building scheme covenant prohibiting subdivision lost the right to enforce the covenant on a subsequent breach. Landowners who wish to maintain the benefit of a restrictive covenant must diligently enforce covenants in a timely, consistent, and equitable (non-discriminatory) manner.

Registration of Restrictive Covenants

In the Land Titles system, a restrictive covenant may be contained in a transfer, or registered separately by Document General in an application to amend the register by entering a restrictive covenant, or registered as part of a subdivision agreement containing a building scheme affecting all subdivision lots. Any owner in the scheme has the right to enforce covenants. Restrictive covenants in a building scheme must be enforced promptly and uniformly against all lots in order to remain legally enforceable. In Land Titles, on occasion, an owner may, at the discretion of the registrar, register a restriction requiring notice to and consent by a named legal person, such as Ontario Housing, prior to registration of a transfer or a mortgage. Once restrictive covenants are registered, a notice of restrictive covenants is entered on the parcel page in the property description line. An application to amend the register by entering a notice of compliance with restrictive covenants may be registered in Land Titles. Applications respecting restrictive covenants are registered by Document General.

Under the Registry system, restrictive covenants may be registered separately by Document General or as part of a deed or subdivision agreement. In the past, in Registry, restrictive covenants may have been included in any document registered within the last 40 years. Restrictive covenants, as with easements, must be re-registered every 40 years by a proscribed notice on both the dominant and the servient tenements for them to remain enforceable. Reference to a restrictive covenant within a document does not constitute notice within the 40-year notice period. (See Chapter 3 for more detail on the 40-year notice period and a discussion of the *Ramsay* case and amending legislation.) Restrictive covenants are discharged by Document General.

A title searcher should record the date of registration, the nature and duration of the restriction, release provisions, complete descriptions of all dominant and servient lands affected, and any right to waive or modify the restriction with or without the consent of other owners who may be benefitting from the restriction. All servient tenements which are subject to a restrictive covenant should be checked for registered notice of the restriction. Expired restrictive covenants, excluding details, should be noted in the search, together with the expiry date.

TITLE INSURANCE AND RESTRICTIVE COVENANTS

Restrictive covenants have the ability to reduce or increase land values. As well, the validity, enforceability, and compliance status of restrictive covenants affect proprietary interests in marketable and insurable title. Unless there is actual notice, standard title insurance covers restrictive covenants running with the land for non-compliance to the closing date. Title insurers do not require compliance inquiries or a statement from the vendor that restrictive covenants have been complied with unless it is a warranty or condition in the agreement of purchase and sale. Although insurers have a duty to defend if a policy owner is named in an action for non-compliance, compensation is the preferred remedy when dealing with restrictive covenant concerns. However, compensation for non-compliance would only cover changes in fair market value and not address the traditional quality of life and non-monetary values so often validated in cases on the modification and termination of restrictive covenants.

CONSERVATION EASEMENTS

Conservation easements are creatures of Federal or Provincial statute. They are part of a patchwork of environmental conservation initiatives. They are governed by statute and do not need to meet the traditional common law requirements. They can be positive covenants and do not require a proximate dominant tenement. They may have an expiry date or continue in perpetuity. Some have a term of 999 years. They are customized to each property and require a close reading to determine their effect on ownership. Although they are called easements, they restrict the use and ownership of land in ways similar to restrictive covenants.

Legal Characteristics of Conservation Easements

A conservation easement is an agreement between a landowner and a "qualified" conservation body for conservation, maintenance, restoration or enhancement of land or the wildlife on the land. Qualified organizations must be designated by government and include, the Crown, organized municipal organizations, government agencies, and conservation trusts or land trusts, such as the Ontario Heritage Foundation, Ontario Nature or a local conservation authority. Conservation easements are registered on title and run with the land. Subsequent owners are subject to the terms of a registered conservation easement. The qualified organization has an access right and monitors the terms of the agreement. Conservation easements do not provide access to the public.

Conservation easements may, for example, protect a wildlife habitat, restrict or prohibit development, mandate agricultural use only, focus on an endangered species or the protection of water sources, place restrictions on future use, or prohibit logging, hunting and trapping, and the removal of native species.

In Ontario, conservation easements fall under the *Conservation Land Act*, R.S.O. 1990, c. C.28, s. 3(6.1), the *Agricultural Research Institute of Ontario Act*, R.S.O. 1990, c. A.13, or the *Ontario Heritage Act*. Easements may affect the entire property or only one feature; for example, a pond, a woodlot, a heritage building or just one stained glass window, or one species of wildflower.

A conveyancer must be careful to distinguish a title transfer disguised as a conservation easement. A conservation agreement may contain a transfer of title to the conservation body or it may transfer title but reserve a "life estate" for the donor and his or her family members who can continue to live on the property subject to the conditions. Some agreements transfer title to a charitable trust in return for regular annuity payments liened on the land. Other agreements transfer ownership and then lease all or a portion of it back for a certain period. The agreement may be a grant of a right of first refusal or an option to purchase to a conservation organization, if and when you decide to sell. A conservation easement, when made in perpetuity, may qualify as an ecological gift under the *Income Tax Act*.

Variation and Termination of Conservation Easements

Conservation easements are an exception to the doctrine of merger and extinguishment by common owner (*Conservation Land Act*, s. 3(6.1)). If a conservation body becomes the owner of the land affected by the conservation easement, the easement is suspended but it does not merge; it is not extinguished. If at a later time, the conservation body conveys the affected land, the easement revives (*Conservation Land Act*, s. 3(6.1)(b)). For policy reasons, recent legislation governing conservation easements has special rules for variation and termination. Common law and equitable rights and remedies relating to the variation and termination of conservation easements continue to govern to the extent that they are not inconsistent with legislation (*Conservation Land Act*, s. 3(9)). For example, s. 3 of Ontario's *Conservation Land Act* sets the following statutory requirements for variation and termination of conservation land easements:

- a conservation easement or covenant may expire on a fixed date or run forever (s. 3(4.1));

- the owner of the land affected requires the consent of the Minister of Natural Resources acting in the public interest to amend the covenant (s. 3(4.2));

- the conservation body requires the consent of the Minister of Natural resources to release the covenant (s. 3(4.3));

- proceedings to amend or release conservation easements require notice to the Minister (s. 3(4.4)); and

- conservation easements do not merge under common ownership; it is suspended and may revive if the conservation body transfers the land (s. 3(6.1)).

Conservation easements are highly vulnerable to political and economic climates such as change of government and government policies, as is environmental policy in general. The political nature of conservation easements may exert a powerful influence on modification and termination policies. It remains to be seen whether public bodies and shifting government priorities will provide enduring protection for land. History suggests that government priorities such as resource utilization and economic impact may outweigh conservation values. Indeed, history provides many examples of poor management of public lands.

ZONING AND BY-LAWS

By-laws registered on title may relate to zoning and property use in general, traffic and parking, animals, seasonal occupation only, water use, trees, fences, the permitted height of lawns, demolition control, site plan control, heritage designations, airports, conservation areas, road dedications, openings or closings, *Planning Act* subdivision control provisions, or a multitude of other increasingly diverse subjects. For example, in Toronto parking garage safety is regulated by an anti-mugging by-law, whereas in Muskoka, by-laws now regulate tree preservation by ensuring no clear-cutting, waterfront density that protects both shorelines and water quality, site preparation that prohibits wholesale blasting, and light pollution by enacting dark sky restrictions in areas such as the Torrens Barrens dark sky park. The City of Toronto is the first city in North America to pass a "green" roof by-law. This innovative by-law requires that every new building with a gross floor area of 2,000 metres or more be built with a green roof according to the Toronto Green Roof Standard. The by-law takes effect on January 31, 2010 for residential and commercial buildings, and on January 31, 2011 for industrial buildings. Contravention of the by-law is an offence and carries a maximum fine of $100,000. The vegetated area may be reduced by solar arrays that are governed by a feed-in tariff (FIT) contact under the *Green Energy Act, 2009.*

Some by-laws, such as *Planning Act* part lot control by-laws, road opening and closing by-laws, and heritage designations are registered in the parcel register in Land Titles or by-law index or abstract index in Registry. By-laws may be summarized or copied as part of a search.

By-laws registered on title should be listed under a separate heading in the search summary.

Restricted Area and Property Standards

Zoning and building by-laws, also referred to as land-use control and property standards by-laws, divide municipalities into specific areas, designate land and building uses, provide set back requirements from the street, side and rear of the lot, and other municipal restrictions.

Lawyers make "off-title" inquiries to the municipality concerning zoning requirements and property compliance. Depending on the municipal response, lawyers may make further specific inquiries of the municipality or independent professional experts in land-use and urban design.

Zoning by-laws should be compared against a survey to determine whether the present use of land conforms to municipal zoning. Historical by-law searches are sometimes necessary to confirm a legal non-conforming use where non-compliance preceded the by-law restriction. Municipal work orders may be registered against land in circumstances of non-compliance.

Although some by-laws may be registered on the parcel or abstract page, or in the by-law index in Registry, it is usually much easier to check zoning directly with the local municipality.

Title Insurance and Building and Zoning Compliance

Title insurance is available to cover many zoning non-compliance risks, and, as a result, may provide an alternative to a survey and basic zoning and building permit and compliance inquiries. Generally, insurance substitutes for searches for building department work orders based on zoning violations. However, title insurers do require certain kinds of zoning searches depending on the nature of the transaction and the nature of the property. Different insurers have different requirements and these requirements change. For example, the conveyancer should check if a property is zoned for year-round occupancy when relevant or for the legality of multi-unit residences when the purchaser relies on the conveyancer for an opinion on the legality or the income from a multi-use building. Usually, insurers require zoning and building searches for transactions of two to six residential units, including properties where the second unit is a boathouse with living accommodation (Stewart Title). Generally, insurers do not require zoning and building compliance searches for single residential dwellings or refinance transactions. Commercial transactions have different requirements based on the value of the transaction for an owner and loan to value ratio for a lender.

As well, a client may wish to confirm a permitted use to allow future plans for the property whether or not these anticipated uses are part of the agreement of purchase and sale, such as building an addition, converting to a business use, or converting a seasonal property to a permanent residence. Lawyers determine the client's needs and expectations in order to advise which searches should be completed and when to rely only on insurance coverage.

Planning Act Subdivision and Part Lot Control By-Laws

Subdivision control by-laws must be registered to affect land. It is necessary to record the description affected, the *Planning Act* section number, and whether the by-law imposes part lot control on certain lands, exempts land from part lot control, cancels the registered subdivision whole lot exemption, or forgives prior subdivision control violations. Check for by-law expiry dates. (See Chapter 11 for more detail.)

Airport Zoning By-Laws

Airport zoning by-laws control the height and lighting of buildings within a certain radius of an airport. The permitted height increases as the distance from the end of the runway increases. The document registered on title contains a large complex map and detailed regulations. As these by-laws are long and complex, record only the basic terms from the abstract or parcel page. A surveyor, an aeronautical engineer, or the federal Department of Transport may be of assistance in interpreting the effect of an airport by-law on a property being purchased.

Ontario Heritage Act

When a municipality designates a property as having historic, architectural, or natural value or interest, a designation by-law must be registered against the property. Check the by-law to determine the exact limit of the designation. The by-law may affect an entire property or merely the coach house, the front door fanlight, or one stained glass keyhole window. Normally, a copy of the by-law is attached to the search.

DEVELOPMENT AGREEMENTS

Development agreements vary greatly in form and content. Conveyancers may be required to summarize important points, such as easements, restrictions, conditions, access rights, or grading restrictions, specifically requested by the lawyer or to attach a copy of the agreement or requested parts of the agreement to the search. Development agreements should be listed under a separate heading in the search summary.

Subdivision Plans and Agreements

Subdivision plans which divide land into numbered building (subdivision) lots, blocks for park and school purposes, and roads, reserves and walkways are registered as part of the development and new subdivision process. Subdivision agreements between developers and municipalities regulate the construction and quality of housing and services such as sewers, lights, streets, sidewalks, curbs and parks within subdivisions. The requirements for these agreements differ from municipality to municipality. Subdivision agreements usually place restrictions on the use of land within their boundaries. Purchasers of lots or houses within a subdivision need to know how the subdivision agreement may affect them. When a release for a subdivision agreement has not been registered on title, check the agreement for the reservation and the nature of easements, restrictive covenants, rights of re-entry, occupancy permit restrictions, zoning, requirements for written approvals from the engineer and architect, potential fees, fines and liens, restrictions that survive release, security lots, and performance bond and discharge privileges for individual lots. Occupancy permits may prohibit a purchaser from taking possession of a new home. Some agreements contain requirements for municipal consent when transferring lots. Subdivision agreements can impose duties on subsequent purchasers. For example, some subdivision agreements require vendors to attach warnings to subsequent agreements of purchase and sale that the water contains high sodium levels and that persons with cardiac conditions should discuss the matter with their doctors.

Note road assumptions as well as the existence and release of one-foot reserves located at the end of access streets because it is important to know whether roads are municipally owned and maintained, and whether a purchaser has access to different traffic routes. The developer first transfers the reserves and some lots to the municipality as an assurance that it will fulfil its commitments under the agreement and not leave the municipality and the subdivision residents with a debt instead of services. Confirm that the municipality owns the reserves and that it has registered a by-law dedicating the reserves as a public highway. The abstract and parcel index pages for roads and reserves, located in the subdivision plan abstract book or register, will record any changes to roads and reserves since the registration of the subdivision. Licence agreements are also registered to permit entry by the developer upon the lands to comply with the subdivision agreement until such time as the municipality accepts the subdivision.

In Land Titles, applications to register or delete a notice of agreement, applications to register a notice of compliance, or applications to register a partial release, are registered by way of Document General. In Registry, agreements and releases are also registered by way of Document General.

Site Plan Control Agreements

Municipalities that have passed a site plan control by-law under s. 41 of the *Planning Act* may require detailed site plan control agreements to be registered as a condition of land development. Detailed provisions contained in these agreements affecting roads, walkways, lighting, buildings, landscaping, *etc.* are binding on subsequent owners.

Other Agreements

You do not know what is in a registered agreement until you read it. For example, it is best not to miss a methane gas venting agreement between the city and the property owner. Contracts for purchase and sale, parking lot lighting and noise provisions, encroachments, easements, options, mortgage postponements and amendments, methane gas management, water flow and flooding rights, and *Planning Act* severance conditions may all lurk behind generic terms, such as agreement and notice, found on the title abstract or register. Thorough conveyancers carefully check and read notice and agreement-type documents on both the lands being purchased and on the adjoining lands.

CROWN GRANT RESERVATIONS AND THE PUBLIC LANDS ACT

All lands in Land Titles and Registry are subject to Crown conditions and reservations found in the original Crown patent. In Registry, Crown rights and reservations are an exception to the 40-year search and notice periods. The *Land Titles Act* provides that land is subject to rights reserved or vested in the Crown in the right of Canada or Ontario.

Original Crown patents frequently reserved minerals, timber, particularly white pines, and 66-foot road and shoreline allowances to the Crown. Unless the Crown patent grants the bed of navigable water or streams bordering on or passing through a parcel of land, title to the waterbed or streams does not pass. Although many of the conditions and reservations relating to minerals and timber are now void as a result of changes in the *Public Lands Act*, original concession, shoreline, and road allowances, and the beds of navigable water remain under Crown ownership. Section 15(6) of the *Public Lands Act* states that:

> In every sale or other disposition of public lands for summer resort locations there shall be reserved to the Crown all mines and minerals thereon or thereunder, and the instrument of sale or other disposition shall so provide.

Section 61(1) of the *Public Lands Act* states that "[i]n the case of land patented before the 6th day of May, 1913, the mines and minerals therein shall be deemed to have passed to the patentee by the letters patent, and every reservation thereof contained in the letters patent or by statute is void". Section 61(3) states that, "[i]n the case of lands patented after the 6th day of May, 1913, mines and minerals pass to the patentee unless expressly reserved by the letters patent". The rules for Crown reservations are different for different categories of land, particularly agricultural and summer resort lands, and the rules vary depending on the date of the Crown grant. It is important to check both the Crown patent and the relevant sections of the *Public Lands Act*.

Practically speaking, practice varies as to whether a conveyancer will always check for the existence and contents of a Crown patent. A title searcher should be given specific instructions on how to deal with the issue of Crown patents in both Land Titles and Registry. It is more common to check when dealing with rural, recreational, waterfront, valuable or development properties. When dealing with a waterfront property always check the patent for the 66-foot shoreline allowance and any restrictions on access or use of the water. It is important as well to determine the exact location of the shoreline allowance. This can only be done with the assistance of a survey as water levels have changed since the time of the patent. Urban properties may receive less attention.

Section 67 of the *Public Lands Act* creates a blanket reservation on the disposition of public lands for water power and adjacent land that "the Minister considers necessary for the erection of buildings and plant and the development and utilization of the power, together with the right to lay out and use such roads as may be necessary for passage to and from such water power or privilege and land".

The federal government is responsible for Crown patents granting lands that were originally vested in the Crown in the right of Canada for Indian reservations. Crown grants may reserve Aboriginal rights although Aboriginal rights may exist independently of Crown grants. The Crown may also have unfulfilled treaty rights that also have the potential to affect the ownership and the use of land.

Only notice of a Crown patent, issued prior to October 1, 1965, is registered in the Registry office. A copy of an actual patent must be obtained from either the provincial or federal government. Copies of Ontario Crown patents are available from the Ministry of Natural Resources. It is important to remember that the law clearly states that land is subject to Crown rights and that all restrictions on title should be reported to the purchaser.

In 1919, the Canada Company quit claimed to the Crown all mineral rights reserved to the company in the original Crown conveyances. As of 1997, s. 180.1 of the *Mining Act* vests these mineral rights in the owners of the surface rights.

Crown and Aboriginal rights are complex and require careful investigation on and off-title. Title insurance does not provide standard coverage for Crown patent issues or Aboriginal title or rights; however, insurers may choose to underwrite specific problems identified by title or off-title inquiries, such as non-compliance with the technical requirements of a Crown patent.

CHAPTER 10

Spousal Rights and the Matrimonial Home

INTRODUCTION

In real property transactions, conveyancers must carefully verify and document clients' identity and spousal status, and whether a property is a matrimonial home for the following reasons:

1. Purchasers, lessees, and mortgagees will take ownership subject to prior spousal interests in the matrimonial home unless a non-titled spouse has consented to the transaction or statements in the conveyance document that the property is exempt from matrimonial home rights. No new homebuyer wants to learn that the seller's spouse has a better right of possession or that his or her title is cluttered with spousal rights of earlier owners!

2. Title insurance claims history indicates a higher risk of title and mortgage fraud based on the impersonation of a spouse, fraudulent statements concerning matrimonial home status, and the fraudulent use of powers of attorney, where one spouse acts on behalf of another spouse.

Section 19 of the *Family Law Act*, R.S.O. 1990, c. F.3 ("the Act") gives both spouses an equal right to the possession of a matrimonial home regardless of whether a spouse has a registered title interest. A spouse's possessory right in the matrimonial home affects the ownership rights of subsequent purchasers, lessees, and mortgagees unless the spouse has consented in writing to the conveyance, a court order or separation agreement has released the spouse's claim, or the spouse has ceased to be a spouse through death or divorce. A spouse is a married person, including a same-sex person. For the purposes of matrimonial home rights and division of assets entitlements, spouse does not include persons living together in common-law relationships.

IDENTITY, SPOUSAL STATUS, AND MATRIMONIAL HOME STATUS INQUIRIES

Title inquiries include a review of spousal status and matrimonial home rights related to prior owners to ensure that the new purchaser takes title clear of pre-existing matrimonial home rights. The Law Society, mortgages lenders, and money-laundering legislation all require lawyers to obtain and keep a record, and sometimes report client identification information, such as client's full name, home and business address, telephone number, and occupation(s). Two pieces of photo identification such as a driver's licence, a passport, or a birth certificate (not including an Ontario health card), and an additional piece of identification are normally required. In addition, lawyers verify and retain spousal status and matrimonial home exemption information, such as photocopies of marriage and divorce certificates, separation agreements, court orders, spousal consent, and powers of attorney. Law Society of Upper Canada By-Law 7.1 (October 31, 2008) sets out rigorous client identification (ID) and verification requirements for Ontario's lawyers and licensed paralegals. It contains sample client ID forms, and rules for out-of-country clients and corporations, trusts and partnerships.

Client ID verifications take place at the beginning of the file. For practical purposes, it is wise to treat real property as having a spousal, matrimonial home claim until proven otherwise; most transfers, leases, and charges must contain carefully verified spousal status and matrimonial home status statements.

MATRIMONIAL HOME RIGHTS

The Act enacts a scheme that provides for the division and equalization of most assets (net family property) acquired by spouses during marriage. The division may take place on marriage breakdown or on the death of a spouse. A spouse's rights in the matrimonial home are accorded special protection. The value of the matrimonial home must be shared unless there is a domestic agreement to the contrary. In addition, s. 19 of the Act creates a possessory right in the matrimonial home for the non-owner spouse. The Act prohibits spouses from contracting out of Part II possessory rights in the matrimonial home by way of a marriage contract. A spouse may hold title to a matrimonial home separately or both spouses may hold title to the matrimonial home jointly.

In addition to the spouse's property right in the division of assets, Part II of the Act sets out special protections regarding disposition (sale), encumbrance (mortgage) and possession of the matrimonial home. Section 21 prohibits a spouse from disposing of or encumbering a matrimonial home without the consent of the non-owner spouse. Section 19 assures each spouse of an equal right of possession in the matrimonial home, irrespective of registered ownership. A spouse's special possessory rights in the matrimonial home are triggered on marriage breakdown or on the death of one of the spouses. In summary, matrimonial home rights must be accounted for during sale, mortgage, and lease transactions.

DEFINITION OF SPOUSE

The Act defines the term "spouse" differently in different Parts. For the purposes of Part II, the matrimonial home provisions, "spouse" is defined in s. 1(1) as follows:

> "spouse" means either of two persons who,
>
> (a) are married to each other, or
>
> (b) have together entered into a marriage that is voidable or void, in good faith on the part of a person relying on this clause to assert any right.

Section 1(2) extends the definition of marriage to include a marriage that is actually or potentially polygamous, if it was celebrated in a jurisdiction whose system of law recognizes it as valid.

Matrimonial home rights and conveyancing procedures apply only to legally married spouses, including persons in polygamous marriages performed in jurisdictions in which they are recognized as valid. They do not apply to persons living in common law relationships.

In the past, rights relating to the division of net family property and the matrimonial home were traditionally limited to legally married, heterosexual couples. The Ontario Court of Appeal in *Halpern v. Canada (Attorney General)*, [2003] O.J. No. 2268 (Ont. C.A.) clearly concluded that the opposite-sex requirement in the definition of marriage creates a formal distinction between opposite-sex and same-sex couples on the basis of sexual orientation, an analogous ground of discrimination under s. 15(1) of the *Canadian Charter of Rights and Freedoms*, Part I of the *Constitution Act, 1982*, being Schedule B to the *Canada Act 1982* (U.K.), 1982, c. 11 ("the Charter"), and is not saved as a justifiable limit in a free and democratic society under s. 1 of the Charter. As a result, the Court declared the *Family Law Act* definition of marriage invalid and reformulated the definition of marriage to be "the voluntary union for life of two persons to the exclusion of all others" (*Halpern*, at para. 148), and ordered "the declaration of invalidity ... and the reformulated definition ... to have immediate effect" (*Halpern*, at para. 156). Court of Appeal cases in Quebec and British Columbia came to the same conclusion. Neither the Government of Canada nor the Province of Ontario expressed an intention to challenge the Court's decision. Following the *Halpern* case, Ontario started issuing marriage licences to same-sex couples.

On July 20, 2005, the federal government enacted the *Civil Marriage Act*, S.C. 2005, c. 33 that stated:

1.   "Marriage, for civil purposes, is the lawful union of two persons to the exclusion of all others" (*Civil Marriage Act*, s. 2); and

2.   "For greater certainty, a marriage is not void or voidable by reason only that the spouses are of the same sex" (*Civil Marriage Act*, s. 4).

The *Family Law Act* was amended by deleting the reference to a "man and a woman" and substituting the word "person". As a result, conveyancers must ensure that all persons, who are legally married, comply with the matrimonial home provisions of the Act.

DEFINITION OF MATRIMONIAL HOME

Section 18 of the Act defines a matrimonial home as being "[e]very property in which a person has an interest and that is or, if the spouses have separated, was at the time of separation ordinarily occupied by the person and his or her spouse as their family residence". Spouses may own one or more matrimonial homes at any given time depending on the ordinary occupation as a family residence at the time of separation. Section 28 of the Act states that Part II applies only to matrimonial homes situated in Ontario.

The Act does not restrict a matrimonial home to real property. "Property" includes both real and personal property (s. 17). Spouses who rent living accommodation have matrimonial home rights in the leased premises. As well, s. 18 allows for a spouse to own more than one matrimonial home at the same time, as long as the matrimonial home was ordinarily occupied by the spouses as a family residence at the time of separation. In effect, a city home, a farm, a cottage, a recreational condominium, a houseboat, a mobile home, a recreational vehicle, and/or a leased apartment could all be treated as matrimonial homes.

Section 18(2) provides that the term matrimonial home includes housing cooperatives and other arrangements in which the ownership of shares of a corporation entitles the owner to occupy a housing unit owned by the corporation. The section may cover the situation in which a spouse directs ownership of a family residence to be placed in the name of a company, which he or she controls, in order to avoid the *Family Law Act* requirement of spousal consent on the sale or mortgage of a matrimonial home. Case law has increasingly pierced the corporate veil when it was used to avoid child and spousal support entitlements (*Wildman v. Wildman*, [2006] O.J. No. 3966 (Ont. C.A.)).

Section 18(3) states that when property is used for both residential and commercial purposes, such as a farm or a flat above a store, "the matrimonial home is only the part of the property that may reasonably be regarded as necessary to the use and enjoyment of the residence".

A matrimonial home need only be "ordinarily occupied" as a family residence at the time of separation. For example, when spouses alternate trips to Australia with summers at the family cottage, the family cottage retains its status as a matrimonial home. Possession need not be regular or frequent, only consistent with the use of the spouses during normal family life. In addition, concurrent ownership, such as joint ownership, tenants in common and partners, does not interfere with matrimonial home status. For example, if a cottage were inherited by two sisters who are both married, as tenants in common, and most summers each sister spends a month at the cottage with her husband and children, then both husbands would be required to sign a spousal consent before the sisters could sell the cottage or even register a mortgage providing funds for major renovations. A spouse's interest in the matrimonial homes ends when he or she ceases to be a spouse, unless a separation agreement or court order provides otherwise (s. 19(2)). Because of this exception, it is important to confirm the contents of the court order or the separation agreement.

Due to the broad definitions of "spouse" and "matrimonial home", and the heightened risk of fraud relating to spousal identity, and spousal and matrimonial home status statements and consents, it is best to treat every property as a matrimonial home until proven conclusively otherwise.

DESIGNATION OF THE MATRIMONIAL HOME

"One or both spouses may designate property owned by one or both of them as a matrimonial home, in the form prescribed by the regulations made under this Act" (s. 20(1)). Designation of Matrimonial Home — Forms, R.R.O. 1990, Reg. 367 contains the required designation forms. These forms are available online in Teraview.

There are two kinds of designations under the *Family Law Act*, and they have different effects in law. In order to be effective, a designation or a cancellation of a designation must be registered in the proper form in the proper land registry office. Designations and cancellations are currently registered by way of document general. As designations affect whether a spousal consent is required on a property, they should be recorded in the search notes, specifically setting out whether they were signed by one or both spouses.

Designation by Both Spouses

When both spouses jointly complete and register a matrimonial home designation, "any other property that is a matrimonial home under s. 18 but is not designated by both spouses ceases to be a matrimonial home" (*Family Law Act*, s. 20(4)). A matrimonial home designation signed by both spouses has the effect of clearing other family properties of the matrimonial home consent and exemption requirements. A designation by both spouses may be cancelled by both spouses. As well, a designation may be cancelled by a decree absolute of divorce or judgment of nullity, a court order, or a proof of death of one of the spouses. Once the cancellation of a joint designation is registered, all other properties regain their status as potential matrimonial homes.

Designation by One Spouse

When a designation is made by one spouse only, then any other property that is a matrimonial home under s. 18 remains a matrimonial home (*Family Law Act*, s. 20(5)). A designation signed and registered by only one spouse acts as a sort of notice to subsequent purchasers and mortgagees of a potential spousal claim in a property. It cannot be registered as a caution as it is not an interest in land. A purchaser or mortgagee must obtain the spouse's consent or the registration of a cancellation of the designation unless they choose to buy subject to a prior, outstanding spousal claim on title. The spouse who registered the original designation may register a cancellation. The cancellation of a single spouse designation has no effect on the status of other properties.

DISPOSITION AND ENCUMBRANCE OF THE MATRIMONIAL HOME

Today, in Ontario, s. 21 of the *Family Law Act* states that no person may dispose of (sell or lease) or encumber (mortgage or charge) an interest in a matrimonial home unless the person is not a spouse, or the property is exempt from the matrimonial home rights for the following reasons:

(a)   the other spouse joins in the instrument or consents to the transaction;

(b)   the other spouse has released all rights under this Part by a separation agreement;

(c)   a court order has authorized the transaction or has released the property from the application of this Part; or

(d)   the property is not designated by both spouses as a matrimonial home and a designation of another property as a matrimonial home, made by both spouses, is registered and not cancelled.

The Act states that subsequent purchasers or mortgagees for value, without notice, may rely on the accuracy of spousal status and matrimonial home exemption statements. If, however, a purchaser or a mortgagee lawyer has reason to suspect that property may be subject to a spousal claim despite the spousal exemption statements, it is necessary to exercise due diligence making careful inquiries and seek independent evidence to confirm the statements. Several Ontario cases dealing with title and mortgage fraud have emphasized that a purchaser or mortgagee may have an opportunity to avoid fraud depending on the transactional proximity to the fraudster. Justice Macdonald in *Reviczky v. Meleknia*, [2007] O.J. No. 4992, 287 D.L.R. (4th) 193 (Ont. S.C.J.), when referring to a fraudulent power of attorney, cautions lawyers against taking a "'business as usual' approach to a transaction which required something more" (*Reviczky*, at para. 68). See also *Lawrence v. Wright*, [2007] O.J. No. 381, 278 D.L.R. (4th) 698 (Ont. C.A.). When the title search of a property or previous dealings with a client reveal potentially contradictory information to the spousal or matrimonial home statements, the lawyer must make further inquiries. The court has the power to set aside a real estate transaction where a spouse acted in contravention of the Act or a subsequent purchaser had notice that the *Family Law Act* statements were false. However, s. 21(2) protects subsequent purchasers and mortgagees who have relied on spousal and matrimonial home statements and acquired the "interest or encumbrance ... for value, in good faith and without notice, at the time of acquiring it or making an agreement to acquire it, that the property was a matrimonial home".

SPOUSAL STATUS AND EXEMPTION STATEMENTS AND SPOUSAL CONSENTS UNDER THE FAMILY LAW ACT

Every Transfer/Deed of Land and every Charge/Mortgage of Land, and certain Documents General that function as Transfers or Charges, are required to include spousal status and exemption statements by the grantor(s) or mortgagor(s). An attorney, on the basis of his or her personal knowledge, may make spousal and matrimonial home statements. Statements as to the age(s) of the transferor(s) and birthdate(s) of the transferee(s) must also be included.

When a person is a non-owner spouse and the property is a matrimonial home that is not exempt, then the spouse must sign and date a spousal consent to the disposition or the encumbrance in the document. A person who has not obtained the consent of the non-owner spouse may instead complete a spousal exemption statement on a disposition or encumbrance in order to satisfy matrimonial home requirements. The Act provides that the following statements by the person making the disposition or encumbrance on registered instruments are deemed to be sufficient proof that the property is not a matrimonial home (s. 21(3)):

    (a) verifying that he or she is not, or was not, a spouse at the time of the disposition or encumbrance;

    (b) verifying that the person is a spouse who is not separated from his or her spouse and that the property was not ordinarily occupied by the spouses as their family residence;

    (c) verifying that the person is a spouse who is separated from his or her spouse and that the property was not ordinarily occupied by the spouses, at the time of their separation, as their family residence;

(d) where the property is not designated by both spouses as a matrimonial home, verifying that a designation of another property as a matrimonial home, made by both spouses, is registered and not cancelled; or

(e) verifying that the other spouse has released all rights under this Part by a separation agreement. ...

The POLARIS (paper) forms and the online Teraview electronic registration forms contain slightly different wording as follows:

1. I am/I am not a spouse.

2. The property transferred (charged, *etc.*) is not ordinarily occupied by me and my spouse, who is not separated from me, as our family residence.

3. I am separated from my spouse and the property transferred (charged, *etc.*) was not ordinarily occupied by us at the time of our separation as a family residence.

4. The property is not designated under s. 20 of the *Family Law Act* as a matrimonial home by me and my spouse, but there is such a designation of another property as our matrimonial home, which has been registered and which has not been cancelled.

5. My spouse has released all rights under Part II of the *Family Law Act* by a separation agreement.

6. This transaction is authorized by court order under s. 23 of the *Family Law Act* registered as Instrument No.__, which has not been stayed.

7. The property transferred (charged, *etc.*) is released from the application of Part II of the *Family Law Act* by court order registered as Instrument No.__, which has not been stayed.

The preceding statements may be relied on by a third party purchaser or mortgagee, for value, in good faith, without notice that the statement is false, when acquiring an interest in land that was a matrimonial home. Case law confirms that lawyers have some duty to consider other information from previous files and title search information when relying on *Family Law Act* statements. For example, if a vendor, when he or she took title or mortgaged land, was shown as being a spouse, then that vendor may have to support a statement that he or she is not a spouse in a subsequent transaction. If, on the other hand, the required statements and/or consents were not completed, then the land disposed of or charged may be subject to a spouse's interest in the matrimonial home. In Land Titles, the parcel register will be marked subject to a spousal interest. In addition, s. 21(2) provides that a transaction respecting a matrimonial home may be set aside by court order under s. 23.

Trustees in bankruptcy, trustees of a religious institution, trustees of a school board, estate trustees selling to pay debts, estate trustees as registered owners, corporations and the sheriff selling pursuant to a writ of seizure and sale (execution) are not required to complete spousal statements. An attorney, pursuant to a power of attorney, may make spousal statements as long as he or she unequivocally bases them on personal, actual knowledge of the circumstances. The Public Guardian and Trustee or a committee may make statements based on knowledge and belief only, for a mentally incompetent person.

The Act requires that spouses be made parties to foreclosure and judicial sale actions and be given notice of power of sale proceedings and evictions from leasehold premises. Court orders respecting preservation, ownership and exclusive possession of the matrimonial home may be registered on title.

When a matrimonial home is held by spouses as joint tenants, one spouse must complete the required *Family Law Act* statements when he or she sells his or her joint tenant's interest to a third party in order to sever a joint tenancy. One joint tenant may sever a joint tenancy in a matrimonial home by signing a conveyance of his or her interest to himself or herself.

Pursuant to s. 21(5) of the *Family Law Act*, liens arising by operation of law, such as liens under s. 48 of the *Legal Aid Services Act, 1998*, S.O. 1990, c. 26 are not subject to the requirements for conveying and encumbering matrimonial homes.

Land dedicated by its owner for a street or public highway is not subject to any claim under Part II of the *Family Law Act* by the spouse of the person by whom it was dedicated.

A title searcher must record all spousal statements, designations, court orders and information relating to spousal status when summarizing documents. This information, recorded in the search notes, should be compared to spousal statements offered in a current transaction's documents, and discrepancies should be diligently investigated.

FAMILY LAW ACT AND AGE STATEMENTS IN ELECTRONIC LAND REGISTRATION

Spousal status and matrimonial home statements under the *Family Law Act* are combined with age statements in the Teraview electronic land registration software. Although similar in content, the wording of the *Family Law Act* statements in Teraview is not identical to the wording set out in the Act. Teraview software pre-populates *Family Law Act* statements directly into the electronic land registration program. For example, when completing a transfer in the electronic land registration system, the user may select an entry screen for required information related to the transferor(s). With the click of a mouse, the user may select the appropriate *Family Law Act* and age statements from a list of all possible options, already on the screen. The Figure below is an example of Teraview's entry screen for transferor information in a standard transfer. When the number of a pre-populated statement is bolded, it indicates that the statement is a statement of law and may only be completed and signed by a lawyer's security key. For example, note that in Figure 10.1, statements 8 and 9 are in bold, and, consequently, are statements of law, which require signing by a lawyer's key. Words in upper case contained in statements (for example, statements 3, 5, 8, 9, 25, 35 and 59) indicate information entry fields. Simply click on the word in capitals and a box opens which allows the user to enter the required information, such as the full proper name of a spouse or the registration details for a matrimonial home designation. All necessary *Family Law Act* and age and power of attorney statements are pre-programmed into the appropriate electronic land registration documents, and, as a result, reduce clerical errors while simplifying document drafting. Supporting documentation for electronic statements, including client authorization and direction to make the electronic statements, as required by the LSUC and the title insurer, must be recorded in the lawyer's file.

Figure 10.1

ELECTRONIC REGISTRATION SCREEN FOR TRANSFEROR(S) FAMILY LAW ACT AND AGE STATEMENTS IN TRANSFER (TERAVIEW VERSION 6)*

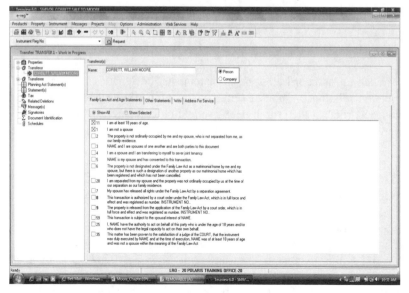

---

*   © Teranet Inc. 2010. Reproduced with permission.

SPOUSAL RIGHTS ON DEATH

Unlike its predecessor, the *Family Law Reform Act*, R.S.O. 1980, c. 152 (repealed S.O. 1986, c. 4, s. 71), the *Family Law Act* legislates division or equalization of net family properties and possessory rights in the matrimonial home, not just on separation, but also on death of a spouse. Estate conveyancing, relating to the estate of a deceased spouse, must be checked for compliance with *Family Law Act* provisions.

SEVERANCE OF THIRD PARTY JOINT TENANCY IN THE MATRIMONIAL HOME

Section 26(1) of the *Family Law Act* states:

> If a spouse dies owning an interest in a matrimonial home as a joint tenant with a third person and not with the other spouse, the joint tenancy shall be deemed to have been severed immediately before the time of death.

Note that this section only applies to matrimonial homes, legally married spouses and a joint tenancy where a spouse is a co-tenant with someone other than his or her one and only spouse. The effect of this section is to sever a joint tenancy, immediately before death, and thus create a tenancy in common instead. As a result, the person who would have been a surviving joint tenant will not inherit by way of survivorship. Instead, the deceased's share in what is now a tenancy in common will fall into the deceased's estate and be distributed according to a will or the rules of intestacy.

Spouses who are married to each other and hold land as joint tenants are not affected by this provision. On death, the deceased spouse's share would, by right of survivorship, vest in the surviving spouse and be documented by a Land Titles survivorship application.

Spousal status of a joint tenant determines who will be the rightful owner(s) of the land on death, *e.g.*, the surviving joint tenant or the estate beneficiaries. Survivorship applications contain statements documenting the spousal status of joint tenants and whether the survivor was a spouse of the deceased joint tenant at the time of death as well as the status of a property as a matrimonial home. Title searchers must be particularly careful when summarizing deeds in joint tenancy and to determine the spousal status of the joint tenants. Title depends upon it.

SURVIVING SPOUSE'S RIGHT TO OCCUPY THE MATRIMONIAL HOME

Section 26(2) of the *Family Law Act* states:

> ... [A] spouse who has no interest in a matrimonial home but is occupying it at the time of the other spouse's death, whether under an order for exclusive possession or otherwise, is entitled to retain possession against the deceased spouse's estate, rent free, for sixty days after the spouse's death.

It was a long-established common law custom that a widow had 60 days to pack and get out before her husband's heirs took possession. Prior to 1978, indeed for centuries, the Dower Acts stated that a widow had a right to tarry in her husband's main house for 60 days following his death.

ESTATE ELECTION BY THE SURVIVING SPOUSE

On the death of a spouse, a surviving spouse has the right to choose between an equalization payment against the net family property under s. 5 of the *Family Law Act*, which includes all property acquired and owned by either spouse during marriage, or his or her share under the will or the law of intestacy. The election form is set out in Election of Surviving Spouse, R.R.O. 1990, Reg. 368. The surviving spouse is allowed six months to file the election with the Ontario Court, General Division (*Family Law Act*, s. 6). Failure to file an election is interpreted as a choice to inherit under the estate rather than make an equalization claim for approximately 50 per cent of the value of the net family property.

A surviving spouse's equalization claim is a claim on the equivalent value of the estate, not a lien against specific property. When land is transferred from the estate, except when it is being distributed directly to beneficiaries, it is unnecessary to require a spousal consent, within the six-month election period. A transfer of land to a beneficiary within the six-month election period requires a spousal consent or a matrimonial home exemption statement.

Survivorship and transmission applications transfer a deceased's land. These documents contain spousal and matrimonial home statements. Estate conveyancing is complicated; fortunately, Teraview includes prescribed electronic documents that contain the required *Family Law Act* statements. It is important to record spousal statements contained in estate conveyances. It is also necessary to record the purpose of the estate transfer and whether the transfer is to an independent third party purchaser, or to a beneficiary as part of a distribution from the estate.

DOWER

Dower represented a one-third possessory life interest in land to which a husband held legal title during marriage and all lands to which a husband died beneficially entitled (*i.e.*, a beneficiary's interest under a trust in a will or land subject to a mortgage). Although dower could be awarded as the use of and income from certain lands for life, usually it was converted to a lump sum payment based on rental evaluations. Dower was meant to protect a widow from becoming destitute should her husband not provide for her adequately on his death.

A widow's dower rights, which had not vested as the result of a husband's death, as of March 31, 1978, were abolished by the *Family Law Reform Act*. Originally, vested dower rights were extinguished ten years after the widow ceased to occupy the land that was subject to dower (*Real Property Limitations Act*, R.S.O. 1990, c. L.15, ss. 25 and 26). As more than 30 years have passed since dower was abolished, although theoretically possible in Registry, it is unlikely that dower is a practical issue today. As of March 31, 1978, land is free of vested dower rights unless a wife has registered a notice of claim on title. Indeed, the *Land Titles Act*, R.S.O. 1990, c. L.5 no longer includes dower as a possible qualification on title in s. 44(1)5 of that Act. Land Titles Conversion Qualified (LTCQ) parcel registers specifically exclude dower as a listed title qualifier (s. 44(1)14). An application to amend the register by deleting dower rights is the way to remove a rare "subject to dower rights" notation that remains on the parcel register.

In the past when a husband transferred land, his wife was required to join in the deed or to specifically bar her dower. A title searcher may still wish to check deeds in Registry, prior to 1978, for outstanding potential dower rights. When land was transferred without a bar of dower, the widow's dower right remained an encumbrance on the land for subsequent purchasers.

Numerous socially archaic exceptions in the now repealed *Dower Act*, R.S.O. 1970, c. 135 (repealed S.O. 1978, c. 2, s. 70(2)) were available to avoid a wife's claim to dower. For example, dower did not attach to land held in joint tenancy, partnership or trust, land held in a state of nature or dedicated as streets, tax sale land, land held to uses, or land purchased subject to a mortgage. Wives who were adulterous, insane (confined to a mental hospital), not resident in Ontario, missing, or later dead or divorced, were ineligible to claim dower. Dower was easily and often avoided by men. All that was required was to add the words "to uses" to a deed, or to change the order of registration between mortgages and deeds. As well, wives were required to elect between their dower rights and their shares under a husband's will where the two rights were inconsistent. Many wills contained a clause requiring a wife to make an election between dower and her estate share. It was possible, although unusual, for a will to contain a clause that allowed a wife to claim both dower and her estate share. The *Estates Administration Act*, R.S.O. 1990, c. E.22 required the registration of a dower election in the general register at the registry office and on the parcel register in land titles.

It was not until the *Family Law Reform Act* came into force in 1978 that family property rights in Ontario were modernized.

THE LAND TITLES ACT AND SPOUSAL RIGHTS

Title, as entered on the Land Titles parcel register, is guaranteed subject to numerous qualifications set out in s. 44 of the *Land Titles Act*. Spousal rights relating to the matrimonial home under Part II of the *Family Law Act* are a qualification to the Land Titles guarantee. When a conveyance does not include a necessary spousal consent or exemption statement, the parcel page will be marked "subject to spousal rights" and, in the past, "subject to dower".

Once a parcel has been made subject to spousal rights, before the land can be conveyed free and clear, the registered owner must register an Application to Delete Spousal Rights by way of Document General. The application will include declaration evidence proving that the land is no longer subject to spousal rights or dower as the case may be.

Dower and spousal rights generated prior to conversion do not apply to LTCQ titles unless they have been carried forward as a "subject to" interest on the new LTCQ parcel register.

A title searcher should continue to check and record spousal status, consents and matrimonial home exemption statements, in dispositions and encumbrances following the date of conversion.

CHANGE OF NAME

The same surname does not necessarily indicate a marital relationship. Similarly, legally married persons may have different surnames. It is unreliable to assume spousal status on the basis of name, although it remains a tradition that a woman adopts her husband's surname on marriage. Change of name on marriage or divorce is the most common reason for change of name documentation in land records. Client ID requirements and checks now require carefully reviewed documentary proof of name changes; such documentation must be retained in the lawyer's file.

When an individual has changed his or her name pursuant to the *Change of Name Act*, R.S.O. 1990, c. C.7, a certified or notarial copy of the Change of

Name Certificate should be registered in the general register in the Registry system. Prior to April 1, 1987, name changes based on marriage required only a statement in a deed as proof of the change. Also, in the past, in the Registry system, statements were included in deeds explaining the reason for the name change. The Registry recital rule allowed conveyancers to rely on historical, factual, change of name statements, when the statement had been registered for more than 20 years.

In Land Titles, a registered owner must use the exact name currently entered on the parcel register in any future dealings with that parcel of land. When a name change, even a minor one caused by error, has taken place, Land Titles requires an Application to Change Name containing the old and the new name and an affidavit explaining the reason for the change often accompanied by a certified or notarial copy of the relevant court order. Change of name documentation must be registered on the parcel register before the registered owner can convey his or her parcel using a different name. A Change of Name Application is registered by way of Document General and includes declaration evidence setting out the reason for the name change. The requirements for change of name registrations in electronic land registration in Land Titles are found in the *Land Registration Reform Act* regulation, Electronic Registration, O. Reg. 19/99. Section 31 of this regulation states that:

> if an application to change a name in the register is submitted for electronic registration, it shall contain,
>
> (a)   the name to be entered in the register; and
>
> (b)   a statement of the authority for the change of name, including the registration number of the document, if any, that sets out the authority.

In electronic land registration, the lawyer completes an existing electronic form in Teraview which contains statements documenting the reasons and authority for the change. The lawyer retains supporting documentation in his or her file. Once the change of name document is registered, the land registrar enters the new name as owner on the parcel register.

When a corporation changes its name, it must register an application to amend the register by changing the name of the corporation. Depending on the nature of the company and the reason for the change, the application contains documentation or statements referring to articles of amendment or amalgamation or orders-in-council for loan and trust corporations.

TITLE INSURANCE SEARCH REQUIREMENTS FOR SPOUSAL STATUS AND MATRIMONIAL HOME RIGHTS

Title insurance does not remove the search requirements for spousal status or spousal rights in the matrimonial home. In Land Titles, it is unnecessary to search behind the parcel register for prior owner spousal rights; however, if the parcel register states that it is subject to spousal rights, then the subject to documents in the thumbnail property description must be reviewed and reported.

Title insurers will not insure a transaction for which Canadian government-issued photo ID has not been obtained, subject to an underwriter's written approval prior to closing. For example, Stewart Title requires its examining counsels to complete the following:

1. obtain Canadian federal or provincial government-issued ID, with a name and signature, for all clients;

2. review and confirm the validity to the best of the examining counsel's ability;

3. not rely on citizenship card as they are easily forged; and

4. keep a legible photocopy in the file.

CHAPTER 11

Adjoining Lands Searches and the Planning Act

INTRODUCTION

Adjoining land searches for access, easements and restrictions, and *Planning Act* contraventions have been and continue to be higher risk practice activities that carry a heightened risk of generating title insurance claims. This chapter is designed to assist the real estate practitioner in risk managing his or her way through adjoining land searches in general and the part lot control provisions in particular.

Adjoining lands searches are an essential part of a full search. They confirm the existence of legal access, the legal enforceability of easements and restrictive covenants, legal description, boundaries, encroachments, and whether prior conveyances or the proposed conveyance on title contravene the subdivision or part lot control provisions of the *Planning Act*, R.S.O. 1990, c. P.13. A *Planning Act* contravention is fatal to the creation of an interest in land; it results in a total failure of consideration. The subdivision and part lot control provisions of the *Planning Act* generate a minefield of legislative amendments, conflicting case law, avoidance schemes, extensive litigation, conveyancing risk, and complicated adjoining land search procedures. Computerization of land records and legal conversion from Registry to Land Titles combined with electronic searching have added more layers of complexity and risk to adjoining land searches.

Adjoining lands searches are time-consuming, technically difficult, and require a strong understanding of several areas of past and present law. They are often more difficult and more costly than the search of the land being conveyed. Title insurance is not a substitute for an adjoining lands search and does not protect clients from problems that can only be revealed by a full search of adjoining lands.

Recent cases such as *Syvan Developments Ltd. v. Ontario (Ministry of Government Services)*, [2006] O.J. No. 3765 (Ont. S.C.J.) where a solicitor did not confirm easement and access rights by searching adjoining lands, and *1390957 Ontario Ltd. v. Acchione*, [2002] O.J. No. 22 (Ont. C.A.) where a solicitor missed a *Planning Act* contravention clearly demonstrate the risks attached to incomplete adjoining land searches. Restrictive covenants, easements, access, and road registrations have not infrequently been missed in the Province of Ontario Land Registration Information

System (POLARIS) automation and conversion, resulting in an increased need to confirm registered rights on dominant and servient tenements. *Registry Act*, R.S.O. 1990, c. R.20 amendments to the 40-year notice and search periods also increase the importance of completing detailed adjoining land searches. For example, easement and restrictive covenants to be legally enforceable must be registered on dominant and servient lands every 40 years by a separate notice document; a reference within a deed is not enough to preserve their validity. Hence, conveyancers must check the registration status/age of covenants and easements on adjoining land as well as the land being purchased and decide when to re-register an existing right in order to avoid automatic termination. Adjoining lands searches are the only way to adequately protect the client, the solicitor, and to meet a solicitor's obligation to the title insurer.

TYPES OF ADJOINING LANDS SEARCHES

As part of his or her search during a purchase or mortgage transaction, a title searcher may be required both to search and subsearch adjoining lands. The ownership characteristics of the land being investigated and the system in which it is registered determine which adjoining lands need to be searched, how far back in time the search must go, what information on adjoining land records is important and the mechanics of the adjoining land search process in general. Adjoining lands may need to be checked for all or some of the following reasons:

1. *Planning Act* subdivision and part lot control contraventions;

2. boundaries, description encroachments, overlaps, gaps, reference plans, and descriptive inconsistencies;

3. easements and restrictive covenants;

4. road widenings, expropriations, laneways, bodies of water, and flooding rights;

5. legal access to land to a public road or highway including one-foot reserves, water access; and

6. any adjoining land information that may interest a particular purchaser, such as environmental non-compliance orders, Aboriginal land claims or environmentally sensitive areas, landfill zoning, *etc.*

Searches of adjoining lands may be short and simple or they may require more time and disbursements than the main property. Adjoining lands searches may uncover a minor boundary encroachment, or a *Planning Act* s. 50 violation which would result in the vendor's inability to convey any interest in land. An urban purchaser may discover that the house next door is subject to a methane gas venting agreement or an environmental clean-up order. A cottage purchaser may discover that the property, intended to become a secluded, year-round, retirement dream home, has water access only, or is subject to a 60-foot right of way in favour of a massive proposed condominium and trailer park development.

Adjoining lands searches should include careful research and documentation as they may reveal title deficiencies and generate contract requisitions equally as serious as principal land searches. The most common and potentially the most serious adjoining lands inquiry is the *Planning Act* s. 50 part lot/subdivision control search.

THE PLANNING ACT

The *Planning Act* ("the Act") was passed in 1946, in response to the optimism of global rebuilding and the ensuing unprecedented growth and development following World War II. The Act delegated power to the municipalities, reviewable by the Ontario Municipal Board, to pass by-laws to regulate the development, subdivision, and general use and enjoyment of land. The Act governs provincial administration and policy statements, local planning administration, official plans, community improvement, land use controls and related administration, and the subdivision of land. The Act delegates the main responsibility for land division (subdivision control) and development decisions to the municipality.

SUBDIVISION AND PART LOT CONTROL

Part VI of the Act currently regulates subdivision control in Ontario. Section 50 creates a complex scheme which restricts the division of existing parcels of land into smaller units. Section 50(3) regulates division of land by way of a subdivision plan. Section 50(5) regulates future division of land within a subdivision, know as part lot control. Any contravention of the s. 50(3) subdivision control or the (s. 50(5)) part lot control provisions will result in a total failure to create or convey any interest in land. In effect, title is extinguished by a *Planning Act* contravention and therefore is not capable of being transferred, in future, to subsequent purchasers or mortgagees until the contravention is cured (s. 50(21)). Municipal consent is required for most divisions of land. Section 50 necessitates a careful search of the ownership of all adjoining, referred to as abutting, lands to ensure that no illegal subdivision of land has previously taken place, or is about to take place.

A detailed familiarity with past and present *Planning Act* subdivision control provisions is required in order to perform competently a *Planning Act* search on adjoining lands. Whenever a searcher is unsure regarding the need for, the process of, or the findings in a *Planning Act* search, he or she should consult the person in charge of the file in order to prevent the serious consequences of a possible subdivision control violation. Keep in mind that it is not always possible to remedy a contravention and that failure to detect one is considered negligence. Unfortunately, the legislation is complex and the cases are ambiguous and restricted to the particular facts of the case. This chapter is meant to provide a practical introduction to the basic principles and procedures involved in completing adjoining lands searches for *Planning Act* and other purposes.

PROHIBITION AGAINST SUBDIVISION OF LAND

Section 50 (formerly ss. 23, 24, 26, 29, or 49) contains a general prohibition against the subdivision of land without either a *Planning Act* consent, also called a severance, or an approval for a new registered plan of subdivision. In addition, s. 50(5) provides a specific prohibition on the subdivision of lots or blocks within a plan of subdivision, usually referred to as part lot control. The combined effect of the section is to prohibit any conveyance that results in the subdivision of land unless that conveyance is exempt under the Act or the municipality grants a consent.

Two basic categories of exemption exist. First, the *Planning Act* lists statutory exemptions to subdivision and part lot control, such as transfer to or from the Crown. As well, it sets out when a violation has been forgiven or cured, for example, by passage of time (forgiveness date) or by a curative by-law, consent, or validation certificate. The most common exemption is the conveyance of one or more whole lots or blocks on a registered plan of subdivision or the whole of a condominium unit on a registered condominium plan. Secondly, the statutory and case law definitions of common ownership and what constitutes abutting or adjoining lands may also determine whether a contravention has taken place, as illegal subdivision may occur only when there is common ownership of adjoining properties.

THE EFFECT OF SECTION 50 OF THE PLANNING ACT

Section 50(3) regulates subdivision control and s. 50(5) regulates part lot control within a plan of subdivision. The sections are similar; however, the whole lot exemption in s. 50(5) is different and s. 50(5) lists additional exemptions. Section 50 makes abutting lands inquiries essential. A *Planning Act* search requires the following:

1. Identify all abutting lands as defined by s. 50;

2. Identify the most recent start date before which contraventions have been forgiven;

3. Identify all conveyances regulated by s. 50 on abutting lands from the start date to present;

4. Check the conveyances in the chain of title to identify common ownership between land being conveyed and abutting lands. Review the definition of common owner under s. 50;

5. If there is a common owner, check for *Planning Act* compliance and review exemptions with particular attention to the effect of consents and by-laws;

6. Complete a sketch illustrating abutting properties;

7. Retain a full record of the *Planning Act* search;

8. Update the search as necessary and prior to registration;

9. Ensure completion of *Planning Act* declarations to shorten and simplify future searches and reduce future risk of contravention; and

10. Depending on the circumstances, search for access, boundaries and description, restrictive covenants, easements, and adjacent bodies of water.

Subdivision and Part Lot Control
Compliance with Section 50 of the Planning Act

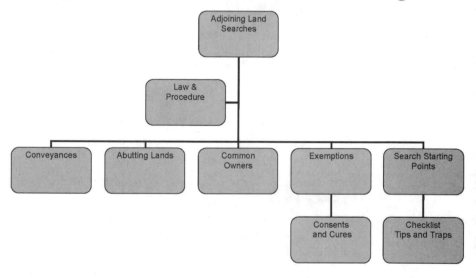

Regulated Conveyances under Section 50(3) and 50(4)

Subdivision control

50(3) No person shall convey land by way of a deed or transfer, or grant, assign or exercise a power of appointment with respect to land, or mortgage or charge land, or enter into an agreement of sale and purchase of land or enter into any agreement that has the effect of granting the use of or right in land directly or by entitlement to renewal for a period of twenty-one years or more unless ... .

This section applies only when an owner of land retains identical ownership rights in any abutting land. The remainder of s. 50(3) outlines exemptions to the main prohibition. Section 50(5) sets out a similar prohibition for part lots or blocks within a registered plan of subdivision. Section 50(3) sets out the different types of transactions that might potentially violate the *Planning Act* subdivision control and part lot control restrictions should they neither fall within an exemption nor be validated by a *Planning Act* consent. The following conveyances have the potential to create a *Planning Act* violation and therefore may require *Planning Act* consent if they result in the division of a parcel of land into two or more separate, smaller parcels of land:

1. deed or transfer;

2. grant, assignment or exercise of a power of appointment that has the effect of transferring an interest in land;

3. conveyance by gift;

4. agreement of sale and purchase unless it is subject to the express condition contained therein that such agreement is to be effective only if the provisions of s. 50 are complied with. Agreement of Purchase and Sale standard forms contain this condition. This allows for the consent to be obtained as part of the purchase transaction;

5. charge or mortgage, including lodgment of title documents;

6. partial discharge of mortgage or partial cessation of charge (s. 50(16));

7. foreclosure or power of sale, including a partial foreclosure or power of sale (s. 15(18));

8. an agreement having the effect of granting the use of or right in land directly or by entitlement to renewal for a period of 21 years or more, including perpetuity, *e.g.*:

    *   a lease for 21 years or more (include options and renewals when calculating the term of the lease);
    *   an easement for 21 years or more (include options and renewals when calculating the term of the easement or right of way). The creation of an easement or right of way over part of a lot must comply with subdivision and part lot control prohibitions. Easements in gross and easements granted by or reserved to condominium corporations do not require *Planning Act* consents;
    *   an easement in perpetuity;
    *   an option to purchase;

9. release or conveyance of an interest in land by a joint tenant or tenant in common to one or more other joint tenants or tenants in common while holding abutting land (s. 50(19));

10. division of land by will if the testator died after July 26, 1990 (s. 50.1(1)). A division of land by will that does not comply with the *Planning Act* will create a tenancy in common of the whole of the land in the devise (s. 50.1(3));

11. simultaneous conveyances of abutting lands under common ownership (s. 50(14)); and

12. order under of the *Partition Act*, R.S.O. 1990, c. P.4 to partition a parcel among co-owners (s. 50(20)).

As a result, all of the above transactions — not just deeds and transfers — have the potential to create a *Planning Act* contravention that will result in the loss of ownership. All transactions must therefore be checked and recorded for all abutting lands in an adjoining lands search in order to avoid any such contraventions.

SUBDIVISION AND PART LOT CONTROL EXEMPTIONS

The *Planning Act* prohibition on subdivision applies to most real property transactions. It applies equally to corporations, partnerships and individual owners. Section 50(3) and 50(5) list transactions that are exempt from the subdivision control prohibition. These exemptions have been interpreted by a large body of complicated and frequently inconsistent, or, at least, ambiguous case law. Any title situation which raises a potential *Planning Act* contravention must be researched carefully in terms of the exact circumstances of the individual case in the context of the legislation at the time of the contravention. When a conveyance falls within a statutory exemption, as interpreted by case law, it is permitted under the subdivision and part lot control prohibitions and does not require a consent.

Conveyances are exempt whenever the owner transfers the whole of the property owned and does not retain the fee (ownership) in any abutting land. Hence, the legal interpretation of "abutting land" becomes crucial. The following exempt transactions neither generate contraventions nor require consents:

Subdivison Plan Exemption

A conveyance where land is described in accordance with and is within a registered plan of subdivision is exempt. The pattern of land division laid out on the subdivision plan has already received governmental approvals (s. 50(3)(a)). Part lots within a plan of subdivision are not exempt. There is no definition of the term "registered plan of subdivision" in the *Planning Act*. The following are not plans of subdivision for the purposes of the subdivision or the part lot control restrictions under s. 50 of the Act:

- reference plans;
- *Boundaries Act* plans;
- Teraview digital maps;

- POLARIS block or property maps;
- composite plans;
- index plans;
- expropriation plans;
- municipal compiled plans;
- judge's compiled plans;
- Registrar's compiled plans; and
- inspector's compiled plan.

Whole Lot or Block within a Registered Plan of Subdivision (M-Plan) Exemption

A conveyance where land is the whole of one or more lots or blocks within one or more registered plans of subdivision is exempt (s. 50(5)). It is necessary to confirm that the plan is a registered plan of subdivision under the registration statute. A plan of subdivision usually identifies itself as a plan of subdivision on the face of the plan. In Land Titles, it is usually referred to as an M-Plan. It is important to remember that this exemption applies only to whole lots or blocks on a registered plan of subdivision and does not offer an exemption for whole concession (also known as farm or township lots), town lots, or lots fronting on rivers, roads, lakes, canals, or natural boundaries. Whole township or farm lots, town lots, road lots, and water lots are not exempt.

A conveyance of a part lot or block within a registered plan of subdivision is also permitted as long as any land abutting the land being conveyed is the whole of one or more lots or blocks within one or more registered plans of subdivision (s. 50(5)(a)). As a result, an owner can sell a part lot and retain abutting land as long as the abutting land is the whole of one or more lots or blocks within one or more registered plans of subdivision.

By-Law Deeming Subdivision Plan Not Registered

The whole lot exemption is lost when a municipality under s. 50(4) deems a plan of subdivision that has been registered for eight years or more not to be a plan of subdivision for the purpose of the whole lot exemption under s. 50(3) of the *Planning Act*. A by-law must be registered deeming the subdivision plan not to be a subdivision plan to cancel the whole lot exemption. As a result, the transfer of a whole lot on a registered plan of subdivision that has been deemed by registered municipal by-law not to be a registered plan of subdivision for the purposes of the *Planning Act* has the potential to create a contravention if the owner of the lot owns abutting land.

Condominium Unit Exemption

A conveyance of a whole condominium unit and common interest is exempt under s. 50 of the *Planning Act*. A parcel of tied land (POTL) in a common elements condominium is not a unit. Easements granted by and reserved to a condominium corporation are exempt as are dealings with the common elements (*Condominium Act*, S.O. 1998, c. 19, s. 9(1)(b)). See below for a review of condominiums and *Planning Act* compliance.

No Interest in Abutting Lands

Where a grantor is transferring all of the land he or she owns and hence does not retain the fee in abutting lands, there is no contravention. See later in the chapter for the definition of abutting lands.

Prior Consent for Identical Parcel Exemption

A conveyance of land for which "a consent is given to convey, mortgage or charge the land or grant, assign or exercise a power of appointment in respect of the land or enter into an agreement in respect of the land" validates the transaction (s. 50(5)(f)). Also, a deed or transfer of land for which a post-March 31, 1979 consent to sever has been given for the conveyance (not a mortgage) of the parcel exempts subsequent conveyances of the identical parcel. A post-March 31, 1979 consent to a transfer of land validates previous and subsequent transactions that involve an identical description unless the consent contains conditions that state the contrary (s. 50(12) and (13)).

Remainder Parcel Exemption

Section 50(6) states where land is the remaining part of a parcel of land, the other part or parts of which parcel have been the subject of a consent given under clause (3)(f) or (5)(f), the whole of the remaining part may be conveyed or otherwise dealt with before the other part or parts are conveyed or otherwise dealt with, provided that the remaining part is conveyed or otherwise dealt with before the consent mentioned above lapses under s. 53(43). Please note that s. 50(6) only applies where the remaining parcel is conveyed *before* the consented to parcel. See the Ontario Court of Appeal decision in *1390957 Ontario Ltd. v. Acchione*, [2002] O.J. No. 22, 57 O.R. (3d) 578 (Ont. C.A.).

Transactions Prior to a Subdivision or Condominium Plan

Transactions including contraventions prior to the registration of a subdivision plan or a condominium description are exempt.

Planning Act Statements

Contraventions prior to the registration of a transfer containing all three (Boxes 13 and 14 on the LRRA forms or electronic statements of law in electronic land registration) completed *Planning Act* statements are forgiven. The curative effect of compliance statements only affects title to land described in the transfer containing the statements. It does not affect title to abutting remainder parcels subject to the same contravention (*White v. Daffern*, [2001] O.J. No. 3841 (Ont. S.C.J.)).

Conveyances To and From the Crown

Land or rights in land acquired or disposed of by a federal, provincial, or municipal government (s. 50(3)(b)) are exempt. For example, road widening conveyances and expropriations are exempt.

Utility Lines Under the *Ontario Energy Board Act*

Land or right in land acquired and declared acquired for the purpose of a utility line within the meaning of the *Ontario Energy Board Act, 1998*, S.O. 1998, c. 15, Schedule B is exempt under s. 50(5)(c). Also, whenever "the land or any use of or right therein was acquired for the purpose of a utility line within the meaning of the *Ontario Energy Board Act, 1998* and is being disposed of to the person from whom it was acquired" (s. 50(5)(g)).

Land Acquired Under the *Conservation Authorities Act*

Land or right in land acquired by the Minister of Natural Resources under s. 24 of the *Conservation Authorities Act*, R.S.O. 1990, c. C.27, and declared acquired by a conservation officer for the purpose of flood control, erosion control, bank stabilization, shoreline management or preservation of environmentally sensitive lands is exempt under s. 50(5)(d).

Remaining Part after Expropriation Exemption

Land that is the "remaining part of a lot or block, the other part of which was acquired by a body that has vested in it the right to acquire land by expropriation" is exempt (s. 50(5)(e)).

Land Acquired Under the *Drainage Act*

An agreement under s. 2 of the *Drainage Act*, R.S.O. 1990, c. D.17 (s. 50(10)) is exempt.

Land Acquired by the Agricultural Rehabilitation and Development Directorate of Ontario

A conveyance or lease from the Agricultural Rehabilitation and Development Directorate of Ontario that comprises all the land that was acquired by the Directorate under one registered deed or transfer is exempt under s. 50(11).

When Partial Discharges of Mortgages/Charges Are Exempt

Partial discharges of mortgage or cessations of charge and like instruments that deal with only part of the mortgaged property are not exempt. However, a partial discharge of mortgage or cessation of charge where the land described relates to one or more whole lots or blocks on a registered plan of subdivision is exempt (s. 50(17)).

When Partial Powers of Sale and Foreclosures Are Exempt

Partial powers of sale and foreclosures that deal with only part of a property are not exempt. A power of sale or foreclosure against part of the land where the land described relates to one or more whole lots or blocks on a registered plan of subdivision is exempt (s. 50(18)). Other standard exemptions apply. See *White v. Daffern*, [2001] O.J. No. 3841 (Ont. S.C.J.) for a recent case that deals with a series of partial powers of sale of abutting part lots under one mortgage.

Vendor Take-Back Mortgage

A vendor take-back mortgage, provided the mortgage or charge applies to all the land described in the purchase, is exempt (s. 50(8)).

Division of Land by Will

A division of land by will where the will was made before the 26th day of July, 1990 and the testator died on or before that date (s. 50.1(2)) is exempt. After July 26, 1990, divisions by will must comply with s. 50 (s. 50.1(1)). If the division in the will violates s. 50, the beneficiaries will take an undivided interest in the whole of the subject land as tenants in common (s. 50.1(3)).

Vesting Orders

Case law establishes that vesting orders under the *Family Law Act*, R.S.O. 1990, c. F.3 or *Trustee Act*, R.S.O. 1990, c. T.23 are exempt.

Quit Claims and Correcting Deeds

A quit claim or correcting deed that is not an actual conveyance of land is exempt.

Mineral Rights In or Under Land

Abutting land excludes mineral rights including tailings in or under land but not on the land. Section 50(2.1) provides that interests in land do not abut when they meet on a horizontal plane only (s. 50(2)). (See *Ginn v. Consolidated Tanager Ltd.*, [1999] O.J. No. 5864 (Ont. Gen. Div.) for a discussion of the mineral rights exemption.)

Part of a Building or Structure

An agreement that has the effect of granting the use or right of an existing building or structure for any period of years, *e.g.*, office building leases (s. 50(9)), is exempt.

Life Lease Housing

Life lease housing is a general term that describes a number of different ownership models, including both leasehold and freehold interests. Life lease housing models where the leasehold interest is for less than 21 years or is based on a right in an existing building or structure for a period of years are exempt. However, if the life lease housing model is based on a freehold life estate, then it requires *Planning Act* approval, probably by way of a consent or an exempting by-law.

Conservation Easement Exemption

Conservation easements and covenants under the *Conservation Land Act*, R.S.O. 1990, c. C.28 are exempt.

Renewable Energy Project

Ontario Bill 150, the *Green Energy and Green Economy Act, 2009*, S.O. 2009, c. 12 received Royal Assent on May 14, 2009. Sections 2(1) and (2) of Schedule K exempt leases for the purposes of renewable energy generation facilities or renewable energy projects from subdivision control and part-lot control under s. 50(3)(d.1) and (5)(c.1) of the *Planning Act* if they are for periods of 50 years or less.

Simultaneous Transactions Are Not Exempt

If an owner conveys two abutting part lots by using simultaneous transactions to separate owners, s. 50(15) confirms that the transaction contravenes the part lot control provisions. If, however, two owners convey abutting part lots to themselves in their same respective capacity, the transaction complies with the part lot control provisions. The owner could convey the whole of the combined two part lots to one new owner as this would not contravene the Act as the owner retained no abutting lands.

By-Law Designation of Lands Not Subject to Part Lot Control

A municipality can designate land within a registered plan of subdivision to be exempt from the part lot control provisions by registering a part lot control exemption by-law (s. 50(7)). As a result, a part lot in a registered plan of subdivision is given the same exempt status as a whole lot. These by-laws may contain automatic expiry dates (s. 50(7.3)); municipal by-laws can also extend the expiry date (s. 50(7.4)). Municipal councils also have the power to amend or repeal these by-laws (s. 50(7.5)). Amendment and repeal by-laws must be registered in the land registry office. It is essential to carefully read exempting by-laws in order to determine their effect on a particular property.

DEFINITION OF ABUTTING LANDS

A legal entity may convey land as long as he, she, or it (*e.g.*, a corporation) does not retain the fee, or control in terms of ownership, over any land that abuts the land that is being conveyed. In other words, no person may convey land that shares a common boundary with abutting land, unless he or she conveys the whole of the parcel owned, including the abutting land or the conveyance is exempt. Should an owner convey land while retaining control over abutting land, then for the transaction to be effective, the owner would be required either to obtain a consent or demonstrate that the conveyance is exempt under the Act. Although the term abutting lands has not been defined by statute, case law provides some guidance. The following situations are not considered to be abutting lands:

1. where land touches at one point only, *e.g.*, a corner: *Herman v. Kalbfleisch*, [1972] O.J. No. 1785, [1972] 2 O.R. 720 (Ont. Co. Ct.);

2. where land abuts on a horizontal plane only, *e.g.*, subsurface and airspace rights (s. 50(2));

3. where mining rights exist in or under land but not on the land (s. 50(2.1));

4. where a grantor holds only an easement right on abutting lands: *Vasey v. Tribee Investments Ltd.*, [1970] O.J. No. 1680, [1971] 1 O.R. 477 (Ont. H.C.J.);

5. where two parcels share only a common right of way: *Hamilton v. Reed*, [1984] O.J. No. 3421, 49 O.R. (2d) 97 (Ont. H.C.J.);

6. where lands are separated by navigable waters; the bed of the water is owned by the Crown (be sure to search and confirm the legal status of navigable waters from the Crown patent to present): *Copley v. Hudson*, [1979] O.J. No. 4432, 26 O.R. (2d) 601 (Ont. Co. Ct.); and

7. where there is an agreement for the use of a part of a building for any period of years, *e.g.*, a lease of office space in a high rise building for more than 21 years (s. 50(9)).

In summary, as long as a person deals with all of the land that he or she owns and does nothing that results in the dividing of a parcel into two or more smaller units, he or she does not contravene s. 50 of the *Planning Act*.

DEFINITION OF COMMON OWNER

Although the concept of common ownership is not defined in the *Planning Act*, some guidance is provided by case law. When the land being transferred and the abutting lands are not held by the grantor in identical capacities, the grantor may be able to convey one of the parcels without contravening s. 50. Depending on the individual facts and circumstances of the case, the following situations are not considered to create common ownership of abutting lands, and, as a result, may not result in a s. 50 contravention:

1. A is the first mortgagee on a parcel of land that abuts land owned by A in fee simple. Consent is not required to convey the land A owns, as the abutting land is held in a different legal capacity, that of mortgagee only (*Redmond v. Rothschild*, [1970] O.J. No. 1670, [1971] 1 O.R. 436 (Ont. C.A.)).

2. An estate trustee sells land pursuant to a will in which he or she is sole beneficiary while owning abutting land in his or her personal capacity.

3. When a partner, joint tenant or tenant in common owns land in concurrent ownership that abuts land that one co-owner is conveying in his or her personal capacity, the transaction does not contravene s. 50 as they are not considered common owners. However, note that s. 50(19) states that when a joint tenant or tenant in common releases or conveys his interest to one or more other joint tenants or tenants in common of the same land while owning abutting land alone or with another person, the transaction does contravene s. 50. Concurrent ownership must be carefully analyzed for potential contraventions.

CURING PLANNING ACT CONTRAVENTIONS

A *Planning Act* contravention results in no title being conveyed to either the current transferee or any subsequent transferees. For title to pass, it is necessary for land to be exempt, not to fall within the definition of abutting land, for the identities of adjoining owners not to be considered identical in law, or to have received a consent to sever. If a *Planning Act* contravention has taken place, then it must be cured before any interest in land can be conveyed.

Planning Act contraventions may be cured by forgiveness legislation, forgiveness by-laws, validation certificates, consents, prescribed statements and conversion into POLARIS as a Land Titles Conversion Qualified title (LTCQ) or an upgrade from LTCQ to Land Titles Absolute Plus title.

Forgiveness Legislation

Section 10(3) of the *Planning Amendment Act, 1967*, S.O. 1967, c. 75 forgave all subdivision and part lot control contraventions that took place prior to June

15, 1967. Section 50(14) of the Act forgives all subdivision and part lot control contraventions that took place prior to the registration of a plan of subdivision or the registration of a condominium description. A consent given under s. 53 of the Act forgives prior subdivision and part lot control contraventions (s. 50(14)).

Validation Certificates and Forgiveness By-Laws

A local municipal council may issue a certificate of validation deeming that no prior contravention has occurred. The municipality may impose conditions on a validation certificate. Forgiveness by-laws and validation certificates should be registered in the Registry office on title to the affected land (s. 57(1)). Conveyancers, when relying on validation certificates, must confirm that conditions have been satisfied. A validation certificate does not affect rights acquired by a person under a prior court order (s. 57(2)). More importantly, a validation certificate is not the same as a consent and does not affect or exempt future transaction. A municipality's discretion to give a validation certificate is more restricted than with a consent (O. Reg. 144/95). A validation certificate is not prospective in effect.

Subdivison and Part Lot Control By-Laws

There are different kinds of subdivision and part lot control by-laws. Some have automatic expiry dates and some do not. It is important to read each by-law for both the content and the duration as non-compliance with these by-laws can be fatal to title. An exempting by-law becomes effective on registration in the registry office (s. 50(27) and (28)).

Designation of Lands Subject to Part Lot Control

Prior to June 27, 1970, the registration of a subdivision control by-law on title was required in order to impose subdivision control on land anywhere in Ontario. This by-law had to be registered on title. Some of these by-laws are now registered prior to the 40-year search period. In theory, it may be necessary to search back for a by-law to determine whether a contravention exists between 1967 and 1970. This applies in Registry and in Land Titles as *Planning Act* contraventions relate to Crown rights. Most properties have a more recent *Planning Act* start date; hopefully, three *Planning Act* statements are completed on the most recent transfer.

Designation of Lands Not Subject to Part Lot Control (Section 50(7) Exempting By-Laws)

A local municipality can pass a by-law that exempts land within a registered plan of subdivision from part-lot control. These by-laws can affect multiple subdivision plans or just parts of one plan. These by-laws can be for an indefinite period or they can contain expiry dates. These by-laws usually apply to more recent, higher density subdivisions that may contain zero lot line development, or attached multi-family units or row housing on part lots set out on reference plans. However, on occasion, an exempting by-law may affect a single structure, such as a duplex.

Designation of Plans of Subdivision Not Deemed Registered (Section 50(4))

A local municipality can pass a by-law that deems the whole or only a part of a plan of subdivision, that has been registered for eight years or more, not to be a registered plan of subdivision for the purposes of subdivision and part lot control. The by-law must be registered in the registry office. The by-law removes the whole lot exemption for the relevant parts of the affected subdivision.

Consents

When the owner of a parcel of land wishes to divide it into smaller units, he or she must apply to the appropriate municipal authority, usually the committee of adjustment, the land division committee, or the Minister of Municipal Affairs and Housing, in order to obtain a consent permitting a legal severance of the land. A consent is good for two years from the date the certificate of consent was issued unless a shorter period is stated (s. 53(43)). The consent must be used within the two-year period or it will lapse. The municipal authority has the power to shorten the lapse date and can also attach conditions to a consent. The *Planning and Conservation Land Statute Law Amendment Act, 2006*, S.O. 2006, c. 23 (Bill 51) expressly authorizes the imposition of a condition for the execution of an agreement imposing terms and conditions as set out in the Committee's decision. This agreement can be registered against the title and enforced against subsequent owners and mortgagees. Consents and agreements may contain conditions such as the transfer of land for park, school, bicycle or pedestrian path, or road purposes. A conveyancer must confirm that the transaction is completed and registered within the prescribed time limits and that all conditions and agreements have been met; otherwise, the transaction will be invalid.

A consent cannot be relied on until appeal periods have expired and appeals have ended. As of January 1, 2007, municipalities that meet prescribed conditions may choose to create independent, local appeal boards to hear minor variance and consent appeals from their Committees of Adjustment, instead of relying on the current appeal to the Ontario Municipal Board.

The Curative Legal Effect of a Consent

The Effect of a Consent on Future Transactions

As of March 31, 1979, where a parcel is conveyed by deed or transfer with a consent given under s. 53, part lot and subdivision control does not apply to a subsequent conveyance of, or other transaction involving, the identical parcel of land unless the certificate of consent states the contrary (s. 50(12) and (13)).

This curative section only applies to consents to a conveyance (for example, a transfer) and not to consents to a mortgage (s. 50(12)). The section applies to consents obtained after March 31, 1979, the date the section was first enacted. This exemption does not apply to the remaining parcel created by the severance.

The Effect of a Consent on the Remainder Parcel

When land is subdivided, one parcel receives a consent to sever and the other parcel becomes the remainder parcel. Only the parcel with the consent on the conveyance can be transferred or mortgaged at a later date as being exempt from the part lot control provisions. This exemption does not apply to the remainder parcel. Unlike the consented to parcel, it would require a consent for future transactions, if in violation of the part lot control provisions.

Special rules apply to remainder parcels. The remainder parcel may be conveyed before the abutting consented to part(s) as long as the remainder is conveyed *before* the consent lapses (s. 50(6)). The recent Ontario Court of Appeal decision in *1390957 Ontario Ltd. v. Acchione*, [2002] O.J. No. 22 (Ont. C.A.) clarifies what has been ambiguous law and practice relating to remainder parcels. Timing is critical. The exemption for a conveyance of a remaining part only applies where the remaining part is conveyed *before* the consented to part. The word "before" is clear and unambiguous and must be interpreted in its grammatical and ordinary sense. An owner's ability to deal with a consented to parcel is very different from his or her ability to deal with the remainder parcel. An owner must carefully consider the consequences of the choice of which property for which to seek consent. Conveyancers must carefully trace and document the sequence of transactions when completing *Planning Act* searches.

Curative Effect on Contraventions Prior to a Consent, a Subdivision Plan, or a Condominium Description

Where land has been conveyed, mortgaged, or charged with a consent granted after December 15, 1978, the consent given has the effect of forgiving prior subdivision and part lot control contraventions of an identical parcel of land (s. 50(14)). Section 50(14) also cures *Planning Act* contraventions prior to the registration of a subdivision plan or a condominium description.

The most common cure for a prior *Planning Act* contravention is to obtain a *Planning Act* consent and register it separately or on a transfer. Keep in mind that *Planning Act* contraventions are both serious and potentially permanent, as applications to obtain consent are not necessarily successful.

The Three *Planning Act* Statements

As of 1984, the *Land Registration Reform Act*, R.S.O. 1990, c. L.4 incorporates the following three optional *Planning Act* compliance statements into transfers:

1. statement by the grantor verifying that, to the best of the grantor's knowledge and belief, the deed or transfer does not contravene this section;

2. statement by the grantor's solicitor, verifying that he or she has explained the effect of this section to the grantor and he or she has made inquiries of the grantor to determine that the deed or transfer does not contravene this section based on the information supplied by the grantor, to the best of the solicitor's knowledge and belief, the deed or transfer does not contravene this section, and he or she is an Ontario solicitor in good standing; and

3. statement by the grantee's solicitor, verifying that he or she has investigated the title to the land and, where relevant, to abutting land he or she is satisfied that the record of title to the land and, where relevant, to abutting land, reveals no existing contravention of this section.

When all three *Planning Act* statements contained in Boxes 13 and 14 of Form 1 (Transfer or Deed under the *Land Registration Reform Act*) are signed by the transferor, the transferor's solicitor and the transferee's solicitor, prior subdivision and part lot control contraventions are cured. Section 50(23) states that "a solicitor is not required to investigate the registered title to the land except with respect to the time since the registration of the most recent deed or transfer affecting the same land and containing" the three prescribed *Planning Act* statements. *Planning Act* compliance statements under s. 50(22) do not validate title to an adjoining parcel subject to the same violation as the curative effect is restricted to the land described in the transfer that contains the statements. In conclusion, a conveyancer may start a *Planning Act* search from the date of the last deed or transfer that contains all three completed *Planning Act* statements.

The vendor's solicitor's statement and the purchaser's solicitor's statement are statements of law which may only be completed by a lawyer. The purchaser's lawyer must have completed a full *Planning Act* search to be entitled to make the statement. Teraview keys are encrypted for use either by a lawyer or a non-lawyer. Only a lawyer's key can sign an electronic transfer containing the vendor's and the purchaser's solicitors' *Planning Act* statements of law. When the case law is ambiguous or conflicting, many lawyers are of the opinion that they can sign a *Planning Act* statement based on their researched legal opinion on compliance with the Act, with the result that the three statements made in good faith will cure a prior contravention should their opinion be found incorrect in subsequent case law. A vendor and purchaser application is the other alternative. Anyone who knowingly makes a false statement is guilty of an offence.

Planning Act statements can have unexpected consequences; they can create new rights. The recent case of *Jacuniak v. Tamburro*, [2002] O.J. No. 1420 (Ont. S.C.J.) illustrates the unexpected impact of *Planning Act* declarations when lawyers have either missed or not dealt directly with *Planning Act* contraventions. *Jacuniak v. Tamburro* dealt with the creation of a right of way in perpetuity by an owner who retained the fee in abutting lands. The owner did not obtain a consent; the conveyance of the right of way contravened the *Planning Act*. Several transactions later, the contravention was cured by the registration of a transfer of the servient lands containing three completed *Planning Act* statements. This case reviews earlier decisions that uphold the curative effect of *Planning Act* statements. The judge warned that it is imprudent to rely on a right of way being legally ineffective because it is void for contravening s. 50. Instead, he recommended that an application declaring the right invalid be obtained and registered on title. Otherwise, *Planning Act* statements could create a new right.

Land Titles Conversion Qualified Title

When Registry land is converted into POLARIS as a Land Titles Conversion Qualified title (LTCQ), all *Planning Act* contraventions prior to the date of conversion are deemed cured by the conversion process. Hence, a title searcher may start a *Planning Act* search from the date of conversion to an LTCQ title. The conveyancer must check for *Planning Act* violations from the date of conversion to LTCQ to present.

This curative provision in the *Land Titles Act*, R.S.O. 1990, c. L.5 (s. 44(1)(11)) applies only to LTCQ land that has been legally converted from Registry into Land Titles. Land Titles and Registry lands that are merely automated such as Land Titles Absolutes and Registry Parcelized Day Forwards are not subject to this curative provision.

Land Titles Absolute Plus

LT PLUS PINs Issued Prior to August 2001

An Application for Absolute Title can upgrade an LTCQ title to a Land Titles Absolute Plus title. Prior to August 2001, this application did not require statements confirming *Planning Act* compliance. Pre-August 2001, when an LTCQ title was upgraded to a Land Titles Absolute Plus title, no new *Planning Act* qualifier was added. The new LT PLUS property identification number (PIN) retained the benefit that any *Planning Act* contravention prior to the date of the original Land Titles conversion was deemed not to have been a contravention of the *Planning Act*. Hence, the search for *Planning Act* compliance on a pre-August 2001 LT PLUS PIN is from the date of conversion to its original LTCQ title to present.

LT PLUS PINs Issued After August 2001

Since August 2001, Applications for Absolute Title usually required a solicitor's statement confirming that there were no *Planning Act* contraventions for the period between the LTCQ conversion and the application. It is important to note that this requirement was not mandatory. When the application contained proof of *Planning Act* compliance, the new LT PLUS PIN was excepted from the standard s. 44(1) *Planning Act* qualifier (similar to the LTCQ, *Planning Act* qualifier). In this situation, any *Planning Act* contravention between the date of the LTCQ conversion and upgrading to a Land Titles Absolute Plus title is deemed cured by the application process. Hence, a conveyancer may start a *Planning Act* search from the date the new LT PLUS PIN was issued.

However, when the application did not contain proof of compliance, then the standard s. 44(1) *Planning Act* qualifier still applies and the conveyancer must start the *Planning Act* search as of the date of conversion to the original LTCQ parcel. In this situation, the conveyancer checks for potential *Planning Act* violations from the date of the original LTCQ title to present. This is the same as the pre-August 2001 search requirement.

It is essential to read very carefully the wording of the *Planning Act* qualifier on an LT PLUS parcel register before deciding where to start the *Planning Act* search.

THE PLANNING ACT SEARCH PERIOD

An illegal subdivision of land in the past can nullify title in the present. As a result, an owner may be prevented from transferring any interest in land to a subsequent purchaser or mortgagee. When checking for good title, it is essential to confirm that no past *Planning Act* violations have taken place affecting the land being transferred. The main property and all abutting lands, as defined by the *Planning Act*, must be checked for both common ownership and the division of land held in common ownership in the past.

Fortunately, legislation has enacted dates and circumstances before which all contraventions have been forgiven, and hence, no longer invalidate current title. The searcher must identify the relevant *Planning Act* forgiveness or starting date for each search and record all owners and s. 50 conveyances from the starting date up to the present.

SIGNIFICANT DATES (WHERE TO START THE SEARCH)

The subdivision and part lot control provisions have changed over the years. Conveyancers need to know past and current provisions to assess whether a contravention exists and also to know the timeframe required for the *Planning Act* search. Amendments to the *Planning Act* and the land registration statutes combined with the POLARIS reforms have provided a number of starting points that depend on the registration system, the documents registered on the property, and the nature of the property. To complete a *Planning Act* search, the conveyancer first identifies and then verifies the most recent *Planning Act* search starting point. The commencement point of the search should be recorded in the search notes. Conveyancers may need to search adjoining lands for compliance with the *Planning Act* as far back as June 15, 1967. All *Planning Act* contraventions were forgiven prior to this date. Since 1967, the Act has provided amendments that cancel potential contraventions prior to a specified event. The definitions for exempt and non-exempt transactions have also changed over the years. A conveyancer needs to understand the significance of the following dates and amendments to determine possible starting points, timeframes, and potential violations that affect a *Planning Act* search.

1. **June 15, 1967** — The *Planning Amendment Act, 1967*, S.O. 1967, c. 75 provided that all subdivision control contraventions prior to this date were forgiven. Subdivision and part lot control provisions only affected land prior to 1970 if a subdivision control by-law was registered prior to this date. If a searcher is unsure where to start, start in 1967. Unfortunately, the 40-year search period in Registry is not an answer to a *Planning Act* contravention, as it involves a Crown right.

2. **A subdivision control by-law registered between June 15, 1967 and June 27, 1970** — Prior to June 27, 1970, the registration of a subdivision control by-law on title was required in order to impose subdivision control on land anywhere in Ontario. The search starts at the date of the by-law when a by-law is registered between 1967 and 1970.

3. **May 2, 1968** — If the land sold and the land retained was ten acres or more. The ten-acre exemption was repealed on May 2, 1968. For a minimum of ten acres property, the search starts at 1968, if there is a registered part lot control by-law.

4. **June 27, 1970** — This is the effective date for province-wide subdivision control. After this date, it was unnecessary to register a subdivision control by-law, as the *Planning Act* automatically implemented subdivision control throughout Ontario. After 1970, it is possible to exempt an area from control by registering an exempting by-law on title.

5. **Registration of a plan of subdivision or a condominium description** — Contraventions prior to the plan of subdivision or the registration of a condominium description (s. 50(14)) are irrelevant. Check to confirm that the plan of subdivision has not been deregistered by by-law.

6. *Planning Act* **consent given on or after December 15, 1978** — Where land has been conveyed, mortgaged, or charged with a consent granted after December 15, 1978, the consent given has the effect of forgiving prior subdivision and part lot control contraventions of an identical parcel of land (s. 50(14)). The conveyancer does not need to go behind a consent given on or after December 15, 1978.

7. *Planning Act* **consent given on or after March 31, 1979** — Where the land now being transferred is identical to the land described in a conveyance for which a consent was given for a transfer on or after March 31, 1979, ss. 50(12) and (13) exempt the subsequent transfer of an iden-

tical parcel from subdivision and part lot control provisions, assuming the consent is not conditional or the conditions have been met, or that the consent was not stipulated to be a one-time only consent. As well, the consent must have been registered within the two-year limit or a shorter limit if specified. This is the "once a consent, always a consent rule". Once the conveyancer has confirmed the effectiveness of the consent and ensured that the parcel is identical, no further search is necessary.

8. ***Land Registration Reform Act* and the *Planning Act* statements, Boxes 13 and 14 on Transfer/Deed, Form 1** — A title searcher need not go behind three properly completed *Planning Act* statements (one by the transferor, one by the transferor's solicitor and one by the transferee's solicitor). Section 50(22) provides that the completion of three prescribed *Planning Act* statements cures previous *Planning Act* contraventions.

9. **By-laws exempting part lots** — These by-laws may have automatic expiry dates. The conveyancer must read the by-law to determine the period of exemption and search time periods that were not exempted by the by-law.

10. **Validation certificate** — Confirm whether conditions exist and have been satisfied (a validation certificate, unlike a consent, does not clear future conveyances of the identical parcel).

11. **Conversion of land to an LTCQ title** — The Land Titles conversion process cures any previous *Planning Act* contraventions. The conveyancer can start the *Planning Act* search from the date of conversion noted on the parcel printout. For LTCQ parcels, *Planning Act* searches are done from the date of conversion to present.

12. **Land Titles Absolute Plus title** — Applications to upgrade an LTCQ to an LT PLUS:

   • **Pre-August 2001** — The *Planning Act* search starts as of the date of the original LTCQ date of conversion. A pre-August 2001, LT PLUS title is subject to *Planning Act* violations from the date of conversion to LTCQ to present.

   • **Since August 2001, when the application contained proof of *Planning Act* compliance** — The new LT PLUS PIN was excepted from the standard s. 44(1) *Planning Act* qualifier (similar to the LTCQ, *Planning Act* qualifier). In this situation, any *Planning Act* contravention between the date of the LTCQ conversion and upgrading to a Land Titles Absolute Plus title is deemed cured by the application process. A conveyancer may start a *Planning Act* search from the date the new LT PLUS PIN was issued.

   • **Since August 2001, when the application did not contain proof of *Planning Act* compliance** — When the application did not contain proof of compliance, then the standard s. 44(1) *Planning Act* qualifier still applies and the conveyancer must start the *Planning Act* search as of the date of conversion to the original LTCQ parcel. In this situation, the conveyancer checks for potential *Planning Act* violations from the date of the original LTCQ title to present. This is the same as the pre-August 2001 search requirement.

HOW TO DO A PLANNING ACT SEARCH

The searcher must confirm whether the land being searched has been held in common ownership with abutting lands at any time within the *Planning Act* search period. Prior common ownership of the subject land and abutting lands raises the spectre of a potential *Planning Act* contravention and resulting failure of title. A *Planning Act* search may be omitted if the land is exempt, *e.g.*, a conveyance to government.

The most common exemption occurs when either the land conveyed or the land retained is composed of one or more whole lots or blocks on a registered plan of subdivision. Whole lots on a registered plan of subdivision lose their whole lot exemption when the local municipality registers a by-law that deems a registered plan of subdivision not to be a registered plan of subdivision for the purposes of s. 50(3) of the *Planning Act*. Searchers must carefully distinguish plans of subdivision from other types of plans such as reference plans, which do not fall under the whole lot on a registered plan of subdivision exemption. In addition, searchers must distinguish between exempt subdivision lots and township, town, river, or other kinds of lots, which are not exempt.

First, the searcher must identify the starting point for the *Planning Act* search period. This requires a review of title, including a reading and recording of documents such as by-laws, consents, and transfers, particularly for ownership and *Planning Act* statements. The searcher must search back on both the main and adjoining properties in order to establish the most recent starting point for the search. Hopefully, the most recent transfer of ownership contains the completed *Planning Act* statements. If not, a final unconditional consent, a subdivision or condominium plan, or a Land Titles conversion or a Land Titles Absolute Plus upgrade may provide a starting date. If a concern exists, it is prudent to do a full *Planning Act* search from June 15, 1967 (if a prior subdivision control by-law had been registered) or June 27, 1970.

Second, to determine the chain of ownership on abutting lands, the searcher must identify the location and description of all adjoining parcels. Plans of subdivision, reference plans, wall maps, POLARIS block and property maps, and Teraview digital maps, for that matter, all available plans maps or other description information in documents, assist the searcher in identifying abutting lands. The process may be simple and involve several subdivision lots, or it may require more time than the main search. Adjoining lands may be in other plans and township lots or, for that matter, they may be registered in different registration systems. They may even be registered in different Registry offices.

A detailed sketch of the subject property and the abutting properties simplifies the search process and illustrates the main land, the adjoining lands, legal access, easements, and boundaries and descriptions. The sketch should indicate lot lines; numbers and dimensions; plans; property dimensions; PINs; and current owner names and the date and instrument number in which they took title. The sketch should outline each property in a different colour (red for the main land) and cross-reference by colour to the respective adjoining owner chain(s) or abstract(s) in the search notes.

In addition to a sketch, an adjoining lands search should include a list or abstract for each adjoining parcel of all documents relating to *Planning Act* and, when relevant, description issues. From a *Planning Act* point of view, the adjoining lands abstract should record all conveyances as defined by the *Planning Act*; subdivision and part lot control and exemption by-laws; by-laws deeming a plan of subdivision not to be a plan of subdivision; and *Planning Act* statements, consents, and validation certificates. The search notes should summarize the nature of the document, dates, legal descriptions, and full names and capacity of owners and *Planning Act* statements. Consents and related agreements are usually photocopied or recorded in full in order to review conditions, appeal dates, and exact descriptions. The adjoining lands search notes and sketch should also include abutting roads, easements, restrictive covenants, and legal access.

When completing the overall search summary, the searcher should include a separate reference to the adjoining lands search, with specific reference to any *Planning Act* by-laws, consents, or POLARIS conversions to Land Titles and upgrades to Land Titles Absolute Plus titles. A searcher who is concerned about a potential *Planning Act* contravention must never rely on the search summary but, instead, communicate the concern directly to the person in charge of the file. Potential *Planning Act* violations must be brought to the attention of the title insurer.

Figure 11.1

ADJOINING LANDS SEARCH SKETCH

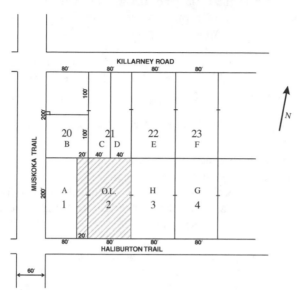

The above illustration is an example sketch of part of Subdivision Plan 649 in the Town of Redrock in the County of Lost Lakes. For the purposes of this example, assume that our client is about to purchase or lease for 21 years or more, the East 20 feet of part Lot 1, Plan 649 and the whole of Lot 2, Plan 649. No *Planning Act* by-laws have been registered against the plan. Lots are represented by numbers, 1, 2, 3, *etc.* and separately owned adjoining properties are represented by letters, A, B, C, *etc.* The land about to be purchased, the main search, is referred to as OL (our land) and indicated by diagonal lines. Note that the sketch includes both roads and the nearest public intersection to confirm public access.

- The abutting lands in this search are A, B, C, D, H, and Haliburton Trail.
- E does not abut the main land being searched as the two parcels touch at one point only, the corner.
- For Haliburton Trail, check the roads page in the abstract index (Registry) for road widenings, closings, encroachments, *etc.* Confirm that streets were dedicated as public on the face of the plan. In POLARIS, road ownership will be indicated in the thumbnail description on a parcel register. There will also be a separate parcel register and PIN for the road.
- Whole lots 3, 4, 22, and 23 are exempt and would not require a *Planning Act* search as they are whole lots on a registered plan of subdivision.

- Lot 2 could be sold without a consent as it is the whole of a lot on a registered plan of subdivision.
- The owner of the main land can sell all (part Lot 1 and Lot 2 combined) he or she owns even though it contains a part lot as long as he or she does not own any of the adjoining lands.

Although fact situations may be similar, it is important to remember that each registration system raises differences in law and procedure related to adjoining lands and *Planning Act* searches.

REGISTRY SYSTEM PLANNING ACT SEARCHES

Registry system searches frequently require adjoining lands searches. Registry, the older system found mostly in southern Ontario, contains older plans often in densely populated regions. Many properties are made up of a combination of whole and part lots. Boundaries may be in question due to the existence of adverse possession and easements by prescription in Registry.

By-laws invoking subdivision and part lot control were common during the 1960s. *Planning Act* searches often go back as far as June 15, 1967 or June 27, 1970. Check *Planning Act* by-laws carefully as it was common for one by-law to both invoke part lot control and deem a subdivision plan to no longer be a subdivision plan for the purposes of the *Planning Act*. As well, exempting by-laws may have automatic expiry dates.

Determine whether a plan is a subdivision plan or a compiled plan or reference plan, as only subdivision plans provide the whole lot exemption. Subdivision plans in Registry are often referred to as registered plans. An examination of the actual plan will normally indicate whether it is indeed a registered plan of subdivision. In Registry, a conveyance may be called by different names, *e.g.*, indenture, deed, mortgage, grant, assurance, lease, order. It is important to investigate all conveyances that may be affected by the *Planning Act*, not just deeds.

LAND TITLES SYSTEM PLANNING ACT SEARCHES

Section 44 of the *Land Titles Act* states that s. 50 of the *Planning Act* is an exception to the Land Titles guarantee. Absolute, leasehold, and qualified titles must all be searched for *Planning Act* contraventions. As in Registry, a *Planning Act* violation in Land Titles will result in a nullity no matter what the register page says.

Fortunately (although not always the case), large portions of Land Titles land are within subdivision or condominium plans. Often, but not always, parcels within a subdivision plan are composed of whole lots. Condominium units are exempt. Parcels of tied land (POTLs) in common elements condominiums are not exempt. Hence, the whole lot or whole unit exemptions may make the *Plan-*

ning Act search unnecessary. However, it is essential to determine what a parcel is made up of prior to deciding whether to complete a *Planning Act* search. A parcel that contains a part lot, which is not otherwise exempt, must be checked for *Planning Act* violations.

Unfortunately, Land Titles parcels are not numbered sequentially and it can be very difficult to find adjoining lands parcel numbers, unless the area is in POLARIS. Some offices make informal unguaranteed indexes available and some do not. Tax information and assessment rolls may be of assistance. POLARIS block and property index maps and Teraview digital maps, when available, are very helpful for identifying adjoining lands, although they are for reference purposes only. They are not guaranteed accurate or to scale and do not indicate boundaries or descriptions. Descriptions on parcel register must be checked to confirm that all adjoining properties have been identified.

Watch for the term "M-Plan", as this indicates a plan of subdivision in the Land Titles system. Never assume that Teraview maps are an accurate illustration of parcel descriptions. Never assume that a lot is a subdivision lot. Lastly, never assume that the whole of a parcel is the same as the whole of a lot.

CONDOMINIUMS AND PLANNING ACT COMPLIANCE

The whole of a condominium unit is exempt under s. 50 of the *Planning Act*. Section 50 does not apply to dealings with common interests in a common elements condominium (s. 142). Easements reserved by or granted by a condominium are also exempt. A condominium purchase, which includes the purchase of one or more units, is exempt. There is no need to search behind the registration of the condominium description. Although the sale or lease of parts of the common elements raises *Planning Act* issues, generally, condominium unit searches are free of *Planning Act* inquiries. Parking spaces and storage space or lockers are usually, but not always, separate units. The declaration and description will indicate whether a parking space is a separate unit or part of another unit.

When dealing with a common elements condominium, the POTL must never be severed or sold separately from the interest in the common elements condominium. POTLs are parcels of freehold land in a common elements condominium; they are not units and are therefore not exempt from s. 50 of the *Planning Act*. The conveyancer must do *Planning Act* compliance searches when dealing with POTLs. POTLs may be exempt as whole lots on an underlying registered plan of subdivision or they may be covered by a part lot control exemption by-law. However, these exemption by-laws are registered to facilitate the launching of the condominium and often expire within two years. Be sure to complete *Planning Act* compliance searches on adjoining lands whenever purchasing, mortgaging, or leasing POTLs. If you are relying on an exemption by-law, be sure to confirm that the by-law was or is in effect at the time of any conveyance where an owner or past owner also retained ownership in an abutting property.

POLARIS AND PLANNING ACT SEARCHES ON TERAVIEW

Land in POLARIS may be in Registry or Land Titles. As a result, Registry, Land Titles, LTCQ, or Land Titles Absolute Plus title rules may apply. Condominiums have one combined condominium register instead of four.

POLARIS greatly simplifies adjoining lands searching. The block and property maps and the digital maps show the location of the main land as well as the location and PINs for adjoining lands and roads. The searcher may call up and print the adjoining lands registers in the automated records using Teraview. When checking past conveyances for possible *Planning Act* violations, the searcher *must* always request deleted transactions; otherwise, past conveyances and potentially contraventions are deleted from both the screen and the printout.

Teraview provides a search feature that allows the searcher to request information from a specific date forward, *e.g.*, the *Planning Act* search start date. Depending on the search start date and the date the land was automated, the searcher may have to search back into the prior paper records to complete the search. Usually, there is a cross-reference back to the old books at the top of the parcel printout.

A Teraview search provides an adjoining land option that produces a map including adjoining lands and a list of adjoining lands and links to parcel information. The searcher may then print a map of the parcel and adjoining lands. In addition, Teraview contains a separate search by map feature that will allow a searcher to identify a larger selection of abutting lands. Using the PINs from the Teraview digital map or the adjoining lands list, the searcher may view or print both main parcel and abutting parcel information. Again, deleted documents *must* be requested. Teraview's list of adjoining lands and its map is for reference purposes only. It does not select on the basis of *Planning Act* requirements. The conveyancer must decide whether the adjoining PINs selected are adequate to complete a *Planning Act* search or to confirm legal access, or easement or restrictive covenant validity. Documents and description information in POLARIS may be viewed online and printed, or faxed and couriered for a price.

Teraview also allows the user to select a specific time period, called a date range, from the parcel register options dialogue box. The user may view the description from the parcel register options box. The conversion date should be checked to decide whether to search back in the paper record. This may be necessary if the land is not LTCQ but merely automated Registry or Land Titles.

LAND TITLES CONVERSION QUALIFIED AND PLANNING ACT SEARCHES

LTCQ titles are searched on Teraview. Contraventions of s. 50 of the *Planning Act* prior to the date of conversion to Land Titles no longer affect title. Note the PIN date of conversion on the parcel register as it provides a new *Planning Act* search start point. As *Planning Act* violations are an exception to the regular Land Titles guarantee, it is still necessary to do a *Planning Act* search from the date of conversion to an LTCQ title up to present. Always request deleted documents.

LAND TITLES ABSOLUTE PLUS TITLE AND PLANNING ACT SEARCHES

When dealing with a pre-August 2001 Land Titles Absolute Plus title, a conveyancer may start a *Planning Act* search from the date of conversion to an LTCQ title. When dealing with a post-August 2001 Land Titles Absolute Plus title, the conveyancer must check the *Planning Act* qualifier on the parcel register. Most post-2001 Land Titles Absolute Plus titles are excepted from the standard s. 44(1) *Planning Act* qualifier (similar to the LTCQ, *Planning Act* qualifier) and as a result, the conveyancer can start the *Planning Act* search at the date the new LT PLUS PIN was issued. Some LT PLUS titles are not excepted from the standard s. 44(1) *Planning Act* qualifier and as a result, the conveyancer must start the *Planning Act* search at the date of conversion for the original LTCQ title. Deleted documents must be requested in order to check conveyances prior to the most recent transfer of ownership in Land Titles. See the section on "significant dates" for more information on LT PLUS titles.

BOUNDARY, ENCROACHMENT, EASEMENT, AND RESTRICTIVE COVENANT SEARCH PROCEDURES

Whenever the law permits possessory rights such as adverse possession and easements by prescription to affect land ownership, it is essential to search adjoining lands for any registration that may affect registered descriptions. Legal descriptions in registered documents for adjoining lands or contained in parcel register thumbnail descriptions must be reconciled in order to identify any overlaps, gaps, or inconsistencies in registered descriptions. Sketches illustrating descriptions can be compared with survey information in order to identify inconsistencies between registered rights and actual physical use or possession. Boundary and encroachment searches are not necessary when the land being conveyed is the whole of one or more lots or condominium units, or the whole of one or more parcels in Lands Titles. However, adjoining land description searches should be done, particularly on part lots in Registry (paper), Parcelized Day Forward Registry, 40-Year Load Registry, and Registry Non-Converts and LTCQ titles. The boundary check may be done separately or together with the *Planning Act* search. The searcher must request deleted documents when searching on Teraview.

Easements and restrictive covenants must be registered on both the dominant and servient lands to be enforceable. When the search reveals an easement or a restrictive covenant, the conveyancer must search all dominant and servient lands to ensure that the easement or restrictive covenant is valid. This is particularly important when the easement or right of way is relied on for legal access by road, to the water, or to a particular street. Special rules apply to building schemes.

Unfortunately, easements, rights of way, restrictive covenants, road, and access rights have not infrequently been missed during the automation and conversion to Land Titles. As a result, it is particularly important to search easements and rights of way and restrictions on both the dominant and servient lands.

The searcher should identify and sketch adjoining lands in the same manner as for the *Planning Act* search. When completing the adjoining lands abstracts, special care should be taken to include all documents that might affect boundaries and descriptions, such as deeds, encroachment agreements, easements and right of ways, restrictive covenants, deposits regarding descriptions and possessory rights, correcting deeds, plans, sketches, reference plans, access agreements, party walls, mutual drives, road widenings, and similar registered interests. Do not decide on document relevance on the basis of a name search, but instead consider description references in the indexes as well as the type of document.

The documents listed on the adjoining land abstracts should be read and summarized, if relevant, as part of the adjoining lands search. Any instrument that appears to create an encroachment on title should be photocopied.

Depending on the level of difficulty, the adjoining lands sketch and description information may be superimposed on a reference plan, a subdivision plan, a Teraview property map, or it may be drafted to scale, using the legal description from the most recent deed. Searchers usually include photocopies of the last registered description on the subject land and the adjoining lands. Some searchers check the first and the last descriptions in the search period. Others stop at the most recent description if it shows no boundary gaps or overlaps. In any case, the sketch should accurately illustrate the main land, as well as all adjoining lands; legal access; easements and rights of way; lot lines; dimensions and numbers; property dimensions and bearings; plans; PINs, if available; north directional arrow; a scale; and names of current owners combined with the date and instrument number by which they took title. Most searchers colour code properties and use that colour to cross-reference to the abstract and related documents. It is useful to compare the adjoining lands sketch with the survey, if available. Check the sketch against the Teraview maps for inconsistencies and bring the inconsistencies to the attention of the Registry Office.

If the adjoining land search reveals a description problem, such as two different owners claiming the same strip of land, it is necessary to search as far back in time as is necessary to discover the cause of the inconsistent claim. Generally, the adjoining land search is limited to the 40-year Registry search period. Remember that gaps in descriptions have the potential to raise *Planning Act* problems. Each land registration system raises differences in law and procedure related to adjoining lands searches.

Registry System

Adverse possession and easements by description may be acquired under the *Registry Act*. Adjoining lands searches, combined with surveys, frequently reveal inconsistent registered legal descriptions, boundary encroachments and possessory rights. Part lots and metes and bounds descriptions are common in Registry. Several properties, with different descriptions, may be registered on the same township or subdivision lot page. Sorting out descriptions in the description and remarks column in an abstract index can be difficult to impossible. Frequently, a searcher must examine a document to decide whether it affects adjoining lands.

Land Titles System

Parcels that are whole lots are outlined and colour coded on M-Plans. A parcel comprised of several parts on a reference plan may be outlined on the reference plan. When part lots are involved, a full sketch to scale may be necessary.

Condominiums

Units, parking, storage space, and exclusive use areas are outlined on the condominium plan.

POLARIS

Land in POLARIS may be in Registry or Land Titles. Registry, Land Titles or LTCQ, or Land Titles Absolute Plus rules may apply. Block and property maps and online Teraview digital maps greatly simplify adjoining lands searches by displaying, adjoining properties, rights of way, and roads. Refer to the *Planning Act* search procedures for POLARIS for more detail.

Land Titles Conversion Qualified

Each LTCQ parcel register warns that title remains subject to any inconsistencies in the description of the property and adjoining properties that existed at the date of conversion. Once converted, however, no new possessory rights may develop. For part lots, a searcher will complete an adjoining lands search for registered descriptions and boundary information. A full description must be obtained from the transfer that represents current ownership at the date of conversion. Once in POLARIS, new transfers do not contain full descriptions. If any boundary inconsistency shows up in the most recent descriptions for main and adjoining lands, the searcher will have to go back behind the conversion into the paper record to find out the cause of the problem. As LTCQ brings forward mature possessory claims from Registry, it may be necessary to track description information back a full 40 years.

Keep in mind that POLARIS block and property maps and Teraview digital maps do not indicate or guarantee property boundaries, but instead act only as an approximate reference. Following conversion, it is even more important for a conveyancer to reconcile document descriptions, POLARIS and Teraview maps, and surveys as part of a title search.

CONFIRMING ACCESS TO LAND

A full search of title includes a search and confirmation of legal access, hopefully by public road. Who would want to buy a "dream home", a peaceful, recreational retreat, or a building for retail sales, and not be able to get to it — with or without title insurance? At some point during either the main search or the adjoining lands search, the searcher should confirm legal access from the property to a public road. The person responsible for the file should also confirm the quality of access to the land being purchased. Access and maintenance of access may be seasonal or year-round. Maintenance of roads may be public or private. A public road may not be maintained by a municipality. Private road maintenance may involve considerable expense.

All plans of subdivision should be checked for notice of dedication for public use of roads and reserves. Reserves are often composed of one-foot strips at the ends of streets, shown on the plan as separate parts. In the past, s. 57 of the *Surveys Act*, R.S.O. 1990, c. S.30 confirmed that roads, lanes, and walkways on a registered plan of subdivision are public unless closed by by-law. As of 2001, s. 26 of the *Municipal Act, 2001*, S.O. 2001, c. 25 states that all road allowances, highways, streets, and lanes shown on a registered plan of subdivision are highways until closed by municipal by-law.

Index books often contain a separate page for roads and reserves. This page should be checked for registrations and by-laws that relate to roads, such as road closings, openings, widenings, extensions, and encroachment agreements. Both the presence and the absence of road pages and registrations should be recorded in the search. In POLARIS, roads and reserves have separate PINs. Print the parcels registers for the road and reserves PINs.

When access is dependent on a registered right of way, be sure to confirm the registration of the right of way on both the property that benefits from the easement (dominant tenement) and all adjoining lands (servient tenements) that the easement crosses out to a public road. The creation of an easement for 21 years or more requires *Planning Act* approval or exemption. In POLARIS, easements and rights of way are included in the property description and noted as being "subject to" or "together with" depending on whether the property is a dominant or a servient tenement. These rights of way and easements should be checked for consistency with adjoining properties and the easement or right of way document should be checked for the extent and nature of and any restrictions on a right that provides access.

POLARIS block and property/PIN maps and Teraview digital maps simplify access and road checks by consolidating plans onto large maps that allow the searcher to trace traffic routes out to the nearest public road. Property maps also refer to instruments affecting roads. Roads and reserves are given separate PINs. A road can be searched by printing the road's PIN and examining the documents listed on the parcel printout. Teraview also contains a search by road feature.

Access has a profound effect on the use and enjoyment and the fair market value of a property. Cottage country access searches can be particularly challenging. The Ontario Court of Appeal delivered at least five decisions on road access to cottages between 2005 and 2008. Entire books have been written on the law relating to roads and access. An ordinary purchaser expects to buy land and access. The conveyancer has a duty to search title to the property and access to the property. For more information about roads and access, refer to Chapter 9.

SUBSEARCH OF ADJOINING LANDS

Subsearches of adjoining lands are required for mortgages as well as transfers. All adjoining lands searched in the original search should be subsearched immediately prior to closing for new registrations that might contravene the *Planning Act*, when the client is relying on the "no abutting lands" exception. The searcher should also subsearch for any new registrations on adjoining lands that might create or affect encroachments, boundaries, access, easements, and restrictive covenants. The adjoining lands subsearch includes all dominant and servient tenements when dealing with easements and restrictive covenants, and requires a search of all properties relied on for access confirming that a right of way ends at a public highway. When subsearching abutting lands, the conveyancer must use the Teraview POLARIS search function. The conveyancer should request deleted documents. The automated subsearch feature in the electronic land registration system (ELRS) only updates the land affected by the registration in progress.

Any new registrations that might create common ownership of main and adjoining lands must be recorded and summarized. Unless the main land searched is the whole of a lot on a registered plan of subdivision or otherwise exempt from the *Planning Act* part lot control provisions, the searcher must ensure that recent registrations do not contravene s. 50 of the *Planning Act*.

Adjoining lands are not permitted to be subsearched as part of the registration process. Searchers must search adjoining lands separately, prior to the registration process. This can be a slow and expensive process. A search summary, containing necessary abstract book, parcel, and PIN references, will avoid wasted time in system indexes. Search procedures vary depending on the registration system in which the land is located. Detailed procedures are included earlier in this chapter.

POLARIS and Teraview maps greatly simplify adjoining lands searching. The property map will outline all adjoining parcels and show their PINs. When searching and subsearching LTCQ lands, it is important to refer to document descriptions, as POLARIS and Teraview digital maps do not guarantee boundaries or illustrate the extent of the parcel.

THE FUTURE OF ADJOINING LANDS SEARCHES

When POLARIS conversion is complete, all land will be Land Titles Absolute, LTCQ, or Land Titles Absolute Plus. Teraview will provide digital maps showing the location of the main land as well as the location and PINs for all adjoining lands and roads. The majority of adjoining lands searches will be shorter because of the new LTCQ and LT PLUS start dates for *Planning Act* purposes. In addition, the property maps will have greatly reduced the difficulty of identifying adjoining parcels. If lawyers, as a group, take advantage of the *Planning Act* statements, the majority of *Planning Act* searches need only be from the most recent transfer up to the present.

Boundary and encroachment searches will remain important when the system is fully automated. Land Titles Conversion Qualified titles remain subject to any inconsistencies in the description of the property and adjoining properties that existed at the date of conversion. Once converted, however, no new possessory rights may develop. Owners have the option of upgrading an LTCQ title to an absolute title, referred to as a Land Titles Absolute Plus title, in order to settle outstanding boundary issues. There has been some discussion as to whether, at some as yet undetermined future date, legislation will stabilize boundaries as they appear within the automated database. As Registry disappears and no new possessory rights are acquired in Land Titles, adverse possession and easements by prescription will become less important. Access and easement searches on adjoining lands remain important to owners, whatever the land recording system.

Title insurer requirements vary between insurers and depending on the nature of the property (residential or commercial) or the policy (loan or owner). These requirements have been and will continue to be subject to change. Title insurer requirements do not necessarily reflect a lawyer's professional due diligence responsibility to a client. Title insurance provides compensation usually estimated by change in fair market value. After the payout and final settlement, depending on the situation, the owner may still have to deal with the title problem and possibly litigation.

TITLE INSURANCE REQUIREMENTS

Residential and commercial search requirements for purchase transactions require a search of title. A full search includes an adjoining lands search, when indicated. Adjoining land searches check for *Planning Act* compliance and easement and restrictive covenant validity. Insurers may not require full searches for residential or commercial mortgage refinance transactions, although they do require an adjoining lands search on commercial refinance transactions over a stated threshold. On residential and some commercial refinances, insurers may accept a verbal inquiry of the borrower that confirms that he, she, or it does not have an interest in adjoining lands. Some insurers on mortgage transactions have only required a search of the most recent adjoining owner on adjoining lands (subsearch). A search of only the last registered owner does not meet *Planning Act* search requirements, and a lawyer who uses this limited type of search cannot complete the purchaser's solicitor's *Planning Act* statement on a deed. A *Planning Act* contravention prevents the creation of an interest in land and results in a total failure of consideration. *Planning Act* searches are time-consuming and require a strong understanding of the law. They are the only way to protect adequately the client, the solicitor, and depending on the policy and the insurer, meet a solicitor's obligation to the title insurer.

Title insurance covers access; however, it does not assure the nature of the access or even if the access is vehicular access. It does not assure that the legal access is sufficient for the insured's current or intended use of the property. Additional endorsements for existing access use, access to particular streets, water access, public highway access, pedestrian access, or private compared to shared access may be arranged or negotiated through an underwriter. It is important to confirm the nature and extent of access for each kind of policy and for individual insurers.

Full adjoining land searches for legal access rights protect purchasers and provide lawyers with the necessary information to arrange appropriate title insurance coverage. Insurers often require a specific confirmation of legal access before issuing additional access endorsements. In addition, conveyancers need to search both dominant and servient tenements when dealing with easements and restrictive covenants in order to confirm their legal validity. Access should be searched to the nearest public road. Disputes over access, ownership and use of driveways, easements allowing others to pass over land, or for that matter, road barricades and checkpoints, often generate intense conflict and potential violence. Access issues have a profound effect on an owner's enjoyment of land as well as affecting fair market value and marketability. Title insurance provides compensation in terms of fair market value. It is not a substitute for a full search of adjoining lands or for professional due diligence standards.

CHECKLIST FOR SEARCHING ADJOINING LANDS

☐ Decide whether the main search requires a full adjoining lands search for *Planning Act* and/or legal descriptions, restrictive covenants, easements and rights of way, and access. (Part lots usually require adjoining lands searches for *Planning Act* purposes.)

☐ Identify the registration system and type of title involved and search accordingly.

☐ Decide whether you are dealing with a subdivision plan or some other kind of plan.
  • "M-Plan" indicates a subdivision plan in Land Titles.
  • "Registered Plan" often refers to a subdivision plan in Registry.
  • Check the information on the face of the plan to determine whether it is a subdivision plan.
  • Reference plans are not subdivision plans.
  • Confirm that the subdivision plan is not subject to a registered *Planning Act* by-law deeming it not to be a registered plan of subdivision for the purposes of the *Planning Act*.

☐ Determine whether you are dealing with a whole lot or block, or a part lot or block on a registered plan of subdivision.

☐ If the land is comprised of one or more whole lots or blocks on a registered plan of subdivision or one or more whole units, then often a full adjoining lands search is not necessary.

☐ If the land is comprised of one or more subdivision part lots, or whole or part township or town lots (they are not exempt), then usually an adjoining lands search is necessary.

☐ Review the exemptions under the *Planning Act* to decide whether the property is exempt and therefore does not require a *Planning Act* search, *e.g.*, a consent or exemption by-law.

☐ Search back on the main and abutting lands in order to establish a *Planning Act* search period start date.

☐ With the help of subdivision plans, reference plans, wall maps, POLARIS and Teraview maps, and description information from the main search index books and documents, identify the location and description of all adjoining parcels.

☐ Consider the definition of abutting lands when identifying all possible adjoining lands.

☐ Include roads in adjoining lands searches.

☐ Confirm access out to the nearest intersection or public road. Indicate access on the sketch.

☐ Check easements and restrictive covenants on the relevant adjoining lands.

☐ Beginning at the *Planning Act* start date, *e.g.*, a deed with three statements, record an abstract of title for each abutting property, up to the present. When in POLARIS, always ask for deleted documents.
  • List all conveyances including leases, easements, foreclosures, *etc.*, not just deeds.
  • Include *Planning Act* by-laws and consents. Read them for conditions and expiry dates.
  • List all documents that might affect boundaries, *e.g.*, quit claims, encroachment agreements, correcting deeds, reference plans, deposits, statutory declarations, and note all *Boundaries Act* plans, *etc.*

- Do not rely on owner names when selecting adjoining lands instruments. Instead, choose on the basis of description reference and the type of document, *e.g.*, quit claim or encroachment agreement.
- Check the first and last descriptions of adjoining lands in the search period, if requested. Many searchers stop at the most recent description if it shows no boundary inconsistencies.

☐ Summarize or photocopy instruments that affect boundaries or the *Planning Act* part lot control provisions and add them to your adjoining lands search notes. Photocopy *Planning Act* consents and by-laws, all plans, encroachments, and the last registered description of abutting lands. These descriptions are useful when plotting the sketch.

☐ Sketch an illustration of the main property and abutting properties.
- Sketch to scale if working with metes and bounds or difficult descriptions.
- A sketch is sometimes superimposed on a subdivision plan, a reference plan, or a POLARIS or Teraview property map.
- The sketch should show the north directional arrow; scale; access; easements; plans; lot numbers; lines and dimensions; property lines and dimensions; bearings; roads, gaps, and overlaps; PINs, and current owner names and the instrument number by which they took title.
- The sketch should illustrate rights of way, easements, and access.
- Colour code properties and use that colour to cross-reference to the respective abstracts, parcel registers, and documents.

☐ Subsearch day books in Registry and, in Land Titles, pencilled-in entries, if in the paper systems, to update the search. Another subsearch of adjoining lands will be made immediately prior to closing.

☐ The search summary or cover page should include:
- a separate reference to the adjoining lands search;
- all *Planning Act* by-laws, consents, statements, and common ownership;
- all easements, restrictive covenants, and encroachments; and
- a separate note on access and roads.

☐ Communicate any concern about a potential *Planning Act* contravention directly to the person in charge of the file.

Tips and Traps

1. Know which system you are in and search accordingly (RPDF, Land Titles Absolute, Land Titles Absolute Plus, or "R" including non-converts).

2. When checking past conveyances in the automated search system, always request deleted documents, otherwise past conveyances are deleted from the parcel printout.

3. POLARIS and Teraview maps do not automatically select adjoining lands as defined in the *Planning Act* any more than they indicate or guarantee legal boundaries. Compare the adjoining lands sketch, the survey, and the POLARIS and Teraview maps for inconsistencies.

4. Identify the most recent starting point. For example, review the last registered transfer for three completed *Planning Act* compliance statements as this can save time.

5. Identify exemptions early.

6. Whole lots and blocks on registered plans of subdivision and whole units in condominiums are exempt from the *Planning Act* subdivision and part lot control provisions, unless there is a by-law to the contrary.

7. The whole of a parcel in Land Titles may contain part lots and therefore may require a *Planning Act* search.

8. Read *Planning Act* by-laws, consents, and validation certificates for content, conditions, and expiry.

CHAPTER 12

Execution (Writ) Searching

INTRODUCTION

Execution searching has traditionally been an area of higher risk for convey-ancers. Missed executions represent one of the more common negligence claims in real estate transactions. In the past, the Land Titles Assurance Fund dealt with more execution-related claims than other aspects of title. Today, the availability of the title insurance coverage has provided an option for managing execution searching risk and greatly removed the need for extensive, particularly histori-cal, execution searches. The title insurance remedy of compensation offers a practical remedy for liens created by executions. As Teranet has now converted most properties in Ontario to Land Titles, Land Titles execution searching is the focus of this chapter. Execution or writ searching is completed online in all of Ontario's Enforcement Offices, be it for land in Registry or Land Titles whether in POLARIS (Province of Ontario Land Registration Information System) or still in a paper record.

The *Execution Act*, R.S.O. 1990, c. E.24 ("the Act") provides a scheme by which a successful plaintiff in a court action, as creditor, may collect a judgment debt against a defendant, now a debtor. The Act permits the execution creditor to file a writ of execution (also referred to as a writ of seizure and sale) with the sheriff in the county or judicial district in which the debtor lives or owns land. Writs of execution are valid for six years in Ontario and federal writs are valid for five years, at which point they must be renewed. A writ renewal may result in a change in the writ file number. Writs of execution filed for liens (charges) under s. 48 of the *Legal Aid Services Act, 1998*, S.O. 1998, c. 26 and s. 1 of the *Bail Act*, R.S.O. 1990, c. B.1 have no automatic expiry date and bind only the land specifically mentioned in the lien. Special rules apply for writs filed under the *Family Responsibility and Support Arrears Enforcement Act, 1996*, S.O. 1996, c. 31 (FRSAEA), allowing amendments to be made by statutory declaration. Ex-amination of the writ summary, called a writ abstract or details, will reveal the terms of the judgment and reconcile old and new file numbers.

The sheriff maintains an index for all writs and renewals of writs. Whenever land is registered under the Land Titles system, the *Land Titles Act*, R.S.O. 1990, c. L.5, s. 136 requires that the execution creditor make a request that the writ, the writ renewal, or certificate of lien be entered in the electronic database that the sheriff maintains for writs of executions that affect Land Titles. A writ of execution only binds land in Land Titles when the writ has been entered in the electronic database and has been linked to Land Titles (s. 136(2)). Once recorded by the sheriff, the writ binds the lands owned by the judgment debtor at the time the writ was entered and any land that the judgment debtor might later acquire in the county in which the writ was filed. In effect, a writ of execution creates a lien against title to land. To satisfy or collect the debt, the sheriff may seize (take possession of) and sell lands owned by the execution debtor, including lands held in trust or in joint tenancy.

The Act also requires that the name of the execution debtor, as set out in the writ, must include a surname and at least one given name in full. Under s. 136(6) of the *Land Titles Act*, a writ of execution has no effect if it is issued against the registered owner under a different name than that under which the owner is registered. In practice, the interpretation of the words "different name" is complex. The Ministry of Consumer and Commercial Relations, Real Property Registration Branch issued *Land Titles Act* Bulletin No. 98003, "Writs of Execution" (December 14, 1998), which lays out the rules for determining whether a name being searched matches a name in the writs database. These rules provide the guidelines for searching and clearing writs of executions in Land Titles. Although the law in Registry is different, these rules have provided some general guidance for practitioners in Registry. A creditor may make an application to amend the name on the writ. When evidence is submitted that a registered owner uses more than one name, for example a birth or a death certificate, both names must be searched.

Executions must be searched any time land ownership is changed or whenever land is used as collateral for a loan to ensure that title is clear of judgment debts. Normally, a full search of executions will be completed at the time of the original title search and an execution subsearch will be performed against the current owners on the day of closing. Execution searches are considered part of financial, credit and collection inquiries and are included in many land-related informational searches. A full search of title will include a completed search of execution, be it in Registry or Land Titles, and whether performed on behalf of a purchaser, a mortgagee, a lessee or sublessee, a financial investigator completing a net worth assessment, or any other interested party.

A conveyancer will complete an execution search, referred to as a WritSearch, and receive either a Certificate of Clearance, where there are no executions, or a Certificate of Execution and a Writ Abstract (Detail) detailing the judgment debt, where an execution is found. A Certificate of Execution, which is issued for the entire day, allows searchers the convenience of completing execution searches early on a closing day. If an execution is found against a particular property, one of two things must occur: (1) the execution must be withdrawn, as evidenced by a sheriff's certificate transmitted to the proper land registrar; or (2) a statutory declaration or electronic land registration compliance statement respecting similar names, attesting to the fact that the owner is not one and the same as the person named in the execution, must be registered. If neither happens, the land will remain encumbered by the execution debt and any new purchaser or mortgagee takes title or takes collateral subject to the execution.

FAMILY RESPONSIBILITY AND SUPPORT ARREARS ENFORCEMENT ACT (FRSAEA) EXECUTIONS

Special rules apply for writs to enforce support orders filed under the FRSAEA. Support orders include court orders and domestic contracts and paternity agreements enforceable by s. 35 of the *Family Law Act*, R.S.O. 1990, c. F.3. FRSAEA has priority over all other civil writs; they do not have an automatic expiry date. A statutory declaration can amend an existing writ to include future support accruals and any name, alias, or spelling variation of any name or alias used by the payor. As a result, when title is subject to a FRSAEA writ, the conveyancer must contact the Family Responsibility Office (FRO) to obtain the current payout figure for all outstanding support arrears. This figure is not the same as the amount on the original writ or the printout of the writ details. FRO has special requirements for release of a FRSAEA writ. The forms and the procedures are available at: <http://www.the FRO.ca>.

For practical reasons it is wise to ask clients if FRSAEA writs exist and then search and follow up on FRSAEA writs early in a transaction. Never rely on the face amount of a support writ and remember to pay out support writs first. FRO has special procedures for similar name executions that require the completion of a FRO form called the *Confirmation of Identity Letter Request* (available at: <http://www.theFRO.ca>). The lawyer will have to obtain and retain both FRO and Law Society of Upper Canada client identification and verification requirements.

FRSAEA or the support recipient may choose to register a support order as a charge against land under s. 42 of the FRSAEA. The charge can be enforced by sale. Special rules apply to the payment, enforcement, and the discharge of a FRSAEA charge.

SEACHING WRITS OF EXECUTION

Ministry of the Attorney General (MAG) writs of execution databases can be searched by debtor name and execution file number using the following online services:

1. the Teraview WritSearch service;

2. within the Teraview electronic land registration system;

3.   the BAR-eX WritSearch service;

4.   BAR-eX's OWL-Ontario Writ Locator service (consolidated search for all 49 Ontario Enforcement Offices); and

5.   ROSCO workstations at land registry offices.

BAR-eX also provides online services for writ issuance, writ filing, and writ withdrawal.

REGISTRY SYSTEM

An execution filed in the sheriff's office of the enforcement jurisdiction in which the land being searched is located creates a lien against the land owned by the person named in the execution at and after the time of filing. Therefore, on completion of a search of title under the *Registry Act*, R.S.O. 1990, c. R.20, a search of executions is required against the registered owners and their predecessors on title throughout the full 40-year search period. If a purchaser is financing a purchase by way of mortgage, then a search of executions should also be completed against the purchaser/mortgagor. In registry, the lawyer decides what names to search and whether a name on title matches a name on a writ of seizure and sale. Detailed rules that apply as to the manner in which owners and predecessors on title are listed on the search inquiry are included later in this chapter in the Debtor Name Execution Search Checklist for Registry. There is uncertainty about what is an identical name, a similar name, or a correct name and when land is affected by an execution. Case law suggests that even when a lawyer has obtained a clear certificate against a name registered on title, the title may still be subject to the execution if the lawyer had actual notice that a similar name was in fact the same person as a registered owner (*Clinton Community Credit Union Ltd. v. Thibert*, [1993] O.J. No. 1579 (Ont. Gen. Div.)). As a result, in registry, it is prudent to search possible similar names and make careful inquiries about the identity of an execution debtor and whether the execution debtor could be the same person as a prior owner.

Outstanding executions should be removed prior to closing. When a certificate of execution reveals an identical name execution, *e.g.*, Jessie Ruth Corbett, a former owner, and Jessie Ruth Corbett, the judgment debtor, you may find that they are not one and the same person. The lawyer who filed the execution will then provide the necessary information to prove that they are not one and the same. The vendor's lawyer should provide a statutory declaration to this effect and deposit it on title.

The same principle applies to similar name executions. Unlike in Land Titles, similar name executions may bind land in registry. A similar name execution occurs when, *e.g.*, William M. Corbett is registered as the owner and the sheriff's office presents an execution against a Bill M. Corbett. Again, a statutory declaration solves the problem, assuming that they are not one and the same person. Should the execution debtor and the registered owner actually be the same person then the vendor's lawyer must arrange for a release of the writ at the sheriff's office. Note that a writ filed against Lewis Hamilton in August 1990 would not affect land he had previously sold in January 1980 and would therefore not require a release or a statutory declaration.

The Law Society of Upper Canada's recent client identification and verification requirements will assist in matching names and identity and hopefully reduce missed executions and execution fraud. As well, conversion of registry lands to land titles reduces risk by setting clearer search standards and title guarantees backed by the Land Titles Assurance Fund. Land Titles is greatly simplified and relates only to current owners and mortgagors as they appear on the parcel register. Lastly extensive title insurance coverage for executions provides compensation for the difficult to manage risk of searching and clearing executions in registry. It is very important to search and follow up on executions early in the transaction.

LAND TITLES SYSTEM

Under the Land Titles system, the only executions that affect a parcel of land are those filed in Land Titles offices by the sheriff in accordance with a paid request by the execution creditor (*Land Titles Act*, s. 136). A writ of execution in Land Titles only affects land when there is an exact name match (identical name) between the name in the search and the registered owner name on the parcel register. In special situations, such as if a death certificate is submitted in which the name is different from the registered deceased owner, a statement is required verifying that it is one and the same person as the name on the parcel register. Both names must then be searched. In most situations, Land Titles requires an application to change the register and change the name on the parcel register.

Problems arise when the name on the judgment does not match the name under which land is registered, particularly as litigation and real estate practice conventions for naming individuals are different. The Land Titles system sets detailed rules for execution searching and for the definition of identical and similar name executions (*Land Titles Act* Bulletin No. 98003, "Writs of Execution"). An Execution Certificate against the identical name as the registered owner should be ordered both as part of the search and on the date of closing or document registration (subject to title insurance alternatives). Conveyancers and subsequent purchasers and mortgagees can rely on system guarantees as long as they meet Land Titles execution requirements (*Land Titles Act*, s. 44(6)).

The *Land Titles Act* does not require execution searches against prior owners unless the parcel register is expressly marked subject to a prior execution (*Land Titles Act*, s. 44(6)). The guarantee against prior executions or executions not properly shown on a Certificate of Clearance is backed by the Land Titles Assurance Fund. Therefore, on completion of a title search under the Land Titles system, a search of executions is required only against the current registered owners, exactly as they are entered on the current parcel register. If a purchaser is financing a purchase by way of a charge, then a search of executions should also be completed against the purchaser, exactly as he or she will be shown on the register as chargor. Executions are also searched when a chargee advances mortgage monies.

Execution (Writ) Name Search Rules

Land Titles Act Bulletin No. 98003 provides the following guidelines for execution search requests:

- Punctuation, accents, and hyphens are ignored.

- Do not include descriptive terms such as estate trustee, executor(rix), personal representative, in trust, trustee, estate of, *etc.*

- Do not include titles such as Mr., Ms, Miss., Mrs., Dr., Jr., "II", *etc.*

- Do not use parts of a surname or spaces in a surname as the name must be an exact match.

- Do not shorten names.

- Do not substitute a different numbering system, such as X for 10.

- Name order for given names has no effect.

- Single letter given names are ignored.

- If you search a given name that has an internal hyphen, the search returns exact matches for the hyphenated name and for each part of the name.

- If you search a given name with an internal space, the search returns exact matches for each part of the name.

When Is a Name an Exact Match?

The following is a summary, taken from *Land Titles Act* Bulletin No. 98003, of when a name will be considered a match in an automated search:

1. Individual names

Where the surname and one forename are identical, the names will be considered to match even if:

a) one name contains initials and the other does not, e.g. John Smith and John A. Smith match.

b) both names contain initials or additional forenames that do not match, e.g. John A. Smith and John B. Smith match, and John A. Smith and John Harold Smith match; or

c) names or initials occur in a different order in each name, e.g. John A. Smith and Andrew John Smith match, and John Andrew Smith and Harold John Smith match.

In the following cases, individual forenames will be considered not to match:

a) where forenames may be interchangeable, e.g. John Smith and Jack Smith do not match;

b) where one forename may be an abbreviation of another forename, e.g. Belle Smith and Isobel Smith do not match;

c) where both forenames may be abbreviations of the same name, e.g. Bill Smith and Willy Smith do not match;

d) where one name may be an Anglicized version of the other, e.g. John Smith and Johan Smith do not match;

e) where there are minor variations in spelling of given names, e.g. Ann Smith and Anne Smith do not match;

f) where a variation may be due to a typographical error, e.g. John Smith and Jhon Smith do not match.

It will be assumed, for search purposes that single letters represent initials and not forenames, unless only single letters are given, e.g. in I. Roberts, the "I" should be considered the forename.

2. Corporate and Partnership Names

Only executions against the exact name of the corporation or partnership as set out in the transfer will be searched. Names will be considered to match only if the name in the parcel register and the name in the writ are identical, except that, where the corporate identifier in one name ("Corporation", "Incorporated", "Limited" or the non-English version in any of these, e.g. "Limitee") is abbreviated in the other name ("Corp.", "Inc.", "Ltd.". "Ltee.") the names will be considered to match. However, where "Limited" or "Ltd." occurs in a corporate name being searched, the name with another corporate identifier, i.e. "Corporation" or "Corp." *will* not be searched (e.g. John B. Smith Limited and John B. Smith Corp. do not match), unless "Corporation" forms part of the corporate name, e.g. "X Corporation Limited".

Names that include a number will be considered to match only if the number is identically set out in both names, e.g. 1000 Yonge Street Ltd. and One Thousand Yonge Street Ltd. do not match.

Bankruptcy

A trustee in bankruptcy conveys title free of writs of execution filed against the bankrupt prior to the date the receiving order was made or the assignment filed as these claims are paid from the proceeds of the sale of the bankrupt's assets. Writs filed after the land vests in the trustee do not affect a purchaser from the trustee. There are special rules for property acquired by a bankrupt subsequent to an assignment. Depending on the circumstances and the conditions in the discharge, subsequently acquired property may or may not be subject to executions against a bankrupt. Refer to the *Electronic Registration Procedures Guide* (Ministry of Government Services, 2008) for details and required statements. Nevertheless, it is necessary to search the bankrupt as there are a number of executions that survive the discharge. The Act provides that the following executions survive discharge:

- any debt or liability arising out of fraud, embezzlement, misappropriation, while acting in a fiduciary capacity;

- any fine or penalty imposed by the court or any debt arising out of a recognizance or bail bond;

- any debt or liability for alimony;

- any debt or liability under a support, maintenance, or affiliation order or under an agreement for maintenance and support of a spouse or child living apart from the bankrupt;

- any debt or liability for obtaining property by false pretences or fraudulent misrepresentation; and

- liability for dividend that a creditor would have been entitled to receive on any provable claim not disclosed to the trustee, unless the creditor has notice or knowledge of the bankruptcy and failed to take reasonable action to prove the claim.

When an Execution Search Is Required

Land Titles requires a search for outstanding writs of execution in the following circumstances (*Land Titles Act* Bulletin No. 98003):

- a transfer of any interest in freehold land, including interspousal, interfamily, self to self, municipally owned, and changes in tenure;

- a transfer of easement;

- a transfer of life estate;

- a transfer of leasehold land;

- a transfer, release, or abandonment of an easement;

- a vesting order;

- a mortgage foreclosure;

- a power of sale transaction;

- a change of name application;

- a survivorship application;

- a transmission application;

- a beneficiary releasing an interest;

- an application to delete debts against a prior deceased owner;

- applications to have beneficiaries registered as owners;

- an application to change name of registered owner;

- plan document — against the registered owner of lands dedicated to the municipality; and

- as required by Land Titles systems procedures.

When the search results in a Certificate of Clearance, the document will be registered clear of executions. If, instead, a search reveals similar or identical name executions against current registered owners, then the conveyancer will obtain a writ abstract or details of the execution. Following an investigation of the relevance of the execution to the registered owner, the lawyer, depending on the circumstances, chooses from the following:

1. pay the execution creditor and lift the execution;

2. register an Application to Amend the Register under s. 75 of the *Land Titles Act* deleting the execution (paper system);

3. register an Application to Delete Execution in Teraview;

4. delete the execution within an electronic transfer by completing electronic statements in Teraview; or

5. register "subject to" a named execution.

Although uncommon, depending on the circumstances, particularly in a non-arm's length transaction, the transferee may register subject to an execution. In that case, the land registrar will make the following note on the parcel register, "subject to execution number ___", if enforceable. An Application to Delete Execution may be registered later to clear title.

More often, a Certificate of Execution involves an identical name (not necessarily the same person) execution that may be deleted at the time of registration by accompanying the transfer with a paper or, when in Teraview, an electronic Statutory Declaration as to Writ of Seizure and Sale. Under the *Land Titles Act*, to clear an execution where the value of the writ is $50,000 or more, the land registrars may accept a statutory declaration by a solicitor; a letter from the solicitor for the registered owner or creditor on the solicitor's letterhead; or an acknowledgment from the execution creditor, setting out the details of the execution and declaring unequivocally that the transferor is not one and the same as the execution debtor. These options are available in electronic land registration by way of electronic solicitors' compliance with law statements.

Where the value of the writ is less than $50,000, the registered owner is permitted to complete a statutory declaration (to be included in the transfer at the time of registration) setting out the details of the execution and declaring unequivocally that, as transferor, he or she is not one and the same as the execution debtor. These statements are available in electronic land registration by way of electronic compliance with law statements. The *Electronic Registration Procedures*, available on the Teraview website, provides detailed instructions on how to complete the electronic documentation.

CONDOMINIUMS

Condominiums are almost always registered in automated Land Titles and hence usually Land Titles execution searching and registration procedures apply. Execution searches of condominium ownership are completed as follows:

- Search executions against the exact names of the registered owners as they appear on the unit register.

- Search the condominium corporation for executions affecting the condominium and the common elements, as s. 23 of the *Condominium Act* states that a judgment against the condominium is a judgment against each owner for its proportionate share in the common interests. A purchaser or lender can require a release from the condominium of a unit's proportionate share liability in an execution.

- Search the purchaser(s) mortgagor(s) as they will appear on title if they are assuming or registering a mortgage. When acting for a lender search the condominium corporation, the registered owners as they appear on the unit register, and the mortgagors as they will appear on the unit register.

- When acting on the purchase of a new as opposed to a resale condominium unit, search the developer who will be the registered owner.

- In Registry, complete an execution search of prior registered owners since the certificate of title.

- Today, title insurance provides alternative coverage and does not require an execution search of the condominium corporation, or of the prior owners in Registry.

- Search executions within ELRS or in WritSearch. You are only able to search and subsearch executions against the registered owners within the electronic land registration system.

POLARIS AND LAND REGISTRATION REFORM

Lands now in the POLARIS database may have been left in the Registry system, continued in Land Titles, or have undergone legal conversion from Registry to Land Titles during the automation process. As a result, Registry, Land Titles or Land Titles Conversion Qualified (LTCQ) rules may apply.

Title searchers should search executions against owners and mortgagors as required by the registration system in which the land is located, keeping in mind that one main goal of Land Registration Reform (POLARIS) is to transfer all land into one system — the Land Titles system. In a fully converted office, such as London, all lands (except for the rare Registry non-converts) are now in Land Titles. This greatly reduces the number of names required to be searched, as Land Titles requires that executions need only be searched against current registered owners and listed executions to which the register has been made "subject to".

Title searchers should be aware that special rules apply when searching LTCQ titles. During the conversion process, executions were searched against former owners of Registry lands. Executions found against prior Registry owners were brought forward and entered at the top of the new parcel register printout by name and by number. These prior executions listed on the current parcel register printout must be searched and resolved in the same manner as any execution found against the current owner(s) shown on the Land Titles Absolute and LTCQ parcel register printout. When executions are renewed, they are issued new numbers. Unfortunately, at this time, these new numbers are not cross-referenced and updated onto the POLARIS parcel registers. If they have been renewed, they must be dealt with in the usual manner. If no longer effective, they can be deleted from the parcel register by using either electronic statements or an electronic application to delete executions. This procedure is outlined later in the chapter.

ONLINE EXECUTION SEARCHING

In the past, in Ontario, executions were registered and searched on a county/district by county/district basis. In addition, executions were registered and searched separately in the Registry system and the Land Titles system. Title searchers were required to complete and submit a Request for Service to the Registry office or Sheriff's office. Long waits for execution certificates were common as title searchers, running between offices, scrambled to close purchases, sales and mortgages, particularly on Fridays and month ends. Complex rules existed as to what constituted a similar name execution, and 40-year Registry searches resulted in the costly duplication of debtor name searches. From a debt collection point of view, anyone attempting to locate executions registered against a particular debtor was confronted with the inefficient, expensive and uncertain task of searching for executions in both registration systems in every county and district in the province.

Today, the MAG Writs of Execution databases may be searched by either debtor name or execution number. MAG execution databases may be accessed directly through Teraview with WritSearch or within electronic land registration, or through BAR-eX with WritSearch or OWL. These computerized online search systems provide official Certificates of Execution, Clear Certificates, and Writ Detail Reports. Execution information may be viewed online or printed.

The following online execution searching and filing services are available throughout Ontario:

- **WritSearch:** Execution searching by name or by number is available in Teraview's WritSearch service. The electronic land registration program also contains a writ searching feature as part of document production and registration. WritSearch covers all of Ontario and may also be accessed directly through BAR-eX. Writsearch searches in only one Enforcement (Registry) Office at a time.

- **OWL:** OWL, the Ontario Writs Locator, is available through BAR-eX at <http://www.bar-ex.com>, and, like Writ-Search, covers all of Ontario. OWL locates executions in all Ontario enforcement jurisdictions in one search. It is useful and very cost effective for corporate/ commercial, creditors' rights, litigation, family, and estates practitioners.

- **BAR-eX:** BAR-eX provides direct access to WritSearch, OWL, and Writfiling services. Lawyers can simultaneously search, issue, file, and release writs of execution in any Ontario enforcement jurisdiction using BAR-eX.

- **ROSCO:**   ROSCO workstations are available in Registry offices and provide access to the MAG Writs (executions) databases. As with Writsearch, the conveyancer can only search one Enforcement (Registry) Office at a time.

HOW TO USE WRITSEARCH

WritSearch is available for all Registry and Land Titles land in Ontario and is accessible through the Teraview Gateway as a separate service or within the ELRS software. It may also be accessed through BAR-eX at <http://www.bar-ex.com>. In addition, WritSearch may be accessed at self-serve terminals in some Registry offices. Most practitioners use WritSearch as part of the electronic land registration process.

WritSearch is user-friendly and contains screens that instruct and prompt users as they proceed through the search steps. WritSearch using Teraview is in a Windows environment complete with drop-down lists and help options. Searching writs in Teraview is detailed in both the Teraview Reference and the Ministry Teraview Procedures Guides.

WritSearch accesses active writs of execution issued by the courts and certificates and warrants for debts, for example, tax arrears, legal aid liens, and family support plan writs.

WritSearch is accessed through the Teraview products menu. It is possible to search executions by either debtor name or by execution number anywhere in Ontario. The Writs of Execution main window allows the user to select a Writs enforcement office and then choose whether to search by debtor name or by writ number (see Figure 12.1). When completing a Writs of Execution Name Search, the user indicates whether he or she is searching a person or a company and enters given names (maximum of three names, up to 50 characters) and surnames (up to 50 characters) (see Figure 12.2). You may search a maximum of 15 names in one inquiry. The searcher next requests that WritSearch print a Writ of Execution Certificate. The system will display and print a Clearance Certificate listing all clear names for which no executions were found or it will display and print a Certificate of Execution listing all executions matching each name searched (see Figure 12.2.1). The latter, when displayed online, is referred to as Writs of Execution Search List (see Figure 12.3). The searcher may view Writ Details from the Writs of Execution Search screen or print a Writ Details report for each execution found (see Figure 12.3.1).

CLEAR EXECUTION CERTIFICATE

```
********************
* CLEAR/LIBRE *
********************
```

CERTIFICATE #:
NO. DE CERTIFICAT:
00000007-0000630B

CERTIFICATE/CERTIFICAT

SHERIFF AT / SHERIF A: LRO#33 Middlesex
DATE OF CERTIFICATE / DATE DU CERTIFICAT : 2009-10 30

THIS CERTIFIES THAT THERE ARE NO WRITS OF EXECUTION, EXTENT OR CERTIFICATES OF LIEN IN MY HANDS AT THE TIME OF SEARCHING AGAINST THE REAL AND PERSONAL PROPERTY OF:

JE CERTIFIE, PAR LA PRESENTE, NE PAS AVOIR DE BREF D'EXECUTION OU DE SAISIE, NI DE CERTIFICAT DE PRIVILEGE EN MA POSSESSION AU MOMENT DE LA RECHERCHE VISANT LES BIENS OU IMMEUBLES DE:

SURNAME / NOM	GIVEN NAMES / PRENOM(S)
(PERSON / PERSONNE)	CORBETT, HAMILTON LEWIS

CAUTION TO PARTY REQUESTING SEARCH:
ENSURE THAT THE ABOVE INDICATED NAME IS THE SAME AS THE NAME SEARCHED. THIS NAME WILL REMAIN CLEAR UNTIL THE CLOSE OF BUSINESS THIS DATE.

AVERTISSEMENT A LA PARTIE QUI DEMANDE LA RECHERCHE:
ASSUREZ-VOUS QUE LE NOM INDIQUE CI-DESSUS EST LE MEME QUE CELUI QUI EST RECHERCHE. CET ETAT DEMEURE VALIDE JUSQU'A LA FIN DE LA JOURNEE DE TRAVAIL.

CHARGE FOR THIS CERTIFICATE: $ 11.00
FRAIS POUR CE CERTIFICAT:

SEARCHER REFERENCE: BUTTERWORTHS
REFERENCE CONCERNANT L'AUTEUR DE LA DEMANDE:

EXECUTION CERTIFICATE

```
********************
* EXECUTION *
********************
```

CERTIFICATE #:
NO. DE CERTIFICAT:
00000007-0000630B

C E R T I F I C A T E / C E R T I F I C A T

SHERIFF AT:
SHERIF A: LRO#33 Middlesex
DATE OF CERTIFICATE: 2009-10-30
DATE DU CERTIFICAT:

THIS CERTIFIES THAT LISTED BELOW ARE ALL WRITS OF EXECUTION, ORDERS AND CERTIFICATES OF LIEN IN MY HANDS AT THE TIME OF SEARCHING AGAINST THE REAL AND PERSONAL PROPERTY OF:

J' ATTESTE PAR LA PRESENTE QU'ENUMERES CI-APRES SONT TOUS LES BREFS D'EXECUTION, LES PRIVILEGES, ET LES ORDONNANCES DONT JE DISPOSAIS AU MOMENT DE LA RECHERCHE FAITE SUR LES BIENS MEUBLES ET IMMEUBLES DE:

SURNAME / NOM	GIVEN NAMES / PRENOM(S)	
(PERSON / PERSONNE)	CORBETT,	JESSIE RUTH
EXECUTION # 09-0649*	CORBETT,	JESSIE
EXECUTION # 09-1694*	CORBETT,	JESSIE SELENA

CAUTION TO PARTY REQUESTING SEARCH:
ENSURE THAT THE ABOVE INDICATED NAME IS THE SAME AS THE NAME SEARCHED. WRITS AND CERTIFICATES MAY BE REMOVED FROM THE SHERIFF'S FILES SUBSEQUENT TO THIS SEARCH AND MAY BE SHOWN AS CLEAR LATER THIS DATE.

AVERTISSEMENT A LA PARTIE QUI DEMANDE LA RECHERCHE:
ASSUREZ-VOUS QUE LE NOM INDIQUE CI-DESSUS EST LE MEME QUE CELUI QUI EST RECHERCHE. IL SE PEUT QUE DES MANDATS ET DES CERTIFICATS SOIENT RETIRES DES DOSSIERS DU SHERIF APRES CETTE RECHERCHE ET PURGES DANS LA JOURNEE.

CHARGE FOR THIS CERTIFICATE: $ 11.00
FRAIS POUR CE CERTIFICAT:

SEARCHER REFERENCE: BUTTERWORTHS
REFERENCE CONCERNANT L'AUTEUR DE LA DEMANDE:

(*)   WRIT REGISTERED AT LAND TITLES.

EXECUTION REPORT / WRIT DETAIL

```
*********************             CERTIFICATE #:
* REPORT/ RAPPORT *              NO. DE CERTIFICAT:
*********************             00000007-0000630B
```

R E P O R T / R A P P O R T

SHERIFF AT: LRO#33 Middlesex
SHERIF A:
DATE OF CERTIFICATE: 2009-04-01
DATE DU CERTIFICAT:

IT IS HEREBY CERTIFIED THAT THE INFORMATION CONTAINED
BELOW IS A TRUE REPRESENTATION OF INFORMATION ON FILE AT
THE TIME OF YOUR REPORT REQUEST.

JE CERTIFIE, PAR LA PRESENTE, QUE LES RENSEIGNEMENTS
CONTENUS CI-APRES REPRODUISENT EXACTEMENT LES RENSEIGNE-
MENTS FIGURANT AU DOSSIER AU MOMENT DE VOTRE DEMANDE
DE RAPPORT.

FILE NUMBER / NO. DE DOSSIER: 2009-1234
ISSUE DATE / DATE DE DELIVRANCE: 2009-04-01
DATE EFFECTIVE: 2009-04-02
DATE D'ENTRÉE EN VIGEUR:

DEBTOR SEARCH NAME(S) / NOM(S) DU (DES) DEBITEUR
RECHERCHE:
(PERSON / PERSONNE) CORBETT,   JESSIE RUTH

DEFENDANT: JESSIE RUTH CORBETT
DEFENDEUSE: For case No. 0408732 – File No. 01234–2009 (612)

ADDRESS: R.R. #3, Neverland, Ont. O2K 1G0
ADDRESSE:

CREDITOR: BANK OF NOVA SCOTIA-ASSIGNOR

CREANCIER: 100-2001 BAY ST.
TORONTO, ONTARIO, M8X 2X3
CANADA MORTGAGE AND HOUSING
CORPORATION-ASSIGNEE
NATIONAL OFFICE
007 MONTREAL RD.
OTTAWA, ONTARIO, K1A 0P7

SOLICITOR: BUTTERWORTHS GLOBE AND MOORE
PROCUREUR: 0649 CHURCH STREET
TORONTO, ONTARIO, M1X 1X2
ATT: M. MOORE
416-111-1111

COMMENTS: RECEIVED "ASSIGNMENT" DATED
SEPTEMBER 23, 2009.

ORIGINAL WRIT: BREF ORIGINAL:	AMOUNT MONTANT	INT RATE TAUX D'INT	START DATE DATE DU DEBUT
JUDGMENT/ JUGEMENT: COSTS/FRAIS:	99,701.16 0.00	7.5000 0.0000	2009-06-07

FINANCIAL TRANSACTIONS:
OPERATIONS FINANCIERES:

TRANS DATE DATE OPER	FEE PAYMENT FRAIS PAIEMENT	REFERENCE OR NOTES REFERENCE OU NOTES
2009-06-07	32.00	FILING
2009-06-07	9.00	LAND TITLES
2009-06-07	63.00	WRIT

CAUTION: ENSURE THAT THE NAME AND FILE NUMBER MATCH YOUR REQUEST.
AVERTISSEMENT: ASSUREZ-VOUS QUE LE NOM ET LE NUMERO DE DOSSIER SONT LES MEMES QUE CEUX QUI SE TROUVENT SUR VOTRE DEMANDE.

CHARGE FOR THIS REPORT: $11.00
FRAIS POUR CE RAPPORT:
REQUESTER REFERENCE: BUTTERWORTHS
REFERENCE CONCERNANT L'AUTEUR DE LA DEMANDE:

Figure 12.1

TERAVIEW WRITS OF EXECUTION ENFORCEMENT OFFICE AND NUMBER SEARCH SCREEN (WRITSEARCH)*

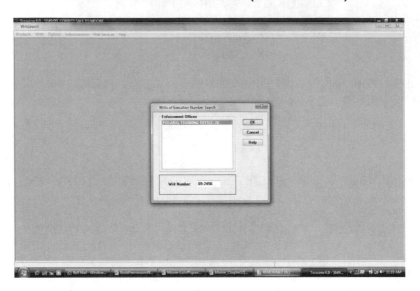

Figure 12.2

TERAVIEW WRITS OF EXECUTION NAME SEARCH SCREEN**

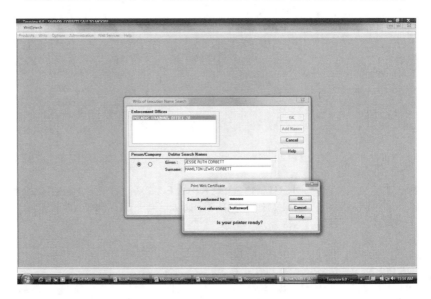

Figure 12.2.1

TERAVIEW EXECUTION CLEAR CERTIFICATE SCREEN*

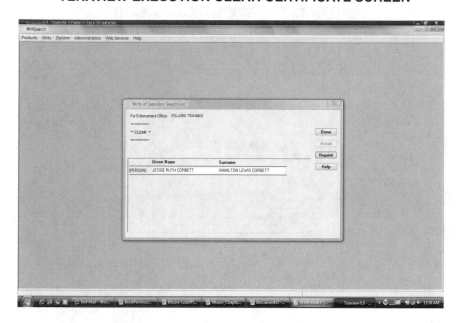

Figure 12.3

TERAVIEW WRITS OF EXECUTION SEARCH LIST**

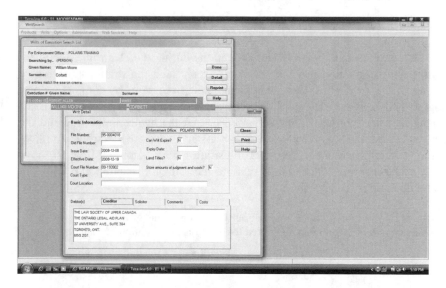

Figure 12.3.1

TERAVIEW WRITS OF EXECUTION SEARCH LIST AND
WRIT DETAIL SCREEN (WRITSEARCH)*

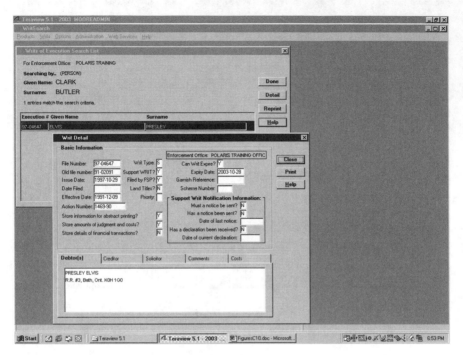

ELECTRONIC LAND REGISTRATION

Lawyers can both search and delete executions during the electronic document drafting and registration process where electronic land registration is available for Land Titles properties. The lawyer can delete executions by completing pre-programmed lawyers' statements which replace sworn, paper declarations affirming that the debt has been discharged or that the owner is not one and the same as the debtor. The lawyer can also register a separate electronic Application to Delete Executions. Electronic Registration Regulation, O. Reg. 19/99, s. 34 (*Land Registration Reform Act*) sets out the rules for deleting executions in electronic registration as follows:

> 34. (1) In addition to the matters set out in sections 4 and 8, if an application to delete a writ of execution is submitted for electronic registration, it shall contain,
>
> (a) particulars of the writ to be deleted including the number, amount and names of the parties to the writ set out in full; and

---

(b) evidence that the writ does not affect the land described in the application.

(2) The evidence mentioned in clause (1) (b) shall be in the form of,

(a) a complete, unconditional and unqualified release from the execution creditor;

(b) a statement by the solicitor for the applicant that the execution debtor has obtained a complete, unconditional and unqualified release from the execution creditor;

(c) a statement by the solicitor for the applicant that the registered owner of the land immediately before the land registrar recorded the writ against the land is not the execution debtor;

(d) a statement by the applicant that the registered owner of the land immediately before the land registrar recorded the writ against the land is not the execution debtor, if the writ of execution is for an amount of less than $50,000; or

(e) a statement by the applicant that the writ of execution,

(i) has expired and has not been renewed,

(ii) has been discharged or withdrawn, or

(iii) describes land other than the land affected by the application.

A search of executions may be performed as part of creating an electronic document. For example, when the solicitor for the purchaser is drafting a transfer, he or she may retrieve writs against the pre-populated names of the registered owner(s) (see Figure 12.4). First, you would select a registered owner from the document tree on the left side of the instrument screen. Next, you would select "Writs" from the "Instrument" menu for each registered owner and then request "Retrieve Writs". The execution search results are displayed within the draft document. You may then print a writ certificate, print and/or view writ detail, add or remove a writ.

EXECUTION CLEARANCE PROCEDURES IN ELECTRONIC LAND REGISTRATION

When the search reveals a writ issued against a judgment debtor with the same surname and one same given name as the name of the registered owner(s), then the parcel register will be marked subject to the writ unless an appropriate execution clearance statement is selected. Pre-programmed statements are available for each transferor and each writ found. It is necessary to select either a statement that clears the writ, or a statement that confirms that the property is subject to the writ. As with paper declarations, an individual may make a statement if the principal amount of the writ is less than $50,000, whereas only a solicitor or a judgment creditor may make a statement if the principal amount of the debt is more than $50,000. A solicitor's statement must be made by a solicitor using a solicitor's Teraview key. The following pre-programmed statements (see Figure 12.5) are available during the document drafting and registration process:

807   This document is supported by evidence.

92   This document is supported by evidence which is indexed at the Land Registry Office as index number ...

803   I am not the party in the writ and the judgment is less than $50,000.

805   The party is not one and the same as the party named in this writ and the judgment was less than $50,000.

814   This property is subject to this writ.

607   There is a writ of execution but the sheriff has not advertised the lands for sale to enforce the writ (for writs against deceased joint tenant).

608   There is a writ of execution but the date of death was within six months of the filing of the writ.

Statements by a solicitor (numbers shown in bold in Teraview)

804   A complete, unconditional and unqualified release from the judgment creditor for the writ has been obtained.

806   The writ does not bind this property as it specifically relates to other land.

813   The judgment creditor(s) states that the registered owner is not one and the same as the party named in this writ.

820   The judgment creditor named in this writ releases any interest under the writ in this parcel.

3524   The party is not one and the same as the party named in this writ.

Application to Delete Executions

If a writ is not cleared on or before closing as part of the transfer registration process, then the transfer may be registered subject to the execution and the parcel is marked subject to the execution. Once the writ of execution is entered on the parcel register, an Application to Delete Executions, containing similar statements is required (see Figure 12.6). An Application to Delete Executions requires one of the following statements:

802   This document is supported by evidence which is indexed at the Land Registry Office as index number____.

Statements by a solicitor (numbers shown in bold in Teraview)

804 A complete, unconditional and unqualified release from the judgment creditor for the writ has been obtained.

806 This writ does not bind this property as it specifically relates to other land.

808 **NAME**, a previous registered owner is not one and the same as the party named in the writ.

809 **NAME(s)**, the judgment creditor(s) states that the registered owner is not one and the same as the party named in writ *writ number*.

810 **NAME**, the deceased is not the party named in writ *writ number*.

820 The judgment creditor named in this writ releases any interest under the writ in this parcel.

3525 The writ has expired and has not been renewed.

3526 The writ is discharged or withdrawn.

DELETING "SUBJECT TO EXECUTION NUMBER" STATEMENT FROM THE PARCEL REGISTER THUMBNAIL

Land Titles Conversion Qualified titles often contain a "subject to execution number ****" statement in the thumbnail description on the parcel register. These are often writs against previous owners from Registry that were not cleared during the POLARIS conversion process. A search of a "subject to" execution often returns the message, "Writ not Found" or "Writ Does Not Exist on File". Usually these writs have expired and or do not affect the current Land Titles title.

The following writs can be deleted by the land registrar without registering an application to delete executions from the register (Bulletin No. 2004-04):

- "Subject To" writ with a "Writ Not Found" search response;

- *Legal Aid Act* writ that does not list the land being transferred or mortgaged; and

- *Bail Act* writ that does not list the land being transferred or mortgaged.

Figure 12.4

RETRIEVE (SEARCH) WRITS IN ELECTRONIC LAND REGISTRATION (TRANSFER)*

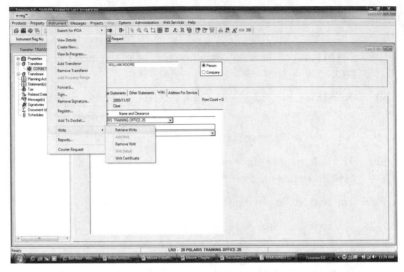

Figure 12.5

REMOVE (DELETE) WRITS IN ELECTRONIC LAND REGISTRATION BY STATEMENT (TRANSFER)**

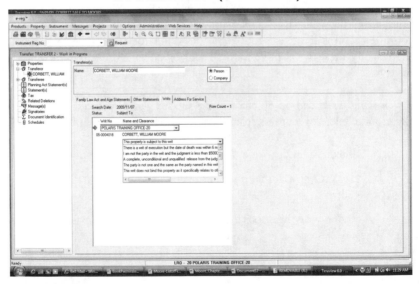

---

* © Teranet Inc. 2010. Reproduced with permission.
** © Teranet Inc. 2010. Reproduced with permission.

Figure 12.6

APPLICATION TO DELETE EXECUTION IN ELECTRONIC LAND REGISTRATION*

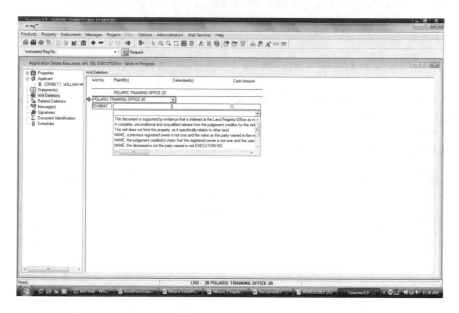

EXECUTION SUBSEARCH

A title searcher may wish to update a certificate or subsearch executions prior to closing a purchase, mortgage or lease transaction. The title searcher will check to see whether any new executions have been filed against the current owners, condominium corporation, or mortgagors since the date of the last execution search. In Registry, execution searches against prior owners need not be repeated as the certificate will validate that their names were clear after they had ceased to be a registered owner.

Subsearches may be completed on WritSearch or as part of the electronic land registration process. An execution certificate is good for the entire day on which it is requested and is often completed early in the day set for closing.

Electronic land registration is available only for Land Titles land already in POLARIS in a registry division which permits or requires electronic land registration. Both the paper and electronic Land Titles registration process require an execution subsearch. It is automatically part of the electronic registration process. There is no additional fee as long as writs are searched within the ELRS

---

document on the same day as executions are searched as part of the registration process. An additional fee will be charged if writs are searched in WritSearch instead of within ELRS on the day of registration. Be sure to retain all certificates or execution information in the file and report all new executions immediately to the individual in charge of the file. Title insurance coverage reduces the requirement for some subsearches (see below).

TITLE INSURANCE AND EXECUTION SEARCHING

The purchase of title insurance changes the requirements for searching writs of execution. The requirements vary from company to company and change depending on risk and claims experience. It is essential to regularly confirm current requirements with the title insurance company.

Insurer execution search requirements are not the same as marketable title execution search requirements. They are a condition of insurance coverage and provide compensation for interests in or encumbrances on land. When title insurance is obtained, it is only necessary to search executions against the vendor(s) and the purchaser(s)/mortgagor(s), if a mortgage is being insured. Some lenders waive the execution search against mortgage guarantors. As a result, it is unnecessary in the registry system to search prior owners on title throughout the 40-year search period. Stewart Title waives the requirement of an execution search for an existing homeowner when the policy is for land in Land Titles but requires an execution search against vendor to the existing owner for land in Registry. Insurers do not require an execution search against a condominium corporation. Execution subsearches may not be required as long as a search of the current owner was completed within a specified time period (for example, at this time, Stewart Title requires ten business days of the transaction's closing date, whereas TitlePLUS requires 14 days). Land Titles Conversion Qualified parcels that are marked subject to execution where a writsearch indicates that the execution has expired or is no longer in the system may receive custom coverage on an assurance that the writ will be removed on closing. Lender coverage for difficult to remove executions, such as when the execution creditor cannot be found may be underwritten on a case-by-case basis.

EXECUTIONS AND THE RISK OF FRAUD

In Registry, the lawyer must independently investigate the validity of an identical or a similar name execution and obtain affidavit evidence from the creditor that the execution does not affect land. Title insurance backs the lawyer's documentation. This requirement reduces the risk of fraud. In Land Titles, the lawyer is allowed to remove an execution under $50,000 based on a sworn statement from the transferor that he or she is not the same person as the judgment debtor named on the writ. The Land Titles system relies on inquiries made by the lawyer and lawyer's statements in the electronic land registration system. As client declarations can be self-serving and raise the risk of a false affidavit by an unscrupulous client, it is necessary for the lawyer to make independent inquiries relating to both the client's and the judgment debtor's identity. Similarly, a lawyer providing a declaration removing an execution over $50,000 must confirm through independent evidence that the judgment debtor is not the same person as the registered owner or mortgagor. Lawyers must retain a record in the file of the inquiries and evidence that support the lawyer's electronic statements that delete executions. The best evidence is a release from the judgment creditor.

In Registry when fraud is present, the transfer or mortgage remains subject to the execution. In Land Titles, once the land registrar has certified the title free of a fraudulently deleted execution, the execution creditor can no longer enforce the execution against a subsequent purchaser or mortgagee. Title insurance provides protection against the increased risk of fraud to purchasers, lenders, and lawyers making inquiries and execution statements in electronic documents.

DEBTOR NAME EXECUTION SEARCH CHECKLIST

Search registered owner name(s) to determine whether there are outstanding executions encumbering the land about to be purchased, mortgaged, leased, or subleased. When an individual or a business is known by different names, be careful to list each name as a separate search name, to obtain maximum protection in the Certificate of Execution. Title insurance coverage changes execution searching requirements. This list outlines the rules on which registered owner names to search, what is considered an identical or a similar name, and how to complete an execution search. Refer to *Land Titles Act* Bulletin No. 98003 for the Ministry's comprehensive statement on when an execution applies to a Land Titles parcel.

Land in Registry

☐ Search current and all prior registered beneficial owners throughout the 40-year search period.

☐ Search current purchaser names, exactly as they will appear on the deed, if the purchase is being financed by a mortgage.

☐ Owner names must be obtained from registered documents, not abstract books. Search any name variations found in the documents. Exact spelling is essential.

☐ If an owner name is spelled several ways in the record, search all spellings.

☐ If the register indicates a change of name, search both former and current names, individual or corporate.

☐ Search all corporate names, all previous corporate names and all amalgamated corporate names.

☐   Search both the names of the partners and the firm name of the partnership property.

☐   Search the names of the general partners and the firm name of a limited partnership.

☐   It is not necessary to search a spouse who joins in a deed only to release a spousal interest or, in the past, to bar dower. Search registered owner spouses only.

☐   Search trustees who appear as registered owners.

☐   Search the deceased owner's name.

☐   Search the name of an estate beneficiary in which estate lands have vested (three-year vesting rule).

☐   Search a beneficiary under a will who releases his or her interest.

☐   It is not usually required to search estate trustees, executors or administrators.

☐   Search executions as of the time that the notice of sale is to be served in a power of sale proceeding and not as of the date that the transfer under the power of sale is registered.

☐   Search executions as of the date that the statement of claim in a foreclosure action was issued and not as of the date the order of foreclosure is registered.

☐   It is not necessary to search the bankrupt or the trustee in bankruptcy when registering a transfer by the trustee in bankruptcy or an application by the trustee to be entered as owner.

Notes:

•   When completing the 40-year search, examine all deposits as they may contain affidavit evidence clearing similar name executions against prior names.

•   Remember that an execution will only attach to land if it is registered prior to or during the judgment debtor's ownership. Always reconcile execution registrations and judgment debtor ownership period dates.

•   Title insurance usually requires execution searches only against the current owners in a residential Registry search.

Land in Land Titles

☐   Search the exact names of the registered owners as they appear on the parcel register.

☐   Be sure to search any "subject to" executions listed in the parcel thumbnail description.

☐   Search the purchaser names, exactly as they will appear on the parcel register, if the purchase is being financed by a mortgage.

☐   It is not necessary to search a spouse who joins in a deed/transfer only to release a spousal interest or, in the past, to bar dower. Search registered owner spouses only.

☐ Search executions against the exact name of a corporation registered as owner, as set out on the parcel register.

☐ Search both the partners and the firm name of a partnership as it appears on the parcel register.

☐ Search both the general partners and the firm name of a limited partnership as it appears on the parcel register.

☐ Search the deceased's name and any beneficiaries releasing their interests when registering a transmission application, a transfer from estate trustees, or when the devisee applies to be registered as owner. When searching the deceased's name, the automated WritSearch system will also search for any capacity of the deceased name, *e.g.*, "Estate of" or "Estate Trustee of the Estate of".

☐ In a survivorship application, search the deceased joint tenant in his or her personal capacity and not the estate. The Sheriff can enforce an execution against the land of a judgment debtor held in joint tenancy unless the joint tenant dies before the Sheriff seizes the land, in which case the joint tenancy share passes by right of survivorship clear of the execution.

☐ Search executions against the registered owner when registering an application to change the name of the registered owner.

☐ Search executions against the registered owner when registering applications to release or abandon an easement.

☐ Search executions against a transferor who is transferring an interest in land from himself or herself to himself or herself.

☐ Search executions for interspousal and interfamily transfers as well as transfers of municipal land.

☐ Search executions as of the time that the notice of sale is to be served in a power of sale proceeding and not as of the date the transfer under the power of sale is registered.

☐ Search executions as of the date that the statement of claim in a foreclosure action was issued and not as of the date of the order of foreclosure is registered.

☐ It is not necessary to search the bankrupt or the trustee in bankruptcy when registering a transfer by the trustee in bankruptcy or an application by the trustee to be registered as owner.

Condominiums

☐ Search exact names of the registered unit owners as they appear on the parcel register.

☐ Search the unit purchasers' names exactly as they will appear on the parcel register, if the purchase is being financed by a mortgage.

☐ Search the condominium corporation (not required for title insurance coverage).

POLARIS

Automated lands records in the POLARIS database may be Land Titles, LTCQ, or still Registry. Take care to determine the type of POLARIS conversion in any particular Registry office. If land records were merely automated, then complete the execution search, as before, according to the registration system in which the subject land is located. If, instead, Teranet completed a full Land Titles conversion during automation, as in London, then search according to Land Titles requirements.

Land Titles Conversion Qualified

☐ Review the top of the LTCQ parcel register printout to determine whether the land was converted subject to executions against prior, though now deleted, Registry owners. These prior executions are listed by number in the thumbnail description. Search these "subject to" executions listed in the parcel thumbnail description.

☐ Search the exact names of the registered owners as they appear on the parcel register printout.

☐ Search the purchasers' names exactly as they will appear on the parcel register, if the purchase is being financed by a mortgage.

☐ Continue the execution search according to Land Titles requirements.

Note: Refer to the *Land Titles Act* Bulletin No. 98003, "Writs of Execution" (December 14, 1998) for detailed procedures.

Title Insurance Execution Searching Requirement

☐ Search only the current vendors.

☐ Search the purchaser(s)/Mortgagor(s), if a mortgage is being insured.

☐ Condominium corporation search not usually required for purchase of a unit.

SYSTEMS COMPARISON CHART

Debtor Name Search

Registry	Land Titles	Condominium	POLARIS Automated Title Database	POLARIS Land Titles Conversion Qualified
• current owners • prior owners during the 40 year title search period	• current owners as per parcel register • executions stated on the parcel register/ "subject to"	• current unit owners as per unit register • executions stated on the parcel register/ "subject to" • condominium corporation	• owners/ mortgagors as required by the registration system in which the land is located • Registry, Land Titles, or Land Titles Conversion Qualified rules may apply	• current owners as per parcel printout • prior owner executions that were brought forward in the title conversion and entered at the top of the parcel printout
• current purchasers/ mortgagors	• current purchasers/ mortgagors as they will appear on the parcel register	• current purchasers/ mortgagors as they will appear on the unit register		• current purchasers/ mortgagors as they will appear on the parcel printout

Subsearch

Registry	Land Titles	Condominium	POLARIS Automated Title Database	POLARIS Land Titles Conversion Qualified
• current owners	• current owners as per parcel register	• current owners as per parcel register • condominium corporation	• current owners as required by the registration system in which the land is located	• current owners as per parcel printout
• current purchasers/ mortgagors	• current purchasers/ mortgagors as they will appear on parcel register	• current purchasers/ mortgagors as they will appear on unit register	• current purchasers/ mortgagors	• current purchasers/ mortgagors as they will appear on the parcel printout

Note: Title insurance may waive the subsearch requirement when the original search was completed within a stated time period.

Remedy

Registry	Land Titles	Condominium	POLARIS Automated Title Database	POLARIS Land Titles Conversion Qualified
• release of writ by judgment creditor	• release of writ by judgment creditor	• release of writ by judgment creditor	• as required by the registration system in which the land is located	• same as Land Titles
• deposit regarding similar name execution on title or in file	• Application to Delete Writ • Statutory Declaration as to Writ accompanying paper transfer or electronic statements in e-transfer	• Application to Delete Writ or statements may be registered electronically in transfer where electronic land registration is available	• Application to Delete Execution or statements may be registered electronically in transfer where electronic land registration is available	• Application to Delete Execution or statements may be registered electronically in transfer where electronic land registration is available
	• transfer subject to Writ	• transfer subject to Writ	• transfer subject to Writ	• transfer subject to Writ

CHAPTER 13

Subsearches

INTRODUCTION

The term subsearch most commonly refers to an update of a previously completed full search, from the date the full search was completed up to and including the date and time immediately preceding the registration of a right or interest in land. In addition, a subsearch may also describe a short search completed for a specific purpose, such as finding the current owner or current legal description. Subsearches may be completed for a specific reason and a limited time period, for example, checking for the registration of a recent construction lien, a notice of claim, or a designation of a matrimonial home by one spouse. Title insurance companies set customized subsearch requirements as a substitute for the traditional full title search when they choose to assume what they have assessed as an acceptable risk. As with legal research, the benefit of the most diligent title inquiries may be lost by not completing a subsearch immediately before registration.

Subsearches are performed on behalf of purchasers of freehold and leasehold titles immediately prior to registration of title or transfer of funds. Financial institutions and private lenders, including vendors taking a mortgage back from a purchaser, search and subsearch the collateral and the borrower (executions) who is financing a purchase by way of a mortgage/charge. A subsearch may be completed to confirm the registration of a discharge of mortgage or a release of an encumbrance or lien, such as an execution. Mortgagees routinely subsearch prior to the assignment of a mortgage, a construction advance, a mortgage amending agreement, or during a periodic review of business loans secured by mortgages. Vendors and mortgagors with common names may search themselves to ensure that no similar or identical name executions exist that might interfere with their right to close a transaction on time. Parties involved in litigation may subsearch to obtain evidence of ownership. Contractors registering construction liens search for current owners and legal description, as well as all outstanding mortgages, construction liens and certificates of action. Proceeds of crime investigators may search specific time periods to collect evidence relating to assets and net worth inference in drug and enterprise crimes.

For the most part, the majority of subsearches are performed on behalf of purchasers immediately prior to registration of a transfer, and by mortgagees immediately prior to the registration of a mortgage as collateral for a loan. However, today, most transactions involve title insurance coverage. Insurers assess and assume certain title risks and set search requirements for policy coverage differently than the underlying legal and due diligence requirements. For example, existing homeowner and refinancing transactions usually require only an insurer-specific customized subsearch. As well, insurers often require subsearches instead of full searches on executions and adjoining lands, and listed off-title inquiries. Insurer-specific requirements vary from time to time and from insurer to insurer. Different requirements apply depending on the category of risk, the nature of the transaction, and the type of policy coverage. Title insurer subsearch requirements are dealt with in more detail later in this chapter under a separate heading.

The extensive use of title insurance is relatively recent in Ontario, becoming the standard over the last 15 years. Title insurance coverage has reduced the need for subsearching in specified transactions and substituted a subsearch requirement for a full title search in others by providing insurance coverage and compensation as an alternative to identifying and dealing with title and off-title problems prior to closing. The insurance alternative both reduces transaction costs and provides a mechanism for closing deals in shortened timelines. Yet, experienced practitioners know that title problems such as boundary and easement conflicts, matrimonial home claims, and indications of fraud may surface shortly before closing, particularly in periods of market downturn.

Whether or not required by the insurer, a careful subsearch immediately before closing is an effective fraud prevention tool. More importantly, a full search of title and off-title claims combined with a survey is the only way to ascertain the extent of the land and the purchaser's rights and restrictions in the property. Title insurance delivers compensation not rights in property. Purchasers who preferred the reduced costs and search requirements of title insurance may find insurance compensation less satisfactory when faced with an actual title defect, such as a boundary dispute, or loss of access to the beach, part of the backyard or even the driveway.

COMMON SUBSEARCHES

The reason for a subsearch, the nature of the land, be it, for example, residential, recreational, agricultural, or commercial, the choice of title or mortgage insurance coverage, and the expectations of the client all guide the lawyer's and the client's decisions regarding the nature and the number of subsearches to be completed. From the perspective of client expectations and satisfaction, a lawyer may, in consultation with the client, choose to complete both title and off-title searches and subsearches beyond the minimum required for insurance coverage. The following are the most commonly completed subsearches:

    1.   title, land purchased, mortgaged or leased;

2. title, adjoining lands:

- for *Planning Act*, R.S.O. 1990, c. P.13 contraventions;

- for boundaries and description encroachments;

- for easements and restrictive covenants;

3. executions;

4. chattel searches: Personal Property Security Registrations (PPSR); and

5. other land-related, off-title searches.

TITLE SUBSEARCHES UNDER THE REGISTRY ACT

Time elapses between the completion of the full search and the closing date of the purchase or mortgage transaction. A title searcher acting for a purchaser, vendor, or chargee/mortgagee will complete a subsearch of title immediately prior to closing to ensure that no document affecting title has been registered since the original search.

Usually, the person who performed the original search will have noted the abstract book number, the page, the last registered document, and the date and time the search was finished, at the top of the search summary. Search summaries are often attached as the first or cover page of a search. Therefore, the search summary provides easy reference to the point of commencement for the subsearch, thus avoiding time-consuming work in Registry office indexes.

When a subsearch reveals that documents, *e.g.*, liens or easements, were registered subsequent to the completion date of the search, you must note and summarize these additional documents and add them to the original search. Immediately advise the individual in charge of the file of any new documents, particularly before proceeding with registrations and releases of funds.

Under the Registry system, a searcher is required to update a full search as follows:

1. Check the abstract index from the time, the date, and the last document noted on the search summary. It may also be necessary to check the abstract pages for adjoining lands for *Planning Act* compliance, easements, restrictive covenants or description conflicts.

2. Check the day book, also known as the fee book, which is a concise recording of all entries that the Registry office clerks did not have time to enter in the abstract book, *e.g.*, "#26432, registered April 1, 2009 — Lot 16, Plan 649, SEVERN BRIDGE". Several copies of the

day book, a series of pages on a clipboard, are available near the registration desk. This may take time on busy days.

3. Check the documents that the clerks did not have time to enter in the day book. These may be in piles behind counters and not easy to review. The searcher is responsible for finding all registrations on title.

4. Check, if possible, documents held by people in the registration line ahead of the person closing the transaction. A lien, mortgage or transfer registered seconds before a closing will have legal priority over the client's registration.

5. Check, during registration, the current day book sheet. Fortunately, in some offices, an informal day book sheet is continuously updated at the registration counter, and the searcher can check for registrations right up to the moment the document is submitted for registration.

6. Note, examine, summarize and report any documents found registered against the client's land. Also, note the last entry on the day book for future reference.

7. Confirm, after registration, that the client's document is entered on the day book. Record the date and registration number of the document on the search and closing memorandum or checklist.

Registry offices organize access to day books differently. POLARIS automation alters subsearch routines. Searchers should familiarize themselves with the procedures in individual offices.

TITLE SUBSEARCHES UNDER THE LAND TITLES ACT (PAPER SYSTEM)

Under the *Land Titles Act*, R.S.O. 1990, c. L.5, a subsearch is less complicated and more reliable. A subsearch of title may be made at the time a document is presented at the registration counter. As part of the registration process, a registration clerk will work with both the parcel register and the new document. A document will not be accepted by the registration clerk if the parcel register indicates that the vendor or chargor named in the document is not identical to the owner indicated on the parcel register.

Under the Land Titles system, a searcher is required to update a full search as follows:

1. Check the parcel register before or during registration to determine if any registrations have taken place since the original search. It may also be necessary to check the register(s) for adjoining lands for *Planning Act* compliance or easements and restrictive covenants.

2. Check the parcel register for pencilled-in notations of documents as these indicate a recent, prior registration in the process of being entered in the parcel register. This pencilled-in, conditional registration will not be legally certified until it has been properly entered into the property register and signed by or on behalf of the registrar. Section 78 of the *Land Titles Act* allows the registrar a maximum of 21 days to accept or reject a Land Titles registration.

3. Note, examine, summarize and report any documents found registered against the client's parcel.

4. Record the date and registration number of the document on the search and closing memorandum or checklist.

5. Confirm the signed, certified entry of the registration. This may require an additional subsearch at a later date. Depending on the circumstances, a searcher may obtain a current copy of the parcel register reflecting the new registration.

CONDOMINIUMS (PAPER SYSTEM)

Since condominiums are almost always registered in Land Titles, the standard Land Titles subsearching procedures as listed above usually apply. In addition, when subsearching a condominium unit in Land Titles, a searcher should check all four condominium registers. As in the original search, the searcher must review the following registers:

1. property parcel register;

2. constitution index;

3. common elements and general index; and

4. one or more unit registers. (The client may purchase a residence, a parking space, and a storage locker. Depending on how the condominium is organized, the purchase might involve one combined unit or three separate units. All relevant units must be subsearched.)

POLARIS has streamlined condominium searching and subsearching by consolidating condominium registrations from all four registers into the unit register. Searchers may wish to subsearch by printing out the unit register. Search screens are designed to allow searchers to start subsearches from a specific date or document. When in the POLARIS database, subsearches may be completed during the electronic land registration process.

TITLE SUBSEARCHES IN POLARIS USING TERAVIEW (LAND REGISTRATION REFORM ACT)

Lands automated in the POLARIS conversion may be in Land Titles, Land Titles Conversion Qualified (LTCQ), Land Titles Absolute Plus, or still in Registry. Care must be taken to determine the nature of the POLARIS conversion in any particular Registry office. If land records have been merely automated, then the subsearch must be completed according to the registration system in which the land being searched is located. If Teranet has completed a full legal conversion to Land Titles, then Land Titles procedures will apply. If, on the other hand, Teranet has simply automated Registry and created Parcelized Day Foreward Registry titles, then the title searcher will complete a Registry subsearch in Teraview using a property identification number (PIN) to access the POLARIS parcel register.

Online searching on Teraview provides the option of subsearching from a particular date or instrument. The previously completed search summary should provide easy reference to the parcel PIN, the last registered transfer number, the name of the vendor, the municipal address, and the description being Part on a reference plan. The searcher may reprint the full parcel register printout or only a parcel printout from the date of the original search forward, accessing the title database by the PIN or the last registered instrument number. Teraview gives the conveyancer the choice of selecting deleted documents as part of an inquiry. The subsearch must include deleted documents; this is also a title insurance requirement.

In addition, both the Land Titles paper registration process and the electronic land registration process include a subsearch of the parcel. For example, the electronic registration system will automatically confirm that the registered owner and the transferor have identical names before processing a registration. Electronic land registration is available for Land Titles only. The electronic land registration program includes a subsearch option as part of the registration process. The registration screen includes a box that provides a request for subsearch. The subsearch box is pre-selected in the registration process. There is no additional charge for this subsearch option. If a conveyancer does not wish to complete a subsearch, he or she must deselect the "subsearch" option. If the subsearch reveals any recent registrations, a box will open containing the relevant details. These instruments would have to be examined and accounted for before finalizing the registration procedure. Following registration, an up-to-date parcel printout confirming the subsearch and the new registration should be obtained. Most conveyancers highlight the new registration on the parcel printout and add the subsearch and registration information to the search.

If purchasing a part lot remember to subsearch adjoining lands for *Planning Act* compliance. The subsearch option in electronic land registration relates only to the PIN on which the new registration is taking place. If you need to subsearch adjoining lands, this must be done separately using the electronic land registration "property" search function. Conveyancers may also subsearch adjoining lands for easements, restrictive covenants, boundary, and access issues. Subsearches for all adjoining parcels should be documented by parcel register printouts and added to the full search.

ADJOINING LANDS

Adjoining lands searched in the original search should be subsearched prior to closing. The searcher will check for any new registrations on adjoining lands that might create or affect boundaries, encroachments, easements and restrictive covenants. The searcher will also check for new registrations that might create common ownership of main and adjoining lands. Unless the main land searched is the whole of a lot on a registered plan of subdivision, the whole of a unit on a registered condominium plan, or otherwise exempt from the *Planning Act* part lot control provisions, the searcher must ensure that recent registrations do not contravene s. 50 of the *Planning Act*.

Adjoining lands are not permitted to be subsearched as part of registration. Conveyancers must search adjoining lands separately, prior to both the paper and the electronic land registration processes. This can be a slow and expensive process. A search summary, containing necessary abstract book, parcel and PIN references, will avoid wasted time in system indexes. Search procedures vary depending on the registration system in which the land is located.

POLARIS and online Teraview maps greatly simplify adjoining lands searching. The property map will outline all adjoining parcels and show their PINs. In Teraview, you may request and print adjoining PINs and their mapping details. When searching and subsearching LTCQ lands, the conveyancer must refer to document descriptions as POLARIS maps do not guarantee boundaries.

EXECUTIONS (WRITS)

A conveyancer may wish to update an execution certificate or subsearch executions prior to closing a purchase, mortgage or lease transaction. The searcher will check to see whether any new executions have been filed against the current owners, the condominium corporation, and/or the mortgagors or guarantors, since the date of the last execution search.

Execution searches against prior owners need not be repeated, as the certificate will validate that their names were clear after they had ceased to be registered owners. When land is in Registry, if executions were not searched against all previous owners at the time of the original search, then they should be searched prior to closing.

An important advantage of electronic land registration is that it simplifies and streamlines the process of execution subsearching in Land Titles. Teraview offers an execution subsearch option within the electronic land registration program. On the day of registration, you may retrieve writs by opening the transferor's branch and selecting "retrieve writs". This request will automatically retrieve the appropriate writs for all registered owners/transferors. You may then view writs results online or print a writs certificate or writs details. If you choose to retrieve writs on the same day as registration, there will be no automatic writs search when the document is registered as the writs search is good for the entire day. On Teraview, it is always possible to use the WritSearch product when subsearching as well as when completing the initial title search. If you use the separate WritSearch product instead of subsearching within ELRS, you will be charged an additional fee. As Teraview only searches against the transferor(s) within the registration program, the conveyancer may, depending on the nature of the transaction, need to do additional searches in WritSearch, for example, against a deceased in an estate conveyance or against a mortgagor when registering a mortgage independent of a conveyance.

If the system shows a new execution, do not register as your document will be made subject to this writ. All new executions should be reported immediately to the individual in charge of the file and all certificates and execution information should be retained in the file. More detailed information on executions and execution searching is found in Chapter 12.

CHATTEL SEARCHES (PERSONAL PROPERTY SECURITY REGISTRATION SYSTEM)

Lenders can register a lien against personal property under the *Personal Property Security Act*, R.S.O. 1990, c. P.10 and the *Repair and Storage Liens Act*, R.S.O. 1990, c. R.25. When the purchaser is also purchasing chattel property of any value (*e.g.*, appliances, equipment, cars, boats, furniture, inventory) which may have been used as collateral for a loan or which has a repair or storage lien on it, the conveyancer may complete a PPSR system search against the vendor and, in some cases, the previous owners, to ensure that no creditor claims a security interest in the chattels. The public can register or search online through a government service called Access Now. As of August 1, 2007, the Minister requires that all PPSRs such as notices of security interests or liens be filed in electronic format. Online filing requires a web account. Conveyancers can search online through ServiceOntario at <http://www.serviceontario.ca> for PPSR liens by using a major credit card or a pre-arranged deposit account set up by the Companies and Personal Property Security Branch. Telephone inquiries are available. Private sector companies such as Cyberbahn and Dye & Durham also provide PPSR services. A conveyancer has the following search options:

1. individual specific/debtor name by first and last names, middle initial, date of birth (IS);

2. individual non-specific/debtor name by first and last names (IN);

3. business debtor name by corporate name, registered partnership name and trade name (BD); or

4. motor vehicle identification number (MV).

OTHER SUBSEARCHES (OFF-TITLE SEARCHES)

Depending on the length of time between the original search and the closing date, as well as the nature of the property and the terms of the agreement of purchase and sale, the lawyer may wish to update or subsearch other inquiries. For example, in a delayed closing, the conveyancer may update tax and utility accounts, answers to outstanding requisitions, and mortgage statements and payments on mortgages being assumed. Although title insurance covers many of these risks, the lawyer in consultation with the client may choose to identify and resolve potential problems prior to closing rather than rely fully on title insurance. In addition, the lawyer, in consultation with the client, chooses which off-title searches and subsearches are needed, particularly regarding risks excluded from insurance coverage such as illegal rent increases, fire retrofit, liens on chattels, arrears of rent on boathouses on Crown land, environmental or water quality problems, Aboriginal rights claims, *etc*. More detailed information on off-title searches is found in Chapter 14.

TITLE INSURANCE AND SUBSEARCH REQUIREMENTS

Title insurers set different title search and subsearch requirements based on the category of risk, the nature of the transaction, and the type of policy coverage. For example, insurers set different search requirements for residential transactions depending on the number of units, for commercial transactions depending on the value of the land, for refinancing transactions, and for existing homeowner policies. Some specialty transactions are dealt with on an individual basis and the search requirements are determined in consultation with an underwriter. As well, the legal principles at work in different jurisdictions and title registration systems determine both risk and search requirements. For example, in Ontario insurers set different requirements based on whether the title is in Registry, Land Titles Absolute, or LTCQ. The requirements vary from company to company and change depending on risk and claims experience. It is essential to regularly confirm current requirements with the title insurance company.

Insurer subsearch requirements are not the same as legal subsearch require-ments. They are a condition of insurance coverage and compensation for inter-ests in land; they do not provide proprietary rights in land or deliver on a pur-chaser's expectations for the use and enjoyment of a newly acquired property. From the perspective of client expectations and satisfaction, a lawyer may, in consultation with the client, choose to complete both title and off-title searches and subsearches beyond the minimum required for insurance coverage. Com-pensation or damages is not always the client's preferred remedy when actually faced with a problem. For centuries, landowners have relied on specific per-formance and injunctions to enforce their rights in land. This traditional expecta-tion remains despite the fact that over the last 15 years lawyers have moved to covering almost all transactions with title insurance.

The subsearch of the full search of title is completed at the time of registration; however, execution subsearches may not be required as long as a search of the current owner was completed within a specified time period (at this time, Stew-art Title requires ten days, whereas TitlePLUS requires 14 days). Some insurers, when dealing with refinance transactions require only a subsearch starting with the current owner on abutting lands when confirming *Planning Act* compliance. Yet, a full abutting land search may be required depending on the insurer and particularly on the value for a commercial transaction. Generally, title insurers waive the full search requirement and require a customized subsearch for exist-ing owner policies and refinances. Search requirements are detailed, subject to change; they vary from insurer to insurer and by property type. It is essential to check search and subsearch requirements on a continuous basis.

Existing Homeowner Policy Search Requirements

Most title insurers only require a subsearch of title containing deleted instru-ments from the date the existing owner acquired title to the date of the policy order. The subsearch should check the current land transfer tax affidavit for as-sumed mortgages. As well, the existing owner must verify any mortgage dis-charges since acquisition. A full search is required if the existing owner acquired the property in a non-arm's length transaction without completing a full search of title. The execution search requirement depends on the land registration sys-tem and the off-title search requirements depend on the nature of the property.

Refinances

On a mortgage refinancing, most title insurers require only a subsearch of title from the last arm's length transfer. A full search is required if the existing owner acquired the property in a non-arm's length transaction without completing a full search of title. A full search, including a full abutting land search, is required for larger commercial transactions. The subsearch must contain deleted instruments and assumed mortgages shown on the current land transfer tax affidavit. As well, the existing owner must verify any mortgage discharges since acquisition. A verbal inquiry of the borrower as to whether he/she owns abutting lands may substitute for an abutting land search. The execution search requirement depends on the land registration system and the off-title search requirements depend on the nature of the property. As long as the refinance/mortgage is registered within, for example, ten days of the subsearch (Stewart Title, 2008), no additional subsearch is required prior to registration.

SUBSEARCH CHECKLIST WHEN ACTING FOR A PURCHASER

Note: When acting on behalf of a lender/mortgagee, subsearches will be similar to those completed on behalf of a purchaser. Title insurance coverage sets search requirements that are different from the traditional marketable title, due diligence standards; this affects subsearch practices (see above).

---

1. Title: Lands Purchased or Morgaged (Main Lands)

Registry System

- ☐ Update abstract book.
- ☐ Check day book including current page at counter, if available.
- ☐ Check previously registered documents not yet entered in day book (behind counter).
- ☐ Check documents held by persons ahead of you in registration lines.
- ☐ Note all registrations found.

Land Titles System

- ☐ Update parcel register.
- ☐ Check any pencilled-in notations for registrations in process.
- ☐ Check parcel register during registration.
- ☐ Note all registrations found.

Condominiums

- ☐ Update all four condominium registers (property parcel register, constitution index, common elements and general index, unit register) despite the fact that changes are usually found in the unit register only.
- ☐ Check one or more unit registers (client may purchase a residence, a parking space, and a storage space as separate units).
- ☐ Check any pencilled-in notations for registrations in process.
- ☐ Check registers during registration.

☐   In POLARIS, print only one condominium register as all four registers were combined in the conversion. This greatly reduces duplication and simplifies searching.

☐   Note all registrations found.

POLARIS

☐   Print up-to-date parcel register using the date forward subsearch option before or on registration.

☐   Subsearch may be completed during the registration process.

2. Adjoining Lands

Registry System

☐   Update all adjoining lands using the same procedures required for main lands.

☐   Check for new registrations that might affect boundaries and use, *e.g.*, easements, restrictive covenants, plans, deposits, quit claims, and encroachment agreements.

☐   From a *Planning Act* point of view, when dealing with a part lot, check for transfers of ownership, *Planning Act* by-laws, consents, and declarations.

☐   Note all registrations found.

Land Titles System

☐   Adjoining lands searches are not required to reconcile boundaries in Land Titles.

☐   Adjoining lands searches, checking for *Planning Act* violations, are much less frequent in Land Titles because the majority of Land Titles parcels are made up of whole lots or blocks on registered plans of subdivision, which are exempt under the *Planning Act* part lot control provisions.

☐   Update all adjoining lands using the same procedures required for main lands.

Condominiums

☐   Condominium units in Land Titles do not require boundary checks.

☐   Condominium units are exempt from the part lot control provisions of the *Planning Act*.

POLARIS

☐ Update according to the procedures of the system in which the land is registered.
☐ POLARIS block maps, Teraview digital maps, and search summaries reference you to the adjoining land PINs.
☐ Land Titles Conversion Qualified lands are in Land Titles; however, conversion does not guarantee boundaries. Update boundaries as in Registry.

3. Executions

Registry System

☐ Search the vendors.
☐ Search all previous registered owners if they were not searched at the time of the original search.
☐ Search the mortgagors (purchasers) and guarantors if the purchase is being financed by way of mortgage.

Land Titles

☐ Search registered owners as they appear on the parcel register.
☐ Search chargors (purchasers) and guarantors as they will appear on the parcel register.

Condominiums

☐ Search registered owners as they appear on the parcel register.
☐ Search the condominium corporation as it appears on the condominium register.
☐ Search chargors (purchasers) and guarantors as they will appear on the parcel register.

POLARIS

☐ Search registered owners, mortgagors/chargers and guarantors as required by the registration system in which the land is located.

4. Chattel Searches: Personal Property Security Registrations

☐ Update individual specific/debtor name (first and last names, middle initial, date of birth).
☐ Update individual non-specific/debtor name (first and last names).
☐ Update business debtor name.

☐ Update vehicle identification number, if part of inventory.

5. Other Land Related Searches

☐ Update inquiries related to nature of land, recreational, farm, *etc*.
☐ Update inquiries related to agreement of purchase and sale.
☐ Update inquiries related to length of time between original search and closing.

SUBSEARCH CHECKLIST WHEN ACTING FOR A VENDOR

☐ Subsearch land being sold in order to answer requisitions.
☐ Search executions against the vendor if the vendor has a common name.
☐ Search executions against the mortgagor/chargor for vendor take-back mortgage/charge.

Table 13.1
TITLE SUBSEARCHES

Registry (paper)	Land Titles	Condominium (paper)	POLARIS Automated Title Database	POLARIS Land Titles Conversion Qualified
Main Lands	**Main Lands**	**Main Lands**	**Main Lands**	**Main Lands**
• abstract book • day book including people in line and documents not entered in day book	• parcel register • pencilled-in entries in parcel register	• unit registers • property parcel register • constitution index • common elements and general index • pencilled-in entries in parcel register • POLARIS combines the four registers into one	• Registry, Land Titles, or Land Titles Conversion Qualified rules may apply • one combined condominium register • parcel printout date forward option or as part of ELRS	• parcel printout using date forward option or as part of ELRS
Adjoining Lands	**Adjoining Lands**	**Adjoining Lands**	**Adjoining Lands**	**Adjoining Lands**
• *Planning Act* part lot control (when the land is comprised of one or more part lots) • boundaries • encroachments • easements, restrictive covenants, and access	• *Planning Act* part lot control (when the parcel is comprised of one or more part lots) • easements, restrictive covenants, and access	• condominium units are exempt under the part lot control provisions	• same as for main lands • Block and property maps and Teraview digital maps will locate parcels	• *Planning Act* part lot control (when the parcel is comprised of one or more part lots) • boundaries (conversion does not guarantee boundaries) • encroachments • easements, restrictive covenants, and access

Table 13.2

EXECUTIONS SUBSEARCH

Registry (paper)	Land Titles	Condominium (paper)	POLARIS Automated Title Database	POLARIS Land Titles Conversion Qualified
• current owners/vendors	• current owners/vendors as per parcel register	• current owners/vendors as per unit register • condominium corporation	• owners/vendors, mortgagors, guarantors as required by the registration system in which land is located	• current owners/vendors as per parcel printout
• purchasers/mortgagors/guarantors	• purchasers/mortgagors/guarantors as they will appear on parcel register	• purchasers/mortgagors/guarantors as they will appear on parcel register	• Registry, Land Titles, or Land Titles Conversion Qualified rules may apply	• purchasers/mortgagors/guarantors as they will appear on the parcel printout
• WritSearch Teraview ELRS/BAR-eX	• WritSearch Teraview ELRS/BAR-eX	• WritSearch Teraview ELRS/BAR-eX	• WritSearch or part of Teraview ELRS/BAR-eX	• WritSearch or part of Teraview ELRS/BAR-eX

CHAPTER 14

Off-Title Inquiries

MANAGING RISK AND OFF-TITLE INQUIRIES

Inadequate off-title inquiries can have catastrophic economic and human consequences. For example, a developer client who purchases property for development purposes needs to know whether the property is affected by Aboriginal title, rights or treaty claims, or environmental contaminants. An individual who unknowingly purchases property that requires environmental clean-up such as a gas station may be destroyed financially. Title insurance excludes these catastrophic risks from residential and most commercial coverages. Even in strong economic climates with available credit, lenders are unlikely to accept what may be a liability rather than an asset. Only a combination of full title searches accompanied by appropriate off-title searches and up-to-date survey information that addresses legal due diligence requirements will reveal title defects in a timely manner, provide lawyers with the ability to make requisitions, prove title, effectively tender on closing, and protect clients and themselves when a deal closes and when a deal does not close. Off-title inquiries serve many purposes. They disclose restrictions on current and future use, outstanding liens, encumbrances and claims, non-compliance with warranties and conditions in the agreement of purchase and sale, work orders, and other potential risks. Lawyers have a duty to disclose and advise on off-title risks and, when necessary, obtain specifically worded waivers from clients who do not wish to pursue off-title inquiries.

Preliminary Considerations

The lawyer's professional responsibility with respect to off-title inquiries is as follows:

1. The lawyer in consultation with the client and considering the impact of alternative or supplemental title insurance coverage, the risks inherent in the specific property, and the expectations associated with the agreement of purchase and sale, directs the nature and the extent of the title and the off-title searches.

2. The lawyer reviews and analyzes the title and off-title searches and in consultation with the client assesses the risk and decides whether to pursue additional title and off-title inquiries.

3. The lawyer reviews the results of title and off-title inquiries and how they relate to the covered risks, conditions, limitations, exclusions, exemptions, and additional coverage options of title insurance policy.

Due Diligence Standards for Off-Title Inquiries

In the Law Society of Upper Canada's *Residential Real Estate Transactions Practice Guidelines*, Guideline 2, "Due Diligence" requires the lawyer to personally review all off-title inquiries and retain search records in the file. Guideline 2 lists the following due diligence standards for off-title inquiries:

☐ The lawyer should discuss with the client and obtain instructions from the client regarding the off-title searches that may be appropriate or advisable in view of the nature of the property, the circumstances of the transaction, the terms of the agreement of purchase and sale and the consequences of not conducting those searches.

☐ Where title insurance is being used, the lawyer should be cognizant of:
- what off-title searches relevant to the client or transaction are not covered by title insurance and make appropriate searches or obtain waivers from the client; and
- the inter-related nature of the following issues: deciding not to make certain off-title searches; allowing the requisition date to pass without the results of those searches being available; the timing of receiving a title insurance binder or commitment (usually after the requisition date has passed); and the policy of the selected title insurer regarding "insure over" requests for adverse circumstances which emerge before closing notwithstanding the lack of a search.

The lawyer must consider the relationship and risks raised by the relationship between the title search, the off-title searches, and the title insurance coverage, specifically exclusions and exemptions. It is important to note that in some situations only an up-to-date survey can reveal title and off-title risks; for example, a swimming pool, costly building or addition built on a road allowance, a hydro easement, a flood plain, or an environmentally sensitive zone. If, for example, the title search reveals that a prior owner operated a dry cleaning business on the property, the lawyer will, in consultation with the client and the underwriting department of the title insurer, consider full environmental off-title searches, arrange an environmental audit, draft client waivers, draft requisitions, require warranties, seek custom title insurance coverage, and take other appropriate measures. The impact of off-title searches can be more serious than the title search itself and may determine whether the transaction closes. Decisions relating to off-title inquiries may be important deciding factors in anticipatory breach of contract, tender, subsequent claims on the title insurance policy, and subsequent litigation including breach of contract or potential negligence claims against the solicitor. Recent cases indicate that clients may choose to sue the lawyer in negligence rather than proceed with a title insurance claim (see Chapter 1).

Title Insurance and Off-Title Inquiries

Title insurance offers an alternative or a back-up supplement for some standard, lower risk residential inquiries and standard and customized commercial risks; it does not provide protection for many serious title and off-title risks. Title insurance provides much needed coverage when it is impossible to complete off-title inquiries within the requisition period or the closing period. As well, title insurance provides much-needed indemnity for the disclaimers of accuracy and liability found in most government responses to inquiries related to government regulation. Title insurance provides cost-effective protection for clients who are resistant to making inquiries because of cost, as title insurance may reduce the cost of specific off-title searches, particularly executions for past owners, corporate searches for past owners, realty taxes, utilities, surveys, common building, zoning, and work order inquiries.

Title insurance is essentially an after-the-fact indemnity. The client has access to compensation based on fair market value differentials and, when financially efficient, the title insurer may negotiate or litigate a remedy on behalf of the client. From a client's perspective, compensation is not necessarily the most appropriate remedy when dealing with a specific property. Compensation may be the preferred remedy for a mortgagee but not for a purchaser who finds himself or herself without a garage or downtown parking space, or a driveway, or access to the beach. A well-informed, conscientious purchaser benefits from knowing the extent of the property and the rights and restrictions that affect the use and enjoyment of property. Families live in homes and escape to cottages; title and off-title problems can have a profound effect on the quality of life that simply cannot be measured by money alone.

Off-title inquiries may reveal problems that would give a purchaser the right to resile from a deal, as well as the evidence needed for tender. Timely off-title inquiries may provide the evidence for proof of title and the defence for a threatened anticipatory breach. Lawyers have the opportunity to offer value-added service when advising and offering quality title, description, and off-title services.

Coverage is subject to change and varies between insurers; it also depends on whether a property is residential, multi-unit residential, or commercial. Some policies may offer or require custom underwriting. Search requirements, listed coverages, exclusions and exceptions, emerging case law which interprets policies, and adjustment process and style must all be reviewed regularly.

SAMPLE TITLE INSURANCE SEARCH REQUIREMENTS

The search requirements of title insurers provide a cost-effective alternative to completing some standard off-title inquiries. Insurers set search requirements that list which searches are not required and which searches are required. Many off-title inquiries are not addressed in either list. The required searches, coverage, exclusions, and exceptions to exclusions vary by insurer and by jurisdiction

(Ontario rules are not the same as Alberta rules), and can change periodically as a result of claims experience and emerging legal requirements and risks. Insurers tend to have separate requirements for residential, commercial, recreational, condominium, and existing owner properties. Search requirements for mortgagees may be different from purchasers, and refinancings have fewer requirements than new mortgages. Examples of search requirements as of the date of writing for residential, commercial, and existing owner policies are contained in the following figures.

Figure 14.1

STEWART TITLE — SEARCH REQUIREMENTS — ONTARIO (RESIDENTIAL)*

Residential Transaction Search Requirements – One to Six Units

Where coverage is provided, title insurance can eliminate the need for certain off-title searches. This results in significant savings to the client, which often outweighs the cost of the title insurance premium. In order to maximize the cost savings, please refer to this list when the transaction is initiated. Please note this information was compiled based on general practices in most jurisdictions. For further information please contact Stewart Title.

IMPORTANT NOTE: It is a requirement of Stewart Title that you obtain Canadian Federal or Provincial Government issued PHOTO ID for all clients, that you review and confirm the validity to the best of your ability, and that you keep a legible photocopy in your file. Due to the ease in which Citizenship Cards may be forged, if you are relying on such a card, we ask that you obtain a second piece of ID that has a name and signature. We will not insure a transaction for which Canadian Federal or Provincial Government issued PHOTO ID is not obtained. If you are unable to obtain Canadian Federal or Provincial Government issued PHOTO ID please contact a Stewart Title underwriter PRIOR to closing.

Title Search Requirements

Registry Properties: A full 40-year search is required including compliance with the Planning Act. Where applicable, the search should include a review of abutting legal descriptions to determine if there are any descriptive inconsistencies resulting in a gap or overlap of legal descriptions.

Land Titles Absolute: Not required to search behind the parcel abstract. However for documents that appear on the parcel register or for which the property is "subject to" we request that you review those documents. Abutting land searches should be done for the current owner as listed in the abstract when you are dealing with a property where the search would normally be required for ascertaining compliance with the Planning Act. **NOTE: Your search must contain deleted instruments.**

Land Titles Conversion Qualified (LTCQ): Not required to search behind the parcel abstract. However, for documents that have been carried forward and appear on the parcel register or for which the property is "subject to" we request that you review those documents. Abutting land searches should be done for the current owner as listed in the abstract when you are dealing with a property where the search would normally be required for ascertaining compliance with the Planning Act. **NOTE: Your search must contain deleted instruments.**

Refinance Transactions – either Registry or Land Titles: Only a sub-search from the last arm's length deed is required (including a review of the LTT affidavit for assumed mortgages). The sub-search may be conducted up to 10 business days prior to the registration of the mortgage without the need to conduct a further search. A verbal inquiry of the borrower must be conducted to determine if they have an interest in an abutting property. **NOTE: For Land Titles transactions your search must contain deleted instruments.**

Not Required off Title Searches

The following searches are **not required** when acting on the purchase of a residential property of up to six units:

(1) **Executions** against anyone other than the *current* vendor(s) and the purchaser(s)/mortgagor(s), if a mortgage is being insured. Similar or same name executions may be underwritten on a case-by-case basis. For both purchase and refinance transactions, the execution search may be conducted up to 10 business days prior to closing without the need to conduct a further execution search on closing.

(2) **Water, Hydro and Gas Certificates/Arrears**. Verbal confirmation is sufficient. If a verbal confirmation is not available these searches are waived. *NOTE: Coverage is provided to the extent the arrears form a lien.*

(3) **Municipal Realty Tax Certificate**. Verbal confirmation, a receipted tax bill or reference in a vendor's Statutory Declaration is sufficient, however, if none of the foregoing can be obtained, we will waive these requirements.

(4) **Corporate Profile/Corporate Status Reports**.

(5) **Subdivision and Development Agreement Compliance**.

(6) **Building and Zoning Compliance** – No search is required for single-family residential dwellings. No search is required for refinance transactions. A building and zoning search is required for transactions for 2 to 6 residential units, where an owner policy is being obtained and coverage for building and zoning matters is requested. Additionally, if your property is located in a municipality where two unit properties must be registered, you must determine if your units are properly registered. For transactions for 2 to 6 residential units where only a lender policy is being obtained, or where the owner does not want coverage for building and zoning matters (contact an underwriter for an exception clause for the owner), the search is not required.

(7) **Unregistered Hydro Easements**, unless the facts known to you suggest the existence of an easement, for example by indication on a survey or by the existence of hydro transmission towers or boxes visible on the property.

(8) **Fire Department Work Orders**. No search is required for single-family residential dwellings. No search is required for refinance transactions. This search is required for transactions of 2 to 6 residential units (including properties where the second unit is a boathouse with living accommodation, where an owner policy is being obtained and coverage for the owner is requested. For transactions of 2 to 6 residential units where only a lender policy is being obtained, or where the owner does not

---

*   © Stewart Title 2010. Reproduced with permission.

Figure 14.1 (cont'd)

want coverage for fire department work orders (contact an underwriter for an exception clause for the owner), the search is not required.

(9) **Septic File Searches.** Our Septic Endorsement is designed to protect the insured regarding the status of the septic system to the extent that a lawyer could do so if the usual septic file search was performed and reviewed. What should be made clear is that neither the policy nor a solicitor's opinion will guaranty that the system is working (it is not a warranty of fitness or quality). Similarly, the coverage does not include protection against defects that would be revealed by a current inspection of the system. It is also worth recognizing that the septic inquiry may provide information which may nonetheless be useful or important to the client. Examples of such issues would include the age of the system or the location of the system on the property. Thus, notwithstanding the comprehensiveness of the Septic Endorsement, it may still be prudent and courteous practice to advise clients of the additional option of ordering a septic inquiry.

(10) **Conservation Authority**, unless you are aware or strongly suspect that the property is subject to conservation authority jurisdiction.

(11) **Parkway Belt Planning and Development Act** for properties in the Niagara Escarpment, unless you are aware or strongly suspect that the property is subject to Parkway Belt Planning or Development Act jurisdiction (Ontario Only).

(12) **Refinance Transactions**: On residential refinancing situations, an Estoppel Certificate/Status Certificate is not required for Condominium transactions. The execution search and sub-search of title may be conducted up to 10 business days prior to the registration of the mortgage without the need to conduct a further execution search or sub-search. For tax status, verbal confirmation, a receipted tax bill or reference in a Statutory Declaration from the Borrower is sufficient, however, if none of the foregoing can be obtained, we will waive these requirements. No building and zoning search is required.

Required Off Title Searches

The following searches **are required** as responses received may reflect issues not covered under the policies:

(1) **Estoppel Certificate/Status Certificate** for Condominiums, *except* for residential refinance transactions. A Status Certificate dated up to 30 days prior to closing is satisfactory and no update is required. For Status Certificates dated 31 – 60 days before closing, an attempt must be made to obtain a verbal update. If a verbal update is not available, we will waive this requirement. For Status Certificates dated 61 - 90 days before closing, a verbal update is required. If a verbal update is not provided, a new Status Certificate should be obtained. For Status Certificates dated greater than 90 days before closing, a new Status Certificate is required.

(2) **Building and Zoning Compliance** – A building and zoning search is required for transactions of 2 to 6 residential units (including properties where the second unit is a boathouse with living accommodation), where an owner policy is being obtained and coverage for building and zoning matters is requested. Additionally, if your property is located in a municipality where two unit properties must be registered, you must determine if your units are properly registered. For transactions of 2 to 6 residential units where only a lender policy is being obtained, or where the owner does not want coverage for building and zoning matters (contact an underwriter for an exception clause for the owner), these searches are not required. No search is required for single-family residential dwellings. No search is required for refinance transactions.

(3) **Fire Department Work Orders.** This search is required for transactions of 2 to 6 residential units, where an owner policy is being obtained and coverage for the owner is requested. For transactions of 2 to 6 residential units where only a lender policy is being obtained, or where the owner does not want coverage for fire department work orders (contact an underwriter for an exception clause for the owner), the search is not required. No search is required for single-family residential dwellings. No search is required for refinance transactions.

(4) **Mining Land Tax Search** with the Ministry of Northern Development & Mines (Ontario) – for applicable properties only.

Additional Considerations Falling outside the Scope of Stewart Title Coverage

(1) **Environmental Clearance** – Any concerns about soil or contamination or toxic pollutants on the property should be addressed by obtaining an environmental audit. Such certification is not usually included in a traditional solicitor's opinion.

(2) **Residential Tenancies Act, 2006 (Ontario)** – Landlord liability for illegal rent increases or other claims arising from residential tenancy legislation are not matters covered by title insurance. Where tenanted properties are concerned, you may want to seek the usual comforts in the form of landlord warranties, tenant acknowledgments and/or a search with the local rent authority.

(3) **Fire Retrofit Issues** – In the cases of tenanted and multi-unit properties, while title insurance does cover the usual work orders and zoning related matters, it does not cover fire retrofit issues such as the sufficiency of smoke alarms or fire barriers, unless they form work orders or are zoning deficiencies which would have been revealed by a regular building and zoning search conducted prior to closing. This is consistent with the principle that title insurance is not a warranty regarding quality or fitness for purpose, but rather a protection regarding matters which can be disclosed by a local authority search.

(4) **Water Potability and Quantity** – If the property is serviced by a well, a solicitor should seek the usual protections to ensure marketability and safety, including confirmation of a water potability certificate (preferably more than one) and a well driller's certificate (if available).

(5) **PPSA Re: Chattels** – Title insurance covers land, not chattels. When significant chattels are included in a purchase or when a transaction involves the likes of a mobile home, consideration should be given to PPSA search and registration.

(6) **Underground Fuel Oil Tanks** – In the event there is an underground fuel oil tank on the property, a solicitor should contact the Technical Safety and Standards Association to determine the tank's registration status for fuel delivery purposes and its compliance with removal, upgrading, and inspection requirements.

(7) **Ministry of Natural Resources Boathouse Leases (Ontario)** - The Ministry of Natural Resources may require that certain boathouses located on Crown Land, including the beds of most waters, must enter into a lease with the Crown and pay rent in order for the boathouse to remain.

Figure 14.2

STEWART TITLE — EXISTING HOMEOWNER POLICY
SEARCH REQUIREMENTS (RESIDENTIAL)*

**Search Requirements
Existing Homeowner Policy**

In order to obtain a policy, Stewart Title requires the completion of a sub-search of title from the date of acquisition of title by the existing owner to the current date of order. Please review the land transfer tax affidavit for a determination of assumed mortgages.

In the event that the existing owner obtained title in a non-arm's length transaction, a full title search must be completed unless you obtain evidence in the form of a legal opinion/reporting letter to the existing owner that confirms a full title search was conducted at the time they obtained title.

No execution search is needed for properties in the Land Titles system. For properties in the Registry system, an execution search for the vendor to the existing owner is required.

If a survey is available, please request a copy from the homeowner and review for obvious defects such as encroachments.

No other searches are required for the issuance of a policy for a single-family residence. For properties of 2-6 units, a building and zoning search should be completed. If the homeowner does not wish to complete this search, contact Stewart Title for an exception clause that will be added to the policy.

Search Information to Be Disclosed to Stewart Title:
In the event that your search determines a title or other defect please consult with a Stewart Title underwriter prior to insuring the transaction. Due to the nature of this policy, known defects will be excepted from the policy. No affirmative underwriting will be given.

In particular, should your search reveal that a mortgage registered at the time of purchase has been discharged, we require that you confirm with the homeowner that this mortgage has indeed been paid.

All registered mortgages must be reported to Stewart Title and will be listed as exceptions to the policy.

Nov 06 – ON

Figure 14.3

STEWART TITLE — SEARCH REQUIREMENTS — ONTARIO (COMMERCIAL)*

Commercial Search Requirements

IMPORTANT NOTE: In addition to your normal corporate due diligence, it is a requirement of Stewart Title that you obtain Canadian/Provincial Government issued PHOTO ID for all private individuals and corporate signing officers for private corporations, that you review and confirm the validity to the best of your ability, and that you keep a legible photocopy in your file. We will not insure a transaction for which acceptable PHOTO ID is not obtained. If you are unable to obtain acceptable PHOTO ID please contact a Stewart Title underwriter PRIOR to closing.

It is imperative that you order your title insurance policy *prior* to the closing date. This ensures all underwriting matters can be considered in the coverage provided for the Insured. Please inform Stewart Title immediately if your deal has been delayed over 30 days.

Where coverage is provided, title insurance can eliminate the need for certain off-title searches. This results in significant savings to the client, which often outweighs the cost of the title insurance premium. In order to maximize the cost savings, please refer to this list when the transaction is initiated. Please note that this information was compiled based on general practices in most jurisdictions. For further information please contact Stewart Title.

Title Search Requirements

Purchase Transactions:

Registry Properties: A full 40-year search is required including compliance with the *Planning Act*.

Land Titles Absolute and Land Titles Conversion Qualified ("LTCQ"): You are not required to search behind the parcel abstract. However for documents that appear on the parcel register or for which the property is "subject to" we request that you review those documents and provide details to Stewart Title. For commercial transactions up to $5,000,000, abutting land searches should be done for the current owner as listed in the abstract when you are dealing with a property where the search would normally be required for ascertaining compliance with the *Planning Act*. A full abutting land search is required for commercial transactions exceeding $5,000,000. **NOTE: Your search must contain deleted instruments.**

Refinances:

Only a Sub-search from the last arm's length deed is required for commercial refinances under $10,000,000. No abutting land searches are required, provided that you make a verbal inquiry of the borrower to determine if they have an interest in an abutting property. (A full search of title is required for commercial refinances over $10,000,000, including a full abutting land search) **NOTE: For Land Titles, your search must contain deleted instruments.**

NOTE: Where a prior opinion is available, the above search requirements may be altered with the approval of a Stewart Title Underwriter. Please contact any of our Underwriters to discuss.

Royal Bank Plaza, North Tower • 200 Bay Street, Suite 2200 • Toronto, ON M5J 2J2
Tel.: (416) 307-3300 • 1-888-667-5151 • Fax.: (416) 307-3305

Figure 14.3 (cont'd)

Survey Requirements

<u>FOR OWNER</u>

Commercial Transactions Under $12,000,000: An up-to-date survey is *not* required to obtain a survey endorsement

Commercial Transactions Over $12,000,000: An up-to-date survey is required to obtain a survey endorsement. Please note, however, that survey coverage may be negotiated for commercial transactions over $12,000,000 in the event that an old survey is available and/or the vendor(s)/mortgagor(s) is willing to provide a Statutory Declaration confirming that there have been no improvements to the subject property, up to the Policy Date.

<u>FOR LENDER</u>

For all Commercial Transactions: An up-to-date survey is *not* required to obtain a survey endorsement.

Off Title Searches

Notes: **i)** **"LTV" = Loan to Value Ratio**

      ii) Where a search is waived for lenders between $10 million and $50 million as set out below a suitable statutory declaration from the vendor (purchase mortgage transaction) or borrower (refinance) must be obtained. Please contact Stewart Title to obtain a sample declaration.

(1)   **Execution Searches** are required against the current vendor(s) and if a mortgage is being insured, against the purchaser(s)/mortgagor(s). Please note that similar name executions may be underwritten on a case-by-case basis. Execution searches are not required against any other parties.

(2)   **Public Utility Certificates/Arrears.**
    For Owner: For transactions under $10,000,000, verbal confirmation, a receipted utility bill or reference in a vendor's Statutory Declaration is sufficient; however, if any of the foregoing cannot be obtained we will require the certificate. Public Utility Certificates are required on transactions over $10,000,000.
    For Lender: Verbal confirmation, a receipted utility bill or reference in a vendor's/mortgagor's Statutory Declaration is sufficient regardless of the mortgage amount; however, if any of the foregoing cannot be obtained we will require the certificate.
    NOTE: Coverage is provided to the extent the arrears form a lien.

(3)   **Municipal Realty Tax Certificate.**
    For Owner: For transactions under $10,000,000, verbal confirmation, a receipted tax bill or reference in a vendor's Statutory Declaration is sufficient; however, if any of the foregoing cannot be obtained we will require the certificate. Tax Certificates are required on transactions over $10,000,000.
    For Lender: Verbal confirmation, a receipted tax bill or reference in a vendor's/mortgagor's Statutory Declaration is sufficient regardless of the mortgage amount; however, if any of the foregoing cannot be obtained we will require the certificate.

(4)   **Corporate Profile Report or Certificate of Status** is required against the vendor(s), and the purchaser(s)/mortgagor(s). They are not required against prior corporate owners.

Royal Bank Plaza, North Tower • 200 Bay Street, Suite 2200 • Toronto, ON M5J 2J2
Tel.: (416) 307-3300 • 1-888-667-5151 • Fax.: (416) 307-3305

Figure 14.3 (cont'd)

(5) **Zoning Compliance.**

For Owner: If the purchase price is under $10,000,000 no report is necessary in order to obtain a zoning endorsement.

For Lender: If the loan amount is under $10,000,000 no report is necessary in order to obtain a zoning endorsement. If the loan amount is between $10,000,000 and $50,000,000 no report is necessary in order to obtain a zoning endorsement provided that we receive confirmation that the LTV is not greater than 75%. With the approval of a Stewart Title Underwriter, the search may be waived for loans over $50,000,000. Please contact any of our Underwriters to discuss.

NOTE: The policy will insure that the Property will be permitted to continue its present use. If the land is vacant or if a change of use is contemplated, the client or solicitor should confirm that zoning corresponds with future plans for development/improvements.

(6) **Municipal Work Orders.**

For Owner: If the purchase price is under $2,000,000 no report is necessary in order to obtain our municipal building department work order coverage.

For Lender: If the loan amount is under $10,000,000 no report is necessary in order to obtain our municipal work order coverage. If the loan amount is between $10,000,000 and $50,000,000 no report is necessary in order to obtain our municipal work order coverage provided that we receive confirmation that the LTV is not greater than 75%.

(7) **Unregistered Hydro Easements.**

For Owner: If the purchase price is under $10,000,000 no search is required unless the property is vacant. Where the property is vacant, this search is required prior to the issuance of an owner's policy regardless of the policy amount. This search is required for purchase prices over $10,000,000.

For Lender: If the loan amount is under $10,000,000, no search is required. If the loan amount is between $10,000,000 and $50,000,000 no search is required provided that we receive confirmation that the LTV is not greater than 75%. For loans over $50,000,000, this search is required.

(8) **Estoppel Certificates/Status Certificates** this search is required for all condominium transactions except for condominium refinances under $2,000,000.

(9) **Orders Under *The Residential Tenancies Act, 2006* (Ontario) Concerning Unlawful Rents** searches are not required for lender policies under $10,000,000. If the loan amount is between $10,000,000 and $50,000,000 no search is required provided that we receive confirmation that the LTV is not greater than 75%. For all owner policies and for lender policies over $50,000,000 no coverage is provided for these matters.

(10) **Subdivision and Development Agreement Compliance**

For Owner: This search is not required for owner policies under $10,000,000 *unless the property is currently under construction*, in which case this search should be completed regardless of the policy amount. For all transactions over $10,000,000, this search is required.

For Lender: This search is not required for lender policies under $10,000,000. If the loan amount is between $10,000,000 and $50,000,000 no search is required provided that we receive confirmation that the LTV is not greater than 75%. For loans over $50,000,000, this search is required.

(11) **Fire Department Compliance** searches are not required for lender policies under $10,000,000. If the loan amount is between $10,000,000 and $50,000,000 no search is required provided that we receive confirmation that the LTV is not greater than 75%. For all owner policies and for lender policies over $50,000,000, no coverage is provided for this matter.

(12) **Electrical Safety Authority** file searches for work orders are not required for lender policies under $10,000,000. If the loan amount is between $10,000,000 and $50,000,000 no search is required

Royal Bank Plaza, North Tower • 200 Bay Street, Suite 2200 • Toronto, ON M5J 2J2
Tel.: (416) 307-3300 • 1-888-667-5151 • Fax.: (416) 307-3305

Figure 14.3 (cont'd)

provided that we receive confirmation that the LTV is not greater than 75%. For loans over $50,000,000, this search is required. For all owner policies no coverage is provided for this matter.

(13) **Technical Standards and Safety Authority** file searches for work orders are not required for lender policies under $10,000,000. If the loan amount is between $10,000,000 and $50,000,000 no search is required provided that we receive confirmation that the LTV is not greater than 75%. For loans over $50,000,000, this search is required. For all owner policies no coverage is provided for this matter.

Items Not Covered By Commercial Policies

Please Note- **Existing Owner and Existing Lender Policies** *are* **not available** *for Commercial Properties*

The following searches may reveal title or other defects which are of relevance to your client and are NOT covered by commercial title insurance policies:

(1) Conservation Authority.
(2) Environmental Clearance.
(3) Residential Tenancies Act, 2006 (Ontario) (except as provided in No. 9 above).
(4) Water Potability and Quantity.
(5) Parkway Belt Planning and Development Act for properties in Niagara Escarpment.
(6) PPSA Re: Chattels.
(7) Estoppel Certificate/Status Certificate for Condominium (except as provided in No. 8 above).
(8) Fire Department Compliance (except as provided in No. 11 above).
(9) Bank Act Issues.
(10) Bankruptcy Act.
(11) Elevator Issues.
(12) Public Health Department Issues.
(13) Septic System.
(14) Electrical Safety Authority (except as provided in No. 12 above).
(15) Technical Standards and Safety Authority (except as provided in No. 13 above).

NOTE: Stewart Title Commercial Policies do not provide coverage for the foregoing matters. This list is for guidance only and is not intended to be an exhaustive list of searches that Solicitors should consider. Solicitors should determine if any of the above or other searches are relevant to the subject transaction and if so, which of the above or other searches need to be conducted to adequately protect their client's interests. Please review the actual policy documents for full particulars of coverage.

Royal Bank Plaza, North Tower • 200 Bay Street, Suite 2200 • Toronto, ON M5J 2J2
Tel.: (416) 307-3300 • 1-888-667-5151 • Fax.: (416) 307-3305

Figure 14.4

TitlePLUS SEARCH REQUIREMENTS[*]

TitlePLUS® purchase policies (up to $2 million) are available for these types of properties[2]:
- new houses and condominiums;
- resale houses and condominiums;
- secondary homes and cottages;
- residential rental (up to 4 units);
- rural;
- farms[3];
- leaseholds[3]; and
- vacant land[4] intended for residential purposes.

Cost savings and peace of mind for you and your clients:
- a TitlePLUS purchase policy = title insurance PLUS legal services coverage[5];
- eliminates the need for up-to-date surveys on most properties: A saving of $600 or more; and
- reduces disbursement costs on many closings by eliminating certain searches[6].

Survey coverage will be provided for all properties in Land Titles (Absolute, Conversion Qualified or Plus); for properties in Registry, survey coverage will be provided when:
- the property is the whole of a lot on a registered plan of subdivision (see below for definition); or
- there is an existing survey which has been reviewed by the purchaser for accuracy or the vendor is providing a statutory declaration commenting on its accuracy; or
- declarations of possession for a 10-year period are available; or
- a surveyor's inspection report is prepared by an Ontario Land Surveyor.

For TitlePLUS purposes, a "whole of a lot on a registered plan of subdivision" includes a property:
- consisting of two or more whole lots on a registered plan of subdivision; or
- consisting of part of a lot on a registered plan of subdivision, where there was a part-lot control exemption by-law registered to allow the initial conveyances in the subdivision; or
- which was the subject of a consent proceeding for severance purposes (either as the parcel to be conveyed or the remaining parcel), provided that the severance occurred in accordance with an up-to-date Reference Plan and any necessary conditions attached to the approval were satisfied; or
- which was the whole of a lot on a registered plan prior to an expropriation, road widening or road closing, resulting in the removal or addition of a part lot.

TitlePLUS policies are also available for the following:
- mortgage-only;
- current owners (OwnerEXPRESS®); and
- new homes enrolled in the TitlePLUS New Home Program.

For information on any of our policy types, visit titleplus.ca or call the TitlePLUS Customer Service Centre.

titleplus.ca   titleplus.lawyerdonedeal.com   1-800-410-1013

[1] The TitlePLUS policy is underwritten by Lawyers' Professional Indemnity Company (LawPRO). Contact LawPRO for brokers in Manitoba, Alberta and Québec.
[2] Please refer to the policy for full details, including actual terms and conditions. Different search requirements apply to transactions over $1 million, please call us for details.

[3] Please call the TitlePLUS Customer Service Centre for assistance with these types of properties.
[4] Some restrictions may apply.
[5] Excluding OwnerEXPRESS policies and Québec policies.
[6] See over for Summary of Searches.

© 2009 Lawyers' Professional Indemnity Company
® Registered trademark of Lawyers' Professional Indemnity Company

Printed on recycled paper. This product can be recycled.

Figure 14.4 (cont'd)

Title✔PLUS Summary of Searches for Residential Purchase Transactions

TYPE OF SEARCH	WHERE REQUIRED	COMMENTS
TITLE SEARCH		
Subject Property	Always	Include deleted instruments in automated title search. Note date of last transfer to insert in TitlePLUS application. If last transfer within past 2 years, note whether transfer at arm's length and if so, insert date and consideration shown in TitlePLUS application. If mortgage discharge registered within last 6 months, indicate in TitlePLUS application.
Servient Tenement re: Easement (if any)	Always	If Registry, confirm that registered title of servient property discloses existence of easement throughout 40 year period or since creation (whichever is shorter). If Land Titles, confirm easement in description for servient property.
Abutting Properties	Sometimes	Where necessary to ascertain subdivision control compliance.
EXECUTION SEARCHES		
Vendor	Always	
Prior Owners	Never	
Condominium Corporation	Never	
Purchaser + Guarantor of Mortgage (if any)	Sometimes	If granting mortgage (other than vendor take-back). Search against guarantor not required if expressly waived by lender.
OFF-TITLE SEARCHES		
Realty Tax and Local Improvements	Always	Where provided, verbal responses or printouts of the municipality's tax records for the property are acceptable; where municipality will **not** provide verbal responses or printouts, any of the following are acceptable: (a) receipted tax bill; (b) confirmation that the prior lender has been paying the taxes; or (c) an unqualified statutory declaration from the vendor that all prior years' taxes have been paid, charges for local improvements (if any) are paid up-to-date and the status for the current year is accurately set out in the Statement of Adjustments; PLUS an undertaking to readjust from the vendor. Where realty taxes for a new house or condo have not yet been separately assessed, you may obtain on closing the builder's undertaking to readjust. For resale of recently constructed houses and condominiums, see titleplus.lawyerdonedeal.com for instructions.
Personal Property Security Act	Never	
Hydro and Gas Arrears	Never	
Water and Sewage Arrears	Sometimes	Need not be done if: (a) included in common expenses for condo; (b) purchaser already in possession and previously paying; (c) in area where water supplier (public or private) has published policy of not pursuing purchaser for arrears; or (d) new home and receiving undertaking to readjust/pay any amounts owing from vendor. The following inquiries are acceptable: (a) verbal responses from suppliers; (b) the most recent bill if it shows that previous bills were paid; or (c) an unqualified Statutory Declaration by the vendor that all such charges have been paid to date, and that the status of payments is accurately set out in the Statement of Adjustments.
Arrears of Charges for Equipment Purchased/Rented from Utility Supplier	Sometimes	Need only be done where: (a) notice of the utility supplier's interest is registered on title; or (b) lawyer or client knows there is equipment which was purchased from utility supplier and is not fully paid for, or is rented.
Technical Standards and Safety Authority (TSSA) (re: registration of underground oil tanks)	Sometimes	Where property heated by oil from an underground oil tank or where the lawyer is otherwise aware that there is an underground oil tank on the property. A verbal response is sufficient.
Zoning	Sometimes	Where: (a) you have reason to believe that year-round occupancy may not be permitted; or (b) where multi-unit property.
Building Department Work Orders	Sometimes	Need not be done where: (a) new home; (b) condo; (c) whole of a lot on a registered plan (see over for definition); (d) vendor giving unqualified warranty to survive closing that there are no work orders; or (e) home inspection done and a copy given to lawyer. Where provided, verbal responses are acceptable.
Electrical Work Orders and Compliance, and Fire Dept. Work Orders and Compliance including Retrofit	Sometimes	Where multi-unit property.
Health Department/Certificate of Approval/Use Permit/Municipal Approval	Sometimes	Where private septic system and Certificate of Approval and Use Permit or municipal approval is not available from vendor. No specific search for work orders on septic system is required, but any information received must be entered in application.
Potability Certificate	Sometimes	Where private water system – client may obtain and deliver.
Unregistered Hydro Easements, Conservation Authority, Controlled/Highway Access	Sometimes	Never required for whole of a lot on a registered plan (see over for definition) or condo; otherwise, required where risk factors apply.
Waterfront Inquiries	Sometimes	Where property fronts on lake or river (e.g., shoreline road allowance, waterbed issues, accretion, etc.).
TARION, Occupancy Approval	Sometimes	Where new home.
Rent Control	Sometimes	Where purchaser wants opinion on legality of rents re: tenancies being assumed.
SEARCHES ARISING FROM TITLE SEARCH		
Corporate Escheats/Limited Partnership	Never	
Subdivision/Development Compliance (as defined)	Never	A "Subdivision/Development Agreement" for TitlePLUS purposes is defined as follows: (a) agreement with a government, government-related body/agency (e.g., school board), or a utility company; (b) imposes the primary obligation on the developer; and (c) requires the developer to post security. Call us or visit titleplus.lawyerdonedeal.com for additional details.
Condo Status Certificate	Sometimes	Where condo or "POTL" with interest in common element condo, obtain and review a current Status Certificate dated no earlier than 60 days prior to closing. If between 60 and 120 days have passed since the date of the Status Certificate, call for instructions.
Restrictive Covenants Compliance	Sometimes	Where have grounds to believe there is non-compliance based on discussion with purchaser and instead of listing alleged non-compliance on Schedule "A", want to attempt to establish that there is in fact compliance.
Reciprocal/Cost-Sharing Agreement	Sometimes	No inquiry necessary where agreement between condominiums; otherwise, must obtain status letter.

Ontario – TPLA79-001 (10/09)

THE NATURE OF OFF-TITLE INQUIRIES

There is a multitude of potential off-title, land-related inquiries which may be completed on behalf of a purchaser, lender, or any other interested person. A law clerk/conveyancer will check for liens, work orders, restrictions on use, compliance or non-compliance with federal, provincial, and municipal (by-laws) regulations, and for information on land and government regulation and programs in general. Client instructions and proposed use, the agreement of purchase and sale, search costs, time restraints, and the search requirements of title insurers when issuing policies all affect the lawyer's decision as to when and whether to conduct off-title inquiries. The type of land involved, for example, urban, residential, commercial, industrial, farm, recreational, vacant, wooded, fronting on water, in a natural state, in an area of mining or oil and gas activity, wetlands, *etc.* also influences the lawyer's decision as to which off-title inquiries are appropriate. Standard searches are done differently from municipality to municipality, ministry to ministry, and government (provincial) to government (federal). Some inquiries are not standard or established searches but instead involve formal research and community consultation such as with Aboriginal claims. The services of a specialist or consultation with a lawyer familiar with the area may be advisable. The question remains: What does a specific purchaser need or want to know, wish to pay for, accept as a risk, or be willing to release in waivers when purchasing a particular property? Purchasers do not like surprises even when they accepted the risk. They tend to see things differently when discussing title in the abstract and focused on costs prior to closing compared to encountering a title problem after closing. Memory is selective and it is all too easy to blame the lawyer. Although title insurance provides much needed though limited protection, lawyers increasingly manage the consistently, identified high-risk activity of title and off-title searching by practising defensive conveyancing. Tightly worded waivers, careful personal communication with clients, and direct supervision of non-lawyer employees protect both clients and lawyers.

CATEGORIES OF AND SELECTION FACTORS FOR OFF-TITLE SEARCHES

Off-title inquiries can be categorized and selected using the following criteria:

- By jurisdiction (often overlapping) or level of government
  - federal searches
  - provincial searches
  - municipal searches
- By type of land
  - urban
  - commercial/industrial
  - recreational
  - rental
  - farm

- o riparian/shoreline/water access
- o mining lands, fish habitat, heritage-designated, environmentally designated
- By location (for example, close to a park, airport, railway, highway, military installation, conservation area, landfill, mining operation (consider the acid drainage impact and particulate depositions))
- By topic (for example docks and boathouses, oil tanks and elevators, *etc.*)
- By type of ownership such as condominium, interval ownership, life lease
- By type of owner such as corporation, partnership, estate, bankruptcy trustee, church, charity
- By availability of up-to-date survey evidence (some off-title searches can only be done when an up-to-date-survey is available)
- By choice of title insurer

METHODS FOR COMPLETING OFF-TITLE INQUIRIES

Off-title inquiries are completed by: letter, personal attendance, phone inquiry and notation on the file (taxes with title insurance coverage), or online search. Increasingly, as with title searching, today most off-title searching is completed online. Some off-title inquiries are sophisticated and may require research by specialists as with Aboriginal rights, railway rights of way, and mining claims. Off-title inquiries may require surveys, inspections, environmental audits, soil or water testing, engineering reports, or consultation with Ministry staff or Band councils. Even with title insurance as a back-up indemnity, off-title searches can carry high levels of risk and be difficult to complete. Off-title searches can be very time consuming and search responses even when they arrive before the requisition or the closing date usually carry a disclaimer as to accuracy and reliability of the response.

COMMON OFF-TITLE INQUIRIES

There is a multitude of potential off-title searches, inquiries, and specialized research. Some are straightforward and done online, and some are by letter, whereas others may require attendance in person, private or government inspections, or an expert researcher in a field such as Aboriginal treaty rights, an archeologist, railway history, or environmental assessment and Brownfields remediation. This chapter addresses the more common kinds of inquiry and is not exhaustive. Consultation with lawyers or government officials in a particular locality or seeking the services of other experts such as in planning may be appropriate.

EXECUTION SEARCHES (WRIT SEARCHES)

Execution searching is done differently depending on whether the property is in Land Titles, Registry, or the Province of Ontario Land Registration Information

System (POLARIS). Title insurance search requirements are different from legal search requirements. Chapter 12 deals in detail with execution searching in all the land registration variations. As well, each chapter on a specific registration system or ownership variation (for example, condominiums) has a section on execution searching, law, and how to remove executions. Although execution searching is technically an off-title inquiry in an independent record system, it is routinely done as part of the title search.

CORPORATE STATUS (EXISTENCE) SEARCHES (CORPORATE ESCHEAT)

The legal requirements for corporate status searches vary depending on the nature of the title and the relevant land registration system. Corporate search requirements and methods including online search providers are addressed under separate heading in the individual search chapters for the specific registration system or ownership variation, be it Registry, Parcelized Day Forward Registry, Land Titles Absolute, Land Titles Conversion Qualified, Land Titles Absolute Plus, or condominiums. Appendix 5 contains contact information for completing corporate status/escheat searches.

When a corporation ceases to exist or dissolves while still owning land, the land escheats or forfeits to the Crown, usually in the right of the Province. As a result, it is necessary to check the status of companies in the chain of title in order to confirm current ownership and the ability of a vendor to transfer or mortgage land to subsequent purchasers or mortgagees. Section 244(3) of the *Business Corporations Act*, R.S.O. 1990, c. B.16 states that a forfeiture of land that occurred more than 20 years before the transfer to the purchaser is registered is no longer effective against a purchaser or mortgagor for value. The *Canada Business Corporations Act*, R.S.C. 1985, c. C-44 also provides for corporate escheat or forfeiture in the right of Canada (s. 228(1)); however, unfortunately, it does not create a time limitation on forfeiture. As a result, in theory, it is necessary to search back to the Crown patent for federal corporate owners unless specific legislation reduces the search requirement.

The *Registry Act*, R.S.O. 1990, c. R.20 has an exception for Crown rights outside the 40-year search and notice periods (s. 113(5)(a)); therefore, in theory, it is necessary to search for corporate owners back to the Crown patent in order to check for federal companies. The risk is low and most conveyancers only check throughout the forty-year period. In POLARIS, Parcelized Day Forward Registry, Non-Converts, and Registry 40-Year Loads are subject to Registry requirements.

The *Land Titles Act*, R.S.O. 1990, c. L.5 also has an exception for Crown rights (s. 44(1)(7)) and as a result, in theory, it is necessary to search for corporate owners back to the Crown patent in order to check for federal companies. From a search point of view, this legal requirement for Land Titles Absolute parcels (in paper format or in POLARIS) is impractical and time-consuming. As a result, most conveyancers check only the current and easily available parcel registers for corporate owners.

Land Titles Conversion Qualified titles (LTCQ) and Land Titles Absolute Plus (LT PLUS) titles are subject to different legal requirements. In an LTCQ, new qualifiers on title state that corporate searches need only go back to the date of conversions. In an LT PLUS title, it is necessary to check the exact wording of the qualifiers on the LT PLUS parcel register. Usually, corporate searches need only go back to the date of registration of the upgrade from the LTCQ to the new absolute title. Some of the early LT PLUS titles did not contain a qualifier that forgave corporate forfeitures prior to upgrade to an absolute title and as a result it is necessary on these parcels to search back to the date of conversion on the parent LTCQ parcel.

Title insurance provides a useful solution to the complexity and legal ambiguity, as well as the administrative difficulty of meeting legal corporate status search requirements. Title insurance provides alternative coverage for the risk of corporate escheat. Title insurance corporate search requirements and coverage are different from legal search requirements. Generally, title insurers do not require corporate profile reports or certificates of status for residential transactions. For commercial transactions, insurers do not require corporate searches for prior corporate owners; however, they do require corporate searches for a corporate vendor or a corporate purchaser/mortgagor.

ABORIGINAL TITLE, RIGHTS, OR TREATY CLAIMS, AND RESERVE LANDS

The *Land Titles Act* and the *Registry Act* do not recognize Aboriginal title or rights claims to be a registerable interest. A title search will not reveal an Aboriginal claim; off-title searches are necessary. Aboriginal land claims are a specific exclusion under standard title insurance policies, although limited, specific coverage may be negotiated on a case-by-case basis for commercial transactions. It is extremely difficult to search for and identity potential Aboriginal claims. Lawyers need to search existing federal and provincial websites for known outstanding claims. In addition, lawyers must determine which Aboriginal group or overlapping groups may have an interest in a particular property. As with environmental risks and searches, available public information in no way guarantees the absence of current or future, potentially economically devastating claims. Today, dealings and the issuance of permits that affect Crown lands will often trigger potential claims issues as well as a duty to give notice of intended use, consult, mitigate, accommodate, and or compensate. Indian and Northern Affairs Canada's (INAC) Public Information Status Report, which is available online, contains a list of current claims, by Province and by date, as well as a summary of the claim and the status of the claim. In addition, municipal, township, or Ministry of Natural Resources offices now usually display land claims on official plan and zoning maps. Chapter 2 and Appendix 5 contain a list of available Aboriginal claims and treaty search resources. The recent Indian and

Northern Affairs Geographic Portal is the best starting point. Note that government websites may not be current.

There is no substitute for personal consultation with the appropriate local Band assuming the client's written authorization. It is necessary to obtain an archeological assessment early in the process, particularly when dealing with an ossuary or when there is uncertainty about the identification of the Aboriginal evidence.

The Reserve Land Register accessed through INAC contains records of reserve lands, certificates of possession, certificates of occupation, and Ministry permits for use by non-Band members.

As with Crown patents, lawyers will assess the risk, advise clients, conduct searches, obtain waivers, and make disclaimers in reports that the property may be subject to claims. Off-title inquiries for Aboriginal claims may include consultations with bands and Aboriginal associations. It is important to remember that Aboriginal claims may affect urban areas; for example, Sarnia, Caledonia, and the Haldimand Tract. Existing legislation such as the *Cemeteries Act (Revised)*, R.S.O. 1990, c. C.4, the *Ontario Heritage Act*, R.S.O. 1990, c. O.18, the *Environmental Protection Act*, R.S.O. 1990, c. E.19 as well as parks legislation contain Aboriginal rights development reviews. In addition, s. 35(1) of the *Constitution Act, 1867* (U.K.), 30 & 31 Vict., c. 3, reprinted in R.S.C. 1985, App. II, No. 5 recognizes that Aboriginal rights may override existing legislation and, in theory, possibly the Crown patent.

The risk is serious and title insurance is not routinely an available alternative; it is possible to negotiate custom coverage in specific commercial circumstances. Aboriginal title and rights claims and treaty claims will continue to be an increasingly important and risky area of off-title inquiries. Lawyers will increasingly take a proactive approach to identifying risks of Aboriginal claims and participate in consultation, negotiation, and accommodation with affected First Nations and the government prior to purchase, particularly when land is being purchased or mortgaged for development purposes.

CANADA NATIONAL PARKS

The Parks Canada Agency (PCA) under the *Canada National Parks Act*, S.C. 2000, c. 32 administers land use planning and development in Canadian Parks. It also administers leases, renewal of leases, restrictions on leasing, and heritage preservation activities.

CROWN PATENTS

The effect of Crown patents on land ownership and searching Crown patents is dealt with in Chapters 1 and 9. It is also addressed in the individual search chapters.

Copies of Crown patents are available at the Ministry of Natural Resources' Peterborough office. Appendix 5 contains contact information for completing Crown patent searches. Crown patents may contain reservations, conditions, and restrictions and may affect any property, including urban property. The decision as to whether to obtain the Crown patent is a decision that must be made in each transaction by the lawyer in consultation with the client and in the context of the risks raised by the particular property. Crown patents may raise issues concerning roads, land adjacent to waterways (retained by the Crown), mines and minerals, timber, use of navigable waters, shoreline (66'), fishery rights, road (shoreline) allowances, beds of navigable waters, hydro-electric rights, military rights and uses, Aboriginal rights, and rights to take a percentage of the property plus materials, without compensation, for the purpose of road construction. Refer to the *Public Lands Act*, R.S.O. 1990, c. P.41 for legislation altering or releasing the original Crown patent terms, particularly reservations concerning timber (white pines) and mineral rights.

Title insurance is not a substitute for Crown patent inquiries.

REALTY TAXES AND RELATED SPECIAL ASSESSMENTS

Municipal taxes are a special lien that attaches to land which has priority over all claims, except for Crown rights (*Municipal Act, 2001*, S.O. 2001, c. 25, s. 349(3)). The *Municipal Act, 2001* provides for the annual current value assessment, collection, arrears, penalties, and sale of realty for unpaid taxes (*Municipal Act, 2001*, Part X). The municipality can register a tax arrears certificate when the taxes are three years in arrears. The municipality may sell the property by public auction one year after the registration of the certificate. Municipalities issue tax certificates. A number of special assessments, listed below, may be added to a tax roll for a particular property. Usually, the additional assessment is revealed by a municipal tax inquiry. However, as with work orders, depending on the stage of the process, the assessment may be in the works but not yet formally added, usually by by-law to the tax roll. Additional inquiries must be made to the municipality as to whether there are projected local improvements or special assessments in process.

Conveyancers obtain tax certificates from municipalities. Depending on the municipality, the request may be by letter, search request form, or online inquiry. Title insurance provides alternative coverage. Insurers normally require verbal confirmation of tax status, a receipted tax bill, or a vendor's statutory declaration that taxes have been paid, when available. In residential transactions, insurers may, on request, waive these requirements and provide coverage. In commercial transactions for smaller amounts, insurers accept verbal confirmation of tax status, a receipted tax bill, or a vendor's statutory declaration that taxes have been paid, or a tax certificate. In larger commercial transactions, insurers require tax certificates. Lender transactions normally require verbal confirmation of tax status, a receipted tax bill, a vendor's statutory declaration that taxes have been paid, or a tax certificate.

Local Improvement Charges

The *Municipal Act, 2001* authorizes municipalities to add local improvement levies for past or present capital works (improvements) such as curbs, sidewalks, sewers, noise abatement, trees or boulevards to the municipal tax bill of benefited, usually (although not always) adjoining properties (s. 5). Local improvements are enforced in the same manner as municipal taxes and have priority lien status. Local improvements are governed by O. Reg. 586/06. Section 1(2) of O. Reg. 586/06 identifies the kinds of work that may be undertaken as a local improvement. Local improvements are implemented by by-law. Conveyancers search for current and pending local improvements.

Provincial Land Tax Act

The *Provincial Land Tax Act, 2006*, S.O. 2006, c. 33, Schedule Z.2 governs areas without municipal organization. Provincial land tax is dealt with later in this chapter under the heading, Areas without Municipal Organization. The Ministry of Municipal Affairs and Housing and the Ministry of Natural Resources have a mandate to facilitate municipal organization in currently unorganized territories.

City of Toronto Act, 2006

The City of Toronto now has special powers to add additional charges to the municipal tax bill. Ontario Regulation 594/06 (under the *City of Toronto Act, 2006*, S.O. 2006, c. 11, Schedule A) provides that Toronto can add fees and charges for the supply of water, the supply of artificial or natural gas, the supply of steam or hot water, the use of a sewage system, the use of a waste management system, and for business improvement initiatives (ss. 1 and 2). These charges have priority lien status and are searched and enforced as municipal taxes. Inquiries about City of Toronto special charges are made to the City of Toronto.

Development Charges Act, 1997

The *Development Charges Act, 1997*, S.O. 1997, c. 27 states that a development charge is payable upon a building permit being issued for a development, an approval of a subdivision plan, or an approval of a *Planning Act* s. 53 consent to sever with a consent agreement, unless a development charge by-law provides otherwise under subsection (s. 26). A municipality may also enter into an agreement, including interest provisions, providing that all or part of the charges be paid before, during, or after issuing the permit or approval (s. 27)).

Unpaid development charges related usually to new construction are added to the municipal tax bill and are enforced and collected as municipal taxes (s. 32(1)). These charges have priority lien status. There may be a by-law on title that exempts an area from development charges. Developers enter into development agreements that include development charges; these agreements are registered on title. Conveyancers inquire of the municipal building department as to the amount, payment terms, and status of the development charges and as to whether the developer is in compliance with the agreements. Municipal tax searches may reveal arrears of development charges.

Drainage Act

Under the *Drainage Act*, R.S.O. 1990, c. D.17, the municipality constructs drainage works at the petition of a majority of owners in the affected area, and then by by-law adds a special assessment to the individual owner's tax bill, similar to local improvements. These charges have priority lien status and are searched and enforced as municipal taxes (s. 61). Inquiries are directed to the municipal clerk. *Drainage Act* loans are also available in territories without municipal organization.

Tile Drainage Act

Under the *Tile Drainage Act*, R.S.O. 1990, c. T.8, owners usually, though not necessarily, of farm property borrow money from the municipality. The loan is authorized by a municipal by-law to be paid over a ten-year period for tiles installed for run-off water (ss. 2 and 3). The municipality adds the tile drainage loan to the property taxes. These charges have priority lien status and are searched and enforced, and collected as municipal taxes. Inquiries are directed to the municipal clerk regarding loan status, payments, and pending loan applications. Title drainage loans are also available in territories without municipal organization.

Shoreline Property Assistance Act

The *Shoreline Property Assistance Act*, R.S.O. 1990, c. S.10 provides for municipal loans authorized by by-law for the construction of retaining walls, cribs, groynes, and similar structures for the protection of shorelines on an owner's property or on adjoining Crown land with the Crown's consent (s. 4). Section 9(2) requires that by-laws which impose annual fees for shoreline improvements be registered on title. These special assessments have priority lien status and are added to the tax roll (s. 9(1)). Inquiries are directed to the municipal clerk regarding loan status, payments, and pending loan applications. Shoreline property assistance loans are also available in territories without municipal organization.

Lakes and Rivers Improvement Act

Under the *Lakes and Rivers Improvement Act*, R.S.O. 1990, c. L.3, the construction, repair, alteration, and use of dams, water crossings including bridges, culverts, fords, and winter ice bridges on lakes and rivers require a permit from the Ministry of Natural Resources (ss. 14-16). "Dam" under the Act means a structure or work forwarding, holding back or diverting water, and includes a dam, tailings dam, dike, diversion, channel alteration, artificial channel, culvert or causeway (s. 1). Conservation authorities administer this Act within their boundaries. Direct inquiries to the Ministry of Natural Resources (MNR) or the local conservation authority.

Non-compliance can generate work orders and fines. These charges have priority lien status and can be added to the tax rolls and enforced as municipal taxes (s. 29). Inquiries are directed to the MNR regarding compliance, work orders, and fines. Territories without municipal organization can also add charges to the tax rolls and enforce as taxes (s. 29(8)).

When activities that fall under the Act have the potential to affect fish or fish habitat, contact the Ministry of Natural Resources, the local conservation authority when available, and Fisheries and Oceans Canada. An authorization under the *Fisheries Act*, R.S.C. 1985, c. F-14 is required when impact on fish habitat is unavoidable.

Weed Control Act

Under the *Weed Control Act*, R.S.O. 1990, c. W.5, an inspector can issue a work order to destroy noxious weeds. If the owner does not comply, the municipality can complete the work. The cost of the work has priority lien status and is added to the tax roll for collection. Inquiries concerning orders to destroy noxious weeds are made to the municipality.

Line Fences Act

Under the *Line Fences Act*, R.S.O. 1990, c. L.17, a fence-viewer's award (boundary fence) and/or certificate of default may be registered on title. Any amount owing may be added to the municipal tax bill (s. 12(7)). Municipalities may opt out of this Act and substitute a by-law.

Managed Forest Tax Incentive Program

The Ontario Forestry Association and the Ontario Woodlot Association administer the Managed Forest Tax Incentive Program (MFTIP) on behalf of the MNR. Owners who are resident in Canada who manage and conserve their forests of four hectares or more under a Managed Forest Plan are eligible for a 25 per cent reduction in property taxes. The purchaser may be responsible for repaying prior tax reductions if the managed forest is not in compliance with the Managed Forest Plan.

The Muncipal Property Assessment Corporation (MPAC) is responsible for the assessment status of properties. MPAC automatically revokes MFTIP assessment status on transfer of land. The new owner may reapply within 90 days of the sale to keep the property in the program. On sale, the vendor should send written notice, a completed Landowner Report, and a copy of the Report of Activities to the managing forest association. The purchaser will need a copy of the Managed

Forest Plan (MFP) from the vendor (property of the vendor). If the vendor has damaged the forest or not complied with the MFP, the purchaser is responsible for repaying prior tax reductions. An MNR field audit will assess whether a managed forest is in compliance with program standards and tax reductions. The agreement of purchase and sale should include terms that protect the purchaser from prior tax liability. The purchaser may keep the property in the program by updating the vendor's MFP or by preparing a new plan for approval by a Managed Forest Plan Approver certified by the MNR, followed by approval by one of the designated associations. The Ontario Managed Forest Tax Incentive Program Guide and application forms and contact information for certified forest plan approvers and associations are available on the MNR website.

Conservation Land Tax Incentive Program

The Conservation Land Tax Incentive Program (CLTIP) provides property tax relief up to 100 per cent exemption of the eligible portion of the property to private landowners of provincially significant conservation lands who agree to protect the natural heritage values of their properties and who are not associated with Conservation Authorities or Conservation Authority properties. CLTIP is an annual program; landowners must apply annually for tax relief. The MNR identifies land eligible for CLTIP annually and sends an inventory of eligible properties to MPAC. Change of ownership removes a property from the program. New owners must reapply for CLTIP tax relief.

The MPAC website provides information about property tax relief, assessment, and property tax status under CLTIP. Section 3(1).25 of the *Assessment Act*, R.S.O. 1990, c. A.31 provides a tax exemption for all or a portion of a property identified by the Natural Heritage Section of the MNR as being provincially significant, eligible conservation land. Section 19(5.2) provides the authority for the valuation of conservation land. Part IV of O. Reg. 282/98 provides the exemption eligibility criteria. In order to qualify for the program, conservation land must be at least 0.5 acres (0.202 hectares), the owner must agree to conserve the land in a natural state, and the land must pass MNR compliance inspections.

Eligible land types are:

1. provincially significant wetland;

2. provincially significant Area of Natural and Scientific Interest (ANSI);

3. habitat of endangered species as listed in O. Reg. 230/08 under the *Endangered Species Act, 2007*, S.O. 2007 c. 6;

4. land designated as escarpment natural area in the Niagara Escarpment Plan; and

5. community conservation land (charitable conservation organizations and conservation authorities).

Information on the CLTIP program is available on the MPAC website and on the MNR website at <http://www.mnr.gov.on.ca/en/Business/CLTIP/index.html>.

Farm Property Class Tax Rate Program (as of 1998; formerly the Farmlands Property Taxation Program and the Farm Tax Rebate Program)

Farm properties that meet the eligibility requirements of the Farm Property Class are taxed at 25 per cent of the municipal residential/farm tax rate. The farm residence and the surrounding one acre are taxed as residential class. On the purchase of farm property under the tax rebate program, a purchaser will need from the vendor the most recent Notice of Property Assessment, the most recent property tax bill, a copy of the completed Farm Property Class tax rate application, and information on what has been done to ensure that the farmland property remains eligible for the 25 per cent tax rate for the next year (*e.g.*, did the vendor register the farm business in the current year, to be eligible for the Farm Property Class next year?).

When a new property owner does not continue to farm the property or changes the use, MPAC issues a supplementary assessment to reclassify the value of the property and places the property in the residential property class for tax rate purposes. The new owner will pay the residential tax rate for the remainder of the taxation year. If the new owner of Farm Property Class land continues farming and meets eligibility requirements, MPAC will continue the Farm Property Class assessment.

When farm property is assessed by MPAC in the Residential Property Class, then a new owner who starts farming the property and meets eligibility requirements can apply to the Ontario Ministry of Agriculture, Food and Rural Affairs for the Farm Property Class tax rate for the remainder of the tax year and future years. MPAC issues assessments based on the Ministry of Agriculture, Food and Rural Affairs approvals.

Education Development Charges

Section 257.54(1) of the *Education Act*, R.S.O. 1990, c. E.2, Division E allows boards to pass by-laws for the imposition of education development charges against land in its area of jurisdiction undergoing residential or non-residential development, where there is residential development in the area of jurisdiction of a board that would increase education land costs. An education development charge by-law expires five years after the day it comes into force. A board can pass a new by-law after the first by-law expires. The by-law requires a research report and is subject to appeal to the Ontario Municipal Board (OMB).

BUILDING AND ZONING COMPLIANCE

Zoning is complex and affects current and future property uses, fair market value, and marketability. Today, most municipal websites contain a wealth on zoning information including zoning maps and official plan information (see Chapter 9 for more on zoning and the *Planning Act*. Non-compliance can generate work orders and fines. Prior non-conforming uses have special status. Direct inquiries to the building department for confirmation of zoning, property standards by-laws, detailed zoning information, proposed amendments to zoning or the official plan, compliance with zoning, whether all necessary permits have been issued, whether permits are in good standing, the existence and results of interim or final inspections, and outstanding work orders and fines are often not available and never guaranteed.

Some municipalities require the registration with the municipality of two unit residential properties. Municipal searches confirm compliance with registration requirements.

Single-family residential and refinance title insurance policies provide compensation for non-compliance for building and zoning without requiring a municipal inquiry. Owner policies for multi-family residential properties, including properties where the second unit is a boathouse with living accommodations, require building and zoning compliance searches. Commercial and lender policies vary, often depending on the value of the transaction and the coverage/endorsements requested. As a result, inquiries for building and zoning compliance — which used to be standard — are often not completed. However, purchaser expectations and plans for future use are important considerations when deciding how thorough an inquiry is needed.

SUBDIVISION AND DEVELOPMENT AGREEMENT COMPLIANCE

Detailed agreements dealing with the provision of subdivision and development services and works (sewers, sidewalks, lighting, drainage, parks, pathways, roads, landscaping, grading), easements and restrictions are registered on title and enforceable against subsequent owners. These agreements are a condition of approval for the development or subdivision. Similar agreements with conditions and restrictions may be required for properties given a consent to sever (*Planning Act*, R.S.O. 1990, c. P.13, s. 45(9.1)). Inquiries concerning compliance, work orders, fines, levies, and performance bond status to the municipality. Some non-compliance issues create priority lien status under the *Planning Act*, such as parking requirement by-law exemptions under s. 40(4). Outstanding charges can be added to municipal tax rolls and collected as taxes.

Residential title policies provide compensation for non-compliance with subdivision and development agreements without requiring a municipal inquiry. As a result, inquiries for subdivision and development agreement compliance, which used to be standard, are often not completed. Purchaser expectations and plans for future use are important considerations when deciding whether to make a subdivision or development inquiry.

MUNICIPAL WORK ORDERS

Municipalities have extensive powers under the *Planning Act* and the *Building Code Act, 1992*, S.O. 1992, c. 23 to plan, regulate, zone, inspect properties, and issue work orders. Municipalities may complete work required by outstanding work orders and add the charges to the municipal tax rolls, to be collected as taxes.

Residential title policies usually provide compensation for municipal work orders without requiring a municipal inquiry. Commercial and lender policies vary, often depending on the value of the transaction and the endorsements requested.

OCCUPANCY PERMITS

Inquiries are directed to the municipal building department as to whether an occupancy permit has been issued.

COMMUNITY IMPROVEMENT PLAN UNDER THE PLANNING ACT

Part IV of the *Planning Act* facilitates community improvement. Community improvement is "the planning or replanning, design or redesign, resubdivision, clearance, development or redevelopment, reconstruction and rehabilitation of a community improvement project area ..." (s. 28(1)). Community improvement includes the provision of affordable housing (s. 28(1.1)). Community Improvement Project Areas are designated by by-law. Section 32 provides for grants or loans to effect community improvement activities and property repairs. These loans including interest are a priority lien on land and can be added to the tax rolls and collected as taxes. The loan is registered as a certificate of loan in the registry office.

DEMOLITION CONTROL AREA UNDER THE PLANNING ACT

Demolition control areas are established by by-law under s. 33(2) of the *Planning Act* for areas with a property standards by-law under s. 15.1 of the *Building Code Act, 1992*. Demolition of the whole or any part of any residential property in the area of demolition control is forbidden unless the person is the holder of a demolition permit. Municipal council issues demolition permits. Inquiries as to the existence of demolition control areas and outstanding permits or refusals for demolition are directed to the building department of the municipality. Section 33(7) sets conditions and time limits on demolition permits regarding the building of a new building with two years or less following demolition. If the building is not completed within the required time on the permit, a penalty specified in the permit limited to no more than $20,000 per residential unit demolished can be added to the tax rolls and collected as municipal taxes. Section 33(9) requires the registration on title of a certificate of the amount added to the municipal tax roll.

Ontario Bill 150, the *Green Energy and Green Economy Act, 2009*, S.O. 2009, c. 12, which received Royal Assent on May 14, 2009, exempts renewable energy undertakings including renewable energy generation facilities, projects, and testing facilities from demolition control by-laws under s. 33 of the *Planning Act*. Section 62.0.2(1)-(5) of the *Planning Act* now states that a by-law passed under s. 33 does not apply to a renewable energy undertaking.

PUBLIC UTILITIES

Conveyancers obtain information and certificates on hydro, water, and gas arrears. Depending on the utility, the request may be by letter, search request form, or online inquiry. Public utilities that are supplied by municipalities have a priority lien status under the *Municipal Act, 2001* and may be added to the tax bill and enforced against current and subsequent owners (ss. 398(2) and 349(3)). Hydro and water are often dealt with in separate municipal departments. Gas and, on occasion, water are supplied by private entities, and these arrears do not create priority liens.

Conveyancers make inquiries of private utilities. It may be necessary to inquire as to the location of utility easements that are not registered on title, particularly when property is bought for development purposes or when building additions are planned. Security deposits and connection fees are standard. Utility arrears in commercial or industrial contexts can be for large amounts. Final readings need to be ordered and utilities require notification of the change of ownership.

Title insurance provides alternative coverage for utility arrears. On residential transactions, title insurers normally require only verbal confirmation of utility status and will waive utility searches and provide coverage when verbal confirmation is not available. Commercial transaction requirements are usually based on transaction value.

UNREGISTERED HYDRO EASEMENTS

Hydro easements were not required to be registered prior to 1998. Conveyancers make inquiries for unregistered hydro easements of local municipal hydro corporations/suppliers and of Hydro One Networks for non-urban areas. The conveyancer should refer to s. 46(1) of the *Electricity Act, 1998*, S.O. 1998, c. 15, Sched. A and s. 48(2), (3) of the soon-to-be repealed *Power Corporation Act*, R.S.O. 1990, c. P.18 for the authority for rights related to unregistered hydro easements. On occasion, there may be additional agreements between prior owners and hydro suppliers that relate to encroachments on and the use and maintenance of easements. Unregistered hydro easements can be searched online at <http://unregeasement.hydroone.com/lvr>. Inquiries require former and current municipal names and original lots and concessions as well as current lots and subdivision plan numbers.

Generally, title insurers for residential policies provide alternative coverage and do not require a search unless indicated by a reference on a survey, other documentation, or the visible physical presence of hydro transmission lines or equipment. Commercial policies may require the search, depending on the value of the property, whether it is vacant, and whether development is planned. Searches are generally required for vacant properties. Requirements for lender policies are similar to commercial requirements and vary depending on loan to equity value.

ELECTRICAL SAFETY AUTHORITY WORK ORDERS

Section 113(11) of the *Electricity Act, 1998* authorizes the issuing of work orders against property for the protection of property and the safety of individuals. Conveyancers make inquiries to the local Electrical Safety Authority for outstanding work orders that relate to the transmission and use of electricity. Title insurance policies require electrical safety work order searches, although some companies allow exceptions for small, conventional loan, lender policies.

FIRE DEPARTMENT WORK ORDERS

The *Fire Protection and Prevention Act, 1997*, S.O. 1997, c. 4 authorizes inspections at reasonable times with or without warrants (s. 19) and work orders (s. 21) that address fire safety. When owners do not comply with work orders, the municipality, with the authorization of the Fire Safety Commission, has a priority lien under the *Municipal Act, 2001* and may add the costs of the work to the municipal tax roll.

Conveyancers may, with the written consent of the client, search for work orders at the local fire department. Searches may trigger mandatory inspections. Fire department work order searches are completed on commercial properties, industrial properties, rental properties, group homes, day cares, schools, new businesses, multi-storey buildings, hotels and motels, fishing lodges, cottage developments, retirement facilities, and whenever the client and the lawyer deem the search prudent.

Title insurance usually provides alternative coverage without a search requirement for single family residential dwellings and some refinance transactions. Title insurers require searches for tenanted, multi-residential, and commercial properties. Title insurance does not cover fire retrofit deficiencies such as the sufficiency of smoke alarms or fire barriers, unless they form work orders or are zoning deficiencies which would have been revealed by a regular building and zoning search conducted prior to closing.

HEALTH UNIT WORK ORDERS

Part III of the *Health Protection and Promotion Act*, R.S.O. 1990, c. H.7 addresses community health protection, including extensive inspection powers (s. 10); Medical Officer of Health orders and deficiency notices related to the occupational and environmental health (s. 12); small drinking water systems (s. 12.1) (dealt with later under the topic "water sources"); food premises (s. 16); and potable water and sanitary facilities required in residential buildings (s. 20). The medical officer of health may require the work done by other than the owner. When work orders are not complied with within 60 days, the work order costs may be added to the municipal tax rolls (s. 15(2) and (3)).

Conveyancers complete searches at the local health unit for work orders on all food premises and facilities that serve food such as, restaurants, retirement homes, boarding houses, day cares, hotels, and rental premises. Commercial and industrial properties may also require searches.

Title insurance does not cover public health unit issues.

TECHNICAL STANDARDS AND SAFETY AUTHORITY

The *Technical Standards and Safety Act, 2000*, S.O. 2000, c. 16 (TSSA) regulates elevating devices, ski lifts, amusement devices (rides), boilers and pressure vessels, and heating and transportation fuels.

Technical standards and safety authority issues are outside of the scope of title insurance owner policies.

TSSA's Fuels Safety Program

Under O. Reg. 213/01, fuel oil tanks must be inspected and registered with the program prior to fuel delivery. Inspections must take place every ten years and suppliers must refuse to deliver fuel to a tank that does not meet TSSA program standards at any time.

Underground Fuel Oil Tanks

Conveyancers should contact the Technical Safety & Standards Association to confirm the registration status for fuel delivery for an underground fuel oil tank and whether it complies with removal, upgrading, and inspection requirements. Underground tanks must be removed within two years of discontinued use. TSSA records can be searched for incident reports, spills, and site contamination. The search requires the municipal address and legal description, and current and former owner and occupier names. Environmental audits may be advisable to determine possible contamination. Inspections may be requested with the client's written consent.

Aboveground Fuel Oil Tanks

Aboveground fuel tanks inside or outside houses must also meet fuel delivery status and inspection requirements. Fuel tanks may be subject to infraction notices and replacement orders. Purchasers of a property that is heated with oil or that was heated with oil in the past should do TSSA searches and request a tank inspection prior to closing.

Elevating Devices Safety Program

The Elevating Devices Safety Program inspects, licences, and registers elevating devices. Periodic inspections take place on a risk-based schedule. Elevating devices include elevators, escalators, moving walks, lifts for persons with physical disabilities, passenger ropeways, dumbwaiters, construction hoists, and ski lifts and tows. Elevating devices require a licence prior to operation (TSSA, s. 6). Authorization for use may be suspended when there is a threat to public safety or for non-payment of fees, penalties, or a *Provincial Offences Act* fine (TSSA, ss. 9 and 13). It is an offence to operate an unlicensed or an unsafe elevating device. Ontario Regulation 209/01 governs the use and safety of elevating devices.

Work order and status report inquiries for elevating devices are directed to the Technical Standards and Safety Authority.

Boilers and Pressure Vessels Safety Program

Ontario Regulation 220/01 regulates boilers and pressure vessels. It is an offence to operate a boiler or pressure vessel without a certificate of inspection. Periodic inspections take place on a risk-based schedule.

Work order, certificate of inspection verification, and inspection report inquiries for boilers and pressure vessels are directed to the Technical Standards and Safety Authority.

Amusement Device Safety Program

The Technical Standards and Safety Authority inspects, licenses (permits), and registers amusement ride designs. A new owner must apply for a permit. Inquiries and applications are directed to the Technical Standards and Safety Authority. Inquiry contact information is included in Appendix 5.

ENVIRONMENTAL SEARCHES AND THE ENVIRONMENTAL PROTECTION ACT

The Ontario Ministry of the Environment, Environment Canada, municipal organizations, the Ontario Ministry of Natural Resources, conservation authorities and similar organizations, Indian and Northern Affairs Canada, local health units, Fisheries and Oceans Canada, the federal Transport, Infrastructure and Communities Portfolio, National Defence and the Canadian Forces, and even the Archives of Ontario and Archives Canada may hold records relating to environmental contamination and risk. The existence of environmental contamination on a property may be revealed by a freedom of information request. Environmental liability falls somewhere between a landmine and a bear trap for the unsophisticated, innocent purchaser. This is a specialist practice area. Buyer beware.

Ontario's *Environmental Protection Act*, R.S.O. 1990, c. E.19 authorizes clean-up orders and the completion of the work as necessary, as well as the addition of the charges to the municipal tax roll as a priority lien that can be collected as taxes (s. 154(2)). The owner or the person who has control of property is liable for the costs; these costs can be catastrophic and far exceed the value or purchase price of the property. Innocent purchasers without notice acquire clean-up liability on acquisition. Generally, commercial transactions focus more on environmental due diligence; however, residential, recreational, and agricultural transactions are also subject to environmental liabilities. On occasion, the title search may indicate that the land investigated or the adjoining lands were once a gas station, landfill, dry cleaning facility, or battery factory. A fish farm, tailings pond, or lake used as a dump may raise serious clean-up risks. For example, wholly inland fish farms generate large quantities of environmental contaminants. Searches are many, costly, slow, and inconclusive, and the Ministry of the Environment (MOE) does not guarantee the accuracy or the completeness of search results. Title insurance does not offer coverage.

Waste Disposal

Direct inquiries to the municipal clerk as to whether the property was used as a waste disposal site, landfill, or sanitary dump, and whether there are records of sewer violations or spills. Old dumps are prohibited from use for 25 years following dump closure unless the MOE issues a permit (s. 46). Old dumps raise additional environmental risks and associated clean-up liabilities long after the 25-year period. There may be a need for Brownfield remediation, multiple environmental assessments, private environmental audits, and consultant reports.

The MOE provides an online *Environmental Bill of Rights, 1993*, S.O. 1993, c. 28 search that contains records regarding waste disposal sites, PCB storage sites, waste manifest and generator information, proposed and finalized certificates of approval, and directions and orders (non-compliance). This searchable MOE register only contains known sites and more recent certificates and orders; it makes no guarantee as to accuracy or completeness. The MOE also issues certificates of property use that restrict the use of land and require remediation and monitoring. Again, the searches are costly, slow, incomplete, and only access existing and limited historical information. In reality, purchasers must draft detailed conditions and warranties in the agreement of purchase and sale, conduct independent environmental audits, obtain independent private sector risk assessments, and, if available, purchase specialty back-up environmental risk insurance. Title insurers do not cover environmental risks. In special circumstances, following audits, risk assessments, and Brownfield requirements, commercial owners and lenders may be able to acquire customized, limited environmental insurance, sometimes only when government wishes to participate in the arrangement. Environmental coverage is usually limited to a ten-year duration.

Part XV.1 of the *Environmental Protection Act* and in particular the Records of Site Condition, O. Reg. 153/04 govern the environmental site registry, environmental site assessment, site condition standards and risk assessments, records of site condition, change of property use, certificates of property use, and dangerous contaminants orders. Purchasers need to investigate this information when a site involves an environmental risk.

Common Environmental Inquiries

Environmental legislation and search requirements are constantly evolving. Common environmental inquiries include the following:

- Environmental Bill of Rights Registry (certificates of property use, certificates of approval, and directions) — This online Ontario record contains approvals for uses such as a future dump site or gravel pit, permits to take water, approvals for discharge into the natural environment, policy statements, exemptions or alterations to minimum standards under the Act for particular companies and more. The register contains information from when the EBR became law in 1994 to present. The Environmental Bill of Rights Registry can be searched by address or keyword and is available at: <http://www.ebr.gov.on.ca/ERS-WEB-External/searchNotice0.jsp?clearForm=true&menuIndex= 1_1&language=en>.
- Brownfields Environmental Site Registry — The *Environmental Protection Act* requires the MOE to keep an Environmental Site Registry, which is online at: <http://www.ene.gov.on.ca/environet/BESR/index. htm> (s. 168.3(1)). Properties that the MOE has certified as meeting its standards for the clean-up of a Brownfield are filed in the MOE Environmental Site Registry as part of the Brownfield remediation process. Additional records of site condition filings are triggered by change of property use (mandatory as of October 1, 2005), municipal change in zoning, or building permit applications. The record of site condition protects the owner, subsequent owners and mortgagees from any additional liability that relates to contamination that existed at the time the Record of Site Condition was issued, although it does not cover a purchaser who changes the use of the land or when contamination has migrated to other locations. The site can be searched on the MOE website, by location, filing number, site property identification number (POLARIS PIN), and filing owner. There is also a

"search by map" function. This search is available at <http://www.ene.gov.on.ca/environet/BESR/index.htm>.

- EcoLog ERIS — EcoLog ERIS is a private search and environmental consultant service. EcoLog ERIS has integrated dozens of federal, provincial, and municipal government records, historical fire insurance plans and reports, aerial photographs, topographical maps, water wells, available title search and survey data, and additional private source records. As well, the EcoLog ERIS search checks records including underground fuel storage tanks, reported toxic spills, waste disposal sites, pesticide use, chemical facilities on or near the site, environmental convictions of current or previous owners, PCB storage sites, manufacturing facilities on or near the site, bore hole data, and much more. EcoLog ERIS provides access to records not otherwise available. Reports include a customized map showing the subject property and all records found that relate to the property and area <http://www.eris.ca/default.aspx>. This search includes adjacent properties up to ¼ km, although from a scientific perspective this distance has limited although useful predictive value. EcoLog ERIS search capacity continues to grow and extend to earlier records. EcoLog ERIS also provides specialized reports, such as the ERIS Loan Risk Assessment Report, including adjacent properties within a 250 metre radius. EcoLog ERIS is dependent on existing government sources. Keep in mind that the source information is not guaranteed accurate or complete.
- Certificate of Approval Request — Direct request for copy of certificate by certificate number to the MOE Approvals Branch.
- Ontario *Freedom of Information and Privacy* — The *Ontario Freedom of Information and Privacy Act*, R.S.O. 1990, c. F.31 (FOI) authorizes requests for general information regarding provincially regulated land (60-day request wait period). FOI requests provide the only way to obtain the complete record of environmental permits, approvals, orders, inspections, directions, reports, consultant's reports, complaints, spills, registration, *etc.* Much of this information is not available through other inquiry services.
- Ministry of Environment Hazardous Waste Information Systems — This program covers hazardous wastes generated by industrial and manufacturing processes, the commercial and institutional sectors, households, including waste acids, contaminated sludges, complex chemicals, biomedical wastes from hospitals, spent photofinishing chemicals, waste pesticides, PCBs, motor oil, unused cleaning products from homes, and discarded batteries.
- Waste Disposal Sites (landfills), Coal Tar Waste Sites, and Coal Gasification Plants (MOE records).
- MOE Index of Record of Orders and Approvals — This index contains orders and approvals under the *Environmental Protection Act*, the *Pesticides Act*, R.S.O. 1990, c. P.11, the *Cosmetic Pesticides Ban Act, 2008*, S.O. 2008, c. 11 (which amended the *Pesticide Act*), the

Ontario Water Resources Act, R.S.O. 1990, c. O.40 and the *Safe Drinking Water Act, 2002*, S.O. 2002, c. 32. Direct written inquiries to the district office. A search requires location, address, legal description, and current and former owner names. Searches date back to 1985. Prior records require a FOI request.

- Environment Canada — Access to Information Requests for general information concerning federally regulated lands.
- National Pollutant Release Inventory — This search is done by company name, location, or substance online at: <http://www.ec.gc.ca>.
- Environment Canada PCB Storage Sites Inventory — This search is by substance, name, or address. Contact the Waste Reduction and Management Division of Environment Canada.
- Ministry of Labour's Health and Safety Division — The Ministry has records and compliance orders on storage, use, spills, worker exposure, and plant contamination. FOI requests are usually necessary. Current and former owner, occupier names, and municipal and legal addresses are needed for an effective inquiry.
- LEED Certification — The Leadership in Energy and Environmental Design (LEED) is administered by the Canada Green Building Council. LEED ranks and measures a building's environmental performance; see online: <http:www.cagbc.org/leed/leed_projects/registered_projects. php>.

ACCESS AND TRANSPORTATION ISSUES

Highways, Roads, Access, and Easements

Check with the local municipality planning department and the Ministry of Transportation about how future growth plans and projected roads will affect the land being purchased. Proximity to highways can both benefit and devastate future development plans, business success, and personal enjoyment of land. For example, consider the creation of virtual ghost towns when once-thriving communities are bypassed by new highways. See Chapter 9 for a full discussion of roads, access, and easements, including possible inquiries.

Highway Entrance Permit Searches

A permit is required for access to a King's highway. A King's highway is designated by an order in council under s. 7(1) of the *Public Transportation and Highway Improvement Act*, R.S.O. 1990, c. P.50. Designations are registered at the local land registry office.

If a purchaser is planning or is relying on plans to build near or create access to a highway, he or she must confirm that a permit exists or will be issued. Inquiries should be made to the Ministry of Transportation.

Public Transportation and Highway Improvement Act Searches

This Act requires permits for buildings, structures, signs, trees, shrubs, and fences within specified distances from highways and intersections (s. 34). The Act also requires permits for the construction or use of a private road or entranceway that accesses the highway. The following uses near a King's highway also require permits:

- the placement or alteration of adjacent buildings, structures, or roads, or the placement of trees, fences, hedges, shrubs, or gas pumps within 45 metres of the highway or within 180 metres of the centre point of an intersection;
- the erection or alteration of power lines, poles, or transmission lines within 400 metres of the highway;
- the sale or exposure of produce or merchandise upon the highway (the Ministry can direct this use to be stopped);
- any sign or advertising device within 400 metres of the highway (size restrictions apply and there are special rules for agricultural signs); or
- the use of land for a shopping mall, fairground, racetrack, drive-in theatre, stadium, or any use that causes people to gather in large numbers within 800 metres of the highway.

Purchasers should inquire of the Ministry of Transportation to confirm current compliance, work orders, and fines, and should seek permits for anticipated uses.

Controlled Access Highways (Expressways and 400 Series Highways)

Larger highways such as expressways and the 400 series highways require special permits for the construction or use of a private road or entranceway that accesses the highway (s. 38). The following uses also require permits:

- the placement or alteration of adjacent buildings, structures, or roads, or the placement of trees, fences, hedges, and shrubs within 45 metres of the highway or within 395 metres of the centre point of an intersection;
- the erection or alteration of power lines, poles, or transmission lines within 400 metres of the highway;
- the sale or exposure of produce or merchandise within 45 metres of the highway or within 395 metres of the centre point of an intersection;
- any sign or advertising device within 400 metres of the highway; or
- use of land for a shopping mall, fairground, racetrack, drive-in theatre, stadium, or any use that causes people to gather in large numbers within 800 metres of the highway.

Address inquiries to the Ministry of Transportation to confirm current compliance, work orders, and fines, and seek permits for anticipated uses.

Local Roads Boards

Local roads boards may determine a tax levy for road creation and maintenance pursuant to the *Local Roads Boards Act*, R.S.O. 1990, c. L.27. Inquire as to existing levies or anticipated levies that may affect tax rolls.

Access over Crown Land

The Ministry of Natural Resources under the *Public Lands Act* requires permits for use of a road or access over Crown lands. Confirm that there is a permit or obtain a permit if access is over Crown lands.

Unopened Original Road Allowances as Unmaintained Access Roads

Use of an unopened road allowance requires permission from municipal council or the road committee in unorganized townships.

Water Access

General inquiries are necessary to confirm whether there is public or private access to water such as a public wharf. Parking is also an issue as parking at public wharfs may be restricted, particularly as to duration.

Air Access

Some smaller lakes and cottage communities or developments place restrictive covenants and contractual restrictions for environmental, noise control, and quality of experience reasons on the use of motors, watercraft, and specific means of transportation over water (for example, float planes).

Airport Zoning By-Laws

Detailed regulations on height, lighting, and other restrictions may require interpretation by an expert. (Searchers should also refer to the *Aeronautics Act*, R.S.C. 1985, c. A-2.)

Railways

Railway rights are an overriding interest under the *Land Titles Act* (s. 44(12)). Railway rights of way, as with road allowances, may not be visible in a physical sense and as a result it is difficult to know when to make an inquiry. Railway rights of way affect adjacent land, similar to highways, and this affects access, buildings, and structures such as signs. In addition, railway uses generate issues of environmental contamination and associated use restrictions, even after the railway no longer exists. Whenever property is traversed by a railway line or is adjacent to a line, sidings, or station, or has been owned by a railway company in the past, make careful inquiries to the Registrar General of Canada (Registry Division) under s. 104 of the *Canada Transportation Act*, S.C. 1996, c. 10. It is the opinion of the author that current environmental and planning pressures will, or at least should, drive extensive rail development in the future, hence careful review of railway rights of way often ignored in the past, is prudent today.

Railway Mortgages and Security Agreements

Sections 104 and 105 of the *Canada Transportation Act* provides that mortgages and security agreements given by railway companies do not need to be registered in the registry office, as long as they are deposited in the office of the Registrar General and published in the *Canada Gazette*. Bill C-11, the *Transportation Amendment Act* removed the requirement for publication in the *Canada Gazette*. In addition, railway rights are an exception to registration statute protections and priorities. As a result, whenever land has been owned by a railway company between the Crown patent and present, it is necessary to search the records of the Registrar General of Canada for outstanding railway mortgages and security agreements.

The Registrar does not conduct searches, subsearches, file inquiries, or issue clearances. The Registrar does not warrant the legal validity of any deposit under the *Canada Transportation Act*. Searches must be conducted in person at the Corporations Canada reception area. The files of all predecessor companies and/or former corporate names of any existing companies should also be searched. Refer to Corporations Canada Policy Statement 16.1, "Procedures pursuant to Sections 104 and 105 of the *Canada Transportation Act*, Office of the Registrar General of Canada" (February 29, 2008).

Heritage Railway Stations Protection Act

The *Heritage Railway Stations Protection Act*, R.S.C. 1985 (4th Supp.), c. 52 gives some limited protection from actions by railway companies to heritage railway stations that are designated under this statute by the federal minister responsible for Parks Canada. Purchasers of retired railway stations need to contact Parks Canada for potential restrictions.

WATER

The use and abuse of water and related activities from shorelines to septic systems is highly regulated and will be increasingly regulated in the future. It is now more broadly understood that ground water and the Great Lakes are for the most part a non-renewable resource. Aboriginal claims and interventions on developments now address water sources and the impact on the environment. Although water has been taken for granted for centuries and the public has often been in the past careless in meeting compliance standards and obtaining permits, lawyers today increasingly take a risk-management and defensive practice approach when drafting water-related conditions and warranties in agreements and making off-title inquiries that relate to water and land adjacent to water.

Permits for Boathouses, Boat Ports, Docks, and Shoreline Interference

Docks and sometimes boathouses are built over navigable waters owned by the Crown in the right of Ontario. As a result, purchasers of land with docks and boathouses should confirm or obtain use permits, work permits, licences, leases, and required annual rental fees from the Ministry of Natural Resources under the *Public Lands Act*. As well, docks and boathouses need to comply with municipal zoning and require municipal building permits. When docks and boathouses are in environmentally sensitive zones, they are often subject to site plan control and require a survey and the registration on title of a site plan agreement. Federally or provincially designated environmentally sensitive zones are strictly regulated and may prohibit or restrict cutting trees, removal of brush or rocks, dredging or dumping of sand, grading and landscaping, or even the building of docks and boathouses.

Shorelines and structures adjacent to shorelines are highly regulated and the Ministry may order the removal of structures that do not comply with standards. The frequent lack of compliance by the public and contractors in obtaining appropriate building and use permits for docks and boathouses or other structures on shoreline allowances (66 feet) does not reduce the risk of regulatory consequences, which include fines and removal. Surveys are important when dealing with shorelines and structures adjacent to shorelines. In addition, full disclosure to the client of the risks accompanied by waivers and special endorsement in the title insurance policy are necessary.

Boathouses and docks require MNR work permits, municipal zoning and building permits, compliance with the *Building Code Act, 1992*, S.O. 1992, c. 23, and Fisheries and Oceans Canada approval in terms of protecting fish habitat. The MNR does not require permits for floating docks or boathouses, cantilever docks where the footings are off-shore, where the total surface area of the supporting structure on the bed of the water is less than 15 m^2, or for the removal of docks or boathouses. Municipal building permits may require prior approval of the MNR and of Fisheries and Oceans Canada when fish habitat may be affected. Municipalities usually do not require prior MNR approval for what appear to be exempt structures or Fisheries and Oceans Canada approval for a floating dock or a dock that does not rest on cribs in excess of 15 m^2.

Inquiries and construction approvals concerning shorelines, spawning beds, and the protection of fish habitat (dredging, fill, beach creation, culverts, diversions, bridges, docks, piers, boathouses, *etc.*) are made to Fisheries and Oceans Canada under the Canada *Fisheries Act*, ss. 35-37.

When a boathouse contains residential facilities and a waste removal system, MOE, local health unit, or Conservation Authority permits, approvals, and inspections are also necessary. In addition, the *Ontario Water Resources Act* requires approvals whenever any work or structure has the potential to impair water quality and drinking water safety. Renewable energy approvals under the *Green Energy and Green Economy Act, 2009* can substitute for an *Ontario Water Resources Act* approval. Furthermore, the *Lakes and Rivers Improvement Act* requires permits whenever construction deposits materials into public waters, and the *Aggregate Resources Act*, R.S.O. 1990, c. A.8 requires permits when topsoil is removed from Crown lands above or below water.

A work permit from the MNR is also required for shoreline interference such as dredging, creating beaches, break walls, groynes, boat slips, boat channels, swimming areas, or rock or aquatic life removal. Permits are required for the installation of water lines, heat loops, or cables for large-scale commercial uses such as marinas and resorts, but not for the installation of a water line, submarine cable, or heat loop for private use.

Parks Canada approvals instead of those from the MNR are required when dealing with federal waterways such as the Trent-Severn, the Rideau Canal Waterways, and Georgian Bay Islands National Park. Parks Canada sets strict standards for applications and permits for boathouses, boat ports, and shoreline interference. Parks Canada requires notice to adjoining owners and may require an environmental screening including impacts on "cultural resources and other heritage values such as viewscapes". Restrictions include one boathouse with no more than two openings per lot, maximum size and footprint, specific design, reduced light pollution, nature blending colours, landscape blending, and restrictions on dredging and shoreline vegetation removal.

Canadian Coast Guard approvals and permits may be required under the *Navigable Waters Protection Act*, R.S.C. 1985, c. N-22 for potential navigable hazards on federal waterways such as dams, booms, bridges, causeways, wharfs, docks, boathouses, and piers. Searches for permits, fill approvals, and declarations of exemption are available from the Canadian Coast Guard District Office.

Refer to MNR Policy PL 3.03.04, *Public Lands Act* Work Permits (Section 14) (August 13, 2003) for detailed information on MNR work permits. Refer to the Parks Canada website for policies on federal waterways: <http://www.pc.gc.ca>.

Title insurance policies vary but usually provide coverage for some non-compliance matters and forced removal. Insurers normally require searches when boathouses contain residential premises. Frequently, removal and compensation for loss in fair market value is the efficient remedy under the title policy. As a result, purchasers may wish to complete searches as removal of docks, boathouses, and decks can have a serious effect on purchaser expectations and enjoyment of the property and on marketability.

In conclusion, structures on or near the water need multiple, time-consuming, detailed inquiries and a careful review of title insurance coverage including potentially customized endorsements. Properties adjacent to water carry higher conveyancing risks.

The 66-Foot Shoreline Allowance

Crown patents for waterfront properties usually reserve a 66-foot shoreline allowance. The municipality or the MNR have records on the location which can be difficult to determine, and the ownership of the shoreline allowance. Shoreline allowances may still be owned by the Crown or may have been conveyed to the adjacent owner by by-law, and the transfer registered in the registry office. The exact location of a purchased shoreline allowance may surprise a purchaser as to how it extends from the property line. The reference plan registered on title will show the exact location. Boathouses, docks, and cottages are often built on the allowance and hence become fixtures for the underlying owner. If the underlying owner is the Crown, the fixtures belong to the Crown and permits for occupation and leases (possibly with rent) and licences are needed.

Navigable Waters

Ontario's *Beds of Navigable Waters Act*, R.S.O. 1990, c. B.4, s. 1 states:

> Where land that borders on a navigable body of water or stream, or on which the whole or a part of a navigable body of water or stream is situate, or through which a navigable body of water or stream flows, has been or is granted by the Crown, it shall be deemed, in the absence of an express grant of it, that the bed of such body of water was not intended to pass and did not pass to the grantee.

The Crown patent will reveal whether or not there was an express grant of a bed of navigable water. When there has not been an express grant of the bed of a body of water, the grant is deemed to exclude the bed. The term express grant includes the wording "together with the bed of navigable water", but does not include the words "woods" and "waters" therein. The Crown may have granted the bed of navigable water in a separate grant to a different owner (water lot) or as part of a grant to an upland owner.

Navigability is determined as of the date of the Crown grant, and subsequent flooding due to artificial means does not alter the size of the privately held parcel. The cases of *Canoe Ontario v. Reed*, [1989] O.J. No. 1293 (Ont. H.C.J.) and *Coleman v. Ontario (Attorney General)*, [1983] O.J. No. 275 (Ont. H.C.J.) are the leading cases on the interpretation of the term navigable and focus on the test of public utility. The *Canoe Ontario* case concludes that "[i]f the waterway serves, or is capable of serving, a legitimate public interest in that it is, or can be, regularly and profitably used by the public for some socially beneficial activity, then, assuming the waterway runs from one point of public access to another point of public access, it must be regarded as navigable and as within the public domain". The *Coleman* case sets out the traditional criteria such as capable of being traversed by large or small craft, not needing to be navigable over all parts, not needing to be continuous, hence allowing seasonal fluctuation, and private purposes such as fishing compared to transportation purposes.

Inquiries to the municipality or the MNR are made to determine whether the body of water is considered to be navigable and whether the Crown claims ownership of the bed. Refer to MNR Policy No. PL 2.02.02, "Ownership Determination - Beds of Navigable Waters" (February 26, 2007).

Boathouses, docks, and cottages are often built on the bed of navigable waters and hence become fixtures for the underlying owner. If the underlying owner is the Crown, the fixtures belong to the Crown and, as with shoreline allowances, permits for occupation and leases (possibly with rent) and licences are needed.

Navigable Waters Protection Act

Canada's *Navigable Waters Protection Act* requires permits for constructing, repairing, or altering any bridge, boom, dam, wharf, dock, pier, tunnel or pipe; for dumping of fill or excavating of materials from the bed of a navigable water; throwing stone, gravel, earth, or any material; for constructing any telegraph or power cable or wire; for any structure, device or thing that may interfere with navigation on, over, under, across, or through a federal navigable water. The Act and its regulations are extensive and cover things such as throwing sawdust, bark, or rubbish of any description that could interfere with navigation.

The Act restricts obstacles and obstruction including equipment, lights, sound signals, buoys, and marks. The Act requires approvals and non-compliance results in offences, fines, work orders, and imprisonment. Approvals have expiry dates ranging from 5 years for aquaculture and fish-rearing facilities; 30 years for marina facilities, breakwalls, and cables; to 35 years for causeways.

Inquiries are directed to Canadian Coast Guard as with docks and boathouses (see above). Refer to the section on boathouses, docks and shoreline interference for inquiries relating to navigable waters in terms of the *Fisheries Act*.

Water Sources

Municipal water systems, surface waters, and wells are all standard water sources. The *Clean Water Act*, S.O. 2006, c. 22 partners municipalities, conservation authorities, communities, and landowners in the protection, identification of risks, and the monitoring of watersheds and water sources, including municipal drinking water sources. Water shortages, consumption issues, and water safety are becoming increasingly problematic. Water sources, particularly wells, are based on the health of the underlying aquifer. Consider the services of a hydrologist when relying on flow requirements. Water issues can have a profound effect on marketability and property values as evidenced by recent American litigation.

Water Quality

Since the Walkerton Inquiry, there has been a heightened awareness about water quality and drinking water safety issues. The Canadian myth of infinite supply of clean water has been refuted. Indeed, environmental and ecosystem health researchers suggest that Canada is facing a water crisis. Title insurers, not surprisingly, generally exclude water issues from coverage, except for potability coverage for lenders on single-family residential properties. Bacterial contamination such as fecal coliform, chemical and industrial contamination such as pesticides, PCBs, and motor oils, and mineral contamination such as lead, mercury, cadmium, and arsenic all require repeated testing in private labs. The local health unit and the MOE provide testing services for bacterial contaminants. Urban properties and municipal water systems, particularly subdivisions before the mid-1960s, may have unsafe levels of lead contamination (there is no safe level for children). Acidification of surface waters can increase heavy mineral leaching. New developments can cause the migration of contaminants into areas previously unaffected. Water quality testing is not just for wells, lakes and rivers, and recreational and agricultural lands.

Permit to Take Water

In Ontario, before well construction begins, a Permit to Take Water must be obtained under the *Ontario Water Resources Act* for the taking of over 50,000 litres per day (with some exceptions such as farming uses, fighting fires, *etc.*). This requirement for permits creates a record of information on groundwater use in an area. Owners must monitor and keep records subject to MOE inspections and renew permits periodically. Domestic uses, such as a well for the private use of the property owner, fall far below 50,000 litres a day and usually do not require a permit to take water. Ontario Regulation 387/04 governs water takings and permits and R.R.O. 1990, Reg. 903 governs wells (both regulations fall under the *Ontario Water Resources Act*).

Welldriller's Certificate

The *Ontario Water Resources Act* regulates wells. Wells must be constructed by licensed contractors. The welldriller's certificate contains the depth of the well, the flow per minute (recovery rate report at the time of installation), and the potability assessment. The Well Installation Report is filed with and available from the MOE or the local health unit. Wells may not meet current construction standards and an inspection by a licensed well contractor is prudent. Water quality testing should be done by a private lab for the presence and the concentration of bacterial, chemical, mineral, or natural contamination. The local health unit and the MOE provide limited testing.

Wells must meet health and safety standards, and an unused or abandoned well must be plugged and sealed (R.R.O. 1990, Reg. 903, s. 21.1). Wells should be maintained, inspected, and tested on a regular basis (R.R.O. 1990, Reg. 903,

s. 20). New wells since August 1, 2003 receive well tags on approval. Improperly maintained wells or wells that do not meet requirements can generate offences, fines, and work orders (*Ontario Water Resources Act*, ss. 83 and 84). Inquiries are directed to the MOE or the local health unit. Work orders, costs, and fines are a priority lien on land and can be added to the municipal tax rolls and collected as taxes (*Ontario Water Resources Act*, s. 88(2)).

Small Drinking Water Systems

Part IV of the *Safe Drinking Water Act* regulates safe drinking water in Ontario. Part IV of the Act regulates municipal and non-municipal drinking water systems, including system approvals, water licences, inspections, testing, emergency response to an imminent drinking water hazard, work orders, fines, and offences. Work orders and costs are a priority lien on land and can be added to the municipal tax rolls and collected as taxes (*Safe Drinking Water Act*, s. 124). Local Services Boards in unorganized territories are subject to similar enforcement procedures.

As of December 1, 2008, the Ministry of Health and Long-Term Care administers the Small Drinking Water Systems (SDWS) program under O. Reg. 319/08 (*Health Protection and Promotion Act*). A SDWS is a system other than a residential municipal drinking water system that offers water to the public, such as seasonal trailer parks, summer camps, motels, bed and breakfasts, gas stations, restaurants, community centres, churches, private cottages, and communal drinking water systems. Children's camps, health care facilities, schools, colleges, universities, and similar facilities are designated not to be SDWSs and therefore are regulated by the MOE. SDWSs require regular sampling for E. coli and total coliforms. Local health units and public health inspectors conduct site-specific risk assessments and customized directives for follow-up for all SDWSs. Prior to the first inspection, transitional rules apply (O. Reg. 318/08).

Owners of SDWSs must retain water testing records and make these records available to the public. Inspectors have broad powers of entry, inspection, and enforcement. Any person who contravenes the Act or a directive under the Act is guilty of an offence and is subject to a fine of not more than $5,000 per day; corporations are subject to $25,000 per day (*Health Protection and Promotion Act*, s. 101).

Flood Plain and Flooding Rights

Federal and provincial Crowns, municipalities, conservation authorities, mining and hydro-electric companies, and even mills may have flooding rights. Flood plains have building and use restrictions. Inquiries are made to the appropriate authority. Parks Canada has records on historical water and power generation rights.

SEPTIC SYSTEMS, WASTEWATER OR SEWAGE SYSTEMS, AND OUTHOUSES

There are six classes of wastewater and sewage disposal systems include pit-privies (outhouses), holding tanks, chemical toilets, grey water or leaching pit systems (only non-human waste), aerobic treatment plant systems, and septic tanks with leaching beds. Septic systems are the most common. Today, permits, inspections, fees, penalties, and work orders apply to all of these disposal systems. The building permit for the residential structure will not be issued without the certificate of approval for the sewage system.

Sewage systems with a capacity of less than 10,000 litres per day are regulated under Part 8 of Division B of the Building Code, O. Reg. 350/06 (*Building Code Act, 1992*, S.O. 1992, c. 23). Sewage systems with a capacity of more than 10,000 litres per day are regulated by the MOE under the *Ontario Water Resources Act*. The *Ontario Water Resources Act* now regulates the licensing of sewage works operators (O. Reg. 129/04), municipal sewage and water and roads class environmental assessment projects (R.R.O. 1990, Reg. 900), and sewage works subject to approval under the *Environmental Assessment Act* (O. Reg. 207/97).

Septic Systems

When dealing with septic systems, confirm with the municipal building department that building permits and certificates of approval were issued and that interim and final inspections were completed for post-April 6, 1998 systems (see Part 8 of Division B of the Building Code). Some municipalities choose to delegate the responsibility for septic systems to the local health unit. Conservation authorities deal with septic systems within their boundaries. For systems pre-April 6, 1998, confirm building permits and certificates of approval and make inquiry of the Ministry of the Environment or local health unit. Lawyers complete file searches for the installation report, which usually contains a sketch and location of the system. Also search for notices of violation and work orders, fines, and complaint records. Search requests require the property description, previous owners and dates of ownership, and the installer's name. Records are most often but not always with the health unit. A written owner consent is required if the purchaser wishes to request an inspection. Title insurer coverage of septic systems is by endorsement and varies among insurers; however, the insurers generally require searches for use permits for older systems, cover compliance, and encroachment issues, but not condition and function issues.

Outhouses

An outhouse (pit-privy) is a Class 1 sewage treatment system and its placement and construction is regulated by the Building Code, although they usually do not require a building permit (below minimum area). There may also be local by-laws that regulate outhouses. Pit-privies must be 15 metres from a drilled well; 30 metres from a dug well or spring used for drinking water; 15 metres from a lake, pond, stream, or reservoir; 3 metres from a property line; and 90 centimetres above the high groundwater table. There are also leaching bed, run-off, and, mercifully, ventilation requirements.

NUTRIENT MANAGEMENT ACT

The *Nutrient Management Act, 2002*, S.O. 2002, c. 4 protects water resources by managing materials containing nutrients (manure). It affects farm properties and is administered by the Ministry of Agriculture, Food and Rural Affairs. Inspectors can issue work orders that are transferred to the municipality for enforcement by adding the amounts and costs to the municipal tax rolls for collection. Farms must have an approved nutrient management strategy for the removal of manure or an approved nutrient strategy plan for the storage or use of manure (O. Reg. 267/03). Conveyancers can make inquiries at the Ministry of Agriculture, Food and Rural Affairs for outstanding work orders. Tax inquiries are directed to the Municipal Property Assessment Corporation.

MINISTRY OF NATURAL RESOURCES

The Ministry of Natural Resources (MNR) administers a number of statutes and programs that relate to lands, forests, water, fish and wildlife, parks, and related health and safety concerns that involve permits, licences, potential fines, and work orders. The MNR is responsible for compliance, investigations, permits, and licensing under the following:

- *Public Lands Act*, R.S.O. 1990, c. P.43: regulates disposition of Crown lands, management and zoning of Crown lands (beaches, water lots, particularly shorelines, boathouses, docks, *etc.*), roads on Crown lands (public and private forest roads), construction and maintenance of dams, and water powers and privileges;
- *Aggregate Resources Act*, R.S.O. 1990, c. A.8: regulates pits, quarries, aspects of beach protection, and some mining activities;
- *Beds of Navigable Waters Act*, R.S.O. 1990, c. B.4;
- *Conservation Land Act*, R.S.O. 1990, c. C.28;
  - **Grants**: the *Conservation Land Act* provides the framework through conservation authorities for the following grants:
    - grants to rural and agricultural landowners to improve water quality, reduce soil erosion, increase natural areas cover, and restore natural areas (s. 2(2)). These programs are in part a response to the Walkerton Inquiry and the initiatives under the *Clean Water Act, 2006*, whereby municipalities, conservation authorities, and communities collaborate to protect, identify risks, and monitor water sources, including municipal drinking water sources;

- grants supporting the conservation of land under the Conservation Land Tax Incentive Program (CLTIP). CLTIP provides property tax relief up to 100 per cent to landowners who agree to protect the natural heritage values of their provincially significant property and who are not associated with Conservation Authorities or Conservation Authority properties (see more on CLTIP earlier in this chapter);

- **Conservation Easements and Covenants** (see Chapter 9): section 3(2) of the *Conservation Land Act* provides that an owner of land may grant an easement to or enter into a covenant with one or more conservation bodies, including the Crown in right of Canada or in right of Ontario; an agency, board, or commission of the Crown in right of Canada or in right of Ontario that has the power to hold an interest in land; a band as defined in the *Indian Act*, R.S.C. 1985, c. I-5; the council of a municipality; a conservation authority; a corporation incorporated under Part III of the *Corporations Act*, R.S.O. 1990, c. C.38 or Part II of the *Canada Corporations Act*, R.S.C. 1970, c. C-32 that is a charity registered under the *Income Tax Act*, R.S.C. 1985 (5th Supp.), c. 1; a trustee of a charitable foundation that is a charity registered under the *Income Tax Act*; or any person or body prescribed by the regulations for the following purposes:
  - for the conservation, maintenance, restoration or enhancement of all or a portion of the land or the wildlife on the land;
  - for the protection of water quality and quantity, including protection of drinking water sources;
  - for watershed protection and management;
    for the conservation, preservation, or protection of the land for agricultural purposes;
  - for the purposes prescribed by the regulations made under the *Conservation Land Act*; or
  - for access to the land for the purposes referred to in clause (a), (b), (c), (d) or (e).

  These covenants may be in perpetuity and run with the land. Compliance is monitored by the authority. Purchasers should inquire whether there has been non-compliance and potentially resulting work orders and fines in relation to conservation easements registered on title;

- *Conservation Authorities Act*, R.S.O. 1990, c. C.27: conservation authorities in partnership with municipalities manage land and water and environmental land use planning (s. 28(1)) within their jurisdiction. Conservation authorities administer "development, interference with wetlands, and alterations to shorelines and watercourses" under O. Reg. 97/04. Conservation authorities also regulate natural and erosion hazards and administer flood control activities in areas prone to flooding. Work or development, including buildings and change in buildings, site grading, temporary or permanent dumping or removal of material that affects or is near lakes, rivers, streams, wetlands, or flood plains requires approvals and inspections from the conservation authority. Non-compliance can generate work orders and fines. Other approvals, such as municipal building permits, approvals under the *Fisheries Act*, zoning, and severances may also be required in addition to a conservation authority approval. Inquiries for regulations, including septic systems within the authority boundaries, approvals/permits, inspections, and outstanding work orders and fines are directed to the conservation authority;

- *Forestry Act*, R.S.O. 1990, c. F.26: administers agreements with landowners including municipalities and conservation authorities for the management of forests;
- *Crown Forest Sustainability Act, 1994*, S.O. 1994, c. 25;
- *Fish and Wildlife Conservation Act, 1997*, S.O. 1997, c. 41: includes licensing of traplines and aquaculture projects, as well as general protection of wildlife;
- *Lakes and Rivers Improvement Act*, R.S.O. 1990, c. L.3: requires approvals for use of water and construction, including dams and maintenance of water levels (see above for details);
- *Mining Act*, R.S.O. 1990, c. M.14: relates to mining, mining claims, rehabilitation and closure of mining lands, and oil and gas (ss. 100-102);
- *Provincial Parks and Conservation Reserves Act, 2006*, S.O. 2006, c. 12: provides for park zoning and specifically controlled use zones, controls mining in parks, and administers tenders and leases for buildings and facilities leases granted in parks;
- *Wild Rice Harvesting Act*, R.S.O. 1990, c. W.7: the harvesting of wild rice requires a licence; and
- *Forestry Workers Lien for Wages Act*, R.S.O. 1990, c. F.28: liens in favour of forestry workers attach to logs or timber on land.

NIAGARA ESCARPMENT PLANNING AND DEVELOPMENT ACT

All construction, site and grade alterations, pond excavations, forestry, and other environmental land alterations in the Niagara Escarpment Plan Area must comply with the *Niagara Escarpment Planning and Development Act*, R.S.O. 1990, c. N.2 and its regulations, and the Niagara Escarpment Plan. Niagara Escarpment landowners must obtain an Escarpment Development Permit for certain types of development and use. Permits are needed for change of use from residential to commercial. Purchasers of land within the Niagara Escarpment Plan Area can obtain information on land use restrictions and confirm whether permits were obtained for existing structures and uses.

GREENBELT ACT, 2005

Under the *Greenbelt Act, 2005*, S.O. 2005, c. 1, the Ministry of Municipal Affairs and Housing regulates environmentally and agriculturally sensitive areas in the Golden Horsehoe, such as the Oak Ridges Moraine Conservation Plan Area, the Niagara Escarpment Plan Area, the protected Countryside Area, and the Parkway Belt West Plan. The Act identifies no urbanization areas. Municipal official plans must comply with Greenbelt restrictions. Municipal applications and permits must comply with the Ontario Greenbelt policy statement. The Ministry of Municipal Affairs and Housing provides online reference maps for the Greenbelt area. These policies can have a profound impact on future development plans, property values, and marketability. They are particularly relevant to commercial transactions.

Greenbelt inquiries should be addressed to the local municipality, the Ministry of Municipal Affairs and Housing, the Oak Ridges Moraine Foundation, or the Niagara Escarpment Commission. Possible Greenbelt inquiries include the following: confirmation that the property is within the Greenbelt boundaries; permitted and restricted uses; whether the property is in a growth area and permitted uses; compliance status of property or development application; designations under the official plan; and proposed changes to the official plan.

The Ministry website has a useful reference chart for 444 Ontario municipalities that gives an "overview of where planning approval authority rests with respect to the approval of official plans and amendments, subdivisions, condominiums, consents, power of sales and validations, either by being directly assigned in the *Planning Act* or prescribed or delegated by the Minister of Municipal Affairs and Housing pursuant to the *Planning Act* for municipalities, planning boards and municipal planning authorities in Ontario": <http://www.mah.gov.on.ca/AssetFactory.aspx?did=1076>.

GREEN ENERGY AND GREEN ECONOMY ACT, 2009

Ontario Bill 150, the *Green Energy and Green Economy Act, 2009* received Royal Assent on May 14, 2009. It amends portions of the *Planning Act*, the *Ontario Water Resources Act*, the *Environmental Protection Act, the Conservation Land Act*, the *Conservation Authorities Act, the Greenbelt Act, 2005*, the *Niagara Escarpment Planning and Development Act*, and the *Public Lands Act*. In general, the Act emphasizes the consideration of environmental benefits and detriments, energy conservation, and the facilitation of green energy initiatives on approval processes under other statutes.

Renewable energy approvals under the Act may provide alternative approvals for or exemptions from other statutes. For example, renewable energy projects are not required to meet official plan and zoning requirements under s. 24 and Part IV of the *Planning Act*. Renewable energy generation facilities, projects, and testing facilities require approvals and may carry conditions and restrictions. This Act, as it takes effect, will generate new inquiries confirming approvals, conditions, restrictions, compliance, and work orders and fines.

Easing of Permitting Requirements for Renewable Energy Projects

The *Green Energy and Green Economy Act, 2009*, S.O. 2009, c. 12 amends the *Planning Act* by effectively eliminating municipal land use planning jurisdiction over "renewable energy undertakings", including the Ontario Power Authority's feed-in-tariff program. Section 62.0.2 of the *Planning Act* states that the following land use planning policies and instruments do not apply to "renewable energy undertakings":

- policy statements relating to matters of provincial interest;
- provincial plans other than the Niagara Escarpment Plan;
- municipal official plans;
- development permit systems;
- municipal by-laws including zoning by-laws, demolition control by-laws, site plan approvals, and minor variances;
- order under the *Ontario Planning and Development Act, 1994*, S.O. 1994, c. 23, Schedule A;
- minister's zoning orders; and
- zoning by-laws and site plan approvals under ss. 113 and 114 of the *City of Toronto Act, 2006* (*Planning Act*, s. 62.0.1(1)).

As well, "renewable energy undertakings" are exempt from the s. 50 subdivision and part lot control restrictions and from public consultation requirements in land use decisions. Approvals for "renewable energy undertakings" may only be challenged on the basis that the undertaking will cause "serious harm to human health or serious and irreversible harm to plant life, animal life or the natural environment" (*Environmental Protection Act*, s. 142.1(3)(a)-(b)). By streamlining the approvals process and creating a renewable energy facilitator, the *Green Energy and Green Economy Act, 2009* has, for practical purposes, generated an "express lane" through the traditional barriers of municipal and provincial land use regulation for renewable energy undertakings.

The Act also proposes that all homeowners provide "information, reports and/or ratings" on energy consumption and efficiency before selling their property. In theory, the cost savings and increased home prices may offset the estimated $300 it will cost for an energy audit, half of which is covered by a government rebate.

MINING CLAIMS, MINING ACT LIENS, AND MINING LANDS TAX SEARCHES UNDER THE MINING ACT

Mining Act Claims

Prospectors can, without the permission of or notice to the property owner, stake a mining claim on land. The *Mining Act* allows a mining company to start exploration work on staked claims with 24 hours' notice and without an environmental assessment. Mining claims are active in the North and the near North, such as the Haliburton Highlands cottage country for graphite and uranium claims. There is inherent conflict between the owners of surface rights and mining claims and mining rights under the Act. Some owners own surface rights only while the Crown retains below-ground mineral rights. These rights may be claimed under the Act or leased by the Crown. Registration records and Crown patents reveal the separation of surface and subsurface rights. Land Titles has separate registers for surface and mineral rights.

It is common in Northern Ontario for surface rights to be separated from below-ground mineral rights; it is uncommon in southern Ontario (about 1.4 per cent) for surface rights to be separated from below-ground mineral rights. Bill 173, the *Mining Amendment Act, 2009*, S.O. 2009, c. 21, received Royal Assent on October 29, 2009 and seeks to modernize the *Mining Act* and balance the competing claims of the mining industry, owners of surface rights, environmental interests, and Aboriginal rights. As of Royal Assent, the Ministry of Northern Development, Mines and Forestry has barred prospecting and claims rights against surface-rights-only private land ownership south of Lake Nipissing, the French River, and the Mattawa River. This decision does not affect claims staked before April 30, 2009. In northern Ontario, private landowners can apply to have Crown-held mineral rights withdrawn from staking. Existing claims and leases are not affected.

The Ministry of Northern Development, Mines and Forestry provides CLAIMaps, a service for the online searching of mining claim information in Ontario. The site is updated nightly. The Ministry of Northern Development, Mines and Forestry also provides an online registry of staked mining claims related to unpatented mining claims in the Province of Ontario. The mining claims information is updated nightly. Conveyancers search to determine the existence and the status of mining claims and mining rights.

Mining Land Tax Searches and Notification of Ownership Change

Large areas of patented lands in Ontario were originally patented under the *Mining Act* or the now-repealed *Gold Mining Act, 1864*, Cap. IX, 27-28 Vict. and the *Gold and Silver Mining Act of 1868*. Part XIII of the *Mining Act* provides for mining land taxes. The patent identifies land as mining land. The legal description often mentions a mining claim or a mining location. Mining rights severed from the surface rights are also subject to mining tax. Land being used for mining purposes, whatever the nature of the original patent, is subject to mining tax. Residential properties may be subject to mining taxes until the mining rights have been surrendered. Mining taxes are a priority lien on mining lands and mining rights (*Mining Act*, s. 200).

Conveyancers complete Mining Land Tax Searches with the Ministry of Northern Development, Mines and Forestry and obtain mining tax certificates for applicable properties. Searches are based on the precise description of the original mining lands. Mining taxes should be adjusted on closing. Purchasers must notify the Ministry of a change in ownership by sending a copy of an updated parcel register or registered transfer in order to receive mining tax bills and avoid arrears. Mining tax searches are required by title insurers.

Forfeiture for Non-Payment of Mining Taxes

If the mining land taxes are two or more years in arrears, the Ministry can start forfeiture of freehold patent or mining rights proceedings under Part XIII of the *Mining Act*, ss. 188, 190, and 197, and Policy L.P. 402-2, "Forfeiture for Non-Payment of Taxes: Patents" (May 1, 2009). Land with a patent that includes mining and surface rights may be subject to provincial lands or municipal tax for surface rights and mining tax for mining rights. In this case, forfeiture would only be for mining rights. A forfeiture notice may be sent six months after non-payment for two years. The owner has another six months to pay the overdue account or forfeit the land to the Crown. The Minister may choose not to take the land by forfeiture, particularly if there are safety or environmental hazards on the land.

Mining Lands or Mining Claim Compensation Liens

Under the *Mining Act*, R.S.O. 1990, c. M.14, as amended, mining entities have the right to use adjoining lands for certain mining purposes such as tailings. The Act requires the mining concern to compensate surface rights holders and adjoining owner(s) for damage to surface rights (s. 175(1)-(3)). Unpaid compensation is a special lien on mining claims and mining lands, and the Commissioner of Mines may also place a stop work order on mining activity until the compensation has been paid. Purchasers must search for special liens and stop work orders when buying mining land, claims, or rights.

NON-RESIDENT OWNERS AND THE INCOME TAX ACT

Section 116 of the *Income Tax Act* places a withholding tax on non-residents when they sell land in Canada. "Non-resident" of Canada is defined in s. 2 and s. 250 of the Act (IT-221R3) as an individual who: normally, customarily, or routinely lives in another country and is not considered a resident of Canada; does not have residential ties in Canada; lives outside Canada throughout the tax year; or stays in Canada for less than 183 days in the tax year. A Canadian government employee, a member of the Canadian Forces or their overseas school staff, or an individual working under a Canadian International Development Agency program are deemed resident. These rules can also apply to dependent children and other family members. A person who is a resident of another country under a tax treaty is usually treated as a non-resident. There are additional deeming residency rules for individuals and for companies, partnerships, and trusts.

Purchasers must obtain evidence that vendors are residents of Canada. In the alternative, the non-resident seller may produce a clearance certificate verifying that the tax has been paid. If a purchaser does not obtain proof that the seller is a resident or a clearance certificate, then the purchaser is required to withhold 25 per cent of the proceeds of disposition and is personally liable for 25 per cent of the purchase price, payable to the Canada Revenue Agency within 30 days after the end of the month in which the property was transferred (s. 116(5)). The purchaser is also liable for a 10 per cent penalty for non-payment and a 20 per cent penalty if the purchaser knowingly failed to report and pay or was grossly negligent. It is also necessary to obtain proof of residency or a clearance for a non-resident owner/mortgagor whose mortgage has gone into default and is now being sold by power of sale.

Goods and Services Tax

It is essential to confirm a purchaser's Goods and Services Tax (GST) registration number on the Canada Revenue Agency GST registry website when the purchaser provides an indemnity and undertaking to pay GST based on the self assessment rule. The vendor is not permitted to rely on a purchaser's statement and runs the risks of being liable for fraudulent or negligent misrepresentations by the purchaser.

SUPER PRIORITY LIENS

Lawyers for purchasers and lenders must determine whether federal or provincial legislation has created a lien in favour of the Crown against real estate for taxpayers who have defaulted on payments (source deductions) to the government. Some statutory liens must be registered on title to affect a new purchaser or lender who has paid value or advanced funds towards the land without notice of the lien. Other liens affect land without being registered and must be investigated by off-title inquiries. Some potential liens can only be dealt with by clauses in the agreement of purchase and sale. The statute determines whether or not registration is required. Government liens usually have priority over private claims. The following claims deem that payments owed are held in trust for the Crown and have absolute priority over a creditor's security interests, including prior security interests and over assets acquired by the tax debtor.

Purchasers and lenders, when purchasing or lending on property that might be affected by a super priority lien, may request and review tax remittance statements and returns and have them reviewed by accountants. Purchasers and lenders include indemnity clauses in agreements of purchase and sale. Lenders insert in loan agreements that super priority liens are an encumbrance and hence a default and can accelerate the loan. In commercial transactions, title insurers will arrange customized coverage for super priority liens.

Income Tax Act

Section 227(4) of the *Income Tax Act* gives a priority lien and deemed trust to the Crown against property of the taxpayer/debtor for amounts deducted or withheld for *Income Tax Act* liabilities. The Canada Revenue Agency will confirm tax compliance but offers no guarantees and can reassess.

Excise Tax Act

Section 221(1) of the *Excise Tax Act*, R.S.C. 1985, c. E-15 gives a priority lien and deemed trust to the Crown against property of the taxpayer/debtor for amounts collected on account of excise tax liabilities.

Canada Pension Plan

Section 23(3) of the *Canada Pension Plan*, R.S.C. 1985, c. C-8 gives a priority lien and deemed trust to the Crown against property of the employer/debtor for amounts an employer has deducted but not remitted from remuneration of an employee as a pension contribution.

Employment Insurance Act

Section 86(2) of the *Employment Insurance Act*, S.O. 1996, c. 23 gives a priority lien and deemed trust to the Crown against property of the employer/debtor for amounts an employer has deducted but not remitted from remuneration of an employee as an employment insurance premium.

Retail Sales Tax Act

Section 22(1) of the *Retail Sales Act*, R.S.O. 1990, c. R.31 gives a priority lien and deemed trust to the Crown against the vendor's/debtor's property for amounts a vendor has collected or are collectable on account of *Retail Sales Act* liabilities. The Ontario government issues binding clearance certificates.

Gasoline Tax Act

Section 18(1) of the *Gasoline Tax Act*, R.S.O. 1990, c. G.5 gives a priority lien and deemed trust to the Crown against the collector's or the registered importer's property for amounts collected or collectable under the Act.

Fuel Tax Act

Section 3.6.1 of the *Fuel Tax Act*, R.S.O. 1990, c. F.35 gives a priority lien and deemed trust against the collector's, distributor's, or registered importer's property to the Crown for amounts collected or collectable under the Act.

Tobacco Tax Act

Section 24.1(1) of the *Tobacco Tax Act*, R.S.O. 1990, c. T.10 gives a priority lien and deemed trust against the collector's, or registered importer's property to the Crown for amounts collected or collectable under the Act.

CEMETERIES

Cemeteries must be licensed. Suspected burial sites must be reported to the police or the coroner.

Section 1(b) of Burial Sites, O. Reg. 133/92 (under the *Cemeteries Act (Revised)*, R.S.O. 1990, c. T.10) provides that when an "unapproved aboriginal peoples cemetery" is identified, the representatives of the deceased shall be "the nearest First Nations Government or other community of Aboriginal people which is willing to act as a representative and whose members have a close cultural affinity to the interred person". The consent of the representative is needed before the remains and associated artifacts can be removed from the cemetery or before scientific analysis of the remains. The owner of the land must comply with the site disposition agreement.

Searches for site disposition agreements and licences are directed to the municipality or the cemeteries regulation unit of the Ministry of Government Services.

HERITAGE PROPERTIES

The *Ontario Heritage Act*, R.S.O. 1990, c. O.18 provides for the designation by municipal by-law of heritage properties (s. 29). Heritage designation by-laws are registered in the registry office. The Act requires that the city clerk maintain a municipal register of designated heritage properties that contains the address, the legal description, the name and address of the current owner, and the reasons for designation. The municipality may provide loans for the maintenance of heritage properties. Repair and property renovation are restricted and may require permissions and inspections. These loans and non-compliance under the Act may create both work orders and liens on the property. These priority liens may be added to the municipal tax roll and collected as taxes (s. 39). Searches relating to heritage properties, including designation and proposed designation, work orders, restrictions on use, and liens are directed to the office of the municipal clerk.

Federal legislation similarly addresses heritage properties as historic places. Address inquiries to Parks Canada.

There are a number of municipal, provincial, and federal registers available online for searching the identification or designation of heritage sites/historic places, including:

1. The Canadian Register of Historic Places — This is an online federal register of heritage properties, including National Historic Sites; registration provides no protection.

2. Heritage Railway Stations — The Minister of Parks Canada can designate heritage railway stations under the federal *Heritage Railway Stations Protection Act*. Designation provides some protection from railway companies for designated stations.

3. The Ontario Heritage Properties Database.

4. The Ontario Ministry of Culture maintains an online comprehensive, searchable database that includes the following protected heritage properties:

    a. properties designated by municipal by-law under Part IV or Part V of the *Ontario Heritage Act*;
    b. properties protected by a municipal heritage conservation easement;
    c. properties owned by the Ontario Heritage Trust (formerly Ontario Heritage Foundation);
    d. properties protected by an Ontario Heritage Trust conservation easement;
    e. properties listed on the Ontario Heritage Bridge List;
    f. properties protected by the federal *Heritage Railway Stations Protection Act*;
    g. properties designated a National Historic Site; and
    h. properties listed in the Canadian Register of Historic Places.

5. Ontario Heritage Conservation Districts (HCDs).

6. The Ontario Ministry of Culture maintains an online record and description of current and proposed (HCD study complete and awaiting by-law) Heritage Conservation Districts. This list contains a reference to the nature of the property and the municipal designation by-law. It also contains a list of areas under study.

7. The Toronto Inventory of Heritage Properties — This online index is searchable alphabetically, by address, by district, or by architect and cross-references designation by-laws.

8. Toronto Heritage Conservation Districts — The City of Toronto maintains an online record and description of current and proposed (HCD study complete and awaiting by-law) Heritage Conservation

Districts. This list contains a reference to the nature of the property and the municipal designation by-law. It also contains a list of areas under study.

Appendix 5 contains website addresses for the above searchable, online heritage site registers.

CONDOMINIUM STATUS CERTIFICATE (ESTOPPEL CERTIFICATE) AND DISCLOSURE STATEMENTS

Chapter 7 addresses the detailed requirements that apply to condominium status certificates and disclosure statements. Title insurers require recent status certificates except for residential refinance transactions (normally within about 30 days of closing).

AIRPORTS AND FEDERAL AIRPORT ZONING REGULATIONS

The *Aeronautics Act*, R.S.C. 1985, c. A-2 is administered by Transport Canada. The Act authorizes the creation of airport sites by order in council published in the *Canada Gazette* and authorizes federal airport zoning regulations that impose restrictions on property owners adjacent to airports. These restrictions limit the height of buildings, structures, and natural growth, prohibit electronic signal interference, regulate lighting, and restrict activities which attract birds that pose a threat to aviation safety. Airport zoning regulations come into force when deposited in the local registry office. These restrictions apply only to new buildings and uses; prior uses are treated as legal non-conforming uses. Land adjacent to proposed airports may also be regulated by a Minister's Zoning Order from the Ministry of Municipal Affairs and Housing. Transport Canada enforces airport zoning regulations and collaborates with municipalities on compatible municipal zoning and enforcement.

Engineering or planning consultants and surveyors can assist in determining whether a development is in compliance with airport zoning. Special rules apply for military airports, aerodromes, aircraft rescue, and fire fighting. For military airports, inquiries are directed to Transport Canada and the Ministry of National Defence and the Canadian Forces.

AREAS WITHOUT MUNICIPAL ORGANIZATION

Provincial Land Tax Act, 2006

Provincial land tax, as regulated by the *Provincial Land Tax Act, 2006*, S.O. 2006, c. 33, Schedule Z.2 is collected on all land in areas located outside of municipal borders and assessed on current values as of 2009. These taxes fund provincial services and are administered by the Ontario Ministry of Revenue. Provincial land taxes contain provincial land tax and education tax, and may contain Local Roads Board and Local Services Board charges depending on whether the Local Roads Board and/or the Local Services Board have opted into the recent one-bill system. Residents may continue to pay separate charges to Local Roads Boards and Local Services Boards. Provincial land tax is a special lien on land (s. 12(3)).

Inquiries and requests for tax certificates are directed to the Provincial Land Tax Office in Thunder Bay.

Northern Services Boards Act

Local services boards under the *Northern Services Boards Act*, R.S.O. 1990, c. L.28 are set up in rural areas to regulate the provision of and the payment for municipal-like services where there is no municipal organization. They supply some or all of the services authorized under the Act, such as water supply, fire protection, garbage collection, sewage works, lighting, recreation, roads, library services, and emergency telecommunications. Municipal-like inquiries are made to local services boards. The Ministry of Northern Development, Mines and Forestry administers the Act.

Local Roads Boards Act

The *Local Roads Boards Act*, R.S.O. 1990, c. L.27 provides for the construction and maintenance of roads in areas without municipal organization. The Ministry of Municipal Affairs and Housing and the Ministry of Transportation administer the Act. The Local Roads Board can levy charges annually on land for road purposes. These charges are a priority lien on land and can be collected like taxes (s. 27(1)). Road charges unpaid for two years can result in forfeiture to the Crown. The Board will register a caution, wait at least 12 months, and then register a certificate of forfeiture. Inquiries are addressed to the Local Roads Board. The Ministry of Transportation provides background on Local Roads Boards.

Zoning in Areas without Municipal Organization

The *Public Lands Act* provides for the designation and administration of restricted areas in unorganized territories similar in function to municipal zoning regulations. Inquiries are directed to the Ministry of Natural Resources concerning the regulation of and restrictions on use, and related permits, work orders, and liens for areas without municipal organization. The MNR will no longer designate new restricted areas in unorganized territories. In future, the Ministry of Municipal Affairs and Housing will exercise zoning powers over unorganized territories by Minister's Zoning Order under s. 47(1) of the *Planning Act*.

Refer to MNR Policy No. PL 2.09.01, "Restricted Areas — Section 13, *Public Lands Act*" (May 9, 2008).

LIQUOR LICENCE ACT

When purchasing a property/business that has a liquor licence, confirm with the Alcohol and Gaming Commission of Ontario whether notices to revoke, suspend, or refuse have been given. (Refer to the *Liquor Licence Act*, R.S.O. 1990, c. L.19.)

WORKPLACE-RELATED INQUIRIES

Under the *Workplace Safety and Insurance Act, 1997*, S.O. 1997, c. 16, Schedule A, purchasers of land and a business are liable for liens for premiums owing of a prior owner/employer registered under the Act. Employers also need clearance certificates for contractors and subcontractors. Clearance certificates must be obtained from the Workplace Safety and Insurance Board.

Under the *Occupational Health and Safety Act*, R.S.O. 1990, c. O.1, inspectors can issue non-compliance orders and fines against employers. Information about the existence and status of work orders can be researched at the Labour Board.

BANK ACT SECURITY AND SECTION 427 SEARCHES

Section 427 of the *Bank Act*, S.C. 1991, c. 46 allows banks to make loans secured on inventory to farming-, forestry-, mining-, and manufacturing-related businesses. Section 427 security requires the filing of a notice of intention with the Bank of Canada to be a preferential lien on property, including crops before or after harvest. Searches are made when purchasing farm, forestry, mining, and business property.

Requests for searches for *Bank Act* security or for clearance certificates can be made to the Bank of Canada registry for *Bank Act* security items or through online service providers such as Dye & Durham, the Canadian Securities Registration System, or Cyberbahn. Searches are made against current and former individual and business, and corporate names.

BANKRUPTCY SEARCHES

Name searches for bankruptcy and insolvency are directed to the Office of the Superintendent of Bankruptcy. *Bankruptcy and Insolvency Act*, R.S.C. 1985, c. B-3 issues are not covered by commercial title insurance policies. Searches are completed for commercial transactions.

GST/HST REGISTRY SEARCH

The Canada Revenue Agency provides an online search for GST/HST that verifies registration and registration numbers fo businesses. Vendors can confirm whether or not a purchaser is GST/HST registered, the availability of tax credits, and whether or not to collect and remit GST/HST or to rely on purchaser self-assessment.

PERSONAL PROPERTY SECURITY ACT SEARCHES

Searches under the *Personal Property Security Act*, R.S.O. 1990, c. P.10 are done for the purchase of land and a related business, and purchases that involve inventory and personal property such as the purchase of a hotel or a restaurant. PPSA searches are addressed in more detail in the title search chapters. Appendix 5 contains contact information for PPSA searches.

ONTARIO NEW HOMES WARRANTIES PLAN ACT

The *Ontario New Homes Warranties Plan Act*, R.S.O. 1990, c. O.31 requires Ontario builders/vendors to register with TARION, enrol every new home prior to the start of construction, and provide new home warranty coverage. TARION is a non-profit corporation which administers the *Ontario New Homes Warranties Plan Act* and manages a guarantee fund that backs builder warranties. TARION protects new home deposits up to a maximum of $40,000 for freehold homes and $20,000 for condominium units and delays in closing or occupancy. New homes have statutory warranty coverage of up to a maximum of $300,000 for claims generated by warranties for one, two (from the builder), and seven years for major structural defects. Builders must complete mandatory pre-delivery inspections (PDI forms). Purchasers must submit 30-day post-possession forms and year-end forms (within the last 30 days of the first year of possession) listing outstanding statutory warranty items to the builder and to TARION.

Direct inquiries to TARION for the builder registration number, builder record, and the new home enrolment number.

RESIDENTIAL TENANCIES ACT AND THE LANDLORD AND TENANT BOARD

Title insurers do not cover residential landlord liability for illegal rent increases or other claims arising from residential tenancy legislation, namely the *Residential Tenancies Act, 2006*, S.O. 2006, c. 17. For tenanted properties, lawyers will need to obtain landlord warranties and directions to pay the new landlord, tenant acknowledgments of lease terms and rent increases and tenant attornment agreements. Purchasers also confirm the legality of rent and the existence of work orders and fines on the property with the local rent authority. In addition, municipal or Ministry inspectors can issue work orders concerning statutory standards and these work orders can be enforced and collected by the municipality. In commercial and lender transactions, title insurers offer coverage to lenders depending on the value of the loan and the loan to value ratios, and to commercial purchasers depending on the value of the transaction and coverage requested.

SPECIALTY STATUTES, SPECIALTY BY-LAWS, AND MISCELLANEOUS REGULATIONS

There is a diverse array of specific regulations that affect specific properties. Increasingly, municipalities pass by-laws that can affect owner expectations by targeting specific interests, such as the preservation of mature trees, light restriction for dark sky preserves, noise restriction, fish habitat and other eco-system health focused by-laws, seasonal use, setbacks from shorelines or other natural locations, protection or buffer zones for endangered species or sensitive areas, or viewscape protections.

The National Energy Board exercises complex approval and permit powers over oil and gas pipelines and hydro transmission lines. Specific specialty statutes dealing with specific harbours, bridges, seaways, the National Capital Commission, universities, museums, institutions, and parks (for example, the *Algonquin Forestry Authority Act*, R.S.O. 1990, c. A.17 or the Seaway Property Regulations, SOR/2003-105 (*Canada Marine Act*)) can limit the use of owners, restrict future plans, and generate work orders, offences, and fines.

FILE MANAGEMENT AND PRACTICE MANAGEMENT TOOLS FOR REAL ESTATE CONVEYANCING

There are a number of real estate file management programs available today in Ontario. Recently available LegalSTEPS from Stewart Title provides cost-effective, state-of-the-art file and practice management, including continuously updated reference information and precedents, risk management, time management, and quality control electronic tools. It also integrates with and imports and exports information to Teraview/ELRS, Ontario's electronic land registration system. In addition, LegalSTEPS provides back-up file storage. The content in file management programs is of special benefit to lawyers who have not yet built years of experience and practice resources. Now that ELRS (Electronic Land Registration System) is a centralized system, lawyers are more likely to be involved in transactions throughout Ontario; LegalSTEPS provides all practitioners with access to current contact information throughout Ontario.

LegalSTEPS is a menu-driven real estate conveyancing file and practice management tool that features a comprehensive list of potential off-title inquiries accompanied by off-title inquiry precedents and full contact information for inquiries in numerous municipalities. LegalSTEPS also offers documentation and precedents used throughout real estate transactions. Stewart Title maintains up-to-date contact information and adds additional jurisdictions and inquiries as they become available. In addition, LegalSTEPS contains standard letters that relate to issues raised by surveys, particularly easements, and has a collection of correspondence and precedents for dealing with executions that affect a property. Inquiry templates can be customized by individual users. Precedents that have been customized by different county law associations, such as standard closing documents, are also available.

LegalSTEPS can export and import transaction information into both ELRS documents and online title insurance policy applications such as StepsOnline. As well, LegalSTEPS links to and provides access to Teraview in conjunction with Ministry access clearances and Teranet's personal security package. Registration continues to take place in Teraview.

The following four figures are the LegalSTEPS off-title inquiries selection screens combined with contact information for Gravenhurst and a sample inquiry letter regarding a permit for a boathouse on Crown land. The first two screens list numerous off-title inquiries, including less routine inquiries such as the Liquor Licence Board/Licence Transfer inquiry. Once selected, the off-title inquiries are generated for the particular municipality and can be stored electronically or in paper form. Although LegalSTEPS contains a comprehensive selection of the routine off-title inquiries and can function as a checklist, individual transactions may require specialized inquiries and research that are not provided for in file management programs.

Figure 14.5.1

COMPLIANCE/OFF-TITLE SEARCHES (BY JURISDICTION) SELECTION CHECKLIST SCREEN, PART 1 (STEWART TITLE: LegalSTEPS)*

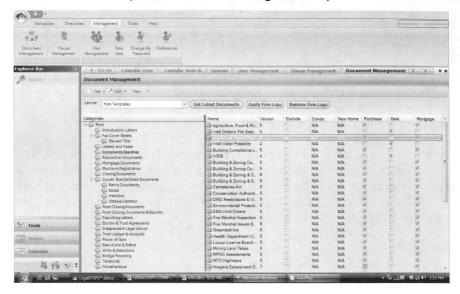

Figure 14.5.2

COMPLIANCE/OFF-TITLE SEARCHES (BY JURISDICTION) SELECTION CHECKLIST SCREEN, PART 2 (STEWART TITLE: LegalSTEPS)*

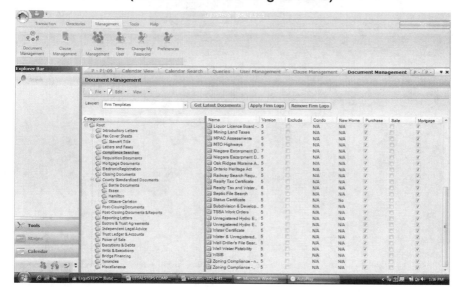

Figure 14.6

COMPLIANCE/OFF-TITLE SEARCHES (BY JURISDICTION) SELECTION CHECKLIST SCREEN (INCLUDING CONTACT INFORMATION) (STEWART TITLE: LegalSTEPS)*

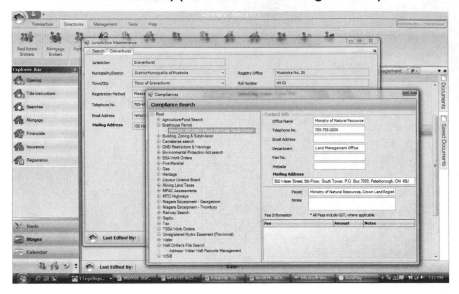

Figure 14.7

COMPLIANCE/OFF-TITLE SEARCHES (BY JURISDICTION) SELECTION CHECKLIST SCREEN (INCLUDING CONTACT INFORMATION) AND SAMPLE INQUIRY LETTER REGARDING PERMIT FOR BOATHOUSE ON CROWN LAND (STEWART TITLE: LEGALSTEPS)*

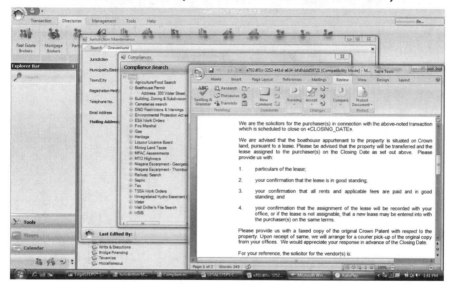

CHAPTER 15

Closing the Transaction

PRACTICE GUIDELINES AND PRACTICE RESOURCES

The Law Society of Upper Canada (LSUC) has developed the *Real Estate Practice Guide*, which includes resources such as the *Residential Real Estate Transactions Practice Guidelines*, *Practice Guidelines for e-reg*, the sample Acknowledgement and Direction and Document Registration Agreement for e-reg, as well as materials on fraud, mortgage due diligence, and cash transactions and money laundering. The LSUC website also contains detailed information on related topics, for example, the new client identification and verification requirements and the use of powers of attorney. These resources have been recently consolidated in the real estate practice portal and are available on the LSUC website at <http://www.lsuc.on.ca>.

The Ontario Government as part of its real estate fraud action plan has set strict new requirements for the following:

1. access to the electronic land registration system including a registration agreement;
2. registration requirements for Transfers including the "Two-Lawyer" requirement for transfers of title to real property; and
3. guidelines for the use of Powers of Attorney in real estate transactions.

Electronic Registration, O. Reg. 19/99 (*Land Registration Reform Act*), the Ministry of Government Services Bulletin No. 2009-01 (January 8, 2009), and Bulletin No. 2009-02 (April 15, 2009) outline the new requirements for access to the electronic land registration system (ELRS), the implementation of the two-lawyer rule in transfers, and the registration requirements for powers of attorney.

The majority of closings now take place in the context of electronic land registration. Practice, documentation, and closing procedures vary depending on location and the nature of the transaction. Some county bar associations such as Ottawa, Essex, Hamilton, and Barrie have adopted standardized closing documentation and procedures. Even something as simple as whether the vendor's or the purchaser's lawyer prepares the transfer may vary between regions and even law firms. Closing responsibilities need to be addressed in the initial letters between lawyers and incorporated into a standard or a modified document registration agreement (DRA). Closings in ELRS always require the client's written authorization in the form of an electronic registration acknowledgment and direction. Closings are complex and this chapter provides only an overview of the basics. Electronic registration procedures are dealt with in Chapter 16. The lawyer is always responsible for the ultimate review of the file and closing documentation.

Almost all closings now involve the placement of a title insurance policy. Delayed closings rely on interim/gap title insurance coverage. Title insurers no longer just set practice requirements for policy coverage but now provide practice resources, continuing education, and training services for both title insurance and transaction management. Comprehensive, "smart", real estate transaction management programs now combine precedents, contact information, practice and time management tools and alerts with the integration of online title insurance and electronic land registration systems. For example, LegalSTEPS generates closing and post-closing documentation as illustrated in the following screen captures.

PRELIMINARY MATTERS: WHAT IS NEW?

The escalating threat of fraud and related risks and the issues of money laundering in real estate transactions has resulted in a cluster of recent developments and added responsibilities in real estate practice.

NEW CLIENT IDENTIFICATION AND VERIFICATION REQUIREMENTS

Part III of By-law 7.1 governs the client identification and verification requirements. These requirements came into effect on December 31, 2008. The requirements are detailed and reference should be made to the by-law for non-routine circumstances. Lawyers must obtain and retain client identification. In addition, verification of identity is required when the transfer of funds is involved except for professional fees, disbursements, and expenses. As real estate transactions involve the transfer of funds and specifically electronic funds transfers, both identification and verification rules apply (By-law 7.1, s. 23(2) and (11)).

Client Identification

Lawyers must obtain client identification and verification documentation for clients and clients' third-party principals and beneficiaries. A lawyer is required to obtain and retain the following client information:

- **Individual Client**: full name, client's home address and home telephone number, occupation or occupations, business address and business telephone number, if applicable;

- **Organization as Client**: other than a financial institution, public body or reporting issuer, the organization's incorporation or business identification number and the place of issue of its incorporation or business identification number, general nature or type of business or businesses or activity or activities engaged in by the client, the name, position and contact information for each individual who gives instructions on behalf of the organization; and
- **Third Party Representation**: Client information as well as the name and occupation or occupations of each director of the organization, other than an organization that is a securities dealer, the name, address and occupation or occupations of each person who owns 25 per cent or more of the organization or of the shares of the organization.

Exemptions from Client Identification and Verification Requirements

There are three basic kinds of exemptions, lawyer exemptions, client exemptions, and funds exemptions. A lawyer is not required to meet identification and verification requirements when a lawyer is acting: on behalf of an employer; as an agent for a lawyer or paralegal who has already verified identity (request confirmation); on referral from another lawyer or paralegal who has already verified identity (request confirmation); when verification of identity has been completed by an employee or other lawyer or paralegal in the firm; when identity verification has been completed on a previous occasion; or as a duty counsel or summary advice provider under the *Legal Aid Services Act, 1998*, S.O. 1998, c. 26, or duty counsel for a not-for-profit. A lawyer does not need to obtain verification of identity for a financial institution, a public body, or a reporting issuer, for example, government, municipal organizations, and hospitals.

The following funds transfers are exempt:

- funds paid to or received from a financial institution, public body or reporting issuer, including funds paid, received, or transferred by electronic funds transfer;
- funds received from the trust account of another licensee or a lawyer;
- funds received from a peace officer, law enforcement agency or other public official acting in an official capacity;
- funds for judicial interim release (bail);
- funds paid or received pursuant to a court order;
- funds paid to pay a fine or penalty;
- funds paid or received as a settlement in a proceeding; and
- funds paid or received for professional fees, disbursements, expenses, or bail.

Verification of Client Identity

Verification of identity is required when a lawyer acts for a client regarding the receiving, payment, or transferring of money. Lawyers must take reasonable steps to verify the identity of clients and third parties represented by clients by obtaining and retaining reliable, independent sources of identification. Verification takes place immediately on offering client services. The lawyer has 60 days to verify the identity of an organization. Independent source identification must be original, government issued, valid and unexpired. The following are independent sources of identification for individuals and organizations:

- driver's licence;
- birth certificate;
- provincial or territorial health card if such use of the card is not prohibited by the applicable provincial or territorial law;
- passport or similar record;
- for a corporate entity or an organization, a written confirmation from a government registry as to the existence, name and address of the organization, which includes the names of the organization's directors such as a certificate of corporate status, a copy obtained from a public body of a record that the organization is required to file annually under applicable legislation, or a copy of a similar record obtained from a public body that confirms the organization's existence; and
- for an organization other than a corporation or society, such as a trust or partnership which is not registered in any government registry, a copy of the organization's constating documents, such as a trust or partnership agreement, articles of association, or any other similar record that confirms its existence as an organization.

For non-face-to-face client verification for a client present in Canada, a lawyer may accept an attestation from a person entitled to administer oaths and affirmations in Canada, a dentist, a physician, a chiropractor, a judge, a magistrate, a justice of the peace, a lawyer, a Quebec notary, a notary public, an optometrist, a pharmacist, an accountant, a professional engineer, a veterinarian, a police officer, a nurse, or a school principal. For clients outside of Canada, a lawyer may retain an agent or obtain an attestation by a commissioner of oaths.

Record Retention and Withdrawal of Service

Lawyers must obtain copies of client identification documents and retain a paper or electronic record of verification for the longer of the lawyer/client service relationship or at least six years following completion of the transfer. Lawyers must withdraw services if the lawyer knows that he/she would be assisting in a fraud or illegal conduct.

THE TWO-LAWYER RULE FOR TRANSFERS

As of April 7, 2008, both a lawyer for the buyer and a lawyer for the vendor must sign a transfer of title. In the electronic land registration system, the two-lawyer rule refers to signing a transfer for completeness. Rule 5.01(3) of the LSUC's *Rules of Professional Conduct* strictly prohibits a lawyer from sharing his or her diskette or pass phrase used to access the ELRS with others including a non-lawyer employee. Signing for release may still be effected by non-lawyers. The lawyers acting for transferors and transferees in transfers of title may be members of the same firm (Rule 2.04.1(2)), although conflict of interest rules still apply and should be considered. Rule 2.04.1 does not apply to mortgage transactions. As long as no conflict of interest exists and a joint retainer has been obtained (Rule 2.04(6-10)), one lawyer may act for both the transferor and the transferee in the following situations:

1. the transferor and the transferee are "related persons" under s. 251 of the *Income Tax Act*, R.S.C. 1985, c. 1 (5th Supp.). "Related Person" is a complex definition. Generally, it includes marriage and common-law partnerships, parents and children (natural, adopted, step) and siblings but not more remote blood relations, dependents, controlling shareholders, controlling related companies, and some trusts and partnerships;

2. the lawyer practises in a remote location and either the transferor or the transferee would suffer undue inconvenience if he/she were required to retain a separate lawyer; or

3. the *Land Registration Reform Act* permits the lawyer to sign for both the transferor and the transferee.

The *Land Registration Reform Act* permits an individual lawyer to act for both the transferor and the transferee in the following circumstances, documented with compliance with law statements (O. Reg. 19/99, s. 5(2), (3)):

1. the transferor and the transferee are the same and the transfer is to effect a change in legal tenure;

2. the transferor and the transferee are the same and the transfer is to effect a severance of land;

3. the transfer is from an estate trustee, or an executor or administrator to a person beneficially entitled to a share in the estate;

4. the transferor or the transferee is a government body, including the Crown in the right of Ontario or Canada, a Crown corporation, agency, board or commission, or a municipal corporation (no required compliance with law statement); or

5.   the transfer of an easement (no required compliance with law statement).

The two-lawyer rule is set out in Rule 2.04.1(1)-(3) of the LSUC's *Rules of Professional Conduct* and has been implemented within the ELRS and the paper POLARIS forms.

CLOSING FUNDS

Fraudulent certified cheque and bank draft schemes, and identity and mortgage frauds are becoming increasingly common. Depending on the situation, the liability may fall on the lawyer personally. It is essential for lawyers to identify when funds deposited in trusts accounts are final and irrevocable. LawPRO recommends that in order to reduce risk, lawyers require a faxed copy of certified cheques and bank drafts and bank verification of electronic transfers as well as bank branch verification of funds received. LawPRO also suggests that lawyers request that banks post remote deposits to trust accounts on receipt rather than waiting for the funds to clear the next business day. Despite lawyer and bank efforts, fraud is becoming more sophisticated and increasingly difficult to detect. The safest approach is to use a large value transaction system wire transfer which provides real-time or same day irrevocable guarantees, particularly when dealing with new clients, off-shore funds, and unusual circumstances. LSUC By-law 9 regulates electronic transfer of trust funds.

Online guaranteed funds (wire) transfer services provide almost real-time finality of payment and reduce the increasing risk and the time involved in certified cheques, bankdrafts, direct deposits and couriers. Financial institutions offer Large Value Transfer System (LVTS) services and Teranet now provides a web-based service called "CLOSURE" that enables the online transfer of guaranteed funds for the closing of real estate transactions, including purchases, mortgage payouts, and agents' commissions. The funds are transferred between participating lawyers, financial institutions, builders, and real estate agents using the LVTS backed by the Bank of Canada. Refer to a recent article by Virginia Tinti available on the Teranet website entitled "10 Reasons Why You Need to Know the Difference between Payments Deposited through the ACSS System and the LVTS System: Required Reading for all Real Estate Practitioners" for a comprehensive discussion of the issues associated with the Automated Clearing Settlement System (ACSS) and LVTS banking system.

The record for an electronic funds transfer must include a "reference number, the name of the financial institution or financial entity sending the funds, the name of the financial institution or financial entity receiving the funds, the date of the transfer of the funds, the amount of funds transferred, the currency of the funds transferred, the name of the holder of the account from which the funds transferred are drawn and the name of the holder of the account to which the funds transferred are deposited" (By-law 7.1, s. 20).

ACSS Funds

Direct deposits, certified cheques, and bank drafts made through the ACSS may not clear and become final until some time during the next business day or later. The timing and finality of ACSS is uncertain and ACSS funds can be returned days after closing. Fraudulent bank drafts and certified cheques in ACSS can be returned up to 90 days after they are received by the drawee bank. A certified cheque with a forged endorsement may be subject to return for up to six years (Tinti). Best practice is to accept only certified cheques from the account holder and confirm all alterations directly with the account holder.

LVTS Funds

Large Value Transaction Funds are finalized on a real-time or same day basis and guaranteed by the Bank of Canada, subject to money-laundering legislation. LVTS is also available for smaller transactions. No system protects against payment to a fraudster and the ever-evolving threat of fraud. As a result, diligent identity verification and due diligence throughout the transaction combined with title insurance and errors and ommissions excepted (E&OE) may provide the most effective protection.

POWERS OF ATTORNEY REQUIREMENTS

The LSUC, the Ministry, and the title insurers have all identified the use of powers of attorney (POA) as an area at higher risk of fraud. The LSUC encourages lawyers to avoid the use of POAs, when possible. As well, the LSUC has created practice guidelines on powers of attorney in real estate transactions and developed checklists and forms for lawyers to use when registering documents signed under the authority of a POA, both when the lawyer has and has not personally prepared the POA. These guidelines, checklists, and forms are available on the LSUC website. The Ministry has passed O. Reg 19/99, under the *Land Registration Reform Act* and published the Ministry of Government Services' Bulletin 2009-01 outlining requirements for powers of attorney. Powers of attorney and revocations of powers of attorney must be registered (original or notarial copy scanned in) in ELRS and documents require a statement as to whether it is signed by way of POA or not. A statement of law is required by any document registered under the authority of a POA. A lawyer's statement of law requires the lawyer to discuss the POA with the client before signing. A statement of law is not required for bank powers of attorney. New statements regarding powers of attorney were introduced in ELRS as of April 7, 2008.

The guidelines encourage lawyers to meet with the donor in person, verify donor identity, prepare the POA personally, review the POA, note restrictions, and attend personally to the signature. When relying on a POA, the lawyer is encouraged to verify the donee's identity, review the POA with the donee, obtain the donee's written approval of the POA's contents, and obtain the donee's written authority to register the POA. Lawyers must register the power of attorney in the land registration system and provide the other side of the transaction with a copy of the POA prior to closing. Powers of attorney must be carefully reviewed for document formalities. In addition, the lawyer should be vigilant for undue influence and duress, particularly when POAs involve related and/or vulnerable persons.

BACKGROUND

Real estate transactions are completed by a process commonly referred to as "closing the deal". In essence, "closing the deal" means that purchase funds are exchanged in return for the registration of a transfer of title and the delivery of keys and possession. Closings are completed on behalf of purchasers, vendors, lessors, lessees, condominium developers, chargees/mortgagees securing collateral, mortgagees selling under power of sale, and mortgagors discharging their mortgages. Closing procedures are detailed and vary greatly depending on the nature of the transaction and whether or not the closing takes place at the Registry office or in ELRS through Teraview.

Closings take place both in the traditional Registry office, paper-based system and in the online POLARIS/Teraview ELRS. Property registered under the Registry system, such as Parcelized Day Forward Registry (PDFR), or property registered in Registry offices that have not been converted to electronic land registration continue to be closed at the Registry office in the traditional manner. Properties registered under the Land Titles system located in a Registry office that has been designated as an electronic land registration area are closed in the electronic land registration system. Although the main elements of a closing remain essentially the same in both situations, the closing documentation and practices vary greatly between a traditional Registry office closing and a closing in electronic land registration. In addition, closing documentation and electronic land registration practices vary from region to region within Ontario. Regional electronic land registration committees have developed recommended documentation and practices that reflect local practice variations. For example, some electronic land registration areas recommend that the solicitor for the vendor initiate the electronic transfer, whereas others prefer that the purchaser initiate the transfer. Document creation and registration of vendor take-back mortgages may be completed by either the solicitor for the vendor or the solicitor for the purchaser depending on the region. Now that POLARIS/Teraview is available in most of Ontario, practice and documentation may standardize as the POLARIS conversion is finalized.

In a traditional, paper-based closing, the lawyer sends a representative (law clerk, title searcher, or student) to the land Registry office to complete subsearches; exchange documents, cheques and keys with a representative of the lawyer acting for the other side of the transaction; and to conduct the necessary registrations.

Electronic registration has transformed file generation and management, drafting and registration of documents, and closing procedures and documentation including the transfer of funds and payment of land transfer tax and registration fees. In an electronic closing, documents are signed electronically by the lawyers pursuant to a signed Acknowledgement and Direction (A&D) from the client. The transaction is then closed and documents are registered in accordance with a Document Registration Agreement (DRA) between the lawyers. In electronic land registration regions, funds are transferred electronically and transactions are closed online, in escrow, usually at the lawyers' offices. However, although not common, the lawyers may also use closing agents or choose to meet at either the Registry office or at the office of either the vendor's or the purchaser's lawyer.

PREPARATION FOR CLOSING

In preparation for closing, the lawyer will review and update file checklists, review the searches and requisitions, review the transaction with the client, complete documentation (including signatures), make arrangements for the exchange of funds and possession, prepare a closing memorandum (checklist), and schedule a time, place, and method for the closing of the transaction.

Electronic registration requires additional documentation and preparation. For a closing in Teraview, the solicitor must complete the following:

Acknowledgement and Direction

The A&D, signed by the client, authorizes the lawyer to enter into the DRA and electronically sign and register the documents. A copy of the DRA should be attached to the A&D. The client acknowledges the content and effect of the electronic documents and gives a warranty as to identity. Law firms must meet client identification and verification requirements in all closings. Teraview generates a standard transaction-specific A&D (as do commercial file management programs) that includes the details of the electronic document. Law firms may develop a customized A&D. For example, the *Family Law Act*, R.S.O. 1990, c. F.3 consent of a non-titled spouse should be added to an A&D and signed by the non-titled spouse. A mortgage guarantor should sign a separate guarantee and a customized A&D. A&Ds are signed by chargees and customized DRAs are used for private mortgages.

Document Registration Agreement

The DRA sets out the arrangements for an escrow closing in electronic land registration. The LSUC website provides a recommended DRA (see Chapter 17). Lawyers often mutually agree to follow the LSUC's DRA in the requisition and requisition reply letters rather than exchanging signed copies. The DRA lists the documents to be registered in Schedule "A". In the DRA, the lawyers agree to hold the closing funds and closing documentation and keys, *etc.* (referred to as the "Requisite Deliveries") in escrow according to the terms of the DRA. The DRA sets the notification requirements for any deficiencies in the "Requisite Deliveries" as well as the practice for the registration of electronic documents. Usually, the purchaser's solicitor registers the electronic documents; however, the lawyers may agree to alternative arrangements, such as when the vendor's (developer's) solicitor registers the sale of new condominium units. The DRA requires the registering lawyer to notify the non-registering lawyer of registration and sets a time for release of funds and keys (6:00 p.m. on closing day, if there is no notice from registering solicitor). It also sets out the alternative arrangements for when registration does not take place. Title insurers now provide gap insurance for delayed registrations and escrow closings.

Figure 15.1

DOCUMENT REGISTRATION AGREEMENT
(STEWART TITLE: LegalSTEPS)*

BETWEEN:

(hereinafter referred to as the "**Purchaser's Solicitor**")

AND:

(hereinafter referred to as the "**Vendor's Solicitor**")

RE:
_____ (the "**Purchaser**") purchase from _____ (the "Vendor") of 69 Jackson Ave, London, ON N6K 1X2 (the "**Property**") pursuant to an agreement of purchase and sale dated April 1, 2009, as amended from time to time (the "Purchase Agreement"), scheduled to be completed on May 24, 2009 (the "**Closing Date**")

FOR GOOD AND VALUABLE CONSIDERATION (the receipt and sufficiency of which is hereby expressly acknowledged), the parties hereto hereby undertake and agree as follows:

Holding Deliveries In Escrow

1. The Vendor's Solicitor and the Purchaser's Solicitor shall hold all funds, keys and closing documentation exchanged between them (the "Requisite Deliveries") in escrow, and shall not release or otherwise deal with same except in accordance with the terms of this Agreement. Both the Vendor's Solicitor and the Purchaser's Solicitor have been authorized by their respective clients to enter into this Agreement. Once the Requisite Deliveries can be released in accordance with the terms of this Agreement, any monies representing payout funds for mortgages to be discharged shall be forwarded promptly to the appropriate mortgage lender.[1]

Advising of Concerns with Deliveries

2. Each of the parties hereto shall notify the other as soon as reasonably possible following their respective receipt of the Requisite Deliveries (as applicable) of any defect(s) with respect to same.

---

* Document reproduced from LegalSTEPS with permission from Stewart Title.

[1] Solicitors should continue to refer to the Law Society of Upper Canada practice guidelines relating to recommended procedures to follow for the discharge of mortgages.

Figure 15.1 (cont'd)

Selecting Solicitor
Responsible for
Registration

3. The Purchaser's Solicitor shall be responsible for the registration of the Electronic Documents (as hereinafter defined) unless the box set out below indicating that the Vendor's Solicitor will be responsible for such registration has been checked. For the purposes of this Agreement, the solicitor responsible for such registration shall be referred to as the "Registering Solicitor" and the other solicitor shall be referred to as the "Non-Registering Solicitor":

Vendor's Solicitor will be registering the Electronic Documents   ☐

Responsibility of
Non-Registering
Solicitor

and

Release of
Requisite Deliveries by
Non-Registering
Solicitor

4. The Non-Registering Solicitor shall, upon his/her receipt and approval of the Requisite Deliveries (as applicable), electronically release for registration the Electronic Documents and shall thereafter be entitled to release the Requisite Deliveries from escrow forthwith following the earlier of:

(a) the registration of the Electronic Documents;

(b) the closing time specified in the Purchase Agreement unless a specific time has been inserted as follows [_____ a.m./p.m. on the Closing Date] (the "**Release Deadline**"), and provided that notice under paragraph 7 below has not been received; or

(c) receipt of notification from the Registering Solicitor of the registration of the Electronic Documents.

If the Purchase Agreement does not specify a closing time and a Release Deadline has not been specifically inserted the Release Deadline shall be 6.00 p.m. on the Closing Date.

Figure 15.1 (cont'd)

Responsibility of Registering Solicitor

5. The Registering Solicitor shall, subject to paragraph 7 below, on the Closing Date, following his/her receipt and approval of the Requisite Deliveries (as applicable), register the documents listed in Schedule "A" annexed hereto (referred to in this agreement as the "**Electronic Documents**") in the stated order of priority therein set out, as soon as reasonably possible once same have been released for registration by the Non-Registering Solicitor, and immediately thereafter notify the Non-Registering Solicitor of the registration particulars thereof by telephone or telefax (or other method as agreed between the parties).

Release of Requisite Deliveries by Registering Solicitor

6. Upon registration of the Electronic Documents and notification of the Non-Registering solicitor in accordance with paragraph 5 above, the Registering Solicitor shall be entitled to forthwith release the Requisite Deliveries from escrow.

Returning Deliveries where Non-registration

7. Any of the parties hereto may notify the other party that he/she does not wish to proceed with the registration of the Electronic Documents, and provided that such notice is received by the other party before the release of the Requisite Deliveries pursuant to this Agreement and before the registration of the Electronic Documents, then each of the parties hereto shall forthwith return to the other party their respective Requisite Deliveries.

Counterparts & Gender

8. This Agreement may be signed in counterparts, and shall be read with all changes of gender and/or number as may be required by the context.

Purchase Agreement Prevails if Conflict or Inconsistency

9. Nothing contained in this Agreement shall be read or construed as altering the respective rights and obligations of the Purchaser and the Vendor as more particularly set out in the Purchase Agreement, and in the event of any conflict or inconsistency between the provisions of this Agreement and the Purchase Agreement, then the latter shall prevail.

Figure 15.1 (cont'd)

Telefaxing
Deliveries
& Providing
Originals if
Requested

10. This Agreement (or any counterpart hereof), and any of the closing documents hereinbefore contemplated, may be exchanged by telefax or similar system reproducing the original, provided that all such documents have been properly executed by the appropriate parties. The party transmitting any such document(s) shall also provide the original executed version(s) of same to the recipient within 2 business days after the Closing Date, unless the recipient has indicated that he/she does not require such original copies.

Dated this 30th day of June, 2010

Name/Firm Name of Vendor's Solicitor

Name/Firm Name of Purchaser's Solicitor

_____

_____

Name of Person Signing

Name of Person Signing

_____

_____

(Signature)

(Signature)

For the purpose of this Agreement, the term "registration" shall mean the issuance of registration number(s) in respect of the Electronic Documents by the appropriate Land Registry Office.

Note: This version of the Document Registration Agreement was adopted by the Joint LSUC-CBAO Committee on Electronic Registration of Title Documents on March 29, 2004 and posted to the website on April 8, 2004.

Teraview Docket (File)

Open a Teraview docket for electronic searching and document creation and registration purposes. Real estate file management programs allow file information to be exported and imported into Teraview. Nevertheless, a conveyancer must still create Teraview dockets and generate and register documents within the Teraview ELRS.

Electronic Documents and Signatures

Documents will be signed and registered on Teraview using a Teraview electronic security access key (PSP) pursuant to the A&D and the DRA. Only lawyers using their personal lawyer access key can sign transfers and documents containing statements of law. For most transactions, two lawyers must sign the transfer. Once transfers and documents containing statements of law have been signed for completeness, they can be released and registered by a non-lawyer employee or agent using his or her personal Teraview PSP.

Detailed information on electronic land registration procedures and example electronic documents and Teraview screen captures are found in Chapter 16.

CLOSING MEMORANDUM

A closing memorandum is prepared following a review of the file, often on the day before closing. Although the format for closing memoranda varies in practice, most lawyers draft the closing memorandum in the form of an annotated checklist identifying the transaction and setting out specific instructions to be followed on closing. Closing memoranda are used in both traditional and electronic closings. A closing memorandum routinely includes the following:

1. the nature of the transaction, the address of the property, the names of the parties and the names and phone numbers of the lawyers on both sides of the transaction;

2. the time, place, and manner of closing as well as the name of the person closing on the other side of the transaction;

3. instructions for confirming closing and returning closing file, especially cheques and keys (Instructions for Requisite Deliveries and notices pursuant to the DRA);

4. instructions on title, execution and other subsearches (the original search summary containing information on when and where to start the subsearch, specifically the last registered instrument number, is attached or noted). Complete search for writs within the electronic transfer on day of closing. Select "subsearch" in the electronic land registration screen and complete a subsearch as part of the registration

process. Writs are also searched as part of the electronic land registration process. Execution subsearches for purchasers/mortgagors must be completed separately in WritSearch;

5. a "Give/Get" list (Requisite Deliveries) setting out documents, cheques, keys, *etc.*, to be given to the other side, as well as documents, cheques, keys, *etc.*, to be received from the other side;

6. instructions listing documents to be registered, by whom and in which order, and a space for completed registration particulars (in electronic land registration attach the registration report printout and the updated parcel register printout);

7. an estimated funds required to close statement, or an itemized list of cheques setting out amounts, payees, and purpose of the cheques (*e.g.*, for payment of land transfer tax); and

8. special instructions that relate to the particular file, such as an agreed-upon undertaking.

A closing memorandum for a traditional Registry office closing can be adapted for use in an electronic closing. Some file management programs include file to do lists, closing/registration screens, and a system of file alerts. The following LegalSTEPS document selection screens illustrate how a file management program can generate the necessary closing documents. Requisite Deliveries are couriered between offices and documents are registered according to the DRA. Fees and taxes and Teraview disbursements are electronically transferred from a designated lawyer's account directly to Teranet at the end of the day. Teranet provides a service called CLOSURE for the electronic transfer of closing funds between participating financial institutions that includes greater protection against fraud than conventional electronic funds transfer.

Figure 15.2

STEWART TITLE: LegalSTEPS DOCUMENT SELECTION SCREEN, PART 1*

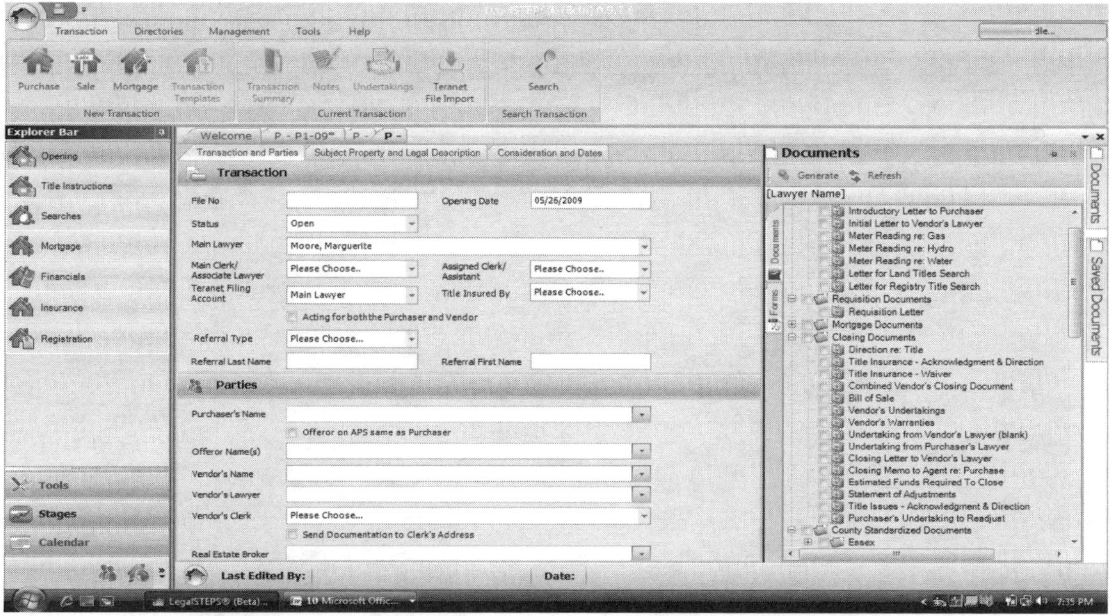

Note Availability of Generic and County Standardized Closing Documents

---

* © Stewart Title 2010. Reproduced with permission.

Figure 15.3

STEWART TITLE: LegalSTEPS DOCUMENT SELECTION SCREEN, PART 2*

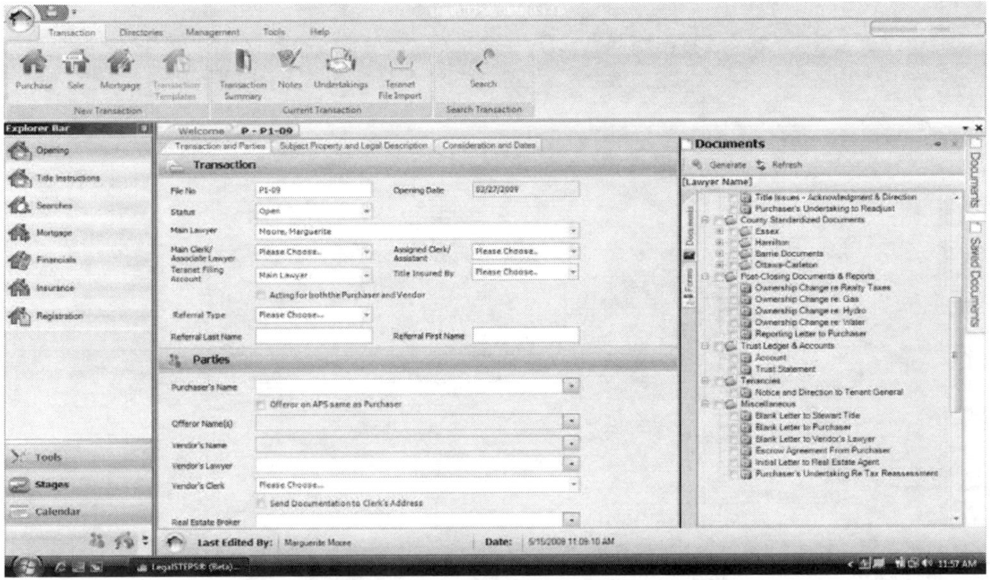

Note Availability of Generic and County Standardized Closing Documents

* © Stewart Title 2010. Reproduced with permission.

Figure 15.4

ESTIMATED FUNDS REQUIRED TO CLOSE
(STEWART TITLE: LegalSTEPS)*

RE: purchase from
           Address:
           Closing Date: June 30, 2010
           Our File No.:   P1-09

Payable to Vendor on closing   **= A**
*(purchase price, less de-
posit(s), with adjustments)*

Ontario land transfer tax   **= B**
(less rebate if applicable)

Estimated legal fees   **$insert amount = E**

Estimated disbursements   **$insert amount = F**

Total estimated legal fees and   **$calculate total = E+F=G**
disbursements

Total estimated amount re-   **$calculate total = A+B+G-D**
quired from you on or before
closing, by certified cheque
or bank draft, payable to
(lawyer), *In Trust*

E. & O. E.

Figure 15.5

PURCHASE CLOSING MEMORANDUM

FILE TO BE RETURNED BY COLLECT COURIER FOLLOWING CLOSING

Date:
To:
Re: _____ purchase from _____
_____Ont.

This transaction is scheduled to close on _____ at _____ with _____from the law office of _____. Telephone # ( ) ___ ____.
As soon as this transaction has closed, please advise me by telephone.

The following cheques are enclosed and are to be given to the solicitor/agent for the vendor(s) and represent the balance due on closing as directed by the vendor:

1. $_____: _____
2. $_____: _____
3. $_____: _____
4. $_____: _____

The enclosed cheques are for the registration(s):

1. $_____: Minister of Finance based on
Land Transfer Tax:
Deed:
Mortgage:
Subsearch:
Total:

2. $_____: Minister of Finance for executions.

Subsearch:

Lot   ____,   Plan   ____,   from Last Instrument # _____

Executions:

Search executions and obtain a certificate against the vendor(s) and the purchaser(s) (if there is a mortgage).

_____
_____

Figure 15.5 (cont'd)

RECEIVE

( )   Deed in duplicate as per the draft
( )   Direction re Payment of Proceeds
( )   Declaration of Possession
( )   Vendor's Undertaking
( )   Vendor's Residency Affidavit
( )   Vendor's Warranty re UFFI
( )   Tax Bill if Available
( )   Mortgage Statement(s)
( )   Bill of Sale
( )   Acknowledgment by Tenants
( )   Directions to Tenants
( )   Undertaking re Mortgage

    Discharge(s)

    (a)_____

    (b)_____

( )   Condominium Documents
( )   TARION Document

Keys: PHONE ME AS SOON
       AS AVAILABLE

Solicitor's Undertakings

REGISTRATION PARTICULARS

( )_____ registered as inst. # _____

DELIVER

( )   Direction re Title
( )   Cheques 1, 2, 3, 4
( )   Mortgage Back to Vendor
( )   Postdated Cheques to
      Vendor
( )   Mortgage Assumption
      Agreement

REGISTER

( )   Deed: Attach L.T.T.
      Affidavit

( )   1st Mortgage:_____

( )   2nd Mortgage:_____

( )   Assignment of Rents

SPECIAL INSTRUCTIONS

_____

_____

Figure 15.6

SALE CLOSING MEMORANDUM
(TRADITIONAL)

GLOBE, MOORE & BUTTERWORTHS,
37 Morrisburg Road, Iroquois, Ontario N6K 2X6
(1-111-111-1111)

FILE TO BE RETURNED BY COLLECT COURIER FOLLOWING CLOSING

File: HANES sale to CORBETT
Closing Date: September 23, 2010
File: 649B
Other Lawyer: _____ Telephone (222) 222-2222
To: _____
The following cheques are to be received from the solicitor/agent for the purchaser(s):

1. $
2. $
3. $

The enclosed cheques are for the following registration(s):

1. $_____Registration of Mortgage to Vendor
2. $_____Registration of Discharges
3. $_____Registration of
4. $_____Execution Certificate

DELIVER   **RECEIVE**

( )   Deed in duplicate   ( )   Direction re Title
( )   GST/ HST Certificate   ( )   Certified Cheques 1, 2, 3, 4
( )   Statement of Adjustments   ( )   Mortgage Back to Vendor
( )   Undertaking/Warranty/
       Bill of Sale/Residency Affi-
       davit
( )   Declaration of Possession
( )   Mortgage Statement   **REGISTER**
( )   Keys   ( )   Mortgage Discharges
( )   Undertaking re Mortgage   ( )   Other: _____
       Discharges
( )   Receipted Tax Bill
( )   Direction re Funds   **OBTAIN**

Figure 15.6 (cont'd)

( )   Redirection re Funds

( )   Solicitor's Undertaking
( )   Acknowledgment by Ten-
        ants
( )   Directions to Tenants
( )   Leases

REGISTRATION PARTICULARS
( )   _____

( )   Registration No. of VTB
        Mortgage

SPECIAL INSTRUCTIONS
_____

registered as inst. # _____

CLOSING SUBSEARCHES

Subsearches are completed immediately prior to closing as time passes between the completion of the search and the closing date of the transaction. See Chapter 13 for a comprehensive review of subsearch procedures and subsearching practice checklists. See Chapter 12 for detailed information on executions and execution searching practice checklists.

Depending on the particular property, all or some of the following subsearches may need to be completed to update the search and the file immediately prior to closing. Check the closing checklist or memorandum for instructions on which subsearches are required.

1. **Title Subsearch:**
    - Update abstract and day books and day sheets prior to registration in Registry.
    - Update parcel register or printout during registration process in Land Titles.
    - Request the automatic subsearch option in the Teraview electronic land registration folder. It is only possible to subsearch the active Property Identification Number (PIN) while in the subsearch option in the electronic land registration document registration folder. In order to subsearch adjoining land, it is necessary to search adjacent lands in the property option.

2. **Adjoining Lands Search:**
    - Subsearch adjoining lands for recent *Planning Act*, R.S.O. 1990, c. P.13 contravention.
    - Subsearch adjoining lands for boundary confirmation, encroachments, easements, restrictive covenants, and access.

3. **Executions:**
    - Obtain execution certificates on WritSearch against the current registered owner(s) and purchaser(s) if financing the purchase by way of a mortgage.
    - Obtain an execution certificate against the condominium corporation as well as the current unit owner(s).
    - In Teraview, update executions against the registered owner(s) while in the work-in-progress electronic transfer. As long as a writ search is completed within the document on the same day as closing, there will be no additional charge for the writ search done by the system as part of the registration process. If the search is completed outside of electronic land registration in WritSearch, an additional fee will be charged. It is only possible to search the current registered owners within an electronic document. When the purchaser is placing a mortgage, purchas-

ers/mortgagors must be subsearched in Writsearch for an additional fee.

4. **Chattel Searches — Personal Property Security Registrations:**
   - When purchasing chattel property of significant value, search the vendor, prior owners and the condominium corporation depending on the circumstances of the file.

5. **Other Subsearches:**
   - corporate searches;
   - partnership searches;
   - off-title inquiries (taxes, utilities, mortgage payments, other depending on transaction *etc.*). See Chapter 14.

CLOSING WHEN ACTING FOR THE PURCHASER (TRADITIONAL CLOSING)

Closing procedures vary depending on the nature of the transaction and the kind of property involved. Closings of commercial transactions, condominiums or specialty conveyances involving power of sale, bankruptcy, or estate administration require additional procedures and documentation. Closing in the electronic environment involves documentation and procedures that are different from that used in a traditional closing.

Review the closing documentation, and with reference to the closing memorandum, complete the following main steps in the standard residential real estate purchase transaction:

1. Perform necessary subsearches and inform the office or person in charge of the file of any problem findings.

2. Meet with the other side.

3. Receive the deed/transfer in duplicate and check and compare with the draft deed.

4. Receive a copy of charge/mortgage statements and the charge/mortgage to be assumed. They should be in accordance with the statement of adjustments, the agreement of purchase and sale and previously produced documentation. The statement should contain the lender reference number and the address for charge/mortgage payments.

5. Receive a discharge of charge/mortgage. Where a discharge of a charge/ mortgage is not available, obtain a charge/mortgage statement showing balance owing, with funds payable to the chargee/mortgagee. Also obtain a solicitor's personal undertaking to obtain and cause to be registered the discharge and provide registration particulars in ac-

cordance with Law Society Guidelines. This procedure should be arranged in advance with the lawyer.

6. Receive vendor's final statement of adjustments and undertaking to readjust taxes, public utilities, insurance premiums and amounts outstanding on charges/mortgages to date of closing. Receive receipted tax and other bills in accordance with the statement of adjustments.

7. Receive direction re: funds as per previous written instructions to the vendor and compare to certified cheques.

8. Receive keys, garage door openers and security system codes.

9. Receive direction re: mortgagee, for the name of the mortgagee in a mortgage back.

10. Receive statutory declaration of possession.

11. Receive vendor's residency declaration re: section 116 of the *Income Tax Act* (Canada).

12. Receive statutory declaration respecting similar name executions.

13. Receive copy of existing survey, if available.

14. Receive leases and assignment of leases and acknowledgments by tenants and directions to tenants to pay future rents to the purchaser, and rent control data, where applicable.

15. Receive warranty re: urea formaldehyde foam and/or asbestos insulation.

16. Receive a copy of the insurance policy and transfer of insurance, if it is transferred (*e.g.*, with a mortgage back). Check the insurance amounts and dates with the statement of adjustments.

17. Receive transfers of service contracts.

18. Receive warranty and bill of sale re: chattel ownership, if transferring chattels.

19. Receive condominium documents, including disclosure package, and status certificate.

20. Receive TARION document (when applicable).

21. Receive warranties from builders and contractors.

22. Receive GST/HST certificate and assignment of GST/HST rebate if buying from a builder (where applicable).

23. Receive occupancy permit if applicable.

24. Receive old title documents (optional).

25. Give certified cheques to be held in escrow by vendor's agent pending registration.

26. Give direction re: title.

27. Give mortgage back, and include proof of sufficient insurance or an assignment of insurance.

28. Give post-dated cheques for mortgage back payments.

29. Give copy of mortgage assumption agreement.

30. Discuss any problems with the office and document telephone instructions on the closing memorandum.

The purchaser's lawyer or lawyer's agent inserts the *Land Transfer Tax Act* Affidavit and attaches the *Planning Act* declaration, registers the deed and other documents in the correct order, and pays the prescribed registration fee and the land transfer tax. Cheques, which have been held temporarily in escrow during registration, are released to the vendor's agent. Following registration in POLARIS, the lawyer may request for file purposes a printout of the parcel register as confirmation of registration. The lawyer is contacted and the file, including duplicate documents and keys, is returned as instructed in the closing memorandum.

ELECTRONIC CLOSING WHEN ACTING FOR THE PURCHASER

Prior to closing, the purchaser's solicitor will arrange for the client to sign the A&D. Pursuant to the DRA, the purchaser's solicitor will receive the vendor's requisite deliveries in escrow on or before the day of closing. The vendor's deliveries will include items such as keys, garage door openers, security system codes and off-title documentation, sometimes referred to as the vendor's closing certificate. The purchaser's solicitor will sign the electronic transfer and deliver the closing funds (certified cheques), as requested by the vendor's direction regarding funds, to the vendor's solicitor to be held in escrow. Closing funds may be transferred electronically or using Teranet's CLOSURE service. If the vendor's solicitor is satisfied with the cheques, he or she signs the transfer for completeness and release and notifies the purchaser's solicitor. If the purchaser's solicitor is satisfied with the deliveries, he or she signs the transfer for completeness and release, subsearches title and registers the transfer and usually a charge. The purchaser's solicitor prints a registration report and an updated parcel register confirming the new registrations. The purchaser's solicitor then notifies the vendor's solicitor that registration is complete. The purchaser's solicitor releases the keys and the vendor's solicitor releases the closing funds. The purchaser's solicitor prints a docket summary and a tax and registration fees summary report on Teraview and arranges to have adequate funds in the solicitor's Teraview transition account in order to cover the transaction's taxes and fees by the end of the day.

Electronic closings are escrow closings conducted by solicitors according to a document registration agreement. This arrangement allows solicitors, if they wish, to exchange documents, cheques and keys prior to closing. The DRA also allows solicitors to sign for both completeness and release prior to the actual closing, should they choose to rely fully on the terms of the DRA. Usually, signing for release takes place on the day of closing as part of the closing process. Solicitors have the ability to customize closing arrangements by mutual amendment of the standard document registration agreement.

SAMPLE RESIDENTIAL PURCHASE CHECKLIST

INITIAL MATTERS	DRAFTED	STATUS	COMMENTS

File:
• **open file**
• **verify client identity**
• **create purchase file docket in Teraview**
• **closing date**
• **requisition date**
• **condition date/waiver**
• **client's address**
• **client's phone no. & e-mail address**
• **vendor's solicitor (in ELRS/e-reg vendor's solicitor's key name)**
• **legal description**
• **PIN**
• **conflict of interest check**
• **review offer**
• **diarize dates**
• **letter re: title insurance**
• **letter re: preliminary matters to discuss with client**
  • **financing arrangements**
  • **title review/title insurance**
  • **survey/title insurance**
  • **insurance**
  • **advise amount of Land Transfer Tax**			

INITIAL MATTERS	DRAFTED	STATUS	COMMENTS
• **value to be assigned to chattels (*)** • **residency** • **client's availability**			
Obtain: • **full given names (required photo-ID/LSUC identification and verification requirements)** • **birthdates** • **spousal status** • **manner of taking title** • **address for service** • **assessment roll no.**			

Searches/Enquiries:
• **search of title**
• **executions**
  • **vendor**
  • **purchaser, if necessary**
  • **predecessors in title**
• **mortgage statement(s)**
• **corporate owners' existence**
• ***Personal Property Security Act* (PPSA) search**
• **off-title inquiries**			

From Vendor's Solicitor: • **response to requisitions** • **in electronic land registration, check DRA confirmation** • **draft transfer** • **in electronic land registration review electronic transfer. Prepare A&D for client's signature.** • **survey** • **statement of adjustments** • **vendor's undertaking to readjust**			

INITIAL MATTERS	DRAFTED	STATUS	COMMENTS
• undertaking to discharge mortgage (together with copy of mortgage statement verifying outstanding amount) • direction re funds/redirection • *Income Tax Act*, s. 116 declaration • *Family Law Act* declaration • undertaking • warranty • bill of sale • declaration of possession • status certificate (condo)			

Financing:
• Note: if also acting for lender of loan, use mortgage checklist
  • obtain conflict letter from purchaser
  • mortgage
  • acknowledgment of standard charge terms
  • direction re funds
  • conflict acknowledgment
• in electronic land registration, create charge and prepare A&D			

Title Insurance: • complete application • submit preliminary information as required • obtain policy number • obtain approval • complete full application • title insurance documents			

INITIAL MATTERS	DRAFTED	STATUS	COMMENTS
• complete fraud litigation reviews • address title qualifiers and underwriting issues • request appropriate endorsements • send mortgagee confirmation of title insurance • insurance binder letter			
Prior to Closing: • draft closing instructions to conveyancer (closing memorandum) • arrange time/method for closing			

Client Interview:
• client signs A&D
• confirm that survey is acceptable
• confirm title encumbrances
• review results of off-title searches
• advise purchaser re funds:
  • amount received from lender
  • land transfer tax amount
  • HST
  • balance to close - amount
• arrange for time and pick-up of all money
• confirm and obtain insurance
• confirm arrangements made with utilities
• inquire where keys to be delivered
• arrange final inspection, if required
• confirm time and method of closing			

INITIAL MATTERS	DRAFTED	STATUS	COMMENTS
Closing: • finalize closing instructions to conveyancer/agent • arrange for transfer/pick-up of mortgage funds and delivery of any documents, as necessary • in electronic land registration, courier/e-transfer funds and off-title documents (Requisite Deliveries to vendor's solicitor) • on receipt of acceptable Requisite Deliveries, sign transfer and mortgage for completeness and release • subsearch title and executions on Teraview • register transfer and charge • print registration report and updated title register • print docket summary and tax and registration fees reports • notify vendor's solicitor of registration of transfer • release keys to purchaser			
After Closing: • arrange key pick-up • advise Municipal Property Assessment Corporation (MPAC) and tax departments of change of ownership (include copy of registered transfer) • report change of ownership to condominium corporation			

INITIAL MATTERS	DRAFTED	STATUS	COMMENTS
• complete ownership change notifications for gas, hydro, water, *etc.* • diarize and complete undertaking(s) still to be fulfilled • ensure payment of interest on deposit • report to title insurer (remit premium) • report to client • report to mortgagee(s) • account • close file • place file in storage			

CLOSING WHEN ACTING FOR THE VENDOR (TRADITIONAL CLOSING)

After reviewing the closing documentation and with reference to the closing memorandum, the vendor's solicitor or agent completes the following procedures, when applicable. As in the closing procedures when acting for the purchaser, closing in the electronic environment for the vendor involves additional procedures and documentation:

1. Receive certified cheque(s) payable to and in the amount set out in the statement of adjustments, or payable to, as set out in a direction signed by the vendor.

2. Receive a direction from the purchaser's lawyer authorizing the vendor's lawyer to describe the purchaser(s) in the deed according to the direction rather than the offer to purchase.

3. Receive charge/mortgage back, where applicable, in accordance with the statement of adjustments and the agreement of purchase and sale. Check the mortgage back against the draft mortgage.

4. Receive post-dated cheques for the vendor take-back mortgage payments.

5. Receive evidence of insurance in the amount of charge/mortgage showing the vendor as first or second chargee/mortgagee.

6. Give the purchaser the closing materials, applicable to the individual file, as listed in the preceding purchaser's closing checklist.

ELECTRONIC CLOSING WHEN ACTING FOR THE VENDOR

The vendor's solicitor creates a sale docket on Teraview, accepts and opens the purchaser's solicitor's message, accepts access to the transfer in progress and assigns the transfer to the vendor's docket. The process is reversed when the vendor initiates the transfer. He or she reviews and completes the transfer and prepares an A&D for the vendor to sign. The vendor's solicitor then delivers the requisite deliveries, including keys and security codes and devices and off-title documentation to the purchaser's solicitor in escrow on or before the closing date. The next step is for the vendor's solicitor to receive the purchaser's requisite deliveries in escrow, including certified cheques and off-title documents. Closing funds are frequently transferred electronically. If the vendor's solicitor is satisfied with the purchaser's deliveries, he or she signs the transfer for completeness and release and notifies the purchaser's solicitor. As soon as the purchaser's solicitor notifies the vendor's solicitor that the transfer has been registered, the vendor's solicitor releases the purchase funds according to the vendor's direction regarding funds. Documents may be signed for completeness prior to closing or signed for both completeness and release immediately prior to closing.

SAMPLE RESIDENTIAL SALE CHECKLIST

INITIAL MATTERS	DRAFTED	STATUS	COMMENT
File: • **verify client identity** • **create sale file docket in Teraview** • **closing date** • **requisition date** • **client** • **client's address** • **client's phone no. and e-mail address** • **purchaser's solicitor (in electronic land registration, purchaser's solicitor's key name)** • **legal description** • **PIN**			
Initial Matters: • **offer reviewed** • **check for client conflicts** • **dates diarized**			

INITIAL MATTERS	DRAFTED	STATUS	COMMENT

Initial Client Discussion:
• **Obtain from Vendor:**
   • **original title documents**
   • **all existing mortgage details**
   • **copies of tax bills and information regarding status of interim payments**
   • **copy of existing title insurance policy**
   • **survey**
   • **whether any ownership of adjoining land**
   • **heating bills**
   • **full given names and copy of required ID**
   • **spousal status and matrimonial home status**
   • **residency**
   • **address for service and forwarding address for final bills**
   • **assessment roll no. (MPAC)**
   • **whether vendor has claimed GST/HST re property**
   • **details of any tenancies**
• **Confirm client's availability**			

Advise Vendor: • **to maintain insurance until closing and review effect of premises being vacant**			

INITIAL MATTERS	DRAFTED	STATUS	COMMENT
• to arrange final readings of utility meters (hydro, water, gas) • arrange for full fuel tank (Note that purchaser may plan to convert to gas)			
Obtain from Purchaser's Solicitors: • direction re title (including date of birth)			
Complete the following: • subsearch title • search executions against vendor (purchaser if mortgage back) • obtain mortgage statements (assumption/discharge), get back promissory note • answer requisitions (in electronic land registration, confirm use of DRA) • register power of attorney, if required (send copy of POA to purchaser's solicitor)			
Prepare and Send to Purchaser's Solicitor: • a response to requisition letter • discuss responsibility for document preparation and use of DRA if in Teraview • deed/transfer • in electronic land registration vendor or purchaser's solicitor may create transfer			

INITIAL MATTERS	DRAFTED	STATUS	COMMENT
• review and complete electronic transfer messaged by purchaser's solicitor • produce A&D for client to sign • direction re funds • vendor's undertaking to readjust or vendor's combined closing certificate • declaration of possession • statement of adjustments • mortgage statement • assignment of contracts • assignment and assumption agreement • undertaking to discharge mortgage • *Income Tax Act*, s. 116 declaration • *Family Law Act* statement • bill of sale • discharge of mortgage • discharge PPSA registrations • release of insurance • notice to tenants • tenant acknowledgment/ direction • warranty for urea formaldehyde and/or asbestos insulation • list any other documents			
If Mortgage Back: • draft mortgage • in electronic land registration create electronic charge • prepare A&D for client to sign • evidence of insurance			

INITIAL MATTERS	DRAFTED	STATUS	COMMENT
• acknowledgment re standard charge terms • post-dated cheques			
If Mortgage Back is Sold: • obtain commitment • prepare assignment			
Client Interview: • List items to cover including: • explain sale documents • in electronic land registration, explain A&D and DRA • obtain client signature • title review • mortgage statement • third party consents • arrange for disbursement of funds • obtain instructions re disbursement of funds • obtain keys • confirm meters read • confirm insurance cancelled • confirm forwarding address			
Closing: • arrange closing time • prepare closing (instructions to agent/conveyancer) memo • in electronic land registration, courier requisite deliveries including keys and off-title closing documentation			

INITIAL MATTERS	DRAFTED	STATUS	COMMENT
• on receipt of acceptable requisite deliveries, including funds and off-title documentation, sign electronic transfer for release and notify purchaser's lawyer • turn over/release keys • in electronic land registration, keys are released by the purchaser's lawyer following registration of transfer			

Post Closing:
• Disburse funds as instructed to:
  • lender
  • real estate commission
  • vendor
  • outstanding taxes, *etc.*
• In ELRS/e-reg funds are disbursed following notification by the purchaser's solicitor that the transfer has been registered
• advise Tax and MPAC/Assessment Departments of sale (include copy of registered deed)
• report to client
• fulfill undertakings (Discharge of Mortgage)
• render account
• close file
• place file in storage			

SPECIALTY CLOSINGS

Closings that involve recreational, new home, condominium, rural, farm, industrial, and commercial properties require additional specialized documentation. As well, closings that involve discharges of mortgage and power of sale proceedings require additional steps and documentation. Special rules and additional forms and procedures apply to private mortgages. The LSUC website contains guidelines for private mortgage transactions. LSUC By-law 9 governs financial transactions and records and contains required form including funds requisition forms for both paper and electronic funds transfers.

DISCHARGE OF MORTGAGE/CHARGE

Closings that contain mortgage/charge discharges raise special difficulties. As a result, the Practice Advisory Service of the LSUC has issued a practice directive for mortgage discharges. This directive, available on the LSUC's website, sets out detailed procedures for mortgage discharges from private lenders, institutional lenders, and blanket and condominium mortgages. Unless the agreement of purchase and sale provides otherwise, these procedures should be followed.

Generally, the lawyer obtains from the mortgagee a mortgage statement for discharge purposes as of the date of closing and informs the mortgagee in writing that the lawyer is relying on the accuracy of the statement and will not be bound by any qualification of the statement whether by use of the abbreviation "E&OE" or otherwise. On closing, the purchaser's lawyer delivers a certified cheque payable to the mortgagee in accordance with the vendor's written direction and the vendor's lawyer gives the purchaser's lawyer his or her personal undertaking to deliver the cheque to the mortgagee, be responsible for any additional monies payable for the discharge as a result of delay in the delivery of the discharge funds and to make every reasonable effort to obtain and register the discharge as soon as possible after closing. The purchaser's lawyer should require the vendor's personal undertaking to pay any additional amounts payable to the mortgagee caused by error or omission in the mortgage statement. Guideline 5 of the Electronic Registration Practice Guidelines reviews the procedures required for discharging charges in ELRS.

CLOSING DOCUMENTATION

Sample closing documentation in this chapter illustrates traditional closing documentation and variations, and precedents available in Stewart Title's real estate practice management program, LegalSTEPS.

UNDERTAKINGS

When it is necessary for lawyers to close transactions prior to completing all the necessary details, one party will promise in writing to complete an outstanding matter after closing. This written promise is called an undertaking. Whenever possible, undertakings should be pre-arranged and exchanged prior to or on closing. Undertakings should be given and accepted only on the lawyer's instructions. Lawyers maintain reminder systems that ensure the timely follow-up on undertakings, particularly undertakings for mortgage discharges.

In general, undertakings should be in writing, clearly drafted, set time limits, provide for contingencies, state clearly whether the client or the lawyer is responsible for completing the undertaking, and provide remedies for non-fulfilment. Lawyers and clients should only give undertakings which are within their ability to fulfil. Undertakings fall into the four categories discussed below.

Solicitor's Personal Undertaking

A solicitor's personal undertaking creates personal liability on the solicitor. These undertakings should only be given or accepted on the solicitor's specific instructions. A solicitor's personal undertaking should only be given or accepted when it is within the ability of the solicitor to fulfil the undertaking and the client has authorized the giving or the accepting of the undertaking in writing.

A solicitor's undertaking is most often given when it is necessary to hold back funds from the sale proceeds to be paid out on stated conditions. For example, the most common solicitor's undertaking is to obtain and register discharges of charges/mortgages, simply because insurance companies, trust companies and banks will not prepare a discharge until they have received the money. An undertaking to discharge a mortgage should not be given or accepted when a private individual is a chargee/mortgagee. A solicitor's personal undertaking to register a discharge of mortgage is prepared in duplicate.

The LSUC's Practice Advisory Service has issued a Directive setting out the guidelines for a solicitor's acceptance of an undertaking to discharge an institutional mortgage. The directive is available on the LSUC's website. Usually, the vendor's solicitor obtains a mortgage (payout) statement for discharge purposes. The vendor directs the purchaser in the direction regarding funds to make a portion of the closing funds payable to the mortgagee as per the payout statement. The vendor undertakes to obtain and cause to be registered a discharge of mortgage as soon as possible, and accepts responsibility for any additional money payable as a result of delay in obtaining the discharge.

When closing a transaction in the electronic land registration environment, the financial institution may prefer to produce and register the electronic discharge of mortgage directly. If the vendor's solicitor is going to register the discharge of mortgage electronically, it is necessary to first obtain a signed acknowledgment and direction from the lender permitting the vendor's solicitor to sign and register the discharge on the mortgagee's behalf. A discharge of mortgage registered pursuant to an acknowledgment and direction is listed as a document to be registered in the document registration agreement.

The vendor's solicitor then gives the purchaser his or her solicitor's personal undertaking to register a discharge of mortgage. The following is an example of a solicitor's undertaking to discharge a title encumbrance.

Figure 15.7

SOLICITOR'S UNDERTAKING

To: PURCHASER(S)

And To: PURCHASER'S SOLICITORS,

His/or her solicitors herein

Re: VENDOR SALE TO PURCHASER

LOT 1, PLAN 1

22 ROBYN ROAD, TEHKUMMAH, ONTARIO

IN CONSIDERATION of the closing of the above-mentioned transaction, we hereby personally undertake as follows:

1.   To deliver your cheque to The Bank of Money, the Mortgagee herein, forthwith after closing;

2.   To be responsible for any additional monies payable for the discharge of Instrument No. BA502001 as a result of any delay in delivery of the discharge funds on the above-noted mortgage; and

3.   To make every reasonable effort to obtain and register a proper form of discharge of the mortgage as soon as possible after closing and if the discharge is not available within 100 days from the date of closing, to make and diligently pursue at our own expense a court application for an order discharging the said mortgage and register such order on title forthwith upon its being granted and indemnify the purchaser and the purchaser's solicitors from and against all direct or consequential claims, costs or damages resulting from a breach of the undertaking or failure to discharge the said mortgage.

DATED at Tehkummah, this 30th day of June, 2010

VENDOR'S SOLICITORS

Per: _____

Lawyer's Name

Solicitor's Best Efforts Undertaking

Case law is unclear on the meaning of the term "best efforts". Best efforts undertakings are given concerning matters that are outside the lawyer's control. It carries the risk of requiring a solicitor to do either more than expected or not being worth the paper it is written on. This type of undertaking is given and accepted with caution in limited circumstances and only with the lawyer's authorization. Best efforts undertakings are rare.

Client's Undertaking(s)

A client's undertaking is signed by the client and creates liability only on the client. The most frequent client's undertaking is the vendor's undertaking to readjust the statement of adjustments. A purchaser gives a reciprocal undertaking to readjust. The following is an example of a vendor's undertaking to readjust the statement of adjustments, which is often combined with warranties, directions, covenants to deliver vacant possession and keys and other closing documentation. A sample Combined Vendor's Closing Document is included at the end of this chapter. An undertaking to discharge a mortgage is always reinforced in an additional solicitor's personal undertaking.

Figure 15.8

VENDOR'S UNDERTAKINGS (STEWART TITLE: LegalSTEPS)*

TO: __________ (the "Purchaser")

AND TO:

RE: purchase from
Address: ___________ (the "Property")
Legal Description: ,
Closing Date: tbd
Our File No.: ____________

In consideration of and notwithstanding the closing of the above-noted transaction, I/we hereby undertake as follows:

1. **POSSESSION & KEYS:** TO provide vacant possession of the Property on the Closing Date and that all keys, entry mechanisms, and access and alarm codes, as applicable, not accompanying this Undertaking, shall be left at the Property.

2. **PROPERTY TAXES:** TO pay all taxes due and all arrears of taxes and penalties, if any, to the Closing Date and as shown on the Statement of Adjustments, and if necessary, to readjust in respect of 20___ **[INSERT YEAR]** realty taxes.

3. **ADJUSTMENTS:** TO readjust, forthwith upon demand, any of the figures as contained in the Statement of Adjustments upon satisfactory evidence that same are found to be incorrect or containing omissions. Acceptance of the Statement of Adjustments by the Purchaser on closing constitutes evidence of the Purchaser's reciprocal agreement to readjust as provided for in this paragraph.

4. **UTILITIES:** TO pay all final accounts, to the Closing Date, for any utilities and services that may form a lien against the Property.

---

* Document reproduced from LegalSTEPS with permission from Stewart Title.

Figure 15.8 (cont'd)

5. **BILL OF SALE:** TO leave on the premises all chattels and fixtures specified in the Agreement of Purchase and Sale, in good working order, free of security interests, encumbrances, liens and claims of any kind whatsoever and in no worse state of repair than at the time of the Purchaser's inspection.

6. **DIRECTION:** TO authorize and direct the Purchaser to make the balance due on closing payable to my/our solicitor as my/our solicitor shall direct in writing.

DATED AT , this 30th day of June, 2010.

Figure 15.9

SAMPLE VENDOR'S UNDERTAKINGS

UNDERTAKING

To: HAMILTON LEWIS CORBETT and

          JESSIE RUTH CORBETT

And To: WILLIAM M. BUTTERWORTHS,

          their solicitor herein

Re: HANES Sale to CORBETT

          69 JACKSON AVENUE, City of Iroquois, Ontario

Closing Date:

UNDERTAKING RE ADJUSTMENTS

IN CONSIDERATION of the closing of the above-noted transaction, I, Maude Selena Hanes, hereby undertake as follows:

To pay all hydro, water and gas charges (if any) on the above-noted property up to the date of closing, and to readjust the items set forth in the Statement of Adjustments and make appropriate payments upon written demand, including realty taxes, if necessary;

To deliver keys to the premises on closing (or other arrangement such as delivered with the undertaking) and deliver up vacant possession of the premises on the day of closing;

To pay out Mortgage/Charge No.___ in favour of ____, and all related instruments in accordance with the attached discharge statement(s) and to cause to be registered the proper form(s) of Discharge of Charge and to delete the Mortgage(s) Charge(s) and all related instruments from the parcel register or the abstract index as soon as reasonably possible following the date of closing and to advise you of the registration particulars thereof. The Vendor will be responsible for any additional amounts payable to the Mortgagee/Chargee by reason of any error, omission or other charge in the mortgage statement (confirmed by a solicitor's personal undertaking);

To fill the tank to capacity and pay for same if the property is heated by fuel oil/propane (I acknowledge that I will receive a credit for the price of a full tank on the statement of adjustments); and

To pay all condominium expenses to the date of closing if the property is a condominium.

Acceptance of the Statement of Adjustments by the Purchaser on closing constitutes evidence of the Purchaser's reciprocal agreement to readjust as provided for in this undertaking.

Figure 15.9 (cont'd)

WARRANTY

I hereby warrant that the home on the above-noted property is not insulated with Urea Formaldehyde Foam Insulation. This warranty will not merge on closing and will continue to be in full force and effect thereafter.

BILL OF SALE

I hereby transfer and convey to the Purchasers the chattels included in this transaction as listed in the Agreement of Purchase and Sale. I covenant that I am the lawful owner of said chattels, that there are no liens, encumbrances or claims affecting the said chattels and that I have the right to transfer and convey same. I confirm that the chattels have been left on the property in a condition similar to that which existed as of the date of the Agreement of Purchase and Sale.

GOODS AND SERVICES TAX / HARMONIZED SALES TAX

I certify that this transaction is not subject to GST/HST as the property is a personal use property or a used home that has been occupied by me or my tenants and that the property does not constitute a "substantially renovated" residential complex as defined under the *Excise Tax Act / Harmonized Sales Tax*.

Date: _____

DECLARATION REGARDING RESIDENCY

I hereby solemnly declare that I am not now and shall not be at the date of closing a non-resident of Canada within the meaning of s. 116 of the *Income Tax Act* of Canada. AND I make this solemn Declaration conscientiously believing it to be true and knowing that it is of the same force and effect as if made under oath.

DECLARED before me at the City of

Iroquois, in the County of Grey Gardens

this 30th day of June, 2010.

_____

Maude Selena Hanes

_____

A Commissioner etc.

Figure 15.10

PURCHASER'S UNDERTAKING TO READJUST (STEWART TITLE: LegalSTEPS)*

TO: ____________

AND TO: ____________

RE:	purchase from	
	Address:	____________
	Legal Description:	
	Closing Date:	tbd
	Our File No.:	«File_No»

In consideration of and notwithstanding the closing of the above-noted transaction, I/we hereby undertake, upon demand, to readjust the statement of adjustments after closing should it be found to contain any errors or omissions.

DATED AT London, this 30th day of June, 2010.

____

* Document reproduced from LegalSTEPS with permission from Stewart Title.

Solicitor's Undertaking on Behalf of the Client

In the client's absence, the solicitor may undertake on the client's behalf with no personal liability. It is preferable to have completed beforehand an undertaking executed by the client. However, when giving or accepting a solicitor's undertaking on behalf of a client, care should be taken that the client has specifically authorized the undertaking, preferably in writing. Always confirm a client's verbal instructions in writing. Be sure that the undertaking contains a clear statement that it is given without personal liability on the solicitor. This undertaking should be signed using the name of the client and always followed by the words, "by his or her solicitor and without personal liability".

REGISTRATION

Following the exchange of documents in a traditional closing, the purchaser's lawyer will register the deed/transfer and mortgage, and the vendor will register a mortgage back. Cheques are held in escrow pending registration. On registration land transfer taxes and registration fees are paid and documents are timed, dated and assigned an instrument number. The person who executes a document must initial content alterations. Likewise, there should be no content alterations to a *Land Transfer Tax Act* Affidavit that has already been sworn, unless initialled by the deponent and the commissioner. Duplicate copies of registered documents are returned to the registering party. In Land Titles, registration may take up to 21 days to be entered into the register. Both Land Titles and Teraview allow the registering party to complete a subsearch as part of the registration process.

In an electronic closing, documents are registered pursuant to the Document Registration Agreement. The purchaser's solicitor usually registers the transfer and the charge online in Teraview, following confirmation by the vendor's solicitor that he or she has received the requisite deliveries and that they are satisfactory. Once both solicitors have confirmed that the requisite deliveries are satisfactory, they sign the transfer for completeness and release. The act of signing provides an automatic check as to whether the document meets registration requirements. If there are deficiencies, Teraview automatically sends an error message setting out the error's nature and location within the electronic document. Any amendment to the transfer automatically removes all digital signatures and the document must be re-signed by both parties. Transfers must be signed for completeness by both lawyers and any document containing a statement of law can only be signed for completeness by a lawyer using the lawyer's personal Teraview PSP and password. The purchaser's lawyer logs onto Teraview and activates the electronic land registration folder. The lawyer can request an automatic subsearch of the active parcel in the registration folder. Writs are searched automatically on the active parcel as part of the registration process. Additional required execution and adjoining land searches, when necessary, are completed online in electronic land registration or in WritSearch for the mortgagor(s) when placing a mortgage. The electronic documents are placed in the electronic registration folder in the proper sequence and registered. A document registration report that contains a copy of the electronic document and the assigned registration number is automatically printed when pre-selected under options in the toolbar. The registration is immediately shown as uncertified on the electronic register.

As in traditional Land Titles, under the *Land Titles Act*, R.S.O. 1990, c. L.5, registration may take up to 21 days to be certified on the electronic register. If a document is rejected during the certification process, it will be messaged on Teraview to the key account that effected the registration. Consequently, it is essential to monitor all messages on Teraview by logging onto Teraview on a regular basis. Most electronic registrations are certified very quickly, almost immediately. Title insurance provides "gap" insurance to cover the risk during initial registration and certification.

Chapter 16 contains example electronic documents and Teraview registration screens and reports.

EXTENDING THE CLOSING DATE

When it is not possible to close and register on the date set for closing, the parties may either agree to extend the closing date or close in escrow. When the closing date is extended, it is necessary to obtain the client's written authorization. An agreement to extend closing should be in writing and contain a new closing date stating that time remains of the essence. If a new time of the essence date is not set, time becomes reasonable time and a new time of the essence date will have to be reset.

The extension agreement should also contain statements as to who is responsible for maintaining insurance and who is responsible for adjustment costs during the extension period. Usually the person requiring the extension is responsible for the costs during the extension. In a short extension, the parties often agree to adjust as of the original closing date and to abide by the terms of the original agreement of purchase and sale.

In an electronic closing, the DRA sets out the arrangements for when a party cannot or does not wish to proceed with registration and closing. Prior to the release of the electronic documents for registration by the registering solicitor, either party may notify the other parties that he or she does not wish to proceed with registration. Notice must be received by the registering solicitor prior to registration. Following notice, the solicitors return their respective deliveries.

When registration does not take place on the contract date, the parties may extend the closing, or close in escrow, particularly when the purchaser is in the process of an actual move and requires immediate possession. On occasion, it may be necessary to tender when one party is either unwilling or unable to close the transaction.

ESCROW CLOSINGS

An escrow closing is a conditional closing pending the resolution of some closing deficiency. Complex commercial transactions are often closed in escrow. Closings in the electronic land registration system are structured as short-term escrow closings and are governed by the Document Registration Agreement between the solicitors. The Client Acknowledgement and Direction authorizes the DRA. Solicitors may agree in writing to extend the existing electronic closing escrow in a manner similar to a traditional escrow closing.

The better organized the file and the sooner the closing documentation is at the Registry office, the less likely it is that a transaction will have to be closed in escrow. When a closing does not take place as scheduled and the purchaser needs possession, the file may be closed in escrow.

In an escrow closing, the purchaser usually takes possession and holds the title documentation in escrow or trust while the vendor holds the cheque in escrow pending registration of the transfer. Escrow agreements should always be in writing and contain solicitors' personal undertakings. They require authorization by the client and the consent of an affected third party, such as a mortgagee. As per a lawyer's instructions, an escrow agreement could contain arrangements for the following:

1. possession of documents, keys, cheques pending the fulfilment of specified conditions, *etc.*;

2. possession of property and liability for damage to property during the escrow period;

3. responsibility, procedures, and date for future registration of documents;

4. provision for dealing with both title and off-title problems that arise during the escrow period;

5. insurance responsibilities and notice to insurer of escrow;

6. mortgage funds and notice to mortgagee of escrow;

7. mortgagee's consent for vendor to hold mortgage funds;

8. notice to title insurer of escrow;

9. revised adjustments, if applicable;

10. agreement of the purchaser to waive any closing objections other than the escrow conditions;

11. notice provisions in a longer term escrow;

12. time limits for the completion of agreed upon responsibilities and an expiration date; and

13. procedures in the event that the escrow does not close for the purchaser giving up possession and responsibility for any damage during the escrow period, return of closing documents, cheques, keys, *etc.*

Usually an escrow closing is for a short period of time. Each escrow closing is unique and must be discussed with and authorized by the lawyer in charge of the file.

TENDER

The act of tender provides evidence that a party to a real estate transaction is ready, willing, and able, and seeks in good faith to close the transaction according to the terms of the contract. Tender acts as evidence if the innocent party seeks compensation for the breach of contract by the defaulting party. Tender must be made during the time and in the manner set for closing in the contract. Tender is evidentiary in nature and although very important is not a prerequisite for recovery.

When attempts to extend or close the deal have failed, it may be necessary to tender all necessary closing documentation on the defaulting party. Tender is unnecessary in the following circumstances:

- when a party has unequivocally repudiated the agreement; (Anticipatory breach may be express or implied and the innocent party may elect to accept or reject the repudiation. The communication of acceptance of an anticipatory breach is irrevocable.)
- when a party has expressly waived in writing the requirement for tender; and
- when the defaulting party has failed to fulfil a condition precedent to the other party's performance under the contract.

Tender should be completed only on instructions from the lawyer and, whenever possible, be observed by an independent witness. The act of tendering provides evidence that while one party is ready, willing and able to close the deal, the other party is not.

When tendering, all the documents necessary to effect closing are exchanged and checked just as on a closing. Confirm with the registration staff that the signed documents are acceptable for registration. Closing documents are then returned to their respective owners and tender has been completed. While in the process of tendering, retain possession of all certified cheques, the signed transfer/deed or charge/mortgage and sworn *Land Transfer Tax Act* Affidavit. Both parties in a tender should make careful notes recording the tender and as soon as possible confirm the tender in writing. Whenever possible, tender should be arranged in advance, supported by written documentation.

In the electronic land registration environment, tender is completed according to both the Document Registration Agreement and the terms in the agreement of purchase and sale. Tender requires the delivery of all "requisite deliveries" pursuant to the DRA as well as the client's A&D. Documents in permanent paper form are often tendered in addition to access to the electronic document. The tendering party must advise the other solicitor that he or she is ready willing and able to close the transaction in accordance with the agreement of purchase and sale. Keys must be made available. The vendor's solicitor must have electronically produced, signed for completeness and given access to the purchaser's solicitor all required electronic documents listed on the DRA. Remember not to sign for release the required electronic documents listed on the DRA. Tender must be completed in person unless both parties have agreed to an alternative arrangement, such as a combination of fax and e-mail. Tender arrangements are confirmed by letter prior to the actual tender or as soon as possible following tender.

POST-CLOSING PROCEDURES

As soon as possible after a traditional closing at the Registry office, the conveyancer contacts the lawyer and the file, including duplicate documents, keys, security codes, cheques, *etc.*, is returned as instructed in the closing memorandum. The person closing the deal should update the closing memorandum by confirming the completion of closing instructions and recording the document registration particulars.

Clients should be contacted immediately and be provided with the keys. Remember that the purchaser is paying the mover by the hour and cares only about getting into the house. The vendor may need the closing funds for another purchase. Pursuant to the Agreement of Purchase and Sale, the law firm pays the real estate agent the balance of the sales commission.

When the transaction is closed in the electronic land registration system, funds must be available by the end of the day in the lawyer's Teraview debit account. The funds are used to cover document registration and *Land Transfer Tax Act* fees, as well as Teraview user fees as itemized in the Teraview docket reports for the docket summary and tax and registration fees. Money is transferred electronically at the end of the business day from the lawyer's debit account directly to Teranet.

All undertakings, particularly ones regarding mortgage discharges, must be followed up and completed as soon as possible. The purchaser's solicitor finalizes the title insurance policy. The purchaser's solicitor will send a report to the mortgage lender and a report and premium payment to the title insurance company when the property has been title insured. As well, the purchaser's solicitor sends written notification of change of ownership for realty taxes, local utilities (gas, water, and hydro) and the condominium corporation, if applicable, thus ensuring that future bills and correspondence will be sent to the purchaser. The fire/house insurer should also be informed of the closing and the first mortgagee should be shown on the policy.

Following closing, the lawyer sends an interim and/or detailed final reporting letter documenting the transaction, reconciles funds, bills the client, and closes the file.

SAMPLE CLOSING DOCUMENTS

The form, content, and organization of closing documentation, referred to as requisite deliveries in electronic closings, vary considerably in different communities. Similarly, closing practices and procedures, whether they are paper or electronic closings, vary considerably from community to community.

Figure 15.11

DIRECTION

To: HAMILTON LEWIS CORBETT and

        JESSIE RUTH CORBETT

And to: WILLIAM M. BUTTERWORTHS,

        their solicitor herein

Re: HANES Sale to CORBETT

        69 JACKSON AVENUE, City of Iroquois, Ontario

I authorize, direct and instruct you to make the balance due on closing in connection with the above transaction payable to my Solicitor, William M. Butterworths in trust or as he may further direct, and for so doing this shall be your good, sufficient and irrevocable authority.

DATED at the City of Iroquois this 30th day of June, 2010.

_____

Maude Selena Hanes

Figure 15.12
RE-DIRECTION AND UNDERTAKING

To: HAMILTON LEWIS CORBETT and

        JESSIE RUTH CORBETT

And to: WILLIAM M. BUTTERWORTHS,

        their solicitor herein

Re: HANES Sale to CORBETT

        69 JACKSON AVENUE, City of Iroquois, Ontario

In consideration of the closing of the above transaction, I authorize, direct and instruct you to pay the balance due on closing in connection with the above transaction, by way of certified funds, in the following manner:

TO: _____ $_____

TO: _____   (Vendor's solicitor, in trust)
$_____

UNDERTAKING TO DISCHARGE

To forward certified funds to the mortgagee(s) named above to discharge at the Vendor's expense the outstanding Mortgage(s) Charge(s) No._____ in favour of _____ (and No._____ in favour of _____) and all related instruments in accordance with the attached discharge statement(s) and to cause to be registered the proper form(s) of Discharge of Charge and to delete the Mortgage(s) Charge(s) and all related instruments from the parcel register or the abstract index as soon as reasonably possible following the date of closing and to advise you of the registration particulars thereof.

The Vendor will be responsible for any additional amounts payable to the Mortgagee/ Chargee by reason of any error, omission or other charge in the mortgage statement.

DATED at the City of Iroquois this 30th day of June, 2010.

_____
Vendor's Solicitor

Figure 15.13

ESTIMATED FUNDS REQUIRED TO CLOSE
(STEWART TITLE: LegalSTEPS)*

RE: purchase from
       Address: 37 Main Street, Geraldton, ON N6K 1X2
       Closing Date: June 30, 2010
       Our File No.:   P1-09

Payable to Vendor on closing $348,000.00 = **A**
(purchase price, less de-
posit(s), with adjustments)

Ontario land transfer tax $0.00 = **B**
(less rebate if applicable)

Estimated legal fees $**insert amount = E**

Estimated disbursements $**insert amount = F**

Total estimated legal fees and $**calculate total =**
disbursements   **E+F=G**

_____

Total estimated amount $**calculate total =**
required from you on or   **A+B+G-D**
before closing, by certified
cheque or bank draft, pay-   _____
able to Marguerite Moore, *In*
Trust

E. & O. E.

Figure 15.14

COMBINED VENDOR'S CLOSING DOCUMENT (STEWART TITLE: LegalSTEPS)*

Vendor's Closing Document

TO: (the "Purchaser")

AND TO:

RE: purchase from
Address: (the "Property")
Legal Description: ,
Closing Date:
Our File No.:

BILL OF SALE

In consideration of the closing of the above-noted transaction, I/we hereby:

1. sell, transfer and convey to the above-noted purchaser(s) the chattels and fixtures included in the purchase price, as specified in the Agreement of Purchase and Sale;
2. covenant that I am/we are the lawful owner(s) thereof; and
3. warrant that I/we have the right to transfer and convey same and that such chattels and fixtures are free of all encumbrances, liens and claims of any kind whatsoever.

WARRANTIES

I/We warrant as follows:

1. THAT since the date of the Purchaser's inspection, no damage has occurred to the Property, to the buildings thereon, or to the chattels and fixtures included in the purchase price.
2. THAT during my/our ownership of the Property, no work, construction or alterations have been carried out on the Property, and no

* Document reproduced from LegalSTEPS with permission from Stewart Title.

Figure 15.14 (cont'd)

material has been supplied, which could result in a lien being registered under the *Construction Lien Act*.

3. THAT any work to be carried out or completed on the Property, as stipulated in the Agreement of Purchase and Sale, shall be completed in a good and workman-like manner prior to the closing date.

4. THAT, as at the closing date, there shall be no work orders or deficiency notices outstanding and/or affecting the Property in relation to same, and if any should exist, they shall be rectified at my/our expense forthwith upon demand.

This Warranty shall survive and not merge on the completion of this transaction.

UNDERTAKINGS

In consideration of and notwithstanding the closing of the above-noted transaction, I/we undertake as follows:

7. **POSSESSION & KEYS:** TO provide vacant possession of the Property on the Closing Date and that all keys, entry mechanisms, and access and alarm codes, as applicable, not accompanying this Undertaking, shall be left at the Property.

8. **PROPERTY TAXES:** TO pay all taxes due and all arrears of taxes and penalties, if any, to the Closing Date and as shown on the Statement of Adjustments, and if necessary, to readjust in respect of 20___ **[INSERT YEAR]** realty taxes.

9. **ADJUSTMENTS:** TO readjust, forthwith upon demand, any of the figures as contained in the Statement of Adjustments upon satisfactory evidence that same are found to be incorrect or containing omissions. Acceptance of the Statement of Adjustments by the Purchaser on closing constitutes evidence of the Purchaser's reciprocal agreement to readjust as provided for in this paragraph.

10. **UTILITIES:** TO pay all final accounts, to the Closing Date, for any utilities and services that may form a lien against the Property.

11. **DELETIONS:** TO make all payments and take all steps necessary to pay off and cause to be discharged any existing mortgages, liens, executions and/or other encumbrances affecting the Property and which are not being assumed by the Purchaser.

12. **BILL OF SALE:** TO leave on the premises all chattels and fixtures specified in the Agreement of Purchase and Sale, in good working order, free of security interests, encumbrances, liens and claims of

Figure 15.14 (cont'd)

any kind whatsoever and in no worse state of repair than at the time of the Purchaser's inspection.

13. **DIRECTION:** TO authorize and direct the Purchaser to make the balance due on closing payable to my/our solicitor as my/our solicitor shall direct in writing.

The execution hereof by the undersigned pertains to the above Bill of Sale, Warranties and Undertakings.

DATED AT , this 30th day of June, 2010.

> **IN THE MATTER OF** title to the property legally described as, and municipally known as _____ (the "Property")
>
> **AND IN THE MATTER OF** purchase from on tbd
>
> **AND IN THE MATTER OF** Goods and Services Tax ("GST") under Part IX of the *Excise Tax Act* (Canada), as amended (the "Act")

I/We, _____, the registered owner(s) of the Property, solemnly declare that:

DECLARATION OF POSSESSION

[PLEASE DELETE THE INAPPLICABLE PARAGRAPH REGARDING UNDISTURBED POSSESSION TO THE PROPERTY; PARAGRAPH ONE: GENERAL STATEMENT OR PARAGRAPH TWO: DETAILED STATEMENT]

1. **POSSESSION:** I am/We are the absolute owner(s) of the Property and throughout my/our period of ownership of the Property, either personally or by tenant(s), have been in actual, peaceable, continuous, exclusive, open, undisturbed and undisputed possession and occupation of the Property, and such possession and occupation of the Property has been undisturbed throughout by any action, suit or other proceedings, or by any claim of adverse possession or otherwise on the part of any person or corporation and that during such

Figure 15.14 (cont'd)

possession and occupation, no acknowledgment of title has been given by me/us or, to the best of my/our knowledge, by anyone else, to any person or corporation in respect of any right, title, interest or claim upon the Property or in any part thereof which may be adverse to or inconsistent with my/our registered title and I/we believe that no such interest exists.

2. **POSSESSION:** I am/We are the absolute owner(s) of the Property and have been since obtaining a conveyance by Instrument No. _____ **[INSERT INSTRUMENT NUMBER WHEN VENDOR TOOK TITLE TO THE PROPERTY]** on _____ **[INSERT DATE WHEN VENDOR TOOK TITLE TO THE PROPERTY]** and throughout my/our period of ownership of the Property, either personally or by tenant(s), have been in actual, peaceable, continuous, exclusive, open, undisturbed and undisturbed possession and occupation of the Property, and such possession and occupation has been undisturbed throughout by any action, suit or other proceedings, or by any claim of adverse possession or otherwise on the part of any person or corporation and that during such possession and occupation, no acknowledgment of title has been given by me/us or, to the best of my/our knowledge, by anyone else, to any person or corporation in respect of any right, title, interest or claim upon the Property or in any part thereof which may be adverse to or inconsistent with my/our registered title and I/we believe that no such interest exists.

[PLEASE DELETE THE INAPPLICABLE PARAGRAPH REGARDING BOUNDARIES AND/OR ADDITIONS/DELETIONS; PARAGRAPH ONE: SURVEY AVAILABLE OR PARAGRAPH TWO: NO SURVEY AVAILABLE]

3. **BOUNDARIES and/or ADDITIONS/DELETIONS:** I/We have examined the plan of survey/surveyor's certificate/plan attached hereto as Schedule "A", as prepared by _____, O.L.S., and dated _____, and that to the best of my/our knowledge and belief, the location of all structure(s) and any fences and other boundary markers on the Property are accurately shown in relation to the boundaries of the Property and that there have been no additions or deletions to same, save and except:

    NONE

4. **BOUNDARIES and/or ADDITIONS/DELETIONS:** To the best of my/our knowledge and belief, the location of all structure(s) and any fences and other boundary markers on the Property are situate

Figure 15.14 (cont'd)

wholly within the boundaries of the Property and that there have been no additions or deletions to same, save and except:

NONE

5. **ENCUMBRANCES:** To the best of my/our knowledge and belief, there are no liens, easements, charges, mortgages or encumbrances affecting the Property, except as disclosed by the registered title.

6. **TITLE DEEDS:** The deeds, evidences of title and other papers which have been produced are all the title deeds, evidences of title and other papers in my/our possession which relate to the title to the Property, and to the best of my/our knowledge and belief, fairly disclose all facts material to the title claimed.

7. **PROPERTY TAXES:** All taxes and any local improvement rates on the Property, including interest and penalties, have been paid to the date set out in the Statement of Adjustments.

8. **CONSTRUCTION LIENS:** There are no construction liens registered against the Property and there has been no work, construction, re-modelling, repairs or improvements made to the premises or materials ordered which could give rise to the right of anyone to claim a lien against the Property pursuant to the *Construction Lien Act*, or any other amendments thereto.

9. **JUDGEMENTS:** There are no judgements or executions against me/us and so far as I/we know, there are none affecting the Property.

10. **BANKRUPTCY:** I/We have neither made an assignment in bankruptcy for the general benefit of my/our creditors, or filed a proposal, or have served upon me/us a petition for such an order, pursuant to the provisions of the *Bankruptcy and Insolvency Act*, nor am/are I/we an undischarged bankrupt under said Act.

11. **BILL OF SALE:** All chattels, as specified in the Agreement of Purchase and Sale, are owned by me/us and are hereby conveyed to the Purchaser free and clear of all security interests, liens or encumbrances and in the condition stated in the Agreement of Purchase and Sale.

12. **PLANNING ACT:** This transaction does not contravene the *Planning Act* because I/we have not retained the fee or the equity of redemption in, or power, or right to grant, assign or exercise a power of appointment with respect to any Property abutting the Property affected by the deed or otherwise dealt with in the current transaction.

Figure 15.14 (cont'd)

13. **RESIDENCY:** I am/We are not and will not be on the day of closing, (a) non-resident(s) of Canada within the meaning of Section 116 of the *Income Tax Act* of Canada.

14. **LINE FENCES ACT, LEASE, RESTRICTION, ETC.:** To the best of my/our knowledge and belief:

    (a) there are no applications pending under the *Line Fences Act* or with respect to local improvement schemes, rezoning, plan amendments, or expropriation proceedings affecting the Property.

    (b) there are no unregistered leases, agreements to lease, or options to purchase the Property.

    (c) the attached Restrictive Covenants registered as Instrument No(s). _____have been complied with.

15. **WORK ORDERS:** I/We have not been served by the municipality with any work orders or deficiency notices affecting the Property.

16. **TENANCIES:** There are no leases or tenancies affecting the Property save and except for:

    NONE

17. **U.F.F.I. WARRANTY:** During the time I/we have owned the Property, I/we have not caused any structure(s) on the Property to be insulated with insulation containing urea formaldehyde and to the best of my/our knowledge and belief, no structure(s) contain or have ever contained such insulation. This warranty shall survive and not merge on the completion of this transaction and if the structure(s) is part of a multiple-unit structure(s), this warranty shall only apply to that part of the structure(s) which are the subject of this transaction.

GST DECLARATION

This transaction is not subject to GST as the Property is a personal use property or a used residential complex occupied by me/us or by persons authorized by me/us for the use and enjoyment of same as a place of residence and the Property does not constitute a "substantially renovated" residential complex, as defined under the Act.

AND I/We make the above solemn Declaration of Possession and GST Declaration conscientiously believing them to be true, and knowing that they are of the same force and effect as if made under oath.

Figure 15.14 (cont'd)

DECLARED before me at the   }
City/Town of Tehkummah,   }
in the Province of Ontario,   }
this 30th day of June, 2010.   }

A COMMISSIONER, ETC.

RESIDENTIAL REAL ESTATE TRANSACTIONS PRACTICE GUIDELINES*

Executive Summary

Purpose

The *Residential Real Estate Transaction Practice Guidelines* contain recommended guidelines or procedures that lawyers should follow when acting for clients in residential real estate transactions. The guidelines focus on six client-centered professional principles: Client/Lawyer Relationship, Due Diligence, Proper Filing and Record-keeping, Document Preparation and Registration, Financial Issues and Extraordinary Matters.

The *Guidelines* are not intended to replace a lawyer's professional judgment or to establish a rigid approach to the practice of law or the conduct of a real estate transaction. Subject to those provisions of the *Guidelines* that incorporate legal, by-law or *Rules of Professional Conduct* requirements, a lawyer should consider the circumstances of the individual transaction and choose and recommend to the client the practice and procedure that best suits the individual transaction. In appropriate circumstances the lawyer may deviate from the *Guidelines*. Whether a lawyer has provided quality service will depend upon the circumstances of each individual transaction.

Terminology

Certain aspects of the Guidelines are mandatory and others are not.

The term "shall" is used in those instances where compliance is mandated by either the By-laws made pursuant to the *Law Society Act* or the *Rules of Professional Conduct*.

The term "should" or the phrase "should consider" connotes a recommendation. The terms refer to those practices or policies that are considered to be a reasonable goal for maintaining or enhancing client service.

The term "may" or the phrase "may consider" convey discretion. Lawyers may or may not pursue these suggested policies or practices depending upon the particular circumstances of the transaction.

Living Document

By their very nature the *Guidelines* are not static: professional requirements, standards, techniques and practices change. The *Guidelines* will be reviewed regularly and revised where necessary to reflect the evolving practice of law.

INTRODUCTION

A lawyer who undertakes to perform legal services on behalf of a client must perform such services to the standard of a competent lawyer. Rule 2.01 provides a definition of the term "competent lawyer". A competent lawyer includes a lawyer who ascertains client objectives, develops and advises the client on appropriate courses of action, communicates with the client at all stages of a matter in a timely and effective manner and complies in letter and in spirit with the *Rules of Professional Conduct*.

A lawyer who undertakes professional services on behalf of a client in a residential real estate transaction should be guided by the following principles.

GUIDELINE 1
CLIENT/LAWYER RELATIONSHIP

Communication

At the commencement of the lawyer-client relationship, the lawyer should ascertain all necessary and relevant information regarding the client, the property and the transaction and clarify and confirm the client's expectations about the lawyer's role and responsibilities in the transaction.

☐ The lawyer should obtain from the client at the outset of the retainer information about the property. This information might include but is not limited to information regarding:

- the number of residential units in the property;
- the manner in which the property is serviced — public or private;
- whether the property is tenanted;
- whether the property is located on a ravine, waterfront or highway or adjacent to any significant physical features;
- whether the property is subject to or near hydro installations; and
- any other matter that may impact on the choice of searches.

☐ The lawyer should communicate with the client at the outset of the retainer to obtain information about the client's intentions regarding the future use of the property.

☐ The lawyer should advise the client of the options available to assure title in order to protect the client's interests and minimize the client's risk. In this regard, the lawyer shall comply with his or her obligations regarding title insurance and real estate conveyancing pursuant to subrules 2.02(10)-2.02(13) of the *Rules*. If the client selects title insurance, the lawyer should advise the client about the searches that the lawyer will not be performing and the type of information that these searches would reveal about the property such as zoning, encroachments or survey issues. Where title insurance is not being used, the lawyer should advise the client about the post closing protections provided by title insurance which the client is not receiving (e.g. regarding post-closing encroachments onto the property and fraud).

☐ Where title insurance is being used, the lawyer should communicate with the client to determine whether the client has any adverse knowledge about the property that could give rise to the insurer relying on the "knowledge" exclusion if the matter is not disclosed and "insured over" pre-closing.

☐ When requested, the lawyer should provide the client or potential client with a timely estimate of the fees and disbursements involved so that the client or potential client is able to make an informed decision on retaining the lawyer. In discussing fees and disbursements with clients, the lawyer:

- should provide a reasonable estimate of the total cost and not an unreasonable estimate designed to garner the client's business;
- should not manipulate fees and disbursements in a manner as to provide a lower fee estimate.

☐ The lawyer should make an early determination whether to advise the client to obtain a survey of the property (for instance, based upon the client's statement of intended use for the property) and should advise the client accordingly.

The lawyer should consider forwarding an initial letter to the client at the commencement of the lawyer-client relationship.

The lawyer may consider including the following topics in the initial letter to the purchaser:

- the name of the lawyer primarily responsible for the matter;
- the name of any person in the firm who will be working on the file and the functions that the person will be performing;
- confirmation that the lawyer will be supervising all non-lawyers who are working on the file and that the lawyer is available to discuss issues with the client;
- information about the various methods of assuring title and the method selected by the client;
- an estimate of fees and disbursements;
- the amount of land transfer tax payable on registration;

- an explanation of the nature of closing adjustments and confirmation that adjustments will be reviewed in detail before closing;
- an explanation of joint retainer issues if the lawyer is acting for more than one client in the transaction (e.g. purchaser and lender), including the inability of the lawyer to keep information confidential as between the two clients;
- a request for instructions regarding title and an explanation of the difference between a joint tenancy and a tenancy in common;
- a request for information regarding the type of property and other relevant information about the property (number of units and approximate age of the property), the type of heating, mortgage and fire insurance policy;
- a request for any available survey and for information on any changes to the property not reflected on the survey, and an explanation of the importance of a survey;
- if the property is a condominium, confirmation of the extent of review of the Status Certificate and attachments;
- instructions regarding arranging utility and other service accounts;
- if the property is a new home, instructions regarding the Tarion inspection, GST and the New Home Rebate and additional types of adjustments that can be expected;
- a request for information regarding the client's proposed mortgage financing;
- instructions regarding the form of funds that will be required shortly before closing (certified cheque or bank draft);
- information regarding the need to produce identification;
- an explanation regarding the requirement for property insurance;
- information regarding how and when keys will be available; and
- any other matter upon which the client has instructed the lawyer or upon which the lawyer must provide information or instruction in order for the lawyer to proceed with the handling of the transaction.

A lawyer may consider including the following topics in the initial letter to the vendor:

- the name of the lawyer primarily responsible for the matter;
- the name of any person in the firm who will be working on the file and the functions that the person will be performing;
- confirmation that the lawyer will be supervising all non-lawyers who are working on the file and that the lawyer is available to discuss any issues with the client;

- an estimate of fees and disbursements;
- a request for the existing transfer, mortgage details (including most recent statement), realty tax bill, most recent utility bills and contact address for after closing;
- a request for any available survey and for information on any changes to the property not reflected on the survey;
- a request for information regarding the manner in which the house is heated;
- if applicable, information regarding the real estate commission payable and prepayment penalties for the discharges of mortgages;
- a request for the name and phone number of the condominium manager if applicable;
- a request for information regarding the client's marital status and residency;
- information regarding the need to produce identification;
- instructions regarding arranging final meter readings;
- an explanation of the statement of adjustments;
- an explanation of GST ; and
- any other matter upon which the client has instructed the lawyer or upon which the lawyer must provide information or instruction in order for the lawyer to proceed with the handling of the transaction.

Responsibility

The lawyer is responsible for carriage of the transaction or client's legal matter and shall have knowledge of legal issues affecting the matter that require a lawyer's expertise to address.

- ☐ The lawyer shall comply with the requirements of Rule 5.01 of the *Rules of Professional Conduct* regarding supervision.
- ☐ While a lawyer may permit a non-lawyer to attend to all matters of routine administration, assist in more complex transactions, draft statements of account and routine documents and correspondence and attend to registrations, the lawyer shall not delegate to a non-lawyer the ultimate responsibility for:

  - review of a title search report or of documents before signing;
  - review and signing of a letter of requisition;
  - review and signing of a title opinion; and
  - review and signing of a reporting letter to the client.

- ☐ A lawyer shall not permit a non-lawyer to:

- provide advice to the client concerning insurance, including title insurance without supervision;
- present insurance options or information regarding premiums to the client without supervision;
- recommend one insurance product over another without supervision;
- provide a legal opinion including without limitation a legal opinion regarding the title insurance coverage obtained.

☐ In transactions using the system for the electronic registration of title documents, only a lawyer can sign for completeness any document requiring compliance with law statements.

☐ If the lawyer has a personalized specially encrypted diskette to access the system for the electronic registration of title documents, the lawyer shall not permit others including a non-lawyer employee or agents to use the lawyer's diskette and shall not disclose his or her personalized e-reg™ pass phrase to others.

Accessibility

The lawyer shall answer with reasonable promptness all communications from other lawyers that require an answer, shall be punctual in fulfilling all commitments and should be reasonably available to speak to clients as well as the lawyer on the other side of the transaction at their request.

Communication Prior to Closing and Reporting

The lawyer shall report in a prompt and clear manner to the client, as reasonably required throughout the transaction on an interim basis and in all cases at the end of a transaction.

☐ Prior to closing, the lawyer should meet with the client where possible and should in any event review with the client and receive written confirmation from the client regarding:

- the manner in which title is being assured;
- the state of title, including the coverage that will be available under the client's title insurance policy, if applicable. The review should include but is not limited to matters such as subdivision/development agreements, easements and restrictive covenants, even if the client is obliged to accept title subject to them;
- where title insurance is being used, whether the client has any adverse knowledge about the property, that could give rise to the insurer relying on the 'knowledge' exclusion if the matter is not disclosed and 'insured over' before closing;

- the manner in which the client is taking title and the implications of joint tenancy or tenancy in common;
- any limitations on the lawyer's retainer, if applicable, regarding private services, condominium documentation, rental property or multi-unit issues;
- any necessary disclosure pursuant to the *Rules of Professional Conduct* regarding payments that the lawyer is receiving from other sources and how that relates, if applicable, to the client's disbursements.

☐ Depending on the nature and type of transaction, it may be appropriate for the lawyer to include the following topics in a reporting letter to a purchaser or mortgagee client:

- details of any waivers given by the client (e.g. instructions on not obtaining an up to date survey of the property or any other material instructions);
- full particulars of any mortgages (e.g. payments, payment dates and privileges);
- information on how title was taken;
- a short description of the closing documentation;
- information regarding the statement of adjustments;
- particulars of property insurance arrangements;
- reference to Tarion, if applicable;
- a description of the various taxes involved such as realty taxes, GST, PST and land transfer tax.
- information on any unusual aspects of the transaction;
- if the property is a condominium, highlights or a reference to the Declaration, By-Laws and status certificate;
- any other information that provides the client with a record of the practical aspects of the property;
- the lawyer's legal opinion on title and the exceptions to which the opinion is subject if title insurance is not being used;
- if title insurance is not being used, advice on the search inquiries conducted and responses received including the status of zoning and building searches, tax account and utility status and other off-title title search inquiries;
- if title insurance is being used, information regarding the title insurance coverage obtained and in a transaction where title insurance has been used to assure title, the reporting letter to the client should not opine on title but should include the title insurance policy issued in favour of the client.

☐ Depending on the nature and type of transaction, it would be appropriate for a lawyer to cover the following topics in a reporting letter to a vendor:

- information regarding the adjustments made on closing;
- particulars of the receipt and disbursement of funds;
- information concerning mortgages or other encumbrances that have been discharged;
- details of real estate commission;
- if the vendor has taken back a mortgage, the details of such mortgage;
- details of any waivers obtained from the client;
- confirmation of payment of realty taxes and other payments;
- a short description of the closing documentation;
- particulars of any undertaking given or received on closing;
- information on any unusual aspect of the transaction; and
- any other information that provides the client with a record of the practical aspects of the property.

GUIDELINE 2
DUE DILIGENCE

The lawyer should employ a well-reasoned approach in determining the level and scope of due diligence involved in any particular transaction and in advising the client regarding due diligence and should conduct title and off-title searches having due regard for the terms of the client's contractual rights and obligations, the time and cost of conducting title and off-title searches and the availability/utility of title insurance.

Title Searches

☐ Performing a proper search requires that the lawyer review all documents on title affecting the client's interest in the property and retain notes on the search of title with respect to every real estate file.

☐ The lawyer should advise a purchaser, borrower or lender client as to the state of title, the location of easements, the impact of restrictive covenants, subdivision and other agreements affecting title.

☐ Due to the increasing risk of fraud in real estate transactions, the lawyer should review:

- the pattern of inactive or deleted instruments on the parcel register and inquire about any suspicious patterns of transfers or discharges;
- the values revealed by arm's-length transfers in the recent past, to determine if there have been any suspicious changes in value.

- The lawyer should report the results of the title search and due diligence process and in particular any suspicious patterns of transfers or discharges and/or any suspicious changes in values revealed by the due diligence process to:

    o the purchaser/borrower if the lawyer is acting for the purchaser/borrower;
    o the lender if the lawyer is acting for the lender; and
    o the title insurer (if applicable).

Off-Title Searches

☐ The lawyer should discuss with the client and obtain instructions from the client regarding the off title searches that may be appropriate or advisable in view of the nature of the property, the circumstances of the transaction, the terms of the agreement of purchase and sale and the consequences of not conducting those searches.

☐ Where title insurance is being used, the lawyer should be cognizant of:

- what off-title searches relevant to the client or transaction are not covered by title insurance and make appropriate searches or obtain waivers from the client; and
- the inter-related nature of the following issues: deciding not to make certain off-title searches; allowing the requisition date to pass without the results of those searches being available; the timing of receiving a title insurance binder or commitment (usually after the requisition date has passed); and the policy of the selected title insurer regarding 'insure over' requests for adverse circumstances which emerge before closing notwithstanding the lack of a search.

Review of Title and Off-Title Searches

☐ A lawyer is responsible for reviewing personally all title search reports, off title search reports and the draft title insurance policy exclusions and exemptions.

Client/Party Identification

☐ Although the lawyer may not be able to guarantee the identity of the client or a party to a document in many circumstances (absent personal, long-term knowledge), the lawyer shall undertake steps to verify that the person retaining the lawyer and/or signing documents under the lawyer's supervision has reasonable identification to substantiate that he/she is the named client/party and should retain details or information about the identification obtained.

Title Insurance

☐ Where title insurance is being relied upon to close a transaction where registration is delayed, there should be an express obligation on the part of the title insurer as part of the binder/commitment pre-closing, addressed to the insured-client(s), to provide coverage to the client for any adverse registrations which occur between releasing the closing proceeds and registration of the title document(s). This obligation may be satisfied by obtaining a draft policy from the title insurer in the name of the insured clients including an endorsement or policy terms providing the coverage described.

☐ The lawyer should review the draft title insurance policy or binder/commitment, to ensure the following:

- Is the insured named correctly?
- Is the legal description correct? Since only the lands described are insured, there may be off-site lands that should be included in the description, so that easements or rights-of-way located on other properties, but benefiting the subject property, and encroachments from the subject property onto other lands, will be covered by the insurance.
- Are there other title issues, not apparent from the insurance commitment, of which the client should be warned? For example, problems may have been found when the search was conducted but the title insurer has not entered them on the Schedule to the policy because those problems are removed from coverage by the standard, pre-printed exceptions.
- In the alternative, have problems emerged with respect to the title that it would be preferable for the owner to have resolved under the terms of the agreement of purchase and sale?
- What coverage is excluded from the commitment/policy?

☐ The lawyer should issue the title insurance policy as soon as possible after closing, to insure that an issued policy exists should the insured-client(s) need to make a claim, and to minimize the risk of the client's being obliged to disclose adverse information obtained between closing and the issuance of the policy.

☐ The issued policy should be compared carefully to the draft policy or binder/commitment received before closing to ensure that there are no discrepancies in coverage.

GUIDELINE 3
PROPER FILING AND RECORD-KEEPING

The lawyer should keep a separate file for each transaction that is consistent with proper management of a transaction including appropriate management of deadlines and the facilitation of information storage and retrieval, while also fulfilling all record-keeping requirements of the *Rules of Professional Conduct* and other regulatory requirements.

☐ Lawyers should maintain a system to follow up on undertakings regarding mortgage discharges and/or other undertakings given or received in the course of the transaction.

☐ Lawyers should approach a post-closing claim relating to an undertaking to re-adjust in good faith, advising clients of their rights and obligations and attempting to resolve the situation (subject to reporting the claim to the purchaser's title insurer, if any, and following the instructions of the insurer).

GUIDELINE 4
DOCUMENT PREPARATION AND REGISTRATION

The lawyer shall utilize appropriate means to ensure the reliable, consistent and legally sound preparation and registration of documents in accordance with evolving professional tools and practices.

Electronic Registration

☐ Where the electronic registration system is being used, the initial letter to the other lawyer should specify:

- who is preparing the electronic transfer;
- whether the Document Registration Agreement ("DRA") is intended to be used and if so, whether it will be signed as a separate document or subscribed to as a protocol (if the latter, additional relevant information and/or changes thereto need to be provided as per the current form of DRA);
- to whom messages should be sent through the system.

☐ Prior to registering electronic documents, lawyers should obtain and retain in their files the client's written authorization.

☐ Lawyers should obtain and retain in their files the evidence upon which compliance with law statements are based, or alternatively ensure that publicly available information to fully support the statements is and remains available.

Review of Documents

☐ A lawyer is responsible for the ultimate review of documents before signing.

GUIDELINE 5
FINANCIAL ISSUES

The lawyer shall maintain appropriate financial records, controls and systems to ensure proper record-keeping and accountability, while also fulfilling all financial requirements of the *Rules of Professional Conduct* and other regulatory requirements.

Transfer of Funds

☐ Due regard should be had to the method of funds transfer. Absent agreement between the law firms and accompanying instructions from the clients, funds should be exchanged in the form provided for in the agreement of purchase and sale.

GUIDELINE 6
EXTRAORDINARY MATTERS

A lawyer should not undertake a matter without honestly feeling competent to handle it or being able to become competent without undue delay, risk or expense to the client.

☐ A lawyer must be alert to recognize any lack of competence for a particular task and the disservice that would be done to the client by undertaking that task. If consulted in such circumstances, the lawyer should either decline the retainer to act or obtain the client's instructions to retain, consult, or collaborate with a lawyer who is competent for that task.

☐ When handling a task on behalf of a client, the lawyer is responsible for keeping up to date with changes in the law and adapting to changing professional requirements, standards, techniques and practices.

☐ When acting for a client in the provision of legal services, the lawyer may be asked for or be expected to give advice on non-legal matters such as business or policy implications involved in the question or the course that the client should choose. If the lawyer expresses views on such matters, the lawyer should where and to the extent necessary point out any lack of experience or qualification in the particular field and should clearly distinguish legal advice from other advice.

CHAPTER 16

Electronic Land Registration System (ELRS)

RECENT DEVELOPMENTS IN ELRS

Real property law and conveyancing practice continue to change at an accelerating pace. Now that the profession and conveyancing practice have shifted to the electronic environment, the focus has reoriented to that of due diligence, fraud avoidance, and risk management for the client, the lawyer, and the insurer. The Law Society of Upper Canada (LSUC) now provides on its website the *Real Estate Practice Guide*, the *Residential Real Estate Transactions Practice Guidelines*, and the *Guidelines for Electronic Registration*.

The Ministry of Government Services' Real Estate Fraud Action Plan has generated significant changes in legislation, practice, and Electronic Land Registration System (ELRS) procedures based on the *Ministry of Government Services Consumer Protection and Service Modernization Act, 2006*, S.O. 2006, c. 34 (Bill 152), which amended parts of the *Land Registration Reform Act*, R.S.O. 1990, c. L.4, the *Land Titles Act*, R.S.O. 1990, c. L.5, and the *Registry Act*, R.S.O. 1990, c. R.20. Ministry Bulletin No. 2009-01 entitled "Access Requirements for ELRS; Registration Requirements for Transfers and Powers of Attorney" (January 8, 2009) and Bulletin No. 2009-02 entitled "Teraview Version 6.0 and Phase 2 System Changes relating to Real Estate Fraud Action Plan" (April 15, 2009) outline the major changes and review the new ELRS statements. All documents now require that individuals signing make a statement that they have the authority to sign and register the document on behalf of the parties to the document. The Ministry has updated its *Electronic Procedures Guide* to reflect the changes in legislation and ELRS and recent Teraview software versions.

Recent developments in real estate conveyancing that affect electronic land registration and closing procedures include the following:

1. strict new government requirements for access authorization to ELRS;

2. new signatory statements for transfers that require both the vendor's and the purchaser's lawyers to sign for completeness and complete:

    a. authorization statements;
    b. unique lawyer statements;
    c. exemption law statements when the two-lawyer rule does not apply;

3. client identification and verification requirements;

4. new power of attorney search capacity;

5. new power of attorney due diligence practice requirements which are re-flected in POA electronic registration statements;

6. additional mandatory fraud risk screening questions in title insurance application;

7. increased title and off-title search requirements for title insurance applications;

8. enhanced import and export capability and integrated access into ELRS from real estate file management software programs; and

9. focus on the security procedures for closing funds and the increasing use of "real time", large value transaction system wire transfers guaranteed by the Bank of Canada (for example, Teraview's CLOSURE service).

In addition, numerous, ongoing revisions are made to electronic form content, particularly the electronic statements. For example, amendments to the *Planning Act* necessitated changes to statements dealing with *Planning Act* consents. The new requirements listed above are reviewed in detail at the beginning of Chapter 15; the new title insurance requirements are outlined in Chapter 18.

LSUC ELECTRONIC REGISTRATION GUIDELINES

Guideline 4 of the *Residential Real Estate Transactions Practice Guidelines* deals with document preparation and electronic registration. The guideline recommends that the initial letter between solicitors specify who will prepare the electronic transfer, whether the lawyers will use the standard document registration agreement or add changes and whether it will be signed or incorporated by reference in letters, and to whom messages should be sent within Teraview. Lawyers must obtain and retain written client authorization. As well, lawyers must retain evidence upon which electronic compliance statements are based. Lawyers may ensure the availability of public information that supports statements, by separate registration. The lawyer is responsible for the ultimate review of documents before signing.

ELECTRONIC SIGNATURES

Special rules apply to electronic/digital signatures in ELRS. In an electronic environment, lawyers may wish to use electronic signatures on non-ELRS documents. When using electronic signatures, lawyers must ensure that security measures exist that prevent unauthorized access, use, or copying of the lawyer's signature; for example, setting guidelines for who may sign which documents under what circumstances. Lawyers who provide employees with their e-signature must supervise the proper use of the signature. The *Personal Information Protection and Electronic Documents Act*, S.C. 2000, c. 5 and the *Electronic Commerce Act, 2000*, S.O. 2000, c. 17 regulate the legality of electronic signatures and electronic documents.

BACKGROUND

The development and implementation of the electronic land registration system represents the final and most ambitious stage of the Province of Ontario Land Registration Information System (POLARIS) initiatives under Part III of the *Land Registration Reform Act*. Electronic land registration is a paperless title searching, document production, and document registration system. The electronic registration feature applies only to Land Titles properties. Electronic searching is available for the few (about 100,000) remaining Registry properties and all Land Titles properties. All registry divisions in Ontario are scheduled to have been converted from the old paper-based system and automated by spring 2010. When the POLARIS conversion of Registry land to Land Titles ownership is complete, ELRS will be available for all properties in Ontario except for a few Registry non-converts and a very small number of low density, difficult to automate areas. These remaining areas are expected to be integrated into POLARIS as they are transferred to new owners. The Ministry has an application process for privately initiated conversion to automated Land Titles.

Ontario is the first jurisdiction in the world to offer a completely automated land registration system. Electronic land registration and WritSearch are available online through Teraview. Lawyers and law clerks work in the online system; they no longer attend at a building called a Registry office. Private individuals will continue to have limited access at the land Registry office using a Teraview kiosk, or at the land Registry office using staff-assisted electronic filing. Electronic land registration has revolutionized real estate practice in that it facilitates the process whereby electronic documents with digital signatures can be registered online from a remote location (usually a lawyer's office), rather than having a person actually attend at a Registry office for closing and registration. Electronic land registration in POLARIS using Teraview provides the following pre-closing and closing services:

1. automated title searching;

2. writ searching in both the WritSearch and ELRS products;

3. subsearching;

4. creation of both draft and registerable documents;

5. automatic electronic calculation and payment of land transfer taxes;

6. communication between lawyers throughout the document production and registration process;

7. review, amendment, and approval of draft documents by lawyers;

8. electronic submission and registration of documents;

9. transfers of funds for registration and *Land Transfer Tax Act* fees;

10. secure private communication network for authorized users;

11. report functions including docket summary, tax and registration fee summary, acknowledgement and direction, document preparation, registration and Land Transfer Tax, deposit account, and account registration and fees activity reports; and

12. confidentiality, security, and an electronic audit trail traceable to the user.

IMPLEMENTATION

The Ministry of Government Services is currently completing the electronic land registration system and implementing Phase 2 system changes relating to the Real Estate Fraud Action Plan. (See Appendix 4 for the completion status of areas in Ontario.) The Ministry initiates the conversion process by filing a regulation making electronic land registration optional in a designated county or district. Training programs and staff-assisted electronic land registration services are available during the transitional period. A second regulation, making electronic land registration mandatory, is filed a minimum of 60 days later, usually about six months later. Once a Registry office is designated as an electronic land registration area under Part III of the *Land Registration Reform Act*, all users will produce and register documents electronically online via Teraview or, on rare occasions, through Teraview customer service (document not suitable for electronic registration) or at the land Registry office using staff-assisted electronic filing. These Registry office services are intended for the occasional user or members of the public. Registry offices are now part of the broader based Service Ontario.

Electronic land registration began with a pilot project in the winter of 1998 in the Middlesex County Land Registry office in London. The first fully electronic land registrations took place on January 25, 1999. Currently, over 99 per cent of documents in mandatory jurisdictions are submitted from a remote location. As of 2003, over 80 per cent of Ontario's properties had been automated and 64 per cent of all land registrations registered electronically. As of 2008, 95 per cent of all properties had been automated. As of 2010, all registration districts are scheduled to be automated and in excess of 95 per cent of registrations are electronic. Almost all searches are done online, although it may be necessary to refer back to pre-conversion records to resolve problems and when dealing with issues affected by historical records such as shorelines, historical boundaries, Aboriginal rights, government claims, or environmental contamination and assessments. The Teraview website maintains an up-to-date Teraview (ELRS) coverage schedule and map, as well as a roll-out schedule for future electronic land registration implementation initiatives. The automation and conversion of Ontario's land registration systems is projected to be substantially complete by spring 2010. As with the development and implementation of title search and execution search automated systems, electronic land registrations and closings will undergo continuous change in the years to come.

ELECTRONIC LAND REGISTRATION RESOURCES

The Ministry of Government Services, Teranet, and the LSUC all actively offer electronic land registration resources. Teranet provides training, including online and on-site training and hardware and software support, as well as call centre and online customer service for electronic land registration (Teraview) clients.

The Teraview website and software offer resources, including newsletters, an interactive e-learning course, a training video/CD, online training modules, a Training System Guide, and a Teraview Reference Guide. The software has an extensive HELP feature. In addition, Teranet provides a Teraview/ELRS online training environment for clients to learn and practise the procedures involved in online title searching and document production and registration.

The Ministry provides an ELRS Procedures Guide and both telephone and online client services for legal issues of either a technical or procedural nature. In addition, the Ministry provides a precedent for a document registration agreement on its website and also maintains a website outlining online services and land registration information which includes orders, forms, bulletins, memos, sample schedules and plans for condominium submissions, and documentation and claims information for the Land Titles Assurance Fund. The website also provides online guides such as the *Certification of Title under the Certification of Titles Act and First Registration under the Land Titles Act*, the *Land Titles Conversion Qualified (LTCQ) to Land Titles Plus (LTplus)*, and the *Boundaries Act Client Guide* (available at <http://www.ontario.ca/en/information_bundle/land_registration/STEL01_130081> under "Residents: Land Registration Information").

The LSUC provides practice directives and recommendations and a suggested document registration agreement. The LSUC also actively regulates the use and supervision of Teraview Personal Security Packages (PSPs) (access diskettes and pass phrases) in the *Rules of Professional Conduct*. In addition, the LSUC has developed the *Practice Guidelines for Electronic Registration of Title Documents* (available on its website).

AUTHORIZATION TO ACCESS THE ELRS FOR ELECTRONIC REGISTRATION OF DOCUMENTS

In 2009, the Ministry as part of its Real Estate Fraud Action Plan introduced a new process for issuing authorization to access ELRS for the electronic registration of documents. The Director has the authority under the *Land Registration Reform Act* to authorize persons to access the electronic land registration system to register documents and establish the manner in which the authorization is assigned to those persons who have access to electronic registration of documents. Applicants for access must meet identity, financial resources (insurance), good character/accountability, and qualifications requirements. The authorization for search-only access requires a lower level of security clearance than electronic document registration. The application for access is available online and is a condition in the Teraview licensing agreement. The LSUC reinforces government and Teraview user access and security requirements through professional practice standards, audits, and errors and omissions excepted (E&OE) fraud reduction initiatives.

PRINCIPLES OF ELECTRONIC LAND REGISTRATION

"Electronic land registration" means registration under the *Land Titles Act* in an electronic format. Electronic documents are created on the Teraview server, accessed between law offices, edited, released, submitted, registered, filed, and maintained, all in an electronic format. Electronic land registration introduced new legal principles, documents, and procedures to real estate conveyancing, such as:

- electronic document production, sharing, and registration

- Ministry access authorization to submit documents for registration in ELRS

- personal security licence and package (Teraview PSP)

- electronic/digital signatures

- acknowledgement and direction report for electronic documents

- compliance with law statements

- signatory statements for transfers that require both the vendor's and the
  purchaser's lawyers to sign for completeness

- general authority (authorization) statements for all electronic signatures

- unique lawyer statements and exemption law statements when the two-lawyer rule does not apply

- power of attorney statements for all documents

- document registration agreements for escrow closings

- escrow closings procedures for electronic land registrations

- secure real-time-guaranteed electronic funds transfers within the ELRS process (CLOSURE)

Electronic documents are signed electronically with digital signatures supported by authorization statements. The client directs the lawyer to sign on his or her behalf by way of a signed Direction and Acknowledgement included in the electronic land registration service. Electronic documents must contain a statement as to whether or not the document was signed by way of a power of attorney. Additional statements are required for documents signed by power of attorney. The electronic document and title record represents the legal document and prevails over any paper form of the document or record. Documents are signed electronically using a Teraview user ID and passphrase and personal security package key or device such as a diskette or USB.

Electronic statements of fact and/or law within the electronic documents replace in most situations required paper supporting evidence; for example, proof of death in survivorship or transmission applications or execution affidavits. Supporting evidence for statements must be retained by the lawyer. Statements that involve an opinion of law are called compliance with law statements. Compliance with law statements, such as *Planning Act* statements, may be selected by a non-lawyer employee but can only be signed for completeness by a lawyer using a lawyer's PSP. Transfers may only be signed by lawyers using a lawyer's PSP. Transfers require the signature of both the lawyer for the transferor and the lawyer for the transferee subject to a number of exceptions. Lawyers may not allow employees to use their keys or passphrases. Transactions must be closed in escrow in the electronic environment. The *Joint Law Society of Upper Canada – Canadian Bar Association Committee on Electronic Registration of Title Documents* has developed a recommended Document Registration Agreement (DRA) that sets out the terms and the procedures for an escrow closing in the electronic environment. The DRA is available on the LSUC website and in Chapter 15.

Personal Security Licence/Package

As of 2009, all users of ELRS must apply for and be issued authorization by the Director to access ELRS for the electronic registration of documents. Public key cryptography, similar to that used with bank cards, controls user access to ELRS services and provides user privacy and security for account information. All users of Teraview must also obtain a personal security licence that includes an encrypted digital signature before they can access ELRS and sign and register documents. The PSP, which contains a personal security disk/USB and a passphrase allowing access to the Teraview Gateway, creates an electronic audit trail for all electronic registration activity.

Rule 5.01(2), (3) and (4) of the LSUC *Rules of Professional Conduct* regulates the use of PSPs issued under a lawyer's Teraview account. Each user of ELRS services under a Teraview account must obtain a separate personalized encrypted disk/USB and passphrase. The access key may be coded for search-only functions, non-lawyer/law clerk functions (cannot sign compliance with law statements or transfers for completeness), or for lawyer functions. All owners of a personal security licence are restricted from sharing keys and passphrases. Only a lawyer's PSP can sign documents containing statements of law and transfers for completeness. Lawyers are forbidden to allow others (for example, a law clerk or legal assistant) to use the lawyer's key, and must never disclose their passphrases to others. Lawyers are responsible for the supervision of non-lawyer employees in terms of use and security of PSPs and passphrases, as well as the contents of any documents signed by a non-lawyer pursuant to their instructions. Law firms must follow strict LSUC guidelines for safeguarding PSPs.

ESCROW CLOSINGS

The implementation of ELRS created changes in the LSUC's *Practice Directions* and *Rules of Professional Conduct* regarding facilitating and standardizing escrow closings, electronic transfer of funds, and law office management.

Under the ELRS system, one lawyer will register the documents on behalf of both parties, subject to a previously agreed-upon arrangement contained in the Document Registration Agreement authorized by an Acknowledgement and Direction signed by the client. As in traditional escrow closings, the lawyers will hold funds in trust until registration and registration undertakings are complete and keys and certified cheques (or electronic transfer of funds) have been exchanged. Standard closing protocols for lawyers to follow before and during ELRS vary from region to region and will continue to develop in the years to come (see Chapter 15).

The electronic transfer of closing funds is reviewed in detail at the beginning of Chapter 15. There has been a steep rise in the risk of fraud regarding certified cheques. Fraudulent certified cheques and bank drafts may be returned up to 90 days following receipt by the drawee bank. A certified cheque with a forged endorsement may be subject to return up to six months. The LSUC has developed practice guidelines for certified cheques. Increasingly, lawyers are moving to online guaranteed by the Bank of Canada funds (wire) transfer services, large value transfer system (LVTS) that provide real time finality of payment. Teraview offers a web-based service within ELRS between participating financial institutions and lawyers and agents called CLOSURE that offers guaranteed real-time LVTS services for real estate closings including purchase funds, mortgage payouts, and real estate agents' commissions.

Acknowledgement and Direction

The Acknowledgement and Direction both confirms the client's approval of the contents of the document and directs and authorizes the lawyer to sign and register documents electronically. It also authorizes the lawyer to enter into a Document

Registration Agreement and close in escrow on behalf of the client. Lawyers may use the Acknowledgement and Direction generated by an ELRS report function or may create an amended Acknowledgement and Direction. It should be signed prior to signing for completeness and completing authorization and unique lawyer statements and must be signed before signing for the release for registration of an electronic document. The Acknowledgement and Direction includes the draft electronic document and frequently the Document Registration Agreement attached as schedules. The client and, when relevant, the non-titled spouse should sign the Acknowledgement and Direction when the transfer contains the *Family Law Act*, R.S.O. 1990, c. F.3 statement confirming that the spouse consents to the transaction. The LSUC website contains a recommended Acknowledgement and Direction and a Document Registration Agreement (DRA). Figure 16.1 is an example of an Acknowledgement and Direction generated in ELRS.

Figure 16.1

ACKNOWLEDGEMENT AND DIRECTION WITH DOCUMENT PREPARATION REPORT INCLUDING LAND TRANSFER TAX ACT STATEMENTS ATTACHED[*]

ACKNOWLEDGEMENT AND DIRECTION

TO: Fanshawe College 40 _____
              (Insert lawyer's name)

AND TO: FANSHAWE COLLEGE _____
              (Insert firm name)

RE: Corbett S/T Moore, 1964 Arameta Trail, Greenstone, 25023-0023 _____ ("the transaction")
              (Insert brief description of transaction)

This will confirm that:

● I/We have reviewed the information set out this Acknowledgement and Direction and in the documents described below (the "Documents"), and that this information is accurate;

● You, your agent or employee are authorized and directed to sign, deliver, and/or register electronically, on my/our behalf the Documents in the form attached.

● You are hereby authorized and directed to enter into an escrow closing arrangement substantially in the form attached hereto being a copy of the version of the Document Registration Agreement, which appears on the website of the Law Society of Upper Canada as of the date of the Agreement of Purchase and sale herein. I/We hereby acknowledge the said Agreement has been reviewed by me/us and that I/We shall be bound by its terms;

● The effect of the Documents has been fully explained to me/us, and I/we understand that I/we are parties to and bound by the terms and provisions of the Documents to the same extent as if I/we had signed them; and

● I/we are in fact the parties named in the Documents and I/we have not misrepresented our identities to you.

● I, _____, am the spouse of _____, the (Transferor/Chargor), and hereby consent to the transaction described in the Acknowledgment and Direction. I authorize you to indicate my consent on all the Documents for which it is required.

DESCRIPTION OF ELECTRONIC DOCUMENTS

        The Document(s) described in the Acknowledgement and Direction are the document(s) selected below which are attached hereto as "Document in Preparation" and are:

■   A Transfer of the land described above.

☐   A Charge of the land described above.

☐   Other documents set out in Schedule "B" attached hereto.

Dated at _____ , this _____ day of _____ , 20___ .

WITNESS

(As to all signatures, if required)

_____   _____

                                               _____

                                               _____

_____

Figure 16.1 (cont'd)

**** NOT VALID - TO BE USED FOR TRAINING PURPOSES ONLY ****

This document has not been submitted and may be incomplete.	yyyy mm dd Page 1 of 2
LRO # 20 Transfer	In preparation on 2009 08 03 at 10:23

Properties

PIN	25023 – 0023 LT *Interest/Estate* Fee Simple
Description	LT 30, PL 649; PT LT 31, PL 649, NW OF SPRUCE ST, AS IN 532743; GREENSTONE FLATS
Address	1964 ARAMETA TRAIL
	HALTON HILLS

Consideration

Consideration $ 300,000.00

Transferor(s)

The transferor(s) hereby transfers the land to the transferee(s).

Name   CORBETT, WILLIAM ELLIS
Acting as an individual

Address for Service   37 Beamish Street, Geraldton, Greenstone, Ontario, POT 2X6

I am at least 18 years of age.

Jessie Ruth Corbett and I are spouses of one another and are both parties to this document

This document is not authorized under Power of Attorney by this party.

Name   CORBETT, JESSIE RUTH
Acting as an individual

Address for Service

I am at least 18 years of age.

William Ellis Corbett and I are spouses of one another and are both parties to this document

This document is not authorized under Power of Attorney by this party.

Transferee(s)   Capacity   Share

Name   MOORE, MARGUERITE ELLEN
Acting as an individual

Date of Birth   1967 04 01

Address for Service   1964 Arameta Trail , Geralton, Greenstone, Ontario POT 2X6

STATEMENT OF THE TRANSFEROR (S): The transferor(s) verifies that to the best of the transferor's knowledge and belief, this transfer does not contravene the Planning Act.

STATEMENT OF THE SOLICITOR FOR THE TRANSFEROR (S): I have explained the effect of the Planning Act to the transferor(s) and I have made inquiries of the transferor(s) to determine that this transfer does not contravene that Act and based on the information supplied by the transferor(s), to the best of my knowledge and belief, this transfer does not contravene that Act. I am an Ontario solicitor in good standing.

STATEMENT OF THE SOLICITOR FOR THE TRANSFEREE (S): I have investigated the title to this land and to abutting land where relevant and I am satisfied that the title records reveal no contravention as set out in the Planning Act, and to the best of my knowledge and belief this transfer does not contravene the Planning Act. I act independently of the solicitor for the transferor(s) and I am an Ontario solicitor in good standing.

Figure 16.1 (cont'd)

**** NOT VALID - TO BE USED FOR TRAINING PURPOSES ONLY ****

This document has not been submitted and may be incomplete.	yyyy mm dd	Page 2 of 2
LRO # 20 Transfer	In preparation on 2009 08 03	at 10:23

Signed By

Fanshawe College 40   acting for   Signed   2009 08 03
                                                     Transferor(s)

Tel

Fax

I am the solicitor for the transferor(s) and I am not one and the same as the solicitor for the transferee(s).

I have the authority to sign and register the document on behalf of the Transferor(s).

Calculated Taxes

Provincial Land Transfer Tax	$2,975.00
Retail Sales Tax	$0.00

File Number

Transferor Client File Number :	S649/2010
Transferee Client File Number :	P1964/2010

Figure 16.1 (cont'd)

**** NOT VALID - TO BE USED FOR TRAINING PURPOSES ONLY ****

LAND TRANSFER TAX STATEMENTS

In the matter of the conveyance of: 25023 – 0023 LT 30, PL 73; PT LT 31, PL 649, NW of SPRUCE ST, AS IN 532743; OGOKI FLATS

BY: CORBETT, WILLIAM ELLIS
CORBETT, JESSIE RUTH
TO: MOORE, MARGUERITE ELLEN %(all PINs)

1. MOORE, MARGUERITE ELLEN

   I am

   ☐ (a) A person in trust for whom the land conveyed in the above-described conveyance is being conveyed;

   ☐ (b) A trustee named in the above-described conveyance to whom the land is being conveyed;

   ☑ (c) A transferee named in the above-described conveyance;

   ☐ (d) The authorized agent or solicitor acting in this transaction for ____ described in paragraph(s) (_) above.

   ☐ (e) The President, Vice-President, Manager, Secretary, Director, or Treasurer authorized to act for ____ described in paragraph(s) (_) above.

   ☐ (f) A transferee described in paragraph ( ) and am making these statements on my own behalf and on behalf of _____ who is my spouse described in paragraph (_) and as such, I have personal knowledge of the facts herein deposed to.

3. **The total consideration for this transaction is allocated as follows:**

(a) Monies paid or to be paid in cash	300,000.00
(b) Mortgages (i) assumed (show principal and interest to be credited against purchase price)	0.00
(ii) Given Back to Vendor	0.00
(c) Property transferred in exchange (detail below)	0.00
(d) Fair market value of the land(s)	0.00
(e) Liens, legacies, annuities and maintenance charges to which transfer is subject	0.00
(f) Other valuable consideration subject to land transfer tax (detail below)	0.00
(g) Value of land, building, fixtures and goodwill subject to land transfer tax (total of (a) to (f))	300,000.00
(h) VALUE OF ALL CHATTELS - items of tangible personal property	0.00
(i) Other considerations for transaction not included in (g) or (h) above	0.00
(j) Total consideration	300,000.00

PROPERTY Information Record

A. Nature of Instrument: Transfer

   LRO 37 Registration No. Date:

B. Property(s): PIN 25023 – 0023 Address 1964 ARAMETA Assessment 4215010 - 00426600
   TRAIL Roll No
   OGOKI FLATS

C. Address for Service: 1964 Arameta Trail , Geralton,
   Greenstone, Ontario POT 2X6

D. (i) Last Conveyance(s): PIN 25023 - 0023 Registration No.

   (ii) Legal Description for Property Conveyed : Same as in last conveyance? Yes ☑ No ☐ Not known ☐

School Tax Support (Voluntary Election)

1. All individual transferees wish to vote for English-Public.

Document Registration Agreement

The DRA standardizes the practice by which lawyers complete escrow closings in the ELRS. The DRA governs the exchange of keys, funds, and off-title documents, as well as registration responsibilities. Lawyers either sign a DRA or agree in writing (often through the letter and reply to the letter of requisitions) to be bound by the terms of the LSUC's recommended DRA. Some law firms and some large vendors work with a customized DRA. Standard agreements of purchase and sale often contain terms relating to the use of the DRA and an acknowledgement by the parties that the solicitors will close in escrow pursuant to the DRA.

The DRA requires that funds, keys, and documents be held in escrow (trust) until the solicitors for both parties have confirmed receipt and approval of their respective (requisite) deliveries. The purchaser's solicitor is usually the "registering solicitor" for the transfer, although the vendor's solicitor may register transfers of new condominium units in bulk closings. Schedule A of the DRA sets out the documents being registered and the order or priority in which they are to be registered. The "non-registering solicitor" electronically releases the electronic document(s) (for example, the transfer) for registration as soon as he or she has received and approved the "requisite deliveries" for closing. The registering solicitor then registers the documents listed in Schedule A and notifies the other solicitor, who may then release the requisite deliveries (for example, the funds) from escrow. The release deadline for closing is 6:00 p.m. on the day of closing unless a different time has been agreed on in the agreement of purchase and sale, the DRA, or between the parties.

Figure 16.2 is the LSUC's recommended DRA.

Figure 16.2

DOCUMENT REGISTRATION AGREEMENT (SCHEDULE A TO THE ACKNOWLEDGEMENT AND DIRECTION)*

DOCUMENT REGISTRATION AGREEMENT

BETWEEN:

_____

(hereinafter referred to as the "**Purchaser's Solicitor**")

AND:

_____

(hereinafter referred to as the "**Vendor's Solicitor**")

RE: _____ (the "**Purchaser**") purchase
from_____ (the "**Vendor**") of _____ (the
"**Property**") pursuant to an agreement of purchase and sale
dated_____ , as amended from time to time (the "**Purchase Agreement**"), scheduled to be completed on
_____ (the "**Closing Date**")

FOR GOOD AND VALUABLE CONSIDERATION (the receipt and sufficiency of which is hereby expressly acknowledged), the parties hereto hereby undertake and agree as follows:

Holding Deliveries In Escrow

1.   The Vendor's Solicitor and the Purchaser's Solicitor shall hold all funds, keys and closing documentation exchanged between them (the "Requisite Deliveries") in escrow, and *shall* not release or otherwise deal with same except in accordance with the terms of this Agreement. Both the Vendor's Solicitor and the Purchaser's Solicitor have been authorized by their respective clients to enter into this Agreement. Once the Requisite Deliveries can be released in accordance with the terms of this Agreement, any monies representing payout funds for mortgages to be discharged shall be forwarded promptly to the appropriate mortgage lender.[1]

[1]   Solicitors should continue to refer to the Law Society of Upper Canada practice guidelines relating to recommended procedures to follow for the discharge of mortgages.

Figure 16.2 (cont'd)

Advising of Concerns with Deliveries

2.   Each of the parties hereto shall notify the other as soon as reasonably possible following their respective receipt of the Requisite Deliveries (as applicable) of any defect(s) with respect to same.

Selecting Solicitor Responsible for Registration

3.   The Purchaser's Solicitor shall be responsible for the registration of the Electronic Documents (as hereinafter defined) unless the box set out below indicating that the Vendor's Solicitor will be responsible for such registration has been checked. For the purposes of this Agreement, the solicitor responsible for such registration shall be referred to as the "Registering Solicitor" and the other solicitor shall be referred to as the "Non-Registering Solicitor":

Vendor's Solicitor will be registering the Electronic Documents   ☐

Responsibility of Non-Registering Solicitor

and

Release of Requisite Deliveries by Non-Registering Solicitor

4.   The Non-Registering Solicitor shall, upon his/her receipt and approval of the Requisite Deliveries (as applicable), electronically release for registration the Electronic Documents and shall thereafter be entitled to release the Requisite Deliveries from escrow forthwith following the earlier of:

a)   the registration of the Electronic Documents;

b)   the closing time specified in the Purchase Agreement unless a specific time has been inserted as follows [_____ a.m./p.m. on the Closing Date] (the "**Release Deadline**"), and provided that notice under paragraph 7 below has not been received; or

c)   receipt of notification from the Registering Solicitor of the registration of the Electronic Documents.

If the Purchase Agreement does not specify a closing time and a Release Deadline has not been specifically inserted the Release Deadline shall be 6.00 p.m. on the Closing Date.

Responsibility of Registering Solicitor

5.   The Registering Solicitor shall, subject to paragraph 7 below, on the Closing Date, following his/her receipt and approval of the Requisite Deliveries (as applicable*)*, register the documents listed in Schedule "A" annexed hereto (referred to in this agreement as the "**Electronic Documents**") in the stated order of priority therein set out, as soon as reasonably possible once same have been released for registration by the Non- Registering Solicitor, and immediately thereafter notify the Non-Registering Solicitor of the registration particulars thereof by telephone or telefax (or other method as agreed between the parties).

Release of Requisite Deliveries by Registering Solicitor

6.   Upon registration of the Electronic Documents and notification of the Non-Registering solicitor in accordance with paragraph 5 above, the Registering Solicitor shall be entitled to forthwith release the Requisite Deliveries from escrow.

Figure 16.2 (cont'd)

Returning
Deliveries where
Non-registration

7.   Any of the parties hereto may notify the other party that he/she does not wish to proceed with the registration[2] of the Electronic Documents, and provided that such notice is received by the other party before the release of the Requisite Deliveries pursuant to this Agreement and before the registration of the Electronic Documents, then each of the parties hereto shall forthwith return to the other party their respective Requisite Deliveries.

Counterparts
& Gender

This Agreement may be signed in counterparts, and shall be read with all changes of gender and/or number as may be required by the context.

Purchase
Agreement
Prevails if
Conflict or
Inconsistency

9.   Nothing contained in this Agreement shall be read or construed as altering the respective rights and obligations of the Purchaser and the Vendor as more particularly set out in the Purchase Agreement, and in the event of any conflict or inconsistency between the provisions of this Agreement and the Purchase Agreement, then the latter shall prevail.

Telefaxing
Deliveries
& Providing
Originals if
Requested

10.   This Agreement (or any counterpart hereof), and any of the closing documents hereinbefore contemplated, may be exchanged by telefax or similar system reproducing the original, provided that all such documents have been properly executed by the appropriate parties. The party transmitting any such document(s) shall also provide the original executed version(s) of same to the recipient within 2 business days after the Closing Date, unless the recipient has indicated that he/she does not require such original copies.

Dated this _____ day of _____, 20_____.

Name/Firm Name of Vendor's Solicitor

Name/Firm Name of Purchaser's Solicitor

_____

_____

_____

_____

_____

_____

Name of Person Signing

Name of Person Signing

_____

_____

(Signature)

(Signature)

---

[2]   For the purpose of this Agreement, the term "registration" shall mean the issuance of registration number(s) in respect of the Electronic Documents by the appropriate Land Registry Office.

Note: This version of the Document Registration Agreement was adopted by the Joint LSUC-CBAO Committee on Electronic Registration of Title Documents on March 29, 2004 and posted to the web site on April 8, 2004.

ELECTRONIC STATEMENTS

ELRS contains a wealth of pre-populated electronic statements. Each document type is pre-populated with a unique selection of legally appropriate statements. All statements are numbered. Some statements are standard to all or a large number of documents, and others are specific to the particular document type or transaction. The *Electronic Registration Procedures Guide* under general requirements contains an extensive review of the requirements for and the effect of electronic statements. Electronic documents contain constantly evolving, prescribed, electronic statements representing the same type of information previously required in paper-based documents in the form of signed statements, affidavits, recitals, and supporting paper evidence. The various types of statements include the following:

- standard statements that form part of the standard document, such as a statement indicating the transferor has agreed to transfer the land and signing authorization statements;
- standard statements required for the parties, such as statements of age, spousal status, and whether the document is being signed by way of power of attorney;
- statements that are required for a particular document, such as *Planning Act* statements or statements that provide estate or bankruptcy information;
- optional or additional, non-standard statements, such as statements concerning supporting evidence filed at the Registry office; and
- standard statements required under the *Land Transfer Tax Act*, R.S.O. 1990, c. L.6 and for the Toronto municipal tax.

ELRS forbids certain types of traditional paper-based statements, such as the vendor is (not) a non-resident pursuant to the *Income Tax Act*, R.S.O. 1990, c. I.2, that the property is being acquired in trust, and that a document was registered without a prior search of title.

Statements regarding legal age, the *Planning Act*, the *Family Law Act*, and signing authority are pre-populated within the electronic form. All documents contain a statement as to whether or not the document is signed by way of power of attorney. In the past, documents such as transmission and survivorship applications, mortgage foreclosures or powers of sale, cautions, applications to delete writs or construction liens, and applications to amend the register based on a court order required the registration of supporting affidavit evidence. Electronic documents permit the solicitor to select the appropriate pre-programmed electronic statement in lieu of registering the supporting evidence. Instead, the supporting evidence must be retained in the solicitor's file. Electronic statements must be supported by careful inquiry and supporting file documentation.

Electronic documents contain both statements of fact and compliance with law statements. Statements of fact do not require a legal opinion, whereas compliance with law statements do require an interpretation or an opinion of law. Only a lawyer can make and sign for completeness documents containing law statements, although statements of law can be completed by a person other than a lawyer. Statements have the same force and effect as earlier paper statements accompanied by signatures or contained in affidavits. All documents now contain signing authorization statements.

Many statements (for example, a statement of age or spousal status) involve a statement of fact based on factual evidence. Section 40(2) of the *Land Registration Reform Act* regulation, Electronic Registration, O. Reg. 19/99 (amended to O. Reg. 200/09) requires that a statement of fact must be made "on the advice of the party to the document containing the statement who has knowledge of the fact". Statements of fact should be confirmed with independent evidence, such as a birth or marriage certificate, and photo-identification. Copies of this evidence should be kept on file.

AUTHORIZATION STATEMENTS

As part of the Real Estate Fraud Action Plan, all documents must have authorization statements which are completed during the signing process. The Teraview account holder signing on behalf of the client/party to the document must obtain and retain evidence of authorization and direction or consent of the property owner or interested person directing the account user to sign and register the electronic document. Authorization is normally obtained by completing the acknowledgement and direction document illustrated in Figure 16.1. Special statements are available when it is an authorization by the Public Guardian and Trustee, a partnership, a corporation, the Crown, a municipality, or pursuant to a power of attorney. Detailed authorization statements related to the use of powers of attorney were revised in 2009 as part of the fraud prevention initiatives.

COMPLIANCE WITH LAW STATEMENTS

The purpose of compliance with law statements is to reduce the amount of paper filed in the Land Titles system. Compliance with law statements involve the practise of law and the giving of a legal opinion. Only an Ontario lawyer in good standing who is a registered Teraview user with a PSP can make a compliance with law statement. Although a non-lawyer employee can select a compliance with law statement, only a lawyer, using the lawyer's diskette or key and personal passphrase, can sign for completeness a document containing a compliance with law statement. For example, a law clerk using a law clerk's key cannot sign for completeness a transfer as it requires at least one and usually two lawyers' signatures. A law clerk cannot use the lawyers PSP to sign a transfer. Similarly, *Planning Act* compliance statements are law statements and therefore only a lawyer can sign for completeness a document containing a *Planning Act* statement. Compliance with law statements are not always separate distinct statements. They may also result from the combined use of a series of related statements, for example, in estate conveyancing. Compliance with law statements are found throughout electronic documents and can be easily identified as the number assigned to a compliance with law statement is always in bold type. All compliance with law statements must be supported by evidence retained in the lawyer's file. The LSUC's *Electronic Registration of Title Documents, Practice Guideline 6* sets out the standards for compliance with law statements. The Ministry's Procedures Guide contains precedents and legal requirements for compliance with law statements.

ELECTRONIC DOCUMENTS

Documents are produced, edited, messaged between participating solicitors, signed, and registered online using Teraview. The document, as a work in progress, is situated on the Teraview server, not in a specific law office. Transactions involving large numbers of documents and/or property identification numbers (PINs), such as condominium creation documents and blanket mortgages, follow special procedures and are referred to as projects.

Pre-Populated Forms

Title information already stored in the POLARIS database will automatically be brought forward and entered into the document creation and registration functions. This process is called pre-population and avoids the need for entering basic information already contained in the register. For example, the names of transferors and chargors, the legal descriptions, and municipal addresses will be automatically contained in the document creation and registration screens and forms.

File management software now has import and export capability. As information entered in file management software may flow through to the ELRS documents in progress, it is essential to enter accurate information in a manner that meets Teraview protocols and naming conventions.

Entry of Title Information

New title information, for example, the names and addresses and capacity of transferees on a transfer, is entered according to a series of user-friendly prompts. Frequently, the user is required to select from a list of pre-programmed statements. For example, when creating a transfer, the user must select from a comprehensive series of pre-programmed statements identifying the capacity in which the transferee takes title, such as beneficial ownership, joint tenancy, tenancy in common, as partnership property, or as estate trustee, *etc.*

Title information can also be entered by the click of a mouse for *Family Law Act* statements, *Planning Act* statements, mandatory power of attorney statements, power of sale statements, corporate execution statements, *etc.* Solicitor compliance with law statements, such as *Planning Act* declarations, will, wherever possible, substitute for supporting documents and evidence in transactions such as transmission applications, mortgage enforcements, and bankruptcy. Supporting documents and evidence such as declarations, postal receipts, court orders, *etc.*, must be retained in the lawyer's file, although in the past it was sometimes submitted separately in paper format and assigned an index number.

The ELRS program automatically warns the user when a draft registration is incomplete, for example, if it lacks a mandatory spousal or power of attorney statement. The signing and registration functions are only permitted after all mandatory information has been submitted and declarations made.

Document Security

Teraview contains security protections regarding access on the document creation and registration levels as well as on the user access (PSP) to the POLARIS database. While new documents are in progress prior to registration, access is restricted to authorized users, pursuant to the grant access procedures. Electronic land registration provides the following three levels of access to documents in progress:

1. Creating/Updating/Editing Documents (Blanket Authority)

2. Completing/Approving/Signing Documents (Update Authority)

3. Releasing/Registering Documents (Release Authority)

The user who initiates a new document can edit and view the document as a work in progress until it has been registered. Documents can be messaged to other lawyers who may or may not be given edit authority. Any change in a document automatically removes all signatures. Once registered, a document is no longer a "work in progress" and cannot be changed. A registered document can only be accessed as part of the property search or view functions.

Blanket Authority

During the document creation and registration process, the user who has created a new document can grant access to other users in the same Teraview account. For example, a solicitor may grant blanket access to the law clerk working on the transaction prior to creating any documents. Blanket authority allows the user the ability to edit, sign, and register documents.

Update Authority

The user who creates the document can grant update authority to another user by way of "messaging". For example, a solicitor acting on behalf of a vendor can grant access for a transfer to the solicitor acting on behalf of the purchaser. This allows the purchaser's solicitor to edit the transfer, sign for completeness and release, and register the document, in accordance with the DRA.

Release Authority

Release authority only allows the user to sign for completeness and release and register the document. Release authority does not permit the user to change the document prior to release.

The solicitor in charge of the file should determine the nature of the access granted both within a law practice and to outside Teraview account holders. The solicitor is responsible for all activity in an account. Access should be granted in accordance with the DRA.

NON-ELECTRONIC DOCUMENTS AND REGISTRATIONS

All documents in the Registry system as well as all documents registered prior to the implementation of electronic land registration are in paper form. Registry documents will continue to be submitted in paper form. Land Titles documents must be submitted in electronic form in the designated ELRS area. As a result, it may still be necessary to obtain and review paper documents as part of the title search and to register paper documents (for example, historical documents and some plans, applications for first registration, and condominium creation documents) even in an electronic land registration environment.

ELECTRONIC DOCUMENT CREATION

Electronic land registration is available for in excess of 100 instrument groups, subgroups, and types. Each main document group expands to offer pre-programmed forms of more specialized forms. For example, the "Transfer" group expands to contain transfers such as Transfer Easement, Transfer by Partnership, Transfer by Easement, Transfer: Power of Sale, and Transfer: Trustee in Bankruptcy. The main instrument groups in ELRS include the following:

- Application (General)
- Application Foreclosure Order
- Application for Vesting Order
- Application Consolidation Parcels

- Application Delete Execution
- Application to Register a Court Order
- By-Laws and Government Order
- Cautions
- Cautions — Land
- Certificate
- Change of Name Application
- Charge
- Transfer of Charge
- Compliance Subdivision Agreements
- Death of Owner Applications
- Discharge of Charge or Other Interest
- Easement
- Release of Easement
- Inhibiting Orders
- Lease or Interest in a Lease Documents
- Liens
- Construction Lien
- Condominium Lien
- Notice of Change of Address for Service
- Notice of Option to Purchase
- Notices
- Plan Document
- Postponement of Interest
- Power of Attorney
- Revocation Power of Attorney
- Projects
- Restrictive Covenants
- Survivorship Application
- Transmission Application
- Title Application Documents
- Application for Absolute Title
- Trustee in Bankruptcy Applications

The creation of a new electronic document requires the choice of a Registry office, the opening of a docket, the granting of access, and the choice of a document type under "Instrument" on the ELRS toolbar. Each document form contains the appropriate content such as parties, description, consideration, statements, *Land Transfer Tax Act* statements, Toronto municipal tax statements, and address for service. Current owners, description information, and sometimes related documents, such as mortgage assignments when creating a discharge, are prepopulated. The content of electronic documents is similar to paper documents except that the standard information and statements are already included. A user who does not choose the correct document type initially must start over. Once a document has been selected, the user will produce the document by following a tree-like checklist on the left side of the screen. A work in progress document can be viewed, edited, saved, signed, or messaged to other users until registration is complete. Any change in a document will automatically remove all signatures. The content and procedures will vary depending on the document type.

Document reports, including the Acknowledgement and Direction, the Document Preparation Report, the Land Transfer Tax schedule, the Registration Report and the Docket Summary and Fees and Taxes reports are printed and retained in the client's file. Figure 16.3 illustrates the background ELRS screen and the "create new form" list.

Figure 16.3

CREATE NEW FORM SCREEN (TRANSFER)*

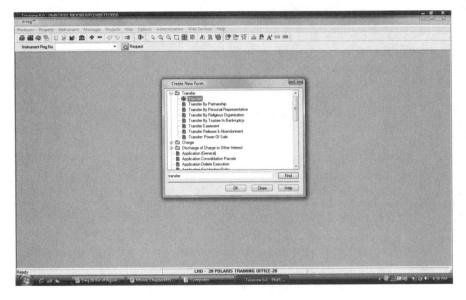

Creating a Transfer

The transfer may be initiated by either the vendor's or the purchaser's lawyer. Practice varies on the region and the law firm. The vendor and vendor's lawyer are familiar with the property and the age and spousal status of the transferors; so, generally, as in the traditional paper transaction, it is more common for the vendor to create the transfer and message update/edit authority to the purchaser's lawyer. The purchaser's lawyer then completes the purchaser's name, birth date, capacity on title, and the *Land Transfer Tax Act* and *Planning Act* compliance statements. Whatever the arrangement, both sides must ensure that the document that is signed for completeness and registered is in the form that protects their respective clients'

---

*   © Teranet Inc. 2010. Reproduced with permission.

interests. Teraview, as a safety feature, removes digital signatures whenever a document is changed by either party. The purchaser's lawyer usually registers the transfer and the charge, subject to DRA amendments.

A transfer is sourced by PIN. The PIN in question is entered into the "Properties" field and the transfer is pre-populated with existing title information, such as the transferors' names and the property's legal description and address. Description changes may also be made. The last name and two given names of the parties, together with an estate qualifier, age and *Family Law Act* statements, power of attorney statements, authorization statements, unique lawyer statements, and transferee birth dates and capacity are entered. Property and service addresses are also added. The *Land Transfer Tax* and Toronto municipal tax statements are completed. The optional, although strongly recommended, *Planning Act* compliance declarations are selected. Document specific schedules and statements are added. Related documents may be deleted, for example, with a Transfer: Power of Sale or Discharge of Mortgage. The document is then given a name and file number for identification purposes; document identification names and file numbers should be easily recognized by both sides of the transaction.

All transfers are signed for completeness by both the lawyer for the transferor(s) and the lawyer for the transferee(s) using a lawyer's PSP device. Other documents must also be signed by both the lawyer for the transferor(s) and the lawyer for the transferee(s) using a lawyer's PSP device, if the document contains a compliance with law statement. The transfer will be messaged to the other solicitor. The other solicitor will be given update or release access depending on the circumstances and the document registration agreement.

Figures 16.4 to 16.18 illustrate the Teraview screens for creating, signing, subsearching, and registering a transfer, including the registration and writ certificate report.

Figure 16.4

TRANSFER SOURCE BY PIN SCREEN*

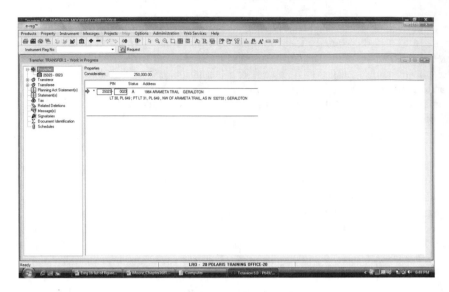

Figure 16.5

TRANSFEROR STATEMENT SELECTION SCREEN**

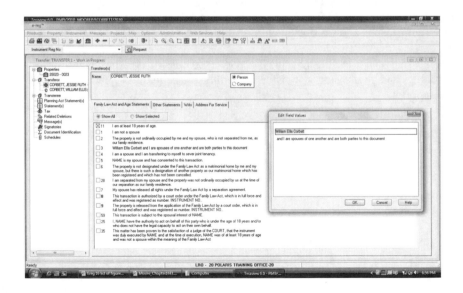

Figure 16.6

TRANSFEROR POWER OF ATTORNEY STATEMENT
SELECTION SCREEN*

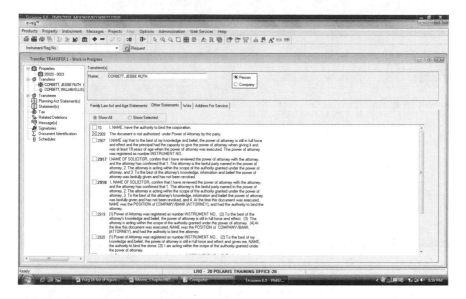

Retrieving Writs

Writs may be searched against the current owners as part of the transfer creation process by selecting "Writs" from the instrument drop-down list and requesting "retrieve writs". The system then displays and prints a Writ Clearance or a Writ Certificate. Writ statements may be added that remove a writ or confirm that the PIN is subject to a writ. Writs are automatically searched as part of the registration process. When writs are searched within the transfer on the same day as registration, only one writ search charge applies. Figure 16.7 illustrates the "retrieve writs" procedure in the transfer creation process.

Figure 16.7

RETRIEVE, DELETE, PRINT WRITS CERTIFICATE SCREEN (TRANSFER)*

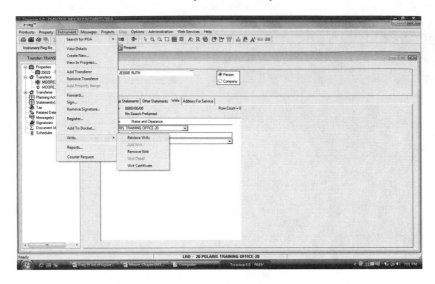

Figure 16.8

PLANNING ACT COMPLIANCE STATEMENTS SELECTION SCREEN (TRANSFER)**

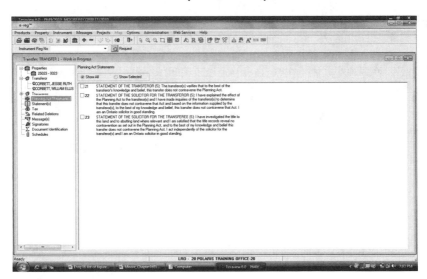

Figure 16.9

TRANSFEREE INFORMATION SCREEN[*]

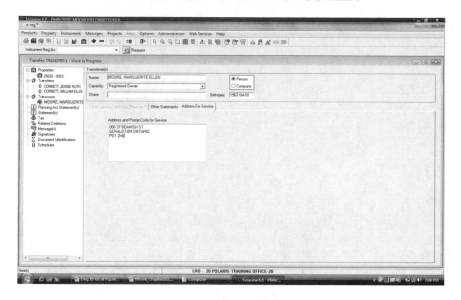

Figure 16.10

TRANSFER DESCRIPTION SCREEN[**]

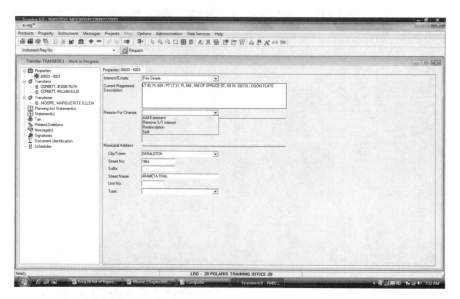

Figure 16.11

DOCUMENT IDENTIFICATION SCREEN (TRANSFER)*

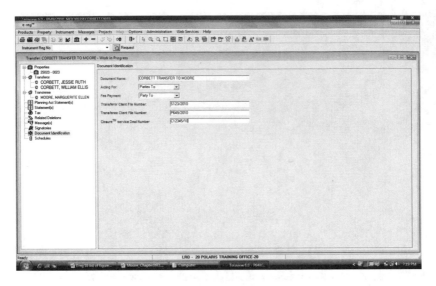

Figure 16.12

TRANSFER SIGNATURE SCREEN**

Figure 16.13

COMPOSE SEND MESSAGE SCREEN (TRANSFER)[*]

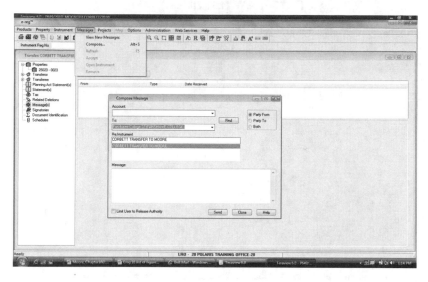

Figure 16.14

RECEIVE MESSAGE, ACCEPT ACCESS, AND OPEN INSTRUMENT SCREEN[**]

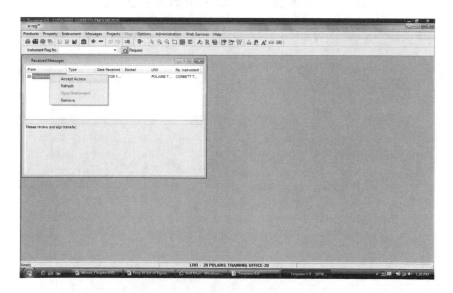

Figure 16.15

SIGNATURE AND UNIQUE LAWYER STATEMENT SCREEN
(TWO-LAWYER RULE)*

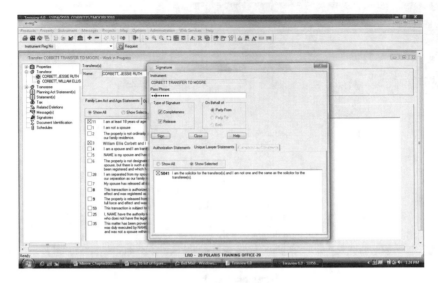

Figure 16.16

REQUEST SCREEN FOR ACKNOWLEDGEMENT AND DIRECTION
AND DOCUMENT PREPARATION REPORTS**

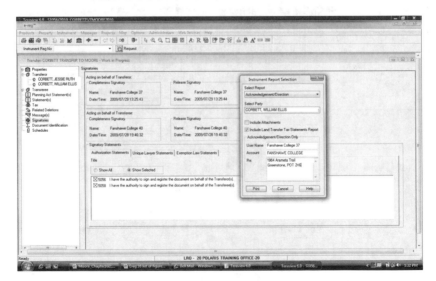

---

*   © Teranet Inc. 2010. Reproduced with permission.
**   © Teranet Inc. 2010. Reproduced with permission.

Registration

The transfer is registered pursuant to the DRA. The registration process offers the option of a subsearch and automatically completes a search for writs against the registered owners (Figure 16.17). An automatic registration report is printed including a paper copy of the registered document, the *Land Transfer Tax Act* statements, and the execution certificate(s) (Figure 16.18).

Figure 16.17

SUBSEARCH AND REGISTRATION REQUEST SCREEN*

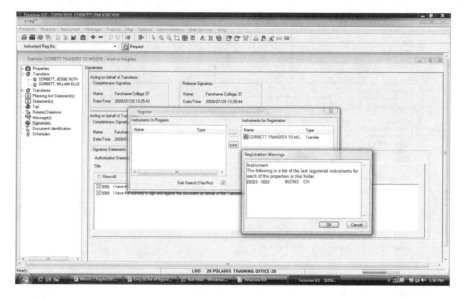

Report Requests

Teraview produces an Acknowledgement and Direction including schedules for a "Transfer in Progress". Schedules include document specific schedules, the Document Preparation report, and the *Land Transfer Tax Act* statements. Teraview also produces a Document Preparation report for the "Transfer in Progress". The client will sign the Acknowledgement and Direction, with the Document Preparation Report attached, thereby authorizing the solicitor to sign on the client's behalf. Figure 16.1 illustrates an Acknowledgement and Direction and attached Document Preparation Report.

Following registration, the law firm will complete docket summary and registration fee and tax charges reports that document disbursements. Figures 16.30 to 16.34 illustrate the Teraview report request screens and administrative reports.

Figure 16.18

REGISTRATION REPORT INCLUDING WRIT CERTIFICATE[*]

**** NOT VALID - TO BE USED FOR TRAINING PURPOSES ONLY ****

This document has not been submitted and may be incomplete.		yyyy mm dd Page 1 of 2
LRO # 20 Transfer		In preparation on 2009 08 03 at 10:23

Properties

PIN	25023 – 0023 LT *Interest/Estate* Fee Simple
Description	LT 30, PL 649; PT LT 31, PL 649, NW OF SPRUCE ST, AS IN 532743; OGOKI FLATS
Address	1964 ARAMETA TRAIL
	GREENSTONE

Consideration

Consideration $ 300,000.00

Transferor(s)

The transferor(s) hereby transfers the land to the transferee(s).

Name   CORBETT, WILLIAM ELLIS

Address for Service   37 Beamish Street, Geraldton, Greenstone, Ontario, POT 2X6

I am at least 18 years of age.

Jessie Ruth Corbett   and I are spouses of one another and are both parties to this document

This document is not authorized under Power of Attorney by this party.

Name   CORBETT, JESSIE RUTH

Address for Service

I am at least 18 years of age.

William Ellis Corbett and I are spouses of one another and are both parties to this document

This document is not authorized under Power of Attorney by this party.

Transferee(s)	Capacity	Share

Name   MOORE, MARGUERITE ELLEN

Date of Birth   1967 04 01

Address for Service   1964 Arameta Trail , Geralton, Greenstone, Ontario POT 2X6

STATEMENT OF THE TRANSFEROR (S): The transferor(s) verifies that to the best of the transferor's knowledge and belief, this transfer does not contravene the Planning Act.

STATEMENT OF THE SOLICITOR FOR THE TRANSFEROR (S): I have explained the effect of the Planning Act to the transferor(s) and I have made inquiries of the transferor(s) to determine that this transfer does not contravene that Act and based on the information supplied by the transferor(s), to the best of my knowledge and belief, this transfer does not contravene that Act. I am an Ontario solicitor in good standing.

STATEMENT OF THE SOLICITOR FOR THE TRANSFEREE (S): I have investigated the title to this land and to abutting land where relevant and I am satisfied that the title records reveal no contravention as set out in the Planning Act, and to the best of my knowledge and belief this transfer does not contravene the Planning Act. I act independently of the solicitor for the transferor(s) and I am an Ontario solicitor in good standing.

---

[*]   © Teranet Inc. 2010. Reproduced with permission.

Figure 16.18 (cont'd)

LRO # 20 Transfer	Receipted as HH37 on 2009 08 04	at 08:50
The applicant(s) hereby applies to the Land Registrar.	yyyy mm dd	Page 2 of 3

Signed By

Fanshawe College 40   acting for Transferor(s)   Signed   2009 08 03

Tel
Fax

I am the solicitor for the transferor(s) and I am not one and the same as the solicitor for the transferee(s).
I have the authority to sign and register the document on behalf of the Transferor(s).

Fanshawe College 37   acting for Transferee(s)   Signed   2009 08 03

Tel
Fax

I am the solicitor for the transferee(s) and I am not one and the same as the solicitor for the transferor(s).
I have the authority to sign and register the document on behalf of the Transferee(s).

Submitted By

FANSHAWE COLLEGE   2009 08 04
Tel
Fax

Fees/Taxes/Payment

Statutory Registration Fee	$60.00
Provincial Land Transfer Tax	$2,975.00
Total Paid	$3,035.00

File Number

Transferor Client File Number :	S649/2010
Transferee Client File Number :	P1964/2010

Figure 16.18 (cont'd)

**** NOT VALID - TO BE USED FOR TRAINING PURPOSES ONLY ****

LAND TRANSFER TAX STATEMENTS

In the matter of the conveyance of: 25023 – 0023 LT 30, PL 73; PT LT 31, PL 649, NW of SPRUCE ST, AS IN 532743; OGOKI FLATS

BY: CORBETT, WILLIAM ELLIS
CORBETT, JESSIE RUTH

TO: MOORE, MARGUERITE ELLEN   %(all PINs)

1. MOORE, MARGUERITE ELLEN

   I am

   ☐ (a) A person in trust for whom the land conveyed in the above-described conveyance is being conveyed;

   ☐ (b) A trustee named in the above-described conveyance to whom the land is being conveyed;

   ☑ (c) A transferee named in the above-described conveyance;

   ☐ (d) The authorized agent or solicitor acting in this transaction for ____ described in paragraph(s) (_) above.

   ☐ (e) The President, Vice-President, Manager, Secretary, Director, or Treasurer authorized to act for ____ described in paragraph(s) (_) above.

   ☐ (f) A transferee described in paragraph ( ) and am making these statements on my own behalf and on behalf of ____ who is my spouse described in paragraph (_) and as such, I have personal knowledge of the facts herein deposed to.

3. The total consideration for this transaction is allocated as follows:

(a) Monies paid or to be paid in cash	300,000.00
(b) Mortgages (i) assumed (show principal and interest to be credited against purchase price)	0.00
(ii) Given Back to Vendor	0.00
(c) Property transferred in exchange (detail below)	0.00
(d) Fair market value of the land(s)	0.00
(e) Liens, legacies, annuities and maintenance charges to which transfer is subject	0.00
(f) Other valuable consideration subject to land transfer tax (detail below)	0.00
(g) Value of land, building, fixtures and goodwill subject to land transfer tax (total of (a) to (f))	300,000.00
(h) VALUE OF ALL CHATTELS - items of tangible personal property	0.00
(i) Other considerations for transaction not included in (g) or (h) above	0.00
(j) Total consideration	300,000.00

PROPERTY Information Record

A. Nature of Instrument: Transfer

LRO 37   Registration No.   Date:

B. Property(s):   PIN 25023 – 0023 Address   1964 ARAMETA   Assessment   4215010 - 00426600
TRAIL   Roll No
OGOKI FLATS

C. Address for Service: 1964 Arameta Trail , Geralton, Greenstone, Ontario P0T 2X6

D. (i) Last Conveyance(s):   PIN 25023 - 0023   Registration No.

(ii) Legal Description for Property Conveyed : Same as in last conveyance? Yes ☑ No ☐ Not known ☐

School Tax Support (Voluntary Election)

1. All individual transferees wish to vote for English-Public.

Figure 16.18 (cont'd)

```
                                                  CERTIFICATE #:
                                                  NO DE CERTIFICAT:
                                                  11228124-6910609B

              CLEAR CERTIFICATE / CERTIFICAT LIBRE

SHERIFF OF /
SHERIF DE: *** NOT VALID - TO BE USED FOR TRAINING PURPOSES ONLY ****

DATE OF CERTIFICATE /
DATE DU CERTIFICAT  : 2009-07-29

THIS CERTIFIES THAT THERE ARE NO WRITS OF EXECUTION, EXTENT OR
CERTIFICATES OF LIEN IN MY HANDS AT THE TIME OF SEARCHING AGAINST
THE REAL AND PERSONAL PROPERTY OF:

JE CERTIFIE, PAR LA PRESENTE, NE PAS AVOIR DE BREF D'EXECUTION,
NI DE CERTIFICAT DE PRIVILEGE, NI D'ORDONNANCE EN MA POSSESSION
AU MOMENT DE LA RECHERCHE VISANT LES BIENS MEUBLES OU IMMEUBLES DE:

                SURNAME / NOM       GIVEN NAME(S) / PRENOM(S)
=================================================================

(PERSON/PERSONNE)  CORBETT, WILLIAM ELLIS
                   CORBETT, JESSIE RUTH

CAUTION TO PARTY REQUESTING SEARCH:
ENSURE THAT THE ABOVE INDICATED NAME IS THE SAME AS THE NAME SEARCHED.
THIS NAME WILL REMAIN CLEAR UNTIL THE CLOSE OF BUSINESS THIS DATE.

AVERTISSEMENT A LA PARTIE QUI DEMANDE LA RECHERCHE:
ASSUREZ-VOUS QUE LE NOM INDIQUE CI-DESSUS EST LE MEME QUE CELUI QUI
EST RECHERCHE.  CET ETAT DEMEURE VALIDE JUSQU'A LA FIN DE LA JOURNEE
DE TRAVAIL.

CHARGE FOR THIS CERTIFICATE /
FRAIS POUR CE CERTIFICAT    : $11.00

SEARCHER REFERENCE /
REFERENCE CONCERNANT L'AUTEUR DE LA DEMANDE:
```

WRIT CERTIFICATE/CLEAR

Creating a Charge

A charge is created in a similar manner to a transfer and includes similar pre-populated core title information. A charge requires the entry of the agreed-upon financial terms (mortgage commitment) and the standard charge terms (acknowledgement of standard charge terms). A charge may only refer to one set of standard charge terms. Additional mortgage terms that are not part of the selected standard charge terms can be keyed in or imported in as schedules. Financial institution charge terms are available on the Teraview website and from the individual financial institution's website. A charge contains chargor statements of age and spousal status as well as power of attorney and signing authorization statements. The charge is signed by the borrower and usually registered by the solicitor for the purchaser or borrower. Teraview produces an Acknowledgement and Direction and a Document Preparation Report for a charge (Figure 16.22). Registration procedures and docket reports are similar to those for a transfer except that executions cannot be searched against the mortgagor(s) within the ELRS mortgage/charge, but must be searched in the separate WritSearch service. Figure 16.20 illustrates the charge creation screen. An automatic registration report is printed, including a paper copy of the registered charge (Figure 16.23).

Figure 16.19

CHARGE SELECTION SCREEN*

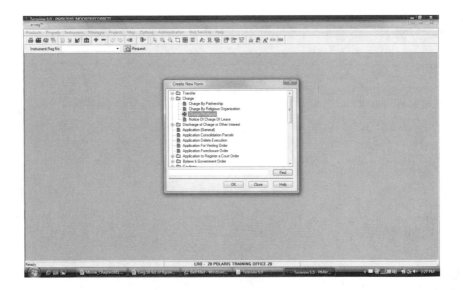

---

* © Teranet Inc. 2010. Reproduced with permission.

Figure 16.20

CHARGE CREATION SCREEN*

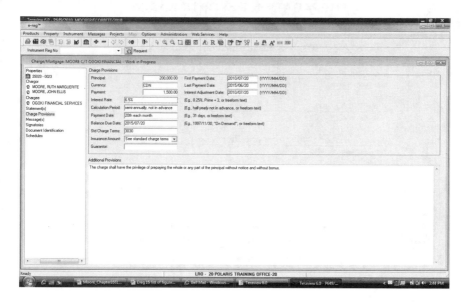

Figure 16.21

ACKNOWLEDGEMENT AND DIRECTION AND DOCUMENT PREPARATION REPORT/CHARGE*

ACKNOWLEDGEMENT AND DIRECTION

TO: Fanshawe College 40
           (Insert lawyer's name)

AND TO: FANSHAWE COLLEGE
           (Insert firm name)

RE: Moore Charge to OGOKI FINANCIAL SERVICES: 1964 Arameta Trail   ("the transaction")
           (Insert brief description of transaction)

This will confirm that:

● I/We have reviewed the information set out this Acknowledgement and Direction and in the documents described below (the "Documents"), and that this information is accurate;

● You, your agent or employee are authorized and directed to sign, deliver, and/or register electronically, on my/our behalf the Documents in the form attached.

● You are hereby authorized and directed to enter into an escrow closing arrangement substantially in the form attached hereto being a copy of the version of the Document Registration Agreement, which appears on the website of the Law Society of Upper Canada as of the date of the Agreement of Purchase and sale herein. I/We hereby acknowledge the said Agreement has been reviewed by me/us and that I/We shall be bound by its terms.

● The effect of the Documents has been fully explained to me/us, and I/we understand that I/we are parties to and bound by the terms and provisions of the Documents to the same extent as if I/we had signed them; and

● I/we are in fact the parties named in the Documents and I/we have not misrepresented our identities to you.

● I, _____, am the spouse of _____, the (Transferor/Chargor), and hereby consent to the transaction described in the Acknowledgment and Direction. I authorize you to indicate my consent on all the Documents for which it is required.

DESCRIPTION OF ELECTRONIC DOCUMENTS

     The Document(s) described in the Acknowledgement and Direction are the document(s) selected below which are attached hereto as "Document in Preparation" and are:

☐   A Transfer of the land described above.

■   A Charge of the land described above.

☐   Other documents set out in Schedule "B" attached hereto.

Dated at _____ , this _____ day of _____ , 20___ .

WITNESS

(As to all signatures, if required)

_____   _____

                                _____

                                _____

Figure 16.21 (cont'd)

**** NOT VALID - TO BE USED FOR TRAINING PURPOSES ONLY ****

This document has not been submitted and may be incomplete.
LRO # 20   Charge/Mortgage

yyyy mm dd   Page 1 of 2
In preparation on 2009 08 02   at 15:01

Properties

PIN	25023 – 0023 LT	Interest/Estate Fee Simple
Description	LT 30, PL 649; PT LT 31, PL 649, NW OF SPRUCE ST, AS IN 532743; OGOKI FLATS	
Address	1964 ARAMETA TRAIL GREENSTONE	

Chargor(s)

The chargor(s) hereby charges the land to the chargee(s). The chargor(s) acknowledges the receipt of the charge and the standard charge terms, if any.

Name	MOORE, RUTH MARGUERITE Acting as an individual
Address for Service	1 Beamish Street, Geraldton, Ontario, P0T 2X6

I am at least 18 years of age.

John Ellis Moore and I are spouses of one another and are both parties to this document

This document is not authorized under Power of Attorney by this party.

Name	MOORE, JOHN ELLIS Acting as an individual
Address for Service	

I am at least 18 years of age.

Ruth Marguerite Moore and I are spouses of one another and are both parties to this document

This document is not authorized under Power of Attorney by this party.

Chargee(s)

	Capacity	Share
Name OGOKI FINANCIAL SERVICES Acting as a company		
Address for Service 1 Ogoki Forest Tower, Nakina, Ontario, P0T 2X6		

Provisions

Principal	$ 200,000.00	Currency	CDN
Calculation Period	semi-annually, not in advance		
Balance Due Date	2015/06/20		
Interest Rate	7.0%		
Payments	$ 1,500.00		
Interest Adjustment Date	2010 07 20		
Payment Date	20th of each month		
First Payment Date	2010 07 20		
Last Payment Date	2015 06 20		
Standard Charge Terms	6490		
Insurance Amount	See standard charge terms		
Guarantor			

Figure 16.21 (cont'd)

**** NOT VALID - TO BE USED FOR TRAINING PURPOSES ONLY ****

This document has not been submitted and may be incomplete.   yyyy mm dd   Page 2 of 2
LRO # 20   Charge/Mortgage   In preparation on 2009 08 02   at 15:01

Additional Provisions

The chargor shall have the privilege of prepaying the whole or any part of the principal hereby secured without notice or penalty.

Signed By

Fanshawe College 40   acting for   Signed   2009 08 02
                                                                                       Chargor(s)

Tel

Fax

I have the authority to sign and register the document on behalf of the Chargor(s).

File Number

Chargor Client File Number :   C123/2010

Chargee Client File Number :   L2001/2010

Figure 16.22

REGISTRATION REPORT/CHARGE[*]

**** NOT VALID - TO BE USED FOR TRAINING PURPOSES ONLY ****

The applicant(s) hereby applies to the Land Registrar.		yyyy mm dd Page 1 of 2
LRO # 20 **Charge/Mortgage**		Receipted as HH27 on 2009 08 02 at 15:10

Properties

PIN	25023 – 0023 LT	Interest/Estate Fee Simple
Description	LT 30, PL 649; PT LT 31, PL 649, NW OF SPRUCE ST, AS IN 532743; OGOKI FLATS	
Address	1964 ARAMETA TRAIL	
	GREENSTONE	

Chargor(s)

The chargor(s) hereby charges the land to the chargee(s). The chargor(s) acknowledges the receipt of the charge and the standard charge terms, if any.

Name	MOORE, RUTH MARGUERITE
Address for Service	1 Beamish Street, Geraldton, Ontario, P0T 2X6

I am at least 18 years of age.

John Ellis Moore   and I are spouses of one another and are both parties to this document

This document is not authorized under Power of Attorney by this party.

Name	MOORE, JOHN ELLIS
Address for Service	

I am at least 18 years of age.

Ruth Marguerite Moore and I are spouses of one another and are both parties to this document

This document is not authorized under Power of Attorney by this party.

Chargee(s)   Capacity   Share

Name	OGOKI FINANCIAL SERVICES
Address for Service	1 Ogoki Forest Tower, Nakina, Ontario, P0T 2X6

Provisions

Principal	$ 200,000.00	Currency	CDN
Calculation Period	semi-annually, not in advance		
Balance Due Date	2015/06/20		
Interest Rate	7.0%		
Payments	$ 1,500.00		
Interest Adjustment Date	2010 07 20		
Payment Date	20th of each month		
First Payment Date	2010 07 20		
Last Payment Date	2015 06 20		
Standard Charge Terms	6490		
Insurance Amount	See standard charge terms		
Guarantor			

Additional Provisions

The chargor shall have the privilege of prepaying the whole or any part of the principal hereby secured without notice or penalty.

Figure 16.22 (cont'd)

**** NOT VALID - TO BE USED FOR TRAINING PURPOSES ONLY ****

The applicant(s) hereby applies to the Land Registrar.		yyyy mm dd	Page 2 of 2
LRO # 20 Charge/Mortgage		Receipted as HH27 on 2009 08 02	at 15:10

Signed By

Fanshawe College 40		acting for Chargor(s)	Signed	2009 08 02
Tel				
Fax				

I have the authority to sign and register the document on behalf of the Chargor(s).

Submitted By

FANSHAWE COLLEGE	2009 08 02
Tel	
Fax	

Fees/Taxes/Payment

Statutory Registration Fee	$60.00
Total Paid	$60.00

File Number

Chargor Client File Number :	C123/2010
Chargee Client File Number :	L2001/2010

Creating a Discharge of Charge

A Discharge of Charge is sourced by the registration number of the charge that is going to be discharged. It requires a statement as to whether the discharge is a partial discharge or a discharge of all of the property (consider the *Planning Act* implications). It contains additional statements concerning whether the charge has been assigned and the nature of the signing authority. A Discharge of Charge contains a section for requesting the deletion of registered documents related to the Charge, such as assignments, postponements, and amendments of the Charge. Figures 16.23 and 16.24 illustrate the Discharge of Charge creation screen and the Source by Charge feature. Registration procedures and docket reports are similar to those for a Transfer. Figure 16.26 illustrates standard statements contained in a Discharge of Charge form. An automatic registration report is printed, including a paper copy of the registered discharge of charge (Figure 16.29).

Teranet now provides a CLOSURE service that notifies the vendor's law firm by e-mail on the next business day of a registration of a mortgage discharge. The notification contains an e-copy of the discharge. CLOSURE facilitates the tracking and completion of solicitor's undertakings to discharge mortgages and inform the purchaser's solicitor.

Figure 16.23

DISCHARGE OF CHARGE CREATION SCREEN*

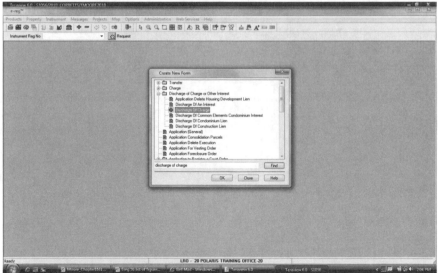

---

* © Teranet Inc. 2010. Reproduced with permission.

Figure 16.24

SOURCE DISCHARGE OF CHARGE BY CHARGE
REGISTRATION NUMBER*

Figure 16.25

FULL OR PARTIAL DISCHARGE OF CHARGE SELECTION SCREEN
(CONSIDER THE PLANNING ACT IMPLICATIONS)**

Figure 16.26

DISCHARGE OF CHARGE STATEMENTS*

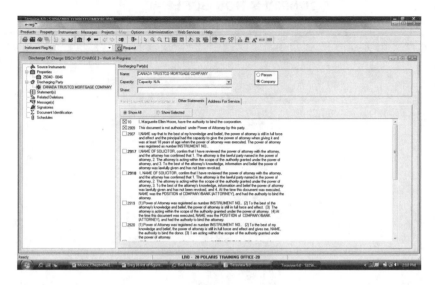

Figure 16.27

DISCHARGE OF CHARGE SIGNATURE, SUBSEARCH, AND REGISTRATION SCREENS**

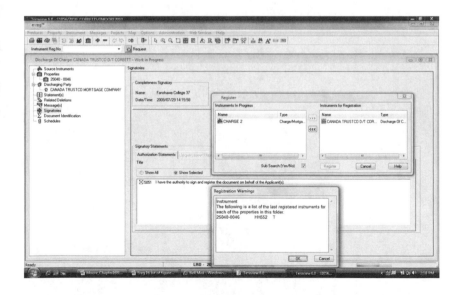

Figure 16.28

DISCHARGE OF CHARGE REGISTRATION
CONFIRMATION SCREEN*

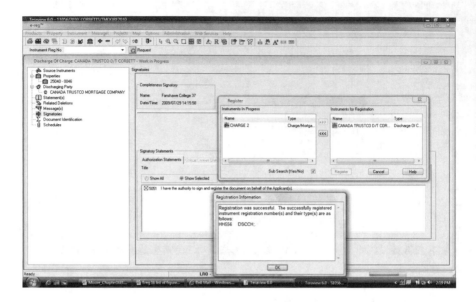

Figure 16.29

REGISTRATION REPORT/ DISCHARGE OF CHARGE˙

**** NOT VALID - TO BE USED FOR TRAINING PURPOSES ONLY ****

The applicant(s) hereby applies to the Land Registrar.	yyyy mm dd Page 1 of 1
LRO # 20 **Discharge Of Charge**	Receipted as HH32 on 2009 08 02 at 16:17

Properties

PIN	25023 – 0023 LT
Description	LT 30, PL 649; PT LT 31, PL 649, NW OF SPRUCE ST, AS IN 532743; OGOKI FLATS
Address	1964 ARAMETA TRAIL
	GREENSTONE

Document to be Discharged

Registration No.	Date	Type of Instrument
HH27	2009 08 02	Charge/Mortgage

Discharging Party(s)

This discharge complies with the Planning Act. This discharge discharges the charge.

Name	OGOKI FINANCIAL SERVICES
Address for Service	1 Ogoki Forest Tower, Nakina, Ontario, POT 2X6

I, Marguerite Ellen Moore, have the authority to bind the corporation.

This document is not authorized under Power of Attorney by this party.

The party giving this discharge is the original chargee and is the party entitled to give an effective discharge

Signed By

Fanshawe College 40	acting for Applicant(s)	Signed	2009 08 02
Tel			
Fax			

I have the authority to sign and register the document on behalf of the Applicant(s).

Submitted By

FANSHAWE COLLEGE	2009 08 02
Tel	
Fax	

Fees/Taxes/Payment

Statutory Registration Fee	$60.00

File Number

Discharging Party Client File Number :	D4035/2010

˙ © Teranet Inc. 2010. Reproduced with permission.

ELRS REPORTS

As long as a document is in progress, Teraview generates the Acknowledgement and Direction and the Document Preparation reports. On registration, Teraview can automatically generate a registration report by printing the document receipted as registered including the new registration number accompanied by the *Land Transfer Tax Act* statements and the writ clearance certificate. Electronic land registration also produces reports that relate to a specific docket (docket summary and docket tax fee summary) or a specific Teraview account (Figures 16.31 and 16.32). Reports can be generated by date range. These reports are particularly useful for client reporting and billing and firm accounting purposes and have export capability. Teraview produces the following reports:

- Docket Specific:
  - Acknowledgement and Direction
  - Document Preparation
  - Registration Report
  - Docket Summary (Figure 16.31)
  - Registration Fees and Tax Charges Summary Report (Figure 16.32)
- Account Specific
  - Account Summary Statement
  - Account Registration Fees Activity Report (Figure 16.33)
  - Account Registration and Land Transfer Tax Report
  - Deposit Account Activity Report (Figure 16.34)
  - Deposit Account Balance

Figure 16.30
REPORT REQUEST LIST[*]

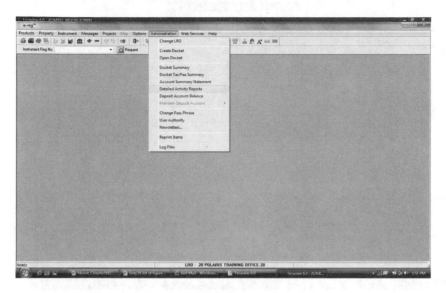

Figure 16.31
REQUEST FOR DOCKET SUMMARY AND REPORT[**]

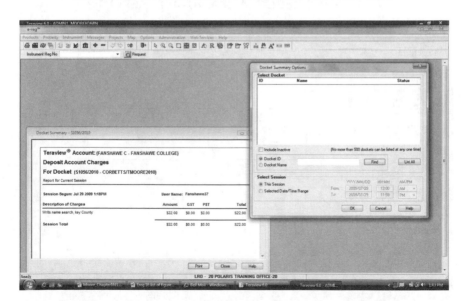

---

[*] © Teranet Inc. 2010. Reproduced with permission.
[**] © Teranet Inc. 2010. Reproduced with permission.

Figure 16.32

DOCKET REGISTRATION FEES AND TAX CHARGES SUMMARY REPORT*

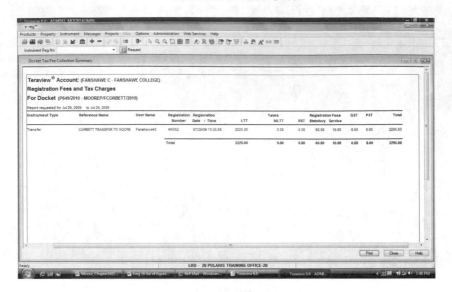

Figure 16.33

ELECTRONIC REGISTRATION ACTIVITY REPORT**

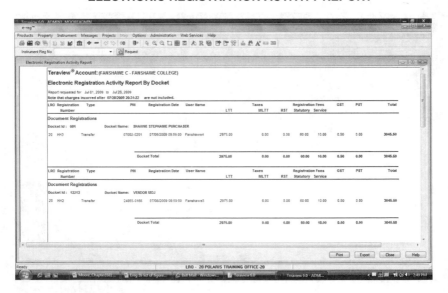

---

*   © Teranet Inc. 2010. Reproduced with permission.
**   © Teranet Inc. 2010. Reproduced with permission.

Figure 16.34
DEPOSIT ACCOUNT ACTIVITY REPORT*

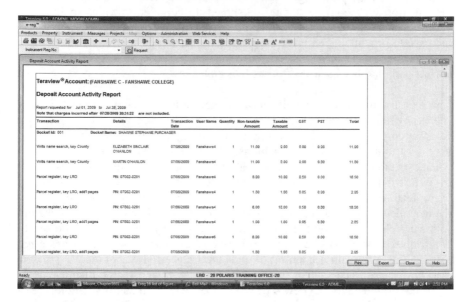

DOCUMENT REGISTRATION AND CLOSING PROCEDURES ON ELRS (E-REG)

The preceding figures illustrate the ELRS subsearch and registration process for a discharge of mortgage.

Registration of documents in ELRS is usually part of a sale, purchase, and/or mortgage transaction, which involves closing procedures within the law firm as well as registration procedures in ELRS. ELRS documents are produced, exchanged (messaged), signed, and registered online instead of at the Registry office. Additional closing documents such as undertakings, cheques, and keys, called the "requisite deliveries", are exchanged and held in escrow at the lawyers' offices. Registration, release of cheques and keys are conducted according to the DRA and, to some extent, local practice. Closing procedures including precedents for either paper transactions at the Registry office or closing procedures for Land Titles transactions involving ELRS are outlined in detail in Chapter 15.

Electronic land registration generates additional software-related conveyancing practices pertaining to document production signing and registration, title and execution subsearching, and the payment of registration fees and taxes. One

---

* © Teranet Inc. 2010. Reproduced with permission.

Teraview docket should contain all the documents for registration in a transaction. They should be positioned in the proper order in the Teraview ELRS folder (screen) so that they are registered in the proper sequence and, ultimately, the proper priority. Documents should be signed for completion which includes an automatic check as to whether the document is properly drafted. If a document is incomplete or contains an error, signing is not permitted by the system and an error message is produced instead. Prior to signing, it is wise to confirm that the correct party has been selected to pay fees and taxes.

The registration process includes an automatic title subsearch (when it is preselected within the registration folder) and an automatic execution search on registration. Depending on the property, for example, a part lot, it may also be necessary to subsearch adjoining lands. The Teraview user is only billed once when executions are subsearched on the day of closing within ELRS instead of in WritSearch. When the Teraview user activates the automatic registration report feature under "Options", a registration confirmation report which includes the document and the document registration number will be printed immediately following closing. In addition, the parcel register may be reprinted in order to confirm registration. Docket and Tax/Fee Summaries are printed and transferred to the client's file and accounting. Funds are transferred electronically into the Teraview deposit account for payment of fees, taxes, and search disbursements at the end of the day. Teraview's recent CLOSURE service now facilitates real-time guaranteed LVTS transfers of purchase and mortgage payout funds.

REJECTED DOCUMENTS

On occasion, documents are returned for corrections any time within 21 days following registration. The uncertified document will be messaged back to the Teraview keyholder who signed the document for completeness. If the document was signed by a non-lawyer employee key, then the rejected document will be messaged back to his or her account. If the document was signed by the lawyer's Teraview key, for example, transfers and whenever the document contained a compliance with law statement such as a *Planning Act* declaration, then the rejected document will be returned by message function to the lawyer's account. Under the *Land Titles Act*, the solicitor has 30 days to correct the problem and message the document back. It is essential to check on a frequent basis for messages on Teraview keys.

A form of title insurance referred to as gap insurance is available for the period between when the document is accepted for registration and appears on the system and when it is certified as registered. Registration and certification is usually almost instantaneous.

ELRS GAPS AND INTERRUPTIONS

The ELRS has statistically very little downtime. Nevertheless, title insurance coverage may be obtained to cover the period between closing and registration; however, Land Titles has in theory up to 21 days to certify documents accepted for registration.

POLARIS IN PERSPECTIVE

Title and mortgage fraud, once uncommon in real property conveyancing and land registration, have become a serious threat. The LSUC, the Province, title insurers, and practitioners have all responded with heightened risk management strategies and practice standards. The *Ministry of Government Services Consumer Protection and Service Modernization Act, 2006* amended the *Land Registration Reform Act*, the *Land Titles Act*, and the *Registry Act* in an attempt to address the growth of title and mortgage fraud and to protect property owners, including easier access to the Land Titles Assurance Fund. Title insurance coverage is now standard and all policy applications contain risk screening questions for fraud.

The security and integrity of Ontario's land records (POLARIS), its land registration system (ELRS), and public confidence are critical. Indeed, reliable land registration systems are in terms of international economic thought considered to be a condition precedent to capitalist structures and the generation of domestic wealth. Not surprisingly, the Ministry of Government Services' Real Estate Fraud Action Plan is the current focus driving the more recent ELRS changes such as the new access licensing process, the two-lawyer rule for transfers, the authorization statements, and the strict registration standards pertaining to powers of attorney, all reflected in Teraview, starting at Version 6.0.

The first electronic land registration took place on January 25, 1999, in the Middlesex County Land Registry office in London. As of 2010, all registration districts will have been automated. Almost all registrations are completed electronically other than a proportionally small number of properties remaining in Registry because of title problems (non-converts), interim conversion practices (Registry Parcelized Day Forward properties), or because their conversion posed administrative difficulties. Teraview software has stabilized, accompanied by periodic mandatory upgrades. Today, over 95 per cent of Land Titles searches and land registrations have moved from an archaic paper-based records system to the most sophisticated fully electronic registration system in the world. The quiet, yet revolutionary, changes in land registration in Ontario, driven by POLARIS and Teranet, reflect not only the legal and technological history of Ontario, but also the political, economic, and social history of a province.

Figure 16.35

GLOSSARY OF ELECTRONIC REGISTRATION TERMS[*]

Account	the person responsible to pay the charges incurred for using the Teraview® system. Also known as the Client of Teranet. The Account name is registered with Teranet and is a maximum of 20 characters long. This is the first piece of information required when accessing the Teraview® system.
Compliance with Law Statements	those statements which call for a conclusion of law and can therefore be made only by a lawyer in good standing, for example - transfers pursuant to a Power of Sale, Planning Act statements.
Desktop	each Teraview® software set is one Desktop and can be installed on only one computer at a time.
Diskette	see "User Diskette"
Docket	a User sets up a Docket and names it in order to create Documents; Dockets roughly equate to files in your office. Each Docket contains a number of Documents; monthly billing statements will contain the name of the Docket.
Document	a Document is "owned" by the person who created it; to allow anyone else to add information to it or change it in some way, the "owner" must give File Access Authority to the other person by sending it to them (see File Access Authority for details).
e-reg [ELRS]	the brand name of the electronic registration process contained in Teraview® release 5.1 being introduced in early 2003.
Electronic Signature	the identifying information contained on a Diskette by which Teranet will: 　1.　Determine that the User is a lawyer, or not; 　2.　Charge usage fees to a specific Account; 　3.　Track activities of that User - including granting of approval for registration of documents, registrations, changes made to documents, etc. - creating an electronic audit trail; and which signature is "affixed" to an electronic document through use of the Teraview® software.
File (Document) Access Authorization	permission you receive from someone else which allows you to access their document; it is available on a document by document basis if you are in another law firm or another Account; inside a law firm, on the same Account, authorization can be granted on a blanket basis (a lawyer authorizes their secretary access to all documents, automatically) or on an individual, document by document basis.
Passphrase	the unique set of characters (words or a phrase are suggested) created by an individual User and subsequently entered by that User, together with their Diskette, in order to gain access to Teraview®; a passphrase must be minimum of 8 characters including at least 1 uppercase and 1 lowercase symbol; Users must change their passphrase periodically.
Personal Security Package	the combination of security access products provided to an individual user to enable that user to access Teraview® it includes the required one-time initial set-up access codes, 1 diskette, 1 PSP handbook and a diskette holder; to obtain a PSP each User must provide personal identifying information and complete a brief application.

---

[*]　© Teranet Inc. 2010. Reproduced with permission.

Figure 16.35 (cont'd)

POLARIS	the acronym for the Province of Ontario Land Registration and Information System, which is a computerized system that stores information on all properties in Ontario.
Prepopulation	the process whereby title information is inserted into a work in progress electronic document usually as a result of the User entering the PIN but in some cases, such as a Discharge of Mortgage, it is as a result of entering the instrument number.
Public Key/ Private Key	transparent to the User, these "keys: are used by Teraview® to ensure the messages and documents sent by an individual accessing the system are encrypted and, if tampered with or altered, such a change will be revealed; the private key is contained on the User Diskette and the public key is in e-reg [ELRS] which uses Entrust Technologies public key infrastructure system.
Teranet	the corporation which is providing remote access to the Ministry of Consumer and Business Services, Teranet was formed in 1991 and is a strategic alliance of equal ownership between the Ontario Government and Teramira Holdings Inc.
Teraview® Application	the contract entered into between an Account holder and Teranet, whereby Teranet agrees to provide the Teraview® software to the Account holder, as a licensee, and the Account holder agrees to pay for access rights to the Teraview® gateware software which provides entry to the POLARIS databases.
User	an individual (lawyer or staff person) registered with Teranet as a person who is permitted to access the system and whose usage will be separately tracked by the Teraview® billing system.
User Diskette	part of the Personal Security Package, the user diskette contains the personal identifying security information required to access Teraview® 5,1,
Username	the combination of characters used by an individual User to sign on to the system and identify themselves. Teranet assigns Usernames in an Account.

Figure 16.36

ABBREVIATIONS WITHIN THUMBNAIL DESCRIPTIONS[*]

#	Number	NW/S	North West Side
'	Minutes	ORIG	Original
"	Seconds	PARKLT	ParkLot
¼	Quarter	PCL	Parcel
½	Half	PK	Park
3/4	Three Quarter	PL	Plan
AV	Avenue	POB	Place of Beginning
BLK	Block	POC	Place of Commencement
BLVD	Boulevard	PREM	Premising
BTN	Between	PROMENADE	Promenade
COMM	Commencing	PT	Part
CON	Concession	RD	Road
COURT	Court	RDAL	Road Allowance
CRES	Crescent	RDWY	Roadway
DEGREES	Degrees	ROW	Right of Way
DR	Drive	S	South
E	East	S/S	South Side
E/S	East Side	S/T	Subject To
ELY	Easterly	SE	South East
EXCEPT	Save & Except	SE/S	South East Side
EXPROP	Expropriation	SEC	Section
EXPWY	Expressway	SLY	Southerly
EXT	Extension	SQUARE	Square
FREEWAY	Freeway	SRO	Surface Rights Only
FT	Feet/Foot	ST	Street
GARDENS	Gardens	ST.	Saint
GATE	Gate	SW	South West
GORELT	Gore Lot	SW/S	South West Side
GROVE	Grove	T/W	Together With
HEIGHTS	Heights	TERRACE	Terrace
HWY	Highway	TOWNLT	Town Lot
INCHES	Inches	TRAIL	Trail
LT	Lot	TWP	Township
MRO	Mineral Rights Only	VIADUCT	Viaduct
N	North	W	West
N/S	North Side	W/S	West Side
NE	North East	WALK	Walk
NE/S	North East Side	WALKWAY	Walkway

NLY	Northerly	WID	Widening
NW	Northwest	WLY	Westerly

CHAPTER 17

Title and Mortgage Fraud

TITLE AND MORTGAGE FRAUD

The growth of title and mortgage fraud over the last 20-year period is unprecedented and exponential in nature. Fraud scenarios increasingly replicate and mutate, like a flu virus. Stakeholders in the conveyancing industry are engaged in continuous response with the focus on fraud prevention. The Ministry of Government Services has initiated its Real Property Fraud Action Plan with the focus on tightened access/licensing for the electronic land registration system, enhanced supervision of the appropriate use of Personal Security Package (PSP) access devices, legislative changes providing greater protection to homeowners, easier access and faster claims processing by the Land Titles Assurance Fund, the requirement that transfers be signed by two lawyers, mandatory authorization statements for electronic signing supported by rigorous client identification and verification requirements, and a comprehensive registration and statements scheme for the use of powers of attorney (POA). In addition, independent mortgage brokers are subject to stricter licensing and disclosure standards.

The courts have responded with heightened due diligence duties and clearly stated that financial institutions and lawyers are remiss when they fall into a business as usual mentality instead of a vigilant examination of all aspects of a transaction. The Law Society of Upper Canada (LSUC) has set new practice guidelines for real estate conveyancing and maintains a section on fraud prevention resources on its website. LawPRO, the Lawyers' Professional Indemnity Company, and TitlePLUS, the LSUC's bar-related title insurer, offer continuing education and regular fraud alerts. The private title insurers offer regular real estate fraud seminars and materials, including regular fraud alerts and underwriter support. In addition, insurers have tightened search requirements, added fraud risk identification and fraud mitigation questions (screening questions) to all policy applications, and initiated practice audits. Law enforcement agencies have dedicated specialized teams to real property fraud investigation and prosecution that collaborate with the LSUC and the title insurers' investigative arms. The courts and the popular CTV investigative news show W-FIVE have commented on the financial industry's apparent lack of participation in the due diligence efforts of the other stakeholders. Teraview has launched a new version for the electronic land registration system (ELRS) that reflects the fraud reduction initiatives and now offers CLOSURE, a Bank of Canada guaranteed large value transaction service (LVTS) that provides a guaranteed, real-time, secure funds transfer service within Teraview. Indeed, title and mortgage fraud — a variation of identity fraud — has become a primary focus for both stakeholders in the real property conveyancing community and the public as illustrated by an abundance of articles in Ontario newspapers claiming that title and mortgage fraud has reached epidemic proportions.

INCREASE IN REAL PROPERTY FRAUD

Since the early 1980s, real property fraud has grown exponentially in Canada. Experts have identified a variety of factors that appear to contribute to or coincide with the increase in title and mortgage fraud. For example, the increasing absence of face-to-face contact in real estate transactions, particularly lending transactions, is frequently raised (*Rabi v. Rosu*, [2006] O.J. No. 4348 (Ont. S.C.J.)). Lenders reduced mortgage underwriting staff and now rely on mortgage brokers for more of the mortgage application process. Standard practices that rely on online applications, e-mail and fax, the instantaneous electronic transfer of large amounts of money, the absence of witness requirements, and the electronic signing and registration of land-related documents by encrypted diskettes or Universal Serial Bus (USB) now provide an anonymous playground for a sophisticated fraudster. The absence of face-to-face contact with the client is reinforced by the absence of physical checks on the nature of the property. In the past, bank appraisals for mortgage purposes and survey requirements resulted in a physical check on a property. Today, valuations based on abstract computer models have replaced site visits and title insurance policies have been substituted for an up-to-date survey. The information age, despite privacy and security efforts, has made masses of personal information, often online, easily available to potential fraudsters anywhere in the world.

Possibly one of the most important factors is the consumer's expectation of immediacy. Fraud appears to be part of the price. Consumers unaware of the potential risks, the complex process of transactions, the extensive nature of land regulation, and the importance of title and due diligence have been encouraged to expect that a residential real estate deal should be closed extremely quickly. Industry players and consumer expectations have caused increased pressure to close deals quickly without traditional safeguards. Reduced or unreasonable timelines limit the ability of real estate professionals to exercise due diligence and delve into the details. Lawyers are often consulted late in the process. It is truly difficult to know your client in a depersonalized, hyper-competitive, frenetic, commercial reality in which long-standing business relationships and consumer loyalty are endangered species. The fraud investigator's perceptive advice of "Know your client" and "Slow down and check the details" is difficult to follow, even for the most diligent of lawyers.

THE FACE OF FRAUD

New variations on title and mortgage fraud are increasingly sophisticated and constantly evolving. The fraud may involve a team of fraudsters, blackmail and duress, sophisticated schemes involving dozens of properties, and collusion by industry insiders, and even an employee co-conspirator. Usually high quality, fake/counterfeit identification (ID) (particularly drivers' licences), letters and documentation, certified cheques, bank drafts, and money orders are involved. Fraudulent corporate minute books and other fake corporate documentation may be created to perpetrate a fraud. Real property fraud may involve organized crime complete with an international component. The proceeds of mortgage fraud have been linked to the financing of terrorist activities. Fraud is most often perpetrated by someone close, or someone trusted. Sadly, fraud is often a family affair.

Recently, fraudsters (often through a person impersonating a bank's loan officer) are retaining lawyers to act on fraudulent matters such as collections, small business loans, and real estate transactions. Marijuana-growing operations target rental units using fraudulent identities for tenants or owners. Fraudsters often time the fraud to coincide with peak periods such as holiday weekends when banks are closed and law firms and banks may be short-staffed and rushed. Unfortunately, title and mortgage fraud usually involve large sums of money as it takes the same amount of work to do a small fraud as a large one. There may be a new scheme by next month.

THE VICTIMS OF FRAUD

Fraud is a crime of many victims. The consequences of title and mortgage fraud can be catastrophic for individuals and practitioners alike, as well as damaging to infrastructure and community. Practitioners involved in a fraud transaction, even as an innocent "dupe", endure labour-intensive, time-consuming investigations and prosecutions. The lawyer will come under close scrutiny by the police, the insurer, and the LSUC in terms of both practice standards and possible collusion. Fraud investigations move slowly and have long-term effects. Fraud threatens the lawyer's reputation; banks may refuse to deal with the lawyer for mortgage loans and clients may view the lawyer with suspicion. Depending on the circumstances, the Ministry of Government Services and Teranet may withdraw access to POLARIS, effectively suspending the lawyer's real estate practice. Fraud and commercial crime, not just violent crime, devastate families and lives. Fraud can kill, just not as quickly or as directly.

TRANSACTIONS AT A HIGHER RISK OF FRAUD

Some properties are more vulnerable to fraud. Title insurers identify higher risk properties during the title insurance application process through the use of fraud screening questions and underwriting reviews for properties that fall into higher risk categories. The following circumstances have traditionally carried a higher risk of fraud.

- any transaction involving a power of attorney;
- transfer or mortgage of properties that are vacant;

- commercial vacant land refinance transactions;
- transfer of unencumbered property free of a mortgage often, but not necessarily, owned by elderly individuals;
- refinance of properties that are mortgage-free where the owner has a good credit rating;
- tenanted properties;
- private lender mortgages; and
- private sales.

TYPES OF TITLE AND MORTGAGE FRAUD

There are numerous, sophisticated variations on a fraud theme. Title theft involves the registration of forged transfer documentation which sets the scene for subsequent fraudulent transfers and mortgages. Mortgage fraud is based on any scheme which deceives a lender into believing that the property is worth more than it is and thereby obtaining more mortgage funds than a lender would have advanced if it had known the true value. Mortgage fraud is often a form of value fraud. It has been frequently suggested that a significant portion of value fraud could be avoided by the lenders conducting on-site due diligence appraisals as they did in the past. Title fraud impersonation, and forgeries, is more difficult to prevent.

In Ontario, most fraudsters are looking for someone with access to a trust account and/or a Teraview access encryption key to Ontario's ELRS. Fraudsters may run a fraudulent certified cheque or bank draft through a lawyer's trust account, obtain real funds from the trust account, leaving the soon-to-be discovered shortfall in the trust account. For these reasons, most fraudsters target lawyers as "dupes" in the scheme. The Ministry's Real Estate Fraud Action Plan and the LSUC see lawyers as the last line of defence against title and mortgage fraud and the Teraview encryption key as the security safeguard for the electronic registration system. The following are examples of typical frauds that affect real property:

- fraudulent transfers where a fraudster impersonates the owner or forges documents and transfers a property to himself without the knowledge of the true owner;
- mortgages obtained by false information or false identity;
- fraudulent discharges;
- identity fraud (individual or corporate);
    - impersonation of vendors, mortgagors, and lawyers;
    - spousal impersonation fraud (a spouse may transfer or mortgage a property such as a matrimonial home, using an accomplice to impersonate the true spouse);
- lawyer/notary taking client funds that were given in trust for discharging a mortgage or purchasing an interest in a property;
- value frauds (the fraudster artificially inflates the true value of the property either by misrepresenting the price, creating fraudulent de-

posits and renovation credits, or through a series of fraudulent flip transactions that repeatedly escalate the price in the transfers and the fraudster then obtains a mortgage based on the fraudulently manipulated price); and

- fictitious law firms.

THE RED FLAGS OF TITLE AND MORTGAGE FRAUD

The presence of a fraud flag does not indicate a fraud, just a higher statistical risk. Fraud flags vary with the nature of the transaction. The following are some of the better recognized red flags for potential fraud:

- a mortgage which advances funds greater than the price needed to obtain title;
- the use of a POA, particularly a POA not drafted by an Ontario lawyer;
  - quality of ID of donor and attorney;
  - international powers of attorney;
  - proceeds paid to the donee of the POA;
  - multiple-use of POA on a property;
  - inter-family transfers, particularly those that involve powers of attorney;
- new "not known" client;
- "flips" or a history of flips on title (recent transfer(s) with unusual increase(s) in property value);
- short turnaround time on mortgage or purchase transaction and urgency to close transaction quickly;
- unusually generous fees;
- unavailability of quality identification (no photo ID);
- clients who do not have personal cheques (counter cheques);
- short-term mortgage;
- recent mortgage(s) and discharge(s);
- no mortgage statement available from vendor for purchaser;
- unusually high mortgage interest rates;
- vulnerable property (vacant, tenanted, mortgage-free);
- large or additional deposits or renovation credits paid directly to the vendor;
- mortgage or purchase funds paid to someone not connected to the property (unusual directions regarding funds);
- denial of policy application by an insurer;
- non-arm's length transaction in combination with other risk factors;
- recent changes to the corporate profile report of a borrower;
- unavailability of minute book and minute book irregularities;
- recent changes in directors, officers or addresses;
- out-of-country service addresses;
- inconsistent personal details (age/income);

- inconsistent financial details (price, *Land Transfer Tax Act* affidavit, mortgage, *etc.*);
- client contact limited to cell phone;
- lawyer changes on other side of transaction;
- lawyer representing multiple clients;
- instructions from other than the parties;
- client unfamiliar with property;
- client will not permit contact with prior lawyer;
- unusual volume of transactions with same parties and real estate agents and mortgage brokers;
- unusually high ratio or "zombie" mortgages; and
- firm member who never takes vacation or sick leave, works unreasonably long hours, refuses to delegate work, or has a sudden change in lifestyle or behaviour.

Stewart Title provides a bulletin to its examining counsels in order to assist them in identifying and avoiding fraud, and in reducing potential claims (see Figure 17.1).

FRAUD REDUCTION STRATEGIES

Fraud, particularly mortgage fraud, is in large part a crime of opportunity. As a result, reducing the opportunity for fraud by the use of comprehensive fraud reduction strategies can have a profound effect. Fraud reduction practices generate multiple benefits. For example, title and mortgage fraud reduction strategies are also effective for identifying money-laundering activities, proceeds of crime, and funds related to terrorist activities. The regulators of the targeted professional groups including lawyers, mortgage brokers, real estate agents, appraisers, and the lenders, the title insurers, and the police are all involved in investigating and prosecuting fraud.

The title insurers have long-term, extensive expertise in identifying, mitigating, and managing the risk of title and mortgage fraud. Some insurers even provide file management software that has fraud reduction practices built in to the structure of the software. Fraud mitigation questions found in title insurance policy applications are designed to flag transactions that merit closer scrutiny and custom underwriting review.

Fraud mitigation strategies include the following:

- Use practice checklists and software that contain fraud reduction features and specifically fraud flag (mitigation) questions.
- Supervise appropriate use and security of PSP and never give anyone your Teranet PSP and password. Keep PSPs in a safe, locked, location. Law clerks must not be given access to a lawyer's ELRS password.

- Comply strictly with LSUC client identification and verification rules under By-Law 7.1.
- Have documents signed in the office.
- Always request deleted documents and investigate any suspicious patterns in recent transactions and changes in values when searching title in POLARIS.
- Review accounting controls particularly in terms of trust accounts and cheques.
- Avoid deals that are just too good to be true. Greed is the hook that fraudsters of all types use to hook the unwary.
- Supervise staff and take an active role in managing the office.
- Screen new staff and complete background checks.
- Obtain second bank-to-bank verification before issuing funds from lawyer's trust account.
- Use LVTS guaranteed by the Bank of Canada, whenever possible.
- Know your bank manager and have contacts within the bank.
- Maintain direct communication with the stakeholders and professionals involved in the transaction.
- Use social networking websites with caution as fraudsters prospect for "dupes" in these sites.

PROFESSIONAL JUDGMENT AND DUE DILIGENCE

A lawyer must apply his or her professional judgment to and make reasonable inquiries related to all aspects of a real estate transaction. A lawyer may not turn a blind eye to suspicious circumstances. The Honourable Justice Randall S. Echlin, in his decision in *Rabi v. Rosu*, [2006] O.J. No. 4348 (Ont. S.C.J.), described in particularly eloquent terms the age-old nature of fraud and the value of due diligence and reasonable inquiry when he stated (at para. 1) that: "Eighteenth century English poet and essayist Dr. Samuel Johnson (1709-1784), once observed, 'Fraud and falsehood only dread examination. Truth invites it.'" Justice Echlin identified the impact of red flags on due diligence when he stated the following (at para. 22):

> Instead, the bank acted pursuant to its "usual procedures" and advanced money to a fraudster in the absence of an interior inspection of the premises to be mortgaged (which would likely have averted the fraud), having chosen to delegate the due diligence to a mortgage broker. It is also extremely curious that the condominium unit in question at 28 Hollywood Avenue was listed as having a locker and two parking units, and yet the fraudulent sale did not refer to these nor did it offer any explanation for the absence of such transfers. Finally, it was odd that there was no deposit. All of these red flags should have raised questions for the lender.

FRAUD REDUCTION RESOURCES

Both the LSUC and the title insurers offer a wealth of fraud reduction resources and fraud reduction training opportunities. The LSUC and the Ontario Bar Association offer regular continuing education opportunities for real estate fraud awareness. The LSUC has specialized investigators as well as practice advisory services. LawPRO provides training seminars and practice resources as part of its risk management initiatives. The real estate practice portal on the LSUC website has an extensive collection of fraud awareness and prevention materials including a checklist that addresses: hiring practices; accounting controls and bookkeeping practices; supervision of staff and segregation of duties and handling money; joint retainers, particularly for mortgage transactions; review of title searches; closing transactions; and the safeguarding of PSP that give access to electronic land registration.

The title insurers also offer reference materials on their websites, regular training seminars, and practice resources, including file management software. Title insurers have in-house expertise in fraud investigation and prosecution; they also share information and collaborate closely with national and international law enforcement agencies. In that the title insurer investigates numerous frauds, it will be aware of persons under suspicion long before the information becomes public. The insurer may recognize names of fictitious law firms, mortgage brokers, loans officers, tenants, and fraudsters and be aware of recent schemes and targeted communities. A phone call to the title insurer in response to nothing more than an uneasy feeling may prevent tremendous expense and disruption to clients, lenders, lawyers, and insurers. When in doubt, call the insurer.

LSUC GUIDELINES FOR DUE DILIGENCE REGARDING FRAUD REDUCTION

The LSUC recommends that lawyers adopt the following practices in order to detect and deter fraud.

Lender Due Diligence

- Meet personally with the client and obtain, verify, and retain two pieces of original identification — at least one must be photo ID.
- Verify information in mortgage loan application with independent sources.
- Verify identity of registered owner and mortgage applicant.
- On-site property visit or appraisal.
- Verify value of property.
- Review all documentation for suspicious circumstances.
- Provide lawyer with all related documentation and a contact at lender.
- Prompt registration of mortgage discharges.

Lawyer Due Diligence in Loan Transaction

- Follow-up on suspicious circumstances with reasonable inquiries, retain records, disclose concerns to all clients in the retainer and withdraw if concerned.
- Follow LSUC verification of client identity rules (see Chapter 15).
- Request deleted documents and review all documents in a search.
- Review transactions in search for suspicious changes in value.
- Review pattern of deleted documents on parcel register for suspicious circumstances.
- Closely scrutinize flips and changes to the agreement of purchaser and sale affecting deposits and payment directions, price reductions, cashbacks, purchaser credits, mortgages larger than purchase price, direct payments to vendor (deposit/down payment), *etc.*
- Verify circumstances surrounding powers of attorney.
- Report suspicious patterns to the purchaser/borrower and the title insurer.
- Investigate inconsistent information regarding the purchaser or the transaction.
- Obtain acknowledgement and direction to sign on client's behalf.
- Provide final mortgage report to the lender within 60 days.

ONTARIO'S REAL ESTATE FRAUD ACTION PLAN

Modernization of the *Land Titles Act*

The purpose of Bill 152, *An Act to Modernize Various Acts Administered or Affecting the Ministry of Government Services, 2006*, S.O. 2006, c. 34 (which came into force on December 20, 2006) is to modernize aspects of the *Land Titles Act*, R.S.O. 1990, c. L.5, the *Land Registration Reform Act*, R.S.O. 1990 c. L.4, and the *Registry Act*, R.S.O. 1990, c. R. 20, particularly as they affect fraudulent instruments registered on or after October 19, 2006. This statute provides the legislative authority for Ontario's Real Estate Fraud Action Plan. The Plan changes the law concerning fraudulent registrations and puts in place a number of procedural safeguards and administrative practices that have made major changes in how conveyancers process mortgages and transfers of land in Land Titles. Bill 152 brought about the changes outlined in the following paragraphs.

The Legal Effect of Fraudulent Registrations

Section 15 of Bill 152 defines "fraudulent instrument" as meaning an instrument:

    (a)   under which a fraudulent person purports to receive or transfer an estate or interest in land,

    (b)   that is given under the purported authority of a power of attorney that is forged,

(c) that is a transfer of a charge where the charge is given by a fraudulent person, or

(d) that perpetrates a fraud as prescribed with respect to the estate or interest in land affected by the instrument. ...

Ontario Regulation 53/07 adds cessations of charge and encumbrances to the definition of fraudulent instrument.

Bill 152 reduces the uncertainty in Canadian case law for fraudulent documents registered on or after October 19, 2006, with respect to the effect of fraudulent registrations on the original true owner and on subsequent, innocent, non-arm's length purchasers, and mortgagees for value, without notice of the fraud. Generally, s. 78(4.1) and (4.2) of the *Land Titles Act* protect property owners from the fraudulent documents; innocent homeowners will not lose their homes because a fraudulent document(s) was registered after October 19, 2006. Therefore, a fraudulent document such as a transfer or a mortgage will have no effect on the register and will not be enforceable against the innocent homeowner. However, documents that are registered subsequent to a fraudulent instrument and that are not fraudulent will be effective. As a result, innocent third-party purchasers for value and without notice who buy from a bona fide or true owner will remain protected under the Act. These legislative changes reflect the principle of deferred indefeasibility.

Bill 152 confirms the established, common law model of deferred indefeasibility as applied in *Lawrence v. Wright*, [2007] O.J. No. 381 (Ont. C.A.), which provides that:

1. a fraudulent registration does not create a valid and enforceable conveyance against the true owner, for example, a transfer, charge, discharge, lease, *etc.*);

2. the person who acquires an interest in land from the party responsible for the fraud is vulnerable to a claim from the true owner because the intermediate owner had an opportunity to avoid the fraud; and

3. a subsequent purchaser or encumbrancer (the deferred owner) did not have an opportunity to avoid the fraud. Consequently, subsequent non-fraudulent registered interests that rely on a fraudulent registration are valid and enforceable. For example, a transfer from an innocent, subsequent owner to an innocent purchaser or mortgagee is valid and enforceable.

The *Lawrence v. Wright* case provides a similar outcome for cases prior to October 19, 2006. Fraud as with money laundering frequently involves a series of intermediaries innocent or otherwise. Consequently, title insurance remains the appropriate comprehensive protection against fraud.

Rectification of the Register in Cases of Fraud

In cases involving fraud, the register may be rectified where the fraudulent registration deprives a person of the property that he or she was legally occupying or for which he or she was receiving rents before the fraudulent registration (*Land Titles Act*, s. 57(13)).

Director's Caution

The Director of Titles may register a caution to prevent any dealings with a property, if it appears that a registered document may be fraudulent (*Land Titles Act*, s. 57(15) and (16)). The Director's caution protects the rights of innocent owners and mortgagees during a fraud investigation.

Access to the Electronic Registration System

The Director of Land Registration may impose conditions and restrictions on users who have access to the electronic registration system by unique access key. Key access is based on an application process that verifies identity, financial resources (errors and omissions excepted (E&OE) or fraud insurance), and good character/accountability (membership in a regulated profession or alternative CPIC-type (Canadian Police Information Centre) checks). Teraview account holders must enter into a registration agreement which makes them responsible for anyone using their account. Each user should have a separate account. Only a lawyer's key permits the signing for completeness of transfers and the making of statements of law. All key-use is traceable to the key holder.

Suspension or Revocation of Access to ELRS

The Director of Titles may suspend immediately the access authorization of a lawyer or other submitter of documents to the ELRS, if it is in the public interest. The Director may act in her or his discretion on reasonable grounds that the lawyer has submitted an electronic document that was not authorized by the true registered owner of the property. There is no right to hearing prior to suspension; however, the suspended person has a right to notice of the suspension. The suspended person has a right to hearing, on written request, before the Director following the suspension and before revocation. The Director must follow timelines and notice requirements in determining whether to lift or maintain the suspension of access pending investigation. There is an appeal of revocation to the Divisional Court. Any suspension of access has a profound business interruption impact on a real estate practitioner.

Changes to the Land Titles Assurance Fund

An applicant/homeowner to the Land Titles Assurance Fund (LTAF) is no longer required to exhaust all other means of remedy before making a compensation claim. The LTAF has ceased to be a fund of last resort. For example, in the past the claimant had to sue the fraudster and potentially the lawyer in negligence as a condition of making a claim. The claimant, however, must have exercised due diligence and not contributed to its loss in order to recover from the fund. The *Syvan* case provides an examination of the Fund's due diligence requirement in the context of a missed access easement (*Syvan Developments Ltd. v. Ontario (Ministry of Government Services)*, [2006] O.J. No. 3765 (Ont. S.C.J.)). The LTAF bars subrogated claims by insurers.

Offences: Fines and Penalties

The maximum fine for a real estate fraud provincial offence has been raised to $50,000 for an individual and $250,000 for a corporation, with the possibility of imprisonment for a term up to two years (*Land Titles Act*, s. 59.2). The court may also order compensation and/or restitution. The *Criminal Code*, R.S.C. 1985, c. C-46 also contains specific real estate fraud offences and sanctions and carries much longer imprisonment terms.

Two-Lawyer Requirement for Transfers (Rule 2.04.1)

Effective April 7, 2008, transfers must be signed by two lawyers prior to being registered electronically. Each signature requires that the lawyer make a statement confirming that he or she has client authorization to sign. Certain exceptions apply and have been covered in earlier chapters on closing transactions (Chapter 15) and the electronic and registration system (Chapter 16).

Verification of Client Identity Requirements

Strict new rules now apply to the verification and retention of client identity records. Special rules apply when a transaction involves a power of attorney. Foreign powers of attorney come under intense scrutiny. These requirements have been dealt with in Chapter 15. Client identity verification requirements are complex; they are posted on the LSUC website.

Powers of Attorney Requirements

Powers of attorney are one of the fraudster's favourite tools, particularly in frauds within families. Both the Ministry and the LSUC have implemented extensive due diligence requirements for the registration of powers of attorney and documents signed by POA. Chapter 15 covers POA requirements. The LSUC posts the *Guidelines on Powers of Attorney in Real Estate Transactions* on its website. The LSUC provides POA checklists in its guidelines for documents signed under power of attorney. Some title insurers include fraud mitigation questions targeting powers of attorney in their policy applications.

The Ministry requires a statement in all electronic documents as to whether or not a document is signed by POA. Powers of Attorney must be registered and can be searched in the electronic POA registers in ELRS. If a document is signed by POA, there are additional statements that describe the circumstances of the POA. The Ministry requires a statement of law when an individual registers a document signed under POA. The statement requires the lawyer to confirm that he or she has discussed the POA with his or her clients.

The Court in *Reviczky v. Meleknia*, [2007] O.J. No. 4992 (Ont. S.C.J.) outlines the due diligence requirements for lawyers who rely on powers of attorney for the authority to sign electronic documents. The case provides an example of how a POA can be used in a fraud and the legal due diligence standards expected of lawyers.

When dealing with powers of attorney, face-to-face contact and identity verification reduce but do not eliminate risk. The common combination of powers of attorney and related persons presents even higher risks. Whenever possible, avoid the use of powers of attorney in real estate transactions.

FRAUD REPORTING

Many frauds are never reported to the authorities. As fraud most often involves insiders. Financial institutions and corporations frequently conduct internal investigations and effectively hide fraud under the cloak of confidentiality agreements. Those who suffer fraud at the hands of a family member may be too hurt or too ashamed to report the crime to the authorities and may never seek compensation from the family member.

Lawyers have a duty to report fraud and suspected fraud in a timely manner to the title insurer and to the LSUC. The registration of fraudulent title documents must be brought to the attention of the Ministry and the Land Registry Office as quickly as possible. The police and the affected financial institution must also be contacted. Title insurers have expertise in investigating fraud and have contacts within law enforcement and the LSUC. The LSUC Practice Advisory and title insurers can provide guidance on reporting and what to do when confronted with the possibility of a mortgage or title fraud.

CASE LAW ON FRAUDULENT REGISTRATIONS

A comprehensive analysis of the case law relating to fraudulent registrations prior to Bill 152 and following Bill 152 is beyond the scope of this chapter. At the time of writing, the Ontario Court of Appeal decision in *Lawrence v. Wright* is the leading authority on the legal effect of fraudulent registrations in Land Titles prior to the enactment of Bill 152. The Court in *Lawrence v. Wright* reviewed the earlier cases and the legal principles of immediate defeasibility and deferred indefeasibility which govern fraudulent registrations in the context of the Land Titles system. The Court confirmed and applied the principle of deferred indefeasibility as being the appropriate law in Ontario. The reasoning in *Lawrence v. Wright* continues to govern the law relating to fraudulent transactions in Land Titles. For two excellent, insightful reviews of the conflicting cases leading up to the *Lawrence v. Wright* decision and an in-depth legal analysis of the case itself, refer to Jeffrey W. Lem, "Immediate Indefeasibility, Deferred Indefeasibility, Double Deferred Indefeasibility, and Infinite Indefeasibility: A Review of the Court of Appeal Decision in *Lawrence v. Wright*" (April 19, 2007), the Fourth Annual Real Estate Law Summit, the Law Society of Upper Canada, and to Professor Bruce Ziff, "Looking for Mr. Wright: A Comment on *Lawrence v. Wright*" (2007) 51 R.P.R. (4th) 22.

Shortly after the *Lawrence v. Wright* decision, the Ontario government enacted Bill 152, *An Act to Modernize Various Acts Administered or Affecting the Ministry of Government Services, 2006*, which expressly incorporated aspects of the *Lawrence v. Wright* decision and the established legal principle of deferred indefeasibility into s. 58 of the *Land Titles Act*. In addition, the Act specifically provides protection to the innocent original homeowner victim of a fraudulent document registered after October 19, 2006 on a residential property. Refer to the previous section on the legal effect of fraudulent registrations.

The impact and the interpretation of the revisions to the *Land Titles Act* on the legal effect of fraudulent registrations and the compensation sections under the LTAF will continue to be examined in future cases. Although the *Land Titles Act* revisions adopt the principle of deferred indefeasibility, they use new language. The future interpretation of the new wording of the *Land Titles Act* sections, combined with the continuing uncertainty in the case law concerning the application of the principle of deferred indefeasibility to different fact situations, remains an open question.

The following cases have been decided since the amendments to the *Land Titles Act*.

Reviczky v. Meleknia expressly confirms that the revised provisions in the *Land Titles Act* should be interpreted in accordance with the theory of deferred indefeasibility. The decision in the *Reviczky* case continues the focus in *Lawrence v. Wright* that the burden of fraud should fall on the party that had the opportunity to avoid the fraud. The judge in *Reviczky* goes on to state that "the opportunity to avoid fraud is now central to the theory of deferred indefeasibility as a rationale for allocating loss among competing parties who claim an interest under the *Land Titles Act*" (*Reviczky*, at para. 44). The decision in *Reviczky* also stressed that the mortgagee/Bank could have avoided the fraud if it had exercised due diligence in reviewing and verifying the validity of a suspicious POA. *Reviczky* indicates that issues of due diligence and the transactional proximity of a party to a fraudster appear relevant to the application of the theory of deferred indefeasibility.

The case of *O'Brien v. Royal Bank of Canada*, [2008] O.J. No. 653 (Ont. S.C.J.) deals with a forged POA by a daughter who then transferred the property to herself and refinanced by a fraudulent mortgage and left the country. The Court in this case followed *Lawrence v. Wright*.

Clients may choose to sue a lawyer in negligence rather than claim under a title insurance policy:

> The general rule is that the existence of insurance will not extinguish a plaintiff's cause of action against a defendant. The mere fact that the plaintiff has an alternate source from which to recover his loss does not extinguish his right to seek recovery from the negligent party. (*Ruksc v. Hussein (c.o.b. Hussein Law Office)*, [2005] O.J. No. 5231 (Ont. S.C.J.))

The duty to defend under a title insurance policy may arise in cases where it eventually turns out that an insured is not entitled to indemnification. The obligation to defend is broader than the obligation to indemnify (*Stewart Title Guarantee Co. v. Zeppieri*, [2009] O.J. No. 322 (Ont. S.C.J.)). The duty to defend does not apply in cases of gross negligence, wilful misconduct, or fraud.

In summary, at this time, the courts and the profession are still exploring the interpretation and application of the new wording of the *Land Titles Act*, as well as the underlying legal principles such as transactional proximity, what is an intermediate compared to a deferred owner, the opportunity to avoid the fraud including mention of fault, complicity, the issue of notice, and a duty to inquire. The case of *Salna v. Chetti*, [2008] O.J. No. 3958 (Ont. S.C.J.) considers whether lenders should be treated differently from owners. Also, see the recent case of *St. Onge v. Willowbay Investments Inc.*, [2008] O.J. No. 3430 (Ont. S.C.J.) for a discussion of intermediate and deferred owners, and the impact of not making reasonable inquiries.

Figure 17.1

REAL ESTATE FRAUD FLAGS FOR LAWYERS*

Bulletin

REAL ESTATE FRAUD FLAGS FOR LAWYERS

To assist your office in identifying fraudulent transactions, Stewart Title has compiled a list of indicators which may signal that the transaction you are working on is fraudulent. We suggest the circulation of this list to your staff.
Please note: This list is not exhaustive. Lawyers should continue to question any transaction which appears unusual and that could involve fraud.

Potential Fraud Indicators:

1. Agreement of Purchase and Sale contains no handwritten amendments on the document.
2. Deposit is paid to the Vendor, not to a real estate agent or lawyer in trust.
3. No real estate agent at all, or there is a real estate agent listed in the agreement, but there is no signature of the agent and no part of purchase funds are directed to the agent.
4. The Agreement of Purchase and Sale stipulates that the Purchaser is to rebate a portion of the agreed upon purchase price to the Vendor from the mortgage advance.
5. A receipt from the Vendor for a significant deposit not called for in the Agreement of Purchase and Sale.
6. Donor's signature on a Power of Attorney does not match the signature on the Donor's I.D. or other available documents.
7. Sale or mortgage funds are NOT made payable to the Donor in a Power of Attorney but to the Attorney alone or a third party.
8. Power of Attorney is not prepared and/or witnessed by a lawyer and does not meet formal requirements with respect to witnesses etc.
9. The I.D. provided by your client does not look similar to legitimate I.D. of your own (i.e. is the last name first?) and the signature on the I.D. does not match your client's signature.
10. The purchaser's identification shows their address as the same as the property being purchased, but they have not moved there yet.
11. The purchaser spells their name inconsistently.
12. The age of the party is inconsistent with how long they appear to have owned the property (i.e. it was purchased prior to the owner being born, or being of legal age).
13. The client is unknown to you and does not come from a usual referral source.
14. The property is mortgage free or vacant land or both.
15. Unusually high brokerage fees.
16. Borrower is a corporation and there have been recent changes to the officers/directors of the company.
17. Corporate records and borrowing resolutions are not available.
18. The direction of funds includes a direction to pay part of the funds to a currency exchange such as cheque cashing/funds transferring locations.
19. A cashback mortgage covering the entire equity in the property.
20. Non-arm's length transfers occurring just prior to the registration of a mortgage.
21. Purchase price appears completely out of line for the area, or with recent transfers of the same property.

Ontario – Head Office	Atlantic Canada	Québec	Western Canada
(888) 667-5151	(888) 757-0078	(866) 235-9152	(866) 515-8401

www.stewart.ca

Figure 17.1 (cont'd)

Bulletin

22. When calculating how much money the purchaser has to bring in to close the deal, it turns out there is a surplus owing to the purchaser.
23. The client needs to close the transaction very quickly.
24. Using a different lawyer on a refinance than the lawyer used on the recent purchase transaction.
25. The Vendor acquires title to the property the same day as it is being transferred to the purchaser, and the first transaction is at a significantly lower purchase price (aka "the flip").
26. The title shows a pattern of mortgages being registered, discharged shortly thereafter, and new mortgage being put on.

Please contact Stewart Title's Underwriting Team prior to insuring any transaction where the above factors appear to indicate a fraudulent transaction may exist.

For more information on fraud, please contact your local Business Development Specialist, or visit www.stewart.ca.

Jan 2010 - NTL

Stewart Title Guaranty Co. is a leader in the Canadian title insurance industry and helps legal professionals increase efficiency and decrease costs by offering value-added title insurance products for residential and commercial transactions. Stewart Title's unwavering philosophy is that the role of a title insurer in Canada should be to underwrite risk, allowing legal professionals to provide legal advice and prepare documents. Stewart Title does not participate in or support programs that reduce or eliminate the lawyer's/notary's role in real estate transactions. To find out more about Stewart Title please visit www.stewart.ca.

Keeping Real Estate Transactions Where They Belong – In Your Office!

Ontario – Head Office	Atlantic Canada	Québec	Western Canada
(888) 667-5151	(888) 757-0078	(866) 235-9152	(866) 515-8401

www.stewart.ca

CHAPTER 18

Title Insurance

INTRODUCTION

The preceding 17 chapters on the mysteries of title searching and land registration have, by now, made it abundantly clear that title investigation and conveyancing are neither simple nor without risk of liability. In fact, real estate transactions, and more particularly title, off-title, execution, and adjoining lands searches, give rise to a disproportionate number of negligence claims against lawyers. In addition, transactions that involve mortgages and powers of attorney present an increased risk of fraud. Traditionally, real estate claims have accounted for almost one half of all claims made annually against LawPRO, the Lawyers' Professional Indemnity Company (formerly LPIC).

When a purchaser or mortgagee has the misfortune to discover that the title to his or her property or investment is defective, then that individual may seek compensation from:

1. LawPRO on the basis of solicitor negligence;

2. the Land Titles Assurance Fund on the basis of error on the record; or

3. a title insurance policy on the contractual basis of insured risks.

When a purchaser or mortgagee has the misfortune to discover that the title to his or her property or investment is defective as a result of fraud, then that individual may seek compensation from:

1. the Land Titles Assurance Fund (limited remedies); or

2. a title insurance policy's fraud coverage.

From a practical point of view, title insurance is the provider of effective, comprehensive fraud coverage for lenders, purchasers, and tenants in longer term leases (for example, a ground lease).

LAWPRO

All lawyers in Ontario must carry mandatory professional negligence insurance. LawPRO provides professional liability insurance to lawyers in private practice in Ontario. LawPRO also provides a bar-related comprehensive title insurance and legal services product called TitlePLUS, described later in this chapter. Since 1995, LawPRO has operated independently of the Law Society of Upper Canada (LSUC). TitlePLUS is available nationally.

LawPRO also offers extensive risk and practice management tools in the form of PracticePRO, including training seminars and practice management software. LawPRO also offers excess insurance. Most lawyers carry additional errors and omissions insurance provided by LawPRO or private insurers. Malpractice insurance provides compensation only when the lawyer has failed to provide a legally required service or has provided legal services that do not meet professional standards of reasonable care and skill.

In Canada, lawyers may give clients a legal opinion as to good and marketable title backed by the lawyer's errors and omissions or malpractice insurance, a certificate of insurable title under a title insurance policy, or a combination of the two. When a lawyer-related error occurs, a purchaser or mortgagee is faced with making a claim in negligence directly against the lawyer, who in turn is insured by LawPRO which would then respond to the claim.

A client must first prove that the lawyer was negligent and failed to meet professional standards before receiving compensation from the lawyer's insurer. This process may involve expensive, time-consuming litigation, complex law, and difficult to prove facts — with no guarantee of success.

THE LAND TITLES ASSURANCE FUND

Revisions to s. 57 of the *Land Titles Act*, R.S.O. 1990, c. L.5 (LTA), driven by the public's concern about title and mortgage fraud, have reformed the Land Titles Assurance Fund (LTAF). Revisions streamline the claims process for innocent homeowner victims of fraud. In the Land Titles system, the government guarantees that title is vested in the current registered owner, subject to registered encumbrances, as shown on the parcel register, and subject to the exceptions and qualifications listed in s. 44 of the LTA. In the event of error, a claim for compensation may be made to the LTAF. Section 57(1) of the LTA states that the LTAF offers compensation to a person wrongfully deprived of land by reason of some other person being registered as owner through fraud or misdescription or other error in an entry on the register. Compensation under the LTAF may include financial losses caused by fraud or error, reasonable legal costs related to the claim, and other reasonable costs related to the claim.

An LTAF claim must be made within six years from the time of having suffered the loss. The LTAF acts as an administrative tribunal with authority to receive and hear evidence and conduct hearings under the *Statutory Powers Procedure Act*, R.S.O. 1990, c. S.22, and its own *Rules of Procedure* (LTA, s. 57(15)). Special rules apply to mining claims (LTA, s. 56).

The Land Titles Assurance Fund is also available for errors made when land is converted under the Province of Ontario Land Registration Information System (POLARIS) into Land Titles and for errors in the electronic title and mapping record. Section 56(1) of the LTA allows for an application to the Director of Titles for financial assistance for surveys and *Boundaries Act*, R.S.O. 1990, c. B.10 plans. The LTAF bars subrogated claims by insurers.

Where land is in Registry, a person is entitled to compensation from the fund when he or she has been wrongfully deprived of land as a result of the deletion by the land registrar of a mortgage or any other related instrument, the deletion by the land registrar of an instrument such as a certificate of pending litigation, or any error or omission in the recording of an instrument. For example, when an instrument such as a mortgage has been ruled out in error in the Registry abstract book by the Registry office staff, the mortgagee might claim compensation against the fund.

Section 16 creates special innocent homeowner protections for individuals who were the registered owners of the land used for residential purposes and for individuals who were purchasers in good faith for valuable consideration of the land used for residential purposes.

Generally, the Act requires that potential claimants must first show that they were unable to recover compensation under the law before claiming against the fund; however, innocent homeowners can apply directly to the fund. As well, a claimant will not be compensated where he or she has caused or substantially contributed to the loss through the claimant's act, neglect, default, and/or omission, such as the failure to register a sufficient caution, notice, or appropriate registration under the Act. The claimant must demonstrate due diligence standards as specified from time to time by the Director. *Syvan Developments Ltd. v. Ontario (Ministry of Government Services)*, [2006] O.J. No. 3765 (Ont. S.C.J.), decided prior to the revisions, provides an examination of the Fund's traditional due diligence requirements.

There are two categories of prescribed claimants or claims before the fund. The claims process has been streamlined for both classes of claimants. The *Rules of Procedure and the Information Document* and all LTAF decisions are available on the Ministry of Government Services website. Ontario Regulation 26/99, as amended by O. Reg. 53/07, sets out the procedures for Claims against the LTAF.

Victims of Fraud (Individual Homeowners)

There is an early payment process for members of a class prescribed by the Director (s. 57(4.1) and (4.2)). The class applies to individual homeowners and innocent, good faith, purchasers of homes for valuable consideration, where a fraudulent document was registered on or after October 18, 2006. The property must have been used for residential, including rental, purposes. The applicant does not have to exhaust all other means of remedy before making a compensation claim. For the individual homeowner, the LTAF has ceased to be a fund of last resort; for example, in the past the claimant had to sue the fraudster and potentially the lawyer in negligence as a condition of making a claim. In legally clear cases, the Director of Title will deliver a decision and compensation within 90 days of registering a Director's Caution on title.

Traditional LTAF Claims

The applicant is required to exhaust all other means of remedy before making a compensation claim to the LTAF. The traditional claim requirements apply to all claims that are not a member of a prescribed class (for example, a bank).

The Director's Due Diligence Standards

The Director has the authority to set by Director's Order standards of due diligence by a claimant required for eligibility to recover under the fund (s. 57(4)(b) and (4.1)(b)). Claimants cannot contribute to their loss by participating or colluding in a fraud (s. 59(d)). The current Director's Order sets different detailed standards for lenders and purchasers (see ODOT-2007-02). Generally, both lenders and purchasers seeking compensation must take reasonable steps that are necessary in the circumstances of the case to verify that the registered owner is in fact selling or mortgaging the property. No specific requirements are currently set for the prescribed class of innocent, good faith homeowners. The Order contains a list of example due diligence steps, but the list is not exhaustive. The hearings officer has the discretion to determine whether due diligence standards have been met in the specific case. Examples of due diligence include the following:

Lenders

- Verify the identity of the mortgagor and the registered owner.
- Meet with the mortgagor in person or require its agent to meet in person with the borrower.
- Require and copy at the time of signing the mortgage original government issued photo identification that contains name, date of birth, and address and at least one other piece of original identification.
- Verify application information by checking references, preferably employer, and consumer reporting.
- Verify that registered owner is selling or mortgaging by obtaining an agreement of purchase and sale.
- Conduct on-site appraisal or visit.
- Complete appropriate title searches.
- Check MLS history and confirm listing details.
- Other requirement(s) appropriate in the circumstances.

Purchasers

- Provide agreement of purchase and sale.
- Instruct completion of appropriate searches.
- Visit or have agent visit the property.
- Other requirement(s) appropriate in the circumstances.

Alternative Protection

The LTAF requirement in non-prescribed classes to seek compensation from other sources such as claims in negligence or professional practice claims can be difficult and expensive to pursue. Title insurance provides a practical, usually non-litigious, cost-effective alternative for protection against fraud or defects in the title or legal services related aspects of a real estate transaction.

THE ROLE OF TITLE INSURANCE

Title insurance first came into being in 1868, in Philadelphia, as a method of providing protection to purchasers and investors from unanticipated title hazards. Today, title insurance is available throughout Canada to purchasers and lenders for both residential and commercial properties. It is available for both freehold and leasehold interests in land. Title insurance is used in varying degrees depending on the Province. In Ontario, title insurance is obtained in virtually all residential transactions and in the majority of commercial transactions. Large, foreign, commercial tenants routinely require title insurance as part of the leasing transaction. Title insurance products are competitive and search requirements for and terms of coverage vary between insurers. Premiums are competitive.

Title insurance protects owners and lenders from title risks and lawyers from claims by clients. In Ontario, since the 1980s, title insurance has become an integral part of the real estate transaction. The LSUC's *Rules of Professional Conduct* specifically acknowledge the role and advisability of title insurance. In addition, the LSUC excludes transactions from the real estate levy surcharge when the transaction is title insured.

Title insurance affects most aspects of a real estate transaction and is no longer a stand-alone topic. As a result, title insurance is dealt with throughout this book in the context of specific topics; for example, access, executions, or the selection of off-title inquiries. Each chapter has a section on title insurance.

The primary function of title insurance is to provide cost-efficient, after-the-fact indemnity protection for purchasers and lenders. It does not guarantee or cure title. Its focus is one of compensation or damages and not specific performance or the uniqueness of specific proprietary rights in land. Title insurance offers insurable title in lieu of the traditional lawyer's opinion on marketable title. It does not provide protection to lawyers or clients for the contract and tort risks associated with anticipatory breach or failure to close. Title insurance is not a replacement for due diligence. It is not a replacement for an up-to-date survey or full-title and off-title searches. At this time, case law indicates that clients may choose whether to sue a lawyer in negligence or seek compensation under a title insurance policy. Title insurance is an alternative or supplement in the convey-ancer's toolbox for managing the complex risks of title conveyancing.

In the future, as a result of the *Land Registration Reform Act*, R.S.O. 1990, c. L.4 conversion into the POLARIS database, all land will be in Land Titles, a register of title system backed by a limited government guarantee in the form of the LTAF. Despite this development, the consideration of title insurance is now a required step in both purchase and lending transactions. Title insurance, which is available for all types of real estate transactions, is a contract for insuring and indemnifying owners or lenders against loss or damage from title risks inherent in real estate transactions. The insured may claim indemnity for actual loss or damage up to the face amount of the policy, including any inflation endorsement.

Title insurance offers a variety of coverage options for protection from defects in either the title or legal services related risks in a real estate transaction, such as conflicting ownership interests, access-related problems, compliance risks, or unmarketable title as well as imperfect legal and conveyancing services pro-vided by lawyers. Title insurance covers reimbursement for legal fees and ex-penses caused by defending the insured's title against litigation generated by a defect in title or legal services. No maximum dollar amount is set for defence of title coverage. In addition, title insurance provides coverage for unforeseeable losses unrelated to a lawyer's negligence; for example, losses caused by forgery, fraud, zoning by-law infractions, or discrepancies not revealed by a property survey.

In effect, title insurance provides owners and lenders with comprehensive no-fault protection against both the title and legal services risks inherent in real estate transactions. A policyholder may claim compensation from the title insurance company rather than suing the lawyer or surveyor and having to prove negligence.

As with other types of insurance, title insurance coverage is subject to numerous detailed exclusions, exemptions, and endorsements depending on the particular insurer and policy involved. Title insurance coverage is available to both pur-chasers and lenders, in either separate or combined policies.

In Ontario, title insurance is currently available through several private title in-surance companies and also from the LSUC's bar-related TitlePLUS product. A list of Canadian title insurers is included later in this chapter under the heading "Title Insurers in Canada".

REGULATION OF TITLE INSURANCE

The Office of the Superintendent of Financial Institutions regulates and licenses title insurance companies which do business in Canada. The Superintendent of Financial Services regulates title insurance in Ontario under the *Insurance Act*, R.S.O. 1990, c. I.8.

Effective April 30, 2007, Ontario legislation broadened the definition of title insurance. Schedule 1 (Classes of Insurance and Definitions for Purposes of the *Insurance Act*) under s. 43 of the *Insurance Act* defines title insurance as insurance against loss or damage caused by:

(a) the existence of a mortgage, charge, lien, encumbrance, servitude or any other restriction on real property;

(b) the existence of a mortgage, charge, lien, pledge, encumbrance or any other restriction on personal property;

(c) a defect in any document that evidences the creation of any restriction referred to in paragraph (a) or (b);

(d) a defect in the title to property; or

(e) any other matter affecting the title to property or affecting the right to the use and enjoyment of property.

Section 139(1) of the *Insurance Act* requires that all title insurance contracts be in writing, that they comply with all requirements prescribed by the Act, and that they expressly limit the liability of the insurer to a sum stated in the contract. Section 139(2) of the *Insurance Act* states that questions arising as to the validity of the title insured or as to the liability of the insurer may be determined by application pursuant to the *Vendors and Purchasers Act*, R.S.O. 1990, c. V.2.

Ontario legislation requires that all title insurance policies require a certificate of title to the property from an independent Ontario lawyer as a condition for issuing the policy. Section 1 of O. Reg. 69/07 of the *Insurance Act* states the following:

> A licence issued to an insurer to undertake title insurance in Ontario is subject to the limitation and condition that no policy of title insurance shall be issued unless the insurer has first obtained a concurrent certificate of title to the property to be insured from a solicitor then entitled to practise in Ontario and who is not at that time in the employ of the insurer.

There has been ongoing advocacy over the last two decades by some title insurers to revoke the requirement of a certificate of title from a solicitor not in the employ of the insurer.

TITLE INSURANCE PRACTICE GUIDELINES

Both the LSUC's *Rules of Professional Conduct* and the *Residential Real Estate Transactions Practice Guidelines* address the use of title insurance in a real estate transaction.

Rules of Professional Conduct

Rules 2.02 and 5.01 of the LSUC's *Rules of Professional Conduct* set out the roles and the responsibilities of lawyers and law clerks regarding the use of title insurance in real estate conveyancing. Rule 2.02 requires lawyers to advise clients as to the role and the advantages and disadvantages of title insurance in all real estate transactions. Lawyers and law clerks must be well-versed in the aspects of any title insurance product and must have taken any training that may be necessary in order to acquire that knowledge before recommending the product to a client:

> A lawyer shall assess all reasonable options to assure title when advising a client about a real estate conveyance and shall advise the client that title insurance is not mandatory and is not the only option available to protect the client's interests in a real estate transaction.
>
> (Rule 2.02(10))

> A lawyer should advise the client of the options available to protect the client's interests and minimize the client's risks in a real estate transaction. The lawyer should be cognizant of when title insurance may be an appropriate option. Although title insurance is intended to protect the client against title risks, it is not a substitute for a lawyer's services in a real estate transaction.
>
> The lawyer should be knowledgeable about title insurance and discuss with the client the advantages, conditions, and limitations of the various options and coverages generally available to the client through title insurance. Before recommending a specific title insurance product, the lawyer should be knowledgeable about the product and take such training as may be necessary in order to acquire the knowledge.
>
> (Rule 2.02 (10), Commentary)

Lawyers and law clerks are not permitted to receive any compensation, whether directly or indirectly, from a title insurer, agent, or intermediary for recommending a specific title insurance product to his or her client. In addition, lawyers and law clerks must disclose to the client that they will receive no commission or fee from any insurer, agent, or intermediary with respect to any title insurance coverage. An insurer may provide a modest policy administration/application fee to the solicitor. The solicitor must inform the client of this fee and may choose to retain the fee or set-off the fee into the client's bill:

The fiduciary relationship between lawyer and client requires full disclosure in all financial dealings between them and prohibits the acceptance of any hidden fees by the lawyer, including the lawyer's law firm, any employee or associate of the firm, or any related entity.

(Rule 2.02(12), Commentary)

Rule 2.02(13) requires that a lawyer or a law clerk must fully disclose the relationship between the legal profession, the LSUC, and LawPRO when discussing the bar-related TitlePLUS insurance with the client.

A non-lawyer is prohibited from giving legal opinions regarding insurance coverage being obtained. Lawyers must supervise staff who inform and advise clients on title insurance options and premiums. Rule 5.01(5) states that law clerks and non-lawyers must not give legal opinions regarding insurance coverage, and, in addition, lawyers must supervise law clerks and non-lawyers when dealing with title insurance in the following situations:

- providing advice to the client concerning any insurance, including title insurance;
- presenting insurance options or information regarding premiums to the client; and
- recommending one insurance product over another.

Section 426 of the *Criminal Code*, R.S.C. 1985, c. C-46 deals with the illegality of accepting secret commissions. A lawyer who arranges title insurance on behalf of a purchaser and who receives a commission from a title insurer of which the purchaser is unaware may have violated the secret commission prohibition under the *Criminal Code*.

Numerous resources are available to lawyers for informing themselves and their clients about the potential benefits of title insurance. The Canadian Bar Association (located in Ontario), in cooperation with the LSUC, offers a brochure for members' clients entitled *Working with a Lawyer When You Buy Your Home*, which explains the role of title insurance in a real estate transaction.

Private title insurance companies provide a variety of print, video, and web-based educational materials for lawyers, financial institutions, and purchasers about the concepts of coverage and risk relating to title insurance. The bar-related product TitlePLUS, sponsored by LawPRO, provides educational videos for lawyers and clients as well as brochures. Both private insurers and TitlePLUS offer training seminars and support to the legal profession.

Residential Real Estate Transactions Practice Guidelines

Guideline 1 of the LSUC's *Residential Real Estate Transactions Practice Guidelines* (concerning the client/lawyer relationship) and Guideline 2 (on due diligence) both directly address the use of title insurance in the residential real estate transaction. Guideline 1 provides that lawyers must advise clients of the "options available to assure title in order to protect the client's interests and minimize the client's risk". This includes title insurance and reinforces the requirements set out in subrules 2.02(10)–2.02(13). The Guidelines contain the following title and off-title search related requirements:

- If the client selects title insurance, the lawyer should advise the client about the searches that the lawyer will not be performing and the type of information that these searches would reveal about the property such as zoning, encroachments or survey issues.
- Where title insurance is not being used, the lawyer should advise the client about the post closing protections provided by title insurance which the client is not receiving (e.g. regarding post-closing encroachments onto the property and fraud).
- Where title insurance is being used, the lawyer should communicate with the client to determine whether the client has any adverse knowledge about the property that could give rise to the insurer relying on the "knowledge" exclusion if the matter is not disclosed and "insured over" pre-closing.

Prior to closing, the lawyer should review the state of the title, including the coverage that will be available under the client's title insurance policy including but not limited to matters such as subdivision/development agreements, easements and restrictive covenants, whether the client has any adverse knowledge about the property that could give rise to the insurer relying on the "knowledge" exclusion if the matter is not disclosed and "insured over", and other title-related matters that might affect the client's rights and obligations under the agreement of purchase and sale and expectations concerning title.

Guideline 1 also provides that the lawyer's reporting letter should contain one of the following:

- the lawyer's legal opinion on title and the exceptions to which the opinion is subject if title insurance is not being used;
- if title insurance is not being used, advice on the search inquiries conducted and responses received including the status of zoning and building searches, tax account and utility status and other off-title title search inquiries;
- if title insurance is being used, information regarding the title insurance coverage obtained and in a transaction where title insurance has been used to assure title, the reporting letter to the client should not opine on title but should include the title insurance policy issued in favour of the client.

The Due Diligence Guideline (Guideline 2) requires lawyers to decide in consultation with the client which title and off-title searches to complete based on:

- due regard for the terms of the client's contractual rights and obligations;
- time and cost of conducting title and off-title searches;
- availability/utility of title insurance;
- nature of the property;

- which searches relevant to the particular transaction are not covered by title insurance and whether to make appropriate searches or obtain waivers; and
- the inter-related nature and risks of deciding which searches to complete, allowing requisition dates to pass, timing of receiving a title insurance binder, or commitment for insure over requests for adverse circumstances.

The Due Diligence Guideline also requires the title insurance policy to provide express coverage for any adverse registrations which occur between releasing the closing proceeds and registration of the title document(s). This is often referred to as Gap coverage. Gap coverage is also available for escrow closings. In addition, lawyers should confirm that the draft (binder/commitment) and final policy contain:

- correct insured's name;
- correct legal description;
- off-site lands that should be included in the description, so that easements or rights-of-way located on other properties, but benefitting the subject property, and encroachments from the subject property onto other lands, will be covered;
- coverage exclusions;
- endorsements; and
- other title matters specific to the policy.

Lawyers should warn clients about title issues, not apparent from the insurance commitment such as standard pre-printed exceptions, for example, environmental risks or Aboriginal rights, title, or treaty rights or problems under the terms of the agreement of purchase and sale. Lawyers should issue title insurance policies as soon as possible after closing. The draft policy or binder/commitment should be reconciled with the issued policy.

The *Residential Real Estate Transaction Practice Guidelines* do not address commercial real estate transactions; however, they may provide a starting point by analogy for commercial transactions despite the custom nature of commercial transaction and commercial policy search requirements.

TITLE INSURANCE

Title insurance policies provide coverage for pre-closing and post-closing fraud. Title insurance provides coverage against loss or damage arising from a title defect covered under the policy, including matters relating to surveys and the legal use of property. Title insurance protects buyers and lenders from title problems related to ownership and the future marketability of the property. Title insurance does not cover risks such as environmental contamination, be it mold or contaminated soil, Aboriginal claims, or water quality.

Title insurance does not insure condition or functionality: it insures title. This concept is frequently misunderstood by the public. For example, title insurance does not cover termite infestation, malfunctioning septic systems, leaky roofs, basements, or foundations. However, if prior to the purchase, a work order or demolition order on title or on record with a public authority was missed by the lawyer, then the missed work order relates to title and may be covered.

TYPES OF TITLE INSURANCE POLICIES

Title insurance policies come in the following categories and subcategories.

Residential

- residential owner policy;
- residential lender policy;
- combined owner/lender policy (TitlePLUS);
- existing owner policy;
- refinance policy; and
- condominium coverage.

Commercial

- commercial owner policy:
  - over a stated coverage amount;
  - under a stated coverage amount;
- commercial lender policy; and
- leasehold policy.

Other

Depending on the insurer, policy endorsements vary for specific types of properties, such as farms or commercial condominiums.

Residential policies usually cover properties with one to six residential units; these policies have standardized terms. Commercial policies start with very basic coverage and then require custom underwriting and negotiated additional endorsements. Commercial policies vary broadly depending on the circumstances and the client preferences. Insurers provide different endorsements and require different searches for lenders compared to owners. Leasehold policies are fact-specific; for example, a ground lease is very different from a shopping centre lease or a long-term commercial lease for a multi-sector, collaborative, research park. The type of policy determines the required searches, the coverages, the endorsements, the exclusions, and the terms of the policy contract generally. Custom endorsements can be negotiated in both residential and commercial policies. Higher risk properties, such as lodging houses, properties that have undergone major renovations, or properties used in the past as grow-ops or drug manufacturing labs, require additional inquiries and receive additional coverage restrictions. Policy coverage and search requirements change regularly and differ among title insurers. Lawyers need to review the details on any individual policy in terms of both coverage and search requirements. As with any insurance policy, the devil is in the details. The combination of title insurance and real estate law is an emerging area of legal specialty.

TITLE INSURANCE POLICY COVERAGE

A title insurance policy is an agreement to indemnify a specific owner(s) of a specific parcel of land for specified, actual losses resulting from title risks covered by the policy up to the policy amount including costs, legal fees, and expenses. The policy coverage is limited by listed exclusions, exceptions, and conditions, and stipulations and may include coverage for specified endorsements. The policy coverage includes risks as of the policy date and does not generally include any risks or events that arise after the policy date unless they are specifically included in the policy. However, policies usually cover certain post-policy events, such as fraud and defence of title; for example, a neighbour builds a deck that encroaches onto the insured property after the policy date. The policy is effective as long as the named insured or his or her spouse, children, heirs, trustees or beneficiaries own the property. Title insurance policies are available to owners of land or lenders. Owner and lender policies are usually issued as separate policies; however, TitlePLUS offers a combined policy when dealing with both the purchase and the mortgage on the same piece of land. When an insured suffers a loss, the insurer may choose whether to correct the title defect or compensate the insured for the loss.

Most title insurance policies contain the following standard terms, although some insurers have simplified policy language by focusing on coverage and exclusions rather than coverage, exclusions, and exceptions to exclusions:

- owner's coverage statement;
- insurance particulars;
- covered title risks;
- insurer's duty to defend (defence coverage);
- exclusions;
- exceptions (often in schedules);
- conditions; and
- endorsements and additional coverages.

OWNER'S POLICY COVERAGE

Owner policies offer defence of title coverage as well as coverage for title defects and fraud. In some circumstances, a property owner may have to demonstrate an actual financial loss before he or she may receive compensation under a title insurance policy. Policy exclusions, unpleasant surprises, loss of expected enjoyment of land, and emotional harm are not included in the coverage. On occasion, insurers may require the commencement of legal action before settling and paying out a claim.

From a "buyer beware" perspective, only a lawyer's opinion on title combined with a surveyor's real property report can disclose the quality and extent of title before a purchaser has transferred funds and completed the purchase. The prudent purchaser who wishes to make a fully informed decision on the purchase of a home must choose whether to purchase a survey or a title insurance policy or both. Title insurance may act as a supplement or as an alternative to the lawyer's inquiries and opinion and a surveyor's real property report. It is important to remember that a lawyer's opinion on title combined with a surveyor's real property report discloses marketable title, whereas a title insurance policy provides financial compensation for insurable title up to the face amount of the policy following an actual financial loss.

LENDER'S POLICY COVERAGE

The title insurance lender's policy and premium remain in effect as long as the mortgage remains on title. It usually covers assignees and renewals. As with other mortgage fees, the borrower is responsible for the payment of title insurance premiums. A mortgage lender's policy provides coverage when, following a default on a loan, a property is foreclosed or sold and the lender is unable to sell the property for the full amount, including fees owing under the mortgage because of a title defect such as a *Planning Act*, R.S.O. 1990, c. P.13 violation. Mortgage lenders are insured for title-related risks and solicitor error.

INSURANCE PARTICULARS

Policies include a schedule setting out the insurance particulars of an individual policy, such as policy name and number; issue date; name of insured(s); description of land; policy amount; premium; title interest insured; lawyer particulars and customized exclusions; exceptions; conditions; and endorsements added to the policy.

COVERED TITLE RISKS

Title insurance policies cover or exclude different risks depending on whether the policy relates to residential, commercial, condominium, rural property, leasehold, residential rental or farm properties, or whether the insured is a lender or a purchaser. As well, different insurers, be they private or bar-related, offer varied coverage. As with any insurance contract, it is essential to read it carefully, especially the fine print describing insured risks, exclusions, exceptions, and endorsements. Generally, title insurance policies may protect against categories of loss caused by the following risks:

- defects in title such as liens, executions, adverse claims, encroachments, unregistered easements, mortgages and other encumbrances, and conflicting claims;
- unmarketability of title in general;
- tax, water, hydro, and gas arrears;
- executions against prior owners;
- corporate status certificates and escheat;
- condominium status certificates (certificate required on purchase);
- septic system violations (work orders);
- compliance risks, such as work orders, non-conforming uses related to zoning, and restrictive covenants;
- compliance risks, related to building and zoning work orders, by-laws, and permits;
- hydro and fire department work orders;
- subdivision and development agreement compliance;
- conservation authority compliance;
- conservation easement compliance;
- unregistered hydro easements;
- hydro corridor building violations and entrance permits;
- forced removal of structures on insured property;
- lack of legal access to the property;
- fraud, forgery, impersonation, duress, mental incompetence, and incapacity;
- authenticity of registered title documents;
- unenforceability of the insured mortgage;
- coverage for mortgage assignability;
- legal services, including lawyer error, lawyer fraud, lawyer death, disbarment, and retirement;
- defence of title;
- defects that would have been revealed by a new survey;
- adverse matters that would have been revealed by a survey, and survey errors;
- contraventions arising out of the *Planning Act*;
- errors in the public record;
- post-closing alterations by mortgagor (lender's policy);
- known defects or risks disclosed to the insurer and covered in the policy;
- gap coverage in lender's policy (when registration of mortgage and advance of mortgage proceeds do not occur at the same time because document certified after received by registration system); and
- re-advances up to original amount of a fluctuating balance mortgage (lender's policy).

Title insurance protection continues as long as the insured retains his or her interest in the insured property. The policy coverage extends to spouses, heirs, and beneficiaries under a trust or successor trustees.

COMPENSATION UNDER TITLE INSURANCE POLICIES

Most title insurance policies provide for the following forms of compensation:

- payment of the lesser of the insured's actual loss or the policy amount in force when the claim is made;
- inflation coverage of up to a contractual maximum set out in the policy (the policy amount may increase based on an increase in the fair market value up to a maximum of twice the original policy amount);
- defence costs including legal fees and other related expenses;
- interim costs including legal fees and related expenses such as a survey; and
- alternative accommodation.

EXCLUSIONS TO COVERAGE UNDER TITLE INSURANCE POLICIES

Title insurers will not assume certain risks that are difficult to anticipate or quantify. These standard exemptions from coverage are called exclusions and are similar to the standard exceptions found in a solicitor's opinion on title. Insurers set out standard exclusions from coverage in the main section of the policy. Exclusions to coverage usually relate to risks that do not appear on the registered title or in public records. The following ownership related risks are routinely excluded in residential title insurance policies:

- condition and functionality;
- title risks that arise or affect the title to the land after the policy date, other than fraud, defence of title, or risks contained in the policy;
- defects disclosed by the examination of title which the insured had accepted at the time the policy was issued;
- any title risk created, accepted, or agreed to by the insured (for example, in the agreement of purchase and sale);
- post-closing changes in government regulation (losses which arise from the exercise of governmental power and the existence or violation of any law, by-law, code, or government regulation, including building and zoning by-laws except for violations which appear in the public records at the policy date);
- the existence of any dangerous or hazardous substance (environmental hazards) on the land, unless express notice of it appears on registered title;
- water potability or quantity;
- legality of rents;
- fire retrofit compliance such as insufficient smoke alarms or fire barriers (multi-unit properties);
- costs of moving fences or boundary walls;
- chattels;

- post-closing expropriations;
- any inability to use the land for other than a single family residential dwelling (the present use can be continued up to use as a six-plex);
- future use should the purchaser change the use of the land or undertake any Aboriginal land claims;
- failure to pay value for the title such as a gift;
- losses created, permitted, agreed to, or resulting from the conduct or collusion of the insured;
- losses resulting from failure to report a claim on a timely basis;
- misrepresentations by the vendor;
- risks known to the insured prior to closing;
- listed exclusions, specific to the property policy;
- failure to close;
- change of use in adjoining lands and amenities (landfill or Walmart built next door); and
- risks that result in no loss.

EXCEPTIONS TO COVERAGE UNDER TITLE INSURANCE POLICIES

Exceptions to coverage are property-specific in nature and are set out in a separate schedule to the policy. They deal with a specific property interest, revealed in the agreement of purchase and sale, or by the title and off-title searches, which affects the ownership of the property being insured. Exceptions are drafted in response to the review of the agreement of purchase and sale and the results of title and related searches completed on the property by the insured's lawyer. Listed exceptions relate directly to the extent and quality of the title to the individual property and will vary from property to property and from insurer to insurer. Existing liens, notices of conditional sales contracts, tax arrears, outstanding mortgages being assumed, easements, leases, encroachments, deficiencies in set-back requirements, non-compliance with restrictive covenants, and development agreements are routinely excepted in most residential title insurance policies. When a title search reveals a problem on title, such as an old, paid-off mortgage or lien for which a required discharge was never registered, an insurer will assess the risk and may agree to cover over the specific exception by an endorsement or an affirmative assurance.

ENDORSEMENTS AND AFFIRMATIVE ASSURANCES

Title insurers will often offer additional protection beyond the basic coverage. They may also offer coverage for a disclosed title deficiency depending on the nature of the deficiency and the risk. The insurer may offer coverage at no additional charge or require an individually assessed additional premium. This form of coverage is called an endorsement. Title insurance policies for residential properties offer standardized coverage, although commercial properties usually offer skeletal coverage subject to additional, custom endorsements. The insured's lawyer is responsible for advising which endorsements may be advisable for a particular title. An insurer may investigate and evaluate a disclosed risk revealed by the title and off-title inquiries, such as an encroachment onto a road allowance. The insurer may then set an individual premium and insure (cover over) the disclosed, known title defect by way of an endorsement or an affirmative assurance.

Insurers offer standard endorsement packages for different types of land and circumstances, such as multi-family dwelling, commercial, condominium, rural, septic system, leasehold, residential rental, farm, and vacant land (future use/improvement) properties. There are also standard endorsements used by specific lender institutions.

RISKS AND BENEFITS OF TITLE INSURANCE

Title insurance insures risks that are not covered by a lawyer's opinion on title or a surveyor's real property report; for example, fraud, forgery, false impersonation, errors appearing in the public record, missing heirs or mental incompetence of the transferor. Title insurance may provide an alternative remedy for title problems, such as minor encroachments and small set-back deficiencies that are often too costly or time-consuming to resolve in a conventional manner. For example, where land boundaries and survey evidence are in dispute, the bank may require title insurance as a condition of advancing funds on a mortgage. With policies for commercial properties, the title insurer may choose to assess the declared risk, provide coverage by way of an endorsement, and set an appropriate premium. Thus, a known title problem that would not otherwise be acceptable to a purchaser or a mortgagee, once covered by insurance, allows the deal to close on time and avoid costly litigation. Title insurers are particularly helpful at solving timing problems and unavoidable delays in a transaction such as the inability to register a discharge of a private mortgage prior to closing.

Title insurance provides a form of no-fault financial compensation for title problems. As a result, an insured may avoid expensive difficult lawsuits in negligence or contract against the lawyer, the Land Titles Assurance Fund, prior owners and persons making competing claims on land. In addition, title insurance may reduce the number of claims against lawyers and the Land Titles Assurance Fund. As of January 1998, when both the purchaser and lender obtain coverage, the LSUC transaction levy (a high-risk surcharge on residential real estate transactions) is waived.

Title insurance may reduce the cost of disbursements in purchase and loan transactions and save the client money by reducing the number of costly low-risk title and off-title searches and eliminating the cost of a new survey. Title insurance may reduce the cost of legal work on mortgage refinancing, and reduce mortgage funding delays. Title insurance offers broader protection than a lawyer's opinion on title combined with reduced risk of malpractice claims. Title insurance saves time by reducing the number of costly low-risk title and off-title searches, although it requires some additional documentation and increased time spent with the client. Title insurance represents the most recent layer to be added to the already overly complex field of real estate conveyancing.

Simple reliance on title insurance as protection against financial loss and a narrowed focus on the bottom line can interfere with a purchaser's awareness of the personal and financial values of being fully informed on all matters relating to land ownership and enjoyment. Let the buyer beware of the consequences of substituting financial compensation, available only for actual loss, for actual knowledge of all matters affecting property ownership.

Title insurance offers service alternatives to lenders, particularly financial institutions, and to owners of land. The effects of Rule 2.02(10) and the increased incidence of land and mortgage related fraud have steadily increased the public's awareness of and demand for title insurance.

New developments in title insurance, the automation of the land records, and the implementation of mandatory electronic land registration present unparalleled change and challenges for professionals involved in the real estate conveyancing field. Title searching will remain an essential step in the purchase transaction, the loan transaction, the completion of a survey, and the placement of a title insurance policy.

TITLE INSURANCE AS BACK-UP FOR LAWYERS' E&OE COVERAGE

Title insurance may provide coverage when a lawyer's E&OE coverage has expired due to death, retirement, disbarment, or simply the expiry of the policy term. The title deficiency may be discovered after both the lawyer and the lawyer's errors and omissions excepted (E&OE) policy have ceased to exist. A retired lawyer's run-off coverage and the lawyer's personal resources may not be adequate to cover the claim. In addition, it is possible for a lawyer to void the E&OE policy by his or her actions.

TITLE INSURANCE SEARCH REQUIREMENTS

Title insurer search requirements are not the same as legal title search requirements. The risks, costs, and potential consequences are different. They are simply a requirement for obtaining title insurance. Title insurance search requirements address title, off-title, and survey and extent of property inquiries. Guideline 2 of the *Residential Real Estate Transaction Practice Guidelines* requires that the lawyer determine in consultation with the client which title and off-title searches will be completed in view of the nature of the property, the circumstances of the transaction, the terms of the agreement of purchase and sale, the expectations of the client, and the extent of the risk of not conducting an inquiry. The lawyer must advise the clients of the difference between insurer search requirements and legal search requirements, the difference in risks, and the differences in available remedies. Client acknowledgements and waivers must be obtained and should reflect and document the expectations and the consequences of risks assumed by decisions not to complete searches such as relying only on title insurer search requirements. Specifically, the lawyer must caution the client about the risks associated with not completing searches prior to the requisition date and closing dates and policy exclusions and exemptions. Earlier chapters, particularly the chapter about off-title inquiries, address the risks and consequences associated with choices concerning search requirements. Decisions that determine which searches will be made may have a profound impact on rights, obligations, and remedies associated with anticipatory breach of contract, tender, title insurance claims, and subsequent litigation based on breach of contract and solicitor negligence. Be aware that recent case law indicates that clients have the right to choose whether to make a title insurance claim or sue the lawyer in negligence.

Title insurer search requirements are competitive and substantially similar between insurers; however, they are not identical. Title insurer search requirements are based on economic efficiency, risk management, claims experience, and changes in law and practice. Insurer requirements are constantly adapting to current risks as demonstrated by recent additional search requirements for properties that are known to have been previously used in the production of illegal substances (grow-ops). Title insurer search requirements are different for residential properties (usually restricted to one to six units), existing homeowner residential properties, and commercial properties. Search requirements may be customized depending on risks associated with specific properties. As well, search requirements are usually different for owner policies compared to loan or refinance policies. Requirements vary from province to province. Depending on search results, properties may be identified for underwriter review and be required to meet custom additional search requirements.

Search Requirements Based on the Nature of Title and the Land Registration System

Changes in law result in changes in insurer search requirements. Search requirements vary depending on the nature of the title and the registration system. For example, there are different requirements depending on whether the search is a Registry including Registry Parcelized Day Forward, a Land Titles Absolute, a Land Titles Conversion Qualified, a condominium, or a leasehold title. Example requirements are dealt with in detail in earlier chapters on searching in specific registration systems. They are also reproduced at the end of this chapter in the figures.

Fraud Risk Identification Inquiries

In addition, title insurers usually require fraud screening inquiries and the completion of standard fraud risk identification questions within all policy applications. These questions correspond closely to the LSUC's practice guidelines, as well as fraud prevention advisories and Ministry fraud prevention recommendations. Insurer fraud screening inquiries are a minimum screening standard. The LSUC recommends more intensive fraud prevention inquiry practices in areas such as powers of attorney. An example of insurer standard fraud screening questions within the policy application is included at the end of Chapter 17.

Fraud is continually evolving and so are risk identification strategies and screening inquiries. The following questions are examples of fraud identification inquiries found in Stewart Title's residential policy applications:

- Will you be obtaining and reviewing prior to closing a Canadian government-issued ID for your purchaser/borrower client and retaining a legible copy in your files?
- Have there been amendments with respect to the purchase price and/or deposits after the date of signing the agreement of purchase and sale (*i.e.*, after the agreement of purchase and sale is firm)?
- Was any portion of the deposit paid directly to the vendor? (It's OK if it was paid directly to a lawyer in trust or to the realtor in trust — answer "No" in this case.)
- Have there been any transfers or mortgage discharges registered in the last six months? Do the transfers/mortgage discharges relate to:
  - a discharge of prior vendor's mortgage;
  - estate conveyance;
  - inter-family transfer where a party was added to title;
  - payment to a spouse under a separation agreement/divorce settlement where your firm acted for one of the spouse in the matrimonial matter;
  - Other (please provide details of the transfer(s) and/or mortgage discharge(s) that have occurred in the last six months).
- Has another title insurer refused to issue a policy of title insurance in respect to this transaction?
- Is a power of attorney being used in this transaction?

Title Insurance Changes the Title Search

When title insurance is obtained in a real estate transaction, both the title search and the off-title searches are affected. Insurer search requirements provide an after-the-fact indemnity alternative to completing costly, low-risk title inquiries. Insurer requirements also provide an indemnity back-up for title inquiries which cannot be completed within contractual timelines and which are subject to the accuracy and liability disclaimers that accompany most government search responses today. For example, title insurers do not require searches for executions against prior owners or the condominium corporation, for corporate escheats and limited partnerships, or for subdivision/development compliance. It is essential to determine for the particular transaction exactly which title searches, execution searches, corporate profile reports, off-title searches, and searches arising from the title search are required by the title insurer.

Title insurers vary in their search requirements, particularly depending on the nature of the transaction. For example, a refinance transaction may require only a subsearch from the last arm's length deed, whereas a purchase in Registry requires a full 40-year search including abutting land searches. LawPRO's TitlePLUS summary of search requirements and Stewart Title's residential, existing owner, and commercial real estate search requirements are included at the end of this chapter as examples of insurer search requirements.

DIFFERING SEARCH REQUIREMENTS AS RISK MANAGEMENT TOOLS

Insurer search requirements, legal title investigation requirements, and current surveyors' real property reports are basic tools used by the lawyer/conveyancer to convey an estate in land and contractual protections that match the transferee's expectations and or legal rights. No one tool in a tool box, no matter how effective, can build a house; no one method of search inquiry can assure the identification and conveyance of the greatest and least encumbered estate in land. A lawyer's approach to title inquiry and choice of search requirements is not a simple either/or choice. Title insurance protects a client after closing; it does not protect a client or lawyer from the risk of litigation when the transaction does not close and it does not protect a client from potentially catastrophic excluded risks such as environmental contamination and Aboriginal claims.

TITLE INSURERS IN CANADA

Title insurers offer title insurance policy coverage for owners and lenders for title and legal services in almost all types of real estate transactions, including residential, residential rental, residential multi-unit, existing owner, commercial, farm, condominium, and leasehold real estate transactions. Policies may be obtained by written request, by phone, or by fax, and are for the most part accessed through online insurer Internet-based services or through the online features in real estate conveyancing, document processing, and file management commercial software programs, such as Stewart Title's LegalSTEPS and STEPSONLINE, Teranet's The Conveyancer, and LawyerDoneDeal and RealtiPLUSWeb associated with TitlePLUS and LawPRO. Today, almost all title insurance policy applications are submitted, pre-approved, processed, and issued online.

The following title insurers are licensed to offer title insurance products in Ontario:

1. The Lawyers' Professional Indemnity Company (also known as LawPRO) offers bar-related TitlePLUS;

2. Stewart Title Guaranty Company works collaboratively with Ontario lawyers through its Examining Counsel Program;

3. First American Title Insurance Company;

4. FCT Insurance Company Limited (also referred to as First Canadian Title Insurance Company);

5. Chicago Title Insurance Company; and

6. Travelers Guarantee Company of Canada.

BAR-RELATED INSURANCE/LAWPRO'S TITLEPLUS

TitlePLUS is a Canadian, bar-related title insurance product combined with a solicitor's legal services policy sponsored by LawPRO. Lawyers must disclose to clients the relationship between TitlePLUS and the Law Society and Law-PRO. The TitlePLUS policy covers title problems as well as legal services problems and states that a lawyer will not be liable for costs, expenses, or legal fees incurred in connection with any claim made under the TitlePLUS policy. Law-PRO also waives all rights of subrogation against the lawyer who gave the opinion on title except for intentional acts or omissions, gross negligence, and fraudulent acts. Legal services related issues would include advice relating to subjects such as how to take title, income, land transfer, HST taxes, the advisability of completing certain off-title inquiries, and agreements of purchase and sale. By combining title insurance and legal services coverage in one policy, clients avoid the risk of potential conflict between multiple insurers disputing whether a claim falls under the contract-based title insurance policy or the negligence-based errors and omissions policy.

Of particular interest and different from commercial policies is the fact that Ti-tlePLUS generates a combined, single fee, combined owner/lender residential title insurance policy which protects both the purchaser and the mortgagee.

TitlePLUS procedures eliminate the need for many low-risk title and off-title letter inquiries. TitlePLUS provides supplemental insurance for inquiries, such as government search responses that disclaim accuracy and liability. TitlePLUS simplifies previously impractical legal title search requirements and generates significant savings for clients for otherwise routine disbursements. TitlePLUS provides software tools that guide lawyers through the required steps in a residential real estate transaction and the application and issuance of a title insurance policy. TitlePLUS search requirements are included as Figure 18.1 and in Chapter 14.

PRIVATE INSURERS

Private insurers offer commercial and residential policies. Separate policies, involving separate premiums, are issued to owners and lenders. Insurers offer a variety of policy ordering alternatives, including online policy processing software incorporated into document processing and file management software programs.

All policies must be checked for the details of coverage, exclusions, exceptions, and endorsements with respect to the particular property and the particular insurer involved. Although private insurers offer standard policies, they also offer extensive experience in analyzing and insuring diverse title risks in non-standard transactions.

As with TitlePLUS, private insurers provide an after-the-fact indemnity alternative for listed, routine, lower risk title and off-title inquiries and, depending on the circumstances, surveys, in real estate transactions. Title insurance offers an alternative of simplified title inquiry requirements, supplemental coverage for certain inquiries and significant savings for clients.

CLAIMS AND THE ADJUSTMENT PROCESS

Title insurers use a variety of creative solutions to resolve claims despite the fact that they primarily provide after-the-fact indemnity. The insurer by contract retains the right to decide whether to compensate the insured financially, negotiate a settlement with the other side, or defend or prosecute the claim in court; for example, challenging the validity of a construction lien or an easement by prescription. The insurer's decision may be affected by time considerations, economic efficiency, the cooperation of the parties involved, or possibly the desire to set or avoid setting a precedent for future client expectations. Generally, insurers value and offer financial compensation for loss; however, they also frequently defend on behalf of the insured, make court applications, obtain *Planning Act* severances, minor variances and zoning changes, correct registered records, relocate driveways, and from time to time, purchase the property from the insured.

Claims Submission

Claims must be submitted in writing as soon as possible after discovering the claim (for example, within 90 days). Claimants may not attempt to resolve a claim without the knowledge and consent of the insurer. Title claims are often divided into routine common claims and non-routine or custom claims. In Ontario, routine claims are usually settled quickly.

Routine Claims

Claims for tax, water arrears, or arrears of condominium common expenses are examples of routine claims. Claims can be made by letter or claim application form setting out contact information, nature and amount of the claim, a copy of the transfer, the agreement of purchase and sale, the copy of adjustments, the vendor's undertaking to readjust, copy of bill showing arrears prior to policy date, information about special or supplemental assessments, and a consent completed by the insured allowing the insurer to obtain additional information on behalf of the claimant. In the case of common expense arrears, the insurer will also require a copy of the condominium status certificate obtained prior to closing and any other correspondence with the condominium confirming that common expense arrears prior to closing.

Other Claims

Fraud claims, missed executions, undischarged mortgages, encroachments, possessory claims, missed construction liens, *Planning Act* contraventions, and access issues are examples of title insurance claims. These non-routine claims require relevant documentation, additional investigation, and customized solutions.

FACTORS IN CHOOSING A TITLE INSURER

Generally, lawyers become comfortable with the policy, search requirements, policy application process and software, underwriting expertise, and sales and customer service support offered by a particular insurer. As a result, they place client policies with the insurer with whom they are most comfortable.

Nevertheless, as with other types of insurance claims, adjustment practices and experience and specifically the risk and record of coverage denial are critical. In addition, as demonstrated by the financial shift in 2008 and bankruptcy of certain American title companies, financial ratings and stability and particularly the existence of healthy reserves are also of critical importance. The discovery of title claims under a policy may take decades, possibly not until the next transfer. The economic sustainability of an insurer, although difficult to predict, is an important consideration. The Ontario Financial Services Commission and the Superintendent of Insurance publish financial statistics for title insurers.

The risk of coverage denial may be reflected in the consistency of longer term patterns in the ratio of claims paid to premiums earned. Numerous variables can affect the ratios for a particular year. Coverage denial risk is historically much higher in the U.S. than in Canada. Generally, in the past, coverage denial has not been a serious concern in Canada. Nevertheless, experience with insurance practice in general illustrates that adjustment policies and practices can change. It remains to be seen how changed economic circumstances and the fact that title insurance is now fully established in Ontario will affect search and practice requirements, adjustment policy, and rates of claim acceptance or denial. As well, once there has been a determination of claim acceptance or claim denial, insurance defence litigators may utilize all available technical and substantive defences. Financial ratings, reserves, and premiums earned and claims paid ratios may provide comparative, predictive criteria and become increasingly important in insurer selection. In addition, as with other kinds of insurance, sophisticated clients are aware that the vigilance of the risk management practices such as those illustrated by fraud screening questions, search requirements, and lawyer support and review combined with consistent, objective adjustment practices and investigative expertise, provide valuable criteria for insurer selection.

THE ROLE OF TITLE INSURANCE IN REAL ESTATE CONVEYANCING

Title insurance provides a cost-effective alternative for managing risk in mortgage and purchase transactions. Title insurance provides a contractual indemnity for specified risks and defects in title. The title insurer decides how to resolve a claim. The insured has a right to compensation and not to having the defect cured or litigated. The case of *Syvan Developments Ltd. v. Ontario (Ministry of Government Services)*, concerning an application to the Land Titles Assurance Fund, illustrates that title insurance requirements do not replace legal or statutory requirements for due diligence.

> Title insurance may provide financial protection from the consequences of a purchaser's failure to exercise what would otherwise be due diligence and, looked at from the standpoint of the purchaser — and of the purchaser's solicitor — it may, in some circumstances, be a substitute for the acts of diligence that would otherwise be required of a prudent business person, or of a solicitor acting for such person. It does not follow that the existence of the insurance should be considered to affect the meaning and application of section 59(1)(c) and what would otherwise be requirements of due diligence under the section. In my opinion, an act or omission that would otherwise be a neglect or default within the meaning of the provision will not cease to be so if it has been insured against. (*Syvan*, at para. 48)

Figure 18.1

TitlePLUS SEARCH REQUIREMENTS*

TitlePLUS® purchase policies (up to $2 million) are available for these types of properties[2]:
- new houses and condominiums;
- resale houses and condominiums;
- secondary homes and cottages;
- residential rental (up to 4 units);
- rural;
- farms[3];
- leaseholds[3]; and
- vacant land[4] intended for residential purposes.

Cost savings and peace of mind for you and your clients:
- a TitlePLUS purchase policy = title insurance PLUS legal services coverage[5];
- eliminates the need for up-to-date surveys on most properties: A saving of $600 or more; and
- reduces disbursement costs on many closings by eliminating certain searches[6].

Survey coverage will be provided for all properties in Land Titles (Absolute, Conversion Qualified or Plus); for properties in Registry, survey coverage will be provided when:
- the property is the whole of a lot on a registered plan of subdivision (see below for definition); or
- there is an existing survey which has been reviewed by the purchaser for accuracy or the vendor is providing a statutory declaration commenting on its accuracy; or
- declarations of possession for a 10-year period are available; or
- a surveyor's inspection report is prepared by an Ontario Land Surveyor.

For TitlePLUS purposes, a "whole of a lot on a registered plan of subdivision" includes a property:
- consisting of two or more whole lots on a registered plan of subdivision; or
- consisting of part of a lot on a registered plan of subdivision, where there was a part-lot control exemption by-law registered to allow the initial conveyances in the subdivision; or
- which was the subject of a consent proceeding for severance purposes (either as the parcel to be conveyed or the remaining parcel), provided that the severance occurred in accordance with an up-to-date Reference Plan and any necessary conditions attached to the approval were satisfied; or
- which was the whole of a lot on a registered plan prior to an expropriation, road widening or road closing, resulting in the removal or addition of a part lot.

TitlePLUS policies are also available for the following:
- mortgage-only;
- current owners (OwnerEXPRESS®); and
- new homes enrolled in the TitlePLUS New Home Program.

For information on any of our policy types, visit titleplus.ca or call the TitlePLUS Customer Service Centre.

titleplus.ca   titleplus.lawyerdonedeal.com   1-800-410-1013

---

[1] The TitlePLUS policy is underwritten by Lawyers' Professional Indemnity Company (LawPRO). Contact LawPRO for brokers in Manitoba, Alberta and Québec.
[3] Please refer to the policy for full details, including actual terms and conditions. Different search requirements apply to transactions over $1 million, please call us for details.

[2] Please call the TitlePLUS Customer Service Centre for assistance with these types of properties.
[4] Some restrictions may apply.
[5] Excluding OwnerEXPRESS policies and Québec policies.
[6] See over for Summary of Searches.

© 2009 Lawyers' Professional Indemnity Company
® Registered trademark of Lawyers' Professional Indemnity Company.

 Printed on recycled paper. This product can be recycled.

Figure 18.1 (cont'd)

Title**PLUS** Summary of Searches for Residential Purchase Transactions

TYPE OF SEARCH	WHERE REQUIRED	COMMENTS
TITLE SEARCH		
Subject Property	Always	Include deleted instruments in automated title search. Note date of last transfer to insert in TitlePLUS application. If last transfer within past 2 years, note whether transfer at arm's length and if so, insert date and consideration shown in TitlePLUS application. If mortgage discharge registered within last 6 months, indicate in TitlePLUS application.
Servient Tenement re: Easement (if any)	Always	If Registry, confirm that registered title of servient property discloses existence of easement throughout 40 year period or since creation (whichever is shorter). If Land Titles, confirm easement in description for servient property.
Abutting Properties	Sometimes	Where necessary to ascertain subdivision control compliance.
EXECUTION SEARCHES		
Vendor	Always	
Prior Owners	Never	
Condominium Corporation	Never	
Purchaser + Guarantor of Mortgage (if any)	Sometimes	If granting mortgage (other than vendor take-back). Search against guarantor not required if expressly waived by lender.
OFF-TITLE SEARCHES		
Realty Tax and Local Improvements	Always	Where provided, verbal responses or printouts of the municipality's tax records for the property are acceptable; where municipality will **not** provide verbal responses or printouts, any of the following are acceptable: (a) receipted tax bill; (b) confirmation that the prior lender has been paying the taxes; or (c) an unqualified statutory declaration from the vendor that all prior years' taxes have been paid, charges for local improvements (if any) are paid up-to-date and the status for the current year is accurately set out in the Statement of Adjustments; PLUS an undertaking to readjust from the vendor. Where realty taxes for a new house or condo have not yet been separately assessed, you may obtain on closing the builder's undertaking to readjust. For resale of recently constructed houses and condominiums, see titleplus.lawyerdonedeal.com for instructions.
Personal Property Security Act	Never	
Hydro and Gas Arrears	Never	
Water and Sewage Arrears	Sometimes	Need not be done if: (a) included in common expenses for condo; (b) purchaser already in possession and previously paying; (c) in area where water supplier (public or private) has published policy of not pursuing purchaser for arrears; or (d) new home and receiving undertaking to readjust/pay any amounts owing from vendor. The following inquiries are acceptable: (a) verbal responses from suppliers; (b) the most recent bill if it shows that previous bills were paid; or (c) an unqualified Statutory Declaration by the vendor that all such charges have been paid to date, and that the status of payments is accurately set out in the Statement of Adjustments.
Arrears of Charges for Equipment Purchased/Rented from Utility Supplier	Sometimes	Need only be done where: (a) notice of the utility supplier's interest is registered on title; or (b) lawyer or client knows there is equipment which was purchased from utility supplier and is not fully paid for, or is rented.
Technical Standards and Safety Authority (TSSA) (re: registration of underground oil tanks)	Sometimes	Where property heated by oil from an underground oil tank or where the lawyer is otherwise aware that there is an underground oil tank on the property. A verbal response is sufficient.
Zoning	Sometimes	Where: (a) you have reason to believe that year-round occupancy may not be permitted; or (b) where multi-unit property.
Building Department Work Orders	Sometimes	Need not be done where: (a) new home; (b) condo; (c) whole of a lot on a registered plan (see over for definition); (d) vendor giving unqualified warranty to survive closing that there are no work orders; or (e) home inspection done and a copy given to lawyer. Where provided, verbal responses are acceptable.
Electrical Work Orders and Compliance, and Fire Dept. Work Orders and Compliance including Retrofit	Sometimes	Where multi-unit property.
Health Department/Certificate of Approval/Use Permit/ Municipal Approval	Sometimes	Where private septic system and Certificate of Approval and Use Permit or municipal approval is not available from vendor. No specific search for work orders on septic system is required, but any information received must be entered in application.
Potability Certificate	Sometimes	Where private water system – client may obtain and deliver.
Unregistered Hydro Easements, Conservation Authority, Controlled/Highway Access	Sometimes	Never required for whole of a lot on a registered plan (see over for definition) or condo; otherwise, required where risk factors apply.
Waterfront Inquiries	Sometimes	Where property fronts on lake or river (e.g., shoreline road allowance, waterbed issues, accretion, etc.).
TARION, Occupancy Approval	Sometimes	Where new home.
Rent Control	Sometimes	Where purchaser wants opinion on legality of rents re: tenancies being assumed.
SEARCHES ARISING FROM TITLE SEARCH		
Corporate Escheats/Limited Partnership	Never	
Subdivision/Development Compliance (as defined)	Never	A "Subdivision/Development Agreement" for TitlePLUS purposes is defined as follows: (a) agreement with a government, government-related body/agency (e.g., school board), or a utility company; (b) imposes the primary obligation on the developer; and (c) requires the developer to post security. Call us or visit titleplus.lawyerdonedeal.com for additional details.
Condo Status Certificate	Sometimes	Where condo or "POTL" with interest in common element condo, obtain and review a current Status Certificate dated no earlier than 60 days prior to closing. If between 60 and 120 days have passed since the date of the Status Certificate, call for instructions.
Restrictive Covenants Compliance	Sometimes	Where have grounds to believe there is non-compliance based on discussion with purchaser and instead of listing alleged non-compliance on Schedule "A," want to attempt to establish that there is in fact compliance.
Reciprocal/Cost-Sharing Agreement	Sometimes	No inquiry necessary where agreement between condominiums; otherwise, must obtain status letter.

Ontario – TPLA78-001 (10/09)

Figure 18.2

STEWART TITLE — RESIDENTIAL SEARCH REQUIREMENTS — ONE TO SIX UNITS*

Residential Transaction Search Requirements – One to Six Units

Where coverage is provided, title insurance can eliminate the need for certain off-title searches. This results in significant savings to the client, which often outweighs the cost of the title insurance premium. In order to maximize the cost savings, please refer to this list when the transaction is initiated. Please note this information was compiled based on general practices in most jurisdictions. For further information please contact Stewart Title.

IMPORTANT NOTE: It is a requirement of Stewart Title that you obtain Canadian Federal or Provincial Government issued PHOTO ID for all clients, that you review and confirm the validity to the best of your ability, and that you keep a legible photocopy in your file. Due to the ease in which Citizenship Cards may be forged, if you are relying on such a card, we ask that you obtain a second piece of ID that has a name and signature. We will not insure a transaction for which Canadian Federal or Provincial Government issued PHOTO ID is not obtained. If you are unable to obtain Canadian Federal or Provincial Government issued PHOTO ID please contact a Stewart Title underwriter PRIOR to closing.

Title Search Requirements

Registry Properties: A full 40-year search is required including compliance with the Planning Act. Where applicable, the search should include a review of abutting legal descriptions to determine if there are any descriptive inconsistencies resulting in a gap or overlap of legal descriptions.

Land Titles Absolute: Not required to search behind the parcel abstract. However for documents that appear on the parcel register or for which the property is "subject to" we request that you review those documents. Abutting land searches should be done for the current owner as listed in the abstract when you are dealing with a property where the search would normally be required for ascertaining compliance with the Planning Act. **NOTE: Your search must contain deleted instruments.**

Land Titles Conversion Qualified (LTCQ): Not required to search behind the parcel abstract. However, for documents that have been carried forward and appear on the parcel register or for which the property is "subject to" we request that you review those documents. Abutting land searches should be done for the current owner as listed in the abstract when you are dealing with a property where the search would normally be required for ascertaining compliance with the Planning Act. **NOTE: Your search must contain deleted instruments.**

Refinance Transactions – either Registry or Land Titles: Only a sub-search from the last arm's length deed is required (including a review of the LTT affidavit for assumed mortgages). The sub-search may be conducted up to 10 business days prior to the registration of the mortgage without the need to conduct a further search. A verbal inquiry of the borrower must be conducted to determine if they have an interest in an abutting property. **NOTE: For Land Titles transactions your search must contain deleted instruments.**

Not Required off Title Searches

The following searches are **not required** when acting on the purchase of a residential property of up to six units:

(1)   **Executions** against anyone other than the *current* vendor(s) and the purchaser(s)/mortgagor(s), if a mortgage is being insured. Similar or same name executions may be underwritten on a case-by-case basis. For both purchase and refinance transactions, the execution search may be conducted up to 10 business days prior to closing without the need to conduct a further execution search on closing.

(2)   **Water, Hydro and Gas Certificates/Arrears**. Verbal confirmation is sufficient. If a verbal confirmation is not available these searches are waived. *NOTE: Coverage is provided to the extent the arrears form a lien.*

(3)   **Municipal Realty Tax Certificate**. Verbal confirmation, a receipted tax bill or reference in a vendor's Statutory Declaration is sufficient, however, if none of the foregoing can be obtained, we will waive these requirements.

(4)   **Corporate Profile/Corporate Status Reports**.

(5)   **Subdivision and Development Agreement Compliance**.

(6)   **Building and Zoning Compliance** – No search is required for single-family residential dwellings. No search is required for refinance transactions. A building and zoning search is required for transactions for 2 to 6 residential units, where an owner policy is being obtained and coverage for building and zoning matters is requested. Additionally, if your property is located in a municipality where two unit properties must be registered, you must determine if your units are properly registered. For transactions for 2 to 6 residential units where only a lender policy is being obtained, or where the owner does not want coverage for building and zoning matters (contact an underwriter for an exception clause for the owner), the search is not required.

(7)   **Unregistered Hydro Easements**, unless the facts known to you suggest the existence of an easement, for example by indication on a survey or by the existence of hydro transmission towers or boxes visible on the property.

(8)   **Fire Department Work Orders**. No search is required for single-family residential dwellings. No search is required for refinance transactions. This search is required for transactions of 2 to 6 residential units (including properties where the second unit is a boathouse with living accommodation, where an owner policy is being obtained and coverage for the owner is requested. For transactions of 2 to 6 residential units where only a lender policy is being obtained, or where the owner does not

---

*   © Stewart Title 2010. Reproduced with permission.

Figure 18.2 (cont'd)

want coverage for fire department work orders (contact an underwriter for an exception clause for the owner), the search is not required.

(9)   **Septic File Searches**. Our Septic Endorsement is designed to protect the insured regarding the status of the septic system to the extent that a lawyer could do so if the usual septic file search was performed and reviewed. What should be made clear is that neither the policy nor a solicitor's opinion will guaranty that the system is working (it is not a warranty of fitness or quality). Similarly, the coverage does not include protection against defects that would be revealed by a current inspection of the system. It is also worth recognizing that the septic inquiry may provide information which may nonetheless be useful or important to the client. Examples of such issues would include the age of the system or the location of the system on the property. Thus, notwithstanding the comprehensiveness of the Septic Endorsement, it may still be prudent and courteous practice to advise clients of the additional option of ordering a septic inquiry.

(10)   **Conservation Authority**, unless you are aware or strongly suspect that the property is subject to conservation authority jurisdiction.

(11)   **Parkway Belt Planning and Development Act** for properties in the Niagara Escarpment, unless you are aware or strongly suspect that the property is subject to Parkway Belt Planning or Development Act jurisdiction (Ontario Only).

(12)   **Refinance Transactions**: On residential refinancing situations, an Estoppel Certificate/Status Certificate is not required for Condominium transactions. The execution search and sub-search of title may be conducted up to 10 business days prior to the registration of the mortgage without the need to conduct a further execution search or sub-search. For tax status, verbal confirmation, a receipted tax bill or reference in a Statutory Declaration from the Borrower is sufficient, however, if none of the foregoing can be obtained, we will waive these requirements. No building and zoning search is required.

Required Off Title Searches

The following searches **are required** as responses received may reflect issues not covered under the policies:

(1)   **Estoppel Certificate/Status Certificate** for Condominiums, *except* for residential refinance transactions. A Status Certificate dated up to 30 days prior to closing is satisfactory and no update is required. For Status Certificates dated 31 – 60 days before closing, an attempt must be made to obtain a verbal update. If a verbal update is not available, we will waive this requirement. For Status Certificates dated 61 - 90 days before closing, a verbal update is required. If a verbal update is not provided, a new Status Certificate should be obtained. For Status Certificates dated greater than 90 days before closing, a new Status Certificate is required.

(2)   **Building and Zoning Compliance** – A building and zoning search is required for transactions of 2 to 6 residential units (including properties where the second unit is a boathouse with living accommodation), where an owner policy is being obtained and coverage for building and zoning matters is requested. Additionally, if your property is located in a municipality where two unit properties must be registered, you must determine if your units are properly registered. For transactions of 2 to 6 residential units where only a lender policy is being obtained, or where the owner does not want coverage for building and zoning matters (contact an underwriter for an exception clause for the owner), these searches are not required. No search is required for single-family residential dwellings. No search is required for refinance transactions.

(3)   **Fire Department Work Orders**. This search is required for transactions of 2 to 6 residential units, where an owner policy is being obtained and coverage for the owner is requested. For transactions of 2 to 6 residential units where only a lender policy is being obtained, or where the owner does not want coverage for fire department work orders (contact an underwriter for an exception clause for the owner), the search is not required. No search is required for single-family residential dwellings. No search is required for refinance transactions.

(4)   **Mining Land Tax Search** with the Ministry of Northern Development & Mines (Ontario) – for applicable properties only.

Additional Considerations Falling outside the Scope of Stewart Title Coverage

(1)   **Environmental Clearance** – Any concerns about soil or contamination or toxic pollutants on the property should be addressed by obtaining an environmental audit. Such certification is not usually included in a traditional solicitor's opinion.

(2)   **Residential Tenancies Act, 2006 (Ontario)** – Landlord liability for illegal rent increases or other claims arising from residential tenancy legislation are not matters covered by title insurance. Where tenanted properties are concerned, you may want to seek the usual comforts in the form of landlord warranties, tenant acknowledgments and/or a search with the local rent authority.

(3)   **Fire Retrofit Issues** – In the cases of tenanted and multi-unit properties, while title insurance does cover the usual work orders and zoning related matters, it does not cover fire retrofit issues such as the sufficiency of smoke alarms or fire barriers, unless they form work orders or are zoning deficiencies which would have been revealed by a regular building and zoning search conducted prior to closing. This is consistent with the principle that title insurance is not a warranty regarding quality or fitness for purpose, but rather a protection regarding matters which can be disclosed by a local authority search.

(4)   **Water Potability and Quantity** – If the property is serviced by a well, a solicitor should seek the usual protections to ensure marketability and safety, including confirmation of a water potability certificate (preferably more than one) and a well driller's certificate (if available).

(5)   **PPSA Re: Chattels** – Title insurance covers land, not chattels. When significant chattels are included in a purchase or when a transaction involves the likes of a mobile home, consideration should be given to PPSA search and registration.

(6)   **Underground Fuel Oil Tanks** – In the event there is an underground fuel oil tank on the property, a solicitor should contact the Technical Safety and Standards Association to determine the tank's registration status for fuel delivery purposes and its compliance with removal, upgrading, and inspection requirements.

(7)   **Ministry of Natural Resources Boathouse Leases (Ontario)** - The Ministry of Natural Resources may require that certain boathouses located on Crown Land, including the beds of most waters, must enter into a lease with the Crown and pay rent in order for the boathouse to remain.

Figure 18.3

STEWART TITLE — EXISTING OWNER RESIDENTIAL SEARCH REQUIREMENTS*

Search Requirements
Existing Homeowner Policy

In order to obtain a policy, Stewart Title requires the completion of a sub-search of title from the date of acquisition of title by the existing owner to the current date of order. Please review the land transfer tax affidavit for a determination of assumed mortgages.

In the event that the existing owner obtained title in a non-arm's length transaction, a full title search must be completed unless you obtain evidence in the form of a legal opinion/reporting letter to the existing owner that confirms a full title search was conducted at the time they obtained title.

No execution search is needed for properties in the Land Titles system. For properties in the Registry system, an execution search for the vendor to the existing owner is required.

If a survey is available, please request a copy from the homeowner and review for obvious defects such as encroachments.

No other searches are required for the issuance of a policy for a single-family residence. For properties of 2-6 units, a building and zoning search should be completed. If the homeowner does not wish to complete this search, contact Stewart Title for an exception clause that will be added to the policy.

Search Information to Be Disclosed to Stewart Title:
In the event that your search determines a title or other defect please consult with a Stewart Title underwriter prior to insuring the transaction. Due to the nature of this policy, known defects will be excepted from the policy. No affirmative underwriting will be given.

In particular, should your search reveal that a mortgage registered at the time of purchase has been discharged, we require that you confirm with the homeowner that this mortgage has indeed been paid.

All registered mortgages must be reported to Stewart Title and will be listed as exceptions to the policy.

Nov 06 – ON

Figure 18.4

STEWART TITLE — COMMERCIAL SEARCH REQUIREMENTS*

Commercial Search Requirements

IMPORTANT NOTE: In addition to your normal corporate due diligence, it is a requirement of Stewart Title that you obtain Canadian/Provincial Government issued PHOTO ID for all private individuals and corporate signing officers for private corporations, that you review and confirm the validity to the best of your ability, and that you keep a legible photocopy in your file. We will not insure a transaction for which acceptable PHOTO ID is not obtained. If you are unable to obtain acceptable PHOTO ID please contact a Stewart Title underwriter PRIOR to closing.

It is imperative that you order your title insurance policy *prior* to the closing date. This ensures all underwriting matters can be considered in the coverage provided for the Insured. Please inform Stewart Title immediately if your deal has been delayed over 30 days.

Where coverage is provided, title insurance can eliminate the need for certain off-title searches. This results in significant savings to the client, which often outweighs the cost of the title insurance premium. In order to maximize the cost savings, please refer to this list when the transaction is initiated. Please note that this information was compiled based on general practices in most jurisdictions. For further information please contact Stewart Title.

Title Search Requirements

Purchase Transactions:

Registry Properties: A full 40-year search is required including compliance with the *Planning Act*.

Land Titles Absolute and Land Titles Conversion Qualified ("LTCQ"): You are not required to search behind the parcel abstract. However for documents that appear on the parcel register or for which the property is "subject to" we request that you review those documents and provide details to Stewart Title. For commercial transactions up to $5,000,000, abutting land searches should be done for the current owner as listed in the abstract when you are dealing with a property where the search would normally be required for ascertaining compliance with the *Planning Act*. A full abutting land search is required for commercial transactions exceeding $5,000,000. **NOTE: Your search must contain deleted instruments.**

Refinances:

Only a Sub-search from the last arm's length deed is required for commercial refinances under $10,000,000. No abutting land searches are required, provided that you make a verbal inquiry of the borrower to determine if they have an interest in an abutting property. (A full search of title is required for commercial refinances over $10,000,000, including a full abutting land search) **NOTE: For Land Titles, your search must contain deleted instruments.**

NOTE: Where a prior opinion is available, the above search requirements may be altered with the approval of a Stewart Title Underwriter. Please contact any of our Underwriters to discuss.

Royal Bank Plaza, North Tower • 200 Bay Street, Suite 2200 • Toronto, ON M5J 2J2
Tel.: (416) 307-3300 • 1-888-667-5151 • Fax.: (416) 307-3305

Figure 18.4 (cont'd)

Survey Requirements

FOR OWNER

Commercial Transactions Under $12,000,000: An up-to-date survey is *not* required to obtain a survey endorsement

Commercial Transactions Over $12,000,000: An up-to-date survey is required to obtain a survey endorsement. Please note, however, that survey coverage may be negotiated for commercial transactions over $12,000,000 in the event that an old survey is available and/or the vendor(s)/mortgagor(s) is willing to provide a Statutory Declaration confirming that there have been no improvements to the subject property, up to the Policy Date.

FOR LENDER

For all Commercial Transactions: An up-to-date survey is *not* required to obtain a survey endorsement.

Off Title Searches

Notes: **i) "LTV" = Loan to Value Ratio**

ii) Where a search is waived for lenders between $10 million and $50 million as set out below a suitable statutory declaration from the vendor (purchase mortgage transaction) or borrower (refinance) must be obtained. Please contact Stewart Title to obtain a sample declaration.

(1) **Execution Searches** are required against the current vendor(s) and if a mortgage is being insured, against the purchaser(s)/mortgagor(s). Please note that similar name executions may be underwritten on a case-by-case basis. Execution searches are not required against any other parties.

(2) **Public Utility Certificates/Arrears.**
For Owner: For transactions under $10,000,000, verbal confirmation, a receipted utility bill or reference in a vendor's Statutory Declaration is sufficient; however, if any of the foregoing cannot be obtained we will require the certificate. Public Utility Certificates are required on transactions over $10,000,000.
For Lender: Verbal confirmation, a receipted utility bill or reference in a vendor's/mortgagor's Statutory Declaration is sufficient regardless of the mortgage amount; however, if any of the foregoing cannot be obtained we will require the certificate.
NOTE: Coverage is provided to the extent the arrears form a lien.

(3) **Municipal Realty Tax Certificate.**
For Owner: For transactions under $10,000,000, verbal confirmation, a receipted tax bill or reference in a vendor's Statutory Declaration is sufficient; however, if any of the foregoing cannot be obtained we will require the certificate. Tax Certificates are required on transactions over $10,000,000.
For Lender: Verbal confirmation, a receipted tax bill or reference in a vendor's/mortgagor's Statutory Declaration is sufficient regardless of the mortgage amount; however, if any of the foregoing cannot be obtained we will require the certificate.

(4) **Corporate Profile Report or Certificate of Status** is required against the vendor(s), and the purchaser(s)/mortgagor(s). They are not required against prior corporate owners.

Last Modification Date: Sept 15 2008
Page 2 of 4

Figure 18.4 (cont'd)

(5) **Zoning Compliance.**

For Owner: If the purchase price is under $10,000,000 no report is necessary in order to obtain a zoning endorsement.

For Lender: If the loan amount is under $10,000,000 no report is necessary in order to obtain a zoning endorsement. If the loan amount is between $10,000,000 and $50,000,000 no report is necessary in order to obtain a zoning endorsement provided that we receive confirmation that the LTV is not greater than 75%. With the approval of a Stewart Title Underwriter, the search may be waived for loans over $50,000,000. Please contact any of our Underwriters to discuss.

NOTE: The policy will insure that the Property will be permitted to continue its present use. If the land is vacant or if a change of use is contemplated, the client or solicitor should confirm that zoning corresponds with future plans for development/improvements.

(6) **Municipal Work Orders.**

For Owner: If the purchase price is under $2,000,000 no report is necessary in order to obtain our municipal building department work order coverage.

For Lender: If the loan amount is under $10,000,000 no report is necessary in order to obtain our municipal work order coverage. If the loan amount is between $10,000,000 and $50,000,000 no report is necessary in order to obtain our municipal work order coverage provided that we receive confirmation that the LTV is not greater than 75%.

(7) **Unregistered Hydro Easements.**

For Owner: If the purchase price is under $10,000,000 no search is required unless the property is vacant. Where the property is vacant, this search is required prior to the issuance of an owner's policy regardless of the policy amount. This search is required for purchase prices over $10,000,000.

For Lender: If the loan amount is under $10,000,000, no search is required. If the loan amount is between $10,000,000 and $50,000,000 no search is required provided that we receive confirmation that the LTV is not greater than 75%. For loans over $50,000,000, this search is required.

(8) **Estoppel Certificates/Status Certificates** this search is required for all condominium transactions except for condominium refinances under $2,000,000.

(9) **Orders Under *The Residential Tenancies Act, 2006* (Ontario) Concerning Unlawful Rents** searches are not required for lender policies under $10,000,000. If the loan amount is between $10,000,000 and $50,000,000 no search is required provided that we receive confirmation that the LTV is not greater than 75%. For all owner policies and for lender policies over $50,000,000 no coverage is provided for these matters.

(10) **Subdivision and Development Agreement Compliance**

For Owner: This search is not required for owner policies under $10,000,000 *unless the property is currently under construction*, in which case this search should be completed regardless of the policy amount. For all transactions over $10,000,000, this search is required.

For Lender: This search is not required for lender policies under $10,000,000. If the loan amount is between $10,000,000 and $50,000,000 no search is required provided that we receive confirmation that the LTV is not greater than 75%. For loans over $50,000,000, this search is required.

(11) **Fire Department Compliance** searches are not required for lender policies under $10,000,000. If the loan amount is between $10,000,000 and $50,000,000 no search is required provided that we receive confirmation that the LTV is not greater than 75%. For all owner policies and for lender policies over $50,000,000, no coverage is provided for this matter.

(12) **Electrical Safety Authority** file searches for work orders are not required for lender policies under $10,000,000. If the loan amount is between $10,000,000 and $50,000,000 no search is required

Royal Bank Plaza, North Tower • 200 Bay Street, Suite 2200 • Toronto, ON M5J 2J2
Tel.: (416) 307-3300 • 1-888-667-5151 • Fax.: (416) 307-3305

Figure 18.4 (cont'd)

provided that we receive confirmation that the LTV is not greater than 75%. For loans over $50,000,000, this search is required. For all owner policies no coverage is provided for this matter.

(13) **Technical Standards and Safety Authority** file searches for work orders are not required for lender policies under $10,000,000. If the loan amount is between $10,000,000 and $50,000,000 no search is required provided that we receive confirmation that the LTV is not greater than 75%. For loans over $50,000,000, this search is required. For all owner policies no coverage is provided for this matter.

Items Not Covered By Commercial Policies

Please Note- **Existing Owner and Existing Lender Policies** *are* **not available** *for Commercial Properties*

The following searches may reveal title or other defects which are of relevance to your client and are NOT covered by commercial title insurance policies:

(1)   Conservation Authority.
(2)   Environmental Clearance.
(3)   Residential Tenancies Act, 2006 (Ontario) (except as provided in No. 9 above).
(4)   Water Potability and Quantity.
(5)   Parkway Belt Planning and Development Act for properties in Niagara Escarpment.
(6)   PPSA Re: Chattels.
(7)   Estoppel Certificate/Status Certificate for Condominium (except as provided in No. 8 above).
(8)   Fire Department Compliance (except as provided in No. 11 above).
(9)   Bank Act Issues.
(10) Bankruptcy Act.
(11) Elevator Issues.
(12) Public Health Department Issues.
(13) Septic System.
(14) Electrical Safety Authority (except as provided in No. 12 above).
(15) Technical Standards and Safety Authority (except as provided in No. 13 above).

NOTE: Stewart Title Commercial Policies do not provide coverage for the foregoing matters. This list is for guidance only and is not intended to be an exhaustive list of searches that Solicitors should consider. Solicitors should determine if any of the above or other searches are relevant to the subject transaction and if so, which of the above or other searches need to be conducted to adequately protect their client's interests. Please review the actual policy documents for full particulars of coverage.

Last Modification Date: Sept 15 2008
Page 4 of 4

Royal Bank Plaza, North Tower • 200 Bay Street, Suite 2200 • Toronto, ON M5J 2J2
Tel.: (416) 307-3300 • 1-888-667-5151 • Fax.: (416) 307-3305

Figure 18.5

STEWART TITLE — POSSIBLE TITLE QUALIFICATIONS*

	Title Qualifications
	November 2006

Access by Water only
- Access is by Water only. Notwithstanding anything else contained in this policy, this policy does not cover lack of pedestrian and vehicular access to and from the land.

Airport Zoning Regulations
- Airport Zoning Regulations registered as Instrument Number(s) _____.
- The Company insures the Insured against loss or damage suffered in the event that Airport Zoning Regulations contained within the above noted Instrument number(s) have not been complied with, up to the policy date.

Assignment of Rents – Active (Loan Policy)
- Assignment of Rents registered as Instrument Number _____.
- Where an Assignment of Rents is being registered in conjunction with the insured mortgage, coverage is provided for said Assignment of Rents as if it were included in Schedule A, Paragraph 4.

Assignment of Rents – Active (Owner Policy)
- Assignment of Rents registered as Instrument Number _____.

Assignment of Rents – Expired (Loan Policy Exception)
- Assignment of Rents registered as Instrument Number _____.

- The Company insures the Insured against loss or damage sustained as a result of the assignee in the above referenced instrument attempting to enforce the above assignment of rents, provided, however, that the Company will not otherwise cover any costs associated with removing this instrument from title, and also provides coverage regarding any loss in marketability as a result of the existence of said assignment of rents.

Assignment of Rents – Expired (Owner Policy Exception)
- Assignment of Rents registered as Instrument Number _____.

- The Company insures the Insured against loss or damage sustained as a result of the assignee in the above named instrument attempting to enforce the above assignment of rents, provided, however, that the Company will not otherwise cover any costs associated with removing this instrument from title. This coverage shall not extend to any loss in marketability as a result of the existence of said assignment of rents. The Company hereby commits to insuring this matter for future purchases on the same basis as set out herein at the then applicable premium.

By-Law
- This title qualification should only be used where upon your review of the by-law you are not aware of any non-compliance.
- By-Law registered as Instrument/Registration Number(s) _____.
- The Company insures the Insured against loss or damage sustained by reason of any violations on the land of any enforceable terms, conditions or obligations contained within the above noted Instrument Numbers(s), up to the policy date.

Common Elements Condominium (Loan Policy Exception)
- When setting out the legal description on Schedule A of the policy, be sure to include reference to the Parcel of Tied Land (POTL) and the Common Elements Condominium Corporation (including both PIN references).
- Terms, Conditions, Agreements, Covenants, Restrictions, Obligations, Reservations, and Easements created by or contained in the Condominium Declaration, including the By-laws and Rules and Regulations annexed thereto, as same may be (further) amended

---

* © Stewart Title 2010. Reproduced with permission.

Figure 18.5 (cont'd)

■ Common Elements Condominium Endorsement is annexed to this policy and applies only to the lands of the Common Elements Condominium and not to the POTL.

Common Elements Condominium (Owner Policy Exception)

▪ When setting out the legal description on Schedule A of the policy, be sure to include reference to the Parcel of Tied Land (POTL) and the Common Elements Condominium Corporation (including both PIN references).

▪ Terms, Conditions, Agreements, Covenants, Restrictions, Obligations, Reservations, and Easements created by or contained in the Condominium Declaration, including the By-laws and Rules and Regulations annexed thereto, as same may be (further) amended. Items disclosed by the Status Certificate, including but not limited to, adequacy of the reserve fund. This does not limit the coverage in paragraph 11(c) of the Gold Comprehensive Protection Owner's Policy.

▪ Common Elements Condominium Endorsement is annexed to this policy and applies only to the lands of the Common Elements Condominium and not to the POTL.

Condominium (Loan Policy Exception)

▪ Terms, Conditions, Agreements, Covenants, Restrictions, Obligations, Reservations, and Easements created by or contained in the Condominium Declaration, including the By-laws and Rules and Regulations annexed thereto, as same may be (further) amended

▪ Condominium Endorsement is annexed to this policy.

Condominium (Owner Policy Exception)

▪ Terms, Conditions, Agreements, Covenants, Restrictions, Obligations, Reservations, and Easements created by or contained in the Condominium Declaration, including the By-laws and Rules and Regulations annexed thereto, as same may be (further) amended. Items disclosed by the Status Certificate, including but not limited to, adequacy of the reserve fund. This does not limit the coverage in paragraph 11(c) of the Gold Comprehensive Protection Owner's Policy.

▪ Condominium Endorsement is annexed to this policy.

Construction Mortgage (Loan Policy Exception)

▪ Notwithstanding the Date of Policy shown in Schedule A, the policy date applicable for all terms and conditions of this policy, including survey coverage, shall be the date of the most recent advance of funds by the Insured.

▪ Pending disbursement of the full proceeds of the loan secured by the mortgage described in Schedule A, this Policy insures only to the extent of the amount actually disbursed, but increases as each disbursement is made in good faith and without knowledge of any defects in or objections to the title, up to the face amount of the Policy. Nothing contained in this paragraph limits any exception or any printed provision of this Policy.

Development Agreement (Optional)

▪ Instrument Number(s) _____ being a Development agreement.

▪ The Company insures the Insured against loss or damage sustained by reason of any violations on the land of any enforceable terms, covenants or conditions contained within the above noted Instrument Number(s), up to the policy date.

Easement

▪ An Easement registered as Instrument/Registration Number(s) _____.

▪ The Company insures the Insured against loss or damage sustained by reason of the owner of the dominant tenement having, prior to the policy date, claimed a legal interest in the title to the servient tenement that is greater than the legal interest provided for in instrument number(s) _____.

Figure 18.5 (cont'd)

Easement - unregistered

- The property is subject to an unregistered easement.
- The Company insures the Insured against loss or damage sustained by reason of the owner of the dominant tenement having, prior to the policy date, claimed a legal interest in the title to the servient tenement that is greater than the legal interest provided for in the unregistered easement.

Encroachment Guidelines:

These rules should be applied to all encroachment boilerplate exceptions:

i)   You must contact Stewart Title where you or the Insured are aware that the principal dwelling encroaches 1 foot or more over the lot lines or if a shed, garage or ancillary improvement appears to encroach more than 3 feet onto neighbouring lands.

ii)   Please do not include fences and/or boundary walls, as they are not covered under the policy. Please see "Fence not on lot line" title qualification.

iii)   Please select the "Encroachment onto subject property" boilerplate exception for all items that encroach onto the subject property.

Encroachment - setback violation (Loan Exception)

- An encroachment of the _____ onto setback requirements.
- This Policy insures the Insured against loss or damage which the Insured shall sustain by reason of the enforced removal of that portion of the above noted item(s) which encroaches onto setback requirements, and also provides coverage regarding any loss in marketability as a result of such encroachment.

Encroachment - setback violation (Owner Exception)

- An encroachment of the _____ onto setback requirements.
- This Policy insures the Insured against loss or damage which the Insured shall sustain by reason of the enforced removal of that portion of the above noted item(s) which encroaches onto setback requirements, however this coverage shall not extend to any loss in marketability as a result of such encroachment. The Company hereby commits to insuring this matter for future purchases on the same basis as set out herein at the then applicable premium.

Encroachment onto neighbouring lands. (Loan Exception)

- An encroachment of the _____ onto neighbouring lands.
- This Policy insures the Insured against loss or damage which the Insured shall sustain by reason of the enforced removal of that portion of the above noted item(s) which encroaches onto neighbouring lands and also provides coverage regarding any loss in marketability as a result of such encroachment.

Encroachment onto neighbouring lands (Owner Exception)

- An encroachment of the _____ onto neighbouring lands.
- This Policy insures the Insured against loss or damage which the Insured shall sustain by reason of the enforced removal of that portion of the above noted item(s) which encroaches onto neighbouring lands, however this coverage shall not extend to any loss in marketability as a result of such encroachment. The Company hereby commits to insuring this matter for future purchases on the same basis as set out herein at the then applicable premium.

Encroachment onto the subject property.

- An encroachment of the _____ onto the subject property.

Figure 18.5 (cont'd)

Execution or Judgment

- Similar or same name Judgments/Executions are not required to be listed in Schedule B of the policy, if you obtain the appropriate affidavits. Please retain an original of the affidavit/declaration for your files. Where there are Judgments/Executions against the actual person, these are not covered and must be listed as an exception on Schedule B.

FOR JUDGMENTS $50,000 OR LESS:

- We will insure over similar or a same name execution (but not the actual person) if you obtain an Affidavit signed by the individual against whom there is a similar or same name execution stating that they are not one and the same person as the judgment debtor.

FOR JUDGMENTS GREATER THAN $50,000:

- We will insure over similar or same name executions (but not the actual person) if you obtain an Affidavit signed by a Solicitor stating that the insured is not one and the same person as the judgment debtor.

Executions/Judgment Not Clear

- Judgment registered against _____ the judgment debtor named in a judgment or execution.

Farm Endorsement

For use only where:
i) the policy amount is up to $2 million;
ii) the property is NOT specifically zoned commercial; and
iii) the property contains a residential house.

- If the property is specifically zoned commercial then a commercial policy must be obtained directly from Stewart Title. If there is no residential house located on the property, the property will be considered vacant land and should be insured according to the guidelines for vacant land set out herein.
- Farm Endorsement to be annexed to this Policy.

Fence – Not on the lot line

The location of a fence does not correspond to the location of the boundary line of the Property.

This policy does not insure against loss or damage which arises from claims relating to title to and/or possession of that portion of the lands between the fence and the boundary line, which loss or damage includes but is not limited to claims arising from loss of use, loss in marketability, and defence of title; furthermore, this policy does not insure against loss or damage arising from the removal or rebuilding of the fence.

Improvement Endorsement (Owner Policy Exception)

If your client is constructing improvements that will increase the value of the land, you may select the Improvement Endorsement if:
i) construction is to commence within 6 months of closing; and
ii) you have a written estimate as to the future value of the land including the improvements (This may be in the form of a certified appraisal or a construction contract). Please note: a realtor's letter of opinion is NOT an acceptable form of appraisal for valuing the improvement in situations where the improvement has not yet been built. We will accept a realtor's letter of appraisal when the improvement is completed.

- The policy amount will be increased to the estimated future value. Additional premiums may apply should the value of the improvements increase the total policy amount to a higher premium pricing threshold. Please contact our office for a complete premium quote as this will not be reflected on your Invoice.

Figure 18.5 (cont'd)

- If construction is to commence <u>after 6 months</u> from closing, the Improvement Endorsement should NOT be selected. The purchaser may contact Stewart Title after 6 months to request that the Improvement Endorsement be issued at that time. An administrative fee will be charged, as well as any additional premium applicable.
- Improvement Endorsement is annexed to this Policy.

Lease/Liens – Expired (Loan Policy)

- Terms and provisions of the lease/lien registered as Instrument/Registration Number(s) _____, which lease/lien is no longer in effect.
- The Company insures the Insured against loss or damage arising from a successful claim against the Property by the lessee/lien claimant in the above noted Instrument Number(s) arising from rights contained in said lease/lien, provided, however, that the Company will not otherwise pay to remove said Instrument(s) from title. The Company also provides coverage regarding any loss in marketability as a result of the existence of said lease/lien.

Lease/Liens – Expired (Owner Policy)

- Terms and provisions of the lease/lien registered as Instrument/Registration Number(s) _____, which lease/lien is no longer in effect.
- The Company insures the Insured against loss or damage arising from a successful claim against the Property by the lessee/lien claimant in the above noted Instrument Number(s) arising from rights contained in said lease/lien, provided, however, that the Company will not otherwise pay to remove said Instrument(s) from title. This coverage shall not extend to any loss in marketability as a result of the existence of said lease/lien. The Company hereby commits to insuring this matter for future purchases on the same basis as set out herein at the then applicable premium.

Mineral and Mining Interest

- Terms and provisions of oil, gas and mineral leases. Mineral and unpatented mining claims, and the royalties, bonuses, rentals and all other rights in connection with these interests, together with the appurtenant rights to use the surface. The Company makes no representation as to the present ownership of these interests.

Municipal Agreement

- Municipal agreement registered as Instrument/Registration Number(s) _____.
- The Company insures the Insured against loss or damage sustained by reason of any violations on the land of any enforceable terms, conditions or obligations contained within the above noted Instrument Number(s), up to the policy date.

Notice of Chattel Lease/Security Interest

- Notice of Chattel Lease/Security Interest registered as Instrument Number(s) _____

Outstanding Taxes

- Outstanding taxes plus applicable penalties and interest.

Restrictions

- Restrictions as more fully set forth in a certain Instrument registered as Instrument/Registration Number(s). _____.
- The Company insures the Insured against loss or damage sustained by reason of any violations on the land of any enforceable restrictive covenants contained within the above noted Instrument/Registration Number(s), up to the policy date.

Figure 18.5 (cont'd)

Right of Re-entry
- Right of Re-entry registered as Instrument/Registration Number(s) _____.
- The Company insures the Insured against loss or damage sustained by reason of any violations on the land of any enforceable terms, conditions or obligations contained within the above noted Instrument/Registration Number(s), up to the policy date.

Right of Way - lands subject to
- The lands are subject to a Right of Way.
- The Company insures the Insured against loss or damage sustained by reason of the owner of the dominant tenement having, prior to the policy date, claimed a legal interest in the title to the servient tenement that is greater than the legal interest provided for in the right of way.

Seasonal Property
- Only for use where the property has been zoned for seasonal use.
- The zoning by-law permits residential use for recreational purposes throughout the year but only continuous residential use during summer months.

Septic System
- Select for properties with a septic system.

- Septic System Endorsement is annexed to this policy.
- Shore Road Allowance/Crown Reservation Abutting Water
- For use where the subject property abuts a shore road allowance (66 foot reservation). In that instance our Shore Road Allowance title qualification must be selected as Stewart Title does not provide coverage for legal title to the shore road allowance. Where cottages or accessory buildings or structures are known to encroach onto the shore road allowance or 66 foot reservation, please contact an Underwriter as custom underwriting is required for these matters.

Please note: when this qualification is selected, our standard title qualification "Water – Property abutting a body of water" should not be used <u>unless</u> you are aware (e.g. upon review of an existing survey) that the old shoreline road allowance is under water and the property does, therefore, in fact, abut the body of water.

Exception (Owner's and Lender's Policy)
- There is a shore road allowance lying between the Property and the body of water adjacent to the shore road allowance. Coverage under this policy does not extend to said shore road allowance or any matter relating thereto unless specifically provided for in this Schedule.

Subdivision Agreement - (Optional)
- Instrument Number(s) _____ being a Subdivision Agreement.
- The Company insures the Insured against loss or damage sustained by reason of any violations on the land of any enforceable terms, covenants or conditions contained within the above noted Instrument Number(s), up to the policy date.

Survey - improvements not shown (Loan Exception)
For use when an improvement is not shown on a survey and the purchaser/mortgagor or lawyer is aware that the improvement either:

i)   did not have a permit; or
ii) there is non compliance with zoning by-laws/regulations.

Figure 18.5 (cont'd)

- This coverage is for survey related issues only. There is NO coverage for the lack of a permit or zoning non compliance. You MUST contact a Stewart Title underwriter prior to closing for an underwriting decision with respect to whether coverage can be given for the lack of a permit or zoning non compliance.
- A _____ not shown on the survey.
- This Policy insures the insured against loss or damage which the insured shall sustain by reason of the enforced removal of the above noted item(s) in the event that said item(s) encroach onto setback requirements, easements, or onto neighbouring lands, and also provides coverage regarding any loss in marketability as a result of such encroachments.

Survey - improvements not shown (Owner Exception)

For use when an improvement is not shown on a survey and the purchaser/mortgagor or lawyer is aware that the improvement either:

i)   did not have a permit; or
ii) there is non compliance with zoning by-laws/regulations.

- This coverage is for survey related issues only. There is NO coverage for the lack of a permit or zoning non compliance. You MUST contact a Stewart Title underwriter prior to closing for an underwriting decision with respect to whether coverage can be given for the lack of a permit or zoning non compliance.
- A _____ not shown on the survey.
- This Policy insures the Insured against loss or damage which the Insured shall sustain by reason of the enforced removal of the above noted item(s) in the event that said item(s) encroach onto setback requirements, easements or onto neighboring lands, however this coverage shall not extend to any loss in marketability as a result of such encroachment. The Company hereby commits to insuring this matter for future purchases on the same basis as set out herein at the then applicable premium.

Tenanted (Any portion) - OWNER

- For use on duplex, triplex etc. properties, and/or single family residences where any portion is not owner occupied.
- Non-owner occupied premises.
- The Company does not provide coverage for any retrofit issues, Residential Rent Regulation Act, Tenant Protection Act, or successor or related legislation issues, any present and future loss in rental income, any necessary eviction procedures, parking requirements, or rental deposits and interest thereon.

Tenanted (Any portion) - LENDER

- For use on duplex, triplex etc. properties, and/or single family residences where any portion is not owner occupied.
- Non-owner occupied premises.
- The Company does not provide coverage for any retrofit issues, Residential Rent Regulation Act, Tenant Protection Act, or successor or related legislation issues, any present and future loss in rental income, any necessary eviction procedures, parking requirements, or rental deposits and interest thereon.

Vacant Land Endorsement

This endorsement is for residential vacant land for both owner and lender. The Vacant Land Endorsement is to be attached to vacant land properties where:

i)   the policy amount is up to $2 million and the zoning is NOT commercial or industrial; or
ii) the policy amount is over $2 million and the land is specifically zoned residential.

Figure 18.5 (cont'd)

- If the property does not fit within i) or ii) above, the policy should be a commercial policy and you must order it directly from Stewart Title.
- Vacant Land Endorsement is annexed to this policy.

Vacant Land Condominium (Loan Policy)

- Terms, Conditions, Agreements, Covenants, Restrictions, Obligations, Reservations, and Easements created by or contained in the Condominium Declaration, including the By-laws and Rules and Regulations annexed thereto, as same may be (further) amended
- Vacant Land Condominium Endorsement is annexed to this policy.

Vacant Land Condominium (Owner Policy)

- Terms, Conditions, Agreements, Covenants, Restrictions, Obligations, Reservations, and Easements created by or contained in the Condominium Declaration, including the By-laws and Rules and Regulations annexed thereto, as same may be (further) amended. Items disclosed by the Status Certificate, including but not limited to, adequacy of the reserve fund. This does not limit the coverage in paragraph 11(c) of the Gold Comprehensive Protection Owner's Policy.
- Vacant Land Condominium Endorsement is annexed to this policy.

Water Potability Endorsement (Loan Policy)

To be attached to Lender policy only where the following criteria are met:
i)   The Land is a residential single family home.
ii) The well is in existence at the Date of Policy.

PLEASE NOTE: There is no coverage for owners for water potability.

- Water Potability Endorsement is annexed to this policy.

Water - Property abutting a body of water

- Title to that portion of the property lying below the high mean water mark.
- Riparian or water rights, claims or title to water whether or not shown by the public records.
- Rights, if any, of the public to use as a public beach or recreation area, any part of any lands abutting any of the subject property which lies between the body of water and the subject property.

Figure 18.6

STEWART TITLE — "GOLD" COMPREHENSIVE PROTECTION OWNER'S POLICY (RESIDENTIAL)*

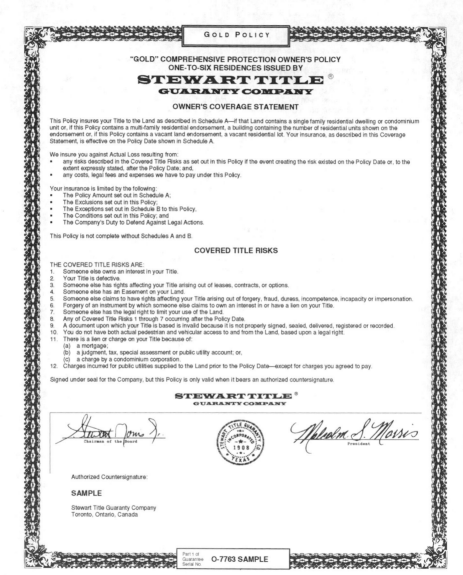

GOLD POLICY

"GOLD" COMPREHENSIVE PROTECTION OWNER'S POLICY
ONE-TO-SIX RESIDENCES ISSUED BY

STEWART TITLE ®
GUARANTY COMPANY

OWNER'S COVERAGE STATEMENT

This Policy insures your Title to the Land as described in Schedule A—if that Land contains a single family residential dwelling or condominium unit or, if this Policy contains a multi-family residential endorsement, a building containing the number of residential units shown on the endorsement or, if this Policy contains a vacant land endorsement, a vacant residential lot. Your insurance, as described in this Coverage Statement, is effective on the Policy Date shown in Schedule A.

We insure you against Actual Loss resulting from:
- any risks described in the Covered Title Risks as set out in this Policy if the event creating the risk existed on the Policy Date or, to the extent expressly stated, after the Policy Date; and,
- any costs, legal fees and expenses we have to pay under this Policy.

Your insurance is limited by the following:
- The Policy Amount set out in Schedule A;
- The Exclusions set out in this Policy;
- The Exceptions set out in Schedule B to this Policy,
- The Conditions set out in this Policy; and
- The Company's Duty to Defend Against Legal Actions.

This Policy is not complete without Schedules A and B.

COVERED TITLE RISKS

THE COVERED TITLE RISKS ARE:
1. Someone else owns an interest in your Title.
2. Your Title is defective.
3. Someone else has rights affecting your Title arising out of leases, contracts, or options.
4. Someone else has an Easement on your Land.
5. Someone else claims to have rights affecting your Title arising out of forgery, fraud, duress, incompetence, incapacity or impersonation.
6. Forgery of an instrument by which someone else claims to own an interest in or have a lien on your Title.
7. Someone else has the legal right to limit your use of the Land.
8. Any of Covered Title Risks 1 through 7 occurring after the Policy Date.
9. A document upon which your Title is based is invalid because it is not properly signed, sealed, delivered, registered or recorded.
10. You do not have both actual pedestrian and vehicular access to and from the Land, based upon a legal right.
11. There is a lien or charge on your Title because of:
    (a) a mortgage;
    (b) a judgment, tax, special assessment or public utility account; or,
    (c) a charge by a condominium corporation.
12. Charges incurred for public utilities supplied to the Land prior to the Policy Date—except for charges you agreed to pay.

Signed under seal for the Company, but this Policy is only valid when it bears an authorized countersignature.

STEWART TITLE ®
GUARANTY COMPANY

Chairman of the Board   President

Authorized Countersignature:

SAMPLE

Stewart Title Guaranty Company
Toronto, Ontario, Canada

Part 1 of Guarantee Serial No.   **O-7763 SAMPLE**

Figure 18.6 (cont'd)

13. There is a lien or charge on your Title because of a local improvement charge, as to that portion of the total amount of the charge which had accrued prior to the Policy Date, unless you agreed to pay the local improvement charge.
14. After the Policy Date a Governmental Authority assesses supplemental real estate taxes not previously assessed against the Land for any period before the Policy Date, unless you agreed to pay the supplemental real estate taxes.
15. Your Land is unmarketable, which allows another person to refuse to perform a contract to purchase, lease or make a mortgage loan because:
    (a) it violates a restriction set out in Schedule B;
    (b) of adverse matters that would have been disclosed by an up-to-date Survey;
    (c) your Land violates an existing zoning by-law or ordinance; or
    (d) your existing structures or any part of them are located on land under the jurisdiction of conservation or similar Governmental Authority without approval.
16. There are construction, builders' or mechanics' liens or rights of priority on your Title, arising now or later, for labour, service or material furnished before the Policy Date—unless you agreed to pay for the labour, service or material.
17. Rights of possession in favour of a spouse under applicable provincial or territorial legislation dealing with matrimonial property rights.
18. Someone else claims an interest in your Title because of a violation of any restriction, covenant, or condition which occurred before you acquired your Title, even if the restriction, covenant or condition is excepted in Schedule B.
19. Your Title is unmarketable, which allows another person to refuse to perform a contract to purchase, to lease or to make a mortgage loan.
20. You are forced by a Governmental Authority (or in the case of 20(a) hereunder, you are forced by the affected neighbour or a party who benefits from the Easement) to remove or remedy your existing structure(s), or any portion thereof, other than a boundary wall or fence, because:
    (a) it extends on to adjoining land or on to any Easement (even if the Easement is excepted in Schedule B);
    (b) it violates a restriction, covenant or condition affecting the Land , even if the restriction, covenant or condition is excepted in Schedule B;
    (c) it violates an existing zoning by-law or ordinance;
    (d) it is located on land under the jurisdiction of a conservation or similar governmental authority without approval;
    (e) of any outstanding notice of violation or deficiency notice;
    (f) any portion of it was built without obtaining a building permit from the proper Governmental Authority, provided a building permit would have been required by such Governmental Authority at the time of construction of the structure or relevant portion thereof.
21. There is a violation of the provisions of a provincial or territorial act which restrict the subdivision of land.
22. Work orders, unless you agreed to be responsible for them.
23. Someone else, after the Policy Date, builds a structure – other than a boundary wall or fence—which encroaches on to your Land.
24. The Land is in violation of a subdivision or development agreement.
25. A residence with the municipal address shown in Schedule A is not located on the Land at the Policy Date.
26. Your existing improvements (or a replacement or modification made to them after the Policy Date) including lawns, shrubbery or trees are damaged because of the future exercise of a right to use the surface of the Land for the extraction or development of minerals, water, or any other substance, even if those rights are excepted or reserved from the description of the Land or excepted in Schedule B.
27. Your existing structure(s) have been damaged because of the exercise of a right to maintain or use any Easement affecting the Land, even if the Easement is excepted in Schedule B.
28. Any incorrectness in a written statement received by you from a Governmental Authority, indicating that there are no defects relating to the Land's compliance with applicable building and zoning by-laws or ordinances at the Policy Date.
29. Any adverse circumstance affecting the Land which would have been disclosed by a Local Authority Search of the Land at the Policy Date.
30. You are forced to correct or remove an existing violation of any restriction, covenant, or condition affecting the Land, even if the restriction, covenant, or condition is excepted in Schedule B.
31. Your Title is lost or taken because of a violation of any restriction, covenant, or condition which occurred before you acquired your Title, even if the restriction, covenant, or condition is excepted in Schedule B.
32. Other defects, liens, charges or encumbrances on your Title.
33. Any defect in or lien or encumbrance on the Title or other matter included in Covered Title Risks 1 through 32 above attaching or created subsequent to Date of Policy and prior to the date and time of registration or recording of the instrument by which you obtained your interest in the Land, unless you agreed to be responsible for them.

COMPANY'S DUTY TO DEFEND AGAINST COURT CASES

We will defend your Title in any court case as to that part of the case that is based on a Covered Title Risk insured against by the Policy. We will pay the covered costs, legal fees, and expenses incurred in that defense.

We can end this duty to defend your Title by exercising any of our options listed in Item 4 of the Conditions.

EXCLUSIONS

In addition to the Exceptions in Schedule B, you are not insured against loss, costs, legal fees, and expenses resulting from:
1. Governmental power, and the existence or violation of any law, by-law, ordinance, order, code or government regulation. This includes laws, by-laws, ordinances, orders, codes or government regulations concerning:
    - building;
    - zoning;
    - land use;
    - land division;
    - improvements on the Land; or,
    - environmental protection.
    This exclusion does not apply to violations or the enforcement of these matters which appear in the Public Records at the Policy Date. This exclusion does not limit the coverage described in Items 10, 15 (b), 15(c), 15(d), 20, 21, 22, 24, 26 of the Covered Title Risks.
2. The right to take the Land by expropriating it, unless:
    - a notice of the right being exercised appears in the Public Records on the Policy Date; or,
    - the expropriation happened prior to the Policy Date and is binding on you if you bought the land without knowing of the expropriation.
3. Risks:
    - that are created, allowed, or agreed to by you;
    - that are actually known to you, but not to us, on the Policy Date;
    - that result in no loss to you; or

2

Figure 18.6 (cont'd)

- that first affect your Title after the Policy Date—this does not limit the coverage described in Items 1-8, 16, 23, and 26 of the Covered Title Risks.
4. Failure to pay value for your Title.
5. Lack of a right:
   - to any land outside the area specifically described and referred to in Item 4. of Schedule A; or,
   - in streets, lanes, or waterways that touch your Land.
   - This exclusion does not limit the coverage described in Items 10 and 20(a) of the Covered Title Risks.
6. Environmental concerns or matters of any kind, including but not limited to, legislation with respect to environmental protection, underground fuel storage tanks, water quality and water quantity.
7. The failure of your existing structure(s) or any part of them to be constructed in accordance with applicable building codes. This exclusion does not apply to violations of building codes if notice of the violation appears in the Public Records at the Policy Date or if the existence of the violation would have been disclosed by a Local Authority Search of the Land at the Policy Date. This exclusion does not limit the coverage described in Item 20(f) or 29 of the Covered Title Risks.
8. A breach of any governmental regulation requiring that improvements on the Land be retrofitted to comply with fire safety requirements.
9. Any matters disclosed in a building inspection report or home inspection report obtained by the Insured prior to the Policy Date.

CONDITIONS

1. DEFINITIONS
   (a) Actual Loss – the difference between the value of the insured estate or interest as insured and the value of the insured estate or interest subject to the defect, lien or encumbrance insured against by the Policy.
   (b) Easement – the right of someone else to use your land for a special purpose.
   (c) Governmental Authority – any department or division of the government of Canada, or any province or territory or of the municipality in which the Land is located which has jurisdiction with respect to matters of building and zoning compliance.
   (d) Land – the land or condominium unit described in Schedule A and any improvements on the land which are real property.
   (e) Local Authority Search – any search of local government records pertaining to the land which customarily be required by a solicitor qualified to practice law in the jurisdiction in which the lands are located in the normal course of a real estate transaction
   (f) Mortgage – a mortgage, charge, trust deed or other security instrument.
   (g) Public Records - records established and maintained by legislation of the province or territory in which the Land is situated for the registration and/ or recording of interests in title.
   (h) Survey – a building location certificate, real property report or certificate of localization prepared by a surveyor qualified to survey land in the province or territory where the Land is located.
   (i) Title – the ownership of your interest in the land, as shown in Schedule A.

2. CONTINUATION OF COVERAGE
   This Policy protects you as long as you own your Title. This Policy also protects you if you take back a mortgage from anyone who buys your land; or are liable for any covenants given by you or implied by statutes relating to the registration of documents in the jurisdiction where the land is located.
   This Policy also protects:
   - anyone who receives your Title because of your death;
   - trustee or successor trustee of a trust, in which you are the trustor/settlor to whom you transfer your Title after the Policy Date;
   - your spouse or child who receives your Title because of a transfer by you where the transfer is for nominal consideration only or in settlement of your obligation under the property division provisions of the matrimonial statutes intended for such a purpose;
   - any successor or assign of a mortgage you took back from anyone who bought your land; and,
   - the beneficiaries to whom the trustee or successor trustee of a trust in which you are the settler, transfers your Title by operation of the terms of the trust.
   We can assert against anyone making a claim under this Policy any of the same rights and defences that we have against anyone previously insured under this Policy.

3. HOW TO MAKE A CLAIM
   (a) You Must Give The Company Notice Of Your Claim. If anyone claims a right against your insured Title, you must notify us promptly in writing. Send the notice to Company Claims Department at Royal Bank Plaza, North Tower, 200 Bay Street, Suite 2200, Toronto, Ontario, Canada, M5J 2J2. Please include the Policy number shown in Schedule A, and the municipality and province where land is located. Our obligation to you could be reduced if:
      - you fail to give prompt notice; and,
      - your failure affects our ability to dispose of or to defend you against the claim.
   (b) Proof Of Your Loss Must Be Given To The Company. You must give us a written statement to prove your claim of loss. This statement must be given to us no later than 90 days after you know the facts which will let you establish the amount of your loss. The statement must have the following facts:
      - the Covered Title Risks which resulted in your loss;
      - the dollar amount of your loss; and
      - the method you used to compute the amount of your loss.
      You may want to provide us with an appraisal of your loss by a professional appraiser as a part of your statement of loss. We may require you to show us your records, cheques, letters, contracts, and other papers which relate to your claim of loss. We may make copies of these papers. We may require you to answer questions under oath. Our obligation to you could be reduced if you fail or refuse to:
      - provide a statement of loss; or,
      - answer our questions truthfully under oath; or,
      - show us the papers we request; and
      - your failure or refusal affects our ability to dispose of or to defend you against the claim.

4. OUR CHOICES WHEN YOU NOTIFY US OF A CLAIM
   After we receive your claim notice or in any other way learn of a matter for which we are liable, we can do one or more of the following:
   (a) Pay the claim against your Title.
   (b) Negotiate a settlement.
   (c) Prosecute or defend a court case related to the claim.

3

Figure 18.6 (cont'd)

(d) Pay you the amount required by the Policy.
(e) Take other action which will protect you, including removing the cause of the claim.
(f) Cancel the Policy by paying the Policy Amount, then in force, and only those costs, legal fees and expenses incurred up to that time which we are obligated to pay.
(g) Pay you the Actual Loss as at the date the defect is discovered.
(h) Pay any amount due you under the Policy to the insured holder of any mortgage shown in this Policy or a later mortgage given by you, and this payment shall be treated as a payment to you under the Policy.
(i) For a claim under Covered Title Risk 20(f), even if the defect is also covered under another Covered Title Risk, we have the following options:
   (i) Where the cost of removing or remedying the portion of the structure built without a permit is less than $50,000, we will pay for the removal or remediation.
   (ii) Where the cost of removing or remedying the portion of the structure built without a permit is greater than $50,000, we may,
      1. Pay for the removal or remediation; or
      2. End the coverage for the claim by paying you your Actual Loss as determined by an appraisal conducted by a member of the Accredited Appraiser Canadian Institute and those costs, legal fees and expenses incurred up to that time which we are obligated to pay. The appraiser will be selected by you from a list of at least 2 appraisers to be provided by us. The appraiser will be instructed by us. We will pay the appraiser's fees and expenses. If we cannot agree on the value of the Actual Loss, we can end all coverage under this Policy by paying you the current fair market value of the Land without regard to the defect insured against by the Policy, and you will transfer your Title to the Land to us.

When we choose the options in paragraph 4 (a), (b), (d), (e), (f), (g), (h) , (i), all our obligation for the claim ends, including our obligation to defend, or continue to defend or prosecute any legal action.

5. HANDLING A CLAIM OR COURT CASE
You must cooperate with us in handling any claim or court case and give us all relevant information. If you do not do so, your coverage under the Policy will be reduced or ended, but only to the extent your failure or refusal to co-operate or give us all relevant information affects our ability to resolve the claim or defend you. We are required to repay you only for those settlement costs, legal fees, and expenses that we approve in advance. When we defend your Title, we have a right to choose the lawyer. We can appeal any decision to the highest court. We do not have to pay your claim until your case is finally decided.

6. LIMITATION OF THE COMPANY'S LIABILITY
(a) We will pay up to (i) your Actual Loss; or (ii) the Policy Amount in force when the claim is made – whichever is less.
(b) If you cannot use any of your land because of a claim against your Title, and you rent reasonable substitute land or facilities, we will repay you for your actual rent until:
   • the cause of the claim is removed; or
   • we settle your claim.
(c) The Policy Amount will be reduced by all payments made under this Policy—except for costs, legal fees and expenses.
(d) The Policy Amount will be reduced by any amount we pay to our insured holder of any mortgage shown in this Policy or a later mortgage given by you.
(e) If you do anything to affect any right of recovery you may have, we can subtract from our liability the amount by which you reduced the value of that right.
(f) Our liability may be reduced or eliminated if you do anything to settle any claim or suit without prior written consent of the Company.
(g) If we remove the cause of the claim with reasonable diligence after receiving notice of it, all our obligations for the claim end, including any obligation for loss you had while we were removing the cause of the claim.
(h) If you have insurance with another insurer for a Covered Title Risk for which you are making a claim under the Policy, we are only liable for that proportion of the your Actual Loss and costs, legal fees and expenses covered by the Policy, that the Policy Amount bears to the total amount of insurance you have with us and the other insurer.

7. TRANSFER OF YOUR RIGHTS
(a) When we settle a claim, we have all the rights you had against any person or property related to the claim. You must transfer these rights to us when we ask, and you must not do anything to affect these rights. You must let us use your name in enforcing these rights.
(b) We will pay any money we collect from enforcing those rights: first to us for costs, legal fees and expenses incurred in enforcing those rights, second to you for your loss that you have not already collected, and third to us for any money paid out under the Policy on account of your claim.
(c) We will not be liable to you if we decide not to pursue these rights, or if we do not recover all amounts that might be recoverable.
(d) If you have rights under contracts to recover all or part of your loss, then all of those rights are transferred to us, even if those contracts provide that those obligated have all of your rights under this Policy.
(e) We have the right to use all information gathered during the underwriting and handling of any claim made under this Policy for the purpose of underwriting, issuing, and administering title insurance policies for future transactions with respect to the Land.

8. OUR LIABILITY IS LIMITED TO THIS POLICY
The Policy, plus any endorsements, are the entire contract between you and the Company. Any claim you make against the Company must be made under this Policy and is subject to its terms.

9. INFLATION COVERAGE
The Policy Amount stated in Schedule A will increase based upon an increase in the fair market value of the land up to a maximum Policy Amount of two hundred percent (200%) of the original Policy Amount.

10. SEVERABILITY.
In the event any provision of this policy is held invalid or unenforceable under applicable law, the policy shall be deemed not to include that provision and all other provisions shall remain in full force and effect.

May 30, 2008

4

Figure 18.7

STEWART TITLE — SCHEDULE B (RESIDENTIAL OWNER)*

STEWART TITLE GUARANTY COMPANY
RESIDENTIAL TITLE INSURANCE POLICY
SCHEDULE B

Royal Bank Plaza, North Tower   416-307-3300
200 Bay Street, Suite 2200   888-667-5151
Toronto, ON M5J 2J2   416-307-3305 fax

File No.
Lawyer File No.
EC No.

Owner Form   Policy Number:

This policy does not insure against loss or damage (and the Company will not pay costs, legal fees, or expenses) which arise by reason of:

1. Environmental concerns or matters of any kind, and any native or aboriginal claims affecting the land.

[Enter all instruments registered on title that would affect good title with the following exceptions: (1) Subdivision Agreements and amendments thereto; and (2) Development Agreements and amendments thereto]:

FOR OFFICE USE ONLY:
File No.

Royal Bank Plaza, North Tower
200 Bay Street, Suite 2200
Toronto, Ontario   M5J 2J2
Tel: (416) 307-3300 Fax: (416) 307-3305

Figure 18.8

STEWART TITLE — "GOLD" COMPREHENSIVE PROTECTION LENDER'S POLICY (RESIDENTIAL)*

GOLD POLICY

"GOLD" COMPREHENSIVE PROTECTION LOAN POLICY
ONE-TO-SIX FAMILY RESIDENCES ISSUED BY

STEWART TITLE ®
GUARANTY COMPANY

LENDER'S COVERAGE STATEMENT

SUBJECT TO THE EXCLUSIONS FROM COVERAGE, THE EXCEPTIONS FROM COVERAGE CONTAINED IN SCHEDULE B AND THE CONDITIONS AND STIPULATIONS, STEWART TITLE GUARANTY COMPANY, a Texas corporation, licensed to carry on business in Canada, herein called the Company, insures, as of Date of Policy shown in Schedule A (or, to the extent expressly stated below, after Date of Policy) against loss or damage, not exceeding one hundred twenty-five percent (125%) of the Amount of Insurance stated in Schedule A, sustained or incurred by the Insured by reason of:

1. Title to the estate or interest described in Schedule A being vested other than as stated therein;
2. Any defect in or lien or encumbrance on the title;
3. Unmarketability of the title;
4. Lack of a right of pedestrian and vehicular access to and from the Land;
5. The invalidity or unenforceability of the Insured Mortgage upon the title;
6. The priority of any lien or encumbrance over the Insured Mortgage;
7. Lack of priority of the Insured Mortgage as to each and every advance of proceeds of the indebtedness secured by the Insured Mortgage, which at Date of Policy the Insured has made or is obligated to make, over any statutory lien for services, labour or material arising from an improvement or work related to the Land, whether or not:
   (a) The statutory lien or liens arise prior to or after Date of Policy; or
   (b) The improvement of work is contracted for or commenced prior to or after Date of Policy;
8. Any assessments for street improvements under construction or completed at Date of Policy which now have gained or hereafter may gain priority over the Insured Mortgage;
9. The invalidity or unenforceability of any assignment of the Insured Mortgage, provided the assignment is shown in Schedule A, or the failure of the assignment shown in Schedule A to vest title to the Insured Mortgage in the named insured assignee free and clear of all liens;
10. The invalidity or unenforceability of the Insured Mortgage upon the title based upon a violation of the usury laws of the jurisdiction where the Land is located;
11. The failure of Land to have the municipal address shown in Schedule A;
12. The failure of the Land to contain a single family residential structure or a condominium, with the municipal address shown in schedule A
13. (a) Any outstanding work orders against the Land; or (b) the failure of the Land to comply with the applicable zoning by laws; or (c) the failure of the land to be zoned to permit a single family residential structure or, if stated in Schedule A, a condominium.
14. The failure of the Land to be a lawfully created parcel according to provincial statutes governing subdivision of Land and local ordinances adopted pursuant thereto;
15. Failure of the existing residential structure, any portion thereof, or a modification thereto or replacement thereof constructed after Date of Policy, to have been constructed with a valid building permit from the appropriate local government issuing office, provided a building permit would have been required by such office or agency at time of construction, modification or replacement of the structure;
16. Any violation, variation, or adverse circumstance affecting the Land that would have been disclosed by an accurate survey, including but not limited to any encroachment of existing improvements located on the Land onto adjoining land and any encroachment onto the Land of existing improvements located on adjoining land, other than boundary walls or fences;
17. The inability to use the existing single family residential structure or condominium or any portion thereof, or any replacement thereof constructed after Date of Policy for residential purposes because that use violates a restriction referred to in paragraph 7 of the Exclusions from Coverage;
18. Encroachment onto the Land of an improvement constructed after Date of Policy by someone other than the then owner of the estate or interest referred to in Schedule A;
19. Any existing improvements, or those constructed after Date of Policy, encroaching upon any easement or right of way referred to in paragraph 7 of the Exclusions from Coverage and the use of that easement or right of way for the purpose granted or reserved interfering with or damaging the improvements, including lawns, shrubbery and trees;

Signed under seal for the Company, but this Policy is only valid when it bears an authorized countersignature.

STEWART TITLE ®
GUARANTY COMPANY

Chairman of the Board

1908

President

Authorized Countersignature:

SAMPLE

Stewart Title Guaranty Company
Toronto, Ontario, Canada

Part 1 of
Guarantee **M-7764 SAMPLE**
Serial No:

Figure 18.8 (cont'd)

20. Any use of the Land for single family residential purposes being affected or impaired by reason of any lease, grant, exception or reservation of minerals or mineral rights referred to in paragraph 7 of the Exclusions from Coverage and damage to existing and future improvements, including lawns, shrubbery and trees resulting from the future exercise of any right to use the surface of the Land for the extraction or development of the minerals or mineral rights referred to in paragraph 7 of the Exclusions from Coverage;
21. The invalidity, unenforceability or lack of priority of the Insured Mortgage resulting from any provisions therein which provide for (i) interest on interest; (ii) changes in the rate of interest; or (iii) the addition of unpaid interest to the principal balance of the loan;
22. Forgery after Date of Policy of any assignment, release, discharge (partial or full), postponement or modification of the Insured Mortgage; or in the event the insured has acquired the estate or interest in the manner described in Section 2(a) of the Conditions and Stipulations and has not conveyed the title, forgery of any instrument by which another claims the title has been conveyed after Date of Policy;
23. The invalidity, unenforceability or lack of priority of the Insured Mortgage as to:
    (a) Advances made after Date of Policy pursuant to the terms of the Insured Mortgage existing at Date of Policy; and
    (b) Advances made and/or changes in the rate of interest charged subsequent to any modification to the terms of the Insured Mortgage made after Date of Policy which are by the terms of the Insured Mortgage, as modified, secured thereby.
24. Any covenants, conditions or restrictions, appearing in the Public Records, under which the Insured Mortgage can be divested, subordinated or extinguished, or its validity, priority or enforceability impaired;
25. Any violations on the Land of any enforceable covenants, conditions or restrictions appearing in the Public Records;
26. Any future violations on the Land of any existing covenants, conditions or restrictions appearing in the Public Records, occurring prior to the acquisition of title to the estate or interest in the Land by the Insured, provided the violations result in:
    (a) invalidity, loss of priority, or unenforceability of the Insured Mortgage; or
    (b) loss of title to the estate or interest in the Land if the Insured acquires title in satisfaction of the indebtedness secured by the Insured Mortgage.
27. Any covenants, conditions or restrictions, appearing in the Public Records, providing for:
    (a) A lien for liquidated damages;
    (b) A private charge or assessment; or
    (c) An option to purchase, a right of first refusal or the prior approval of a future purchaser or occupant.
28. Any adverse circumstance affecting the Land which would have been disclosed by a Local Authority Search of the Land at Date of Policy.

The Company will also pay the costs, legal fees and expenses incurred in the defence of the title or the charge against the title contained in the Insured Mortgage, as insured, but only to the extent provided in the Conditions and Stipulations.

EXCLUSIONS FROM COVERAGE

The following matters are expressly excluded from the coverage of this policy and the Company will not pay loss or damage, costs, legal fees or expenses which arise by reason of:
1. (a) Any law, by-law, ordinance, code or governmental regulation (including but not limited to building and zoning by-laws restricting, regulating, prohibiting or relating to (i) the occupancy, use, or enjoyment of the Land; (ii) the character, dimensions or location of any improvement now or hereafter erected on the land; (iii) a separation in ownership or a change in the dimensions or area of the Land or any parcel of which the Land is or was a part; or (iv) environmental protection, or the effect of any violation of these laws, by-laws, ordinances or governmental regulations, except to the extent that a notice of the enforcement thereof or a notice of a defect, lien or encumbrance resulting from a violation or alleged violation affecting the Land has been recorded in the Public Records at Date of Policy. This exclusion does not limit the coverage provided under insuring provisions 13, 14, 15, 16 and 17 of this policy.
   (b) Any governmental power not excluded by (a) above, except to the extent that a notice of the exercise thereof or a notice of a defect, lien or encumbrance resulting from a violation or alleged violation affecting the Land has been registered in the Public Records at Date of Policy. This exclusion does not limit the coverage under insuring provisions 13, 14, 15, 16 and 17 of this policy.
2. Rights of expropriation unless notice of the exercise thereof has been registered in the Public Records at Date of Policy, but not excluding from coverage any expropriation for which notice has been given prior to Date of Policy which would be binding on the rights of a purchaser for value without Knowledge.
3. Defects, liens, encumbrances, adverse claims or other matters:
   (a) created, suffered, assumed or agreed to by the Insured Claimant;
   (b) not Known to the Company, not registered in the Public Records at Date of Policy, but Known to the Insured Claimant and not disclosed in writing to the Company by the Insured Claimant prior to the date the Insured Claimant became an Insured under this policy;
   (c) resulting in no loss or damage to the Insured Claimant;
   (d) attaching or created subsequent to Date of Policy (this paragraph (d) does not limit the coverage provided under insuring provisions 7, 8, 15, 17, 18, 19, 20, 22, 23 and 26; or
   (e) resulting in loss or damage which would not have been sustained if the Insured Claimant had paid value for the Insured Mortgage.
4. Unenforceability of the Insured Mortgage because of the inability or failure of the Insured at Date of Policy, or the inability or failure of any subsequent owner of the indebtedness, to comply with applicable doing business laws of the jurisdiction in which the Land is situated.
5. Invalidity or unenforceability of the Insured Mortgage, or claim thereof, which arises out of the transaction evidenced by the Insured Mortgage and is based upon any Consumer Protection Law. This exclusion does not limit the coverage provided under insuring provision 10 of this Policy.
6. Taxes or assessments of any taxing or assessment authority which become a lien on the Land subsequent to Date of Policy.
7. Any covenants, conditions, restrictions, easements, rights of way, statutory building schemes, and regarding minerals and mineral rights, any lease, grant, exception or reservation, appearing in the Public Records. This exclusion does not limit the coverage provided under insuring provisions 17, 19, 20, 24, 25, 26, and 27 of this policy.
8. The overvaluation of the Insured Land as of the Policy Date.

CONDITIONS AND STIPULATIONS

1. DEFINITION OF TERMS.
   The following terms when used in this policy mean:
   (a) "Consumer Protection Law": any law designed or intended to give protection to a borrower in respect of the terms and conditions of the loan including without limitation, any laws requiring disclosure of interest rates, any laws specifying a maximum rate of interest and any

Figure 18.8 (cont'd)

laws relating to un-conscionability, misleading advertising or consumer protection.

(b) "Insured": the Insured named in Schedule A. The term "Insured" also includes (i) the owner of the indebtedness secured by the Insured Mortgage and each successor in ownership of the indebtedness except a successor who is an obligor under the provisions of Section 12(c) of these conditions and Stipulations (reserving, however, all rights and defences as to any successor that the Company would have had against any predecessor Insured, unless the successor acquired the indebtedness as a purchaser for value without Knowledge of the asserted defect, lien, encumbrance, adverse claim or other matter insured against by this policy as affecting title to the estate or interest in the Land); (ii) any governmental agency or crown corporation or private corporation which is an insurer or guarantor under an insurance contract or guarantee insuring or guaranteeing the indebtedness secured by the Insured Mortgage, or any part thereof, whether named as an Insured herein or not; or (iii) the parties designated in Section 2(a) of these Conditions and Stipulations.

(c) "Insured Claimant": an Insured claiming loss or damage.

(d) "Knowledge" or "Known": actual knowledge, or notice, but not knowledge or notice which may be imputed to an Insured by reason of the Public Records as defined in this policy or any other records which impart actual notice of matters affecting the Land.

(e) "Land": the land described or referred to in Schedule A, and improvements affixed thereto which by law constitute real property. The term "Land" does not include any property beyond the lines of the area described or referred to in Schedule A, nor any right, title, interest, estate or easement in abutting streets, roads, avenues, alleys, lanes, ways or waterways, but nothing herein shall modify or limit the extent to which a right of access to and from the Land is insured by this policy.

(f) "Mortgage": mortgage, charge, trust deed, or other security instrument.

(g) "Public Records": records established and maintained by legislation of the province or territory in which the Land is situated for the registration and or/ recording of interests in title.

(h) "Unmarketability of the title": an alleged or apparent matter affecting the title to the land, not excluded or excepted from coverage, which would entitle a purchaser of the estate or interest described in Schedule A or the Insured Mortgage to be released from the obligation to purchase by virtue of a contractual condition requiring the delivery of marketable title.

(i) "Local Authority Search": any search of local government records pertaining to the Land which would customarily be required by a solicitor qualified to practice law within the jurisdiction, in the normal course of a real estate transaction.

2. CONTINUATION OF INSURANCE.

(a) After Acquisition of Title. The coverage of this policy shall continue in force as of Date of Policy in favour of (i) an Insured who acquires all or any part of the estate or interest in the Land by foreclosure, trustee's sale, conveyance in lieu of foreclosure, or other legal manner which discharges the Insured Mortgage; (ii) a transferee of the estate or interest so acquired from an Insured corporation, provided the transferee is the parent or wholly-owned subsidiary of the Insured corporation, and their corporate successors by operation of law and not by purchase, subject to any rights or defences the Company may have against any predecessor Insureds; and (iii) any governmental agency or crown corporation or private corporation which acquires all or any part of the estate or interest pursuant to a contract of insurance or guarantee insuring or guaranteeing the indebtedness secured by the Insured Mortgage.

(b) After Conveyance of Title. The coverage of this policy shall continue in force as of Date of Policy in favour of an Insured only so long as the Insured retains an estate or interest in the Land, or holds an indebtedness secured by a purchase money Mortgage given by a purchaser to the Insured, or only so long as the Insured shall have liability by reason of covenants implied by any Provincial statute governing the conveyance of real property, or covenants contained in the terms of the Mortgage, made by the Insured in any transfer or conveyance of the estate or interest. This policy shall not continue in force in favour or any purchaser from the Insured of either (i) an estate or interest in the Land, or (ii) an indebtedness secured by a purchase money Mortgage given to the Insured.

(c) Amount of Insurance. The amount of insurance after the acquisition or after the conveyance shall in neither event exceed the least of

(i) One hundred twenty-five percent (125%) of the Amount of Insurance stated in Schedule A,

(ii) the amount of the principal of the indebtedness secured by the insured Mortgage, at the time of acquisition of the estate or interest, interest thereon, expenses of foreclosure, amounts advanced pursuant to the insured Mortgage to assure compliance with laws or to protect the Insured Mortgage prior to the time of acquisition of the estate or interest in the Land and secured thereby and reasonable amounts expended to prevent deterioration of improvements, but reduced by the amount of all payments made; or

(iii) the amount paid by a governmental agency or crown corporation or private corporation, if the agency or corporation is the Insured Claimant, in the acquisition of the estate or interest in satisfaction of its insurance contract or guarantee.

3. NOTICE OF CLAIM TO BE GIVEN BY INSURED CLAIMANT.

The Insured shall notify the Company promptly in writing (i) in case of any litigation as set forth in Section 4(a) below, (ii) in case Knowledge shall come to an Insured hereunder of any claim of title or interest which is adverse to the title to the estate or interest of the Insured Mortgage, as insured, and which might cause loss or damage for which the Company may be liable by virtue of this policy, or (iii) if title to the estate or interest or the Insured Mortgage, as insured, is rejected as unmarketable. If prompt notice shall not be given to the Company, then as to the Insured all liability of the Company shall terminate with regard to the matter or matters for which prompt notice is required; provided, however, that failure to notify the Company shall in no case prejudice the rights of any Insured under this policy unless the Company shall be prejudiced by the failure and then only to the extent of the prejudice.

4. DEFENCE AND PROSECUTION OF ACTIONS; DUTY OF INSURED CLAIMANT.

(a) Upon written request by the Insured and subject to the options contained in Section 6 of these Conditions and Stipulations, the Company, at its own cost and without unreasonable delay, shall provide for the defence of an Insured in litigation in which any third party asserts a claim adverse to the title or interest as insured, but only as to those stated causes of action alleging a defect, lien or encumbrance or other matter insured against by this policy. The company shall have the right to select counsel of its choice (subject to the right of the Insured to object for reasonable cause) to represent the Insured as to those stated causes of action and shall not be liable for and will not pay the fees of any other counsel. The Company will not pay any fees, costs or expenses incurred by the Insured in the defence of those causes of action which allege matters not insured against by this policy.

(b) The Company shall have the right, at its own cost, to institute and prosecute any action or proceeding or to do any other act which in its opinion may be necessary or desirable to establish the title to the estate or interest or the lien of the Insured Mortgage, as insured, or to prevent or reduce loss or damage to the Insured. The Company may take any appropriate action under the terms of this policy, whether or not it shall be liable hereunder, and shall not thereby concede liability or waive any provision of this policy. If the Company shall exercise its rights under this paragraph, it shall do so diligently.

(c) Whenever the Company shall have brought an action or filed a defence as required or permitted by the provisions of this policy, the Company may pursue any litigation to final determination by a court of competent jurisdiction and expressly reserves the right, in its sole discretion, to appeal from any adverse judgment or order.

3

Figure 18.8 (cont'd)

(d)   In all cases where this policy permits or requires the Company to prosecute or provide for the defence of any action or proceeding, the Insured shall secure to the Company the right to so prosecute or provide defence in the action or proceeding, and all appeals therein, and permit the Company to use, at its option, the name of the Insured for this purpose. Whenever requested by the Company, the Insured at the Company's expense, shall give the Company all reasonable aid (i) in any action or proceeding, securing evidence, obtaining witnesses, prosecuting or defending the action or proceeding, or effecting settlement, and (ii) in any other lawful act which in the opinion of the Company may be necessary or desirable to establish the title to the estate or interest or the Insured Mortgage, as insured. If the Company is prejudiced by the failure of the Insured to furnish the required cooperation, the Company's obligations to the Insured under the policy shall terminate, including any liability or obligation to defend, prosecute, or continue any litigation, with regard to the matter or matters requiring such cooperation.

5.   PROOF OF LOSS OR DAMAGE.
      In addition to and after the notices required under Section 3 of these Conditions and Stipulations have been provided by the Company, a proof of loss or damage signed and sworn to by the Insured Claimant shall ascertain the facts giving rise to the loss or damage. The proof of loss or damage shall describe the defect in, or lien or encumbrance on the title, or other matter insured against by this policy which constitutes the basis of loss or damage and shall state, to the extent possible the basis of calculating the amount of the loss or damage. If the Company is prejudiced by the failure of the Insured Claimant to provide the required proof of loss or damage, the Company's obligations to the Insured under the policy shall terminate, including any ability or obligation to defend, prosecute or continue any litigation, with regard to the matter or matters requiring such proof of loss or damage.
      In addition, the Insured Claimant may reasonably be required to submit to examination under oath by any authorized representative of the Company and shall produce for examination, inspection and copying, at such reasonable times and places as may be designated by any authorized representative of the Company, all records, books, ledgers, checks, correspondence and memoranda, whether bearing a date before or after Date of Policy, which reasonably pertain to the loss or damage. Further, if requested by any authorized representative of the Company, the Insured Claimant shall grant its permission, in writing, for any authorized representative of the Company to examine, inspect and copy all records, books, ledgers, checks, correspondence and memoranda in the custody or control of a third party, which reasonably pertain to the loss or damage. All information designated as confidential by the Insured Claimant provided to the Company pursuant to this Section shall not be disclosed to others unless, in the reasonable judgment of the Company, it is necessary in the administration of the claim. Failure of the Insured Claimant to submit for examination under oath, produce other reasonably requested information or grant permission to secure reasonably necessary information from third parties as required in this paragraph, unless prohibited by law or governmental regulation, shall terminate any liability of the Company under this policy as to that claim.

6.   OPTIONS TO PAY OR OTHERWISE SETTLE CLAIMS; TERMINATION OF LIABILITY.
      In case of a claim under this policy, the Company shall have the following options:
      (a)   To Pay or Tender Payment of One Hundred Twenty-five percent (125%) of the Amount of Insurance or to Purchase the Indebtedness.
              (i)   To pay or tender payment of one hundred twenty five percent (125%) of the amount of insurance under this policy together with any costs, legal fees and expenses incurred by the Insured Claimant, which were authorized by the Company, up to the time of payment or tender of payment and which the company is obligated to pay; or
              (ii)   To purchase the indebtedness secured by the Insured Mortgage for the amount owing thereon together with any costs, legal fees and expenses incurred by the Insured Claimant which were authorized by the Company up to the time of purchase and which the Company is obligated to pay.
              If the Company offers to purchase the indebtedness as herein provided, the owner of the indebtedness shall transfer, assign and convey the indebtedness and the Insured Mortgage, together with any collateral security, to the Company upon payment therefor.
              Upon the exercise by the Company of either of the options provided for in paragraphs (a) (i) or (ii), all liability and obligations to the Insured under this policy, other than to make the payment required in those paragraphs, shall terminate, including any liability or obligation to defend, prosecute, or continue any litigation, and the policy shall be surrendered to the Company for cancellation.
      (b)   To Pay or Otherwise Settle With Parties Other than the Insured or With the Insured Claimant.
              (i)   To pay or otherwise settle with other parties for or in the name of an Insured Claimant any claim insured against under this policy, together with any costs, legal fees and expenses incurred by the Insured Claimant which were authorized by the Company up to the time of payment and which the Company is obligated to pay; or
              (ii)   To pay or otherwise settle with the Insured Claimant the loss or damage provided for under this policy, together with any costs, attorneys' fees and expenses incurred by the Insured Claimant which were authorized by the Company up to the time of payment and which the Company is obligated to pay.
              Upon the exercise by the Company of either of the options provided for in paragraphs (b) (i) or (ii), the Company's obligations to the Insured under this policy for the claimed loss or damage, other than the payments required to be made, shall terminate, including any liability or obligation to defend, prosecute or continue any litigation.

7.   DETERMINATION AND EXTENT OF LIABILITY.
      This policy is a contract of indemnity against actual monetary loss or damage sustained or incurred by the Insured Claimant, who has suffered loss or damage by reason of matters insured against by this policy and only to the extent herein described.
      (a)   The liability of the Company under this policy shall not exceed the least of: (i) One hundred twenty-five percent (125%) of the Amount of Insurance stated in Schedule A, or, if applicable, the amount of insurance as defined in Section 2(c) of these Conditions and Stipulations; (ii) the amount of the unpaid principal indebtedness as defined in 2(c)(ii) secured by the Insured Mortgage as limited or provided under Section 8 of these Conditions and Stipulations or as reduced under Section 9 of these Conditions and Stipulations, at the time the loss or damage insured against by this policy occurs, together with the interest thereon; or (iii) the difference between the value of the insured estate or interest as insured and the value of the insured estate or interest subject to the defect, lien or encumbrance insured against by this policy; provided, however, that this Section 7(a)(iii) shall not apply when the defect, lien, encumbrance or other matter insured against by this policy results in a total failure of the Insured Mortgage to attach to the insured estate or interest.
      (b)   In the event the Insured has acquired the estate or interest in the manner described in Section 2(a) of these Conditions and Stipulations or has conveyed the title, then the liability of the Company shall continue as set forth in Section 7(a) of these Conditions and Stipulations.
      (c)   The Company will pay only those costs, legal fees and expenses incurred in accordance with Section 4 of these Conditions and Stipulations.

8.   LIMITATION OF LIABILITY.
      (a)   If the Company establishes good and marketable title, or removes the alleged defect, lien or encumbrance, or cures the lack of a right of access to or from the Land, or cures the claim of Unmarketability of title, or otherwise establishes the Insured Mortgage, all as insured, in a

4

Figure 18.8 (cont'd)

reasonably diligent manner by any method, including litigation as the completion of any appeals therefrom, it shall have fully performed its obligations with respect to that matter and shall not be liable for any loss or damage caused thereby.

(b) In the event of any litigation, including litigation by the Company or with the Company's consent, the Company shall have no liability for loss or damage until there has been a final determination by a court of competent jurisdiction and disposition of all appeals therefrom, adverse to the title or interest of the Insured or to the Insured Mortgage, as insured.

(c) the Company shall not be liable for loss or damage to any Insured for liability voluntarily assumed by the Insured in settling any claim or suit without the prior written consent of the Company.

(d) The Company shall not be liable for: (i) any indebtedness created subsequent to Date of Policy except for advances covered under insuring provision 23 and those made to protect the Insured Mortgage and secured thereby and reasonable amounts expended to prevent deterioration of improvements; or (ii) construction loan advances made subsequent to the Policy Date, except for construction loan advances made subsequent to Date of Policy for the purpose of financing in whole or in part the construction of an improvement to the Land which at Date of Policy were secured by the Insured Mortgage and which the Insured was and continued to be obligated to advance at and after Date of Policy.

9. REDUCTION OF INSURANCE; REDUCTION OR TERMINATION OF LIABILITY.

(a) All payments under this policy, except payments made for costs, legal fees and expenses, shall reduce the amount of insurance accordingly. However, any payments made prior to the acquisition of title to the estate or interest as provided in Section 2(a) of these Conditions and Stipulations shall not reduce accordingly the amount of insurance afforded under this policy except to the extent that the payments reduce the amount of the indebtedness secured by the Insured Mortgage.

(b) Payment in part by any person of the principal of the indebtedness, or any other obligation secured by the Insured Mortgage, or any voluntary partial satisfaction or release of the Insured Mortgage, to the extent of the payment, satisfaction or release, of the Insured Mortgage, to the extent of the payment, satisfaction or release, shall reduce the amount of insurance accordingly. The amount of insurance may thereafter be increased by accruing interest and advances made pursuant to the terms of the Insured Mortgage and secured thereby, with interest thereon, provided in no event shall the amount of insurance be greater than one hundred twenty-five percent (125%) of the Amount of Insurance stated in Schedule A.

(c) Payment in full by any person or the voluntary satisfaction of release of the Insured Mortgage shall terminate all liability of the Company except as provided in Section 2(a) and Section 9(b) of these Conditions and Stipulations.

10. LIABIILITY NONCUMULATIVE.

If the Insured acquires title to the estate or interest in satisfaction of the indebtedness secured by the Insured Mortgage, or any part thereof, it is expressly understood that the amount of insurance under this policy shall be reduced by any amount the Company may pay under any policy insuring a Mortgage to which exception is taken in Schedule B or to which the Insured has agreed, assumed, or taken subject, or which is hereafter executed by an Insured and which is a charge or lien on the estate or interest described or referred to in Schedule A, and the amount so paid shall be deemed a payment under this policy.

11. PAYMENT OF LOSS.

(a) No payment shall be made without producing this policy for endorsement of the payment unless the policy has been lost or destroyed, in which case proof of loss or destruction shall be furnished to the satisfaction of the Company.

(b) When liability and the extent of loss or damage has been definitely fixed in accordance with these Conditions and Stipulations, the loss or damage shall be payable within 30 days thereafter.

12. SUBROGATION UPON PAYMENT OR SETTLEMENT.

(a) The Company's Right of Subrogation. Whenever the Company shall be settled and paid a claim under this policy, all rights of subrogation shall vest in the Company unaffected by any act of the Insured Claimant. The Company shall be subrogated to and be entitled to all rights and remedies which the Insured Claimant would have had against any person or property in respect to the claim had this policy not been issued. If requested by the Company, the Insured Claimant shall transfer to the Company all rights and remedies against any person or property necessary in order to perfect this right of subrogation. The Insured Claimant shall permit the company to sue, compromise or settle in the name of the Insured Claimant and to use the name of the Insured Claimant in any transaction or litigation involving these rights or remedies. If a payment on account of a claim does not fully cover the loss of the Insured Claimant, the Company shall be subrogated to all rights and remedies of the Insured Claimant after the Insured Claimant shall have recovered its principal, interest, and costs of collection.

(b) The Insured's Rights and Limitations. Notwithstanding the foregoing, the owner of the indebtedness secured by the Insured Mortgage, provided the priority of the Insured Mortgage or its enforceability is not affected, may release or substitute the personal liability of any debtor or guarantor, or extend or otherwise modify the terms of payment, or release a portion of the estate or interest from the Insured Mortgage, or release any collateral security for the indebtedness. When the permitted acts of the Insured Claimant occur and the Insured has Knowledge of any claim of title or interest adverse to the title to the estate or interest or the priority or enforceability of the lien of the Insured Mortgage, as insured, the Company shall be required to pay only that part of any losses insured against by this policy which shall exceed the amount, if any, lost to the Company by reason of the impairment by the Insured Claimant of the Company's right of subrogation.

(c) The Company's Rights Against Non-Insured Obligors. The Company's right of subrogation against non-insured obligors shall exist and shall include, without limitation, the rights of the Insured to indemnities, guarantees, other policies of insurance or bonds, notwithstanding any terms or conditions contained in those instruments which provide for subrogation rights by reason of this policy. The Company's right of subrogation shall not be avoided by acquisition of the Insured Mortgage by an obligor (except an obligor described in Section 1(b) (ii) of these Conditions and Stipulations) who acquires the Insured Mortgage as a result of an indemnity, guarantee, other policy of insurance, notwithstanding Section 1(b) (i) of these Conditions and Stipulations.

13. ARBITRATION.

Unless prohibited by applicable law, either the Company or the insured may demand arbitration in accordance with the legislation of the Province or Territory in which the Land is situated. Arbitrable matters may include, but are not limited to, any controversy or claim between the Company and the insured arising out of or relating to this policy, any service of the Company in connection with its issuance or the breach of a policy provision or other obligation. All arbitrable matters shall be arbitrated only when agreed to by both the Company and the Insured. Arbitration pursuant to this policy shall be binding upon the parties. The award may include legal fees. Judgment upon the award rendered by the Arbitrator(s) may be entered in any court having jurisdiction thereof. The law of the Province or Territory in which the Land is situated shall apply to an arbitration under this Policy. A copy of the Rules may be obtained from the Company upon request.

5

Figure 18.8 (cont'd)

14. LIABILITY LIMITED TO THIS POLICY; POLICY ENTIRE CONTRACT.
   This policy together with all endorsements, if any, attached hereto by the Company is the entire policy and contract between the Insured and the Company in interpreting any provision of this policy, this policy shall be construed as a whole. (b) Any claim of loss or damage, whether or not based on negligence, and which arises out of the status of the Insured Mortgage or of the title to the estate or interest covered hereby or by any action asserting such claim, shall be restricted to this policy. (c) No amendment of, or endorsement to, this policy can be made except by a writing endorsed hereon or attached hereto signed by either the President, Vice-President, the Secretary, an Assistant Secretary, or validating officer or authorized signatory of the Company.

15. SEVERABILITY
   In the event any provision of this policy is held invalid or unenforceable under applicable law, the policy shall be deemed not to include that provision and all other provisions shall remain in full force and effect.

16. NOTICES, WHERE SENT
   All notices required to be given the Company and any statement in writing required to be furnished the Company shall include the number of this policy and shall be addressed to the Company at Royal Bank Plaza, North Tower, 200 Bay Street, Suite 2200, Toronto, Ontario, Canada, M5J 2J2.

6

Figure 18.9

STEWART TITLE — SCHEDULE B (RESIDENTIAL LENDER)*

STEWART TITLE GUARANTY COMPANY RESIDENTIAL TITLE INSURANCE POLICY SCHEDULE B	Royal Bank Plaza, North Tower 200 Bay Street, Suite 2200 Toronto, ON M5J 2J2	416-307-3300 888-667-5151 416-307-3305 fax

File No.
Lawyer File No.
EC No.

Loan Form   Policy Number:

This policy does not insure against loss or damage (and the Company will not pay costs, legal fees, or expenses) which arise by reason of:

1.   Environmental concerns or matters of any kind.

[Enter all instruments registered on title that would affect good title with the following exceptions: (1) Subdivision Agreements and amendments thereto; (2) Development Agreements and amendments thereto.]:

[In the event this policy is issued to a second mortgagee, registration particulars of the first mortgage should be set out.]

FOR OFFICE USE ONLY:
File No.

Royal Bank Plaza, North Tower
200 Bay Street, Suite 2200
Toronto, Ontario   M5J 2J2
Tel: (416) 307-3300 Fax: (416) 307-3305

Figure 18.10

STEWART TITLE — COMMERCIAL OWNER POLICY OF TITLE INSURANCE*

COMMERCIAL OWNER POLICY OF TITLE INSURANCE ISSUED BY

STEWART TITLE ®
GUARANTY COMPANY

SUBJECT TO THE EXCLUSIONS FROM COVERAGE, THE EXCEPTIONS FROM COVERAGE CONTAINED IN SCHEDULE B AND THECONDITIONS AND STIPULATIONS, STEWART TITLE GUARANTY COMPANY, a Texas corporation, licenced to carry on business in Canada, having its Canadian operations headquartered in Toronto, Ontario, herein called the Company, insures, as of Date of Policy shown in Schedule A, against loss or damage, not exceeding the Amount of Insurance stated in Schedule A, sustained or incurred by the insured by reason of:

1. Title to the estate or interest described in Schedule A being vested other than as stated therein;

2. Any defect in or lien or encumbrance on the title;

3. Unmarketability of the title;

4. Lack of a right of access to and from the land.

5. The forced removal of the existing structure (other than a boundary wall or fence) for violation of an existing zoning by law, or the inability of the Insured to use the land as a single residential dwelling;

6. Any rights arising from tenancies, contracts, options, or rights of possession under the *Family Law Act.*

The Company will also pay the costs, legal fees and expenses incurred in defence of the title, as insured, but only to the extent provided in the Conditions and Stipulations.
IN WITNESS WHEREOF, Stewart Title Guaranty Company has caused this policy to be signed and sealed by its duly authorized officers as of Date of Policy shown in Schedule A.

EXCLUSIONS FROM COVERAGE

The following matters are expressly excluded from the coverage of this policy and the Company will not pay loss or damage, costs, legal fees or expenses which arise by reason of:

1. (a)   Any law, by-law, order, notice or governmental regulation (including but not limited to building and zoning laws, but excluding subdivision control legislation) restricting, regulating, prohibiting or relating to (i) the occupancy, use, or enjoyment of the land; (ii) the character, dimensions or location of any improvement now or hereafter erected on the land; (iii) a separation in ownership or a change in the dimensions or area of the land or any parcel of which the land is or was a part; (iv) environmental concerns or matters of any kind, or, (v) the effect of any violation of these laws, ordinances or governmental regulations, except to the extent that a notice of the enforcement thereof or a notice of a defect, lien or encumbrance resulting from a violation or alleged violation affecting the land has been recorded in the public records at Date of Policy.

(b)   Any governmental power not excluded by (a) above, except to the extent that a notice, lien or encumbrance resulting from a violation or alleged violation affecting the land has been recorded in the public records at Date of Policy.

2.   Rights of expropriation unless notice of the exercise thereof has been registered in the public records at Date of Policy, but not excluding from coverage any taking which has occurred prior to Date of Policy which would be binding on the rights of a purchaser for value without knowledge.

3.   Defects, liens, encumbrances, adverse claims or other matters:

(a) created, suffered, assumed or agreed to by the insured claimant;
(b) not known to the Company, not registered in the public records at Date of Policy, but known to the insured claimant and not disclosed in writing to the Company by the insured claimant prior to the date the insured claimant became an insured under this policy;
(c) resulting in no loss or damage to the insured claimant;
(d) attaching or created subsequent to Date of Policy; or
(e) resulting in loss or damage which would not have been sustained if the insured claimant had paid value for the estate or interest insured by this policy.

STEWART TITLE ®
GUARANTY COMPANY

Chairman of the Board

President

Authorized Countersignature:

Stewart Title Guaranty Company
Toronto, Ontario, Canada

Part 1 of Guarantee Serial No.	O-7761

Figure 18.10 (cont'd)

4. Any claim, which arises out of the transaction vesting in the Insured the estate or interest insured by this policy by reason of the operation of bankruptcy, insolvency, or other creditors' rights laws, that deem the transaction fraudulent or preferential, or subordinate to the interest of another person or entity.

CONDITIONS AND STIPULATIONS

1. DEFINITION OF TERMS.
The following terms when used in this policy mean:

(a)   "insured": the insured named in Schedule A, and, subject to any rights or defences the Company would have had against the named insured, those who succeed to the interest of the named insured by operation of law as distinguished from purchase including, but not limited to, heirs or survivors.
(b)   "insured claimant": an insured claiming loss or damage
(c)   "knowledge" or "known": actual knowledge, not constructive knowledge or notice which may be imputed to an insured by reason of the public records as defined in this policy or any other records which impart constructive notice of matters affecting the land.
(d).   "land": the land described or referred to in Schedule A, and improvements affixed thereto which by law constitute real property. The term "land" does not include any property beyond the lines of the area described or referred to in Schedule A, nor any right, title, interest, estate or easement in abutting streets, roads, avenues, alleys, lanes, ways or waterways, but nothing herein shall modify or limit the extent to which a right of access to and from the land is insured by this policy.
(e)   "mortgage": mortgage, deed of trust, trust deed, or other security instrument
(f)   "public records": records established and maintained by legislation of the province or territory in which the land is situated, for the registration and or recording of interests in land.
(g)   "unmarketability of the title": an alleged or apparent matter affecting the title to the land, not excluded or excepted from coverage, which would entitle a purchaser of the estate or interest described in Schedule A to be released from the obligation to purchase by virtue of a contractual condition requiring the delivery of good, registerable, proper or marketable title.

2. CONTINUATION OF INSURANCE AFTER CONVEYANCE OF TITLE.
The coverage of this policy shall continue in force as of Date of Policy in favor of an insured only so long as the insured retains an estate or interest in the land, or holds an indebtedness secured by a vendor take-back mortgage given by a purchaser from the insured, or only so long as the insured shall have liability by reason of covenants of warranty made by the insured in any transfer or conveyance of the estate or interest. This policy shall not continue in force in favor of any purchaser from the insured of either (i) an estate or interest in the land, or (ii) an indebtedness secured by a vendor take-back mortgage given to the insured.

3. NOTICE OF CLAIM TO BE GIVEN BY INSURED CLAIMANT.
The insured shall notify the Company promptly in writing (i) in case of any litigation as set forth in Section 4(a) below, (ii) in case knowledge shall come to an insured hereunder of any claim of title or interest which is adverse to the title to the estate or interest, as insured, and which might cause loss or damage for which the Company may be liable by virtue of this policy, or (iii) if title to the estate or interest, as insured, is rejected as unmarketable. If prompt notice shall not be given to the Company, then as to the insured all liability of the Company shall terminate with regard to the matter or matters for which prompt notice is required; provided, however, that failure to notify the Company shall in no case prejudice the rights of any insured under this policy unless the Company shall be prejudiced by the failure and then only to the extent of the prejudice.

4. DEFENCE AND PROSECUTION OF ACTIONS; DUTY OF INSURED CLAIMANT TO COOPERATE.
(a)   Upon written request by the insured and subject to the options contained in Section 6 of these Conditions and Stipulations the Company, at its own cost and without unreasonable delay, shall provide for the defence of an insured in litigation in which any third party asserts a claim adverse to the title or interest as insured, but only as to those stated causes of action alleging a defect, lien or encumbrance or other matter insured against by this policy. The Company shall have the right to select counsel of its choice (subject to the right of the insured to object for reasonable cause) to represent the insured as to those stated causes of action and shall not be liable for and will not pay the fees of any other counsel. The Company will not pay any fees, costs or expenses incurred by the insured in the defence of those causes of action which allege matters not insured against by this policy.
(b)   The Company shall have the right, at its own cost, to institute and prosecute any action or proceeding or to do any other act which in its opinion may be necessary or desirable to establish the title to the estate or interest, as insured, or to prevent or reduce loss or damage to the insured. The Company may take any appropriate action under the terms of this policy, whether or not it shall be liable hereunder, and shall not thereby concede liability or waive any provision of this policy. If the Company shall exercise its rights under this paragraph it shall do so diligently.
(c)   Whenever the Company shall have commenced an action or filed a defence as required or permitted by the provisions of this policy, the Company may pursue any litigation to final determination by a court of competent jurisdiction and expressly reserves the right, in its sole discretion, to appeal from any adverse judgment or order.
(d)   In all cases where this policy permits or requires the Company to prosecute or provide for the defence of any action or proceeding, the insured shall secure to the Company the right to so prosecute or provide defence in the proceeding, and all appeals therein, and permit the Company to use, at its option, the name of the insured for this purpose. Whenever requested by the Company, the insured, at the Company's expense, shall give the Company all reasonable aid (i) in any action or proceeding, securing evidence, obtaining witnesses, prosecuting or defending the action or proceeding, or effecting settlement, and (ii) in any other lawful act which in the opinion of the Company may be necessary or desirable to establish the title to the estate or interest as insured. If the Company is prejudiced by the failure of the insured to furnish the required cooperation, the Company's obligations to the Insured under the policy shall terminate, including any liability or obligation to defend, prosecute, or continue any litigation, with regard to the matter or matters requiring such cooperation.

5. PROOF OF LOSS OR DAMAGE.
In addition to and after the notices required under Section 3 of these Conditions and Stipulations have been provided the Company, a proof of loss or damage signed and sworn to by the insured claimant shall be furnished to the Company within 90 days after the insured claimant shall ascertain the facts giving rise to the loss or damage. The proof of loss or damage shall describe the defect in, or lien or encumbrance on the title, or other matter insured against by this policy which constitutes the basis of loss or damage and shall state, to the extent possible, the basis of calculating the amount of the loss or damage. If the Company is prejudiced by the failure of the insured claimant to provide the required proof of loss or damage, the Company's obligations to the insured under the policy shall terminate, including any liability or obligation to defend, prosecute, or continue any litigation, with regard to the matter or matters requiring such proof of loss or damage.

Figure 18.10 (cont'd)

In addition, the insured claimant may reasonably be required to submit to examination under oath by any authorized representative of the Company and shall produce for examination, inspection and copying, at such reasonable times and places as may be designated by any authorized representative of the Company, all records, books, ledgers, checks, correspondence and memoranda, whether bearing a date before or after Date of Policy, which reasonably pertain to the loss or damage. Further, if requested by any authorized representative of the Company, the insured claimant shall grant its permission, in writing, for any authorized representative of the Company to examine, inspect and copy all records, books, ledgers, checks, correspondence and memoranda in the custody or control of a third party, which reasonably pertain to the loss or damage. All information designated as confidential by the insured claimant provided to the Company pursuant to this Section shall not be disclosed to others unless, in the reasonable judgment of the Company, it is necessary in the administration of the claim. Failure of the insured claimant to submit for examination under oath, produce other reasonably requested information or grant permission to secure reasonably necessary information from third parties as required in this paragraph shall terminate any liability of the Company under this policy as to that claim.

6. OPTIONS TO PAY OR OTHERWISE SETTLE CLAIMS; TERMINATION OF LIABILITY.
In case of a claim under this policy, the Company shall have the following additional options:

(a)   **To Pay or Tender Payment of the Amount of Insurance.**
(i)   To pay or tender payment of the amount of insurance under this policy together with any costs, legal fees and expenses incurred by the insured claimant, which were authorized by the Company, up to the time of payment or tender of payment and which the Company is obligated to pay.
(ii)   Upon the exercise by the Company of this option, all liability and obligations to the insured under this policy, other than to make the payment required, shall terminate, including any liability or obligation to defend, prosecute or continue any litigation, and the policy shall be surrendered to the Company for cancellation.
(b)   **To Pay or Otherwise Settle With Parties Other than the Insured or With the Insured Claimant.**
(i)   To pay or otherwise settle with other parties for or in the name of an insured claimant any claim insured against under this policy, together with any costs, legal fees and expenses incurred by the insured claimant which were authorized by the Company up to the time of payment and which the Company is obligated to pay; or
(ii)   To pay or otherwise settle with the insured claimant the loss or damage provided for under this policy, together with any costs, legal fees and expenses incurred by the insured claimant which were authorized by the Company up to the time of payment and which the Company is obligated to pay.
Upon the exercise by the Company of either of the options provided for in paragraphs (b)(i) or (ii) the Company's obligations to the insured under this policy for the claimed loss or damage, other than the payments required to be made, shall terminate including any liability or obligation to defend, prosecute or continue any litigation.

7. DETERMINATION, EXTENT OF LIABILITY.
This policy is a contract of indemnity against actual monetary loss or damage sustained or incurred by the insured claimant who has suffered loss or damage by reason of matters insured against by this policy and only to the extent herein described.

(a)   The liability of the Company under this policy shall not exceed the least of:
(i)   the Amount of Insurance stated in Schedule A, or,
(ii)   the amount of the unpaid principal indebtedness secured by the insured mortgage as limited or provided under Section 8 of these Conditions and Stipulations or as reduced under Section 9 of these Conditions and Stipulations, at the time the loss or damage insured against by this policy occurs, together with interest thereon; or
(iii)   the difference between the value of the insured estate or interest as insured and the value of the insured estate or interest subject to the defect, lien or encumbrance insured against by this policy.
(b)   In the event the insured has acquired the estate or interest in the manner described in Section 2(a) of these Conditions and Stipulations or has conveyed the title, then the liability of the Company shall continue as set forth in Section 7(a) of these Conditions end Stipulations.
(c)   The Company will pay only those costs, legal fees and expenses incurred in accordance with Section 4 of these Conditions and Stipulations.

8. APPORTIONMENT.
If the land described in Schedule A consists of two or more parcels which are not used as a single site, and a loss is established affecting one or more of the parcels but not all, the loss shall be computed and settled on a pro rata basis as if the amount of insurance under this policy was divided pro rata as to the value on Date of Policy of each separate parcel to the whole, exclusive of any improvements made subsequent to Date of Policy, unless a liability or value has otherwise been agreed upon as to each parcel by the Company and the insured at the time of the issuance of this policy and shown by an express statement or by an endorsement attached to this policy.

9. LIMITATION OF LIABILITY.
(a)   If the Company establishes the title, or removes the alleged defect, lien or encumbrance, or cures the lack of a right of access to or from the land, or cures the claim of unmarketability of title, all as insured, in a reasonably diligent manner by any method, including litigation and the completion of any appeals therefrom, it shall have fully performed its obligations with respect to that matter and shall not be liable for any loss or damage caused thereby.
(b)   In the event of any litigation, including litigation by the Company or with the Company's consent, the Company shall have no liability for loss or damage until there has been a final determination by a court of competent jurisdiction, and disposition of all appeals therefrom, adverse to the title as insured.
(c)   The Company shall not be liable for loss or damage to any insured for liability voluntarily assumed by the insured in settling any claim or suit without the prior written consent of the Company.

10. REDUCTION OF INSURANCE; REDUCTION OR TERMINATION OF LIABILITY.
All payments under this policy, except payments made for costs, legal fees and expenses, shall reduce the amount of the insurance by the amount of such payment.

11. LIABILITY NONCUMULATIVE.
It is expressly understood that the amount of insurance under this policy shall be reduced by any amount the Company may pay under any policy insuring a mortgage to which exception is taken in Schedule B or to which the insured has agreed, assumed, or taken subject, or which is hereafter executed by an insured and which is a charge or lien on the estate or interest described or referred to in Schedule A, and the amount so paid shall be deemed a payment under this policy to the insured owner.

3

Figure 18.10 (cont'd)

12. PAYMENT OF LOSS.

(a)   No payment shall be made without producing this policy for endorsement of the payment unless the policy has been lost or destroyed, in which case proof of loss or destruction shall be furnished to the satisfaction of the Company.

(b)   When liability and the extent of loss or damage has been definitely fixed in accordance with these Conditions and Stipulations, the loss or damage shall be payable within 30 days thereafter.

13. SUBROGATION UPON PAYMENT OR SETTLEMENT.

(a)   **The Company's Right of Subrogation.**

Whenever the Company shall have settled and paid a claim under this policy, all rights of subrogation shall vest in the Company unaffected by any act of the insured claimant.

The Company shall be subrogated to and be entitled to al rights and remedies which the insured claimant would have had against any person or property in respect to the claim had this policy not been issued. If requested by the Company, the insured claimant shall transfer to the Company all rights and remedies against any person or property necessary in order to perfect this right of subrogation.   The insured claimant shall permit the Company to sue, compromise or settle in the name of the insured claimant and to use the name of the insured claimant in any transaction or litigation involving these rights or remedies.

If a payment on account of a claim does not fully cover the loss of the insured claimant, the Company shall be subrogated to these rights and remedies in the proportion which the Company's payment bears to the whole amount of the loss.

If loss should result from any act of the insured claimant, as stated above, that act shall not void this policy, but the Company, in that event, shall be required to pay only that part of any losses insured against by this policy which shall exceed the amount, if any, lost to the Company by reason of the impairment by the insured claimant of the Company's right of subrogation.

(b)   **The Company's Rights Against Non-Insured Obligors.**

The Company's right of subrogation against non-insured obligors shall exist and shall include, without limitation, the rights of the insured to indemnities, guarantees, other policies of insurance or bonds, notwithstanding any terms or conditions contained in those instruments which provide for subrogation rights by reason of this policy.

14. ARBITRATION.

Unless prohibited by applicable law, either the Company or the insured may demand arbitration in accordance with the legislation of the Province or Territory in which the land is situated. Arbitrable matters may include, but are not limited to, any controversy or claim between the Company and the insured arising out of or relating to this policy, any service of the Company in connection with its issuance or the breach of a policy provision or other obligation. All arbitrable matters shall be arbitrated only when agreed to by both the Company and the insured.   Arbitration pursuant to this policy shall be binding upon the parties. The award may include legal fees. Judgment upon the award rendered by the Arbitrator(s) may be entered in any court having jurisdiction thereof. The law of the Province or Territory in which the Land is situated shall apply to an arbitration under this Policy.   A copy of the Rules may be obtained from the Company upon request.

15. LIABILITY LIMITED TO THIS POLICY; POLICY ENTIRE CONTRACT.

(a)   This policy together with all endorsements, if any, attached hereto by the Company is the entire policy and contract between the insured and the Company. In interpreting any provision of this policy, this policy shall be construed as a whole.

(b)   Any claim of loss or damage, whether or not based on negligence, and which arises out of the status of the title to the estate or interest covered hereby or by any action asserting such claim, shall be restricted to this policy.

(c)   No amendment of or endorsement to this policy can be made except by a writing endorsed hereon or attached hereto signed by either the President, a Vice President, the Secretary, an Assistant Secretary, or validating officer or authorized signatory of the Company.

16. SEVERABILITY.

In the event any provision of the policy is held invalid or unenforceable under applicable law, the policy shall be deemed not to include that provision and all other provisions shall remain in full force and effect.

17. NOTICES, WHERE SENT.

All notices required to be given the Company and any statement in writing required to be furnished the Company shall include the number of this policy and shall be addressed to the Company at Royal Bank Plaza, North Tower, 200 Bay Street, Suite 2200, Toronto, Ontario, Canada, M5J 2J2.

Figure 18.11

STEWART TITLE — COMMERCIAL LOAN POLICY OF TITLE INSURANCE*

COMMERCIAL LOAN POLICY OF TITLE INSURANCE ISSUED BY

STEWART TITLE ®
GUARANTY COMPANY

SUBJECT TO THE EXCLUSIONS FROM COVERAGE, THE EXCEPTIONS FROM COVERAGE CONTAINED IN SCHEDULE B AND THE CONDITIONS AND STIPULATIONS, STEWART TITLE GUARANTY COMPANY, a Texas corporation, herein called the Company, insures, as of Date of Policy shown in Schedule A, against loss or damage, not exceeding the Amount of Insurance stated in Schedule A, sustained or incurred by the insured by reason of:

1. Title to the estate or interest described in Schedule A being vested other than as stated therein;
2. Any defect in or lien or encumbrance on the title;
3. Unmarketability of the title;
4. Lack of a right of access to and from the land;
5. The invalidity or unenforceability of the insured mortgage upon the title;
6. The priority of any lien or encumbrance over the insured mortgage;
7. Lack of priority of the insured mortgage to a lien for the supply of services, labor or material to the land;
8. The invalidity or unenforceability of any assignment of the insured mortgage, provided the assignment is shown in Schedule A, or the failure of the assignment shown in Schedule A to vest title to the insured mortgage in the named insured assignee free and clear of all liens.
9. Any outstanding municipal work orders against the land and that the use of the property at the policy date for one to four residential units is permitted by the municipality.

The Company will also pay the costs, legal fees and expenses incurred in defense of the title or the lien of the insured mortgage, as insured, but only to the extent provided in the Conditions and Stipulations.

IN WITNESS WHEREOF, Stewart Title Guaranty Company has caused this policy to be signed and sealed by its duly authorized officers as of Date of Policy shown in Schedule A.

EXCLUSIONS FROM COVERAGE

The following matters are expressly excluded from the coverage of this policy and the Company will not pay loss or damage, costs, legal fees or expenses which arise by reason of:

1. (a) Any law, by-law, order, notice, ordinance or governmental regulation (including but not limited to building and zoning laws, ordinances, or regulations but excluding subdivision control legislation) restricting, regulating, prohibiting or relating to (i) the occupancy, use, or enjoyment of the land; (ii) the character, dimensions or location of any improvement now or hereafter erected on the land; (iii) a separation in ownership or a change in the dimensions or area of the land or any parcel of which the land is or was a part; (iv) environmental matters of any nature; or (v) the effect of any violation of these laws, by-laws, orders, notices, ordinances or governmental regulations, except to the extent that a notice of the enforcement thereof or a notice of a defect, lien or encumbrance resulting from a violation or alleged violation affecting the land has been recorded in the public records at Date of Policy.

   (b) Any governmental power not excluded by (a) above, except to the extent that a notice of the exercise thereof or a notice of a defect, lien or encumbrance resulting from a violation or alleged violation affecting the land has been registered in the public records at Date of Policy.

2. Rights of expropriation unless notice of the exercise thereof has been registered in the public records at Date of Policy, but not excluding from coverage any taking which has occurred prior to Date of Policy which would be binding on the rights of a purchaser for value without knowledge.

3. Defects, liens, encumbrances, adverse claims or other matters:
   (a) created, suffered, assumed or agreed to by the insured claimant;
   (b) not known to the Company, not registered in the public records at Date of Policy, but known to the Insured claimant and not disclosed in writing to the Company by the insured claimant prior to the date the insured claimant became an insured under this policy;
   (c) resulting in no loss or damage to the insured claimant;
   (d) attaching or created subsequent to Date of Policy (except to the extent that this policy insures the priority of the insured mortgage over any statutory lien for services, labor or material); or
   (e) resulting in loss or damage which would not have been sustained if the insured claimant had paid value for the insured mortgage.

4. Unenforceability of the insured mortgage because of the inability or failure of the insured at Date of Policy or the inability or failure of any subsequent owner of the insured mortgage to comply with applicable laws of doing business laws of the province or territory in which the land is situated.

Signed under seal for the Company, but this Policy is only valid when it bears an authorized countersignature.

STEWART TITLE ®
GUARANTY COMPANY

Chairman of the Board　　　　　　　　　　　　　　　　　　_President_

Authorized Countersignature:

Stewart Title Guaranty Company
Toronto, Ontario, Canada

Part 1 of Guarantee Serial No **M-7762**

---

* © Stewart Title 2010. Reproduced with permission.

Figure 18.11 (cont'd)

5.   Invalidity or unenforceability of the insured mortgage, or claim thereof, which arises out of the transaction evidenced by the insured mortgage and is based upon any consumer credit protection legislation.

6.   Any statutory lien for services, labor or materials (or the claim of priority of any statutory lien for services, labor or materials over the insured mortgage) arising from an improvement or work related to the land which is contracted for and commenced subsequent to Date of Policy and is not financed in whole or in part by proceeds of the indebtedness secured by the insured mortgage which at Date of Policy the insured has advanced or is obligated to advance.

7.   Any claim, which arises out of the transaction creating the interest of the mortgagee insured by this policy, by reason of the operation of bankruptcy, insolvency, or similar creditors' rights or equitable laws, that deem the transaction fraudulent or preferential, or subordinate to the interest of another person or entity.

CONDITIONS AND STIPULATIONS

1.   DEFINITION OF TERMS.

The following terms when used in this policy mean:

(a)   "insured": the insured named in Schedule A. The term "insured" also includes:

(i)   the owner of the indebtedness secured by the insured mortgage and each successor in ownership of the indebtedness except a successor who is an obligor under the provisions of Section 12(c) of these Conditions and Stipulations (reserving, however, all rights and defenses as to any successor that the Company would have had against any predecessor insured, unless the successor acquired the indebtedness as a purchaser for value without knowledge of the asserted defect, lien, encumbrance, adverse claim or other matter insured against by this policy as affecting title to the estate or interest in the land);

(ii)   any governmental agency or crown corporation which is an insurer or guarantor under an insurance contract or guarantee insuring or guaranteeing the indebtedness secured by the insured mortgage, or any part thereof, whether named as an insured herein or not;

(iii)   the parties designated in Section 2(a) of these Conditions and Stipulations.

(b)   "insured claimant": an insured claiming loss or damage.

(c)   "knowledge" or "known": actual knowledge, not constructive knowledge or notice which may be imputed to an insured by reason of the public records as defined in this policy or any other records which impart constructive notice of matters affecting the land.

(d)   "land": the land described or referred to in Schedule [A], and improvements affixed thereto which by law constitute real property. The term "land" does not include any property beyond the lines of the area described or referred to in Schedule [A], nor any right, title, interest, estate or easement in abutting streets, roads, avenues, alleys, lanes, ways or waterways, but nothing herein shall modify or limit the extent to which a right of access to and from the land is insured by this policy.

(e)   "mortgage": mortgage, charge or other instrument securing an interest in land.

(f)   "public records": records established and maintained by legislation of the province or territory in which the land is situated, for the registration and/or recording of interests in land.

(g)   "unmarketability of the title": an alleged or apparent matter affecting the title to the land, not excluded or excepted from coverage, which would entitle a purchaser of the estate or interest described in Schedule A or the insured mortgage to be released from the obligation to purchase by virtue of a contractual condition requiring the delivery of good, registrable, proper or marketable title.

2.   CONTINUATION OF INSURANCE.

(a)   **After Acquisition of Title.** The coverage of this policy shall continue in force as of Date of Policy in favor of (i) an insured who acquires all or any part of the estate or interest in the land by foreclosure, trustee's sale, quit claim, or other legal manner which discharges the insured mortgage; (ii) a transferee of the estate or interest so acquired from an insured corporation, provided the transferee is the parent or wholly-owned subsidiary of the insured corporation, and their corporate successors by operation of law and not by purchase, subject to any rights or defences the Company may have against any predecessor insureds; and (iii) any governmental agency or crown corporation which acquires all or any part of the estate or interest pursuant to a contract of insurance or guarantee insuring or guaranteeing the indebtedness secured by the insured mortgage.

(b)   **After Conveyance of Title.** The coverage of this policy shall continue in force as of Date of Policy in favor of an insured only so long as the insured retains an estate or interest in the land, or holds an indebtedness secured by a vendor take-back mortgage given by a purchaser from the insured, or only so long as the insured shall have liability by reason of covenants of warranty made by the insured in any transfer or conveyance of the estate or interest or implied by legislation of the province or territory in which the land is situated. This policy shall not continue in force in favor of any purchaser from the insured of either (i) an estate or interest in the land, or (ii) an indebtedness secured by a vendor take-back mortgage given to the insured.

(c)   **Amount of Insurance.** The amount of insurance after the acquisition or after the conveyance shall in neither event exceed the least of:

(i)   the amount of Insurance stated in Schedule A;

(ii)   the amount of the principal of the indebtedness secured by the insured mortgage as of Date of Policy, interest thereon, expenses of foreclosure, amounts advanced pursuant to the insured mortgage to assure compliance with laws or to protect the insured mortgage prior to the time of acquisition of the estate or interest in the land and secured thereby and reasonable amounts expended to prevent deterioration of improvements, but reduced by the amount of all payments made; or

(iii)   the amount paid by any governmental agency or crown corporation, if the agency or crown corporation is the insured claimant, in the acquisition of the estate or interest in satisfaction of its insurance contract or guarantee.

3.   NOTICE OF CLAIM TO BE GIVEN BY INSURED CLAIMANT.

The insured shall notify the Company promptly in writing (i) in case of any litigation as set forth in Section 4(a) below, (ii) in case knowledge shall come to an insured hereunder of any claim of title or interest which is adverse to the title to the estate or interest or the lien of the insured mortgage, as insured, and which might cause loss or damage for which the Company may be liable by virtue of this policy, or (iii) if title to the estate or interest or insured mortgage, as insured, is rejected as unmarketable. If prompt notice shall not be given to the company, then as to the insured all liability of the Company shall terminate with regard to the matter or matters for which prompt notice is required; provided, however, that failure to notify the Company shall in no case prejudice the rights of any insured under this policy unless the Company shall be prejudiced by the failure and then only to the extent of the prejudice.

4.   DEFENSE AND PROSECUTION OF ACTIONS; DUTY OF INSURED CLAIMANT TO COOPERATE.

(a)   Upon written request by the insured and subject to the options contained in Section 6 of these Conditions and Stipulations, the Company, at its own cost and without unreasonable delay, shall provide for the defence of an insured in litigation in which any third party asserts a claim adverse to the title or interest as insured, but only as to those stated causes of action alleging a defect, lien or encumbrance or other matter insured against by this policy. The Company shall have the right to select counsel of its choice (subject to the right of the insured to object for reasonable cause) to represent the insured as to those stated causes of action and shall not be liable for and will not pay the fees of any other counsel. The Company will not pay any fees, costs of expenses incurred by the insured in the defence of those causes of action which allege matters not insured against by this policy.

(b)   The Company shall have the right, at its own cost, to institute and prosecute any action or proceeding or to do any other act which in its opinion may be necessary or desirable to establish the title to the estate or interest or the lien of the insured mortgage, as insured, or to prevent or reduce loss or damage to the insured. The Company may take any appropriate action under the terms of this policy, whether or not it shall be liable hereunder, and shall not thereby concede liability or waive any provision of this policy. If the Company shall exercise its rights under this paragraph, it shall do so diligently.

2

Figure 18.11 (cont'd)

(c) Whenever the company shall have commenced an action or filed a defence in a proceeding as required or permitted by the provisions of this policy, the Company may pursue any litigation to final determination by a court of competent jurisdiction and expressly reserves the right, in its sole discretion, to appeal from any adverse judgment or order.

(d) In all cases where this policy permits or requires the Company to prosecute or provide for defence in any proceeding, the insured shall secure to the Company the right to so prosecute or provide defence in the proceeding, and all appeals therein, and permit the company to use, at its option, the name of the insured for this purpose. Whenever requested by the Company, the insured, at the Company's expense, shall give the Company all reasonable aid (i) in any action or proceeding, securing evidence, obtaining witnesses, prosecuting or defending the action or proceeding, or effecting settlement, and (ii) in any other lawful act which in the opinion of the Company may be necessary or desirable to establish the title to the estate or interest of the insured. If the Company is prejudiced by the failure of the insured to furnish the required cooperation, the Company's obligations to the insured under the policy shall terminate, including any liability or obligation to defend, prosecute, or continue any litigation, with regard to the matter or matters requiring such cooperation.

5. PROOF OF LOSS OR DAMAGE.

In addition to and after the notices required under Section 3 of these Conditions and Stipulations have been provided the company, a proof of loss or damage signed and sworn to by the insured claimant shall be furnished to the Company within 90 days after the insured claimant shall ascertain the facts giving rise to the loss or damage. The proof of loss or damage shall describe the defect in, or lien or encumbrance on the title, or other matter insured against by this policy which constitutes the basis of loss or damage and shall state, to the extent possible, the basis of calculating the amount of the loss or damage. If the Company is prejudiced by the failure of the insured claimant to provide the required proof of loss or damage, the Company's obligations to the insured under the policy shall terminate, including any liability or obligation to defend, prosecute, or continue any litigation, with regard to the matter or matters requiring such proof of loss or damage.

In addition, the insured claimant may reasonably be required to submit to examination under oath by any authorized representative of the Company and shall produce for examination, inspection and copying, at such reasonable times and places as may be designated by any authorized representative of the Company, all records, books, ledgers, checks, correspondence and memoranda, whether bearing a date before or after Date of Policy, which reasonably pertain to the loss or damage. Further, if requested by an authorized representative of the Company, the insurance claimant shall grant its permission, in writing, for any authorized representative of the Company to examine, inspect and copy all records, books, ledgers, checks, correspondence and memoranda in the custody or control of a third party, which reasonably pertain to the loss or damage. All information designated as confidential by the insured claimant provided to the Company pursuant to this Section shall not be disclosed to others unless, in the reasonable judgment of the Company, it is necessary in the administration of the claim. Failure of the insured claimant to submit for examination under oath, produce other reasonably requested information or grant permission to secure reasonably necessary information from third parties as required in this paragraph shall terminate any liability of the Company under this policy as to that claim.

6. OPTIONS TO PAY OR OTHERWISE SETTLE CLAIMS; TERMINATION OF LIABILITY.

In case of a claim under this policy, the Company shall have the following additional options:

(a) **To Pay or Tender Payment of the Amount of Insurance or to Purchase the Indebtedness.**

(i) to pay or tender payment of the amount of insurance under this policy together with any costs, legal fees and expenses incurred by the insured claimant, which were authorized by the Company, up to the time of payment or tender of payment and which the Company is obligated to pay; or

(ii) to purchase the indebtedness secured by the insured mortgage for the amount owing thereon together with any costs, legal fees and expenses incurred by the insured claimant which were authorized by the Company up to the time of purchase and which the Company is obligated to pay.

If the Company offers to purchase the indebtedness as herein provided, the owner of the indebtedness shall transfer, assign, and convey the indebtedness and the insured mortgage, together with any collateral security, to the Company upon payment therefor.

Upon the exercise by the Company of either of the options provided for in paragraphs a(i) or (ii), all liability and obligations to the insured under this policy, other than to make the payment required in those paragraph, shall terminate, including any liability or obligation to defend, prosecute, or continue any litigation, and the policy shall be surrendered to the Company for cancellation.

(b) **To Pay or Otherwise Settle With Parties Other than the Insured or With the Insured Claimant.**

(i) to pay or otherwise settle with other parties for or in the name of an insured claimant any claim insured against under this policy, together with any costs, legal fees and expenses incurred by the insured claimant which were authorized by the company up to the time of payment and which the company is obliged to pay; or

(ii) to pay or otherwise settle with the insured claimant the loss or damage provided for under this policy, together with any costs, attorneys' fees and expenses incurred by the insured claimant which were authorized by the Company up to the time of payment and which the Company is obligated to pay. Upon the exercise by the Company of either of the options provided for in paragraphs b(i) or (ii), the Company's obligations to the insured under this policy for the claimed loss or damage, other than the payments required to be made, shall terminate, including any liability or obligation to defend, prosecute or continue any litigation.

7. DETERMINATION AND EXTENT OF LIABILITY.

This policy is a contract of indemnity against actual monetary loss or damage sustained or incurred by the insured claimant who has suffered loss or damage by reason of matters insured against by this policy and only to the extent herein described.

(a) The liability of the Company under this policy shall not exceed the least of:

(i) the Amount of Insurance stated in Schedule A, or, if applicable, the amount of insurance as defined in Section 2 (c) of these conditions and Stipulations;

(ii) the amount of the unpaid principal indebtedness secured by the insured mortgage as limited or provided under Section 8 of these Conditions and Stipulations, or as reduced under Section 9 of these Conditions and Stipulations at the time the loss or damage insured against by this policy occurs, together with interest thereon; or

(iii) the difference between the value of the insured estate or interest as insured and the value of the insured estate or interest subject to the defect, lien or encumbrance insured against by this policy.

(b) In the event the insured has acquired the estate or interest in the manner described in Section 2(a) of these Conditions and Stipulations or has conveyed the title, then the liability of the Company shall continue as set forth in Section 7(a) of these Conditions and Stipulations.

(c) The Company will pay only those costs, legal fees and expenses incurred in accordance with Section 4 of these Conditions and Stipulations.

8. LIMITATION OF LIABILITY

(a) If the Company establishes the title, or removes the alleged defect, lien or encumbrance, or cures the lack of a right of access to or conditions and stipulations continued and concluded from the land, or cures the claim of unmarketability of title, or otherwise establishes the insured mortgage, all as insured, in a reasonably diligent manner by any method, including litigation and the completion of any appeals therefrom, it shall have fully performed its obligations with respect to that matter and shall not be liable for any loss or damage caused thereby.

(b) In the event of any litigation, including litigation by the Company or with the Company's consent, the Company shall have no liability for loss or damage until there has been a final determination by a court of competent jurisdiction, and disposition of all appeals therefrom, adverse to the title or, the insured mortgage, as insured.

(c) The Company shall not be liable for loss or damage to any insured for liability voluntarily assumed by the insured in settling any claim or proceeding without the prior written consent of the Company.

Figure 18.11 (cont'd)

(d)   the Company shall not be liable for: (i) any indebtedness created subsequent to Date of Policy except for advances made to protect the insured mortgage and secured thereby and reasonable amounts expended to prevent deterioration of improvements; or (ii) construction loan advances made subsequent to Date of Policy, except for advances made to protect the insured mortgage and secured thereby and reasonable amounts expended to prevent deterioration of improvements; or (ii) construction loan advances made subsequent to Date of Policy, except construction loan advances made subsequent to Date of Policy for the purpose of financing in whole or in part the construction of an improvement to the land which at Date of Policy were secured by the insured mortgage and which the insured was and continued to be obligated to advance at and after Date of Policy.

9.   REDUCTION OF INSURANCE; REDUCTION OR TERMINATION OF LIABILITY.

(a)   All payments under this policy, except payments made for costs, legal fees and expenses, shall reduce the amount of the insurance by the amount of such payments. However, any payments made prior to the acquisition of title to the estate or interest as provided in Section 2(a) of these Conditions and Stipulations shall not reduce by the amount of such payments the amount of the insurance afforded under this policy except to the extent that the payments reduce the amount of the indebtedness secured by the insured mortgage.

(b)   Payment in part by any person of the principal of the indebtedness, or any other obligation secured by the insured mortgage, or any voluntary partial satisfaction or release of the insured mortgage, to the extent of the payment, satisfaction or release, shall reduce the amount of insurance by such payment. The amount of insurance may thereafter be increased by accruing interest and advances made to protect the lien of the insured mortgage and secured thereby, with interest thereon, provided in no event shall the amount of insurance be greater than the Amount of Insurance stated in Schedule A.

(c)   Payment in full by any person or the voluntary satisfaction or release of the insured mortgage shall terminate all liability of the Company except as provided in Section 2(a) of these Conditions and Stipulations.

10.   LIABILITY NONCUMULATIVE.

If the insured acquires title to the estate or interest in satisfaction of the indebtedness secured by the insured mortgage, or any part thereof, it is expressly understood that the amount of insurance under this policy shall be reduced by any amount the Company may pay under any policy insuring a mortgage to which exception is taken in Schedule B or to which the insured has agreed, assumed, or taken subject, or which is hereafter executed by an insured and which is a charge or lien on the estate or interest described or referred to in Schedule A, and the amount so paid shall be deemed a payment under this policy.

11.   PAYMENT OF LOSS.

(a)   No payment shall be made without producing this policy for endorsement of the payment unless the policy has been lost or destroyed, in which case proof of loss or destruction shall be furnished to the satisfaction of the Company.

(b)   When liability and the extent of loss or damage has been definitely fixed in accordance with these Conditions and Stipulations, the loss or damage shall be payable within 30 days thereafter.

12.   SUBROGATION UPON PAYMENT OR SETTLEMENT.

(a)   **The Company's right of Subrogation.**

Whenever the Company shall have settled and paid a claim under this policy, all rights of subrogation shall vest in the Company unaffected by any act of the insured claimant. The Company shall be subrogated to and be entitled to all rights and remedies which the insured claimant would have had against any person or property in respect to the claim had this policy not been issued. If requested by the Company, the insured claimant shall transfer to the company all rights and remedies against any person or property necessary in order to perfect this right of subrogation. The insured claimant shall permit the company to sue, compromise or settle in the name of the insured claimant and to use the name of the insured claimant in any transaction or litigation involving these rights or remedies. If a payment on account of a claim does not fully cover the loss of the insured claimant, the Company shall be subrogated to all rights and remedies of the insured claimant after the insured claimant shall have recovered its principal, interest, and costs of collection.

(b)   **The Insured's Rights and Limitations.**

Notwithstanding the foregoing, the owner of the indebtedness secured by the insured mortgage, provided the priority of the insured mortgage or its enforceability is not affected, may release or substitute the personal liability of any debtor or guarantor, or extend or otherwise modify the terms of payment, or release a portion of the estate or interest from the insured mortgage, or release any collateral security for the indebtedness. When the permitted acts of the insured claimant occur and the insured has knowledge or any claim of title or interest adverse to the title to the estate or interest or the priority of enforceability of the insured mortgage, as insured, the Company shall be required to pay only that part of any losses insured against by this policy which shall exceed the amount, if any, lost to the Company by reason of the impairment by the insured claimant of the Company's right of subrogation.

(c)   **The Company's Rights Against Non-Insured Obligors.**

The Company's right of subrogation against non-insured obligors shall exist and shall include, without limitation, the rights of the insured to indemnities, guaranties, other policies of insurance or bonds, notwithstanding any terms or conditions contained in those instruments which provide for subrogation rights by reason of this policy. The Company's right of subrogation shall not be avoided by acquisition of the insured mortgage by an obligor (except an obligor described in Section 1(a)(ii) of these conditions and Stipulations) who acquires the insured mortgage as a result of an indemnity, guarantee, other policy of insurance, or bond and the obligor will not be an insured under this policy, notwithstanding Section 1(a)(i) of these Conditions and Stipulations.

13.   ARBITRATION.

Unless prohibited by applicable law, either the Company or the insured may demand arbitration in accordance with the legislation of the Province or Territory in which the land is situated. Arbitrable matters may include, but are not limited to, any controversy or claim between the Company and the insured arising out of or relating to this policy, any service of the Company in connection with its issuance or the breach of a policy provision or other obligation. All arbitrable matters shall be arbitrated only when agreed to by both the Company and the insured. Arbitration pursuant to this policy shall be binding upon the parties. The award may include legal fees. Judgement upon the award rendered by the Arbitrator(s) may be entered in any court having jurisdiction thereof. The law of the Province or Territory in which the land is situated shall apply to an arbitration under this Policy. A copy of the Rules may be obtained from the Company upon request.

14.   LIABILITY LIMITED TO THIS POLICY; POLICY ENTIRE CONTRACT.

(a)   This policy together with all endorsements, if any, attached hereto by the Company is the entire policy and contract between the insured and the Company. In interpreting any provision of this policy, this policy shall be construed as a whole.

(b)   Any claim of loss or damage, whether or not based on negligence, and which arises out of the status of the insured mortgage or of the title to the estate or interest covered hereby or by any action asserting such claim, shall be restricted to this policy.

(c)   No amendment of or endorsement to this policy can be made except by a writing endorsed hereon or attached hereto signed by either the President, a Vice President, the Secretary, an Assistant Secretary, or validating officer or authorized signatory of the Company.

15.   SEVERABILITY.

In the event any provision of this policy is held invalid or unenforceable under application law, the policy shall be deemed not to include that provision and all other provisions shall remain in full force and effect.

16.   NOTICES, WHERE SENT.

All notices required to be given the Company and any statement in writing required to be furnished the Company shall include the number of this policy and shall be addressed to the Company at Royal Bank Plaza, North Tower, 200 Bay Street, Suite 2200, Toronto, Ontario, Canada, M5J 2J2.

Figure 18.12

STEWART TITLE — MULTI-UNIT RESIDENTIAL ENDORSEMENT (OWNER POLICY)*

ENDORSEMENT TO TITLE POLICY
Attached to and forming part of Policy No. O-7763

Charge $Nil

ISSUED BY

STEWART TITLE
GUARANTY COMPANY
HEREIN CALLED THE COMPANY

MULTI-UNIT RESIDENTIAL ENDORSEMENT
Owner Policy

The within Policy is hereby amended as follows:

1.   Covered Title Risk #20 is hereby deleted and replaced with the following:

"You are forced by a Governmental Authority (or in the case of 20(a) hereunder, you are forced by the affected neighbour or a party who benefits from the Easement) to remove or remedy your existing structure(s), or any portion thereof, other than a boundary wall or fence, or it cannot be used for _____ residential dwelling units because:

     a)   it extends on to adjoining land or on to any Easement (even if the Easement is excepted in Schedule B);

     b)   it violates a restriction, covenant or condition affecting the Land, even if the restriction, covenant or condition is excepted in Schedule B;

     c)   it violates an existing zoning by-law or ordinance;

     d)   it is located on land under the jurisdiction of a conservation or similar governmental authority without approval;

     e)   of any outstanding notice of violation or deficiency notice;

     f)   any portion of it was built without obtaining a building permit from the proper Governmental Authority, provided a building permit would have been required by such Governmental Authority at the time of construction of the structure or relevant portion thereof.

This Endorsement is made a part of the policy and is subject to all the terms and provisions thereof and of any prior endorsements thereto. Except to the extent expressly stated, this Endorsement neither modifies any of the terms and provisions of the policy and any prior endorsements, nor does it extend the effective date of the policy and prior endorsements, nor does it increase the face amount thereof. Signed under seal for the Company, but this Endorsement is to be valid only when it bears an authorized countersignature, dated 10 February, 2010.

Chairman of the Board

President

1908

Countersigned:

Authorized Countersignature
Stewart Title Guaranty Company
Toronto, Ontario, Canada

Figure 18.13

STEWART TITLE — MULTI-UNIT RESIDENTIAL ENDORSEMENT (LENDER POLICY)*

ENDORSEMENT TO TITLE POLICY
Attached to and forming part of Policy No. M-7764

Charge $Nil

ISSUED BY

STEWART TITLE
GUARANTY COMPANY
HEREIN CALLED THE COMPANY

MULTI-UNIT RESIDENTIAL ENDORSEMENT
Lender Policy

The policy is hereby amended as follows:

1. Covered Title Risk #12 is hereby deleted and replaced with the following:

    "The failure of the land to contain _____ residential dwelling units, with the municipal address(es) shown in schedule A."

2. Covered Title Risk #13(c) is hereby deleted and replaced with the following:

    "The failure of the Land to be zoned to permit _____ residential dwelling units."

3. Covered Title Risk #17 is hereby deleted and replaced with the following:

    "The inability to use the existing _____ residential dwelling units, or any portion thereof, or any replacement thereof constructed after Date of Policy for residential purposes because that use violates any restrictions referred to in paragraph 7 of the Exclusions from Coverage."

4. Covered Title Risk #20 is hereby deleted and replaced with the following:

    "Any use of the land for _____ residential dwelling units being affected or impaired by reason of any lease, grant, exception or reservation of minerals or mineral rights referred to in paragraph 7 of the Exclusions from Coverage and damage to existing and future improvements, including lawns, shrubbery and trees resulting from the future exercise of any right to use the surface of the Land for the extraction or development of the minerals or mineral rights referred to in paragraph 7 of the Exclusions from Coverage."

This Endorsement is made a part of the policy and is subject to all the terms and provisions thereof and of any prior endorsements thereto. Except to the extent expressly stated, this Endorsement neither modifies any of the terms and provisions of the policy and any prior endorsements, nor does it extend the effective date of the policy and prior endorsements, nor does it increase the face amount thereof. Signed under seal for the Company, but this Endorsement is to be valid only when it bears an authorized countersignature, dated 10 February, 2010.

Chairman of the Board

President

Countersigned:

Authorized Countersignature
Stewart Title Guaranty Company
Toronto, Ontario, Canada

Figure 18.14

STEWART TITLE — SEPTIC ENDORSEMENT (OWNER POLICY)*

ENDORSEMENT TO TITLE POLICY
Attached to and forming part of Policy No. O-7763

Charge $Nil

ISSUED BY

STEWART TITLE
GUARANTY COMPANY
HEREIN CALLED THE COMPANY

SEPTIC ENDORSEMENT
Owner Policy

1.   The Company insures the Insured against loss or damage arising from any outstanding notice of violation, deficiency notice or work order issued as of the Policy Date affecting the septic system which services the land.

2.   The Company also insures the Insured against loss or damage in the event that a local authority search would have disclosed:

       a)   that the certificate of approval and/or the use permit issued for the private septic system servicing the land does not conform with the current as-built nature of construction; or

       b)   that a certificate of approval and/or a use permit had not been issued at the time the system was constructed and a certificate and/or use permit was required at the time of construction.

3.   The Company does not insure against any loss or damage related to the functionality and/or age of the system unless such loss or damage arises from an issue covered under paragraphs 1 and 2 above.

4.   Item #29 under the Covered Title Risks section of the Gold Owner's Policy shall not apply in respect to any septic systems save and except as set out in this Endorsement.

5.   Coverage under this Endorsement applies provided that the governmental authority having jurisdiction over the regulation of the septic system would respond to requests for certificates of approval, use permits and/or work orders, if requested.

This Endorsement is made a part of the policy and is subject to all the terms and provisions thereof and of any prior endorsements thereto. Except to the extent expressly stated, this Endorsement neither modifies any of the terms and provisions of the policy and any prior endorsements, nor does it extend the effective date of the policy and prior endorsements, nor does it increase the face amount thereof. Signed under seal for the Company, but this Endorsement is to be valid only when it bears an authorized countersignature, dated 10 February, 2010.

Chairman of the Board

President

Countersigned:

Authorized Countersignature
Stewart Title Guaranty Company
Toronto, Ontario, Canada

---

*   © Stewart Title 2010. Reproduced with permission.

Figure 18.15

STEWART TITLE — SEPTIC ENDORSEMENT (LENDER POLICY)*

ENDORSEMENT TO TITLE POLICY
Attached to and forming part of Policy No. M-7764 -

Charge $Nil

ISSUED BY

STEWART TITLE
GUARANTY COMPANY
HEREIN CALLED THE COMPANY

SEPTIC ENDORSEMENT
Lender's Policy

1. The Company insures the Insured against loss or damage arising from any outstanding notice of violation, deficiency notice or work order issued as of the Policy Date affecting the septic system which services the land.

2. The Company also insures the Insured against loss or damage in the event that a local authority search would have disclosed:

    a) that the certificate of approval and/or the use permit issued for the private septic system servicing the land does not conform with the current as-built nature of construction; or

    b) that a certificate of approval and/or a use permit had not been issued at the time the system was constructed and a certificate and/or use permit was required at the time of construction.

3. The Company does not insure against any loss or damage related to the functionality and/or age of the system unless such loss or damage arises from an issue covered under paragraphs 1 and 2 above.

4. Coverage under this Endorsement applies provided that the governmental authority having jurisdiction over the regulation of the septic system would respond to requests for certificates of approval, use permits and/or work orders, if requested.

This Endorsement is made a part of the policy and is subject to all the terms and provisions thereof and of any prior endorsements thereto. Except to the extent expressly stated, this Endorsement neither modifies any of the terms and provisions of the policy and any prior endorsements, nor does it extend the effective date of the policy and prior endorsements, nor does it increase the face amount thereof. Signed under seal for the Company, but this Endorsement is to be valid only when it bears an authorized countersignature, dated 10 February, 2010.

Chairman of the Board

President

Countersigned:

Authorized Countersignature
Stewart Title Guaranty Company
Toronto, Ontario, Canada

Figure 18.16

STEWART TITLE — WATER POTABILITY ENDORSEMENT (LENDER POLICY)*

ENDORSEMENT TO TITLE POLICY
Attached to and forming part of Policy No(s). M-7764

Charge $Nil

ISSUED BY

STEWART TITLE GUARANTY COMPANY
HEREIN CALLED THE COMPANY

WATER POTABILITY ENDORSEMENT
Lender's Policy

The Company insures the Insured against loss or damage resulting from water supplying the Land not being potable as of the Date of Policy according to the standards of the Department of Environment to service the Land, provided, however, that nothing in this Endorsement or the Policy itself shall be construed as coverage for health issues related to the potability of the water.

This Endorsement applies only if the Land is a residential single family home.

This Endorsement is made a part of the policy and is subject to all the terms and provisions thereof and of any prior endorsements thereto. Except to the extent expressly stated, this Endorsement neither modifies any of the terms and provisions of the policy and any prior endorsements, nor does it extend the effective date of the policy and prior endorsements, nor does it increase the face amount thereof. Signed under seal for the Company, but this Endorsement is to be valid only when it bears an authorized countersignature, dated 10 February, 2010.

Chairman of the Board

President

Countersigned:

Authorized Countersignature
Stewart Title Guaranty Company
Toronto, Ontario, Canada

---

* © Stewart Title 2010. Reproduced with permission.

Figure 18.17

STEWART TITLE — IMPROVEMENT ENDORSEMENT (OWNER POLICY)*

ENDORSEMENT TO TITLE POLICY
Attached to and forming part of Policy No. O-7763

Charge $Nil

ISSUED BY

STEWART TITLE
GUARANTY COMPANY
HEREIN CALLED THE COMPANY

IMPROVEMENT ENDORSEMENT
OWNER'S POLICY

1. The Company hereby insures the Insured:

   a. That in the event of a loss otherwise insured against by this policy, such loss shall include the interest of the Insured in any improvements located on the Land, however such improvements shall not include personal property or improvements not characterized as fixtures, and the definition of "Land" as set out in the within policy shall be extended to include such improvements.

   b. That at such time when the erection of improvements contemplated upon the Land herein shall be commenced, liability under this policy shall increase, as the improvements progress, in the amount equal to the greatest of (i) the cost of the improvements, or (ii) the value of the improvements, but in each case only up to the face amount of the policy, as amended in Schedule B to this Policy.

2. Notwithstanding the additional coverage contained within this Endorsement, and notwithstanding any other provisions of this Policy, the Company is not liable for and will not pay any loss or damage related to the inability of the Insured:

   a. to have constructed any improvements on the Land;
   b. to legally use any improvements on the Land constructed after the Policy Date; or
   c. to have constructed on the Land a single family residence.

This Endorsement is made a part of the policy and is subject to all the terms and provisions thereof and of any prior endorsements thereto. Except to the extent expressly stated, this Endorsement neither modifies any of the terms and provisions of the policy and any prior endorsements, nor does it extend the effective date of the policy and prior endorsements, nor does it increase the face amount thereof. Signed under seal for the Company, but this Endorsement is to be valid only when it bears an authorized countersignature, dated 2 February, 2010.

Chairman of the Board

President

Countersigned:

Authorized Countersignature
Stewart Title Guaranty Company
Toronto, Ontario, Canada

---

*   © Stewart Title 2010. Reproduced with permission.

Figure 18.18

STEWART TITLE — FARM RESIDENTIAL ENDORSEMENT (OWNER POLICY)*

ENDORSEMENT TO TITLE POLICY
Attached to and forming part of Policy No(s).

Charge $Nil

ISSUED BY

STEWART TITLE
GUARANTY COMPANY
HEREIN CALLED THE COMPANY

FARM RESIDENTIAL ENDORSEMENT
Owner Policy

The within Policy is hereby amended as follows:

All of the provisions of our Gold Owner's Policy shall apply, except as waived, varied, amended, deleted or added herein. The within Endorsement supersedes our Septic Endorsement, and applies to farm properties where the Policy Amount is $2 million or under.

1. The Company insures the Insured against loss or damage arising from any outstanding notice of violation, deficiency notice or work order issued as of the Policy Date affecting the septic system which services the private residence on the land.

2. The Company also insures the Insured against loss or damage in the event that a local authority search would have disclosed:

    a) that the certificate of approval and/or the use permit issued for the private septic system servicing the private residence on the land does not conform with the current as-built nature of construction; or

    b) that a certificate of approval and/or a use permit had not been issued at the time the private residence system was constructed and a certificate and/or use permit was required at the time of construction.

3. The Company does not insure against any loss or damage related to the functionality and/or age of the system unless such loss or damage arises from an issue covered under paragraphs 1 and 2 above.

4. Item #29 under the Covered Title Risks section of the Gold Owner's Policy shall not apply in respect to any septic systems save and except as set out in this Endorsement.

This Endorsement is made a part of the policy and is subject to all the terms and provisions thereof and of any prior endorsements thereto. Except to the extent expressly stated, this Endorsement neither modifies any of the terms and provisions of the policy and any prior endorsements, nor does it extend the effective date of the policy and prior endorsements, nor does it increase the face amount thereof. Signed under seal for the Company, but this Endorsement is to be valid only when it bears an authorized countersignature, dated 10 February, 2010.

Chairman of the Board

President

Countersigned:

Authorized Countersignature
Stewart Title Guaranty Company
Toronto, Ontario, Canada

---

* © Stewart Title 2010. Reproduced with permission.

Figure 18.18 (cont'd)

Farm Endorsement – Page 2

5. Coverage under sections 1, 2 & 3 of this Endorsement applies provided that the governmental authority having jurisdiction over the regulation of the residential septic system would respond to requests for certificates of approval, use permits and/or work orders, if requested.

6. The Company does not insure against any loss or damage arising from any outstanding notice of violation, deficiency notice, work order issued, lack of a permit or failure of the permit to conform with the current as-built nature of construction relating to any septic system on the subject property other than the septic system which services the private residence on the land.

7. The Company does not insure against any loss or damage arising from any legislation relating to farm or agricultural operations on the land and, without limiting the generality of the foregoing, does not insure against any loss or damage arising from non-compliance with or contravention of the following Statutes and their Regulations as amended from time to time and any successor Legislation: *Forestry Act; Environmental Protection Act; Farm Debt Mediation Act; Farm Income Protection Act; Drainage Act; Health Protection & Promotion Act; Weed Control Act; Cemeteries Act; Conservation Authorities Act and Ontario Water Resources Act*, or comparable local legislation.

8. The addition of a new insuring provision "#34" which shall read:

   The following use is allowed as of the Policy Date under the zoning classification applicable to the Property – continuation of present use as agricultural and/or residential.

STEWART TITLE GUARANTY COMPANY

By:_____
Authorized Countersignature

Residential Farm Endorsement

Figure 18.19

STEWART TITLE — VACANT LAND ENDORSEMENT (OWNER POLICY)[*]

ENDORSEMENT TO TITLE POLICY
Attached to and forming part of Policy No(s).

Charge $Nil

ISSUED BY

STEWART TITLE
GUARANTY COMPANY
HEREIN CALLED THE COMPANY

VACANT LAND ENDORSEMENT
Owner Policy

The within Policy is hereby amended as follows:

All of the provisions of our Gold Residential Owner Policy shall apply, except as waived, varied, amended, deleted or added herein.

1. The addition of a new insuring provision "#34" which shall read:

   The following use is allowed as of the Policy Date under the zoning classification applicable to the Property – continuation of the present use as at the Date of Policy.

2. Notwithstanding the additional coverage contained within this Endorsement and notwithstanding any other provisions of this Policy, the Company is not liable for and will not pay any loss or damage related to the inability of the Insured:

   a) to have constructed any improvements on the Land;
   b) to legally use any improvements on the Land constructed after the Policy Date; or
   c) to have constructed on the Land a single family residence.

This Endorsement is made a part of the policy and is subject to all the terms and provisions thereof and of any prior endorsements thereto. Except to the extent expressly stated, this Endorsement neither modifies any of the terms and provisions of the policy and any prior endorsements, nor does it extend the effective date of the policy and prior endorsements, nor does it increase the face amount thereof. Signed under seal for the Company, but this Endorsement is to be valid only when it bears an authorized countersignature, dated 10 February, 2010.

Chairman of the Board

President

Countersigned:

Authorized Countersignature
Stewart Title Guaranty Company
Toronto, Ontario, Canada

[*]　© Stewart Title 2010. Reproduced with permission.

Figure 18.20

STEWART TITLE — VACANT LAND ENDORSEMENT (LENDER POLICY)*

ENDORSEMENT TO TITLE POLICY
Attached to and forming part of Policy No(s).

Charge $Nil

ISSUED BY

STEWART TITLE
GUARANTY COMPANY
HEREIN CALLED THE COMPANY

VACANT LAND ENDORSEMENT
Lender Policy

The within Policy is hereby amended as follows:

All of the provisions of our Gold Residential Loan Policy shall apply, except as waived, varied, amended, deleted or added herein.

1. The addition of a new insuring provision "#29" which shall read:

    The following use is allowed under the zoning classification applicable to the Property as of the Policy Date – continuation of the present use as at the Date of Policy.

2. Notwithstanding the additional coverage contained within this Endorsement, the Company is not liable for and will not pay any loss or damage related to the inability of the Insured:

    a) to have constructed any improvements on the Land;
    b) to legally use any improvements on the Land constructed after the Policy Date; or
    c) to have constructed on the Land a single family residence.

    This provision does not limit the coverage in insuring provisions 13, 15, 17, and 19 of the Gold Residential Loan Policy.

This Endorsement is made a part of the policy and is subject to all the terms and provisions thereof and of any prior endorsements thereto. Except to the extent expressly stated, this Endorsement neither modifies any of the terms and provisions of the policy and any prior endorsements, nor does it extend the effective date of the policy and prior endorsements, nor does it increase the face amount thereof. Signed under seal for the Company, but this Endorsement is to be valid only when it bears an authorized countersignature, dated 10 February, 2010.

Chairman of the Board

President

Countersigned:

Authorized Countersignature
Stewart Title Guaranty Company
Toronto, Ontario, Canada

Figure 18.21

STEWART TITLE — CONDOMINIUM ENDORSEMENT[*]

ENDORSEMENT TO TITLE POLICY
Attached to and forming part of Policy No(s). O-7763 O-7763 1949748
M-7764 2093602

$Nil

Charge

ISSUED BY

STEWART TITLE
GUARANTY COMPANY
HEREIN CALLED THE COMPANY

CONDOMINIUM ENDORSEMENT

The Company hereby insures against loss or damage by reason of:

1. The failure of the unit identified in Schedule A and its common elements to be part of a condominium within the meaning of the condominium statutes of the jurisdiction in which the unit and its common elements are located.

2. The failure of the documents required by said condominium statutes to comply with the requirements of said statutes to the extent that such failure affects the title to the unit and its common elements.

3. Present violations of any restrictive covenants which restrict the use of the unit and its common elements and which are contained in the condominium documents provided that said restrictive covenants do not contain any provisions which will cause a forfeiture or reversion of title.

4. The failure of the unit and its common elements to be entitled by law to be assessed for real property taxes as a separate parcel.

5. Any obligation to remove any improvements which exist at date of policy because of any present encroachment or because of any future unintentional encroachment of the common elements upon any unit or of any unit upon the common elements or another unit.

6. The owner of the dominant tenement having, prior to the policy date, claimed a legal interest in the title to the servient tenement that is greater than the legal interest provided for in any easements to which the Property is subject.

7. Violations on the land of any enforceable terms, conditions, covenants, restrictions, obligations or reservations contained within registered instruments to which the municipality, a utility company , the developer, the builder, or the Condominium Corporation are parties, up to the policy date, save those specifically excluded in Schedule "B".

This Endorsement is made a part of the policy and is subject to all the terms and provisions thereof and of any prior endorsements thereto. Except to the extent expressly stated, this Endorsement neither modifies any of the terms and provisions of the policy and any prior endorsements, nor does it extend the effective date of the policy and prior endorsements, nor does it increase the face amount thereof. Signed under seal for the Company, but this Endorsement is to be valid only when it bears an authorized countersignature, dated 10 February, 2010.

Chairman of the Board

President

Countersigned:

Authorized Countersignature
Stewart Title Guaranty Company
Toronto, Ontario, Canada

Figure 18.22

STEWART TITLE — COMMON ELEMENTS CONDOMINIUM ENDORSEMENT*

ENDORSEMENT TO TITLE POLICY
Attached to and forming part of Policy No(s).

Charge $Nil

ISSUED BY

STEWART TITLE
GUARANTY COMPANY
HEREIN CALLED THE COMPANY

COMMON ELEMENTS CONDOMINIUM ENDORSEMENT

The Company hereby insures against loss or damage by reason of:

1. The failure of the common elements to be part of a common elements condominium within the meaning of the condominium statutes of the jurisdiction in which the common elements are located.

2. The failure of the documents required by said condominium statutes to comply with the requirements of said statutes to the extent that such failure affects the title to the common elements.

3. Present violations of any restrictive covenants which restrict the use of the common elements and which are contained in the condominium documents provided that said restrictive covenants do not contain any provisions that will cause a forfeiture or reversion of title.

4. The failure of the common elements to be entitled by law to be assessed for real property taxes as a separate parcel.

5. Any obligation to remove any improvements which exist at date of policy because of any present encroachment or because of any future unintentional encroachment of the common elements upon any Parcel of Tied Land ("POTL") or of any POTL upon the common elements.

6. The owner of the dominant tenement having, prior to the policy date, claimed a legal interest in the title to the servient tenement that is greater than the legal interest provided for in any easements to which the Property is subject.

7. Violations on the land of any enforceable terms, conditions, covenants, restrictions, obligations or reservations contained within instruments registered against the common elements condominium to which the municipality, a utility company, the developer, the builder, or the Condominium Corporation are parties, up to the policy date, save those specifically excluded in Schedule "B".

This endorsement applies only to that portion of the insured Property that constitutes a common elements condominium within the meaning of the condominium statutes of the jurisdiction in which the common elements are located and has no applicability to the freehold POTL.

This Endorsement is made a part of the policy and is subject to all the terms and provisions thereof and of any prior endorsements thereto. Except to the extent expressly stated, this Endorsement neither modifies any of the terms and provisions of the policy and any prior endorsements, nor does it extend the effective date of the policy and prior endorsements, nor does it increase the face amount thereof. Signed under seal for the Company, but this Endorsement is to be valid only when it bears an authorized countersignature, dated 10 February, 2010.

Chairman of the Board

President

Countersigned:

Authorized Countersignature
Stewart Title Guaranty Company
Toronto, Ontario, Canada

---

* © Stewart Title 2010. Reproduced with permission.

Figure 18.23

STEWART TITLE — VACANT LAND CONDOMINIUM ENDORSEMENT (OWNER POLICY)[*]

ENDORSEMENT TO TITLE POLICY
Attached to and forming part of Policy No(s). O-7763

Charge $Nil

ISSUED BY

STEWART TITLE
GUARANTY COMPANY
HEREIN CALLED THE COMPANY

VACANT LAND CONDOMINIUM ENDORSEMENT
Owner's Policy

The Company hereby insures against loss or damage by reason of:

1. The failure of the unit identified in Schedule A and its common elements to be part of a condominium within the meaning of the condominium statutes of the jurisdiction in which the unit and its common elements are located.

2. The failure of the documents required by said condominium statutes to comply with the requirements of said statutes to the extent that such failure affects the title to the unit and its common elements.

3. Present violations of any restrictive covenants which restrict the use of the unit and its common elements and which are contained in the condominium documents provided that said restrictive covenants do not contain any provisions which will cause a forfeiture or reversion of title.

4. The failure of the unit and its common elements to be entitled by law to be assessed for real property taxes as a separate parcel.

5. Any obligation to remove any improvements which exist at date of policy because of any present encroachment or because of any future unintentional encroachment of the common elements upon any unit or of any unit upon the common elements or another unit.

6. Loss or damage sustained by reason of the owner of the dominant tenement in any easement(s) or right(s) of way registered against the unit or the common elements having, prior to the date of policy, claimed a legal interest in the title to the servient tenement that is greater than the legal interest provided for in the easement(s) or right(s) of way.

7. Violations on the land of any enforceable terms, conditions, covenants, restrictions, obligations or reservations contained within registered instruments to which the municipality, a utility company, the developer, the builder, or the Condominium Corporation are parties, up to the date of policy, save those specifically excluded in Schedule "B".

This Endorsement is made a part of the policy and is subject to all the terms and provisions thereof and of any prior endorsements thereto. Except to the extent expressly stated, this Endorsement neither modifies any of the terms and provisions of the policy and any prior endorsements, nor does it extend the effective date of the policy and prior endorsements, nor does it increase the face amount thereof. Signed under seal for the Company, but this Endorsement is to be valid only when it bears an authorized countersignature, dated 10 February, 2010.

Chairman of the Board

President

Countersigned:

Authorized Countersignature
Stewart Title Guaranty Company
Toronto, Ontario, Canada

---

[*] © Stewart Title 2010. Reproduced with permission.

Figure 18.23 (cont'd)

ENDORSEMENT TO TITLE POLICY
Attached to and forming part of Policy No(s). O-7763

Charge $Nil

ISSUED BY

STEWART TITLE
GUARANTY COMPANY
HEREIN CALLED THE COMPANY

Where the condominium unit does not contain a dwelling as at the date of the policy, the within Policy is hereby further amended as follows:

All of the provisions of our Gold Residential Owner Policy shall apply, except as waived, varied, amended, deleted or added herein.

1. The addition of a new insuring provision "#34" which shall read:

    The following use is allowed as of the Date of Policy under the zoning classification applicable to the Property – continuation of the present use as at the Date of Policy.

2. Notwithstanding the additional coverage contained within this Endorsement and notwithstanding any other provisions of this Policy, the Company is not liable for and will not pay any loss or damage related to the inability of the Insured:

    a) to have constructed any improvements on the Land;
    b) to legally use any improvements on the Land constructed after the Date of Policy; or
    c) to have constructed on the Land a single family residence.

This Endorsement is made a part of the policy and is subject to all the terms and provisions thereof and of any prior endorsements thereto. Except to the extent expressly stated, this Endorsement neither modifies any of the terms and provisions of the policy and any prior endorsements, nor does it extend the effective date of the policy and prior endorsements, nor does it increase the face amount thereof. Signed under seal for the Company, but this Endorsement is to be valid only when it bears an authorized countersignature, dated 10 February, 2010.

Chairman of the Board

President

Countersigned:

Authorized Countersignature
Stewart Title Guaranty Company
Toronto, Ontario, Canada

Figure 18.24

STEWART TITLE — VACANT LAND CONDOMINIUM ENDORSEMENT (LENDER POLICY)*

ENDORSEMENT TO TITLE POLICY
Attached to and forming part of Policy No(s). M-7764

Charge $Nil

ISSUED BY

STEWART TITLE
GUARANTY COMPANY
HEREIN CALLED THE COMPANY

VACANT LAND CONDOMINIUM ENDORSEMENT
Lender's Policy

The Company hereby insures against loss or damage by reason of:

1. The failure of the unit identified in Schedule A and its common elements to be part of a condominium within the meaning of the condominium statutes of the jurisdiction in which the unit and its common elements are located.

2. The failure of the documents required by said condominium statutes to comply with the requirements of said statutes to the extent that such failure affects the title to the unit and its common elements.

3. Present violations of any restrictive covenants which restrict the use of the unit and its common elements and which are contained in the condominium documents provided that said restrictive covenants do not contain any provisions which will cause a forfeiture or reversion of title.

4. The failure of the unit and its common elements to be entitled by law to be assessed for real property taxes as a separate parcel.

5. Any obligation to remove any improvements which exist at date of policy because of any present encroachment or because of any future unintentional encroachment of the common elements upon any unit or of any unit upon the common elements or another unit.

6. Loss or damage sustained by reason of the owner of the dominant tenement in any easement(s) or right(s) of way registered against the unit or the common elements having, prior to the date of policy, claimed a legal interest in the title to the servient tenement that is greater than the legal interest provided for in the easement(s) or right(s) of way.

7. Violations on the land of any enforceable terms, conditions, covenants, restrictions, obligations or reservations contained within registered instruments to which the municipality, a utility company, the developer, the builder, or the Condominium Corporation are parties, up to the date of policy, save those specifically excluded in Schedule "B".

This Endorsement is made a part of the policy and is subject to all the terms and provisions thereof and of any prior endorsements thereto. Except to the extent expressly stated, this Endorsement neither modifies any of the terms and provisions of the policy and any prior endorsements, nor does it extend the effective date of the policy and prior endorsements, nor does it increase the face amount thereof. Signed under seal for the Company, but this Endorsement is to be valid only when it bears an authorized countersignature, dated 10 February, 2010.

Chairman of the Board

President

Countersigned:

Authorized Countersignature
Stewart Title Guaranty Company
Toronto, Ontario, Canada

Figure 18.24 (cont'd)

ENDORSEMENT TO TITLE POLICY
Attached to and forming part of Policy No(s). O-7763

ISSUED BY

Charge $Nil

STEWART TITLE
GUARANTY COMPANY
HEREIN CALLED THE COMPANY

Where the condominium unit does not contain a dwelling as at the date of the policy, the within Policy is hereby further amended as follows:

All of the provisions of our Gold Residential Owner Policy shall apply, except as waived, varied, amended, deleted or added herein.

1. The addition of a new insuring provision "#34" which shall read:

   The following use is allowed as of the Date of Policy under the zoning classification applicable to the Property – continuation of the present use as at the Date of Policy.

2. Notwithstanding the additional coverage contained within this Endorsement and notwithstanding any other provisions of this Policy, the Company is not liable for and will not pay any loss or damage related to the inability of the Insured:

   a) to have constructed any improvements on the Land;
   b) to legally use any improvements on the Land constructed after the Date of Policy; or
   c) to have constructed on the Land a single family residence.

This Endorsement is made a part of the policy and is subject to all the terms and provisions thereof and of any prior endorsements thereto. Except to the extent expressly stated, this Endorsement neither modifies any of the terms and provisions of the policy and any prior endorsements, nor does it extend the effective date of the policy and prior endorsements, nor does it increase the face amount thereof. Signed under seal for the Company, but this Endorsement is to be valid only when it bears an authorized countersignature, dated 10 February, 2010.

Chairman of the Board

President

Countersigned:

Authorized Countersignature
Stewart Title Guaranty Company
Toronto, Ontario, Canada

Figure 18.25

STEWART TITLE — LEASEHOLD ENDORSEMENT (OWNER POLICY)[*]

ENDORSEMENT TO TITLE POLICY
Attached to and forming part of Policy No.

Charge $Nil

ISSUED BY

STEWART TITLE
GUARANTY COMPANY
HEREIN CALLED THE COMPANY

LEASEHOLD ENDORSEMENT
(Owner's Policy)

1.　As used in this endorsement, the following terms shall mean:

　　a.　"Evicted" or "Eviction": (a) the lawful deprivation, in whole or in part, of the right of possession insured by this policy, contrary to the terms of the Lease or (b) the lawful prevention of the use of the land or the Tenant Leasehold Improvements for the purposes permitted by the Lease, in either case, as a result of a matter covered by this policy.

　　b.　"Lease": the lease agreement described in Schedule A.

　　c.　"Leasehold Estate": the right of possession for the Lease Term.

　　d.　"Lease Term": the duration of the Leasehold Estate, including any renewal or extended term if a valid option to renew or extend is contained in the Lease, subject to any provisions in the Lease which limit the right of possession.

　　e.　"Personal Property": chattels located on the land and property which, because of their character and manner of affixation to the land, can be severed from the land without causing appreciable damage to themselves or to the land to which they are affixed.

　　f.　"Remaining Lease Term": the portion of the Lease Term remaining after the insured has been Evicted as a result of a matter covered by this policy.

　　g.　"Tenant Leasehold Improvements": Those improvements, including landscaping, required or permitted to be built on the land by the Lease that have been built at the insured's expense or in which the insured has an interest greater than the right to possession during the Lease Term.

This Endorsement is made a part of the policy and is subject to all the terms and provisions thereof and of any prior endorsements thereto. Except to the extent expressly stated, this Endorsement neither modifies any of the terms and provisions of the policy and any prior endorsements, nor does it extend the effective date of the policy and prior endorsements, nor does it increase the face amount thereof. Signed under seal for the Company, but this Endorsement is to be valid only when it bears an authorized countersignature, dated 10 February, 2010.

Chairman of the Board

President

Countersigned:

Authorized Countersignature
Stewart Title Guaranty Company
Toronto, Ontario, Canada

---

[*]　© Stewart Title 2010. Reproduced with permission.

Figure 18.25 (cont'd)

LEASEHOLD ENDORSEMENT   Page 2
(Owner's Policy)

2.   Valuation of Estate or Interest Insured

If, in computing loss or damage, it becomes necessary to value the estates or interests insured by this policy as the result of a covered matter that results in an Eviction, then that value shall consist of the value for the Remaining Lease Term of the Leasehold Estate and any Tenant Leasehold Improvements valued either as a whole or separately. In either event, this determination of value shall take into account rent and other consideration no longer required to be paid for the Remaining Lease Term.

3.   Additional items of loss covered by this endorsement:

If the insured is Evicted, the following items of loss, if applicable, shall be included in computing loss or damage incurred by the insured, but not to the extent that the same are included in the valuation of the estates or interests insured by this policy.

a.   The reasonable cost of removing and relocating any Personal Property that the insured has the right to remove and relocate, situated on the land at the time of Eviction, the cost of transportation of that Personal Property for the initial one hundred kilometers incurred in connection with the relocation, and the reasonable cost of repairing the Personal Property damaged by reasons of the removal and relocation.

b.   Rent or damages for use and occupancy of the land prior to the Eviction which the insured as owner of the Leasehold Estate may be obligated to pay to any person having paramount title to that of the lessor in the Lease.

c.   The amount of rent that, by the terms of the Lease, the insured must continue to pay to the lessor after Eviction with respect to the portion of the Leasehold Estate and Tenant Leasehold Improvements from which the insured has been Evicted.

d.   The fair market value, at the time of the Eviction, of the estate or interest of the insured in any lease or sublease made by the Tenant as lessor of all or part of the Leasehold Estate or the Tenant Leasehold Improvements.

e.   Damages that the insured is obligated to pay to the lessees or sublessees on account of the breach of any lease or sublease made by the Tenant as lessor of all or part of the Leasehold Estate or the Tenant Leasehold Improvements caused by the Eviction.

f.   Reasonable costs incurred by the insured to secure a replacement leasehold equivalent to the Leasehold Estate.

g.   If Tenant Leasehold Improvements are not substantially completed at the time of Eviction, the actual cost incurred by the insured, less the salvage value, for the Tenant Leasehold Improvements up to the time of Eviction. Those costs include costs incurred to obtain land use, zoning, building and occupancy permits, architectural and engineering fees, construction management fees, costs of environmental testing and reviews, and landscaping costs.

STEWART TITLE GUARANTY COMPANY

BY: _____   Authorized Countersignature

APPENDICES

APPENDIX 1

Conversion of Imperial to Metric

The following are the conversion factors by which the number of imperial units is to be multiplied in order to obtain the SI equivalent.

LENGTH

1 chain (66 feet)	=	20.1168 m
1 foot	=	0.3048 m
1 inch	=	0.0254 m
1 link	=	0.2012 m
1 mile (5280 feet)	=	1.609344 km
1 mile (1760 yards)	=	1 609.344 m
1 perch (16.5 feet)	=	5.0292 m
1 pole (16.5 feet)	=	5.0292 m
1 rod (16.5 feet)	=	5.0292 m
1 yard	=	0.9144 m
1 furlong (660 feet)	=	201.168 m

AREA

1 acre	=	4 046.856 m^2
1 acre	=	0.4046856 ha
1 square foot	=	0.09290304 m^2
1 square mile	=	2.589988 km^2
1 square yard	=	0.8361274 m^2

In order to convert from SI units to imperial units, the only step necessary is to divide the number of SI units by the conversion factors given above. Fortunately, most modern calculators provide a metric conversion feature.

APPENDIX 2

Metric Linear Units Most Frequently Used

UNITS OF LENGTH

Metric linear units most frequently used:

millimetre	(mm)
centimetre	(cm)
metre	(m)
kilometre	(km)

The relationships between these four linear units are:

1 cm	=	10 mm
1 m	=	100 cm = 1 000 mm
1 km	=	1 000 m

On metric plans of survey and in descriptions the metre (m) and decimals thereof are used exclusively to express distances, except for the occasional use of the kilometre (km) on key plans.

UNITS OF AREA

The following units of area will be commonly used:

square centimetre	(cm^2)
square metre	(m^2)
hectare	(ha)
square kilometre	(km^2)

The relationships between these units are:

$1 \ m^2$	=	$10 \ 000 \ cm^2$
1 ha	=	$10 \ 000 \ m^2$
$1 \ km^2$	=	100 ha

APPENDIX 3

Surveyors' Measure

MEASUREMENTS

7.92 inches	=	1 link
25 links (16.5 feet)	=	1 rod, pole, or perch (all of equal length)
100 links	=	1 chain
100 links	=	4 rods
66 feet	=	1 chain
22 yards	=	1 chain
4 rods	=	1 chain
100 links	=	1 chain
80 chains	=	1 mile
625 square links	=	1 square rod
16 square rods	=	1 square chain
10 square chains	=	1 acre
43,560 square feet	=	1 acre
4,840 square yards	=	1 acre
160 square rods	=	1 acre
640 acres	=	1 square mile

APPENDIX 4

Significant Dates Related to Title Searching

1921 June 1	Land Transfer Tax Affidavit.
1922 June 13	Impossible to acquire prescriptive title against municipal roads after this date (*Real Property Limitations Act*, R.S.O. 1990, c. L.15, s. 16).
1929 June 1	Affidavit of Celibacy.
1937 January 1	All documents, when registered, perforated with the term "registered".
1939 June 25	Affidavit of Age and Marital Status for men required in a Deed or Mortgage when a wife joined to bar dower.
1954 April 30	Affidavit of Mortmain (revoked for Ontario companies June 23/65; Quebec companies exempt January 1/69).
1957 April 1	Affidavit of Age for men and women (except joint tenants) in Deed and Mortgage.
	Affidavit of Marital Status for men in a Deed or Mortgage if no one joins in or signs as a wife.
1958 March 1	Affidavit of Age for all Grantors except Executors, Administrators, Trustees under a Will or the Public Trustee.
1959 January 1	Dominion Estate Tax Consents required for estates (revoked January 1/72).
1959	Assets of Canadian Farm Loan Board vested in Farm Credit Corporation.
1961 March 29	Planning Board Consent.
1964 May 8	Retail Sales Tax Clearance (repealed April 1976).
1964 July 1	Affidavit of Age required in Powers of Attorney, Leases, Assignments of Leases and Mortgages.
	Affidavit of Marital Status may be made by men or women.
	Grantees other than corporations must be shown on documents as having at least one given name and a surname.
1965 May 3	Power of granting *Planning Act* (s. 29) consents transferred from Planning Board to Committee of Adjustment, Land Division Committee, or Department of Municipal Affairs (*Planning Amendment Act, 1964*, S.O. 1964, c. 90).
1965 June 23	Affidavit of Mortmain requirement for Ontario companies repealed.

1967 January 1	Affidavit of Age required on a Discharge of Mortgage. Deed to Uses legislation.
1967 June 1	*Planning Act* (remedial legislation).
1967 June 15	All violations of *Planning Act* subdivision and part lot control restrictions (s. 29) prior to this date are retroactively forgiven (*Planning Amendment Act, 1967*, S.O. 1967, c. 75, s. 10(3)).
1968 January 1	Capacity of officer signing for corporation.
1968 May 3	Parcels of more than 10 acres are no longer exempt from *Planning Act* (s. 29) subdivision control provisions (*Planning Amendment Act, 1968*, S.O. 1968, c. 96).
1969 May 13	Affidavit of Marital status any time wife joins in or signs the document.
1970 January 1	Succession Duty Consent required for estates (revoked April 10/79).
1970 June 27	*Planning Act* subdivision and part lot control in force throughout Ontario unless a municipal by-law is registered exempting an area.
1971 September 1	Age of majority changed to 18 from 21 years.
1972 January 1	Affidavit of Residence requirement (*Income Tax Act* (Canada), s. 116). Dominion Estate Tax Consents no longer required. Federal *Estate Tax Act* repealed.
1973 January 1	All new plans of subdivision must be registered in Land Titles, if available.
1973 April 1	Reference Plans required for all *Planning Act* severances.
1973 July 1	Tax Certificates under the *Municipal Affairs Act* and conveyances under the *Assessment Act* and *Municipal Act* confirmed to this date by the *Tax Sales Confirmation Act* (1974).
1973 August 1	Registration of Notice, or Assignment of Agreement of Purchase and Sale, or Option to Purchase valid for one year under the *Registry Act*.
1974 January 9	*Planning Act* severance not required when mortgage held on adjoining land.
1974 April 10	Land Transfer Tax Affidavit of Residence by grantee inserted in deed. Land Speculation Tax Affidavit or Clearance stamped on or included in deed (repealed October 24/78).
1976 April 1	Requirement for Retail Sales Tax Clearance in deed repealed.
1977 July 12	Succession Duty Release not required for Discharges of Mortgage.

1978 January 19	Succession Duty Release not required for documents by surviving joint tenant (affidavit must confirm joint tenancy) (*Succession Duty Act*, O. Reg. 44/78).
1978 March 31	*Family Law Reform Act, 1978*, S.O. 1978, c. 2, s. 70. New Affidavit of Spousal Status containing *Family Law Reform Act* statements. A wife's right to dower abolished except when previously vested. A right of possession in the matrimonial home in favour of either spouse created.
1978 December 15	*Planning Act* subdivision control violations prior to the registration of a subdivision plan, a condominium plan or a consent are forgiven except when court order to the contrary.
1978 October 24	*Land Speculation Tax Act* repealed.
1979 March 31	Once a *Planning Act* unconditional consent is granted, future conveyances of the identical description will not require another consent.
1979 November 30	Corporation Tax Lien effective only if registered on title.
1980 January 1	No claim against land for mortgage if discharge registered more than 10 years. Similarly no claim against land for *Lis Pendens*, Construction Lien, or Certificate of Action, Notice of Conditional Sale, Gas or Oil Lease, or Notice of Security Interest, if registered for more than two years (*Registry Act*, s. 65(1)).
1980 July 1	Registration requirement for Estate Tax Consents repealed.
1981 June 26	*Planning Act* consent required for partition orders (s. 49(20)).
1982 January 1	As of January 1, 1982, all new plans of subdivision must be investigated and certified pursuant to the *Certification of Titles Act* before they can be accepted for registration in the Registry system. A certificate of title registered for lands registered in the Registry system eliminates the 40-year search requirement for Registry system lands. This Act does not apply to land registered in the Land Titles system.
1982 June 15	*Mortmain and Charitable Uses Act* repealed.
1983 April 2	*Construction Lien Act, 1983*, S.O. 1983, c. 6 in force [now R.S.O. 1990, c. C.30].
1983 August 1	*Planning Act, 1983*, S.O. 1983, c. 1 provided an exemption for a grant of a remaining parcel and a remaining parcel after an expropriation where consent obtained to convey an abutting parcel (s. 49(6)).
1984 November 1	Part I of *Land Registration Reform Act, 1984* introduced in Oxford County.

	All affidavits except residence and value of the consideration replaced with statements.
	Where *Planning Act* statements signed, the conveyance and all prior conveyances deemed to comply with s. 49 of *Planning Act, 1983*, and predecessors.
	Second given name of purchaser required.
1985 January 1	*Municipal Tax Sales Act.*
	Part I of *Land Registration Reform Act, 1984* in force throughout Ontario.
1985 January 1	An easement can no longer be created as part of a charge (*Land Registration Reform Act*).
1986 March 1	*Family Law Act* revised statements with respect to the matrimonial home and abolished the creation of any new dower interests, *Dower and Miscellaneous Abolition Act* (*Family Law Act, 1986*, S.O. 1986, c. 4, s. 71(4)).
1988 March 31	Vested dower rights abolished unless notice of claim registered.
1991	Ontario Government and a private sector consortium (Teramira Holdings Inc.) form a strategic alliance called Teranet to automate land registration and convert Registry titles to Land Titles titles.
1995 March 31	Ontario *Business Corporations Act* was amended so as to limit the requirement for corporate searches to no more than 20 years before registration of a transfer to a subsequent purchaser for value (s. 244(3)).
1998	Hydro One Networks is required to register hydro easements.
1999 January 25	Land Titles documents registered electronically by remote registration for the first time in Middlesex County.
1999 June 18	The *Red Tape Reduction Act, 2000*, S.O. 2000, c. 26 creates special rules for LT cautions based on agreements of purchase and sale, including a 60-day expiry. The Act creates two kinds of cautions: one that allows dealings and one that prohibits dealings.
2000 July 6	Electronic registration is introduced in the Regional Municipality of Halton on an optional basis.
2000 October 23	Electronic registration is introduced in the Region of Hamilton-Wentworth on an optional basis.
2000 October 25	Electronic registration is introduced in the Region of Peel on an optional basis.
2001 January 29	Electronic registration is mandatory in the Region of Hamilton-Wentworth.
2001 February 21	Electronic registration is introduced in Dufferin County on an optional basis.
2001 April 25	Electronic registration is mandatory in the Regional Municipality of Halton.

2001 May 5	*Condominium Act, 1998*, S.O. 1998, c. 19 proclaimed, and provides for new forms of condominium ownership, such as leasehold, vacant land, phased, and common elements condominiums.
2001 June 20	Electronic registration is introduced in Durham County on an optional basis.
2001 August	For LTPLUS titles registered prior to August 2001, a *Planning Act* compliance search is required back to the date of conversion on the LTCQ parcel. In Applications for Absolute Title since August 2001, the solicitor for the applicant was usually required to make a statement regarding *Planning Act* and corporate escheat for the period between the conversion to LTCQ and the Application creating a new *Planning Act* start date at the date of registration of the LTPLUS.
2001 September 17	Electronic registration is introduced in the Ottawa Region on an optional basis.
2001 October 24	Electronic registration is mandatory in the Region of Peel.
2001 November 21	Electronic registration is mandatory in Dufferin County.
2001 December 12	Electronic registration is mandatory in York Region.
2002	OWL (Ontario Writs Locator), available through BAR-eX, searches all 49 enforcement offices in a single writs search. OWL and WritFiling provide for the online searching, issuing, and filing of writs of execution.
2002 February 13	Electronic registration is introduced in Simcoe County on an optional basis.
2002 March 19	Electronic registration is mandatory in Durham County.
2002 May 23	Electronic registration is mandatory in Ottawa.
2002 July 10	Electronic registration is introduced in Brant County on an optional basis.
2002 July 17	Electronic registration is introduced in Wellington County on an optional basis.
2002 November 20	Electronic registration is mandatory in Simcoe County.
2002 December 11	Electronic registration is mandatory in Wellington County.
2002 December 12	Electronic registration is mandatory in Brant County.
2002 September 23	Electronic registration is introduced in Metropolitan Toronto on an optional basis.
2002 November 29	The one millionth e-reg registration using Teraview software.
2003 January 13	Electronic registration is introduced in Lanark County on an optional basis.
2003 January 13	Electronic registration is introduced in Renfrew County on an optional basis.
2003 January 13	Electronic registration is introduced in Russell County on an optional basis.

2003 February 10	Electronic registration is introduced in Huron County on an optional basis.
2003 February 10	Electronic registration is introduced in Perth County on an optional basis.
2003 April 7	Electronic registration is introduced in Essex (Windsor) on an optional basis.
2003 May 14	Electronic registration is mandatory in Perth County.
2003 May 14	Electronic registration is mandatory in Huron County.
2003 May 31	Teraview access to TitlePLUS policies is discontinued.
2003 June 9	Electronic registration is mandatory in Lanark County.
2003 June 10	Electronic registration is mandatory in Russell County.
2003 June 10	Electronic registration is mandatory in Renfrew County.
2003 July 7	Electronic registration is optional in Niagara North.
2003 July 7	Electronic registration is optional in Niagara South.
2003 September 9	Electronic registration is mandatory in Essex.
2003 December 9	Electronic registration is mandatory in Toronto.
2004 February 10	Electronic registration is mandatory in Waterloo.
2004 September 16	Electronic registration is mandatory in Niagara South.
2004 September 16	Electronic registration is mandatory in Niagara North.
2004 November 22	Electronic registration is mandatory in Rainy River.
2005 February 22	Electronic registration is mandatory in Cochrane.
2005 March 15	Electronic registration is mandatory in Sudbury.
2005 May 19	Electronic registration is mandatory in Thunder Bay.
2005 June 9	Electronic registration is mandatory in Nipissing.
2005 October 1	Mandatory site condition filings in application Brownfields Environmental Site Registry for change of use, zoning, and building permit application.
2006 February 9	Electronic registration is mandatory in Timiskaming.
2006 February 23	Electronic registration is mandatory in Kenora.
2006 October 19	Section 78 of the *Ministry of Government Services Consumer Protection and Service Modernization Act, 2006*, S.O. 2006, c. 34 (Bill 152) clarifies the effect of fraud on innocent homeowners. The true registered owner will not lose title as a result of a fraudulent document registered on or after October 19, 2006.
2006 December 20	The *Ministry of Government Services Consumer Protection and Service Modernization Act, 2006* amended the *Registry Act*, requiring registration of easements, restrictive covenants, and claims, by separate document every 40 years. Reference to claims in subsequent documents does not constitute notice.
2006 December 20	**CHANGES TO THE LAND TITLES ASSURANCE FUND** The *Ministry of Government Services Consumer Protection and Service Modernization Act, 2006* created two categories of claimant. Innocent residential purchasers

and homeowners who are victims of fraud can go directly to the fund. Due diligence conditions are implemented for other claimants.

2007 May 22	Electronic registration is mandatory in Elgin.
2007 August 20	Electronic registration is mandatory in Peterborough.
2007 September 24	Electronic registration is mandatory in Lambton.
2007 September 24	Electronic registration is mandatory in Norfolk.
2007 October 15	Electronic registration is mandatory in Algoma.
2007 November 19	Electronic registration is mandatory in Muskoka.
2007 December 11	Electronic registration is mandatory in Prince Edward.

2008   **REAL ESTATE FRAUD ACTION PLAN**

The Ministry of Government Services implemented several fraud avoidance strategies, including:

- two-lawyer rule for transfers;
- tightened ELRS access requirements;
- changes in power of attorney requirements; and
- changes to the Land Titles Assurance Fund.

2008   The Law Society of Upper Canada launched new client identification requirements.

2008 March 10	Electronic registration is mandatory in Lennox.
2008 March 20	Electronic registration is mandatory in Haldimand.

2008 April 7   New **POWER OF ATTORNEY RULES**

The *Ministry of Government Services Consumer Protection and Service Modernization Act, 2006* amended the law relating to the registration requirements for powers of attorney. The Ministry's Real Estate Fraud Action Program identified powers of attorney as a real estate fraud "hotspot" (see also O. Reg. 19/99, s. 4).

2008 April 21	Electronic registration is mandatory in Bruce.
2008 June 16	Electronic registration is mandatory in Stormont.

2008 September 30   New **ACCESS REQUIREMENTS FOR ELRS**

The Ministry's Real Estate Fraud Action Plan reviewed access of all ELRS users and completes new identity, financial resources, and good character/accountability checks as a condition of continuing ELRS access.

2008 November   **TWO-LAWYER RULE**

Both the lawyer for the transferee and the lawyer for the transferor must sign a transfer in the ELRS, subject to listed exceptions. The two-lawyer rule created new statements in transfers. Ontario Regulation 76/08, filed April 7, 2008, incorporated these changes into O. Reg. 19/99. See Bulletin No. 2009-01.

2008 December 15   Electronic registration is mandatory in Hastings.

2009	Ontario's Feed-In Tariff Renewable Energy Generation Program (FIT) under the *Green Energy Act, 2009*, S.O. 2009, c. 12, Sched. A.
2009 April 20	Electronic registration is mandatory in Northumberland.
2009 May 11	Electronic registration is optional in Dundas.
2009 May 25	Electronic registration is mandatory in Leeds.
2009 August 10	Electronic registration is mandatory in Dundas.
2009 August 17	Electronic registration is optional in Grenville.
2009 October 1	FIT program accepts applications.
2009 November 2	Electronic registration is mandatory in Glengarry.
2009 December 7	Electronic registration is mandatory in Grey.
2009 December 7	Electronic registration is mandatory in Parry Sound.
2009 December 29	New Brownfields regulation (O. Reg. 153/04, under the *Environmental Protection Act*, R.S.O. 1990, c. E.19) filed for Phase I and II Environmental Site Assessments (revisions are extensive and take effect in stages).
2010 January 31	City of Toronto Green Roof By-Law No. 583-2009 for larger buildings in effect.
2010 February	FIT program offers FIT contracts.
2010 March 22	Electronic registration is mandatory in Victoria.
2010 April 19	Electronic registration is mandatory in Prescott.
2010 December 21	Domestic content requirements rise for FIT applications.
2010 December 31	The *Energy Conservation Responsibility Act, 2006* requires all condominium units to have individual smart meters.

As of February 2010, the following Registry offices remain optional:

2005 April	Frontenac
2006 January	Oxford
2006 March	Kent
2006 October	Haliburton
2007 January	Manitoulin

POWERS OF ATTORNEY SEARCHES

LRO #01 Algoma	April 24, 2006
LRO #02 Brant	December 12, 2002
LRO #03 Bruce	June 19, 2006
LRO #04 Ottawa	September 14, 2001
LRO #06 Cochrane	August 23, 2004
LRO #07 Dufferin	November 21, 2001
LRO #11 Elgin	March 21, 2006
LRO #12 Essex	July 2003
LRO #13 Frontenac	July 24, 2003
LRO #14 Glengarry	October 5, 2009

LRO #16 Grey	May 23, 2006
LRO #18 Haldimand	December 19, 2005
LRO #20 Halton	1998
LRO #21 Hastings	June 2004
LRO #22 Huron	May 14, 2003
LRO #23 Kenora	November 27, 2005
LRO #24 Kent	January 1, 2004
LRO #25 Lambton	July 10, 2006
LRO #27 Lanark	January 13, 2003
LRO #28 Leeds	October 23, 2006
LRO #29 Lennox	January 23, 2006
LRO #30 Niagara North	1997
LRO #31 Manitoulin	November 20, 2006
LRO #33 Middlesex	January 25, 1999
LRO #35 Muskoka	April 18, 2005
LRO #36 Nipissing	March 2005
LRO #39 Northumberland	May 8, 2006
LRO #40 Durham	June 20, 2001
LRO #41 Oxford	June 1990
LRO #42 Parry Sound	September 18, 2006
LRO #43 Peel	October 25, 2000
LRO #44 Perth	May 14, 2003
LRO #45 Peterborough	March 8, 2004
LRO #46 Prescott	April 28, 2006
LRO #47 Prince Edward	July 24, 2006
LRO #48 Rainy River	August 9, 2004
LRO #49 Renfrew	February 1, 2003
LRO #50 Russell	August 2002
LRO #51 Simcoe	February 13, 2002
LRO #52 Stormont	May 23, 2006
LRO #53 Sudbury	August 16, 2004
LRO #54 Temiskaming	November 21, 2005
LRO #55 Thunder Bay	November 29, 2004
LRO #57 Victoria	May 24, 2005
LRO #58 Waterloo	February 9, 2004
LRO #59 Niagara South	2000
LRO #61 Wellington	2001
LRO #62 Hamilton-Wentworth	January 2001
LRO #65 York	December 12, 2001
LRO #80 Toronto	September 23, 2002

APPENDIX 5

Useful Websites, Resources, and Contact Information

In an age of continuous private sector reorganization and federal, provincial, and municipal government restructuring combined with incessant regulatory and technological change, e-mail and mailing addresses, telephone and fax numbers, contact information, and regulatory responsibilities are in a state of constant change. The following references provide frequently used resources for the real estate practitioner.

REAL ESTATE AND LEGAL SERVICES INFORMATION

Law Society of Upper Canada's Practice Resource Centre's Real Estate Practice Portal

This portal provides access to a large collection of real estate current awareness practice tools and materials on electronic land registration, professional practice standards, real estate fraud, title insurance, and links to case law, Continuing Legal Education, commentary, forms and precedents, legal research resources (often a commercial account and password are required), risk management strategies, and news and practice alerts (hot topics). The portal contains the following:

1. Residential Real Estate Transactions Practice Guidelines

2. Real Estate Practice Guide

3. Fighting Real Estate Fraud: Reference Materials

4. Electronic Registration of Title Documents including an example Document Registration Agreement (DRA) and an ELRS Acknowledgement and Direction

Internet: <http://rc.lsuc.on.ca/library/research_portals_realestate.htm>

E-Laws (Ontario legislation, statutes and regulations, and bills)

Internet: <http://www.e-laws.gov.on.ca>

Laws of Canada (Federal statutes and regulations)

Internet: <http://laws.justice.gc.ca>

Registry Divisions, O. Reg. 427/99 (under the *Registry Act*, R.S.O. 1990, c. R.20)

This much-amended regulation sets out a schedule of Registry divisions, the location of land Registry offices, and a short description of the lands recorded in all the Registry divisions. Note that where a road allowance forms the boundary between Registry divisions, the centre line of the allowance is the boundary between the Registry divisions.

Service Ontario

This is the portal to Government of Ontario services and publications. It cross-references contact information and services under the provincial ministries.

Internet: <http://www.serviceontario.ca>

- Under "Services for Businesses", it links to an online **PPSR registration** and search service. The Guide to the Personal Property Security Registration and Searching is available at: <http://www.ontario.ca/en/services_for_business/access_now/ONT04_020917>

- Under "Services for Residents", select **Land Registration Informtion** <http://www.ontario.ca/en/information_bundle/land_registration/STEL01-130081>

- **Land Registration Information** contains the following:

  - Application for Access to ELRS
  - Index to bulletins, memos, and forms
  - Registry Offices contact information
  - Client guides and checklists
  - Information on real estate fraud
  - Land Titles Assurance Fund applications, procedures, and searchable database of prior claims decisions <http://www.ontario.ca/en/information_bundle/land_registration/STEL01-130081>

    Office of the Director of Titles
    Ministry of Government Services
    Policy and Regulation Branch
    Suite 420, Box 117
    20 Dundas Street West
    Toronto, Ontario
    M5G 2C2
    Telephone: (416) 314-4882
    Fax: (416) 314-4878
    E-mail: Director_of_Titles@ontario.ca

Service Ontario INFO-GO

This website provides an online searchable directory of Ontario government offices and services descriptions. INFO-GO also contains an online government telephone directory of positions, names, phone numbers, addresses, and e-mail addresses.

Internet: <http://www.infogo.gov.on.ca/infogo/mainPage.do>

Teranet Inc.

Teranet is an extensive legal technology solutions provider that offers a suite of products and services including Teraview, BAR-eX, CLOSURE, Conveyancer, and Dye & Durham products. Teranet provides exclusive access to Ontario's Electronic Land Registration System (ELRS).

Internet: <http://www.teranet.ca>

1 Adelaide St. E.
Suite 600
Toronto, Ontario
M5C 2V9
Telephone: (416) 360-5263
Toll-free: 1-800-208-5263
Fax: (416) 360-0871
E-mail: info@teranet.ca

Teraview and ELRS

This online software download centre provides online customer service, online system status check, online reference and resource information, online training manuals and demonstrations. The following guides are available online at the Teraview website:

- Teraview Training System Guide
- Teraview Reference Guide
- Electronic Registration Procedures Guide

Internet: <http://www.teraview.ca/>
E-mail: info@teraview.ca

BAR-eX: Legal Services and Resources Portal

BAR-eX is part of Teranet. The BAR-eX website provides access to legal information, software, and the following services:

- **WritSearch**: provides access to the Ontario Ministry of the Attorney General writs of execution databases by name, number, county, district, region.
- **OWL** (Ontario Writs Locator): provides the ability to search writs for all of Ontario at once.
- **WritFiling**: provides the ability to issue and file a writ of execution (form 60A) into any Ontario enforcement jurisdiction.
- **POLARIS search**: enables the user to search the Ontario government's POLARIS land titles database.
- **Current Awareness**: alerts and career postings.
- **BAR-eX search**: a Canadian legal search engine indexing approximately 250,000 webpages and full text documents selected for their relevancy to Canadian legal issues.

Internet: <http://www.bar-ex.com>

Corporate Inquiries

Corporate status certificates, PPSA, Business and Partnership Names, and NUANS searches for Ontario corporations are available through online service providers such as Cyberbahn, OnCorp Direct, Dye & Durham, now associated with Teranet, or at the Companies Branch, Ministry of Government Services, Government of Ontario ONBIS electronic searching. Corporate certificate of compliance and certificate of existence searches for companies under the *Canada Business Corporations Act* are made at Corporations Canada.

Internet: Cyberbahn <http://www.cyberbahngroup.com/CyberbahnCMS/>
   OnCorp Direct <http://www.oncorp.com/>
   Dye & Durham <http://dyedurham.ca>

Enhanced Search Report/Corporate

Teranet now offers an enhanced search report that provides an executive search summary of the following corporate information:

- Certificate of Status
- PPSA uncertified
- Official receiver/Bankruptcy
- *Bank Act*
- Writs of Execution

- Bulk Sales
- Litigation

Crown Land Records, Management Board Secretariat, Archives of Ontario, Ministry of Government Services

The Ontario Land Records Index, specifically the Crown Lands records, on this website contains documents relating to the grant, sale, or lease of Crown lands. Most of these records originated in the Office of the Surveyor General or the Crown Lands department. Land patent indices created by the provincial Secretary's Official Documents section as well as records of the Heir and Divisee Commission are included in the Index.

Internet: <http://www.archives.gov.on.ca/english/interloan/l-intro.htm#patents>

Copies of Crown patents may be obtained through the following:

> Ministry of Natural Resources
> Lands & Natural Heritage Branch
> Land Management Section
> Crown Land Registry
> 300 Water Street
> P.O. Box 7000
> Peterborough, Ontario
> K9J 8M5
> Telephone: (705) 755-2193
> Fax: (705) 755-2181

Hydro One Networks Inc. Unregistered Easements

It is now possible to search online all of Hydro One's unregistered easements province-wide and receive an up-to-date answer within minutes.

Internet: <http://unregeasement.hydroone.com/lvr/welcome.html>

ONLINE MAPPING AND DESCRIPTION RESOURCES

Land Information Ontario, Ministry of Natural Resources

The Government of Ontario has established Land Information Ontario (LIO) for the collection and management of land information in the Province of Ontario. LIO oversees data for use in maps and geographic information systems regarding:

- property boundaries, and boundaries of cities and towns
- zoning, land-use, assessments, and mining rights information

- population information (*e.g.*, demographics and census data)
- topographic features (*e.g.*, elevation, contours, streams)
- information about water, soils, plants, trees, fish, and wildlife
- water and air quality information
- roads and civic addressing data
- structures built on the land, such as utilities and buildings

Internet: <http://www.mnr.gov.on.ca/en/Business/LIO/index.html>

The Ontario Parcel Network

Internet: <http://www.ontarioparcel.ca/english/pages/generalinfo/overview.asp>

Ontario's Crown Use Policy Atlas (Ministry of Natural Resources)

Internet: <http://crownlanduseatlas.mnr.gov.ca/clupa.html>

Natural Resources Canada Mapping

Natural Resources Canada provides online topographic maps, aerial photography, satellite imagery, geological maps, mining maps, forest maps, wetlands, groundwater and drainage pattern maps, and other geographic information system (GIS) and global positioning system (GPS) data.

Internet: <http://atlas.nrcan.gc.ca>

Canada Centre for Cadastral Management (Natural Resources Canada)

This website contains maps for First Nations Land Management Areas, Indian Lands Registry Plans, Land Claim Settlement Maps, Canada Lands Index Maps, and other Canada Lands Survey System (CLSS) maps.

Internet: <http://clss.nrcan.gc.ca/googledata-donneesgoogle-eng.php>

The Association of Ontario Land Surveyors

This website includes a searchable database listing surveyors available by region. It also contains a description of the different types of surveys and surveying methods such as cadastral, hydrographic, or photogrammetric surveying. There is no substitute for an up-to-date survey.

Internet: <http://www.aols.org>

Land Survey Records Inc.

Internet: <http://www.landsurveyrecords.com/index.asp>

INDIAN TREATY MAPS AND CLAIMS INFORMATION

Indian and Northern Affairs Canada Geographic Portal

This comprehensive, integrated geographic portal is under development. It will provide location-based data and geographic map visualization available to Canadians and First Nations communities with an interest in geomatics. The INAC GeoPortal project will contain the location of First Nations reserves, treaty boundaries, and claims area for Aboriginal title and rights.

Internet: <http://geoviewer.inac.gc.ca>

First Nation Information Project

Internet: <http://www.aboriginalcanada.com/firstnation/dirfnont.htm>

First Nations and Reserves

Internet: <http://www.chiefs-of-ontario.org>

Natural Resources Canada (Maps of Treaty and Reserve Lands)

Canada Lands Survey System's GeoBase now contains an Aboriginal lands data layer, including a new First Nations land management map edition.

Internet: <http://clss.nrcan.gc.ca>

LAND-RELATED REGULATORY RESOURCES

Ontario Ministry of Municipal Affairs and Housing

This website provides:

- names, addresses, and phone numbers for Ontario municipalities and regional municipal portals
- resources and guides on municipal planning, Brownfield development, greenbelts, housing and Landlord and Tenant Board, and building regulation, including the *Ontario Building Code*.

Internet: <http://www.mah.gov.on.ca>

Conservation Authorities

This website deals with conservation authority searches relating to approvals for development, interference with wetlands, and alterations to shorelines and watercourses, including buildings and changes to building under O. Reg. 97/04 (*Conservation Authorities Act*, R.S.O. 1990, c. C.27). Conservation authority jurisdictions and contact information is available online.

Internet: <http://www.conservation-ontario.on.ca>

Niagara Escarpment Commission

Provides development and permit applications and searches, and compliance and enforcement procedures.

Internet: <http://www.escarpment.org/home/index.php>

Conservation Land Tax Incentive Program

CLTIP provides property tax relief up to 100 per cent to landowners who agree to protect the natural heritage values of their property and who are not associated with Conservation Authorities or Conservation Authority properties. It is available for:

- wetlands
- Areas of Natural and Scientific Interest (ANSI)
- Niagara Escarpment Endangered Species
- community conservation natural areas
- habitat of lands

Internet: <http://www.mnr.gov.on.ca/en/Business/CLTIP>

Managed Forest Tax Incentive Program (MFTIP) (see *Conservation Authorities Act*, s. 21)

An MPAC search will reveal if a property is under the MFTIP and has been taxed at 25 per cent of the municipal tax rate set for residential properties. A purchaser may be liable for past tax rebates if the vendor did not need eligibility requirements.

Internet: <http://www.mnr.gov.on.ca/en/Business/Forests/2ColumnSubPage/STEL02_166346.html>

Farm Property Class Tax Rate Program

Formerly the Farmland Taxation Policy Program (formerly the Farm Tax Rebate Program), the program ensures that eligible farm properties will be taxed at 25 per cent of the municipal residential/farm tax rate. This program is maintained by the Ontario Ministry of Agriculture, Food, and Rural Affairs. OMAFRA approves applications for the Farm Property Class reduced rate, and the Municipal Property Assessment Corporation maintains a record of eligible properties.

Internet: <http://www.omafra.gov.on.ca>

Ontario Ministry of Agriculture, Food and Rural Affairs
Property Tax and Farm Finance Unit
1 Stone Road West
Guelph, Ontario
N1G 4Y2
Telephone: (519) 826-3446
Toll-free: 1-800-469-2285
Fax: (519) 826-3170
E-mail: farmtax.omafra@ontario.ca

Municipal Property Assessment Corporation

The Municipal Property Assessment Corporation maintains a list of properties eligible for tax reduction status as well as property assessment and value of the property information. It has a searchable database for property assessment and tax status.

Internet: <http://www.mpac.on.ca>
Telephone: 1-866-296-6722 (toll-free)

Ontario Ministry of Natural Resources/Public Lands Act

For more information on work permits and exemptions, shorelines, Crown lands, docks, boathouses, *etc.*, contact the Ontario Ministry of Natural Resources.

Internet: <http://www.mnr.gov.on.ca/en/Business/CrownLand>

Mining Claims (Ministry of Northern Development Mines and Forestry)

The website for the Mining Lands section of the Ministry of Northern Development, Mines and Forestry provides:

- online searching of mining claims information and claim maps

- polygon coverage of mining claim, disposition, and alienation layers with associated claim number and all administrative boundaries (township and unorganized areas)
- base data, including general drainage, roads, and provincial outline

Internet: <http://www.mndm.gov.on.ca/mines/lands>

Natural Resources Canada

For federally regulated waters, contact Natural Resources Canada.

Trent-Severn Waterway Office (boathouses, boat ports, docks, shorelines, *etc.*)

P.O. Box 567
2155 Ashburnham Drive
Peterborough, Ontario,
K9J 626
Telephone: (705) 755-4900
Internet: <http://www.pc.gc.ca/eng/docs/r/poli/page06_e.asp>

Rideau Canal Waterway Office (boathouses, docks, shorelines, *etc.*)

34A Beckwith Street
Smith Falls, Ontario
K7A 2B3
Telephone: (613) 283-5170

HERITAGE PROPERTIES

Ontario Heritage Properties Database

Internet: <http://www.hpd.mcl.gov.on.ca/scripts/hpdsearch/English/default.asp>

Ontario Heritage Conservation Districts

Internet: <http://www.culture.gov.on.ca/english/heritage/conservation/conservation_list.htm>

Ontario Heritage Tool Kit

Internet: <http://www.culture.gov.on.ca/english/heritage/Toolkit/toolkit.htm>

Toronto Inventory

Internet: <http://app.toronto.ca/HeritagePreservation/setup.do?action=init>

Toronto Heritage Conservation Districts

Internet: <http://www.toronto.ca/heritage-preservation/heritage_districts.htm>

Canadian Register of Historic Places

This federal register contains heritage properties and National Historic Sites.

Internet: <http://www.historicplaces.ca>

Heritage Railway Stations Protection Act: The Historic Sites and Monuments Board of Canada

Parks Canada has a list of heritage railway stations designated under the *Heritage Railway Stations Protection Act*, R.S.C. 1985 (4th Supp.), c. 52. The Board also has a searchable database for Historic Sites and Monuments.

Internet: <http://www.pc.gc.ca>

ENVIRONMENTAL ISSUES/BROWNFIELDS AND TECHNICAL SAFETY RESOURCES

Technical Standards and Safety Act, 2000

The TSSA 2000 regulates the following:

- Fuel safety program (underground and aboveground fuel tanks), elevating devices, boilers and pressure vessels, and amusement rides.
- Outstanding work orders, certificates of inspection, permits and licences, inspections, compliance, infractions, and prosecutions.

Public Information Services
Technical Standards & Safety Authority
14th Floor, Centre Tower
3300 Bloor Street West
Toronto, Ontario
M8X 2X4
Telephone: (416) 734-3300
Toll-free: 1-877-682-TSSA (8772)
Fax: (416) 231-1626
E-mail: publicinformationservices@tssa.org (written requests)
        customerservices@tssa.org (verbal confirmations)

Brownfields Environmental Site Registry

Internet: <http://www.ene.gov.on.ca/environet/BESR/index.htm>

Ontario's Environmental Registry under Ontario's Environmental Bill of Rights (EBR)

The Registry contains certificates of property use, certificates of approval, directions, notices, licences, and court actions.

Internet: <http://www.ebr.gov.on.ca>

National Pollutant Release Inventory

Internet: <http://www.ec.gc.ca>

EcoLog ERIS

EcoLog Eris is a private, broad-spectrum, environmental search provider.

Internet: <http://www.eris.ca>

Brownfield Property Resources

- Records of Site Condition Regulation, O. Reg. 153/04 (*Environmental Protection Act*, R.S.O. 1990, c. E.19)
- Records of Site Condition process: <http://www.ene.gov.on.ca/envision/land/decomm/condition.htm>
  - A Guide on Site Assessment, the Cleanup of Brownfield Sites and the Filing of Records of Site Condition (2004)
  - Procedures for the Use of Risk Assessment under Part XV.1 of the *Environmental Protection Act*
  - Protocol for Analytical Methods Used in the Assessment of Properties under Part XV.1 of the *Environmental Protection Act* (March 9, 2004)
  - Soil, Ground Water and Sediment Standards for Use under Part XV.1 of the *Environmental Protection Act* (March 9, 2004)
- Proposed New Standards and Guidelines for Consultant Archaeologists: Important Information for Property Developers <http://www.culture.gov.on.ca/english/heritage/archaeology/arch_sng.htm>
- Companies that provide environmental goods and services including remediation, legal support and insurance, see Ontario Environment Business Directory: <http://www.envirodirectory.on.ca>
- Companies and organizations representing the environment industry in Ontario, see Ontario Environment Industry Association: <http://www.oneia.ca>
- Companies active in property remediation, see aboutRemediation: <http://www.aboutremediation.com>

- Worker health and safety, see Ontario Ministry of Labour: <http://www.labour.gov.on.ca>

OTHER DIRECTORIES

Michael L. Young, Ontario Municipal Service Directory: A Comprehensive Guide for Real Estate Professionals

Published annually by Canada Law Book, this directory lists Registry offices, sheriffs' offices, municipal addresses and contacts, clearances including tax certificates, water arrears, outstanding work orders, and zoning compliance, utilities, fire safety inspections, conservation authorities, septic system clearances, *etc.*

Vernon's City Directories

This directory was published annually by city, and included names, addresses, street layout, telephone numbers, and other municipal information. They can be useful for historic searches and are often available online through local libraries.

Telephone Directory Blue Pages

Lists federal, provincial, and municipal government services.

Online 411 Lookup

Internet: <http://www.411.ca>

Canada Post: Find a Postal Code

Internet: <http://www.canadapost.ca/business/tools>

Index